CIVILIZATION IN THE WEST

VOLUME II SINCE 1555

MARK KISHLANSKY
University of Chicago

PATRICK GEARY
University of Florida

PATRICIA O'BRIEN
University of California, Irvine

 HarperCollins*Publishers*

Executive Editor: Bruce Borland
Development Editor: Betty Slack
Project Coordination: The Wheetley Company, Inc.
Cover Design: Lucy Lesiak Design, Inc.: Lucy Lesiak
Text Design: Debbie Costello
Photo Research: Sandy Schneider
Cartographer: Paul Yatabe. Maps produced by Mapping Specialists, Inc.
Production: Michael Weinstein
Compositor: Dayton Typographic Services
Printer and Binder: R.R. Donnelley & Sons Company
Cover Printer: The Lehigh Press, Inc.

For permission to use copyrighted material, grateful acknowledgment is made to the copyright holders on pp. 993-994, which are hereby made part of this copyright page.

Cover: Details from the cycle of frescos depicting *The Legend of the True Cross* by Piero della Francesca, c. 1450s. In the church of San Francesco, Arezzo. Courtesy Superintendence of Cultural, Architectural, Artistic and Historical Welfare of Arezzo.

Civilization in the West, Volume II Since 1555

Library of Congress Cataloging-in-Publication Data
Kishlansky, Mark A.
    Civilization in the West / Mark Kishlansky, Patrick Geary,
Patricia O'Brien.
        p.   cm.
    Includes bibliographical references and index.
    Contents: v. I. To 1715 -- v. II. Since 1555.
    ISBN 0-673-46389-3 (v. 1 : student ed.). -- ISBN 0-673-53602-5 (v.
1 : teacher ed.). -- ISBN 0-673-46390-7 (v. 2 : student ed.). --
ISBN 0-673-53603-3 (v. 2 : teacher ed.)
    1. Civilization, Occidental--History. I. Geary, Patrick J.,
1948- . II. O'Brien, Patricia, 1945- . III. Title.
CB245.K546 1991b
909 .09821--dc20   90-23786
                                                             CIP

90 91 92 93   9 8 7 6 5 4 3 2 1

Contents

Maps *ix*
Charts, Tables, and Figures *x*
Preface *xi*
Acknowledgments *xiv*
Supplements *xv*
About the Authors *xvi*

15 Europe at War, 1555-1648 449

The Massacre of the Innocents *450*
The Crises of the Western States *452*
  The French Wars of Religion *452*
SPECIAL FEATURE:
THE MONSTROUS REGIMENT
OF WOMEN *456*
  One King, Two Faiths *458*
  The World of Philip II *460*
  The Burgundian Inheritance *461*
  The Revolt of the Netherlands *463*
The Reorganization of Northeastern
Europe *465*
  The Struggles in the East *466*
  The Rise of Sweden *469*
The Thirty Year's War *472*
  The Bohemian Revolt *473*
  The War Widens *474*
  The Long Quest for Peace *477*
  Suggestions for Further Reading *480*

16 The Royal State 481

Fit for a King *482*
The Rise of the Royal State *484*
  Divine Kings *484*
  The Court and the Courtiers *486*
  The Drive to Govern *488*
  Taxing Demands *490*
The Crises of the Royal State *492*
  The Need to Resist *492*
  The Right to Resist *494*
  The English Civil Wars *497*
  The English Revolutions *499*
SPECIAL FEATURE:
KING CHARLES' HEAD *500*
The Zenith of the Royal State *503*
  Absolute Monarchy *504*
  Absolutism in the East *505*
  The Origins of French Absolutism *508*
  Louis Le Grand *509*
  Suggestions for Further Reading *512*

17 Conquering the Material World 513

Rembrandt's Lessons *514*
The New Science *516*
  Heavenly Revolutions *517*
  The Natural World *519*

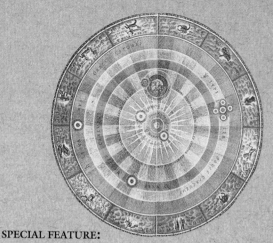

SPECIAL FEATURE:
THE TRIALS OF GALILEO *520*
Science Enthroned *524*
Empires of Goods *525*
The Marketplace of the World *526*
Consumption Choices *529*
Dutch Masters *531*
Mercantile Organization *533*
The Wars of Commerce *535*
The Mercantile Wars *535*
The Wars of Louis XIV *537*
The Colonial Wars *541*
Suggestions for Further Reading *544*

18 *The New European Powers* 545

Calling the Tune *546*
Europe in 1714 *548*
The West *549*
The East *552*
The Rise of Russia *554*
Russia Turns West *555*
Life in Rural Russia *557*
The Enlightened Empress *558*
SPECIAL FEATURE:
CATHERINE BEFORE SHE WAS GREAT *560*
The Two Germanies *562*
The Prussian Miracle *563*
Austria Survives *565*
The Politics of Power *567*

The Greatness of Britain *569*
The British Constitution *570*
Parties and Ministers *570*
America Revolts *573*
Suggestions for Further Reading *576*

19 *High and Low in the Eighteenth Century* 577

Happy Families *578*
The Nobility *580*
All That Glitters *581*
The Enlightenment *582*
Three Enlightenment Figures *584*
The Impact of the Enlightenment *588*
The Bourgeoisie *590*
Urban Elites *591*
The Charm of the Bourgeoisie *592*
Family Life *594*
The Masses *596*
Breaking the Cycle *597*
Daily Bread *599*
SPECIAL FEATURE:
GIVING BIRTH TO THE EIGHTEENTH CENTURY *600*
The Plight of the Poor *603*
Popular Culture *605*
Suggestions for Further Reading *607*

20 *The French Revolution and the Napoleonic Era, 1789-1815* 609

"Let Them Eat Cake" *610*
The Crisis of the Old Regime in France, 1715-48 *612*
Louis XV's France *612*
The End of the Old Regime *613*
The Three Estates *615*
The French Revolution and the End of the Old Regime *618*

Taking Politics to the People 619
Convening the Estates-General 620
The Storming of the Bastille 622
The Revolution of the Peasantry 623
Women's Actions 624
The Revolution Threatened 625

Experimenting With Democracy 627
Declaring Political Rights 627
The Second Revolution: The Revolution of
the People 628
"Terror is the Order of the Day" 629

SPECIAL FEATURE:
**THE GUILLOTINE AND
REVOLUTIONARY JUSTICE** 630
The End of the Revolution 633

The Reign of Napoleon, 1799-1815 634
Bonaparte Seizes Power 634
War and More War 635
Peace At Home 636
Decline and Fall 637
Suggestions for Further Reading 639

21 Industrial Europe 641

Portrait of an Age 642
The Traditional Economy 644
Farming Families 645
Rural Manufacture 646
The Agricultural Revolution 649

The Industrial Revolution in Britain 652
Britain First 653
Minerals and Metals 655
Cotton Is King 658
The Iron Horse 660
Entrepreneurs and Managers 663
The Wages of Progress 665

SPECIAL FEATURE:
**INDUSTRY AND THE
ENVIRONMENT** 666

The Industrialization of the Continent 669
Industrialization Without Revolution 670
Industrialization and Union 673
The Lands That Time Forgot 675
Suggestions for Further Reading 678

22 Social Transformations and Political Upheavals, 1815-1850 679

Potato Politics 680
Europe in 1815 682
The Congress of Vienna 683
The Alliance System 686

The New European Society 686
Urban Life 687
The Social Question 688
Family Life 689

The New Ideologies 692
Liberalism 692
Nationalism 693
Romanticism 694
Conservatism 696
Socialism 696

Protest and Revolution 698
The Revolutions of 1830 699
Reforming Great Britain 702
Workers Unite 704
The Revolutions of 1848 705

SPECIAL FEATURE:
PARIS IN 1840 706
Europe in 1850 711
Suggestions for Further Reading 712

23 State-Building and Social Change In Europe, 1850-1871 713

The Birth of the German Empire 714
Building Nations: The Politics of Unification 716
  The Crimean War 716
  Unifying Italy 719
SPECIAL FEATURE:
A WORKING WOMAN 720
  Unifying Germany 723
  Nationalism and Force 725
Reforming European Society 726
  The Rise and Fall of the Second Empire in France, 1852-70 726
  The Victorian Compromise 730
  Reforming Russia 732
  The Politics of Leadership 735
Changing Values and the Force of New Ideas 736
  The Politics of Homemaking 737
  The New World of Realism in the Arts 740
  Charles Darwin and the New Science 742
  Karl Marx and the Science of Society 742
  A New Revolution? The Siege of Paris and the Commune 745
  Suggestions for Further Reading 748

The Jewish Question and the Zionist Solution 767
Workers and Minorities on the Margins 769
Shaping the New Consciousness 771
  The Authority of Science 771
  Establishing the Social Sciences 773
  The "New Woman" and the New Consciousness 774
SPECIAL FEATURE:
SIGMUND FREUD, EXPLORER OF DREAMS 776
  The New Consumption 778
  Suggestions For Further Reading 780

24 The Crisis of European Culture, 1871-1914 749

Speeding to the Future 750
European Economy and the Politics of Mass Society 752
  Regulating Boom and Bust 753
  Challenging Liberal England 755
  Political Struggles in Germany 758
  Political Scandals and Mass Politics in France 760
  Defeating Liberalism in Austria 762
Outsiders in Mass Politics 764
  Feminists and the State 764

25 Europe and the World, 1870-1914 781

Mapping the World and Measuring Time 782
The New Imperialism 784
  The Technology of Empire 784
  Motives for Empire 787
The European Search for Territory and Markets 790
  Scrambling for Africa 791
  Imperialism in Asia 794

Conflicts in Empires 797

Results of a European-Dominated World 801

A World Economy 801

Race and Culture 802

Women and Imperialism 803

SPECIAL FEATURE:

THE POWER OF WORDS 804

Ecology and Imperialism 806

New Imperial Contenders 807

Critiquing Capitalism 808

Conflict at Home: The European Balance of Power 809

The Geopolitics of Europe 809

The Instability of the Alliance System 810

Suggestions for Further Reading 813

26 *War and Revolution, 1914-1920* 815

Selling the Great War 816

The War Europe Expected 818

The Alliance System 819

Military Timetables 820

Assassination at Sarajevo 821

The War Europe Got 823

Technology and the Trenches 823

The Battle of the Marine 826

War on the Eastern Front 827

War on the Western Front 829

War on the Periphery 831

Adjusting to the Unexpected: Total War 832

Mobilizing the Home Front 833

War Governments 835

The Turning Point and Victory, 1917-18 836

Reshaping Europe: After War and Revolution 838

Settling the Peace 838

Revolution in Russia, 1917-20 840

SPECIAL FEATURE:

THE WOMEN WHO STARTED THE RUSSIAN REVOLUTION 842

Suggestions for Further Reading 847

27 *Searching for Stability: Europe, 1920-1932* 849

Buildings for the Future 850

Mapping International Politics in 1920s Europe 852

East Central Europe 853

Germany 854

Western Europe 856

The United States in Europe 857

Economic Nationalism in the 1920s 858

Reparations and Debts 859

Trade and Reparations 861

SPECIAL FEATURE:

THE SCHOOL OF HARD KNOCKS AND INFLATION 862

The Soviet Union's Separate Path 865

The Soviet Regime at the End of the Civil War 865

The New Economic Policy 866

Stalin's Rise to Power 868

Women and the Family in the New Soviet State 872

The Promise of Fascism 874

Mussolini's Italy 874

The Failure of Democracy in Germany 877

The Beginnings of the Nazi Movement 880

Cultural Experimentation and Economic Collapse 881

Cultural Experimentation in the 1920s 882

The Great Depression 884

Suggestions for Further Reading 885

28 Crisis and Global Conflict, 1933-1945 887

The Screams From Guernica 888
Political Polarization in the 1930s 890
  Dictatorships in Control 890
  Hitler and the Third Reich 893
  Democracies in Crisis 898
The Coming of World War II 902
  Hitler's Foreign Policy and Appeasement 903
  Hilter's War, 1939-41 904
Racism and Destruction 908
  The Destruction of Europe's Jews 909
  Who Knew? 912
Allied Victory 914
  The Soviet Union's Great Patriotic War 914
  The United States Enters the War 917
  The Fate of Allied Cooperation. 1945 920
  Suggestions for Further Reading 921
SPECIAL FEATURE:
THE ATOMIC WASTELAND 922

29 Postwar Recovery and Crisis: From the Cold War to the New Europe, 1945-1968 925

Sex and Drugs and Rock 'N' Roll 926
Regulating the Cold War 928
  Atomic Politics 928
  Decolonization 930
  The Two Germanies and the World in Two Blocs 933
Reconstructing Europe 938
  The Problem: Europe in Ruins 939
  The Solution: The Marshall Plan 940
  Administering the Plan 942
  Western European Economic Integration 943
Creating the Welfare State 944
  Prosperity and Consumption in the West 945
SPECIAL FEATURE:
UTOPIA LOST 946
  The Eastern Bloc and Recovery 949
  Family Strategies 950

Youth Culture and the Generation Gap 953
  Sex and Drugs and Protest 954
  The Protests of 1968 955
  Suggestions for Further Reading 957

30 Europe Faces the Future: Hope and Uncertainty, 1968 to the Present 959

Toppling Communism 960
Ending the Cold War 962
  Soviet Dissent 962
  Detente: The Soviets and the West 963
  The Gorbachev Phenomenon 964
Eastern and Central Europe Since 1968 970
Solidarity in Poland 970
SPECIAL FEATURE:
TELEVISION AND REVOLUTIONS 972
  Emancipation in Eastern Europe 974
  The Two Germanies Since 1968 976
  Toward One Germany 978
Unity and Diversity in Western Europe 980
  Eurocommunism 980
  A New Working Class: Foreign Workers 981
  Women's Changing Lives 984
  Terrorism and Contemporary Society 986
  Toward a Single European Community: Europe 1992 989
  Suggestions for Further Reading 991

Map Credits 993
Photo Credits 993
Index 995

Maps

Page

453 Religious Divisions in France
461 The Habsburg Empire Under Philip II
464 The Revolt of the Netherlands
466 Northeastern Europe, ca. 1550
469 The Rise of Russia
471 The Rise of Sweden
477 Population Loss in Germany During the Thirty Year's War
478 The Peace of Westphalia, Europe 1648
499 The English Civil War
507 Russia Under Peter the Great
527 Dutch Trade Routes, ca. 1650
538 France Under Louis XIV
540 War of the Spanish Succession
541 The Treaty of Utrecht, Europe 1714
542 The Seven Years' War
548 Tour of Europe: Europe in 1714 — Overview
549   North America
550   India and the East Indies
550   Great Britain and the Low Countries
551   France and Spain
552   The Holy Roman Empire
553   Russia and Sweden
564 The Expansion of Prussia
569 The Partition of Poland
573 The British Empire, ca. 1763
602 Cereal Crops
618 Revolutionary France
634 Napoleon's Empire
646 Population Growth in Europe, 1800–1850
648 The European Linen Industry
653 Canals and Navigable Rivers
654 Coal and Iron Ore Deposits
660 Textile Centers
662 Railroads, ca. 1850
663 Manufacturing Centers
676 The Industrial Revolution on the Continent

Page

682 Tour of Europe: Europe in 1815 — Overview
683   France
684   United Netherlands
684   Italy
684   The German Federation
685   Poland
685   Saxony
686 The Quadruple Alliance
686 The Holy Alliance
708 The Revolutions of 1830 and 1848
718 The Crimean War
722 The Unification of Italy
725 The Unification of Germany
733 Russian Serfs
747 The Siege of Paris and the Paris Commune
768 Jewish Migration
791 Africa 1914
794 India 1858–1914
798 South Africa
802 European Foreign Investments, ca. 1878
812 Linguistic Groups in the Balkans
818 European Alliances on the Eve of World War I
819 Linguistic Groups in Austria-Hungary
820 The Schlieffen Plan
828 World War I
839 Europe After World War I
844 Revolution and Civil War in Russia, 1914–20
852 Tour of Europe: Europe in 1918 — Overview
853   East Central Europe
855   Germany
857   Western Europe
890 Europe: Types of Government
901 The Spanish Civil War
906 World War II in Europe

Page
907 The Division of France, 1940-44
909 The Holocaust
920 World War II in the Pacific, 1941–45
929 Territorial Gains of the USSR
930 The Cold War: U.S. and Soviet Alliances
932 Decolonization

Page
935 The Division of Germany
939 European Migrations After World War II
968 Republics of the Soviet Union
974 Events in Eastern Europe, 1989-90
980 United Germany
991 Europe 1992

Charts, Tables, and Figures

Page
458 The Houses of Valois and Bourbon
460 Chronology: The French Wars of Religion
462 The Family of Charles V
465 Chronology: Revolt of the Netherlands
468 The Jagiellon Monarchy of Poland
471 The House of Vasa of Sweden
479 Chronology: The Thirty Year's War
492 European Population, 1550–1700
502 War and Peace in Europe, 1598–1650
506 Tsars of Russia
516 Epicycles and Eccentric Circles
530 Tea Imports in England
539 The Spanish Succession
543 Chronology: War and Peace, 1648–1763
574 Chronology: The New European Powers
589 Major Works of the Enlightenment

Page
633 Chronology: The French Revolution
639 Chronology: The Reign of Napoleon
650 Yield Ratios
800 Chronology: The New Imperialism in Africa and Asia
813 Chronology: European Crises and the Balance of Power
864 Indices of Manufacturing Production, 1913–1925
895 Defense Expenditures
910 The "Final Solution"
914 Jewish Population Loss, 1939–1945
918 Tank Production
978 The Two Germanies
989 Aggregate Economic Indicators

$\mathcal{P}$reface

We have tried to write a book that students would *want* to read. Throughout three years of planning, writing, revising, rewriting, and numerous meetings together, this was our constant overriding concern. Would students read this? Would it be effective in conveying information while stimulating imagination? Would it work across the variety of Western civilization courses, with the different levels and formats that make up this fundamental course? It was not easy to keep this concern in the forefront through the long months of composition, but it was easy to receive the reactions of scores of reviewers to this single questions: "Would students *want* to read these chapters?" Whenever we received a resounding "no!" we began again—not just rewriting, but rethinking how to present material that might be complex in argument or detail or that might simply seem too remote to engage the contemporary student. Though all three of us were putting in long hours in front of word processors, we quickly learned that we were engaged in a teaching rather than a writing exercise. And though the work was demanding, it was not unrewarding. We hope that you will recognize and come to share with us the excitement and enthusiasm we experienced in creating this text. We have enjoyed writing this book, and we want students to enjoy reading it.

$\mathcal{A}$pproach

We made a number of decisions early in the project that we feel contributed to our goal. First, we were *not* writing an encyclopedia of Western civilization. Information was not to be included in a chapter unless it fit within the themes of that chapter. There was to be no information for information's sake, and each of us was called upon to defend the inclusion of names, dates, and events whenever we met to critique our chapters. We found, to our surprise, that by adhering to the principle that information included must contribute to or illustrate a particular point or dominating theme, we provided as much, if not more, material than books that habitually list names, places, and dates without any other context.

Secondly, we were committed to integrating the history of ordinary men and women into our narrative. We believe that isolated sections, placed at the end of chapters, that deal with the experiences of women or minority groups in a particular era profoundly distort historical experience. We called this technique *cabooing*, and whenever we found ourselves segregating women or families or the masses, we stepped back and asked how we might recast our treatment of historical events to account for a diversity of actors. How did ordinary men, women, and children affect the course of world historical events? How did world historical events affect the fabric of daily life for men and women and children from all walks of life? We tried to rethink critical historical problems of civilization as gendered phenomena. To assist us in this endeavor, we engaged two reviewers whose sole responsibility was to evaluate our chapters for the integration of these social groups into the themes of our chapters.

We took the same approach to the coverage of central and eastern Europe that we did to women and minorities. Even before the epochal events of 1989 that returned this region to the forefront of international attention, we realized that in too many textbooks the Slavic world was treated as "marginal" to the history of Western civilization. Thus, with the help of a specialist reviewer, we worked to integrate more of the history of eastern Europe into our text than is found in most others, and to do so in a way that presented these regions, their cultures and their institutions, as integral rather than peripheral to Western civilization.

To construct a book that students would *want* to read, we needed to develop fresh ideas about how to involve them with the material, how to transform them from passive recipients to active participants. We borrowed from computer science both the language and the concept of "user-friendly." We wanted to find ways to stimulate the imagination of the student, and the more we experimented with different techniques, the more we realized that the most effective way to do this was visually. It is not true that contemporary students cannot be taught effectively by the written word; it is only true that they cannot be taught *as* effectively as they can by the combination of words and images. From the beginning, we realized that a text produced in full color was essential to the features we most wanted to use: the pictorial chapter openers; the large number of maps, some inset directly into the text for maximum effectiveness; the geographical tours of Europe with their specially designed maps; and the two-page special feature in each chapter, each with its own illustration.

Features

It is hard to have a new idea when writing a textbook—so many authors have come before, each attempting to do something more effective, more innovative than his or her predecessor. It is probably the case that somewhere there has been a text that has used a chapter-opening feature similar to the one we use here. What we can say with certainty is that nothing else we experimented with, no other technique we attempted, has had such an immediate and positive impact on our readers or has so fulfilled our goal of involving the students in learning as our **pictorial chapter openers**. An illustration—a painting, a photograph, a picture, an artifact, an edifice—appears at the beginning of each chapter, accompanied by text through which we explore the picture, guiding students across a canvas or helping them see in an artifact or a piece of architecture details that are not immediately apparent. It is the direct combination of text and image that allows us to achieve this effect, to "unfold" both an illustration and a theme. In some chapters we highlight details, pulling out a section of the original picture to take a closer look. In others we attempt to shock the viewer into the recognition of horror, or of beauty. Some chapter-opener images are designed to

transport students back into time, to make them ask the question, "What was it like to be there?" All of the opening images have been chosen to illustrate a dominant theme within the chapter, and the dramatic and lingering impression they make helps reinforce that theme.

We have taken a similar image-based approach to our **presentation of geography**. When teachers of Western civilization courses are surveyed, no single area of need is cited more often that geographical knowledge. Students simply have no mental image of Europe, no familiarity with those geophysical features that are a fundamental part of the geopolitical realities of Western history. We realized that maps, carefully planned and skillfully executed, would be an important component of our text. To complement the standard map program of the text, we have added a special geographical feature. Six times throughout the book, we pause in the narrative to take a tour of Europe. Sometimes we follow an emperor as he tours his realm; sometimes we examine the impact of a peace treaty; sometimes we follow the travels of a merchant. Whatever the thematic occasion, our intention is to guide the student around the changing contours of the geography of Western history. In order to do this effectively, we have worked with our cartographer to develop small inset, or thumbnail, maps to complement the overview map that appears at the beginning of each tour section. We know that only the most motivated students will turn back several pages to locate on a map a place mentioned in the text. Using the small inset map allows us to integrate the map directly into the relevant text, thus relieving the student of the sometimes frustrating experience of attempting to locate not only a specific place on a map but perhaps even the relevant map itself. The great number of maps throughout the text, the specially designed tour-of-Europe geographical feature, and the ancillary programs of map transparencies and workbook exercises combine to provide the strongest possible program for teaching historical geography.

The third technique we have employed to engage students with historical subjects is the two-page **special feature** that appears in each chapter. These special features focus on a single event or personality chosen to enhance the student's sense that history is something that is real and alive. These features are written more dramatically or sympathetically or with a greater sense of wonder than would be appropriate in the body of the text. The prose style and the accompanying illustration are designed to captivate the reader. Three of the features concern utopias (Plato's *Republic*, More's *Utopia*, and Orwell's *Animal Farm*), posing questions about the ways in which different societies dream. Three of the features focus on Paris at various points in its history (the medieval period, the early modern age, and the modern era), tracing the development of the quintessential European city over a millennium. Accounts of the discovery of King Tut's tomb, of the fall of Constantinople, or of tsarist cavalry trampling women protesters place the student squarely in the middle of a historical event.

There are many new features in our text, and much that is out of the ordinary. But there are important traditional aspects of the narrative itself that also require mention. **Civilization in the West** is a mainstream text in which most energies have been placed in developing a solid, readable narrative of Western civilization that integrates coverage of women and minorities into the discussion. We have highlighted personalities while identifying trends. We have spotlighted social history, both in sections of chapters and in separate chapters, while maintaining a firm grip on political developments. We hope that there are many things in this book that teachers of Western civilization will find valuable. But we also hope that there are things here with which you will disagree, themes that you can develop better, arguments and ideas that will stimulate you. A textbook is only one part of a course, and it is always less important than a teacher. What we hope is that by doing our job successfully, we have made the teacher's job easier and the student's job more enjoyable.

Mark Kishlansky
Patrick Geary
Patricia O'Brien

Acknowledgments

We want to thank the many conscientious historians who reviewed our manuscript and gave generously of their time and knowledge. Their valuable critiques and suggestions have contributed greatly to the final product. We are grateful to the following:

Meredith L. Adams, *Southwest Missouri State University*
John W. Barker, *University of Wisconsin*
William H. Beik, *Northern Illinois* University
Lenard R. Berlanstein, *University of Virginia*
Raymond Birn, *University of Oregon*
Donna Bohanan, *Auburn University*
Werner Braatz, *University of Wisconsin at Oshkosh*
Thomas A. Brady, Jr., *University of Oregon*
Anthony M. Brescia, *Nassau Community College*
Elaine G. Breslaw, *Morgan State University*
Daniel Patrick Brown, *Moorpark College*
Ronald A. Brown, *Charles County Community College*
Edward J. Champlin, *Princeton University*
Stephanie Evans Christelow, *Western Washington University*
Gary B. Cohen, *University of Oklahoma*
John J. Contreni, *Purdue University*
Samuel E. Dicks, *Emporia State University*
Frederick Dumin, *Washington State University*
Margot C. Finn, *Emory University*
Allan W. Fletcher, *Boise State University*
Elizabeth L. Furdell, *University of North Florida*
Thomas W. Gallant, *University of Florida*
Joseph J. Godson, *Hudson Valley Community College*
Eric Haines, *Bellevue Community College*
David A. Harnett, *University of San Francisco*
Paul B. Harvey, Jr., *Pennsylvania State University*
Daniel W. Hollis, *Jacksonville State University*
Kenneth G. Holum, *University of Maryland*
Charles Ingrao, *Purdue University*
George F. Jewsbury, *Oklahoma State University*
Donald G. Jones, *University of Central Arkansas*
William R. Jones, *University of New Hampshire*
Richard W. Kaeuper, *University of Rochester*
David Kaiser, *Carnegie-Mellon University*
William R. Keylor, *Boston University*

Joseph Kicklighter, *Auburn University*
Charles L. Killinger, III, *Valencia Community College*
David C. Large, *Montana State University*
Roberta T. Manning, *Boston College*
Lyle McAlister, *University of Florida*
Therese M. McBride, *College of the Holy Cross*
Robert Moeller, *University of California at Irvine*
Pierce C. Mullen, *Montana State University*
Thomas F. X. Noble, *University of Virginia*
Dennis H. O'Brien, *West Virginia University*
Peter E. Piccillo, *Rhode Island College*
Marlette Rebhorn, *Austin Community College*
John P. Ryan, *Kansas City Kansas Community College*
Steven Schroeder, *Indiana University of Pennsylvania*
Bonnie Smith, *University of Rochester*
Peter N. Stearns, *Carnegie-Mellon University*
Darryl R. Sycher, *Columbus State Community College*
Steven Vincent, *North Carolina State University*
Richard A. Voeltz, *Cameron University*
Eric Weissman, *Golden West College*

Each author also received invaluable assistance and encouragement from many colleagues, friends, and family members over the years of research, reflection, writing, and revising that went into the making of this text.

Mark Kishlansky wishes to thank Ann Adams, Robert Bartlett, Ray Birn, David Buisseret, Ted Cook, Frank Conaway, Constantine Fasolt, Katherine Haskins, Richard Hellie, Matthew Kishlansky, Donna Marder, Mary Beth Rose, Jeanne Thiel, The Staff of the Joseph Regenstein Library and the Newberry Library.

Patrick Geary wishes to thank Mary Geary, Catherine Geary, and Anne Geary for their patience, support, and encouragement as well as Anne Picard and Dale Scofield for their able assistance throughout the project.

Patricia O'Brien thanks Jon Jacobson for his constant support and for sharing his specialized knowledge and his historical sense. She also wishes to thank Elizabeth Bryant for her encouragement and enthusiasm throughout the project; Robert Moeller for his keen eye for organization and his suggestions for writing a gendered history; and Katherine Turley for her unflagging assistance with bibliographic issues.

All the authors would also like to thank, though words are but a poor expression of our gratitude, Barbara Muller, Bruce Borland, and Betty Slack, the editors of our project. If ever authors have had more felicitous experiences with their editors than we have had with ours, they have been lucky indeed. The authors also extend sincere appreciation to Michael Weinstein, Elizabeth Gabbard, Susan Ritchey, Lucy Lesiak, Sandy Schneider, and Paul Yatabe, who contributed their skills and expertise to the editorial, design, photo research, and cartographic processes involved in the production of this book.

Supplements

The following supplements are available for use in conjunction with this book:

For the Student

Student Study Guide in two volumes. Volume 1 (chapters 1-16) prepared by Steven Schroeder, Indiana University of Pennsylvania, and Volume 2 (chapters 15-30) prepared by Werner Braatz, University of Wisconsin at Oshkosh. Includes learning objectives, an overview of each chapter, glossary terms, and sample study exercises, including identification questions, chronology exercises, multiple-choice questions, and historical thinking/essay questions. Each volume also contains the essay, "Writing About History," a brief guide to writing a history research paper.

Mapping Western Civilization: Student Activities workbook by Gerald Danzer, University of Illinois at Chicago. Features numerous map skill exercises written to enhance students' basic geographical literacy. The exercises provide ample opportunities for interpreting maps and analyzing cartographic materials as historical documents. The instructor is entitled to one free copy of **Mapping Western Civilization: Student Activities** for each copy of the text purchased from HarperCollins.

Sources of the West by Mark Kishlansky, a collection of primary source documents available in two volumes, features a well-balanced selection of constitutional documents, political theory, intellectual history, philosophy, literature, and social description. Review questions follow each selection. Each volume includes the introductory essay, "How to Read a Document," which leads students step by step through the experience of using historical documents.

SuperShell Computerized Tutorial, an interactive program for computer-assisted learning, prepared by Paul A. Bischoff, Oklahoma State University. Features multiple-choice, true-false, and completion quizzes, comprehensive chapter outlines, "Flash Cards" for key terms and concepts, and diagnostic feedback capabilities. Available for IBM computers.

Historical Geography for Western Civilization: Computerized Atlas by William Hamblin, Brigham Young University. Computerized atlas and historical geography tutorial for the Macintosh.

For the Instructor

Instructor's Resource Manual by Margot C. Finn of Emory University. Includes units on Teaching the Western Civilization Course, Teaching with Primary Sources, Teaching Through Film, and Teaching Through Maps as well as a chapter-by-chapter guide to each chapter of the text. The chapter-by-chapter guides contain a chapter synopsis, a list of key terms, and sample questions for class discussion or writing assignments.

Test Bank prepared by Daniel Patrick Brown, Moorpark College, Paul A. Bischoff, Oklahoma State University, and Darryl R. Sycher, Columbus State

Community College. A total of 1500 questions, 50 per text chapter, including both objective and essay questions. Each test item is referenced by topic, type, and text page number. Available in print and computerized format.

TestMaster Computerized Testing System, test-generation software package available for the IBM, Apple, and Macintosh. Allows users to add, edit, and create graphics. Test questions are translatable to word processing software. Available free to adopters.

Visual Archives of Western Civilization—Video Laser Disc includes a "Portrait Gallery" of fine art and photos, over 300 still images and 29 minutes of full-motion film clips. Crisp detail and remote-control access make this supplement especially useful in large lecture halls. An accompanying **Instructor's Guide** contains fully referenced user's notes keyed to the text, a frame-by-frame list of images, and a brief tutorial on using the laser disc in the classroom.

Discovering Western Civilization Through

Maps and Views by Gerald Danzer, University of Illinois at Chicago, and David Buisseret, Newberry Library, Chicago. This set of 100 four-color transparencies from selected sources is bound in a three-ring binder and available free to adopters. Also contains an introduction on teaching history with maps and a detailed commentary on each transparency. The collection includes cartographic and pictorial maps, views, and photos, urban plans, building diagrams, classic maps, and works of art.

The Winner's Circle Video Program, a collection of ten prize-winning films and videos for Western Civilization. Available for loan exclusively to adopters of the text.

The Integrator, a cross-referencing guide to all print, software, and media supplements accompanying the text.

Grades, a grade-keeping and classroom management system maintains date for up to 200 students.

About the Authors

Mark Kishlansky

Recently appointed to the Committee on Social Thought at the University of Chicago, Mark Kishlansky is among today's leading young scholars. After receiving his Ph.D. at Brown University, Professor Kishlansky joined the University of Chicago faculty where he has taught since. A Fellow of the Royal Historical Society, his primary area of expertise is seventeenth-century English political history. Among his main publications are *Parliamentary Selection: Social and Political Choice in Early Modern England* and *The Rise of the New Model Army*. He is the editor of the *Journal of British Studies* and the recipient of the 1989 Most Distinguished Alumnus Award from SUNY Stony Brook.

Patrick Geary

Holding a Ph.D. in Medieval Studies from Yale University, Patrick Geary is both a noted scholar and teacher. Named outstanding undergraduate history teacher for the 1986-87 year at the University of Florida, where he currently teaches, Professor Geary

has also held academic positions at the Ecole des hautes etudes en sciences sociales, Paris, the Universitat Wien, and Princeton University. A member of the Institute for Advanced Study, his many publications include *Readings in Medieval History, Before France and Germany: The Creation and Transformation of the Merovingian World, Aristocracy in Provence: The Rhone Basin at the Dawn of the Carolingian Age*, and *Furta Sacra: Medieval Narratives of Stolen Relics*.

Patricia O'Brien

An Associate Professor at the University of California, Irvine, and Assistant Vice Chancellor in the Office of Research and Graduate Studies, Professor O'Brien holds a Ph.D. from Columbia University in modern European history. Among her many publications are *The Promise of Punishment: Prisons in 19th Century France, l'Embastillement de Paris: The Fortification of Paris During the July Monarchy, Crime and Punishment as Historical Problem*, and Michel Foucault's *History of Culture*.

15

Europe at War, 1555–1648

The Massacre of the Innocents

"War is one of the scourges with which it has pleased God to afflict men," wrote Cardinal Richelieu (1585–1642), the French minister who played no small part in spreading the scourge. War was a constant of European society and penetrated to its very core. It dominated all aspects of life. It enhanced the power of the state, it defined gender roles, it consumed lives and treasure and commodities ravenously. War affected every member of society from combatants to civilians. There were no innocent bystanders. Grain in the fields was destroyed because it was food for soldiers; houses were burned because they provided shelter for soldiers. Civilians were killed for aiding the enemy or holding out against demands for their treasure and supplies. Able-bodied men were taken forcibly to serve as conscripts, leaving women to plant and harvest as best as they could.

There was nothing new about war in the middle of the sixteenth century. The early part of the century had witnessed the dynastic struggle between the Habsburgs and the House of Valois as well as the beginnings of the religious struggle between Catholics and Protestants. But the wars that dominated Europe from 1555 to 1648 brought together the worst of both of these conflicts. War was fought on a larger scale, it was more brutal and more expensive, and it claimed more victims, civilians and combatants alike. During this century war extended throughout the Continent. Dynastic strife, rebellion, and international rivalries joined together with the ongoing struggle over religion. Ambition and faith were an explosive mixture. The French endured forty years of civil war; the Spanish eighty years of fighting with the Dutch. The battle for hegemony in the east led to dynastic strife for decades on end, as Poles, Russians, and Swedes pressed their rival claims to each other's crowns. Finally, in 1618 these separate theaters of war came together in one of the most brutal and terrifying episodes of destruction in European history, the Thirty Years' War.

Neither the ancient temple nor the Roman costume can conceal the immediacy of the picture on the facing page. It is as painful to look at now as it was when it was created over 350 years ago. Painted by Nicolas Poussin (1594–1665) at the height of the Thirty Years' War, the *Massacre of the Innocents* remains a horrifying composition of power, terror, and despair. The cruel and senseless slaughter of the innocent baby which is about to take place is echoed throughout the canvas. Between the executioner's legs can be seen a mother clasping her own child tightly and anticipating the fall of the sword. In the background on the right another mother turns away from the scene and carries her infant to safety. In the foreground strides a mother holding her dead child. She tears at her hair and cries in anguish. To a culture in which the image of mother and child—of Mary and Jesus—was one of sublime peacefulness and inexpressible joy, the contrast could hardly be more shocking.

The picture graphically displays the cruelty of the soldier, the helplessness of the child, and the horror of the mother. By his grip on the mother's hair and his foot on the baby's throat, the warrior shows his brute power. The mother's futile effort to stop the sword illustrates her powerlessness. She scratches uselessly at the soldier's back. Naked, the baby boy raises his hands as if to surrender to the inevitable, as if to reinforce his innocence.

To study Europe at war, we must enter into a world of politics and diplomacy, of issues and principles, of judgment and error. We must talk about armies in terms of their cost and numbers, of generals in terms of their strategy and tactics, of battles in terms of winners and losers. There can be no doubt that the future of Europe was decisively shaped by this century of wholesale slaughter during which dynastic and religious fervor finally ran its course. The survival of Protestantism, the disintegration of the Spanish empire, the rise of Holland and Sweden, the collapse of Poland and Muscovy, the fragmentation of Germany—these were all vital transformations whose consequences would be felt for centuries. We cannot avoid telling this story, untangling its causes, narrating its course, revealing its outcome. But neither should we avoid facing its reality. Look again at the painting by Poussin.

The Crises of the Western States

"*Un roi, une foi, une loi*"—one king, one faith, one law. This was a prescription that members of all European states accepted without question in the sixteenth century. Society was an integrated whole, equally dependent upon monarchical, ecclesiastical, and civil authority for its effective survival. A European state could no more tolerate the presence of two churches than it could the presence of two kings. But the Reformation had created two churches. The coexistence of both Catholics and Protestants in a single realm posed a stark challenge to accepted theory and traditional practice.

In Germany, where the problem first arose, the Peace of Augsburg (1555) enacted the most logical solution. The religion of the ruler was to be the religion of the subjects. Princes, town governments, or bishops would determine faith. Not surprisingly, this was a policy more convenient for rulers than for the ruled. Sudden conversions of princes, a hallmark of Protestantism, threw the state into disarray. Those closely identified with Catholicism as well as those who firmly believed in its doctrines had no choice but to move to a neighboring Catholic community and begin again. Given the dependence of ordinary people upon networks of kin and neighbors, enforced migration was devastating. Protestant minorities in Catholic states suffered the same fate. The enmity between the two groups came as much from bitter experience as from differences of belief.

The problem proved intractable because it admitted only one solution: total victory. There could be no compromise for several reasons. Religious beliefs were profoundly held. Religious controversy was a life-and-death struggle, but it was a struggle between everlasting life and eternal damnation. What happened on earth was of less consequence than what happened in the hereafter. Both Catholics and Protestants revered their martyrs, and in the sixteenth century each religion obliged the other by making new ones. The willingness to die for one's religious beliefs was extremism only to those who did not believe in the extreme importance of religion. Thus compromises that might have brought Protestants back into a reformed Catholic church were doomed from the start.

Doomed too was the practical solution of toleration. To the modern mind, toleration seems so logical that it is difficult to understand why it took over a century of bloodshed before it came to be grudgingly accepted by those countries most bitterly divided. But toleration was not a practical solution in a society that admitted no principle of organization other than one king, one faith. In such a world, toleration was more threatening than warfare. Pope Clement VIII (1592–1605) described liberty of conscience as "the worst thing in the world." Those who advocated limited forms of toleration were universally despised. Those occasions during which toleration was a reluctant basis for a cease-fire were moments for catching breath before resuming the struggle for total victory. Only Poland-Lithuania, Hungary, and a few German states experimented with religious toleration during the sixteenth century.

The crises of the western European states that stretched from the middle of the sixteenth century to the middle of the seventeenth were as much internal and domestic as they were external and international. In France, a half-century of religious warfare sapped the strength of both the monarchy and the nation. In Spain, the protracted revolt of the Netherlands drained men, money, and spirit from the most powerful nation in Europe. Decades of intermittent warfare turned the golden age of Spain to lead and hastened the decline of the Spanish empire. Each crisis had its own causes and its own history. Yet it was no coincidence that they occurred together or that they starkly posed the conflict between the authority of the state and the conscience of the individual. The century between the Peace of Augsburg (1555) and the Peace of Westphalia (1648) was the century of total war.

The French Wars of Religion

No wars are more terrible than civil wars. They tear at the very fabric of society, rending its institutions and destroying the delicate web of relationships that underlie all communal life. The nation is divided; communities break into factions; families are destroyed. At every level of organization the glue that binds society together comes unstuck. Civil wars are wars of passion. The issues that bring them on are not easily resolved because they can rarely be compromised. Something so fundamental is at stake that neither side can yield, something important enough to be worth risking all. Issues become elevated into causes, into principles that form the rallying cry of heroic self-sacrifice or wanton destruction. Civil wars feed on themselves. Each act of war becomes an outrage to be revenged, each act of revenge a new outrage. Passions run deep and, however primitive, the rules for the civilized conduct of war are quickly broken. The loss of lives and property is staggering but the loss of communal identity is greater still. Generations pass before societies recover from their civil wars.

Such was the case with the French wars of religion. For nearly half a century civil war tore France apart. Massacres of Catholic congregations matched massacres of Protestant ones. Assassinations of Catholic leaders followed assassinations of Protestant ones. Kings of France died at the hands of their subjects. Leaders of Protestant and Catholic movements died by the order of the king. Aristocratic armies roamed the country wreaking havoc on friend and foe alike. Indeed, the religious causes that brought the wars about were soon forgotten.

Protestantism came late to France. The unyielding hostility of the monarchy had prevented Lutheran reforms from making much headway there. Through a series of concessions made by the papacy in the fifteenth century, and codified in the Concordat of Bologna (1516), the French kings had gained the right to make ecclesiastical appointments and thus controlled much of the wealth of the Church. Lutheranism held little attraction for Francis I (1515–47) and he rigorously suppressed it, sending John Calvin, among others, into exile. The Catholic church directed by the monarchy proved even more resistant to reform than had the Catholic church directed by the papacy. It was not until after Calvin reformed the church in Geneva and began to export his brand of Protestantism that French society began to divide along religious lines. Calvinist pastors received a warm reception in many French towns. They soon found that they could hardly meet the demand for preaching and instruction from newly formed congregations. By

Religious Divisions in France

1560 there were over two thousand Protestant congregations in France, whose membership totaled nearly 10 percent of the French population. Calvin and his successors concentrated their efforts on large provincial towns and had their greatest success among the middle ranks of urban society, merchants, traders, and craftsmen. They also found a receptive audience among aristocratic women, whose conversions were a turning point in the movement. These women sheltered the fledgling Calvinist congregations before they were able to fend for themselves. Eventually, they also converted their husbands and their sons. By 1560 between one third and one half of the French lesser nobility professed Calvinism.

The wars of religion, however, were brought on by more than the rapid spread of Calvinism. Equally important was the vacuum of power that had been created when Henry II (1547–59) died in a jousting tournament. Surviving Henry were his extraordinary widow, Catherine de Médicis, three daughters, and four sons, the oldest of whom, Francis II (1559–60), was only fifteen. At the best of times the leaders of the French nobility played a high-stakes game for influence with the king. A strong monarch balanced the aristocratic factions at court and made sure that each raked in an occasional pot. Now the accession of a malleable and sickly teenager intensified the competition. Though the aristocracy no longer contested for the throne, it remained inherently dangerous to the crown. High offices were found for all of the leaders of the greatest families and all were kept at court under the watchful eyes of the monarch.

It had taken four kings of France nearly a century to quell the ambitions of the aristocracy. It took Francis II less than a year to revive them. Under the influence of his beautiful young wife, Mary, Queen of Scots, Francis II allowed the Guise family to dominate the great offices of state and to exclude their rivals from power. The Guises controlled the two most powerful institutions of the state, the army and the Church. Two of the Guises were cardinals, and Francis, Duc de Guise, was France's greatest general. The Guises were staunchly Catholic and among their enemies were the Bourbons, princes of the blood with a direct claim to the French throne but also a family with powerful Protestant members. The revelation of a Protestant plot to remove the king from Paris provided the Guises with an opportunity to eliminate their most potent rivals. The Bourbon Duc de Condé, the leading Protestant peer of the realm, was sentenced to death. But five days before Condé's execution, Francis II died and Guise power evaporated. The new king, Charles IX (1560–74) was only ten years old and firmly under the grip of his mother, Catherine de Médicis, who now declared herself regent of France. (See Special Feature, "The Monstrous Regiment of Women," pp. 456–457.)

The diverse elements of Calvinist zeal, monarchical weakness, and aristocratic ambition now combined. Condé's death sentence convinced him that the Guises would stop at nothing to gain their ambitions. Force would have to be met with force. Protestants and Catholics alike raised armies and in 1562 civil war ensued. As was to be the case for nearly four decades, the initial battles were indecisive. Protestant strength lay in the south and west of France, Catholic strength in Paris and the northern portions of the country. Though destructive, aristocratic armies were too weak to wage an offensive war. At best, they could fortify the towns that were under their control and retreat to them in times of danger. In holding Paris, the Catholics held the monarch and this

was their ultimate advantage. But like the Protestant leaders, Catherine de Médicis feared the power of the Guises. Throughout the wars she followed only one principle, to protect the succession of her sons and the authority of the monarchy. However duplicitous were her policies, her purpose was singular.

Because of the tangle of motives among the participants, each side in the struggles had different objectives. Catherine wanted peace and was willing to accept almost any strategy for securing it. War weakened the state and weakened loyalty to the monarch. At first she negotiated with the Bourbons, but she was ultimately forced to accept the fact that the Guises were more powerful. The Guises wanted to suppress Protestantism and eliminate Protestant influence at court. They were willing to undertake the task with or without the king's express support. Once the wars began, the leading Protestant peers had fled the court, but the position of the Guises was not altogether secure. Henry Bourbon, king of Navarre, was the next in line to the throne should Charles IX and his two brothers die without male heirs. Henry had been raised in the Protestant faith by his mother, Jeanne d'Albret, whose own mother, Marguerite of Navarre, was among the earliest protectors of the French Protestants. The objectives of the Huguenots, as the French Calvinists came to be called, were less clear-cut. The townsmen wanted the right to practice their faith, the clergy wanted the right to preach and make converts, and the nobility wanted their rightful place in local government. Almost from the beginning, the Huguenots were on the defensive, fighting to preserve what they already had and to avoid annihilation.

The inconclusive nature of the early battles might have allowed for the pragmatic solution sought by Catherine de Médicis had it not been for the assassination of the Duc de Guise in 1563 by a Protestant fanatic. This act added a personal vendetta to the religious passions of the Catholic leaders. When Charles IX issued the Edict of Amboise (1563), which allowed free worship for Protestant noblemen and restricted worship for all other Huguenots, Catholic leaders deliberately undermined royal policy. They encouraged the slaughter of Huguenot congregations and openly planned the murder of Huguenot leaders. Protestants gave as good as they got, though their movement was limited to a number of fortified towns. Catherine de Médicis looked with horror upon the warfare that physically divided the country and made mockery of the power of the monarchy. In open defiance of Valois dynastic interests, the Guises courted support from Spain, while the Huguenots imported Swiss and German mercenaries to fight in France. Noble factions and irreconcilable religious differences were together pulling the government apart.

By 1570 Catherine was ready to attempt another reconciliation. She blamed the Guises for the failure of the Edict of Amboise and informed Protestant leaders that they would be welcomed back to court and would be placed in positions of trust in the government. Charles IX was nearly twenty years old, and if he lacked the substance of a great monarch, now at least he could make the show of one. Through him Catherine announced her plans for a marriage between her daughter Margaret and Henry of Navarre, a marriage that would symbolize the spirit of conciliation between the crown and the Huguenots. The marriage was to take place in Paris during August 1572, and preparations that befit a royal wedding were under way all that summer. Huguenot lead-

The scene below depicts the mistreatment of French Catholics by the Protestants in the town of Angoulême. They were deprived of all nourishment, dragged over a taut rope, and then slowly roasted at the stake.

ers who had not seen the capital for years came to celebrate the union of Valois and Bourbon as well as the dawn of a new era of peace.

But preparations for the wedding festival were not the only plans being made that summer. The arrival of Huguenot leaders from all over France presented an opportunity of a different kind to the Guises and their supporters. If leading Huguenots could be assassinated in Paris, the Protestant cause might collapse and the truce that the wedding signified might be turned instead into a Catholic triumph. It is not altogether clear how Catherine de Médicis and Charles IX were persuaded to support this reckless plan. The murder of Huguenot leaders had been discussed before, both as an effective policy and as revenge for the killing of the Duc de Guise. What Catherine undoubtedly did know was that her plans to bring a halt to open warfare and to give her son the opportunity to establish his authority depended upon Catholic cooperation. After ten years of civil war it was clear that the Huguenots could not win and the Guises would not accept toleration. Catherine may actually have believed that the death of a few Huguenot leaders might satiate the Catholics. Desperate problems called for desperate solutions.

Saint Bartholomew was the apostle that Jesus described as a man without guile. Ironically it was on his feast day that the Huguenots who had innocently come to celebrate Henry's marriage were led like lambs to the slaughter. The attempt on the life of the first Huguenot leader failed; he was merely wounded by a musket shot. When news of the Guise plot spread, the Huguenots threatened retaliation. These threats were used to justify the subsequent massacre. "Kill them all, the King commands it," was the order given by the young Duc de Guise, intent on revenge for the murder of his father. On 24 August 1572 the streets of Paris ran red with Huguenot blood. Though frenzied, the slaughter was inefficient. Henry of Navarre and a number of other important Huguenots escaped the carnage and returned to their urban strongholds. In the following weeks the violence spread from Paris to the countryside and thousands of Protestants paid for their beliefs with their lives. Until the French Revolution, no event in French history would evoke as much passion as the memory of the Saint Bartholomew's Day massacre.

The Monstrous Regiment of Women

"To promote a woman to bear rule, superiority, dominion or empire above any realm, nation, or city is repugnant to nature, contumely to God, and the subversion of good order, of all equity and justice." So wrote the Scottish theologian John Knox (1513–72) in *The First Blast of the Trumpet Against the Monstrous Regiment of Women* (1558). Though he made his points more emphatically than many others, Knox was only repeating the commonplace notions of his day. He could quote Aristotle and Aquinas as well as a host of secular authorities to demonstrate female inadequacies: "Nature, I say, doth paint them forth to be weak, frail, impatient, feeble, and foolish." He could quote Saint Paul along with the ancient Fathers of the Church to demonstrate the "proper" place of women—"Man is not of the woman, but the woman of the man."

But no stacking up of authorities, no matter how numerous or revered, could erase the fact that all over Europe in the sixteenth century women could and did rule. In the Netherlands Mary, Queen of Hungary (1531–52) and Margaret of Parma (1559–67) were successful regents. Jeanne d'Albret (1562–72) was queen of the tiny state of Navarre, territory claimed by both France and Spain but kept independent by this remarkable woman. Catherine de Médicis (1560–89), wife of one king of France and mother of three others, was the effective ruler of that nation for nearly thirty

years. Mary, Queen of Scots (1542–87) was the nominal ruler of Scotland almost from her birth. England was ruled by two very different women, the Catholic Mary I (1553–58) and her Protestant half-sister Elizabeth I (1558–1603).

The problems faced by this long list of queens and regents were more than just the ordinary cares of government. The belief that women were inherently inferior in intelligence, strength, and character was so pervasive that for men like Knox, a woman ruler was almost a contradiction in terms.

Yet this was not the view taken by everyone, and female rule had its defenders as well as its detractors. One set of objections was overcome by the traditional medieval theory of the two bodies of the monarch. This argument was developed to reconcile the divine origins and functions of monarchs with their very real human frailties. In the theory of the two bodies, there was the body natural and the body politic. Both were joined together in the person of the ruler but the attributes of each could be separated. Rule of a woman did nothing to disrupt this notion. In fact, it made it easier to argue that the frailties of the body natural of a woman were in no way related to the strengths of the body politic of a monarch.

While such ideas might help a female ruler win the acceptance of her subjects, they did little to invigorate her own sense of her role. Female rulers often strained against the strait-

jacket that definitions of gender placed them in. When angered, Elizabeth I would proclaim that she had more courage than her father, Henry VIII, "though I am only a woman." Mary, Queen of Scots, once revealed that her only regret was that she "was not a man to know what life it was to lie all night in the fields or to walk with a buckler and a broadsword." Some queens assumed masculine traits, riding in armor or leading forces to battle. Elizabeth's presence in armor at the threat of the landing of the Spanish Armada was viewed as one of the heroic moments of her reign. Other women rulers mixed together characteristics that were usually separated by gender definitions. Margaret of Parma was considered one of the most accomplished horse riders of her day. After leading her courtiers through woods and fields at breakneck speed, she would then attend council meetings and work on her needlepoint. Mary, Queen of Scots, loved hawking, a traditional kingly sport in the Scottish wilds. After relishing the hawk's destruction of its prey, she liked to negotiate matters of state by beginning with tears and entreaties and ending with accusations and threats. The effect was more than discomforting.

Women were no more nor less successful as rulers than were men. Women's achievements, like men's, depended upon strength of character and the circumstances of the times. All the women rulers of the sixteenth century had received

outstanding educations. Whether raised Catholic or Protestant, each was trained in Latin as well as modern languages, in the liberal arts, and in fine arts. Mary and Elizabeth Tudor of England wrote poetry and played musical instruments with considerable accomplishment. Mary, Queen of Scots, who was raised at the court of France, was considered particularly apt at learning, praise not often accorded a foreigner by the French. Catherine de Médicis, orphaned as an infant, was raised in convents and instructed in the new learning by Italian nuns. It was said that her political instincts were in her blood. Machiavelli had dedicated *The Prince* to her father. Marguerite of Navarre chose one of the leading French humanists to supervise the training of her daughter, Jeanne d'Albret.

Mary, Queen of Scots, was the only one of these female rulers born to rule. She was the sole survivor of her father, who died shortly after her birth. Mary and Elizabeth Tudor came to their thrones after the death of their younger brother

Edward VI; Mary of Hungary and Margaret of Parma came to theirs as princesses of the House of Habsburg. The rule of Catherine de Médicis was the most unexpected of all. Her vigorous husband, Henry II, died during a jousting tournament and her eldest son, Francis II, husband of Mary, Queen of Scots, died the following year. Instead of retirement as a respected queen dowager—the widow of a previous king— Catherine de Médicis was forced into the vortex of French politics to protect the rights of her ten-year-old son, Charles IX.

Unfortunately, the accomplishments of women rulers did little to dispel prejudices against women as a whole or to alter the definition of gender roles. Except for Mary, Queen of Scots, whose principal achievement was to provide an heir to the English throne, all the queens and regents of the sixteenth century were successful rulers. Margaret of Parma steered the careful middle course in the conflict between Spain and the Netherlands. She opposed the intervention of the Duke of Alba, and had her advice been followed, the eighty years of war between Spain and the Netherlands might have been avoided. Catherine de Médicis held the crown of France on the heads of her sons, navigated the treacherous waters of civil war, and provided the model for religious toleration that finally was adopted in the Edict of Nantes. Elizabeth I of England became one of the most beloved rulers

in that nation's history. A crafty politician who learned to balance the factions at her court and who turned the aristocracy into a service class for the crown, she brought nearly a half-century of stability to England at a time when the rest of Europe was in flames.

For most of these queens and regents, marriage was of central importance to their position. Both Mary, Queen of Hungary, and Mary, Queen of Scots, married kings whose reigns were exceedingly brief. Lewis of Hungary died at the battle of Mohács in 1526, just four years after Mary had become his queen. Mary, Queen of Scots, was widowed even sooner and throughout the rest of her remarkable career schemed for remarriage. To strengthen her claim to the throne of England, she married the Scottish Lord Darnley. When he proved unsatisfactory to her plans, she plotted his murder and then married one of his assassins. When this husband died, she sought a match with a powerful English lord who might help her capture Elizabeth's throne. These intrigues finally led to her execution in England in 1587. Mary Tudor married Philip II of Spain in hope of reestablishing Catholicism in England through a permanent alliance with the most powerful Catholic state in Europe. Her dreams went unfulfilled when she failed to produce an heir and the throne passed to her sister Elizabeth who, alone among the women rulers of the period, did not marry.

One King, Two Faiths

The Saint Bartholomew's Day massacre was a transforming event in many ways. In the first place it prolonged the wars. A whole new generation of Huguenots now had an emotional attachment to the continuation of warfare. Their fathers and brothers had been mercilessly slaughtered. By itself the event was shocking enough. But in the atmosphere of anticipated reconciliation created by the wedding, it screamed out for revenge. And the target for retaliation was no longer limited to the Guises and their followers. By accepting its results, the monarchy sanctioned the massacre and spilled Huguenot blood on itself. For over a decade Catherine de Médicis had maintained a distance between the crown and the leaders of the Catholic movement. That distance no longer existed.

Nor could the Huguenots continue to maintain the fiction that they were fighting against the king's evil advisors rather than against the king. After Saint Bartholomew's Day, Huguenot theorists began to develop the idea that resistance to a monarch whose actions violated divine commandments or civil rights was lawful. For the first time, Huguenot writers provided a justification for rebellion. Perhaps most importantly, a genuine revulsion against the massacres swept the nation. A number of Catholic peers now joined with the Huguenots to protest the excesses of the crown and the Guises. These Catholics came to be called the *politiques* from their desire for a practical settlement of the wars. They were led by the duc d'Anjou, next in line to the throne when Charles IX died in 1574 and Henry III (1574–89) became king.

There can be no doubt that whatever strategy had led to the massacres, it had backfired. The defection of important Catholic noblemen from the court further weakened the monarchy. Joining forces with the Huguenots, Anjou inflicted a humiliating defeat upon the new king in 1576, and the authority of the crown was openly flouted. The extreme Catholic party again organized its strength, but it no longer made any pretense of being led by the king. In Paris and a number of other towns the Catholic League was formed, a society that pledged its first allegiance to religion. The League took up where the Saint Bartholomew's Day massacre left off, and the slaughter of ordinary people who unluckily professed the wrong religion continued. Matters grew worse in 1584 when Anjou died. With each passing year it was becoming apparent that Henry III would produce no male heir. After Anjou's death, Henry of Navarre was the next in line for the throne, and he was a Huguenot. The leaders of the Catholic League had little interest in the niceties of the lawful succession. They were

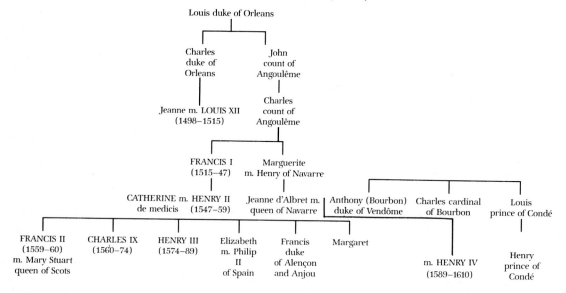

THE HOUSES OF VALOIS AND BOURBON OF FRANCE (to 1610)

interested only in ensuring that the crown of France rested on a Catholic head.

The bolder the League became, the more desperate was the position of the crown. Though Catherine de Médicis had frequently advocated a policy similar to that supported by the *politiques*, after the Saint Bartholomew's Day massacre she had little credit with the Huguenots. Catholic Leaguers talked openly of altering the royal succession and began to develop their own theories of lawful resistance to monarchical power. By 1585, when the final civil war began—the war of the three Henrys, named for Henry III, Henry Guise, and Henry of Navarre—the crown was in the weakest possible position. Paris and the Catholic towns were controlled by the League, the Protestant strongholds by Henry of Navarre. The king could not abandon his capital or his religion, but neither could he gain control of the Catholic party. The extremism of the Leaguers kept the *politiques* away from court, and without the *politiques*, there could be no settlement. To make matters worse, Henry III's military forays against the Huguenots always ended in humiliation while those of Henry Guise ended in triumph. Desperate problems demanded desperate solutions.

In December 1588 Henry III summoned Henry Guise and Guise's brother to a meeting in the royal bedchamber. There they were murdered by the king's order. But the elimination of the leaders of the League did not secure Catholic support for the king. A tactic that might have worked a decade earlier, when the Guises still claimed to represent the crown, now served only to invigorate the League. The *politiques* were blamed for the murders—revenge was taken on a number of them—and Henry III was forced to flee his capital. Paris was still firmly in the hands of the League and Henry was in danger of becoming a king without a country. He made a pact with Henry of Navarre and together royalist and Huguenot forces besieged Paris. All supplies were cut off from the city and only the arrival of a Spanish army prevented its fall. In 1589 Catherine de Médicis died, her ambition to reestablish the authority of the monarchy in shambles, and in the same year a fanatic priest gained revenge for the murder of the Guises by assassinating Henry III.

Finally, Henry of Navarre came into his inheritance. After nearly thirty years of continuous civil war it was certain that a Huguenot could never rule France. The League had already proclaimed a Catholic rival as king, and the pope excommunicated Henry of Navarre and absolved France from loyalty to him. If Henry was to become king of all France, he would have to become a Catholic king. It is not clear when Henry made the decision to accept the Catholic faith—"Paris is worth a mass," he reportedly declared—but he did not announce his decision at once. Rather he strengthened his forces, tightened his bonds with the *politiques*, and urged his countrymen to expel the Spanish invaders. He finally made his conversion public and in 1594 was crowned Henry IV (1589–1610). A war-weary nation was willing to accept the sincerity of its new king rather than endure a seemingly endless struggle. Even the Leaguers were exhausted. Their claimant to the throne had died, and they were now seen as rebels rather than patriots. War had sapped both their treasuries and their spirit. Most of the leading peers on both sides were nearly bankrupt, and Henry IV was willing to pay large cash settlements to all those who would return to their estates and pledge allegiance to him.

Resistance to the reestablishment of the monarchy continued for several years, but Henry IV was a strong and capable ruler. He declared war on Spain to unite his nation against foreign aggression, and he carefully reestablished the balance of aristocratic factions at his court. The league collapsed and moderate Catholics rallied around the king. Though Huguenots and Calvinists everywhere were shocked by Henry's conversion, they were hardly in a position to wage a successful war against their former leader. Henry's accession gave them their first real hope for an enduring settlement with the crown.

In 1598 Henry proclaimed the Edict of Nantes, which granted limited toleration to the Huguenots. It was the culmination of decades of attempts to find a solution to the existence of two religions in one state. It was a compromise that satisfied no one, but it was a compromise that everyone could accept. One king, two faiths was as apt a description of Henry IV as it was of the settlement. Yet neither Henry's conversion nor the Edict of Nantes stilled the passions that had spawned and sustained the French wars of religion. Sporadic fighting between Catholics and Huguenots continued and fanatics on both sides fanned the flames of religious hatred. Henry IV

The French Wars of Religion

1559   Death of Henry II

1560   Protestant Duc de Condé sentenced to death

1562   First battle of wars of religion

1563   Catholic Duc de Guise assassinated

Edict of Amboise grants limited Protestant worship

1572   Saint Bartholomew's Day massacre

1574   Accession of Henry III

1576   Formation of Catholic League

1584   Death of Duc d'Anjou makes Henry of Navarre heir to throne

1585   War of the three Henrys

1588   Duc de Guise murdered by order of Henry III

1589   Catherine de Medicis dies; Henry III assassinated

1594   Henry IV crowned

1598   Edict of Nantes

survived eighteen attempts on his life before he was finally felled by an assassin's knife in 1610. But by then he had reestablished the monarchy and brought a semblance of peace to France.

The World of Philip II

By the middle of the sixteenth century Spain was the greatest power in Europe. The dominions of Philip II (1556–98) of Spain stretched from the Atlantic to the Pacific: his continental territories included the Netherlands in the north and Milan and Naples in Italy. In 1580 Philip became king of Portugal, uniting all the states of the Iberian peninsula. With the addition of Portugal's Atlantic ports and its sizable fleet, Spanish maritime power was now unsurpassed. Spain was also a great cultural and intellectual center. The fashions and tastes of its golden age dominated all the courts of Europe. The expansion of Spanish dominion and the increase in Spain's wealth and prestige was reflected in a self-conscious spirit of

national pride that could be seen even in the story of Don Quixote, the knight who tilted at windmills in search of greatness in the novel published by Miguel de Cervantes (1547–1616) between 1605 and 1615.

Great power meant great responsibilities, and few monarchs took their tasks more seriously than did Philip II. Trained from childhood for the cares of office, he exceeded all expectations. Philip II earned his reputation as "King of Paper" by maintaining a grueling work schedule. Up at eight and at mass soon afterwards, he met with his advisers and visitors on official business until noon. After a brief lunch, he began the real business of the day, the study of the mountains of papers that his empire generated. Though summaries were prepared of the hundreds of documents he handled each day, Philip II frequently read and annotated the longer originals. No detail was too small to escape his attention. His work day often lasted ten hours or longer. Even when he was traveling, his secretaries carried huge chests of state papers that Philip studied in his carriage and annotated on a portable desk that always accompanied him.

There was good reason why this slightly stooped king appeared as if he had the weight of the world on his shoulders. In the Mediterranean, Spain alone stood out against the expansion of Ottoman power. The sultan's navy continually threatened to turn the Mediterranean into a Turkish lake, while his armies attempted to capture and hold Italian soil. All Europe shuddered at the news of each Ottoman advance. Popes called for holy wars against the Turks but only Philip heeded the cry. From nearly the moment that he inherited the Spanish crown he took up the challenge of defending European Christianity. For over a decade Philip maintained costly coastal garrisons in North Africa and Italy and assembled large fleets and larger armies to discourage or repel Turkish invasions. This sparring could not go on indefinitely, and in 1571 both sides prepared for a decisive battle. A combined Spanish and Italian force of over three hundred ships and eighty thousand men met an even larger Ottoman flotilla off the coast of Greece. The Spanish naval victory at Lepanto was considered one of the great events of the sixteenth century, celebrated in story and song for the next three hundred years. Though the Turks continued to menace the Mediterranean islands, Lepanto marked the end of Ottoman advances.

If Philip II saw himself as a Christian monarch fending off the advance of the infidel, he also saw himself as a Catholic monarch fending off the spread of heresy. There can be no doubt of Philip's personal devotion to Catholicism or of his oft-expressed conviction that "I would prefer to lose all my dominions and a hundred lives if I had them [rather] than be lord over heretics." The lives that were to be lost in battling heretics were numbered not in hundreds, but in hundreds of thousands. Philip II came to the throne at just the moment that Calvinism began its rapid growth in northern Europe. He supported the Catholic cause in France throughout the civil wars, sending money, advisers, and ultimately an army to relieve Paris. His ambassadors urged Catherine de Médicis and her sons to take the most repressive measures against the Huguenots, including the Saint Bartholomew's Day massacre.

Philip was equally aggressive against English Protestants. For a brief time he had been king in England through his marriage to Mary I (1553–58). He encouraged Mary's efforts to restore the Catholic church in England and supported her policies of repression. When Mary died and Elizabeth I (1558–1603) rejected his marriage proposal, his limited rule in England came to an end. From then on England and Spain entered a long period of hostility. English pirates raided Spanish treasure ships returning to Europe and Elizabeth covertly aided both French and Dutch Protestants. Finally in 1588 Philip decided upon invasion. A great fleet set sail from the Portuguese coast to the Netherlands, where a large Spanish army stood waiting to be conveyed to England.

The Spanish Armada comprised over 130 ships, many of them the pride of the Spanish and Portuguese navies. They were bigger and stronger than anything possessed by the English, whose forces were largely merchant vessels hastily converted for battle. But the English ships were faster and more easily maneuverable in the unpredictable winds of the English Channel. They also contained guns that could easily be reloaded for multiple firings, while the Spanish guns were designed to discharge only one broadside before hand-to-hand combat ensued. With these advantages the English were able to prevent the Armada from reaching port in the Netherlands and to destroy many individual ships as they were blown off course. The defeat of the Spanish Armada was less a military than a psychological blow to Philip II. He could more easily replace ships than restore confidence in Spanish power.

The Burgundian Inheritance

This confidence was all the more necessary when Philip II faced the gravest crisis of his reign: the revolt of the Netherlands. Though Philip's father, Charles V, amassed a great empire, he had begun only as the Duke of Burgundy. Charles' Burgundian inheritance encompassed a diverse territory in the northwestern corner of Europe. The seventeen separate provinces of this territory were called the Netherlands or the Low Countries because of the flooding that kept large portions of them under water. The Netherlands was one of the richest and most populous regions of Europe, an international leader in manufacturing, banking, and above all, commerce. Antwerp and Amsterdam were bustling port cities with access to the North Sea; inland were the prosperous industrial towns of Ghent and Brussels. The preeminence of the Netherlands was all the more remarkable because the provinces themselves were divided geographically, culturally, and linguistically. Rivers, lakes, and flooded plains separated the southern provinces, where French was the background and language of the inhabitants, from the northern ones where Germans had settled and Dutch was spoken. Charles V attempted to unify the provinces by removing them from the

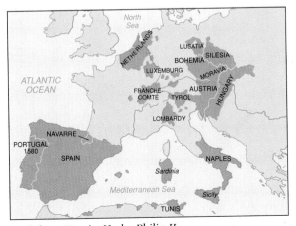

Habsburg Empire Under Philip II

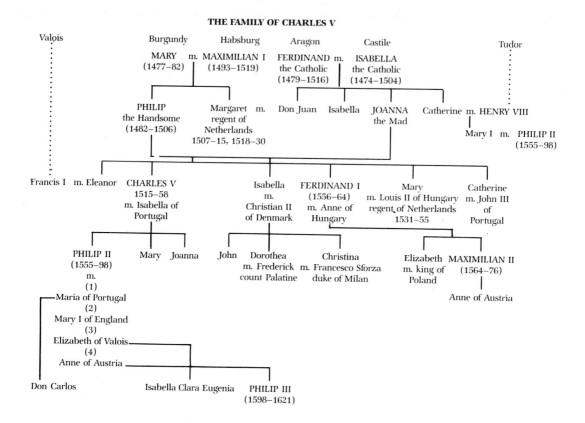

THE FAMILY OF CHARLES V

jurisdiction of the Holy Roman Empire and establishing a separate regency under his eldest son, Philip II. Thus the future of the Netherlands was tied to Spain and the New World when Philip II set sail for Castile in 1559 to claim the crown of Spain.

Though Philip II had every intention of returning to the Low Countries, in fact the Netherlands had seen the last of their king. Philip left his half-sister, Margaret of Parma, as regent and provided her with a talented group of Spanish administrators to carry out policies that were to be formulated in Madrid. As Philip's own grasp on the affairs of the Netherlands loosened, so did the loyalty of the native nobility to the absent monarch. The resentments that built up were the traditional ones—hostility to foreigners, distrust of royal advisors, and contempt for policies that lacked understanding of local conditions. All of these discontents came together over Philip's religious policies. The Low Countries had accepted the Peace of Augsburg in a spirit of conciliation in which it was never intended. Here Catholics, Lutherans, Anabaptists, and Calvinists peaceably coexisted. Though the laws against

heresy promulgated by Charles V and Philip II ostensibly pertained to the Low Countries, local magistrates rarely enforced them.

As in France, this situation changed dramatically with the spread of Calvinism. In their cat-and-mouse game with Catholic authorities, French Calvinists crossed back and forth along the borders of the provinces. The heavy concentration of urban populations in the Low Countries provided the natural habitat for Calvinist preachers, who made converts across the entire social spectrum. While in France Calvinism survived as a religion of the nobility and middle classes, in the Netherlands it attracted peasants, laborers, and artisans as well. As Holy Roman Emperor, Charles V may have made his peace with Protestants, but as king of Spain he had not. Charles V had maintained the purity of the Spanish Catholic church through a sensible combination of reform and repression. Philip II intended to pursue a similar policy in the Low Countries. With papal approval he initiated a scheme to reform the hierarchy of the Church by expanding the numbers of bishops, and he invited the Jesuits to establish schools for orthodox learning. Simultaneously, he strengthened the power of the Inquisition and ordered the enforcement of the decrees of the Council of Trent.

Philip's intended reforms ran into immediate difficulties. In the first place there were the Protestants, not only aggressive Calvinists, but also settled Lutherans and Anabaptists who lived quietly in their own communities. They sought the protection of their local nobility who, Catholic or Protestant, had their own reasons for opposing the strict enforcement of heresy laws. Philip's harsh dictates threatened the uneasy peace that kept religious extremists from each other's throats. Moreover, the imposition of the Inquisition robbed local governors of their long-established powers. Provincial nobility and magistrates resented both the policies that were being pursued and the fact that they disregarded local autonomy. Town governors and noblemen refused to cooperate in implementing the new laws. Leading Protestants like Prince William of Orange, one of the largest landholders in the Netherlands, and Count Egmont, an outstanding military leader, urged Margaret to adopt a policy of toleration along the lines of the Peace of Augsburg and made clear that they would resign from office rather than support anything else.

The Revolt of the Netherlands

The passive resistance of nobles and magistrates was soon matched by the active resistance of the Calvinists. Unable to enforce Philip's policy, Margaret and her advisers agreed to a limited toleration. But in the summer of 1566, before it could be put into effect, bands of Calvinists unleashed a storm of iconoclasm in the provinces, breaking stained glass windows and statues of the Virgin and the saints, which they claimed were idolatrous. Catholic churches were stormed and turned into Calvinist meeting houses. Local authorities were helpless in the face of determined Calvinists and apathetic Catholics; they could not protect Church property. Iconoclasm gave way to open revolt. Fearing social rebellion, even the leading Protestant noblemen took part in suppressing these riots. But they could not escape blame for having encouraged the weakening of royal resolve. Many found it prudent to retire to estates outside the Netherlands. It was a prudence that saved their lives.

In Spain, the events in the Netherlands were treated for what they were: open rebellion. Despite the fact that Margaret had already restored order, Philip II was determined to punish the rebels and enforce the heresy laws. A large military force under the command of the Duke of Alba (1507–82), Philip's ablest general, whose record of success was matched only by his record of brutality, was sent from Spain as an army of occupation. As befit a warrior who had made his reputation leading imperial troops against the Lutherans, Alba gave no quarter to the Protestants of the Netherlands. Like Machiavelli, he believed that terror was more effective than mercy: "Everyone must be made to live in constant fear of the roof breaking down over his head," he wrote.

Alba lured Count Egmont and other Protestant noblemen to Brussels, where he publicly executed them in 1568. He also established a military court to punish participants in the rebellion, a court that came to be called the Council of Blood. The Council handed down over nine thousand convictions, a thousand of which carried the death penalty. As many as sixty thousand Protestants fled beyond Alba's jurisdiction, swelling the Protestant population of France and the northern provinces. Alba next made an example of several small towns that had been implicated in the iconoclasm. He allowed his soldiers to pillage the towns at will before slaughtering their entire populations and razing them to the ground. By the end of 1568 royal policy had gained a sullen acceptance in the Netherlands, but the hostilities did not end. For the next eighty years, with only occasional truces, Spain and the Netherlands were at war.

Like the French civil wars, the Dutch revolts fed upon themselves. Alba's policies drove Protestants into rebellion. This forced the Spanish government to maintain its army by raising taxes from those provinces that had remained loyal. Soon the loyal provinces too were in revolt, not over religion, but over taxation and local autonomy. In 1571 a number of southern provinces staged a tax strike against Alba's plan to collect the "tenth penny," a 10 percent levy on trade. Tax resistance and fear of an invasion from France left Alba unprepared for the series of successful assaults Protestants launched in the northern provinces during 1572. Though their forces were never a match for Alba's battle-tested veterans, the Protestant generals were able to take advantage of the geography of the provinces to capture coastal towns and establish a permanent base in the northwestern provinces of Holland and Zeeland. By 1575 the Protestants had gained a stronghold that they would never relinquish. Prince William of Orange assumed the leadership of the two provinces that were now united against the tyranny of Philip's rule. Though neither province had been predominantly Calvinist at the beginning of the revolts, both became progressively so as exiles from the south fled Spanish persecution. Spanish persecution of Protestants in the south was matched by Calvinist persecution of Catholics in the north. Despite sincere efforts by William—who himself had been Catholic, Lutheran, and Calvinist—the newly united provinces were no more tolerant of religious differences than was the old Habsburg one.

Spanish government was collapsing all over the Netherlands. William ruled in the north, and the States-General, a parliamentary body composed of representatives from the separate provinces, ruled in the south. Margaret of Parma had resigned in disgust at Alba's tactics, and Alba had been relieved of his command when his tactics had failed. No one was in control of the Spanish army. The soldiers, who had gone years with only partial pay, now roamed the southern provinces looking for plunder. Brussels and Ghent both had been targets, and in 1576 the worst atrocities of all occurred when mutinous Spanish troops sacked Antwerp. One of the wealthiest cities in Europe, home to the most important mercantile and banking establishments in the world, Antwerp was torn apart like a roasted pig. The rampage lasted for days. When it ended over seven thousand people had been slaughtered and nearly a third of the city burned to the ground.

The "Spanish fury" in Antwerp effectively ended Philip's rule over his Burgundian inheritance. The Protestants had established a permanent home in the north—whose borders would shift continually over the next thirty years. The States-General had established its ability to rule in the south, and Spanish policy had been totally discredited. To achieve a settlement, the Pacification of Ghent of 1576, the Spanish government conceded local autonomy in taxation, the central

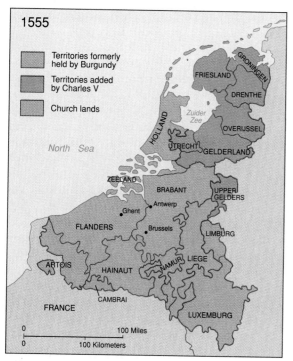

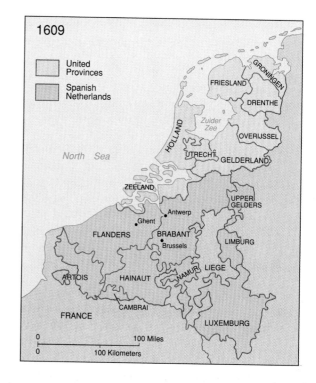

The Revolt of the Netherlands

Revolt of the Netherlands

1559 Margaret of Parma named regent of the Netherlands

1566 Calvinist iconoclasm begins revolt

1567 Duke of Alba arrives in Netherlands and establishes Council of Blood

1568 Protestant Count Egmont executed

1571 "Ten Penny" revolt begins

1572 Protestants capture Holland and Zeland

1573 Alba relieved of his command

1576 Sack of Antwerp

Pacification of Ghent

1581 Catholic and Protestant provinces split

1585 Spanish forces under Alexander Farnese take Brussels and Antwerp

1609 Twelve Years' Truce

role of the States-General in legislation, and the immediate withdrawal of all Spanish troops from the Low Countries. Five southern provinces pledged to remain Catholic and to accept the authority of the king's regent. This rift among the provinces was soon followed by a permanent split. In 1581 one group of provinces voted to depose Philip II while a second group decided to remain loyal to him.

The cost of the revolts was staggering. Commerce and agriculture throughout the Low Countries had been permanently disrupted and vast movements of population had occurred. All this tore at the fabric of Burgundian society. For Spain the price was reckoned in gold—pounds and pounds of South American specie went to finance year after year of indecisive military campaigns. Though as early as the 1570s it was clear that the war could not be won, decade after decade it continued. Philip II refused to accept the dismemberment of his inheritance and refused to recognize the independent Dutch state that now existed in Holland. Throughout the 1580s and 1590s military expeditions attempted to reunite

the southern provinces and to conquer the northern ones. Appointed commander of Spanish forces in 1578, Alexander Farnese, Margaret of Parma's son, brought the southern and eastern provinces back under Spanish control. He took Ghent in 1584, Brussels and Antwerp in 1585. But Spanish military successes in the south were outweighed by the long-term failure of their objectives in the north. In 1609 Spain and the Netherlands concluded the Twelve Years' Truce, which tacitly recognized the existence of the state of Holland. By the beginning of the seventeenth century Holland was not only an independent state, it was one of the greatest rivals of Spain and Portugal for the fruits of empire.

The Reorganization of Northeastern Europe

In eastern Europe dynastic struggles outweighed the problems created by religious reform. Muscovy remained the bulwark of Eastern Orthodox Christianity, immune from the struggles over the Roman faith. Protestantism did spread into Poland-Lithuania, but unlike in the west, the Polish state tolerated its presence. The spread of dissent was checked not by repression, but by a vigorous Catholic reformation led by the Jesuits. The domestic crises in the east were crises of state rather than of church. The biological failure of the Jagiellon monarchy in Poland ended that nation's most successful line of kings. Without a natural heir, the Polish nobility and gentry, who officially elected the monarch, had to peddle their throne among the princes of Europe. In Muscovy, the disputed succession that followed the death of Ivan the Terrible plunged the state into anarchy and civil war. Centuries of conflict between Poland-Lithuania and Muscovy came to a head with the Poles' desperate gamble to seize control of their massive eastern neighbor. War between Poland-Lithuania and Muscovy inevitably dominated the politics of the entire region. The Baltic states, of which Sweden was to become the most important, had their own ambitions for territory and economic gain. They soon joined the fray, making alliances in return for concessions and conquering small pieces of the mainland.

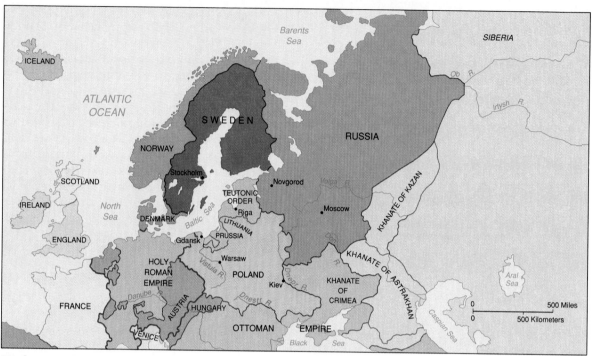

Northeastern Europe, ca. 1550

Religious conflict may not have been a national problem in eastern Europe, but it was an international one. The persistent warfare between the Roman-dominated Christianity of Poland-Lithuania and the Eastern Orthodox Christianity of Muscovy always had a religious tinge to it. Along the Baltic Sea, the Roman Catholic settlements of the Knights of the Teutonic Order crusaded for religious converts. Adherents of both Roman and Eastern Christianity belonged to the Lithuanian aristocracy. Sometimes these nobles were subject to Polish rule, at other times to Muscovite. Poland had a large minority of Eastern Christians. The Poles saw themselves as the bulwark of Roman Catholicism in Europe and justified their offensive wars against Muscovy as efforts to defend and to spread the true faith.

But the most important source of religious conflict in northeastern Europe resulted from the rise to prominence of the Lutheran state of Sweden. Before religious reformation swept Sweden, the country's traditional enemies had been the Danes and the Russians, who kept the Swedes hemmed in by the Baltic Sea. Security rather than religion motivated these hostilities. In 1587 the heir to the Swedish crown, Sigismund Vasa, was

elected king of Poland. Though he lived in a Lutheran land, Sigismund had a Jesuit upbringing and strongly supported Jesuit reforms in Poland. When Sigismund inherited the Swedish crown in 1592, the Lutheran nobility faced a new threat to its religious and national independence. To protect both, the Swedes were forced into an active role in European affairs, a role that propelled their tiny nation into one of the greatest powers of the seventeenth century.

The Struggles in the East

In 1572 Sigismund II (1548–72) of Poland died without an heir. Though the Polish monarchy was elective rather than hereditary, during the centuries of rule by the Jagiellon family the electoral process had more form than substance. Sons succeeded their fathers to the throne and the Jagiellons regarded the Polish and Lithuanian crowns as their rightful inheritance. But now there were no heirs and the nobility and gentry of Poland-Lithuania had to select their king from among the princes of Europe. In fact, the next three Polish kings were so chosen, giving the Polish crown successively to a prince of France, a prince of Transylvania, and finally a prince of Sweden. Each was bound more tightly than his predecessor to a set of constitutional and religious restrictions that protected the power and privileges of the nobility and gentry. Matters of war and peace, of taxation, and of reform were placed under the strict supervision of the Polish Diet, a parliamentary body that represented the Polish landed elite. The Diet also carefully controlled religious policy. Roman Catholicism was the principal religion in Poland but the state tolerated numerous Protestant and Eastern creeds. In the Warsaw Confederation of 1573 the Polish gentry vowed "that we who differ in matters of religion will keep the peace among ourselves," a remarkable pledge that was honored by kings and subjects for over a half of a century. Poland was the only state in Europe where religious toleration was practiced as well as preached.

Until the end of the sixteenth century, Poland-Lithuania was the dominant power in the eastern part of Europe. It was economically healthy and militarily strong. Through its Baltic ports, especially Gdansk, Poland played a central role in international commerce and a dominant role in the northern grain trade. Poland's agricultural surplus nourished the Netherlands during the long years of civil war. The vast size of the Polish state made defense difficult, and during the course of the sixteenth century it had lost lands to Muscovy in the east and to the Crimean Tartars in

An assembly of the Polish Diet, the parliamentary body composed of the landed elite. On the throne is Sigismund III. Rivalry among the magnates weakened the Diet, and conflicts with the elected monarchs were frequent.

the south. But the permanent union with Lithuania in 1569 and the gradual absorption of the Baltic region of Livonia more than compensated for these losses. The Poles were able to raise and maintain large armies, and when the Polish Diet thought that the prize was worth fighting for, it could finance long and costly campaigns.

When Sigismund III (1587–1632) was elected to the Polish throne in 1587, he was also heir to the crown of Sweden. His Jesuit upbringing, under the direction of his Polish mother, was an ideal background for extending the Catholic reformation in Poland. Sigismund accepted the prohibitions against religious repression outlined in the Warsaw Confederation, but he actively encouraged the establishment of Jesuit schools, the expansion of monastic orders, and the strengthening of the Roman Catholic church. During his reign the numbers and importance of Protestant gentry declined significantly.

All of these policies enjoyed the approval of the Polish ruling classes. But the Diet would not support Sigismund's efforts to gain control of the Swedish crown, which he inherited in 1592 but from which he was deposed three years later. The Polish gentry had little to gain and much to lose from their king's success in Sweden. They were uninterested in the spoils to be taken from Sweden's poor agrarian economy and unimpressed by the prospect of converting the Swedes to Roman Catholicism. If Sigismund triumphed in Sweden, all Poland would get was a part-time monarch. The Polish Diet consistently refused to give the king the funds necessary to invade Sweden successfully. Nevertheless, Sigismund mounted several unsuccessful campaigns against the Swedes, campaigns that sapped Polish money and manpower.

If their king was to be militarily aggressive, the leaders of the Diet preferred that he look east rather than north. Before the seventeenth century there was little history of hostility between Poland and Sweden; between Poland and Muscovy there was no history of anything else. The wars of Ivan the Great and Ivan the Terrible in the fifteenth and sixteenth centuries were waged to secure agricultural territory in the west and a Baltic port in the north. Both objectives came at the expense of Poland-Lithuania. But following the death of Ivan the Terrible in 1584, the Muscovite state began to disintegrate. For years it had been held together only by conquest and fear—the military service class received prizes of captured territory; the boyars, or hereditary nobility, were cowed by Ivan's brutal policies. Ivan's conflicts with the boyars created an aristocracy unwilling and unable to come to the aid of his successors. Landowners and merchants retreated eastward beyond Ivan's grasp, leaving the center of the country depopulated. Siberia was colonized and its riches discovered by those who preferred the Arctic's frigid winters to Ivan's torrid temper. Near-anarchy prevailed in the south as Tartars raided Russian settlements for slaves and bands of Cossacks pillaged them for food. Peasant revolts followed harvest failures as the fragile agrarian economy broke down.

By 1601 the crown was plunged into a crisis of legitimacy known as the Time of Troubles. Ivan had murdered his heir in a fit of anger and left his half-witted son to inherit the throne. This led to a vacuum of power at the center as well as a struggle for the spoils of government. Private armies ruled great swaths of the state and pretenders to the crown—all claiming to be Dimitri, the lost brother of the last legitimate tsar—appeared everywhere. Ambitious groups of boyars backed their own claimants to the throne. So, too, did ambitious foreigners who eagerly sought to carve up Muscovite possessions.

Muscovy's Time of Troubles was Poland's moment of opportunity. While anarchy and civil war raged—perhaps as many as two and a half million people perished in one decade—Poland looked to regain the territory that it had lost to Muscovy over the previous century. Sigismund abandoned war with Sweden in order to intervene in the struggle for the Russian crown. Polish forces crossed into Muscovy and Sigismund's generals backed one of the strongest of the false Dimitris. They provided him with Jesuits for religious instruction and a Polish princess for a wife. Their plan to put him on the throne failed when he was assassinated. Sigismund used the death of the last false Dimitri as a pretext to assert his own claim to the Muscovite crown. More Polish forces poured across the frontier. In 1610 they took Moscow and Sigismund proclaimed himself tsar, intending to unite the two massive states.

The Russian boyars, so long divided, now rose against the Polish enemy. The Polish garrison in Moscow was starved into submission and a native Russian, Michael Romanov (1613–45) was chosen tsar by an assembly of landholders, the Zemsky Sobor. He made a humiliating peace with the Swedes—who had also taken advantage of the Time of Troubles to invade Muscovy's Baltic provinces—in return for Swedish assistance against the Poles. Intermittent fighting continued for another twenty years. In the end, Poland agreed to peace and a separate Muscovite state, but only in exchange for large territorial concessions. Peace allowed Tsar Michael to establish the legitimacy of his rule, rebuild his shattered state and to plot his revenge.

THE JAGIELLON MONARCHY OF POLAND

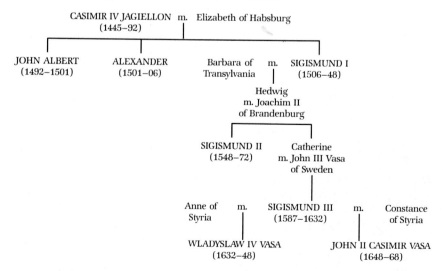

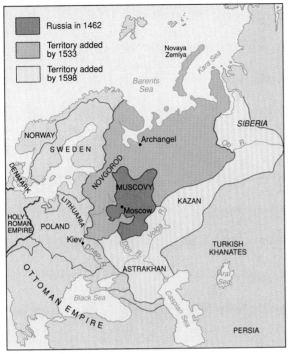

Russia in 1462

Territory added
by 1533

Territory added
by 1598

The Rise of Russia

The Rise of Sweden

Sweden's rise to power during the seventeenth century was as startling as it was swift. Until the Reformation, Sweden had been part of the Scandinavian confederation ruled by the Danes. Although the Swedes had a measure of autonomy, they were very much a junior partner in Baltic affairs. Denmark controlled the narrow sound that linked the Baltic with the North Sea, and its prosperity derived from the tolls it collected on imports and exports. When, in 1523, Gustavus Vasa led the uprising of the Swedish aristocracy that ended Danish domination, he won the right to rule over a poor, sparsely populated state with few towns or developed seaports. Its internal economy was based almost entirely on barter and most of its vast territory, which included Lapland in the north and Finland in the east, was uninhabitable.

The Vasas ruled Sweden in conjunction with the aristocracy. Although the throne was hereditary, the part played by the nobility in elevating Gustavus I Vasa (1523–60) gave the nobles a powerful voice in Swedish affairs. Through the council of state, known as the Rad, the Swedish nobility exerted a strong check on the monarch.

Still, the active engagement of the nobility in civil government meant that the king could count on their resources in times of crisis. This became increasingly important as Sweden took a greater interest in Baltic affairs.

Sweden's aggressive foreign policy began accidentally. When in the 1550s the Teutonic Knights found themselves no longer capable of ruling in Livonia, the Baltic seaports that had been under their dominion scrambled for new alliances. Muscovy and Poland-Lithuania were the logical choices, but the town of Reval, an important outlet for Russian trade near the mouth of the Gulf of Finland, asked Sweden for protection. After some hesitation, since the occupation of territory on the southern shores of the Baltic would involve great expense, Sweden fortified Reval in 1560. A decade later, Swedish forces captured Narva, farther to the east, and consolidated their hold on the Livonian coast. By occupying the most important ports on the Gulf of Finland, Sweden could control a sizable portion of the Muscovite trade.

Having gained so much so soon, the Swedes yearned to gain more. Only two obstacles prevented them from dominating trade with Muscovy: Archangel in the north and Riga in the south. In the 1580s, as the Muscovites pushed eastward across their immense territories, they established a port at Archangel on the White Sea. With this new port they opened a trading route to the west, around northern Scandinavia. There were two advantages of the Arctic route; it made direct trade between Muscovy and the west possible and it avoided the Danish tolls in the Baltic. In the west, England and the Low Countries benefited from the White Sea trade, being directly in its route. In the east, Sweden benefited by claiming the northern portions of the Scandinavian peninsula necessary to make the trade secure. In all of their dealings with Muscovy the Swedes sought further privileges at Archangel while laying plans for its conquest. Riga was a problem of a different sort. It was the most important port in Livonia, providing easy access to the Lithuanian and Russian hinterland. Under Polish domination it was the center for Poland's eastern trade. As the Swedes secured the northern Livonian ports, more of the Muscovy trade moved to the south and passed through Riga. It, too, would have to be captured or blockaded if the Swedes were to control commerce in the eastern Baltic.

Surprisingly, it was not Swedish belligerence that initiated the near continuous warfare of the next half-century. Though the ambition may have been to control the Muscovy trade, Sweden had very little prospect of actually doing so. Poland was far too strong to be challenged over Livonia, and Denmark also laid claim to the northern Scandinavian coast. But the fact that Sweden aspired to power in the Baltic made Livonia a more attractive target than ever before. Because Sigismund III, king of Poland, was also heir to the Swedish crown, it became possible that a combination of Swedish and Polish forces would challenge Danish dominion in the Baltic. Yet it soon became clear that the Swedes were far more interested in their religious liberty and national freedom than they were in the spoils of commerce. Sigismund's aggressive alliance with the Polish Jesuits persuaded the Swedish nobility that he would undermine their Lutheran church. Sigismund was deposed in favor of his uncle Charles IX (1604–11). Soon Sweden was fighting simultaneously with the Poles and the Danes.

Both conflicts were initially disastrous. War with Poland resulted from Sigismund's efforts to regain the Swedish crown. The Swedes used the opportunity to blockade Riga and to occupy more Livonian territory. The Swedish navy was far superior to any force that the Poles could assemble, but on land Polish forces were masters. The Swedish invasion force suffered a crushing defeat and had to retreat to its coastal enclaves. The Poles now had an opportunity to retake all of Livonia but, as always, the Polish Diet was reluctant to finance Sigismund's wars. Furthermore, Sigismund had his eyes on a bigger prize. Rather than follow up its Swedish victory, Poland invaded Muscovy.

Meanwhile, the blockade of Riga and the assembly of a large Swedish fleet in the Baltic threatened Denmark. The Danes continued to claim sovereignty over Sweden and took the opportunity of the Polish-Swedish conflict to reassert it. In 1611, under the energetic leadership of the Danish king Christian IV (1588–1648), Denmark invaded Sweden from both the east and the west. The Danes captured the towns of Kalmar and Alvsborg and threatened to take Stockholm. The loss of Alvsborg was of critical importance. A large part of the Swedish fleet was anchored there, and it was the only Swedish port that let out

A Livonian peasant. Livonia was conquered by Ivan the Terrible in his campaign of 1563, but was soon reclaimed by the Poles. In 1660 Livonia became part of the Swedish empire. Livonia was originally inhabited by the Livs, a Finnish people.

directly on the North Sea. To end the Danish war, Sweden accepted humiliating terms in 1613. Not only did Sweden renounce all claims to the northern coasts and recognize Danish control of the Arctic trading route, but Alvsborg remained in Danish possession for six years until a huge ransom had been paid.

Paradoxically, these setbacks became the springboard for Swedish success. Fear of the Danes led both the English and the Dutch into alliances with Sweden. The countries all shared Protestant interests, and the English were heavily committed to the Muscovy trade, which was still an important part of Swedish commerce. It was the Dutch who financed the ransom of Alvsborg. In exchange for Swedish iron and copper, the Dutch provided credit to meet the stiff annual payments. Fear of the Poles had a similar effect upon Muscovy. In 1609 the Swedes agreed to send five thousand troops to Muscovy to help repel the Polish invasion. In return, Muscovy agreed to cede to Sweden its Baltic possessions. This was accomplished in 1617 and gave Sweden complete control of the Gulf of Finland.

In 1611, during the middle of the Danish war, Charles IX died and was succeeded by his son Gustavus Adolphus (1611–32). Unlike his father and cousin before him, who had come by chance to the Swedish throne, Gustavus Adolphus was raised to be king. Gruff and affable by turns, he was one of the leading Protestant princes of his day, in every way a match for Christian IV of Denmark. Gustavus' greatest skills were military. He inherited an ample navy and an effective army. Unlike nearly every other European state, Sweden raised its forces from its own citizens. Gustavus' predecessors had made important innovations in the training of soldiers and in their battlefield tactics. These the new king improved upon. He introduced new weapons like the light mobile gun and reshaped his army into standard-size squadrons and regiments, which were easier to administer and deploy.

The calamitous wars inherited from his father occupied Gustavus during the early years of his reign. He was forced to conclude the humiliating peace with the Danes in 1613 and to go to war with the Russians in 1614 to secure the Baltic coastal estates that had been promised in 1609. Gustavus' first military initiative was to resume war with Poland in order to force Sigismund to renounce his claim to the Swedish throne. In 1621 Gustavus landed in Livonia and in two weeks captured Riga, the capstone of Sweden's Baltic ambitions. Occupation of Riga increased Swedish control of the Muscovy trade and it deprived Den-

The Rise of Sweden

mark of a significant portion of its customs duties. Gustavus now claimed Riga as a Swedish port and successfully demanded that ships sailing from there pay tolls to Sweden rather than Denmark. The capture of Riga firmly established Sweden as a co-equal Baltic power.

By the mid-seventeenth century, the Sweden of Gustavus Adolphus was well on its way to international prominence. The capture of Riga gave Sweden complete control of the eastern Baltic and ended Polish pretensions to the Swedish

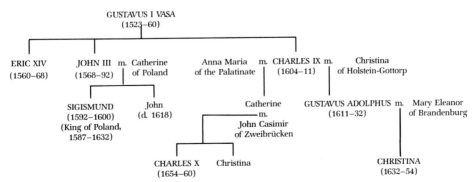

THE HOUSE OF VASA OF SWEDEN

GUSTAVUS I VASA
(1523–60)

ERIC XIV
(1560–68)

JOHN III   m.   Catherine
(1568–92)   of Poland

SIGISMUND
(1592–1600)
(King of Poland,
1587–1632)

John
(d. 1618)

CHARLES X
(1654–60)

Christina

Anna Maria   m.   CHARLES IX   m.   Christina
of the Palatinate   (1604–11)   of Holstein-Gottorp

Catherine
m.
John Casimir
of Zweibrücken

GUSTAVUS ADOLPHUS   m.   Mary Eleanor
(1611–32)   of Brandenburg

CHRISTINA
(1632–54)

throne. In 1619 Alvsborg returned to Swedish hands and immediately began a prosperous trade with the Dutch. A negotiated settlement with the Danes over the collection of tolls enhanced Swedish prestige and increased Sweden's commercial prosperity. Moreover, Gustavus' marriage into the family of the Protestant rulers of Prussia gave Sweden a presence in Germany as well. For the time being Sweden faced east. But the storm clouds of religious warfare were already bursting over the Holy Roman Empire. Gustavus Adolphus now took his place among the Protestant princes of Europe, and Sweden ranked among the leading Protestant powers.

Gustavus Adolphus of Sweden, shown at the Battle of Breitenfeld in 1631. The battle was the first important Protestant victory of the Thirty Years' War. Gustavus died on the battlefield at Lützen in the following year.

The Thirty Years' War

Perhaps it was just a matter of time before the isolated conflicts that dotted the corners of Europe were joined together. At the beginning of the seventeenth century the battle lines were clearly drawn. Two great forces swelled against each other: the religious struggle between Catholics and Protestants and the dynastic struggle between the Habsburgs and their enemies. At times they intersected, as in the revolt of the Netherlands, where Protestantism could be defended and the Habsburgs attacked. Other times they diverged, as in the support that Catholic France provided to the Protestant enemies of Spain and the Holy Roman Empire. This mixture of religion and politics was extremely volatile. Some princes hid their dynastic ambitions beneath the cloak of religious conviction. Others pursued holy war without regard for the well-being of their state. In this battle for the glory of God and the glory of man there could be no end, only occasional interruptions.

It was one such interruption that claimed the attention of the European powers at the beginning of the seventeenth century. In 1609 Spain and the Dutch Republic had signed a truce that was to last until 1621. In over forty years of nearly continuous fighting the Dutch had carved out a state in the northern Netherlands. They used the truce to consolidate their position and increase their prosperity. A maritime state, Holland expanded overseas, largely at the expense of Spain and Portugal.

Thus to the insult of rebellion was added the injury of commercial competition. Spain had reluctantly accepted Dutch independence, but Philip III (1598–1621), like his father before him, never abandoned the objective of recovering his Burgundian inheritance. By the opening of the seventeenth century Philip had good reasons for hope. Beginning in the 1580s, Spanish forces had reconquered the southern provinces of the Netherlands. The prosperous towns of Brussels, Antwerp, and Ghent were again under Spanish control, and they provided a springboard for another invasion.

The Twelve Years' Truce gave Spain time to prepare for the final assault. During this time Philip III attempted to resolve all of Spain's other European conflicts so that he could then give full attention to a resumption of the Dutch war. Circumstance smiled upon his efforts. In 1603 the pacific James I (1603–25) came to the English throne. Secure in his island state, James I desired peace among all Christian princes. He quickly concluded the war with Spain that had begun with the invasion of the Spanish Armada, and he entered into negotiations to marry his heir to a Spanish princess. In 1610 the bellicose Henry IV of France was felled by an assassin's knife. French plans to renew war with Spain were abandoned with the accession of the eight-year-old Louis XIII (1610–43). As the sands of the Twelve Years' Truce ran out, Spain and the Netherlands readied for war. Towns were fortified and cannons were cast. Mercenaries offered their services to the highest bidder. But not even the greatest empire in Europe could control its own destiny. War was in the air all over the Continent, and not everyone could wait until 1621.

The Bohemian Revolt

The Peace of Augsburg had served the German states well. The principle that the religion of the ruler was the religion of the state complicated the political life of the Holy Roman Empire, but it also pacified it. Though rulers had the right to enforce uniformity on their subjects, in practice many of the larger states tolerated more than one religion. By the beginning of the seventeenth century Catholicism and Protestantism had achieved a rough equality within the German states, symbolized by the fact that of the seven electors who chose the Holy Roman Emperor, three were Catholic, three Protestant, and the seventh was the emperor himself, acting as king of Bohemia. This situation was not unwelcome to the leaders of the Austrian Habsburg family who succeeded Emperor Charles V. By necessity, the eastern Habsburgs were more tolerant than their Spanish kinfolk. Protestants fought the Ottomans with as much zeal as did Catholics, and the Ottomans were the empire's more potent enemy. The unofficial policy of toleration not only helped the Austrian Habsburgs defend their state, it allowed them to expand it. The head of their house was elected king of Bohemia and king of Hungary, both states with large Protestant populations.

But the delicate religious balance in central Europe presented difficulties as well as advantages. The appearance of Calvinism in Germany led to more Protestant converts, the appearance of the Counter-Reformation to more Catholic reconversions. Each change heightened anxieties. Every diplomatic marriage or contested inheritance threatened to upset the balance. Protestant and Catholic states, fearful of the power of their rivals, formed separate defensive alliances. The arming of one camp incited the arming of the other. The military temperature rose along with the religious and the political.

Matters came to a head in 1617 when Mathias, the childless Holy Roman Emperor, began making plans for his cousin, Ferdinand Habsburg, to succeed him. In order to ensure a Catholic majority among the electors, the emperor relinquished his Bohemian title and pressed for Ferdinand's election as the new king of Bohemia. Ferdinand was Catholic, very devout and very committed. He had been educated by Jesuits and practiced what had been preached to him. On his own estates, Ferdinand abandoned the policy of toleration. Jesuit schools were founded and the precepts of the Council of Trent were enforced. Protestant preachers were barred from their offices, Protestant books were publicly burned, and thousands of common people were forced to flee, many into nearby Bohemia, where Protestants constituted the majority of the population.

Thus Ferdinand's election as king of Bohemia was no foregone conclusion. Though in the end the Protestant nobles of Bohemia could not prevent his election, they forced the new king to accept the strictest limitations upon his political and religious powers. But once elected Ferdinand had not the slightest intention of honoring the provisions that had been thrust upon him. His opponents were equally strong willed. When Ferdinand violated Protestant religious liberties, a group of noblemen marched to the royal palace in Prague in May 1618, found two of the king's chief advisers, and hurled them out of an upper-story window. The officials' lives, if not their dignity, were preserved by the pile of manure in which they landed.

The Defenestration of Prague, as this incident came to be known, initiated a Protestant counteroffensive throughout the Habsburg lands. Fear of Ferdinand's policies led to Protestant uprisings in Hungary as well as Bohemia. Those who seized control of the government declared Ferdinand deposed and the throne vacant. But they had no candidate to accept their crown. The stakes were extremely high. Whatever their religion, princes were always uneasy about the overthrow of a lawful ruler. There had been nothing improper about Ferdinand's election. His policies may have been impolitic, but they were not illegal. Whoever came to be called king of Bohemia in place of

Ferdinand would also be called rebel of the empire. And his rebellion would have to face the combined might of the Habsburgs. Philip III of Spain saw with great clarity that a successful Protestant revolt in central Europe would threaten his plans to resume the war in the Netherlands. A successful Protestant revolt would win the Dutch new allies and might sever the vital supply lines through the Alps. Spain again would be forced to fight a war on two fronts. Suppression of the Bohemian revolt would have to precede resumption of the Dutch war.

These considerations weighed heavily upon the Protestant princes of Germany who, one by one, declined the offer of the Bohemian crown. When Emperor Mathias died in 1619, the stalemate was broken. Ferdinand succeeded to the imperial title as Ferdinand II (1619–37) and Frederick V, one of the Protestant electors, accepted the Bohemian crown. Frederick was a sincere but weak Calvinist whose credentials were much stronger than his abilities. His mother was a daughter of Prince William of Orange and his wife, Elizabeth, a daughter of James I of England. It was widely believed that it was Elizabeth's resolution that she would "rather eat sauerkraut with a King than roast meat with an Elector," that decided the issue. No decision could have been more disastrous for the fate of Europe. Frederick ruled a geographically divided German state known as the Palatinate. One hundred miles separated the two segments of his lands, but both were strategically important. The Lower Palatinate bordered on the Catholic Spanish Netherlands and the Upper Palatinate on Catholic Bavaria.

Once Frederick accepted the Bohemian crown, he was faced with a war on three fronts. It was over almost before it began. Ferdinand II had no difficulty enlisting allies to recover the Bohemian crown, since he could pay them with the spoils of Frederick's lands. Spanish troops from the Netherlands occupied the Lower Palatinate, and Bavarian troops occupied the Upper Palatinate. Frederick, on the other hand, met rejection wherever he turned. Neither the Dutch nor the English would send more than token aid—both had advised him against breaking the imperial peace. The Lutheran princes of Germany would not enter into a war between Calvinists and Catholics, especially after Ferdinand II promised to protect the Bohemian Lutherans.

At the battle of the White Mountain in 1620, Ferdinand's Catholic forces annihilated Frederick's army. Frederick and Elizabeth fled north, first to Denmark and then to Holland. Bohemia was left to face the wrath of Ferdinand, the victorious king and emperor. The retribution was horrible. Mercenaries who had fought for Ferdinand II were allowed to sack Prague for a week. Elective monarchy was abolished and Bohemia became part of the hereditary Habsburg lands. Free peasants were enserfed and subjected to imperial law. Those nobles who had supported Frederick lost their lands and their privileges. Calvinism was repressed and thoroughly rooted out, consolidating forever the Catholic character of Bohemia. Frederick's estates were carved up and his rights as elector transferred to the Catholic duke of Bavaria. The battle of the White Mountain was a turning point in the history of central Europe.

The War Widens

Yet the Catholic triumph may have been too complete. For the Habsburgs, religious and dynastic interests were inseparable. Ferdinand II and Philip III of Spain fought for their beliefs and for their patrimony. Their victory gave them more than they could have expected. Ferdinand swallowed up Bohemia and strengthened his position in the empire. Philip gained possession of a vital link in his supply route between Italy and the Netherlands. The Habsburgs were now more dangerous than ever. Ferdinand's aggressive Catholicism threatened the Protestant princes of Germany, who prudently began to seek allies outside the empire. Spanish expansion threatened France. The occupation of the Lower Palatinate placed a ring of Spanish armies around the French borders from the Pyrenees to the Low Countries. The French too searched for allies; in one diplomatic maneuver Louis XIII's sister, Henrietta Maria, was married to the heir to the English throne. But French opinion remained divided over which was the greater evil: Spain or Protestantism.

Frederick, now in Holland, refused to accept the judgment of battle. He lobbied for a grand alliance to repel the Spaniards from the Lower Palatinate and to restore the religious balance in the empire. Though his personal cause met with little sympathy, his political logic was impeccable, especially after Spain again declared war upon the Dutch. A grand Protestant alliance— secretly supported by the French—brought together England, Holland, a number of German states, and Denmark. It was the Danes who led this potentially powerful coalition. In 1626 a large Danish army under the command of King Christian IV engaged imperial forces on German soil.

But the Danes received little effective support from their allies. For three years they were the chief hope of Protestant Europe, and each year that hope grew dimmer. Danish forces could not match the superior numbers and the superior leadership of the Catholic mercenary forces under the command of the ruthless and brilliant Count Albrecht von Wallenstein (1583–1634). In each successive campaign Wallenstein inflicted heavy defeats upon the Danish armies and exacted even heavier retribution from the German population that stood in his path. In 1629 the Danes withdrew from the empire and sued for peace. Their grand Protestant alliance fell apart and Danish ambitions to lead international Protestantism were crushed.

If the Catholic victory at the White Mountain in 1620 threatened the well-being of German Protestantism, the Catholic triumph over the Danes threatened its survival. More powerful than ever, Ferdinand II determined to turn the religious clock back to the state of affairs that had existed when the Peace of Augsburg was concluded in 1555. He demanded that all lands that had then been Catholic but had since become Protestant must now be returned to the fold. He also proclaimed that as the Peace of Augsburg made no provision for the toleration of Calvinists, they would no longer be tolerated in the empire. These policies together constituted a virtual revolution in the religious affairs of the German states, and they proved impossible to impose. Ferdinand succeeded in only one thing—he united Lutherans and Calvinists against him. As long as the main Protestant creeds had been divided, Ferdinand had had little difficulty in undermining their alliances and defeating their armies. He also had little need to compromise with his own German allies, whose leaders were increasingly nervous about Spanish occupation of the Lower Palatinate and Ferdinand's confrontational policies. By demanding the restitution of Catholic lands and the suppression of Calvinism, Ferdinand II strengthened every position but his own.

This direct challenge to the survival of Protestantism was met from an unexpected quarter. Twelve years of fighting had devastated much of the empire. Marauding armies cared little for the distinctions of friend and foe, but it was the Protestant north that had borne the brunt of the destruction. After the defeat of the Danes, Catholic policy was to secure a beachhead on the Baltic from which a fleet could be built that would disrupt Protestant, and especially Dutch, shipping. Though these efforts were unsuccessful, they threatened the security of Sweden, which had recently concluded a long war with the Poles for control of the Baltic. In 1630 King Gustavus Adolphus of Sweden decided to enter the German conflict. To protect Swedish interests, he reasoned, he must defend the Protestant states of northern Germany. Moreover, France was willing to pay much of the cost of a war against Ferdinand. The French too felt the pressure of increasing imperial and Spanish power.

Gustavus Adolphus had more success gaining the support of Catholic France than he did gaining the support of the Protestant German princes. Saxony and Brandenburg, the two largest states, feared the consequences of renewed war. Though both suffered under Ferdinand's policies, they were fearful of his wrath. It was hard to forget what had happened to Frederick. Nor did they think that the Swedes would succeed where the Danes had failed. But in fact the situation in 1630 was far different than it had been five years earlier. Ferdinand's alliances were coming unraveled, both for fear of his power and dislike of his policies. The costs of the war were heavy even for the victors. Wallenstein, who had over 130,000 men in arms, would no longer take orders from anyone, and Ferdinand II was forced to dismiss him from service. The loss of Wallenstein reduced imperial military might just at the moment that the empire was to face its greatest challenge.

Moreover, the Swedes were not the Danes. The Swedish army was composed of battle-tested veterans used to the conditions of land war. Their king and commander, Gustavus Adolphus, was a military leader of considerable talent and verve. He had continued Swedish innovations in military tactics and he had already proven himself an able strategist. Gustavus believed that he could defend the north German states from Ferdinand's aggression and by doing so protect Sweden's Baltic empire. "I seek not my own advantage in this war, nor any gain save the security of my Kingdom," he lectured the reluctant Germans. It was a far-sighted strategy. In fact, the only thing he could not foresee when he landed in Germany early in 1630 was how successful his intervention would be.

While Gustavus Adolphus struggled to construct his alliance, imperial forces continued their triumphant progress. In 1631 they besieged, captured, and put to the torch the town of Magdeburg. In a war noted for cruelty between combatants and atrocities against civilians, the destruction of Magdeburg set new standards. Perhaps three-fourths of the forty thousand inhabitants of the town were slaughtered—"in the midst of a horrible din of heart-rending shrieks and cries they were tortured and put to death in so cruel a manner that no words would suffice to describe nor no tears to bewail it," was the report in one pamphlet. The sack of Magdeburg marked a turning point in Protestant fortunes. It gave the international Protestant community a unifying symbol that enhanced Gustavus' military efforts. Hundreds of pamphlets, woodcuts, and news-

paper accounts brought the horror of Magdeburg home to Protestants throughout the Continent. Brandenburg and Saxony joined Gustavus Adolphus, not only enlarging his forces, but allowing him to open a second front in Bohemia. He would soon have 140,000 men under his command, only 13,000 of whom were Swedish. In the autumn of 1631 this combination overwhelmed the imperial armies. Gustavus won a decisive triumph at Breitenfeld, while the Saxons occupied Prague. For the first time since 1618, Protestant forces were ascendant, and they brought the war into the Catholic heartland of the empire.

Gustavus Adolphus lost no time in pressing his advantage. While Ferdinand II pleaded with Wallenstein to resume his command, the Swedes marched west to the Rhine, easily conquering the richest of the Catholic cities and retaking the Lower Palatinate. In early 1632 Protestant forces plundered Bavaria. It was the Bavarian ruler Maximilian who had gained most from the years of war. His troops had occupied the Upper Palatinate, and he had received Frederick's rights as imperial elector in return for support of Ferdinand. It was Maximilian who had insisted on the dismissal of Wallenstein and Maximilian who had played a double game of negotiating with the French for neutrality and with the emperor for the spoils of victory. So there was poetic justice when Maximilian's state was invaded, his castles looted, and his lands plundered. There was poetic justice, too, when Wallenstein resumed his com-

The siege of Magdeburg, 1631. The sack of the city by the Imperial troops of Tilly's army was one of the most barbarous incidents of a brutal war.

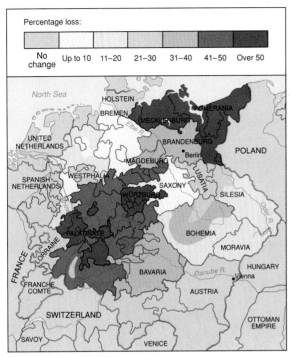

Percentage loss:

| No change | Up to 10 | 11–20 | 21–30 | 31–40 | 41–50 | Over 50 |

Population Loss in Germany

mand and chose to chase the Saxons from Bohemia rather than the Swedes from Bavaria. But there was no justice at all for the wretched inhabitants of this stronghold of German Catholicism. Town and countryside were laid waste. Not until the winter of 1632 did the armies of Gustavus and Wallenstein finally meet. At the battle of Lutzen the Swedes won the field but lost their beloved king. Wounded in the leg, the back, and the head, Gustavus Adolphus died. In less than two years he had decisively transformed the course of the war and the course of Europe's future. Protestant forces now occupied most of central and northern Germany. Ferdinand's ability to redraw the religious map of the empire was at an end.

The Long Quest for Peace

The Thirty Years' War was barely half over when Gustavus Adolphus fell at Lutzen. But from that time forward its central European phase receded in importance. The final stages of the war involved the resumption of the century-old struggle between France and Spain. When the Twelve Years' Truce expired in 1621, Spain again declared war upon the Dutch. Philip III's hopes of concentrating all his resources against Holland had been disappointed by the outbreak of war in central Europe. Not until after the Bohemian revolt had been repressed did the Spanish army begin the long, laborious process of besieging the well-fortified and well-defended towns of the Netherlands. There were successes and failures. But now Dutch strategy was not only to protect the homeland. Dutch naval power was considerable and the Dutch took the war to the far reaches of the globe, attacking Portuguese settlements in Brazil and in the East and harassing Spanish shipping on the high seas. In 1628 the Dutch captured the entire Spanish treasure fleet as it sailed from the New World. Not since the defeat of the Armada in 1588 had Spain suffered such a blow to its prestige. But the dent in its pride was nothing compared to the dent in its pocketbook. Spain had declared bankruptcy in 1627, and the loss of the whole of the next year's treasure from America exacerbated an already catastrophic situation. The golden age of Spain had melted away.

These reversals, combined with the continued successes of Habsburg forces in central Europe, convinced Louis XIII and his chief minister, Cardinal Richelieu, that the time for active involvement in European affairs was now at hand. Throughout the early stages of the war, France had secretly aided anti-Habsburg forces. From 1624 it had provided a subsidy to the Dutch and from 1630 one to the Swedes. French support for princes in a number of small states situated in the passages of the Alps continually threatened the Spanish supply route to the Netherlands and had more than once nearly led to open warfare. Gustavus Adolphus' unexpected success dramatically altered French calculations. Now it was evident that the Habsburgs could no longer combine their might, and Spanish energies would be drained off in the Netherlands and in central Europe. The time had come to take an open stand. In 1635 France declared war on Spain.

Neither country was prepared for large-scale military action, and neither could afford it. The war resembled nothing so much as two punch-drunk fighters pounding each other, both receiving as much punishment as they inflicted. France took the offensive first, invading the Spanish Netherlands. In 1636 a Spanish army struck back, pushing to within twenty-five miles of Paris before

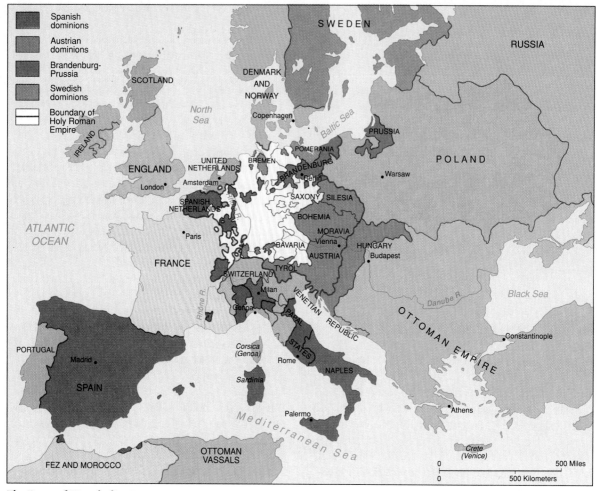

The Peace of Westphalia, Europe 1648

it was repelled. Both sides soon began to search for a settlement, but pride prevented them from laying down their gloves. Spain toppled first. Its economy in shambles and its citizens in revolt over high prices and higher taxes, it could no longer maintain its many-fronted war. The Swedes again defeated imperial forces in Germany, the Dutch destroyed much of Spain's Atlantic fleet in 1639, and the Portuguese rose up against the union of crowns that had brought them nothing but expense and the loss of crucial portions of their empire. In 1640 the Portuguese regained their independence. In 1643 Spain gambled once more on a knockout blow against the French. But at the battle of Rocroi, exhausted French troops held out and the Spanish invasion failed.

By now the desire for peace was universal. Most of the main combatants had long since per-

ished: Philip III, ever optimistic, in 1621; Frederick V, an exile to the end, in 1632; Gustavus Adolphus, killed at Lutzen in the same year; Wallenstein, murdered by order of Ferdinand II in 1634; Ferdinand himself in 1637; and Louis XIII in 1643, five days before the French triumph at Rocroi. Those who succeeded them had not the same passions, and after so many decades the longing for peace was the strongest emotion on the Continent. But the tangle of wars and alliances was not easily unsnarled, and those who saw themselves as victors at one stage or another still sought desperately for their spoils. Some wanted to reconstruct the political world as it had existed in 1618, others to reestablish it as it was after the first round of Catholic victories in 1627. The Swedes, who had gained most from the struggle—they now occupied much of northern Germany and, after a brief war with Denmark, much territory in the western Baltic as well—wished to settle things largely as they stood. Fighting persisted as each effort to reach a universal peace failed. Finally, at the beginning of 1648 Spain and the Netherlands concluded their eighty years of fighting. This bilateral agreement broke the log jam. One by one the combatants agreed to end their hostilities with one another, and soon the stage was set for a Continent-wide settlement.

A series of agreements, collectively known as the Peace of Westphalia, established the outlines of the political geography of Europe for the next century. Its focus was on the Holy Roman Empire and it reflected Protestant successes in the final two decades of war. It was the powers who had been brought into the war in central Europe that benefited most from the peace. Sweden gained further territories on the Baltic, making it master of the north German ports. Along with the territorial concessions it had won from Denmark, Sweden was now an international power. France, too, gained in territory and prestige. It kept the vital towns in the Lower Palatinate through which Spanish men and material had moved and, though it did not agree to come to terms with Spain immediately, France's fear of encirclement was at an end. The Dutch gained statehood though official recognition by Spain and through the power they had displayed in building and maintaining an overseas empire.

Settlement in the empire also reflected Protestant successes. Territorial boundaries were reestablished as they had existed in 1624, giving the Habsburgs control of both Bohemia and Hungary. But the independence of the Swiss cantons was now officially recognized as were the rights of Calvinists to the protection of the Peace of Augsburg, which again was to govern the religious affairs of the empire. Two of the larger German states were strengthened as a counterweight to the emperor's power. Bavaria was allowed to retain the Upper Palatinate, and Brandenburg, which ceded some of its coastal territory to Sweden, gained extensive territories in the east. The emperor's political control over the German states was also weakened. German rulers were given independent authority over their states and the imperial diet, rather than the emperor, was empowered to settle disputes. Thus weakened, future emperors ruled in the Habsburg territorial

The Thirty Years' War

1618	Defenestration of Prague
1619	Ferdinand Habsburg elected Holy Roman Emperor
	Frederick of the Palatinate accepts the crown of Bohemia
1620	Catholic victory at battle of White Mountain
1621	End of Twelve Years' Truce; war between Spain and Netherlands
1626	Danes form Protestant alliance under Christian IV
1627	Spain declares bankruptcy
1630	Gustavus Adolphus leads Swedish forces into Germany
1631	Sack of Magdeburg
	Protestant victory at Breitenfeld
1632	Protestant victory at Lutzen; death of Gustavus Adolphus
1635	France declares war on Spain
1640	Portugal secedes from Spain
1643	Battle of Rocroi; French forces repel Spaniards
1648	Peace of Westphalia

lands with little ability to control, or influence, or even arbitrate German affairs. The judgment that the Holy Roman Empire was neither holy, Roman, nor an empire was now irrevocably true.

The Peace of Westphalia put the pieces of the map of European states back together. Protestantism and Catholicism now coexisted and there was to be little further change in the geography of religion. The northwest of Europe—England, Holland, Scandinavia, and the north German states—was Protestant, the south was Catholic. The empire of the German peoples was now at an end, the Austro-Hungarian empire at a beginning. Holland and Sweden had become international powers, Spain and Denmark faded from prominence. Muscovy began a long period of isolation from the west, attempting to restore a semblance of government to its people. But if the negotiators at Westphalia could resolve the political and religious ambitions that gave rise to a century of nearly continuous warfare, they could do nothing to eradicate the effects of war itself. The devastation of humanity in the name of God with which the reform of religion had begun was now exhausted. The costs were horrific. The population of Germany fell from 15 million in 1600 to 11 million in 1650. The armies brought destruction of all kinds in their wake. Plague again raged in Europe—the town of Augsburg lost eighteen thousand inhabitants in the early 1630s. Famine, too, returned to a continent that fifty years earlier had been self-sufficient in grain. The war played havoc with all of the economies that it touched. Inflation, devaluation of coinage, huge public and private debts were all directly attributable to the years of fighting. And the toll taken on the spirit of those generations that never knew peace is incalculable.

Suggestions for Further Reading

General Reading

* J. H. Elliott, *Europe Divided 1559–1598* (New York: Harper & Row, 1968). An outstanding synthesis of European politics in the second half of the sixteenth century.

* Geoffrey Parker, *Europe in Crisis 1598–1648* (London: William Collins and Sons, 1979). An up-to-date study of European states in the early seventeenth century.

* Richard Dunn, *The Age of Religious Wars 1559–1715* (New York: Norton, 1979). A well-written survey of early modern society.

* H. G. Koenigsberger, *Early Modern Europe* (London: Longmans, 1987). A general overview designed for beginning students.

The Crises of the Western States

J. H. M. Salmon, *Society in Crisis* (New York: St. Martin's Press, 1975). The best single-volume account of the French civil wars; difficult but rewarding.

N. M. Sutherland, *The Massacre of St. Bartholomew and the European Conflict* (London: Macmillan, 1973). Argues the case for the importance of Spanish influence on the massacre and the course of the wars of religion.

Robert Kingdon, *Myths About the St. Bartholomew's Day Massacres 1572–76* (Cambridge, MA: Harvard University Press, 1988). A study of the impact of a central event in the history of France.

David Buisseret, *Henry IV* (London: George Allen & Unwin, 1984). A stylish biography of a problematic personality.

* Mark Greengrass, *France in the Age of Henri IV* (London: Longmans, 1984). An important synthesis of French history in the early seventeenth century.

Geoffrey Parker, *Philip II* (Boston: Little, Brown, 1978). The best introduction.

* Garrett Mattingly, *The Armada* (Boston: Houghton Mifflin, 1959). Still the classic account despite recent reinterpretations.

Colin Martin and N. G. Parker, *The Spanish Armada* (London: Hamilton Press, 1988). A recent study based on archaeological finds and a fresh look at the evidence.

John Lynch, *Spain Under the Hapsburgs, Vol. II. Spain and America* (Oxford: Oxford University Press, 1969). A full treatment of Spanish history with sections on society and culture as well as politics.

* Henry Kamen, *Spain 1469–1714* (London: Longmans, 1983). A recent survey with up-to-date interpretations.

* Geoffrey Parker, *The Dutch Revolt* (London: Penguin Books, 1977). An outstanding account of the tangle of events that comprised the revolts of the Netherlands.

* Pieter Geyl, *The Revolt of the Netherlands* (London: Ernest Benn, 1962). Still worth reading for its passion and enthusiasm.

The Reorganization of Northeastern Europe

W. F. Reddaway, et al., eds., *The Cambridge History of Poland to 1696* (Cambridge: Cambridge University Press, 1950). A difficult but thorough narrative of Polish history.

S. F. Platonov, *The Time of Troubles* (Lawrence, KS: University Press of Kansas, 1970). A good narrative of the disintegration of the Muscovite state.

Michael Roberts, *Gustavus Adolphus and the Rise of Sweden* (London: English Universities Press, 1973). A highly readable account of Sweden's rise to power.

Michael Roberts, *The Swedish Imperial Experience* (Cambridge: Cambridge University Press, 1979). Reflections on Swedish history by the preeminent historian of early modern Sweden.

The Thirty Years' War

* C. V. Wedgwood, *The Thirty Years' War* (New York: Doubleday, 1961). A heroic account; the best narrative history.

Geoffrey Parker, *The Thirty Years' War* (London: Routledge and Kegan Paul, 1984). A multi-authored account that views the war from a variety of vantage points.

* Peter Limm, *The Thirty Years' War* (London: Longmans, 1984). An excellent brief survey with documents.

J. H. Elliott, *Richelieu and Olivares* (Cambridge: Cambridge University Press, 1984). A comparison of statesmen and statesmanship in the early seventeenth century.

* Indicates paperback edition available

16

The
Royal State

Fit for a King

Behold Versailles: the greatest palace of the greatest king of the greatest state in seventeenth-century Europe. Everything about it was stupendous, a reflection of the grandeur of Louis XIV and of France. Sculptured gardens in dazzling geometric forms stretched for acres, scenting the air with exotic perfumes. Nearly as beautiful as the grounds were the 1,400 fountains, especially the circular basins of Apollo and Latona, the sun god and his mother. The hundreds of water jets that sprayed at Versailles defied nature as well as the

senses, for the locale was not well irrigated and water had to be pumped through elaborate mechanical works all the way from the Seine. Gardens and fountains provided the setting for the enormous palace with its hundreds of rooms for both use and show. Five thousand people, a tenth of whom served the king alone, inhabited the palace. Thousands of others flocked there daily. Most lived in the adjacent town, which had grown from a few hundred to over forty thousand in a single generation. The royal stables quartered twelve thousand

horses and hundreds of carriages. The cost of all of this magnificence was equally astounding. Fragmentary accounts indicate that construction costs were over 100 million French pounds. Louis XIV ordered the official receipts burned.

Like the marble of the palace, nature itself was chiseled to the requirements of the king. Forests were pared to make leafy avenues or trimmed to conform to the geometric patterns of the gardens. In spring and summer groves of orange trees grown in tubs were every-

where; in winter and fall they were housed indoors at great expense. Life-size statues and giant carved urns lined the carefully planned walkways that led out to breathtaking views or into sheltered grottoes. A cross-shaped artificial canal, over a mile long, dominated the western end of the park. Italian gondolas skimmed along its surface, carrying visitors to the zoo and aviary on one side or to the king's private château on the other.

But this great pile of bricks and stone, of marble and precious metals expressed the contradictions of its age as well as its grandeur. The seventeenth century was an era when the rich got richer and the poor got poorer. It was a time when the monarchical state expanded its power and prestige even as it faced grave challenges to its very existence. It was an epoch of unrelenting war amid a nearly universal desire for lasting peace. Thus it was fitting that this prodigious monument was uncomfortable to live in, so unpleasant that Louis had a separate château built on the grounds as a quiet retreat. His wife and his mistresses com-

plained constantly of accommodations in which all interior comforts had been subordinated to the external façade of the building. Versailles was a seat of state as well as the home of the monarch, and it is revealing that the private was sacrificed to the public.

The duc de Saint-Simon, who passed much of his time at Versailles, was well aware of the contradictions. "The beautiful and the ugly were sown together, the vast and the constricted." Soldiers, tradesmen, and the merely curious clogged the three great avenues that led from Paris to the palace. When the king dined in public, hordes of Parisians drove out for the spectacle, filing past the monarch as if he were an exhibit at a museum. The site itself was poorly drained. "Its mud is black and stinking with a stench so penetrating that you can smell it for several leagues around." The orange groves and the stone urns filled with flower petals were more practical than beautiful: they masked the stench of sewage that was particularly noxious in the heat and the rain. Even the gardens were too vast to be enjoyed. In the planted areas, the smell of flowers was overpowering while the acres of mown lawn proved unattractive to an aristocracy little given to physical exercise. "The gardens were admired and avoided," Saint-Simon observed acidly. In these contrasts of failure amid achievement Versailles stands as an apt symbol of its age: a gaudy mask to hide the wrinkles of the royal state.

The Rise of the Royal State

The religious and dynastic wars that dominated the early part of the seventeenth century had a profound impact upon the western European states. Not only did they cause terrible suffering and deprivation but they also demanded efficient and better-centralized states to conduct them. War was both a product of the European state system and a cause of its continued development. As armies grew in size, the resources necessary to maintain them grew in volume. As the battlefield spread from state to state, defense became government's most important function. More and more power was absorbed by the monarch and his chief advisers, more and more of the traditional privileges of aristocracy and of towns were eroded. At the center of these rising states, particularly in western Europe, were the king and his court. In the provinces were tax collectors and military recruiters.

Divine Kings

"There is a divinity that doth hedge a king," wrote Shakespeare. Never was that hedge more luxuriant than in the seventeenth century. In the early sixteenth century, monarchs treated their states and their subjects as personal property. Correspondingly, rulers were praised in personal terms, for their virtue, their wisdom, or their strength. By the early seventeenth century, the monarchy had been transformed into an office of state. Now rulers embodied their nation and, no matter what their personal characteristics, they were held in awe because they were monarchs.

Thus as rulers lost direct personal control over their patrimony, they gained indirect symbolic control over their nation. This symbolic power was everywhere to be seen. By the beginning of the seventeenth century, monarchs had set permanent seats of government attended by vast courts of officials, place seekers, and servants. The idea of the capital city emerged, with Madrid, London, and Paris as the models. Here, the grandiose style of the ruler stood proxy for the wealth and glory of the nation. Great display bespoke great pride, and great pride was translated into great strength.

Portraits of rulers in action and in repose conveyed the central message. Elizabeth I was depicted bestriding a map of England or clutching a rainbow and wearing a gown woven of eyes and ears to signify her power to see and hear her subjects. The Flemish painter Sir Anthony Van Dyck (1599–1641) created powerful images of three generations of Stuart kings of England. He was court painter to Charles I, whose qualities he portrayed with great sympathy and not a little exaggeration. Diego Velázquez (1599–1660) was court painter to Philip IV of Spain. His series of equestrian portraits of the Habsburgs—kings, queens, princes, and princesses—exude the spirit of the seventeenth-century monarchy, the grandeur and pomp, the power and self-assurance. Peter Paul Rubens (1577–1640) represented twenty-one separate episodes in the life of Marie de Médicis, queen regent of France.

The themes of artists were no different than those of writers. Monarchy was glorified in a variety of forms of literary representation. National history, particularly of recent events, enjoyed wide popularity. Its avowed purpose was to draw the connection between the past and the present glories of the state. One of the most popular French histories of the period was entitled *On the Excellence of the Kings and the Kingdom of France.* Francis Bacon (1561–1626), who is remembered more as a philosopher and scientist, wrote a laudatory history of Henry VII, founder of the Tudor dynasty. Artistic enterprise flourished across the Continent. The century between 1550 and 1650 was one of the richest periods of high culture in European history.

In England it was a period of renaissance. Poets, playwrights, historians, and philosophers by the dozens gravitated to the English court. One of the most remarkable of them was Ben Jonson (1572–1637). He began life as a bricklayer, fought against the Spanish in Flanders, and then turned to acting and writing. His wit and talent brought him to court, where he made his mark by writing and staging masques, light entertainment that included music, dance, pantomime, and acting. Jonson's masques were distinguished by their lavish productions and exotic costumes and the inventive set designs of the great architect Inigo

Queen Elizabeth I of England. This portrait was commissioned by Sir Henry Lee to commemorate the Queen's visit to his estate at Ditchley. Here the queen is the very image of Gloriana—ageless and indomitable.

Jones (1573–1652). They were frequently staged at Christmastime and starred members of the court as players. The masques took the grandeur of England and its rulers for their themes.

The role of William Shakespeare (1564–1616) in the celebration of monarchy was more ambiguous. Like Jonson, Shakespeare came from an ordinary family, had little formal education, and began his astonishing career as an actor and producer of theater. He soon began to write as well as direct his plays and his company, the King's Players, received royal patronage. He set many of his plays at the courts of princes and even comedies like the *Tempest* (1611) and *Measure for Measure* (1604) centered on the power of the ruler to dispense justice and to bring peace to his subjects. Both were staged at court. His history plays focused entirely on the character of kings. In *Richard II* (1597) and *Henry VI* (3 parts, 1591–94) Shakespeare exposed the harm that weak rulers inflicted on their states, while in *Henry IV* (2 parts, 1598–1600) and *Henry V* (1599) he highlighted the

benefits to be derived from strong rulers. Shakespeare's tragedies made this point in a different way. The tragic flaw in the personality of rulers exposed the world around them to ruin. In *Macbeth* (1606) this flaw was ambition. Macbeth killed to become a king and had to keep on killing to remain one. In *Hamlet* (1602) the tragic flaw was irresolution. The inability of the "Prince of Denmark" to act decisively and reclaim the crown that was his by right brought his state to the brink of collapse. Shakespeare's plays were viewed in London theaters by members of all social classes, and his concentration on the affairs of rulers helped reinforce their dominating importance in the lives of all of their subjects.

The political theory of the divine right of kings further enhanced the importance of monarchs. This theory held that the institution of monarchy had been created by God, and the monarch functioned as God's representative on earth. One clear statement of divine right theory was actually written by a king, James VI of Scotland, who later became James I of England (1603–25). In *The True Law of Free Monarchies* (1598) James instructed the leaders of the Scottish nobility and the Scottish church on their duties to their king. He recalled the Old Testament story of how the Israelites begged the Lord to create a king to rule over them. Thus, James reasoned, God had placed kings on earth to rule, and he would judge them in heaven for their transgressions.

The idea of the divine origin of monarchy was uncontroversial, and it was espoused not only by kings. One of the few things that the French Estates-General actually agreed upon during its meeting in 1614—the last for over 175 years—was the statement that "the king is sovereign in France and holds his crown from God only." This sentiment echoed the commonplace view of French political theorists. The greatest writer on the subject, Jean Bodin (1530–96), called the king "God's image on earth." In *The Six Books of the Commonwealth* (1576), Bodin defined the essence of the monarch's power: "The principal mark of sovereign majesty is essentially the right to impose laws on subjects generally without their consent."

Though at first glance the theory of the divine right of kings appears to be a blueprint for arbitrary rule, in fact it was yoked together with a number of principles that restrained the conduct of the monarch. As James I pointed out, God had charged kings with the obligations "to minister justice; to establish good laws; and to procure peace." By these standards would kings ultimately be judged; failure would be met with the wrath of God. For a king who viewed himself as father of his nation, or as head of the body politic, there was no contradiction between his power and his subjects' welfare. *Rex est Lex; Lex est Rex*: "the king is the law and the law is the king." Kings were bound by the law of nature and the law of nations. They could not deprive their subjects of their lives, their liberties, or their property without due cause established by law. As one French theorist held, "while the kingdom belongs to the king, the king also belongs to the kingdom."

Wherever they turned, kings were instructed in the duties of kingship. In tracts, in letters, and in literature they were lectured on the obligations of their office. "A true king should be first in government, first in council, and first in all the offices of state." If such advice appealed to strong personalities like Philip II of Spain, Henry IV of France, or Elizabeth I of England, it burdened their weaker successors. Louis XIII (1610–43) loved nothing more than to hunt in the French countryside and hated nothing more than the daily burdens of affairs of state. James I may have embraced the theory of his divine office, but he recoiled from the London crowds that jostled for a glimpse of him whenever he set foot outside his palace. Both kings had speech impediments that led them to shy away from public ceremonies. They nervously endured obligations like the "royal touch," during which people afflicted with certain diseases hoped for a miraculous cure from the hands of the king. The nine-year-old Louis XIII touched over nine hundred supplicants following his coronation in 1610 and remarked with great pride that he had sickened only slightly and "never let it show."

The Court and the Courtiers

For all of the bravura of divine-right theory, far more was expected of kings than they could possibly deliver. They were to be soldiers in times of war and statesmen in times of peace. They were to administer the affairs of society, legislate the affairs of state, and adjudicate the affairs of jus-

tice. "I am neither a god nor an angel but a man like any other," James I proclaimed in a moment when he wasn't thinking about his divine right. Small wonder that seventeenth-century kings built palaces in which to hide.

The increase in the power of the monarchy required an increase in the effectiveness of the monarch. The day-to-day affairs of government had grown beyond the capacity of any monarch to handle them. The expansion in the powers of the western states absorbed more officials than ever. At the beginning of the sixteenth century the court of Francis I employed 622 officers; at the beginning of the seventeenth century the court of Henry IV employed over 1,500. Yet the difference was not only in size. Members of the seventeenth-century court were becoming servants of the state as well as of the monarch.

Expanding the court was one of the ways in which monarchs co-opted potential rivals within the aristocracy. In return, those who were favored enhanced their power by royal grants of titles, lands, and income. As the court expanded so did the political power of courtiers. Royal councils—a small group of leading officeholders who advised the monarch on state business—grew in significance. Not only did the council assume the management of government, it also began to advocate policies for the monarch to adopt.

Yet, like everything else in seventeenth-century government, the court revolved around the monarch. The monarch appointed, promoted, and dismissed officeholders at will. As befit this type of personal government, most monarchs chose a single individual to act as a funnel for private and public business. This was the "favorite," whose role combined varying proportions of best friend, right-hand man, and hired gun. Some favorites, like the French Cardinal Richelieu and the Spanish Count-Duke Olivares, were able to transform themselves into chief ministers with a political philosophy and a vision of government. Others, like the English Duke of Buckingham, simply remained royal companions. Favorites walked a not very tight rope. They could retain their balance only as long as they retained their influence with the monarch. Richelieu claimed that it was "more difficult to dominate the four square feet of the king's study than the affairs of Europe." Ministers acted as a safety valve for the monarchy. When royal policy suc-

This portrait of Richelieu by Philippe de Champaigne shows the cardinal's intellectual power and controlled determination.

ceeded it was the king's success; when royal policy failed it was the minister's failure. Critics could attack the influence of "evil advisers" without attacking the king. The parallel careers of Richelieu, Olivares, and Buckingham neatly illustrate the dangers and opportunities of the office.

Cardinal Richelieu (1585–1642) was born into a noble family of minor importance. A younger son, he trained for the law and then for a position that his family owned in the Church. After skillful participation in the meeting of the Estates-General of 1614, Richelieu was given a court post through the patronage of Queen Marie de Médicis, mother of Louis XIII. He gradually established his own relationship with the king. Richelieu was sixteen years older than Louis XIII and he often acted toward him as a parent to a child, roles to which neither the celibate cardinal nor the fatherless monarch were well suited. Still the two men made a good match. Louis XIII hated the work of ruling and Richelieu loved little else. Though Richelieu received great favor from the king—he became a duke and amassed the largest private fortune in France—his position rested upon his managerial abilities. Richelieu never enjoyed a close personal relationship with his monarch, and he never felt that his position was secure. In 1630, Marie de Médicis turned against him and he was very nearly ousted from office. His last years were filled with suppressing plots to undermine his power or to take his life. Yet in 1642 he died in the arms of the king whom he had served with near total devotion for almost two decades.

The Count-Duke Olivares (1587–1645) was a younger son of a lesser branch of a great Spanish noble family. Though Olivares trained for a career in the Church, by the time he was twenty he had outlived his father and two elder brothers. He was thus able to become a courtier with a title, a large fortune, and most unusually, a university education. Olivares was soon the favorite courtier of the prince, and when Philip III suddenly died in 1621, Olivares became the favorite of the new king, Philip IV (1621–65. He was elevated to the highest rank of the nobility and lost no time consolidating his position. He moved into rooms directly adjoining those of the monarch and served personally as one of the grooms of the chamber who helped the king to dress.

Olivares used his closeness to the monarch to gain court appointments for his relatives and political supporters, but he was more interested in establishing political policy than in building a court faction. His objective was to maintain the greatness of Spain, whose fortunes, like the Count-Duke's moods, waxed and waned. Like Richelieu, Olivares attempted to further the process of centralizing royal power, which was not very advanced in Spain. And like his French counterpart, he was unable to overcome entrenched opposition. Olivares' plans for a nationally recruited and financed army ended in disaster. His efforts at tax reform went unrewarded. He advocated the aggressive foreign policy that mired Spain in the Thirty Years' War in Europe and the eighty years of war in the Netherlands. As domestic and foreign crises mounted, Philip IV could not resist the pressure to dismiss his chief minister. In 1643 Olivares was removed from office and two years later, physically exhausted and mentally deranged, he died.

The Spanish master Diego Velázquez painted this portrait of the Count-Duke Olivares.

George Villiers, duke of Buckingham. The royal favorite virtually ruled the country between 1618 and 1628. The general rejoicing at his death embittered the king and helped bring about the eleven years' rule without Parliament.

The Duke of Buckingham (1592–1628) was also a younger son, but not of the nobility. He received the aimless education of a country gentleman, spending several years in France learning the graces of fashion and dancing. Reputedly one of the most handsome men in Europe, Buckingham hung about the fringes of the English court until his looks and charm brought him to the attention of Queen Anne, James I's wife. She recommended him for the office of cupbearer, a minor official who carried drinks to the royal table. Frequently in the king's presence, Buckingham quickly caught the eye of James I. Soon

James would have no one else at his side, and Buckingham's rise was meteoric. In less than seven years he went from commoner to duke, the highest rank of the English nobility.

Along with his titles, Buckingham acquired political power. He assumed a large number of royal offices, among them Admiral of the Navy, and placed his relatives and dependents in many others. Buckingham took his obligations seriously. He began a reform of naval administration, for example, but his rise to power was so sudden that he found enemies at every turn. These increased dramatically when James I died in 1625. There was to be no new broom to sweep away the duke and his supporters. He succeeded where so many others had failed by becoming the favorite and chief minister of the new king, Charles I (1625–49). His accumulation of power and patronage proceeded unabated, as did the enmity he aroused. Buckingham became the symbol of everything that was wrong with the nation. But Charles I stood firmly behind him. A discontented naval officer finally accomplished what the most powerful men in England could not. In 1628 Buckingham was assassinated. While Charles I wept inconsolably at the news, ordinary Londoners drank to the health of his killer.

The Drive to Govern

Richelieu, Olivares, and Buckingham met very different ends. Yet in their own ways they shared a common goal, to extend the authority and control of the monarch over his state.

One of the chief means by which kings and councilors attempted to expand the authority of the state was through the legal system. Administering justice was one of the sacred duties of the monarchy. The complexities of ecclesiastical, civil, and customary law gave trained lawyers an essential role in government. As legal experts and the demands for legal services increased, royal law courts multiplied and expanded. In France, the Parlement of Paris, the main law court of the state, became a powerful institution that contested with courtiers for the right to advise the monarch. The number of regional parlements increased, bringing royal justice to the farthest reaches of the realm. Members of the Parlement of Paris and of the expanding provincial parlements were known as nobility of the robe, from the long gowns worn by lawyers and judges. In Spain the *letrados*—university-trained lawyers who were normally members of the nobility—were the backbone of royal government. Formal legal training was a requirement for many of the administrative posts in the state. In Castile members of all social classes frequently used the royal courts to settle personal disputes. The expansion of a centralized system of justice thus joined the interests of subjects and the monarchy.

In England the legal system expanded differently. Central courts situated in the royal palace of Westminster grew and the lawyers and judges who practiced in them became a powerful profession. They were especially active in the House of Commons of the English Parliament, which along with the House of Lords had extensive advisory and legislative powers. More important than the rise of the central courts, however, was the rise of the local ones. The English Crown extended royal justice to the counties by granting legal authority to members of the local social elite. These justices of the peace, as they were known, became agents of the Crown in their own localities. Justices were given power to hear and settle minor cases and to imprison those who had committed serious offenses until the assizes, the semiannual sessions of the county court.

Assizes combined the ceremony of rule with its process. Royal authority was displayed in a great procession to the courthouse that was led by the judge and the county justices, followed by the grand and petty juries of local citizens who would hear the cases, and finally by the carts carrying the prisoners to trial. Along with the legal business that was performed, assizes were occasions for edifying sermons, typically on the theme of obedience. Their solemnity, marked by the black robes of the judge, the Latin of the legal proceedings, and the public executions with which assizes invariably ended, all served to instill a sense of the power of the state in the throngs of ordinary people who witnessed them.

Efforts to integrate center and locality extended to more than the exercise of justice. The monarch also needed officials who could enforce royal policy in those localities where the special privileges of groups and individuals remained strong. The best strategy was to appoint local leaders to royal office. But with so much of the aristocracy resident at court, this was not always an effective course. In France, the provincial governors were traditionally members of the ancient nobility who enjoyed wide powers in matters of military recruitment, revenue collection, and judicial administration. But many governors spent far more time in Paris than in the locality that they were to administer and often opposed the exactions demanded by the monarch. By the beginning of the seventeenth century, the French monarchy began to rely on new central officials known as *intendants* to perform many of the tasks of the provincial governors. Cardinal Richelieu expanded the use of the intendants and by the middle of the century they had become a vital part of royal government.

The Lords Lieutenant were a parallel institution created in England. Unlike every other European state, England had no national army. Every English county was required to raise, equip, and train its own militia. Lords Lieutenant were in charge of these trained bands. Since the aristocracy was the ancient military class in the state, the lieutenants were chosen from the greatest nobles of the realm. But they delegated their work to members of the gentry, large local landholders who took on their tasks as a matter of prestige rather than profit. Perhaps not surprisingly, the English military was among the weakest in Europe and nearly all its foreign adventures ended in disaster.

Efforts to centralize the affairs of the Spanish monarchy could not proceed so easily. The separate regions over which the king ruled maintained their own laws and privileges. Attempts to apply Castilian rules or implant Castilian officials always drew opposition from other regions. Olivares frequently complained that Philip IV was the king of Castile only and nothing but a thorough plan of unification would make him the king of Spain. This he proposed in 1625 to attempt to solve the dual problems of military manpower and military finance. After 1621, Spain was again deeply involved in European warfare. Fighting in the Netherlands and in Germany demanded large armies and larger sums of money. Olivares launched a plan for a Union of Arms to which all the separate regions of the empire, including Mexico and Peru in the west, Italy in the east, and the separate regions in Iberia would contribute. He envisioned an army of 140,000 but soon lowered his sights. Not all of the Iberian provinces were persuaded to contribute. Catalonia, stood upon its ancient privileges and refused to grant either troops or funds. But Olivares was able to establish at least the principle of unified cooperation.

Taxing Demands

More than anything else, war propelled the consolidation of the state. Whether offensive or defensive, continuous or intermittent, successful or calamitous, war was the irresistible force of the seventeenth-century monarchy. War taxation was its immovable object. Perhaps half of all revenue of the western states went to finance war. To maintain its armies and navies, its fortresses and outposts, the state had to squeeze every penny from its subjects. Old taxes had to be collected more efficiently, new taxes had to be introduced and enforced. As one Spanish jurist observed in a familiar refrain, "there can be no peace without arms, no arms without money, and no money without taxation." On the other side, the unprecedented demands for money on the part of the state were always resisted. The privileged challenged the legality of levying taxes, the unprivileged did whatever they could to avoid paying them.

The claims and counterclaims were very strong. In the first place, armies were bigger and more expensive. In 1625 Philip IV had nearly three hundred thousand men in arms throughout his empire. The expense of maintaining Spanish fortresses alone had quintupled since the time of Philip II. Not only were there more men to pay, equip, and supply, but the cost of war materials continued to rise with inflation. Similarly, the cost of food and fodder rose. Marauding armies might be able to plunder sufficient grain during the spring and autumn, but they still consumed massive amounts of meat and drink that could not be supplied locally.

The economic hardships caused by the ceaseless military activity touched everyone. Those in the direct path of battle had little left to feed themselves, let alone to provide to the state. The disruption of the delicate cycle of planting and harvesting devastated local communities. Armies plundered ripened grain and trampled seedlings as they moved through fields. The conscription of village men and boys removed vital skills from the community and upset the gender-based division of labor. Peasants were squeezed by the armies for crops, by the lords for rents, and by the state for taxes.

In fact, the inability of the lower orders of European society to finance a century of warfare was clear from the beginning. In Spain and France, the principal problem was that so much of the wealth of the nation was beyond the reach of traditional royal taxation. The nobility and many of the most important towns had long achieved exemption from basic taxes on consumption and wealth. European taxation was regressive, falling most heavily upon those least able to pay. Rulers and subjects alike recognized the inequities of the European system of taxation. Regime after regime began with plans to overhaul the national system of taxation before settling for propping up new emergency levies against the rotting foundations of the old structure. Nevertheless, the fiscal crisis that the European wars provoked did result in an expansion of state taxation.

In France, for example, royal expenditures rose 60 percent during the first two decades of the seventeenth century, while the yield from the *taille,* the crown's basic commodity tax, remained constant. Thus the crown was forced to search for new revenues, the most important of which was the *paulette,* a tax on officeholding. To raise money, especially in emergencies, the crown had been forced to sell government offices, until by the seventeenth century a majority of offices had been obtained by direct purchase. The sale of an office provided a one-time windfall for the crown, but after that the cost of salaries and benefits was a perpetual drain. So, too, were the administrative costs of potentially inefficient officeholders. Many purchased their posts as an investment and treated them as personal property. For an annual payment of 1/60 the value of the office, the *paulette* allowed the current holder to sell or bequeath it as desired. Henry IV instituted the *paulette* in 1604, and it became a vital source of royal revenue as well as an acute source of aristocratic and legal complaint. In the early 1620s, revenue from the sale of offices amounted to one-third of the crown's income. The purchase of office was inherently corrupt, but it was not necessarily inefficient. Sons who were to inherit offices could be trained for their posts, if for no other reason than to operate them profitably. The crown received money from classes in society that were generally beyond the reach of taxation, while members of these classes received power, prestige, and experience in public service. As long as profit and efficiency went hand in hand, both officeholder and monarch might be well served. Unfortunately, it was the king rather than his officers who had the greatest incentive to manipulate the system. The more offices that could be created, the larger the income from the *paulette*. During fiscal emergencies this was a temptation to which all French monarchs succumbed.

Fiscal emergency was just another name for the routine problems of the Spanish monarchy. As the greatest military power in Europe, Spain necessarily had the greatest military budget and thus the most extensive system of taxation. The crown taxed both domestic and imperial trade and took a healthy share of the gold and silver that continued to be mined in America. But all these revenues fell short of the state's needs. In the 1590s Philip II established an important new source of internal taxation. In an agreement with the Cortes of Castile he introduced the *milliones*, a tax on consumption that was to yield millions of ducats a year for war costs. An extremely regressive measure, the *milliones* taxed the sale of meat, wine, and oil, the basic elements of diet. It was a tax that hit urban areas particularly hard and was originally designed to last only six years. But the crises that the crown pleaded in the 1590s were even deeper at the turn of the century. The *milliones* became a permanent tax and a permanent grievance throughout Castile.

By contrast, the English crown was never able to persuade Parliament to grant permanent additional revenues. Though uninvolved in the European conflicts, England was not immune from military spending. War with Ireland in the 1590s and with Spain between 1588 and 1604 depleted the reserves that the crown had obtained when Henry VIII dissolved the monasteries. Disasterous wars against France and Spain in the 1620s provoked fiscal crisis for a monarchy that had few direct sources of revenue. While the great wealth of the kingdom was in land, the chief sources of revenue for the crown were in trade. In the early seventeenth century customs duties, or impositions, became a lucrative source of income when the judges ruled that the king could determine which commodities could be taxed and at what rate. Impositions fell heavily upon the merchant classes and upon urban consumers, but unlike the *milliones*, impositions were placed on luxury import goods rather than basic commodities.

Because so much of the crown's revenues derived from commerce and because foreign invasion could only come from the sea, the most pressing military need of the English monarchy was for naval defense. Even during the Armada crisis, the largest part of the English fleet had been made up of private merchant ships pressed into service through the emergency tax of Ship Money. This was a tax on each port town to hire a merchant ship and fit it out for war. In the 1630s, Charles I revived Ship Money and extended it to all English localities. His innovation aroused much opposition from the gentry, especially after his refusal to call Parliament into session to have the tax confirmed.

War finance was like an all-consuming monster. No matter how much new revenue was fed into it, its appetite grew for more. New taxes and increased rates of traditional taxation created suffering and a sense of grievance throughout the western European states. Opposition to taxation was not based on greed. The state's right to tax was not yet an established principle. Monarchs received certain forms of revenue in return for grants of immunities and privileges to powerful groups in their state. The state's efforts to go beyond these restricted grants was viewed as theft of private property. In the Ship Money case challengers argued that the king had no right to what belonged to his subjects except in a case of national emergency. This was a claim that the king accepted, arguing that such an emergency existed in the presence of pirates who were attacking English shipping. But if Charles I did not make a convincing claim for national emergency, the monarchs of France and Spain, the princes of Germany, and the rulers of the states of eastern Europe all did.

The Crises of the Royal State

The expansion of the functions, duties, and powers of the state in the early seventeenth century was not universally welcomed in European societies. The growth of central government came at the expense of local rights and privileges held by corporate bodies like the Church and the towns or by individuals like provincial officials and aristocrats. The state proved a powerful competitor, especially in the contest for the meager surplus produced on the land. As rents and prices stabilized in the early seventeenth century, after a long period of inflation, taxation increased, slowly at first and then at a pace with the gathering momentum of the Thirty Years' War. State exactions burdened all segments of society. Peasants lost the small benefit that rising prices had conferred upon producers. The surplus that parents had once passed on to children was now taken by the state. Local officials, never altogether popular, came to be seen as parasites and were easy targets for peasant rebellions. Larger landholders, whose prosperity depended upon rents and services from an increasingly impoverished peasantry, suffered along with their tenants. Even the great magnates were appalled by the state's insatiable appetite.

It was not only taxation that aroused opposition. Social and economic regulation meant more laws. More laws meant more lawyers and agents of enforcement. State regulation may have been more efficient—though many believed it was more efficient only for the state—but it was certainly disruptive. It was also expensive at a time when the fragile European economy was in a phase of decline. The early seventeenth century was a time of hunger in most of western Europe. Subtle changes in climate reduced the length of growing seasons and the size of crops. Bad harvests in the 1620s and 1640s left disease and starvation in their wake. And the wars ground on. Armies brought misery to those who were forcibly recruited to fight, those who were taxed into destitution, and those who simply had the misfortune to live in the path of destruction.

By the middle of the seventeenth century, a Europe-wide crisis was taking shape, though its timing and its forms differed from place to place.

Rural protests, like grain riots and mob assaults on local institutions, had a long history in all of the European states. Popular revolt was not the product of mindless despair, but rather the natural form of political action for those who fell outside the institutionalized political process. Bread riots and tax revolts became increasingly common in the early seventeenth century. More importantly, as the focus of discontent moved from local institutions to the state, the forms of revolt changed. So, too, did the participants. Members of the political elite began to formulate their own grievances against the expansion of state power. A theory of resistance, first developed in the French wars of religion, came to be applied to political tyranny and posed a direct challenge to the idea of the divine right of kings. By the 1640s all of these forces converged and rebellion exploded across the Continent. In Spain the ancient kingdoms of Catalonia and Portugal asserted their independence from Castilian rule; in France members of the aristocracy rose against a child monarch and his regent. In Italy, revolts rocked Naples and Sicily. In England, a constitutional crisis gave way to civil war and then to the first political revolution in European history.

The Need to Resist

Europeans lived more precariously in the seventeenth century than in any period since the Black Death. One benchmark of crisis was population decline. In the Mediterranean, Spanish population fell from 8.5 to 7 million and Italian population from 13 to 11 million. The ravages of the Thirty Years' War were most clearly felt in central Europe. Germany lost nearly a third of its people, Bohemia nearly half. Northwestern Europe—

European Population Data (in millions)							
Year	1550	1575	1600	1625	1650	1675	1700
England	3		4	4.5		5.8	5.8
France		20					19.3
Italy	11	13	13	13	12	11.5	12.5
Russia	9		11	8	9.5	13	16
Spain	6.3		7.6		5.2		7
All Europe	85	95	100	100	80	90	100

that is, England, the Netherlands, and France—was hardest hit in the first half of the century and only gradually recovered by 1700. Population decline had many causes and, rather remarkably, direct casualties from warfare were a very small component. The indirect effects of war, the disruption of agriculture, and the spread of disease were far more devastating. Spain alone lost a half million people at the turn of the century and another half million between 1647 and 1652. Severe outbreaks in 1625 and in 1665 hit England, while France endured three consecutive years of epidemics from 1629 to 1631.

All sectors of the European economy from agriculture to trade stagnated or declined in the early seventeenth century. Not surprisingly, peasants were hardest hit. The surplus from good harvests did not remain in rural communities to act as a buffer for bad ones. Tens of thousands died during the two great subsistence crises in the late 1620s and the late 1640s. In England, starvation was most common in the north, where scrubland had been put under the plow to accommodate the expanding population. Northern Italy lost nearly a third of its inhabitants between 1628 and 1630 with the simultaneous appearance of bad harvests, plague, and marauding armies. Even the weather became a scourge. The entire period from 1647 to 1653 was the worst ever in parts of France. Five consecutive bad harvests decimated the countryside. A Spanish official observed: "many places which a few years ago had 500 inhabitants now have barely 100. There are numerous families who go one or two days without a full meal and others live on herbs and roots from the fields."

Predictably, acute economic crisis led to rural revolt. As the French peasants reeled from visitations of plague, frost, and floods, the French state was raising the *taille*, the tax that fell most heavily upon the lower orders. A series of French rural revolts in the late 1630s focused on opposition to tax increases. The Nu-Pieds—the barefooted—rose against changes in the salt tax, others rose against new levies on wine. These revolts began in the same way, with the murder of a local tax official, the organization of a peasant militia, and the recruitment of local clergy and notables. The rebels forced temporary concessions from local authorities, but they never achieved lasting

The Plague in Milan, *a painting by Caspar Crayer of the seventeenth-century Flemish school. The victims of the epidemic are shown being consoled by a priest.*

reforms. Each revolt ended with the reimposition of order by the state. In England the largest rural protests, like the Midland Revolt of 1607, centered upon opposition to the enclosure of grain fields and their conversion to pasture.

The most spectacular popular uprisings occurred in Spanish-occupied Italy. In the spring of 1647 the Sicilian city of Palermo exploded under the pressure of a disastrous harvest, rising food prices, and relentless taxation. A city of 130,000 inhabitants, Palermo imported nearly all of its foodstuffs. As grain prices rose, the city government subsidized the price of bread, running up huge debts in the process. When the town governors could no longer afford the subsidies, they decided to reduce the size of the loaf rather than increase its price. This did not fool the women of the city, who rioted when the first undersized loaves were placed on sale. Soon the entire city was in revolt. "Long live the king and down with taxes," became the rebel slogan. Commoners who were not part of the urban power structure led the revolt in Palermo. For a time they achieved the abolition of Spanish taxes on basic foodstuffs. Their success provided the model for a similar uprising in Naples, the largest city in Europe. The Neapolitan revolt began in 1647 after the Spanish placed a tax on fruit. A crowd gathered to protest the new imposition, burned the customs house, and murdered several local officials. The protesters were led first by a fisherman and then by a blacksmith, and again the rebels achieved the temporary suspension of Spanish taxation. But neither of the Italian urban revolts could attract support from the local governors or the nobility. Both uprisings were eventually crushed.

The Right to Resist

Rural and urban revolts by members of the lower orders of European society were doomed to failure. Not only did the state control vast military resources, but it could count upon the loyalty of the governing classes to suppress local disorder. It was only when local elites rebelled and joined their social and political discontent to the economic grievances of the peasants that the state faced a genuine crisis. Traditionally, aristocratic rebellion centered upon the legitimacy rather than the power of the state. Claimants to the throne initiated civil wars for the prize of the crown. By the early seventeenth century, however, hereditary monarchy was too firmly entrenched to be threatened by aristocratic rebellions. When Elizabeth I of England died without an heir, the throne passed to her cousin, James I, without even a murmur of discontent. The assassination of Henry IV in 1610 left a child on the French throne, yet it provoked little more than intrigue over which aristocratic faction would advise him. The principles of hereditary monarchy and the divine right of kings laid an unshakable foundation for royal legitimacy. But if the monarch's right to rule could no longer be challenged, was the method of rule equally unassailable? Were subjects bound to their sovereign in all cases whatsoever?

Luther and Calvin had preached a doctrine of passive obedience. Magistrates ruled by divine will and must be obeyed in all things, they argued. Both left a tiny crack in the door of absolute submission, however, by recognizing the right of lesser magistrates to resist their superiors if divine law was violated. It was during the French civil wars that a broader theory of resistance began to develop. In attempting to defend themselves from accusations that they were rebels, a number of Huguenot writers responded with an argument that accepted the divine right of kings but that limited royal power. They claimed that kings were placed on earth by God to uphold piety and justice. When they failed to do so, lesser magistrates were obliged to resist them. As God would not institute tyranny, oppressive monarchs could not be acting by divine right. Therefore, the king who violated divine law could be punished. In the most influential of these writings, *A Defense of Liberty Against Tyrants* (1579), Philippe Duplessis-Mornay (1549–1623) took the critical next step and argued that the king who violated the law of the land could also be resisted.

In the writings of both Huguenot and Dutch Protestants there remained strict limits to this right to resist. These authors accepted all the premises of divine right theory and restricted resistance to other divinely ordained magistrates. Obedience tied society together at all levels. Loosening any of the knots might unravel everything. In fact, one crucial binding had already come loose when the arguments used to justify resistance in matters of religion came to be applied to of matters of state. Logic soon drove the argument further. If it was the duty of lesser magistrates to resist monarchical tyranny, why was it not the duty of all citizens to do so? This was a question posed not by a Protestant rebel, but by a Jesuit professor, Juan de Mariana (1536–1624). In *The King and the Education of the King* (1598), Mariana described how human government developed from the need of individuals to have leaders to act for their convenience and well-being. These magistrates were first established by the people and then legitimated by God. Magistrates were nothing other than the people's representatives, and if it was the duty of magistrates to resist the tyranny of monarchs, then it must also be the duty of every individual citizen. "If the sacred fatherland is falling into ruins, he who tries to kill the tyrant will be acting in no ways unjustly."

Mariana was careful to specify that only the most willful and deliberate lawbreakers were actually tyrants. He also advocated the use of national assemblies rather than individual assassins to make the decision to punish them. But there was no escaping the implications of his argument. If anyone could judge the conduct of kings, then there would be no standards of judgment. As Cardinal Richelieu observed succinctly: "tyranny is monarchy misliked." In 1605 a Catholic conspiracy to murder James I of England was foiled by government agents at the last moment. In 1610 a religious fanatic assassinated Henry IV of France. The right of individuals to resist tyrants was rapidly developing into the right of subjects to overthrow their monarchs.

In fact, there remained one more vital link in the chain. This was supplied by the great English poet John Milton (1608–74) in his defense of the English Revolution. Milton built upon traditional resistance theory as it had developed over the previous fifty years. Kings were instituted by the people to uphold piety and justice. Lesser magistrates had the right to resist monarchs. An unjust king forfeited his divine right and was to be punished as any ordinary citizen. In *The Tenure of Kings and Magistrates* (1649), Milton expanded upon the conventional idea that society was formed by a covenant, or contract, between ruler and ruled. The king in his coronation oath promised to uphold the laws of the land and to rule for the benefit of his subjects. The subjects promised to obey. Failure to meet obligations—by either side—broke the contract.

By the middle of the seventeenth century, resistance theory provided the intellectual justification for a number of quite different attacks upon monarchical authority. In 1640 simultaneous rebellions in the ancient kingdoms of Portugal and Catalonia threatened the Spanish monarchy. The Portuguese successfully dissolved the rather artificial bonds that had been created by Philip II and resumed their separate national identity. Catalonia, the easternmost province of Spain, which Ferdinand of Aragon had brought to the union of crowns in the fifteenth century, presented a more serious challenge. Throughout the 1620s, Catalonia, with its rich Mediterranean city of Barcelona, had consistently rebuffed Olivares' attempts to consolidate the Spanish provinces.

The Catalonian Cortes—the representative institution of the towns—refused to make even small contributions to the Union of Arms or to successive appeals for emergency tax increases. Catalonian leaders feared that these demands were only the thin edge of the wedge. They did not want their province to go the way of Castile, where taxation was as much an epidemic as was plague.

Catalonia relied upon its ancient laws to fend off demands for contributions to the Spanish military effort. But soon the province was embroiled in the French war and Olivares was forced to bring troops into Catalonia. The presence of the soldiers and their conduct inflamed the local population. In the spring of 1640 an unconnected series of peasant uprisings took place. Soldiers and royal officials were slain, and the Spanish viceroy of the province was murdered. But the violence was not only directed against outsiders. Attacks upon wealthy citizens raised the specter of social revolt.

It was at this point that a peasant uprising broadened into a provincial rebellion. The political leaders of Barcelona not only decided to sanction the rebellion, they decided to lead it. They declared that Philip IV had violated the fundamental laws of Catalonia and that in consequence their allegiance to the crown of Spain was dissolved. Instead they turned to Louis XIII of France, offering him sovereignty if he would preserve their liberties. In fact, the Catalonians simply exchanged a devil they knew for one they did not. The French happily sent troops into Barcelona to repel a Spanish attempt to crush the rebellion. Now two armies occupied Catalonia. The Catalan rebellion lasted for twelve years. When the Spanish finally took Barcelona in 1652, both rebels and ruler were exhausted from the struggle.

The revolt of the Catalans posed a greater external threat to the Spanish monarchy than it did an internal one. In contrast, the French Fronde, an aristocratic rebellion that began in 1648, was more directly a challenge to the underlying authority of the state. It too began in response to fiscal crises brought on by war. Throughout the 1640s the French state had tottered on the edge of bankruptcy. It had used every means of creative financing that its ministers could devise, mortgaging as much of the future as anyone would buy. Still it was necessary to raise traditional taxes and to institute new ones. The first tactic revived

A episode from the second Fronde, one of the two French civil wars that occurred during the minority of Louis XIV.

peasant revolts, especially in the early years of the decade; the second led to the Fronde.

Louis XIV (1643–1715) was four years old when he inherited the French throne. His mother, Anne of Austria (1601–66), ruled as regent with the help of her Italian advisor, Cardinal Mazarin (1602–61). In the circumstances of war, agricultural crisis, and financial stringency, no regency government was going to be popular, but Anne and Mazarin made the worst of a bad situation. They initiated new taxes on officeholders, Parisian landowners, and the nobility. Soon all three united against them, led by the Parlement of Paris, the highest court in the land, in which new decrees of taxation had to be registered. In 1648 the Parlement refused to register a number of the new taxes proposed by the government and soon insisted upon the right to control the crown's financial policy. When Anne and Mazarin struck back by arresting a number of leading members of the Parlement, barricades went up in Paris, and the court, along with the nine-year-old king, fled the capital. As the in-group of courtiers scurried out of Paris, the out-group hustled into it. Quickly the Fronde—which took its name from the slingshots that children used to hurl stones at carriages—became an aristocratic revolt aimed not at the king, but at his advisers. Demands for Mazarin's resignation, the removal of the new taxes, and greater participation in government by nobles and Parlement were coupled with profuse statements of loyalty to the king. Even the Parisian population, who took the opportunity of the dis-

order to settle old scores with the tax collectors, wanted little more than the stable rule of the boy king.

Had the Fronde taken place during a period of international peace, Mazarin might have succeeded in isolating Paris and starving the rebels into submission. Instead the French got a taste of the medicine they had served up to the Spanish in the Catalonian revolt. The Duc de Condé, leader of the Parisian insurgents, courted Spanish aid against Mazarin's forces, and the cardinal was forced to make concessions to prevent another Spanish invasion of France. The leaders of the Fronde agreed that the crown must overhaul its finances and recognize the rights of the administrative nobility to participate in formulating royal policy. But they had no concrete proposals to accomplish either aim. Nor could they control the deteriorating political situation in Paris and a number of provincial capitals where urban and rural riots followed the upper-class attack upon the state. The catastrophic winter of 1652, with its combination of harvest failure, intense cold, and epidemic disease, brought the crisis to a head. Louis XIV was declared old enough to rule and his forces recaptured Paris, where he was welcomed as a savior. Born of frustration, fear, and greed, the Fronde accomplished little. Like the Catalonian revolt, it revealed the fragility of the absolute state on the one hand, yet its underlying stability on the other. In neither France nor Spain was there ever any real alternative to royal rule.

The English Civil Wars

On the surface, it is difficult to understand why the most profound challenge to monarchical authority took place in England. Among the nations of Europe, England alone enjoyed peace in the early seventeenth century. Except for a brief period around 1620, the English economy sputtered along. The monarchy itself was stable. James I had succeeded his cousin Elizabeth I without challenge and already had as many children as the Tudors had produced in nearly a century.

James I was not a lovable monarch but he was capable, astute, and generous. In the eyes of his critics he had two great faults: he succeeded a legend and he was Scottish. There was little he could do about either. Elizabeth I had ruled England successfully for over forty years. As the economy soured and the state tilted toward bankruptcy in the 1590s, the queen remained above criticism. She sold off royal lands worth thousands of pounds and ran up huge debts at the turn of the century. Yet the gleaming myth of the glorious virgin queen tarnished not the least bit. When she died, the general population wept openly and the governing elite breathed a collective sigh of relief. There was so much to be done to set things right.

At first, James I endeared himself to the English gentry and aristocracy by showering them with the gift of social elevation. On his way to London from Scotland, the first of the Stuart kings knighted thousands of gentlemen who had waited in vain for favor from the queen. He promoted peers and created new titles to meet the pent-up demands of decades of stinginess. But he showered favor equally on his own countrymen, members of his royal Scottish court who accompanied him to England. A strong strain of ethnic prejudice combined with the disappointed hopes of English courtiers to generate immediate hostility to the new regime. If Elizabeth could do no wrong, James could do little right. Though he relied upon Elizabeth's most trusted ministers to guide state business, James was soon plunged into financial and political difficulties. He never escaped from either.

His financial problems resulted directly from the fact that the tax base of the English monarchy was undervalued. For decades the monarchy had staved off a crisis by selling lands that had been confiscated from the Church in the mid-sixteenth century. But this solution reduced the crown's long-term revenues and made it dependent upon extraordinary grants of taxation from Parliament. Royal demands for money were met by parliamentary demands for political reform, and these differing objectives provoked unintentional political controversies in the 1620s. The most significant, in 1628, during the reign of Charles I, led to the formulation of the Petition of Right, which restated the traditional English freedoms from arbitrary arrest and imprisonment (habeas corpus), from nonparliamentary taxation, and from the confiscation of property by martial law.

Religious problems mounted on top of economic and political difficulties. Demands were made for thoroughgoing church reforms by groups and individuals who had little in common other than the name given to them by their detractors: Puritans. One of the most contentious issues raised by Puritans was the survival in the Anglican church of the Catholic hierarchy of archbishops and bishops. They demanded the abolition of this episcopal form of government and its replacement with a presbyterial system similar to that in Scotland, in which congregations nominated their own representatives to a national assembly. As the king was the supreme head of the English church, an attack upon church structure was an attack upon the monarchy. "No bishop, no king," James I declared as he rejected the first formal attempts at reform. But neither James I nor his son, Charles I, opposed religious reform. They too wanted a better educated clergy, a plain and decorous worship service, and godly citizens. But to achieve their reforms they strengthened episcopal power. In the 1620s Archbishop William Laud (1573–1645) rose to power in the English church by espousing a Calvinism so moderate that many denied it was Calvinism at all. Laud preached the beauty of holiness and strove to reintroduce decoration in the church and a formal decorum in the service. One of Laud's first projects after he was appointed archbishop of Canterbury was to establish a consistent divine service in England and Scotland by creating new prayer books.

It fell to the unfortunate dean of St. Giles Cathedral in Edinburgh Cathedral to introduce the new Scottish prayer book in 1637. The reaction was immediate: someone threw a stool at his head and dozens of women screamed that "popery" was being brought to Scotland. There were riots by citizens and resistance to the use of the new prayer book by clergy and the nobility. To Charles I the opposition was rebellion and he began to raise forces to suppress it. But Scottish soldiers were far more determined to preserve their religious practice than were English soldiers to impose the king's. By the end of 1640 a Scottish army had successfully invaded England.

Now the fiscal and political problems of the Stuart monarchs came into play. For eleven years Charles I had managed to do what he was in theory supposed to do, live from his own revenues. He had accomplished this by a combination of economy and the revival of ancient feudal rights that struck hard at the governing classes. He levied fines for unheard-of offenses, expanded traditional taxes, and added a brutal efficiency to the collection of revenue. While these expedients sufficed during peacetime, now that an army had to be raised and a war fought, Charles I was again dependent upon grants from Parliament, which he reluctantly summoned in 1640.

The Long Parliament, which met in November 1640 and sat for thirteen years, saw little urgency in levying taxes to repel the Scots. After all, the Scots were resisting Laud's religious innovations and there were many Englishmen who believed that they should be resisted. More to the point, members of Parliament had a host of political grievances to be redressed before they granted the king his money. Parliament proposed a number of constitutional reforms that Charles I reluctantly accepted. The Long Parliament would not be dismissed without its own consent. In the future Parliaments would be summoned once in every three years. Due process in common law would be observed and the ancient taxes that the crown had revived would be abolished. To show its seriousness of purpose, Parliament, as the highest court in the land, tried and executed Charles' leading political adviser, the Earl of Strafford, and imprisoned Archbishop Laud.

At first Charles I could do nothing but bide his time and accept these assaults upon his power and authority. Once he had crushed the Scots he would be able to bargain from a position of strength. But as the months passed it became clear that Parliament had no intention of providing him with money or forces. Rather, the members sought to negotiate with the Scots themselves and to continue to demand concessions from the king as long as the Scottish threat remained. By the end of 1641 Charles' patience had worn thin. He bungled an attempt to arrest the leaders of the House of Commons, but he successfully spirited his wife and children out of London. Then he too left the capital and headed north where, in the summer of 1642, he raised the royal standard and declared the leaders of Parliament rebels and traitors. England was plunged into civil war.

Parliament had finally pushed too hard and its members now found themselves in the unprecedented situation of having to fight a war against their sovereign, a war that few of them wanted and that hardly anyone believed they could win. One of the Parliament's generals summed up the futility of the situation: "If we defeat the king ninety-nine times, yet still he is king. But if he defeat us once we will all be hanged as traitors." Nevertheless, there were strong passions on both sides. Parliamentarians believed that they were fighting to defend their religion, their liberties, and the rule of law. Royalists believed they were fighting to defend their monarch, their church, and social stability. After nearly three years of inconclusive fighting, in June 1645 Parliament won a decisive victory at Naseby and brought the war to an end the following summer. The king was in captivity, bishops had been abolished, a Presbyterian church had been established, and limitations were placed on royal power. All that remained necessary to end three years of civil war was the king's agreement to abide by the judgment of battle.

But Charles I had no intention of surrendering either his religion or his authority. Despite the rebels' successes, they could not rule without him, and he would concede nothing as long as opportunities to maneuver remained. In 1647 there were opportunities galore. The war had proved ruinously expensive to Parliament. It owed enormous sums to the Scots, to its own soldiers, and to the governors of London. Each of these elements had its own objectives in a final settlement of the war and they were not altogether compatible. London feared the parliamentary army, unpaid

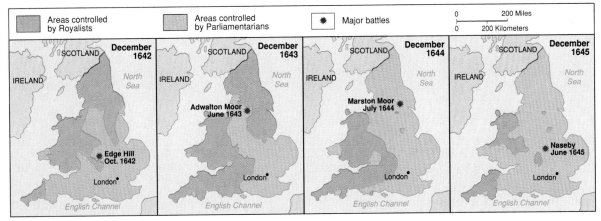

The English Civil War

and camped dangerously close to the capital. The Scots and the English Presbyterians in Parliament feared that the religious settlement already made would be sacrificed by those known as Independents, who desired a more decentralized church. The Independents feared that they would be persecuted just as harshly by the Presbyterians as they had been by the king. In fact, the war had settled nothing.

The English Revolutions

Charles I happily played both ends against the middle until the army decisively ended the game. In June 1647 soldiers kidnaped the king and demanded that Parliament pay their arrears, protect them from legal retribution, and recognize their service to the nation. Those in Parliament who opposed the army's intervention were impeached, and when London Presbyterians rose up against the army's show of force, troops moved in to occupy the city. The civil war, which had come so close to resolution in 1647, had now become a military revolution. Religious and political radicals flocked to the army and encouraged the soldiers to support their programs and to resist disbandment. New fighting broke out in 1648 as Charles encouraged his supporters to resume the war. But forces under the command of Sir Thomas Fairfax (1612–71) and Oliver Cromwell (1599–1658) easily crushed the royalist uprisings in England and Scotland. The army now

demanded that Charles I be brought to justice for his treacherous conduct both before and during the war. When the majority in Parliament refused, still hoping against hope to reach an accommodation with the king, the soldiers again acted decisively. In December 1648 army regiments were sent to London to purge the two houses of Parliament of those who opposed the army's demands. The remaining members, contemptuously called the Rump Parliament, voted to bring the king to trial for his crimes against the liberties of his subjects. On 30 January 1649, Charles I was executed and England was declared to be a commonwealth. (See Special Feature, "King Charles' Head," pp. 500–501.) The monarchy and the House of Lords were abolished and the nation was to be governed by what was left of the membership of the House of Commons.

For four years the members of the Rump Parliament struggled with proposals for a new constitution while balancing the demands of moderate and radical reformers and an increasingly hostile army. It achieved little other than to raise the level of frustration. In 1653 Oliver Cromwell, with the support of the army's senior officers, forcibly dissolved the Rump and became the leader of the revolutionary government. At first he ruled along with a Parliament handpicked from among the supporters of the commonwealth. When Cromwell's Parliament proved no more capable of governing than had the Rump, a written constitution, The Instrument of Government (1653) established a new polity. Cromwell was

King Charles' Head

They could have killed him quietly: the executioners slipping away silently in the night, unauthorized, unknown. It was the quickest way and it would end all doubts. Since June 1647, Charles I had been prisoner of the parliamentary army, and there had been more than one moment in which his elimination would have settled so many vexing problems. They could have let him escape: a small boat, an unlocked door, a guard conveniently asleep. Let him take his chances on the open sea. Let him live out his life in exile. Dangerous, perhaps, but still he would be gone and a new government in the name of the people could get on with creating a new order. They could have done it quietly.

Instead the leaders of Parliament and the army decided on a trial, a public presentation of charges against the king, a public judgment of his guilt. A high court of justice, enforcing the laws of England, would try its king for treason against the state. The logic was simple: if Parliament had fought for the preservation of the liberties of all Englishmen, then they could only proceed against the king by law. If they followed any other course, they were open to the charge that they were usurpers, that they ruled by the power of might rather than by the power of law. But if the logic was simple, everything else was hopelessly complex. English law was a system of precedents, one case stacking upon another to produce the weighty judgments of what was and was not law-

ful. Never had there been a treason case like this one. Indeed, how could the king commit treason, how could he violate his own allegiance? Always before the king acted as prosecutor, the king's judges had rendered decisions, and the king's executioner had carried out sentences. Not one of these precedents was now in the least way useful.

Nor was it clear what court had jurisdiction over this unprecedented case. The royal judges would have no part of it; neither would the House of Lords. The House of Commons was forced to create its own high court of justice, 135 supporters of the parliamentary cause drawn from its own members, from the army, and from among the leading citizens of London. Barely half attended any of the sessions. Judge John Bradshaw, who presided over two provincial royal courts, was chosen to preside at the king's trial after several of his more distinguished col-

leagues tactfully declined the post. Bradshaw took the precaution of lining his hat with lead against the chance that he would be shot at from the galleries rather than the floor.

These shortcomings did not deter the leaders of the parliamentary cause. These were unprecedented times and the ossified procedures of lawyers and law courts could not be allowed to detract from the undeniable justice of their cause. Charles I had committed treason against his nation. He had declared war on his people. He had brought Irish and Scottish armies into England to repress Parliament, and when that had failed he had negotiated with French, Danish, and Dutch troops for the same purpose. Even when he had been defeated in battle, when the judgment of God was clear for all to see, even then he plotted and he tricked. His lies were revealed by his own hand, his captured correspondence detailing how he intended to double-cross those to whom he swore he would be faithful. Cromwell called him "a man against whom the Lord had witnessed," and the prosecution needed no better testimony than that. If there were no precedents, then this trial would set one.

Nevertheless, the makeshift nature of the court provided the king with his line of attack. If there was to be a public display, then Charles I was determined to turn it to his advantage. Even as his royal palace was being converted into a courtroom and an execution platform was being hastily erected on one of its balconies, even now the king could not conceive that the nation could be governed without him. Royal government had guided England for a millennium and for all he could see would do so for another. Rather he feared that he would be deposed and replaced, and against that eventuality he had secured the escape of his two elder sons. They were safe in France and only his youngest child was in the hands of these savage parliamentarians.

About the trial itself, he worried not at all. There could be no court in the land that could try its king, no authority but his own that could determine a charge of treason. When it was read out that he was a tyrant and traitor, he burst out laughing. "Remember, I am your king, your lawful king and what sins you bring upon your heads and the judgment of God upon this land, think well upon it," he told his accusers.

The trial began on Saturday, 20 January 1649. Armed soldiers in battledress cleared the floor of the large chamber. Curious onlookers packed the galleries. Despite the fact that all former royalists had been ordered out of the city before the trial began, the king had more than one supporter well placed to heckle the commissioners. The king wore the enormous golden star of the Order of the Garter on his cloak but was allowed no other symbol of royalty to overawe his accusers.

The charge of "treason and high misdemeanors" had been carefully prepared. The king was accused of making war on his people "whereby much innocent blood of the free people of this nation hath been spilt." When the resounding indictment concluded, all eyes turned toward Charles I. Now he would have to answer the charge, guilty or not guilty, and in answering show the line of his defense. But the king chose a different strategy. Rather than answer the charge, he questioned the authority of the court. "I would know by what power I am called hither, a king cannot be tried by any superior jurisdiction here on earth." This was the weakest point of the parliamentary strategy. Judge Bradshaw could only assert that the court represented the free people of England. But Charles was relentless. He demanded precedents and refused to be silenced by the assertion that his objections were overruled.

The prosecutors had prepared a case against the king and were ready to call their witnesses. They hoped to place the king's evil conduct before the eyes of the nation. But in English law, a defendant who refused to plead was presumed to have pleaded guilty. Thus the king's trial ended as soon as it had begun. After three fruitless sessions, and much behind-the-scenes maneuvering, it was decided that the king should be condemned and sentenced to die. On 27 January, Judge Bradshaw appeared in the scarlet robes of justice and issued the sentence. Charles had prepared a statement for maximum effect and waited patiently to deliver it. Now it was the king's turn to be surprised. After pronouncing sentence, Bradshaw and the commissioners rose from the bench. "Will you not hear me a word, Sir," called a flustered Charles I. "No," replied the judge. "Guards, withdraw your prisoner."

Tuesday, 30 January, dawned cold and clear. It had been a bitter winter. Charles put on two shirts so that if he trembled from the cold it would not be interpreted as fear. In fact he made a very good end. The chopping block had been set very low, and great iron staples were driven in the platform to pin down the king's arms if he attempted to resist his fate. But those who exercised such caution understood little of the man they had opposed for the last seven years. Charles was more than ready to accept his fate. He spoke briefly and to the point, denying that he had acted against the true interests and rights of his subjects. Then he lay down on the platform, placed his head upon the block, and prayed. As the axe fell, one witness recorded "such a groan as I never heard before and hope never to hear again," broke forth from the crowd. The English Revolution had begun.

given the title Lord Protector, and he was to rule along with a freely elected Parliament and an administrative body known as the Council of State.

Cromwell was able to hold the revolutionary cause together through the force of his own personality. A member of the lesser landed elite who had opposed the arbitrary policies of Charles I, he was a devout Puritan who believed in a large measure of religious toleration for Christians. As both a member of Parliament and a senior officer in the army, he had been able to temper the claims of each when they conflicted. Cromwell saw God's hand directing England toward a more glorious future and he believed that his own actions were divinely ordained: "No man climbs higher than he that knows not whither he goes." Though many urged him to accept the crown of England and begin a new monarchy, Cromwell steadfastly held out for a government in which fundamental authority resided in Parliament. Until his death he defended the achievements of the revolution and held its conflicting constituents together.

But a sense that only a single person could effectively rule a state remained too strong for the reforms of the revolutionary regimes to have much chance of success. When Cromwell died in

1658 it was only natural that his eldest son Richard should be proposed as the new Lord Protector despite the fact that Richard had very little experience in either military or civil affairs. Nor did he have the sense of purpose that was his father's greatest source of strength. Without an individual to hold the movement together, the revolution fell apart. In 1659 the army again intervened in civil affairs, dismissing the recently elected Parliament and calling for the restoration of the monarchy, to provide stability to the state. After a period of negotiation in which the king agreed to a general amnesty with only a few exceptions, the Stuarts were restored when Charles II (1649–85) took the throne in 1660.

Twenty years of civil war and revolution had their effect. Parliament became a permanent part of civil government and now had to be managed rather than ignored. Royal power over taxation and religion was curtailed, though in fact Parliament proved more vigorous in suppressing religious dissent than the monarchy ever had. England was to be a reformed Protestant state though there remained much dispute about what constituted reform. Absolute monarchy had become constitutional monarchy with the threat of revolution behind the power of Parliament and

War and Peace in Europe, 1598–1650

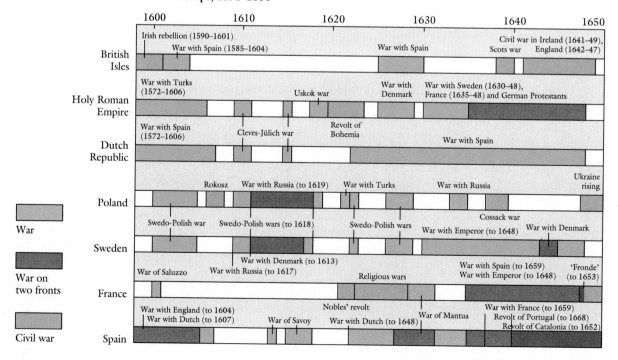

the threat of anarchy behind the power of the crown.

Both threats proved potent in 1685 when James II (1685–88) came to the throne. A declared Catholic, James attempted to use his power of appointment to foil the constraints that Parliament imposed upon him. He elevated Catholics to leading posts in the military and in the central government and began a campaign to pack a new Parliament with his supporters. This proved too much for the governing classes, who entered into negotiations with William, Prince of Orange, husband of Mary Stuart, James' eldest daughter. In 1688 William landed in England with a small force. Without support, James II fled to France, the English throne was declared vacant, and William and Mary were proclaimed king and queen of England. There was little bloodshed in England and little threat of social disorder, and the event soon came to be called the Glorious Revolution. Its achievements were set down in the Declaration of Rights (1689), which was presented to William and Mary before they took the throne. The Declaration reasserted the fundamental principles of constitutional monarchy as they had developed over the previous half-century. Security of property and the regularity of Parliaments were guaranteed. The Toleration Act (1689) granted religious freedom to nearly all groups of Protestants. The liberties of the subject and the rights of the sovereign were to be in balance.

The events of 1688 in England reversed a trend toward increasing power on the part of the Stuarts. This second episode of resistance resulted in the development of a unique form of government which, a century later, would spawn dozens of imitators. John Locke (1632–1704) was the theorist of the Revolution of 1688. He was heir to the century-old debate on resistance and he carried the doctrine to a new plateau. In *Two Treatises on Civil Government* (1690), Locke developed the contract theory of government. Political society was a compact that individuals entered into freely for their own well-being. It was designed to maintain each person's natural rights—life, liberty, and property. Natural rights were inherent in individuals; they could not be given away. The contract between rulers and subjects was an agreement for the protection of natural rights. "Arbitrary power cannot consist with the ends of society and government. Men would not quit the

freedom of the state of nature were it not to preserve their lives, liberties, and fortunes and by stated rules to secure their peace and happiness." When rulers acted arbitrarily, they were to be deposed by their subjects, preferably in the relatively peaceful manner in which James II had been replaced by William III.

The Zenith of the Royal State

The mid-century crises tested the mettle of the royal states. Over the long term, the seventeenth-century crises had two different consequences. First they provided a check to the exercise of royal power. Fear of recurring rebellions had a chilling effect upon policy, especially taxation. Reforms of financial administration, long overdue, were one of the themes of the later seventeenth century. Even as royal government strengthened itself, it remained concerned about the impact of its policies. On the other hand, the memory of rebellion served to control the ambitions of factious noblemen and town oligarches.

If nothing else, these episodes of opposition to the rising royal states made clear the universal desire for stable government, which was seen as the responsibility of both subjects and rulers. By the second half of the seventeenth century, effective government was the byword of the royal state. As Louis XIV proclaimed, rule was a trade that had to be constantly studied and practiced. The natural advantages of monarchy had to be merged with the interests of the citizens of the state and their desires for wealth, safety, and honor. After so much chaos and instability, the monarchy had to be elevated above the fray of day-to-day politics, elevated to become a symbol of the power and glory of the nation. Control no longer meant the greedy grasp of royal officials but their practiced guidance of affairs.

In England, Holland, and Sweden a form of constitutional monarchy developed in which rulers shared power, in varying degrees, with other institutions of state. In England it was Parliament, in Holland the town oligarchies, and in Sweden the nobility. But in most other states in Europe there developed a pure form of royal government known as absolutism. Absolute monarchy revived the divine right theories of kingship and added to them a cult of the personality of the ruler. Absolutism was practiced in states as dissimilar as Denmark, Brandenburg-Prussia, and Russia. It reached its zenith in France under Louis XIV, the most powerful of the seventeenth-century monarchs.

Absolute Monarchy

Locke's theory of contract provided one solution to the central problem of seventeenth-century government: how to balance the monarch's right to command and the subjects' duty to obey. By establishing a constitutional monarchy, in which power was shared between the ruler and a representative assembly of subjects, England found one path out of this thicket. But it was not a path that many others could follow. The English solution was most suited to a state that was largely immune from invasion and land war. Constitutional government required a higher level of political participation of citizens than did an absolute monarchical one. Greater participation in turn meant greater freedom of expression, greater toleration of religious minorities, and greater openness in the institutions of government. All were dangerous. The price that England paid was a half-century of governmental instability.

The alternative to constitutional monarchy was absolute monarchy. It, too, found its greatest theorist in England. Thomas Hobbes (1588–1679) was one of many Englishmen who went into exile in France during the course of the English civil wars. In his greatest work, *Leviathan* (1651), Hobbes argued that before civil society had been formed, humans lived in a savage state of nature, "in a war of every man against every man." This was a ghastly condition without morality or law—"the notions of right and wrong, of justice and injustice have there no place." People came together to form a government for the most basic of all purposes: for self-preservation. Without government they were condemned to a life that was "solitary, poor, nasty, brutish, and short." To escape the state of nature, individuals pooled their power and granted it to a ruler. The terms of the Hobbesian contract were simple. Rulers agreed to rule; subjects agreed to obey. When the contract was intact, people ceased to live in a state

of nature. When it was broken, they returned to it. With revolts, rebellions, and revolutions erupting in all parts of Europe, Hobbes' state of nature never seemed very far away.

For most states of Europe in the later seventeenth century, absolute monarchy became not only a necessity but an ideal. The consolidation of power in the hands of the divinely ordained monarch who, nevertheless, ruled according to principles of law and justice, was seen as the perfect form of government. Absolutism was an expression of control rather than of power. If the state was sometimes pictured as a horse, the absolute monarch gripped the reins rather than the whip most tightly. "Many writers have tried to confound absolute government with arbitrary government. But no two things could be more unlike," wrote Bishop Jacques Bossuet (1627–1704), who extolled absolutism in France. The absolute ruler ruled in the interests of his people:

The title page of the first edition of Thomas Hobbes' Leviathan, *published in 1651. The huge figure composed of many tiny human beings symbolizes the surrender of individual human rights to those of the state.*

"the prince is the public person, the whole state is included in him, the will of all the people is enclosed within his own."

The main features of absolute monarchy were all designed to extend royal control. As in the early seventeenth century, the person of the monarch was revered. Courts grew larger and more lavish in an effort to enhance the glory of the monarchy and thereby of the state. *L'état, c'est moi*—"I am the state"—Louis XIV was supposed to have said. No idea better expresses absolutism's connection between governor and governed. As the king grew in stature, his competitors for power all shrank. Large numbers of nobles were herded together at court under the watchful eye of monarchs who now ruled rather than reigned. The king shed the cloak of his favorites and rolled up his own sleeves to manage state affairs. Representative institutions, especially those that laid claim to control over taxation, were weakened or cast aside for obstructing efficient government and endangering the welfare of the state. Monarchs needed standing armies, permanent forces that could be drilled and trained in the increasingly sophisticated arts of war. Thus the military was expanded and made an integral part of the machinery of government. The military profession developed within nations, gradually replacing mercenary adventurers who had fought for booty rather than for duty.

Yet the absolute state was never as powerful in practice as it was in theory. Nor did it ever exist in its ideal shape. Absolutism was always in the making, never quite made. Its success depended upon a strong monarch who knew his own will and could enforce it. It depended upon unity within the state, upon the absence or ruthless suppression of religious or political minorities. The absolute ruler needed to control information and ideas, to limit criticism of state policy. Ultimately, the absolute state rested upon the will of its citizens to support it. The seventeenth-century state remained a loose confederation of regions, many acquired by conquest and whose loyalty was practical rather than instinctive. There were no state police to control behavior or attitudes, no newspapers or mass communication to spread propaganda. Censorship might restrict the flow of forbidden books, but it could do little to dam up the current of ideas.

Absolutism in the East

Frederick William, the Great Elector of Brandenburg-Prussia (1640–88), was one of the European princes who made the most effective use of the techniques of absolutism. In 1640 he inherited a scattered and ungovernable collection of territories that had been devastated by the Thirty Years' War. Brandenburg, the richest of his possessions, had lost nearly half of its population. The war had a lasting impact upon Frederick William's character. As a child he had hidden in the woods to escape bands of marauding soldiers; as a teenager he had followed to its burial the corpse of Gustavus Adolphus, the man he most admired and wished to emulate. A long stay in Holland during the final stages of the Dutch Revolt impressed upon him the importance of a strong army and a strong base of revenue to support it.

Frederick William had neither. In 1640 his forces totaled no more than 2,500 men, most of them, including the officers, the dregs of German society. Despite the fact that he was surrounded by powerful neighbors—Sweden and Poland both claimed sovereignty over parts of his inheritance—the territories under his control had no tradition of military taxation. The nobility, known as *die Junker,* enjoyed immunity from almost all forms of direct taxation, and the towns had no obligation to furnish either men or supplies for military operations beyond their walls. When Frederick William attempted to introduce an excise—the commodity tax on consumption that had so successfully financed the Dutch Revolt and the English Revolution—he was initially rebuffed. But military emergency overcame legal precedents. By the 1650s Frederick William had established the excise in the towns though not on the land.

With the excise as a steady source of revenue, the Great Elector could now create one of the most capable standing armies of the age. He built his forces in stages, careful not to frighten his powerful eastern neighbors. The geographical scattering of his territory was a benefit. He could raise and train his troops in the west without endangering his security in the east. The strictest discipline was maintained in the new army, and the Prussian army developed into a feared and

TSARS OF RUSSIA

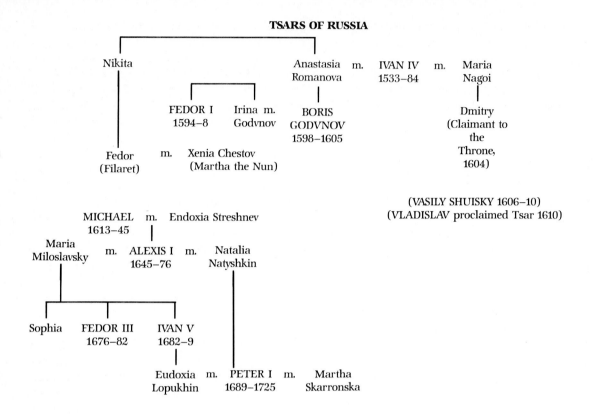

(VASILY SHUISKY 1606–10)
(VLADISLAV proclaimed Tsar 1610)

efficient fighting machine. Frederick William organized one of the first departments of war to oversee all of the details of the creation of his army, from housing and supplies to the training of young officer candidates. This department was also responsible for the collection of taxes. By integrating military and civilian government, Frederick William was able to create an efficient state bureaucracy that was particularly responsive in times of crisis. By the time that Frederick William died, the army had grown to over thirty thousand and state revenues had tripled. The creation of the Prussian army was the force that led to the creation of the Prussian state.

The same materials that forged the Prussian state led to the transformation of Russia. Soon after the young tsar Peter I (1682–1725) came to the throne, he realized that he could compete with the western states only by learning to play their game. In 1697 Peter visited the west, ostensibly to build an alliance against the Turks but actually to learn as much as he could about western military technology. He worked as an apprentice shipbuilder in Holland and as a blacksmith in

an arms foundry in England. Everywhere he went he tried to learn about the systems of taxation, the structure of administration, and, above all, the organization of the military. His stay in Germany led him to admire the reforms of the Great Elector and his son, especially the bureaucratic control of the army.

When Peter returned to Russia he attempted to implement at once all that he had learned. It is impossible to describe Peter's various personalities or to do justice to his ever changing character. He was ruthless and brutal in the tradition of Ivan the Terrible but far-sighted and determined in the tradition of Ivan the Great. Despite the fact that he was nearly seven feet tall, Peter attempted to walk the streets of Moscow in disguise so that he could gauge the impact of his reforms. He loved novelty, introducing new agricultural products like wine and potatoes to his subjects. When he determined that Russians should no longer wear beards, he took a hand in cutting them off. When he was persuaded of the benefits of dentistry, he practiced it himself upon his terrified subjects. His campaign to westernize

Russia frequently confused the momentous with the inconsequential, but it had an extraordinary impact at all levels of government and society.

Like those of Frederick William, Peter's greatest reforms were military. Peter realized that if Russia were to flourish in a world dominated by war and commerce it would have to reestablish its hold on the Baltic ports. This meant dislodging the Swedes from the Russian mainland and creating a fleet to protect Russian trade. Neither goal seemed likely. The Swedes were one of the great powers of the age, constant innovators in battlefield tactics and military organization. Peter studied their every campaign. His first wars against the Swedes ended in humiliating defeats, but with each failure came a sharper sense of what was needed to succeed.

First Peter introduced a system of conscription that resulted in the creation of a standing army. Conscripts were branded to inhibit desertion, and a strict discipline was introduced to prepare the soldiers for battle. Peter unified the military command at the top and stratified it in the field. He established promotion based on merit. For the first time Russian officers were

given particular responsibilities to fulfill during both training and battle. Peter created military schools to train cadets for the next generation of officers. Finally in 1709 Peter realized his ambitions. At the Battle of Poltava the Russian army routed the Swedes, wounding King Charles XII, annihilating his infantry, and capturing dozens of his leading officers. That night Peter toasted the captured Swedish generals. He claimed that everything he knew about warfare he had learned from them and he congratulated them on their success as teachers. After the Battle of Poltava, Russia gradually replaced Sweden as the dominant power in the Baltic.

Like everything else about him, Peter the Great's absolutism was uniquely his own. In Russia there was little to be made of the distinction between absolute and arbitrary power. Peter consciously borrowed from the west, but he adapted western ideas to Russian conditions. He created a series of regions that were to be controlled from the center by officers similar to the French intendants. He also borrowed from the Prussian example by establishing departments of state, especially to control the organization and finance

Russia under Peter the Great

of the military. Peter confirmed his intention of establishing a "window to the west" by building a new port city on the Baltic at Saint Petersburg. Here he helped construct the Russian navy, actually working on the docks for a time. Though Peter's power was unlimited, it was not uncontested. He secularized the Russian Orthodox church, subjecting it to the control of state power and confiscating much of its wealth in the process. He broke the old military service class, which attempted a coup d'etat when he was abroad in the 1690s. By the end of his reign, the Russian monarchy was among the strongest in Europe.

The Origins of French Absolutism

Nowhere was absolutism as successfully implanted as in France, and nowhere was it less likely to have grown. Not since Francis I (1515–47) had there been a king who was able to consolidate power, develop a policy of government, and attempt to carry it through. Henry IV (1589–1610) hoped to do all three. He was a vigorous and powerful man who exuded the qualities of a king. He literally bought peace from Catholic and Huguenot competitors, granting enormous sums to those aristocratic leaders willing to lay down arms and give their undivided allegiance to the monarchy. Under the watchful eye of his capable finance minister, the Duc de Sully, he began a program of fiscal reforms, which included taxing the sale of offices. He also looked to secure French interests against the expanding power of the Habsburgs. But the assassin's knife cut short the reinvigoration of the monarchy. Louis XIII (1610–43) was only eight years old when he came to the throne, and he grew slowly into his role under the tutelage of Cardinal Richelieu.

It was Richelieu's vision that stabilized French government. As chief minister, Richelieu saw clearly that the prosperity and even the survival of France depended upon strengthening royal power. He preached a doctrine of *raison d'etat*— reason of state—in which he placed the needs of the nation above the privileges of its most important groups. "One must be inflexible in punishing those who fail to obey," Richelieu wrote in his *Political Testament* (1646). Richelieu saw three threats to stable royal government, "the Huguenots shared the state, the nobles conducted themselves as if they were not subjects, and the most powerful governors in the provinces acted as if they were sovereign in their office."

Richelieu took measures to control all three. The power of the nobles was the most difficult to attack. The nobles' long tradition of independence from the crown had been enhanced by the wars of religion. Perhaps more importantly, the ancient aristocracy, the nobility of the sword, felt themselves in a particularly vulnerable position. Their world was changing and their traditional roles were becoming obsolete. Professional soldiers replaced them at war; professional administrators at government. Mercantile wealth threatened their economic superiority, the growth of the nobility of the robe—lawyers and state officials—threatened their social standing. They were hardly likely to take orders from a royal minister like Richelieu, especially when he attacked one of the great symbols of their power, the duel. Dueling was the traditional method of settling affairs of honor. Hand-to-hand combat with large, unwieldy swords provided satisfaction for perceived affronts as much through exhaustion as anything else. But at the same time that the nobility became more self-conscious about its honor, and thus more ready to perceive insults, technology changed the game. The introduction of the rapier made dueling deadly serious. A single thrust with the razorlike blade, skillful or lucky, bled the nation of hundreds of nobles. Richelieu banned the duel and executed the first noblemen to violate the ban.

To limit the power of local officials, Richelieu used intendants to examine their conduct and to reform their administration. He made careful appointments of local governors and brought more regions under direct royal control. Against the Huguenots, Richelieu's policy was more subtle. He was less interested in challenging their religion than their autonomy. In 1627 when the English sent a force to aid the Huguenots against the government, Richelieu and Louis XIII abolished the Huguenots' privileges altogether. They were allowed to maintain their religion but not their special status. They would have no privileges other than to be subjects of the king of France.

Richelieu's program was a vital prelude to the development of absolute monarchy in France. But the cardinal was not a king. While it is clear that Richelieu did not act without the full support of

Louis XIII, and clear that the king initiated many reforms for which the cardinal received credit, there can be no doubt that Richelieu was the power behind the throne. Louis XIII hated the business of government and even neglected his principal responsibility of providing the state with an heir. For years he and his wife slept in separate palaces and only a freak rainstorm in Paris forced him to spend a night with the queen, Anne of Austria, in 1637. It was the night of the conception of Louis XIV. Louis XIII and Richelieu died within six months of each other in 1642–43, and the nation again endured the turmoil of a child king. Richelieu's aggressive policy to curb the nobility as well as his stringent financial program in the 1630s helped precipitate the Fronde. Louis XIV (1643–1715) was never to forget the terror of the aristocratic rebellion in Paris: how he was forced to flee the capital in the dead of night, how he endured the penury of exile, how he suffered the humiliation of being bossed about by the rebels. He would never forget, and he would have a long time to remember.

Louis le Grand

While most seventeenth-century monarchs received a humanist education as preparation for rule, Louis XIV learned statecraft by the seat of his pants. Not quite five years old when he came to the throne, he was tutored by Cardinal Jules Mazarin (1602–61), Richelieu's successor as chief minister. If anything, Mazarin was more ruthless and less popular than his predecessor. An Italian from a modest background, Mazarin won the money to launch his career at the gaming table. Good fortune seemed to follow him everywhere. He gambled with his life and his career and each time he raked in the stakes. He died with the largest private fortune that had ever been accumulated by a French citizen, easily surpassing the fortune of Richelieu. Despite his foreign background and his connections with the papal court at Rome—either of which would normally have been debilitating—Mazarin rose to the pinnacle of French government. Like Richelieu, whom he emulated, Mazarin was an excellent administrator who had learned well the lessons of *raison d'etat*. At the conclusion of the Thirty Years' War, for example, Mazarin refused to make peace with

Spain, believing that the time was ripe to deliver a knockout blow to the Spanish Habsburgs. Even during the Fronde, France fought on, ultimately winning back small pieces of strategic territory. The peace treaty of 1659 was sealed by the marriage of Louis XIV to one of the heirs to the Spanish throne, a match that brought further territorial gains for France. Mazarin taught the boy king many valuable lessons in how to deal from positions of weakness as well as from positions of strength.

In order to pacify the rebellious nobility, who opposed Mazarin's power, Louis XIV was declared to have reached his majority at the age of thirteen. But it was not until Mazarin died ten years later in 1661 that the king began to rule. Then, he astounded his court by announcing that he would be his own chief minister and guide the affairs of state with his own hand. It was a momentous decision that at the time was thought to be catastrophic, but it was a decision that Louis XIV never had cause to regret. In fact, Louis was blessed with able and energetic ministers. The two central props of his state—money and might—were in the hands of dynamic men, Jean-Baptiste Colbert (1619–83) and the Marquis de Louvois (1639–91). Colbert, to whom credit belongs for the building of the French navy, the reform of French legal codes, and the establishment of national academies of culture, was Louis' chief minister for finance. Colbert's fiscal reforms were so successful that in less than six years a debt of 22 million French pounds had become a surplus of 29 million. Colbert achieved this astonishing feat not by raising taxes but by increasing the efficiency of their collection. Until Louis embarked upon his wars, the French state was solvent.

To Louvois, Louis' minister of war, fell the task of reforming the French army. During the Fronde, royal troops were barely capable of defeating the makeshift forces of the nobility. Louis XIV inherited an army of less than 20,000 whose officers were noblemen who had purchased their commissions as much for status as for use. By the end of the reign, the army had grown to 400,000 and its organization had been thoroughly reformed. Louvois introduced new ranks for the field officers who actually led their men into battle, and promotions were distributed by merit rather than purchase. He also solved one of the most serious logistical problems of the age by establishing storehouses of arms and ammunition throughout the realm. The greatest achievements of the reign were built on the backs of fiscal and military reforms, which were themselves a product of the continuing sophistication of French administration.

Louis XIV furthered the practice of relying upon professional administrators to supervise the main departments of state and to offer advice on matters of policy. He created a nearly complete separation between courtiers and officeholders and largely excluded the nobility of the sword from the inner circles of government. These were composed of ministers of departments and small councils that handled routine affairs. These councils were connected to the central advisory body of government, the secret council of the king. Within each department, ministers furthered the process of professionalization that led to the advancement of talented clerks, secretaries, and administrators. Though there still remained a large gulf between the promulgation of policy at Versailles and its enforcement in the provinces, it was now a gulf that could be measured and ultimately bridged. Louis XIV built upon the institution of the intendant that Richelieu had developed with so much success. Intendants were now a permanent part of government, and their duties expanded from their early responsibilities as coordinators and mediators into areas of policing and tax collection. It was through the intendants that the wishes of central government were made known in the provinces.

Though Louis XIV was well served, it was the king himself who set the tone for French absolutism. "If he was not the greatest king, he was the best actor of majesty that ever filled the throne," wrote an English observer. The acting of majesty was central to Louis' rule. His residence at Versailles was the most glittering court of Europe, renowned for its beauty and splendor. It was built on a scale never before seen, and Louis took a personal interest in making sure it was fit for a king. When the court and king moved there permanently in 1682, Versailles became the envy of the Continent. But behind the imposing facade of Versailles stood a well-thought-out plan for domestic and international rule.

Louis XIV attempted to tame the French

This Hyacinthe Rigaud portrait of Louis XIV in his coronation robes shows the splendor of the Roi Soleil (Sun King), who believed himself to be the center of France as the sun is the center of the solar system.

nobles by requiring their attendance at his court. Though not all provincial nobles hurried to Versailles, the more attractive the honey, the more numerous were the flies drawn to it. Louis established a system of court etiquette so complex that constant study was necessary to prevent humiliation. While the nobility studied decorum, they could not plot rebellion. At Versailles one never knocked on a door, one scratched with a fingernail. This insignificant custom had to be learned and remembered—it was useless anywhere else—and practiced if one hoped for the favor of the king. Leading noblemen of France rose at dawn so that they could watch Louis be awakened and hear him speak his first words. Dozens followed him from hall to gallery and from gallery to chamber as he washed, dressed, prayed, and ate. There was no greater concern than the king's health, unless it was the king's mood, which was as changeable as the weather.

This aura of court culture was equally successful in the royal art of diplomacy. For Louis XIV image was everything. In fact, we know very little about his private personality. Even his love letters to his mistresses appear to have been written for effect. "I prefer fame above all else, even life itself," he wrote in his memoirs. It was the fame of Versailles that stamped him with the power to dominate international affairs. During his reign, France replaced Spain as the greatest nation in Europe. Massive royal patronage of art, science, and thought brought French culture to new heights. The French language replaced Latin as the universal European tongue. France was the richest and most populous European state, and Louis' absolute rule finally harnessed these resources to a single purpose. France became a commercial power rivaling the Netherlands, a naval power rivaling England, and a military power without peer. It was not only for effect that Louis took the image of the sun as his own. In court, in the nation, and throughout Europe everything revolved around him.

France's rise to preeminence in Europe was undoubtedly the greatest accomplishment of the absolute monarchy of Louis XIV. But it did not come without costs. The strength of absolutism was that it harnessed the energies of the state to the purpose of the monarch. Its weakness was that it required a level of wisdom and foresight that was not very common among either monarchs or subjects. Louis XIV made his share of mistakes, which were magnified by the awe in which his opinions were held. His aggressive foreign policy ultimately bankrupted the crown. But without doubt, his greatest error was to persecute the Huguenots. As an absolute ruler, Louis believed that it was necessary to have absolute conformity and obedience. The existence of the Huguenots, with their separate communities and distinct forms of worship, seemed an affront to his authority. Almost from the beginning, Louis

allowed the persecution of Protestants, despite the protection provided by the Edict of Nantes. Protestant churches were pulled down, conversions to Catholicism were bought with the lure of immunities from taxation, children were separated from their families to be brought up in Catholic schools. Finally, in 1685 Louis XIV revoked the Edict of Nantes. All forms of Protestant worship were outlawed and the ministers who were not hunted down and killed were forced into exile. Despite a ban on Protestant emigration, over two hundred thousand Huguenots fled the country, many of them carrying irreplaceable skills with them to Holland and England in the west and to Brandenburg in the east.

Supporters of the monarchy celebrated the revocation of the Edict of Nantes as an act of piety. Religious toleration in seventeenth-century Europe was still a policy of expediency rather than of principle. Even the English, who prided themselves on developing the concept, and the Dutch, who welcomed Jews to Amsterdam, would not officially tolerate Catholics. But the persecution of the Huguenots was a social and political disaster for France. Those who fled to other Protestant states spread the stories of atrocities that stiffened European resolve against Louis. Those who remained became an embittered minority who pulled at the fabric of the state at every chance. Nor did the official abolition of Protestantism have much effect upon its existence. Against these policies, the Huguenots held firm to their beliefs. There were well over a million French Protestants, undoubtedly the largest religious minority in any state. Huguenots simply went underground, practicing their religion secretly and gradually replacing their numbers. No absolutism, however powerful, could succeed in eradicating religious beliefs.

Louis XIV gave his name to the age that he and his nation dominated, but he was not its only towering figure. The Great Elector, Peter the Great, Louis the Great: so they were judged by posterity, kings who had forged nations for a new age. Their style of rule showed the royal state at its height, still revolving around the king but more and more dependent upon permanent institutions of government that followed their own imperatives. The absolute state harnessed the economic and intellectual resources of the nation to the political will of the monarch. It did so to ensure survival in a dangerous world. But while monarchs ruled as well as reigned, they did so by incorporating vital elements of the state into the process of government. In England the importance of the landholding classes was recognized in the constitutional powers of Parliament. In Prussia the military power of *die Junker* was asserted through command in the army, the most important institution of the state. In France, Louis XIV co-opted many nobles at his court, while he made use of a talented pool of lawyers, clergymen, and administrators in his government. A delicate balance existed between the will of the king and the will of the state, a balance that would soon lead these continental powers into economic competition and military confrontation.

Suggestions for Further Reading

General Reading

A. L. Moote, *The Seventeenth Century* (Lexington, MA: D. C. Heath, 1970). A comprehensive survey.

* William Doyle, *The Old European Order* (Oxford: Oxford University Press, 1978). An important synthetic essay bristling with ideas.

* Geoffrey Parker, *Europe in Crisis 1598–1648* (London: William Collins and Sons, 1979). The best introduction to the period.

Perry Anderson, *Lineages of the Absolutist State* (London: NLB Books, 1974). A sociological study of the role of absolutism in the development of the western world.

The Rise of the Royal State

* Graham Parry, *The Golden Age Restor'd* (New York: St. Martin's Press, 1981). A study of English court culture in the reigns of James I and Charles I.

J. H. Elliott and Jonathan Brown, *A Palace for a King* (New Haven, CT: Yale University Press, 1980). An outstanding work on the building and decorating of a Spanish palace.

* J. N. Figgis, *The Divine Right of Kings* (Cambridge: Cambridge University Press, 1914). Still the classic study of this central doctrine of political thought.

* J. H. Elliott, *The Count-Duke of Olivares* (New Haven, CT: Yale University Press, 1986). A massive and massively important study of the leading statesman of Spain.

* Roger Lockyer, *Buckingham* (London: Longman, 1984). A stylish biography of the favorite of two monarchs.

The Crises of the Royal State

* Quentin Skinner, *The Foundations of Modern Political Thought*, 2 vols. (Cambridge: Cambridge University Press, 1978). A seminal work on the history of ideas from Machiavelli to Calvin.

* Perez Zagoin, *Rebels and Rulers*, 2 vols. (Cambridge: Cambridge University Press, 1982). A good survey of revolutions, civil war, and popular protests throughout Europe.

* Trevor Aston, ed., *Crisis in Europe 1600–1660* (Garden City, NY: Doubleday, 1967). Essays on the theme of a general crisis in Europe by distinguished historians.

G. Parker and L. Smith, eds., *The General Crisis of the Seventeenth Century* (London: Routledge & Kegan Paul, 1978). A collection of essays on the problem of the general crisis.

* Lawrence Stone, *The Causes of the English Revolution* (New York: Harper & Row, 1972). A vigorously argued explanation of why England experienced a revolution in the mid-seventeenth century.

* J. S. Morrill, *The Revolt of the Provinces* (London: Longman, 1980). An outstanding essay on the importance of the localities in the English civil war.

* D. E. Underdown, *Pride's Purge* (London: Allen and Unwin, 1985). The most important work on the politics of the English Revolution.

The Zenith of the Royal State

* H. W. Koch, *A History of Prussia* (London: Longman, 1978). A comprehensive study of Prussian history with an excellent chapter on the Great Elector.

* Paul Dukes, *The Making of Russian Absolutism* (London: Longman, 1982). A thorough survey of Russian history in the seventeenth and eighteenth centuries.

* Vasili Klyuchevsky, *Peter the Great* (Boston: Beacon Press, 1984). A classic work, still the best study of Peter.

* W. E. Brown, *The First Bourbon Century in France* (London: University of London Press, 1971). A good introduction to French political history.

* William Beik, *Absolutism and Society in Seventeenth Century France* (Cambridge: Cambridge University Press, 1985). The single best study of the government of a French province in the seventeenth century.

Victor Tapié, *France in the Age of Louis XIII and Richelieu* (Cambridge: Cambridge University Press, 1984). A translation of the classic narrative of events in the reign of Louis XIII.

John Wolf, *Louis XIV* (New York: Norton, 1968). An outstanding biography of the Sun King.

* Indicates paperback edition available.

17

Conquering the Material World

Rembrandt's Lessons

By the early seventeenth century interest in scientific investigation had spread out from narrow circles of specialists to embrace educated men and women. One of the more spectacular demonstrations of new knowledge was public dissection, by law performed only on the corpses of criminals. Here the secrets of the human body were revealed both for those who were in training as physicians and for those who had the requisite fee and strong stomach. Curiosity about the human body was becoming a mark of education. New publications, both scientific and popular, spread ancient wisdom as well as the controversial findings of the moderns. Pictures drawn on the basis of dissections filled the new medical texts like the one on the stand at the feet of the corpse in *The Anatomy Lesson of Dr. Nicolaes Tulp* (1632) by Rembrandt van Rijn (1606–69).

Dr. Tulp's anatomy lesson was not meant for the public. In fact, those gathered around him in various poses of concentration were not students at all. They were members of the Amsterdam company of surgeons, the physicians' guild of the early seventeenth century. The sitters had commissioned the picture, which was a celebration of themselves as well as of the noted Professor Tulp. They hired the young Rembrandt to compose the picture with the assurance that each of the sitters (whose names are written on the paper one of them holds in his hand) would appear as if he alone were the subject of a portrait. Rembrandt succeeded beyond expectation. Each individual was given his due. The expressions on their faces as much as their physical characteristics mark each one out from the group. Yet the portraits were only one part of the painting. The scene that Rembrandt depicted unified them. They became a group by their participation in the anatomy lesson. Rembrandt has chosen a moment of drama to stop the action. Dr. Tulp is about to make some point before cutting the tendons of the arm on the gruesome cadaver. The central figures of the group are rapt in attention though only one of them is actually observing the procedure of the anatomy. Each listens to Tulp, comparing his own experience and knowledge to that of the professor and the text that stands open.

The Anatomy Lesson established the twenty-five-year-old Rembrandt as one of the most gifted and fashionable painters in Amsterdam. If any people could be said to be consumers of art in seventeenth-century Europe, it was the Dutch. Artists flourished and pictures abounded. Travelers were struck by the presence of artwork in both public and private places and in the homes of even moderately prosperous people. The group portrait, which Rembrandt brought to new levels of expression, was becoming a favorite genre. It was used to celebrate the leaders of Dutch society who, unlike the leaders of most other European states, were not princes and aristocrats, but rather merchants, guild officials, and professionals. Rembrandt captured a spirit of civic pride in his group portraits. Here it was the surgeons' guild; later it would be the leaders of the cloth merchants' guild, another time a militia company.

Like the leaders of the surgeons' guild who commissioned their own portrait, which hung in their company's hall, the Dutch Republic

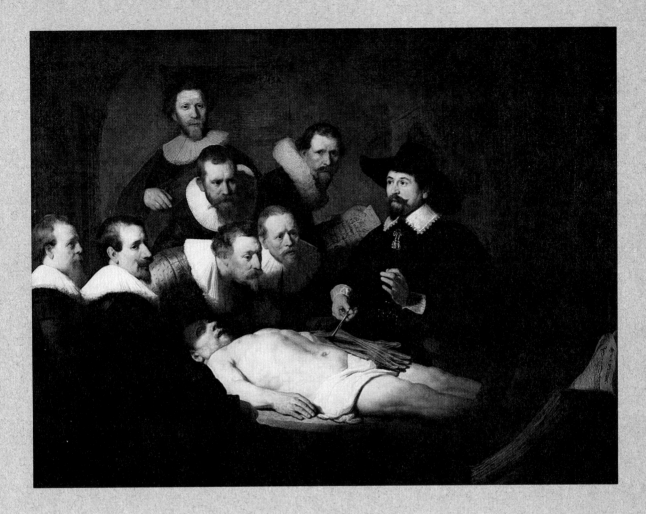

swelled with pride in the seventeenth century. Its long war with Spain
was finally drawing to a close and it was time to celebrate the birth of
a new state. The Dutch were a trading people and their trade
flourished as much in times of war as in times of peace. Their ships
traveled to all parts of the globe and they dominated the great luxury
trades of the age. Bankers and merchants were the backbone of the
Dutch Republic. Yet this republic of merchants was also one of the
great cultural centers of the Continent. Intellectual creativity was
cultivated in the same manner as was a trading partner. In the
burgeoning port of Amsterdam, the fastest growing city in Europe,
artists, philosophers, and mathematicians lived cheek by jowl. The
free exchange of ideas made Amsterdam home to those exiled for
their beliefs. The Dutch practiced religious toleration as did no one
else. Catholics, Protestants, and Jews all were welcomed to the
Republic and found that they could pursue their own paths without
persecution. Freedom of thought and freedom of expression helped
develop a new spirit of scientific inquiry, like that portrayed in *The
Anatomy Lesson of Dr. Nicolaes Tulp.*

The New Science

"And new Philosophy calls all in doubt,/ The element of fire is quite put out;/ The sun is lost and the earth, and no man's wit/ Can well direct him where to look for it." So wrote the English poet John Donne (1572–1631) about one of the most astonishing yet perplexing moments in the history of Western thought: the emergence of the new science. It was astonishing because it seemed truly new. The discoveries of the star-gazers, like those of the sea explorers, challenged people's most basic assumptions and beliefs. Men dropping balls from towers or peering at the skies through a glass claimed that they had disproved thousands of years of certainty about the nature of the universe. "And new Philosophy calls all in doubt." But it was perplexing because it seemed to loosen the moorings of everything that educated people thought they knew about their world. Nothing could be more disorienting than to challenge common sense. One needed to do little more than wake up in the morning to know that the sun moved from east to west while the earth stood still. But mathematics, experimentation, and deduction were needed to understand that the earth was in constant motion and that it revolved around the sun. "And no man's wit/ Can well direct him where to look for it."

The scientific revolution was the opening of a new era in European history. After two centuries of classical revival, European thinkers had finally come against the limits of ancient knowledge. Ancient wisdom had served Europeans well, and it was not to be discarded lightly. But one by one, the certainties of the past were being called into question. The explanations of the universe and the natural world that had been advanced by Aristotle and codified by his followers no longer seemed adequate. There were too many contra-dictions between theory and observation, too many things that did not fit. Yet breaking the hold of Aristotelianism was no easy task. If there is anything as powerful as an idea whose time has come, it is one whose time has gone. A full century was to pass before even learned people would accept the proofs that the earth revolved around the sun. Even then, the most famous of them had to recant these views or be condemned as a heretic.

The two essential characteristics of the new science were that it was materialistic and mathe-matical. Its materialism was contained in the realization that the universe is composed of matter in motion. This meant that the stars and planets were not made of some perfect ethereal substance but of the same matter that was found on earth. They were thus subject to the same rules of motion as were earthly objects. The mathe-matics of the new science was contained in the realization that calculation had to replace common sense as the basis for understanding the universe. Mathematics itself was transformed with the invention of logarithms, analytic geome-try, and calculus. More importantly, scientific experimentation took the form of measuring repeatable phenomena. When Galileo attempted to develop a theory of acceleration, he rolled a brass ball down an inclined plane and recorded the time and distance of its descent one hundred times before he was satisfied with his results.

The new science was also a Europe-wide movement. The spirit of scientific inquiry flour-ished everywhere. The main contributors to astronomy were a Pole, a Dane, a German, and an Italian. The founder of medical chemistry was

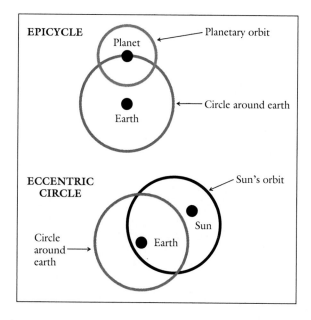

EPICYCLE

Planet

Planetary orbit

Earth

Circle around earth

ECCENTRIC CIRCLE

Sun's orbit

Sun

Circle around earth

Earth

Swiss, the best anatomist was Belgian. England contributed most of all—the founders of modern chemistry, biology, and physics. By and large, these scientists operated outside the traditional seats of learning at the universities. Though most were university trained and not a few taught the traditional Aristotelian subjects, theirs was not an academic movement. Rather it was a public one made possible by the printing press. Once published, findings became building blocks for scientists throughout the Continent and from one generation to the next. Many discoveries were made in the search for practical solutions to ordinary problems, and what was learned fueled advances in technology and the natural sciences. The new science gave seventeenth-century Europeans a sense that they might finally master the forces of nature.

Heavenly Revolutions

There was much to be said for Aristotle's understanding of the world, for his cosmology. For one thing, it was harmonious. It incorporated a view of the physical world that coincided with a view of the spiritual and moral one. The heavens were unchangeable and therefore they were better than the earth. The sun, moon, and planets were all faultless spheres, unblemished and immune from decay. Their motion was circular because the circle was the perfect form of motion. The earth was at the center of the universe because it was the heaviest planet and because it was at the center of the great chain of being, between the underworld of spirits and the upperworld of gods. The second advantage to the Aristotelian world view was that it was easily incorporated into Christianity. Aristotle's description of the heavens as being composed of a closed system of crystalline rings that held the sun, moon, and planets in their circular orbits around the earth left room for God and the angels to reside just beyond the last ring. There were many passages of Scripture that described heaven and earth in just this way. Aristotle was both a philosopher and a scientist, for natural philosophy was the branch of knowledge devoted to understanding the physical world.

There were, of course, problems with Aristotle's explanation of the universe as it was preserved in the work of Ptolemy, the greatest of the Greek astronomers. For one thing, if the sun revolved in a perfect circle around the earth, then why were the seasons not perfectly equal? If the planets all revolved around the earth in circles, then why did they look nearer or farther, brighter or darker at different times of year? To solve these problems, a host of ingenious hypotheses were advanced. Perhaps the sun revolved around the earth in an eccentric circle, that is, a circle not centered on the earth. This would account for the differing lengths of seasons. Perhaps the planets revolved in circles that rested on a circle around the earth. Then when the planet revolved within the larger circle, it would seem nearer and brighter, and when it revolved outside it, it would seem farther away and darker. This was the theory of epicycles. Yet in order to account for the observable movement of all the known planets, there had to be fifty-five of these epicycles, of these circles within circles. As ingeniously complex as they were, the modifications of Aristotle's views made by the theories of eccentric circles and epicycles had one great virtue: they accurately predicted the movements of the planets. Though they were completely hypothetical, they answered the most troubling questions about the Aristotelian system.

The Polish University of Kraków had one of the leading mathematical faculties in Europe. There they taught the latest astronomical theories and vigorously debated the existence of eccentric circles and epicycles. In the 1490s, Nicolaus Copernicus (1473–1543) came to Kraków for a liberal arts education before pursuing a degree in Church law. He became fascinated by astronomy and puzzled by the debate over planetary motion. Copernicus believed, like Aristotle, that the simplest explanations were the best. If the sun were at the center of the universe and the earth simply another planet in orbit, then many of the most elaborate explanations of planetary motion were unnecessary. "At rest, in the middle of everything is the sun," Copernicus wrote in *On the Revolutions of the Heavenly Spheres* (1543). "For in this most beautiful temple who would place this lamp in another or better position than that from which it can light up the whole thing at the same time?"

Though Copernicus had discovered the key to

This chart of the heavens was engraved by Andreas Cellarius in 1660. It portrays the heliocentric universe described by Nicolaus Copernicus and accepted by Galileo. Earth and Jupiter are shown with moons orbiting them.

understanding the planetary system, he was never satisfied with his findings. When he was finally persuaded to publish his results at the end of his life, he already knew that he had created more problems than he had solved. Because Copernicus accepted most of the rest of the traditional Aristotelian explanation, especially the belief that the planets moved in circles, his sun-centered universe was only slightly better at predicting the position of the planets than the traditional earth-centered one.

Copernicus' idea stimulated other astronomers to make new calculations. Under the patronage of the king of Denmark, Tycho Brahe (1546–1601) built a large observatory to study planetary motion. In 1572, Brahe discovered a nova, a brightly burning star that was previously unknown. This discovery challenged the idea of an immutable universe composed of crystalline rings. In 1577 the appearance of a comet cutting through the supposedly impenetrable rings punched another hole into the old cosmology. Brahe's own views were a hybrid of old and new. He believed that all planets but the earth revolved around the sun and that the sun and the planets

revolved around a fixed earth. To demonstrate this theory, Brahe and his students compiled the largest and most accurate mathematical tables of planetary motion yet known. From this research, Brahe's pupil, Johannes Kepler (1571–1630), one of the great mathematicians of the age, formulated laws of planetary motion. Kepler discovered that planets orbited the sun in an elliptical rather than a circular path. This accounted for their movements nearer and farther from the earth. More importantly, he demonstrated that there was a precise mathematical relationship between the speed with which a planet revolved and its distance from the sun. Kepler's findings supported the view that the galaxy was heliocentric and that the heavens, like the earth, were made of matter that was subject to physical laws.

What Kepler demonstrated mathematically, the Italian astronomer Galileo (1564–1642) confirmed by observation. Creating a telescope by using magnifying lenses and a long tube, Galileo saw parts of the heavens that had never been dreamt of before. In 1610 he discovered four moons of Jupiter, proving conclusively that all heavenly bodies did not revolve around the earth. He observed the landscape of the earth's moon and described it as full of mountains, valleys, and rivers. It was of the same imperfect form as the earth itself. He even found spots on the sun, which suggested that it, too, was composed of ordinary matter. Through the telescope, Galileo gazed upon an unimaginable universe: "the Galaxy is nothing else but a mass of innumerable stars," he wrote. Galileo's greatest scientific discoveries had to do with motion—he was the first to posit a law of inertia—but his greatest contribution to the new science was his popularization of the Copernican theory. He took the debate over the structure of the universe to the public, popularizing the discoveries of scientists in his vigorous Italian tracts.

As news of his experiments and discoveries spread, Galileo became famous throughout the Continent, and his support for heliocentrism became a celebrated cause. In 1616 the Roman Catholic church cautioned him against promoting his views. In 1633, a year after publishing his *A Dialogue Between the Two Great Systems of the World*, Galileo was tried by the Inquisition and forced specifically to recant the idea that the earth moves. He spent the rest of his life under house arrest, where Europeans of all nations came to pay him homage—both Hobbes and Milton were taken to see him when touring Italy. Galileo insisted that there was nothing in the new science that was anti-Christian. He rejected the view that his discoveries refuted the Bible, arguing that the words of the Bible were often difficult to interpret and that nature was another way in which God revealed himself. In fact, Galileo feared that the Church's opposition to what he deemed as scientific truth could only bring the Church into disrepute. (See Special Feature, "The Trials of Galileo," pp. 520–521.)

The Natural World

The new science originated from a number of traditions that were anything but scientific. Inquiry into nature and the environment grew out of the discipline of natural philosophy and was nurtured by spiritual and mystical traditions. Much of the most useful medical knowledge had come from the studies of herbalists; the most reliable calculations of planetary motion had come from astrologers. Though the first laboratories and observatories were developed in aid of the new science, practice in them was as much magical as experimental. For those attempting to unlock the mysteries of the universe, there was no separation between magic and science. Some of the most characteristic features of modern science, such as the stress on experimentation and empirical observation, developed only gradually. What was new about the new science was the determination to develop systems of thought that could help humans understand and control their environment. Thus there was a greater openness and spirit of cooperation about discoveries than in the past, when experiments were conducted secretly and results were kept hidden away.

Aristotelianism was not the only philosophical system to explain the nature and composition of the universe. During the Renaissance the writings of Plato attracted a number of Italian humanists, most notably Marsilio Ficino (1433–99) and Pico della Mirandola (1463–94). At the Platonic Academy in Florence they taught Plato's theory that the world was composed of ideas and forms, which were hidden by the physical properties of objects. These Neoplatonic humanists believed that the architect of the universe possessed the spirit of a geometrician and that the

perfect disciplines were music and mathematics. These elements of Neoplatonism created an impetus for the mathematically based studies of the new scientists. They were especially important among the astronomers, who used both calculation and geometry in exploring the heavens. But they served as well to bolster the sciences of alchemy and astrology. Alchemy was the use of fire in the study of metals, an effort to find the essence of things through their purification. While medieval alchemists mostly attempted to find gold and silver as the essence of lead and iron, the new experimentation focused on the properties of metals in general. Astrology was the study of the influence of the stars on human behavior, calculated by planetary motion and the harmony of the heavenly spheres. Astrologers made careful calculations based on the movement of the planets and were deeply involved in the new astronomy.

The Neoplatonic emphasis upon mathematics also accorded support for a variety of mystical sciences based on numerology. These were efforts to predict events from the combination of particular numbers. Arcane calculations of ancient prophecies were combined with the years and dates of significant occurrences in the lives of individuals to yield lucky or unlucky numbers. The most influential of these mystical traditions was that associated with Hermes Trismegistus (Thrice Greatest), an Egyptian who was reputed to have lived in the second century A.D. and to have known the secrets of the universe. A body of writings mistakenly attributed to Hermes was discovered during the Renaissance and formed the basis of a Hermetic tradition. The core of Hermetic thinking centered on the idea of a universal spirit that was present in all objects and that spontaneously revealed itself. Kepler was one of many of the new scientists influenced by Hermeticism. His efforts to understand planetary motion derived from his search for a unifying spirit.

A combination of Neoplatonic and Hermetic traditions was central to the work of one of the most curious of the new scientists, the Swiss alchemist Paracelsus (1493–1541). The son of a Zurich doctor, Paracelsus spent some of his youth working in the mines, where he gained knowledge in metallurgy. He studied with a leading German alchemist before following in his father's footsteps by becoming a physician. Paracelsus led an

The Trials of Galileo

For eight years he had held his peace. Since 1616 he had bided his time, waiting for a change in the attitudes of the Catholic authorities or, as he believed, waiting for reason to prevail. For a time he had even abandoned his astronomical investigations for the supposedly safer fields of motion and physics. Even there Aristotle had been wrong. No matter what he touched, his reason showed him that the conclusions of Aristotle, the conclusions adopted and supported by the Roman Catholic Church, were wrong. Now finally, with the accession of Pope Urban VIII, old Cardinal Barbarini, who was himself a mathematician, Galileo felt confident that he could resume his writing and publishing.

Galileo's rebellion began early, when he decided to study mathematics rather than medicine. Galileo was fascinated with the manipulation of numbers and by the age of twenty-five was teaching at the University of Pisa. There he began to conduct experiments to measure rates of motion. Galileo was soon in trouble with his colleagues and was forced to leave Pisa for Padua.

It was in Padua that his real difficulties began. After seeing a small prototype made in Holland, Galileo developed a telescope that could magnify objects to thirty times their size, which made it possible to see clearly the stars and planets that had been only dimly perceptible before. In 1610 Galileo had looked at the moon and discovered that its properties were similar to those of the earth. He had seen four moons of Jupiter, the first conclusive proof that there were heavenly bodies that did not revolve around the earth. Even before he had gazed at the stars, Galileo was persuaded that Copernicus must be right in arguing that the earth revolved around the sun. Now he believed he had irrefutable proof, the proof of his own eyes. From the publication of the *Starry Messenger* in 1610, Galileo became the most active and best known advocate of the Copernican universe.

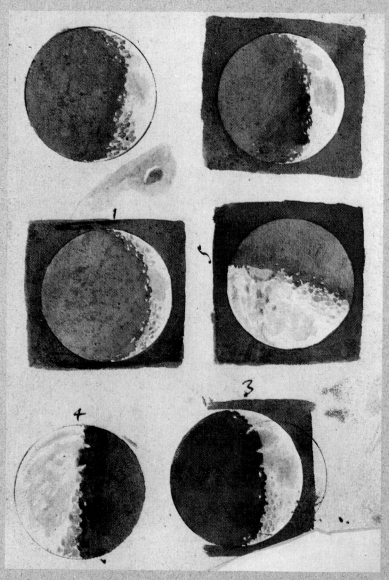

In 1616 he was called to Rome and warned about his opinions. Belief in the theories of Copernicus was heresy, he was told. If Galileo held or maintained them, he would incur a heavy penalty. The Church accepted unequivocally the Ptolemaic explanations of the structure of the universe and could cite innumerable passages in the Bible to support them. It was willful and stubborn to oppose official doctrine, doctrine that had been frequently and fully examined. At first it looked like Galileo would be silenced, but the erudite Cardinal Bellarmine, to whom the case had been assigned, wished only to caution him. Galileo might still examine the Copernican hypotheses; he might still discuss them with his learned colleagues, as long as he did not hold or maintain them to be true.

For eight years he kept his peace. When he decided to write again, it was with the belief that things were changing. He created a dialogue between a Ptolemaist and a Copernican. Let the one challenge the other on the most basic points just as if they were in formal academic dispute. How did each explain the most difficult things that there were to explain, the existence of spots on the sun or the movement of the tides. Especially the tides. If the earth stood still and the sun moved, why were there tides in the seas that moved with such regularity that they could be predicted?

Galileo was no heretic. He had no desire to challenge the Church. He would not print his tract anonymously in a Protestant country. Rather he would create a true dialogue, one with which not even the most narrow-minded censor of the Roman church could find fault. He submitted his book to the official censor in Rome for approval, then to the official censor in Florence. The censors struck out passages, changed some words, and deleted others. They demanded a new preface, even a new title: *A Dialogue Between the Two Great Systems of the World*. Finally, in 1632 the book went to press and it was an immediate success.

Indeed it was a success that could not be ignored. The Jesuits, who regarded learning and education as their special mission, demanded that action be taken against Galileo. Their teachings had been held up to ridicule; their official astronomers had been challenged; their doctrines had been repudiated. There was much at stake. Galileo's book had not been the vigorous academic dispute that he promised and it had not concluded with the triumph of Church doctrine over the speculations of Copernicus. No, it had been advocacy. Anyone could see where the author's true sympathies lay. The character chosen to speak the part of Aristotle was not named Simplicio for nothing. Though this was the name of an ancient Aristotelian, it was also a perfect description for the arguments that the speaker advanced. Especially in the matter of the tides, Galileo had reduced the Aristotelian position to nonsense. The Jesuits brought their case directly to the pope and won an investigation, an investigation that they knew would end with Galileo's condemnation.

Though initially Pope Urban VIII was reluctant to prosecute the seventy-year-old astronomer, "the light of Italy," ultimately he had no choice. The great war to stamp out heresy was going badly for the Church. The pope needed the support of the Jesuits in Vienna and in Madrid much more than he needed the support of a scientist who had seen the moons of Jupiter. Nevertheless, when the case was turned over to the Inquisition, it proved weak in law. Galileo had only to present the book itself to show that he had received the official sanction of not one, but two censors of the Roman Catholic Church. If there was still anything in his book that offended, could the fault be his alone? The argument stymied the prosecutors, who were forced to find evidence where none existed. Resurrecting the agreement between Galileo and Bellarmine, they attempted to make it say that Galileo was under an absolute ban from even discussing the Copernican theories. Either Galileo would agree to recant his views, admit his errors, and beg the forgiveness of the Church or he would be tried and burned as a heretic. But though he could be forced to recant his view that the earth orbits the sun, Galileo could not be forced to change his mind.

After his recantation, Galileo was sentenced to live out his days under house arrest. Five years after his death in 1642, his greatest scientific work, *The Two New Sciences*, was smuggled out of Italy and printed anonymously in Holland in 1648.

unsettled life, moving from town to town in the Swiss cantons and German states. His rash temper and unusual behavior marked him wherever he went. Though he worked as a doctor, his true vocation was alchemy, and he conducted innumerable experiments designed to extract the essence of particular metals. After his death stories began to circulate attributing miraculous cures to Paracelsus's secret remedies. Masses of his papers were discovered and published, though most were an entirely incoherent blend of astrology, philosophy, alchemy, and his own unique terms for the substances he had created. Paracelsus taught that all matter was composed of combinations of three principles: salt, sulfur, and mercury. This view replaced the traditional belief in the four elements of earth, water, fire, and air. Paracelsus also believed that the properties of things were contained in their forms. Like the Hermetic magician, he saw inherent properties in the remedies he prescribed. "The Syderica bears the image and form of a snake on each of its leaves, and thus it gives protection against any kind of poisoning."

Though the Paracelsian system was peculiar, it transformed ideas about chemistry and medicine. Paracelsus rejected the theory that disease was caused by an imbalance in the humors of the body, the standard view of Galen, the great Greek physician of the second century A.D. Instead, Paracelsus argued that each disease had its own cause, which could be diagnosed and remedied. Where traditional doctors treated disease by bloodletting or sweating to correct the imbalance of humors, Paracelsus prescribed the ingestion of particular chemicals, especially distilled metals like mercury, arsenic, and antimony, and he favored administering them at propitious astrological moments.

Paracelsus' experimentation with metals and his practice of diagnostic medicine gave a practical turn to the study of alchemy. Efforts to cure new diseases like syphilis led to the continued study of the chemical properties of substances and to a new confidence about medical science. Although established physicians and medical faculties rejected Paracelsian cures and methods, his influence spread among ordinary practitioners. It ultimately had a profound impact on the studies of Robert Boyle (1627–91), an Englishman who helped establish the basis of the science of chem-

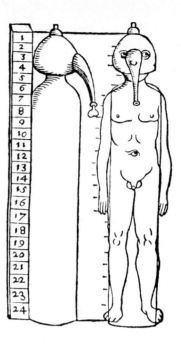

Paracelsus devised this "anatomical furnace" in which a patient's urine was distilled in a measuring cylinder, the parts of which correspond in length and width to those of the human body. Thus the body was "chemically dissected" for the benefit of the patient.

istry. Boyle devoted his energies to raising the study of medical chemistry above that of merely providing recipes for the cure of disease. He worked carefully and recorded each step in his experiments. Boyle's first important work, *The Sceptical Chymist* (1661), attacked both the Aristotelian and Paracelsian views of the basic components of the natural world. Boyle rejected both the four humors and the three principles. Instead he favored an atomic explanation in which matter "consisted of little particles of all sizes and shapes." Changes in these particles, which would later be identified as the chemical elements, resulted in changes in matter. Boyle's most important experiments were with gases—a word invented by Paracelsus. He formulated the relationship between the volume and pressure of a gas (Boyle's Law) and invented the air pump.

The new spirit of scientific inquiry also affected medical studies. The study of anatomy through dissection had helped the new scientists reject many of the descriptive errors in Galen's texts. The Belgian doctor Andreas Vesalius (1514–64), who was physician to the Emperor Charles V, published the first modern set of anatomical drawings in 1543, the same year that Copernicus published his work. But accurate knowledge of the composition of the body did not also mean better understanding of its operation. Dead bodies didn't easily yield the secrets of life. Much of what was known about matters as common as reproduction was a combination of ancient wisdom and practical experiences of midwives and doctors. Both were woefully inadequate.

One of the greatest mysteries was the method by which blood moved through the vital organs. It was generally believed that the blood originated in the liver, traveled to the right side of the heart, and then passed to the left side through invisible pores. Anatomical investigation proved beyond doubt that there was blood in both sides of the heart, but no one could discover the pores through which it passed. William Harvey (1578–1657), an Englishman who had received his medical education in Italy, offered an entirely different explanation. Harvey was employed as royal physi-

Tenth "Muscle plate" from Adreas Vesalius' De Humani Corporis Fabrica (Concerning the Fabric of the Human Body), published in 1543. The muscles of the back of the body are laid bare.

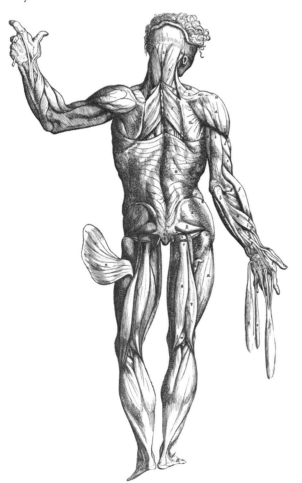

cian to both James I and Charles I and had one of the most lucrative medical practices in Europe. His real interest, however, was in studying the anatomy of the heart. Harvey examined hearts in more than forty species before concluding that the heart worked like a pump ør, as he put it, a water bellows. Harvey observed that the valves of the heart chambers allowed the blood to flow in only one direction. He thus concluded that the blood was pumped by the heart and circulated throughout the entire body.

The greatest of all English scientists was the mathematician and physicist Sir Isaac Newton (1642–1727). It was Newton who brought together the various strands of the new science. He merged the materialists and Hermeticists, the astronomers and astrologers, the chemists and alchemists. He made stunning contributions to the sciences of optics, physics, astronomy, and mathematics, and his magnum opus, *Mathematical Principles of Natural Philosophy* (1687), is one of a handful of the most important scientific works ever composed. Most importantly, Newton solved the single most perplexing problem: if the world was composed of matter in motion, what was motion?

Newton came from a moderately prosperous background and was trained at a local grammar school before entering Cambridge University. There was little in his background or education to suggest his unique talents and in fact his most important discoveries were not appreciated until years after he had made them. Newton was the first to understand the composition of light, the first to develop a calculus, the first to build a reflecting telescope. Though Newton became a professor at Cambridge, he spent much of his time alone. He made a great study of Hermetic writings and from them revived the mystical notions of attraction and repulsion.

Though Galileo had first developed a theory of inertia, the idea that a body at rest stays at rest, most materialists believed that motion was inherent in objects. In contrast, Newton believed that motion was the result of the interaction of objects and that it could be calculated mathematically. From his experiments he formulated the concept of force and his famous laws of motion: (1) that objects at rest or of uniform linear motion remain in such a state unless acted upon by an external force; (2) that changes in motion are proportional to force; and (3) that for every action there is an equal and opposite reaction. From these laws of motion, Newton advanced one step further. If the world was no more than matter in motion and if all motion was subject to the same laws, then the movement of the planets could be explained in the same way as the movement of an apple falling from a tree. There was a mathematical relationship between attraction and repulsion, a universal gravitation as Newton called it, that governed the movement of all objects. Newton's theory of gravity joined together Kepler's astronomy and Galileo's physics. The mathematical, materialistic world of the new science was now complete.

Science Enthroned

By the middle of the seventeenth century, the new science was firmly established throughout Europe. Royal and noble patrons supported the enterprise by paying some of the costs of equipment and experimentation. Royal observatories were created for the astronomers, colleges of physicians for the doctors, laboratories for the chemists. Both England and France established royal societies of learned scientists to meet together and discuss their discoveries. The French Académie des Sciences (1666) was composed of twenty salaried scientists and an equal number of students, divided among the different branches of scientific learning. They met twice weekly throughout the year and each worked on a project of his own devising. The English Royal Society (1662) boasted some of the greatest minds of the age. It was there that Newton first made public his most important discoveries. Scientific bodies were also formed outside the traditional universities. These were the so-called mechanics colleges, like Gresham College in London, where the practical applications of mathematics and physics were studied and taught. Navigation was a particular concern of the college, and the faculty established close ties with the Royal Navy and with London merchants.

The establishment of learned scientific societies and practical colleges fulfilled part of the program advocated by Sir Francis Bacon (1561–1626), one of the leading supporters of scientific research in England. In the *Advancement of Learning* (1605) Bacon proposed a scientific method through inductive, empirical experimentation. Bacon believed that experiments should be carefully recorded so that results were both reliable and repeatable. He advocated the open world of the scientist over the secret world of the magician. In his numerous writings he stressed the practical impact of scientific discovery and even wrote a utopian work in which science appeared as the savior of humanity. Though he was not himself a scientific investigator, Bacon used his considerable influence to support scientific projects in England.

Bacon's support for the new science contrasts markedly with the stance taken by the Roman Catholic church. Embattled by the Reformation and the wars of religion, the Church had taken the offensive in preserving the core of its heritage. By the early seventeenth century the missionary work of the Jesuits had won many reconversions and had halted the advance of Protestantism. Now the new science appeared to be another heresy. Not only did it confound ancient wisdom and contradict Church teachings, but it was also a lay movement that was neither directed nor controlled from Rome. The trial of Galileo slowed the momentum of scientific investigation in Catholic countries and starkly posed the conflict between authority and knowledge. But the stand taken by the Church was based on more than narrow self-interest. Ever since Copernicus had published his views, a new skepticism had emerged among European intellectuals. Every year new theories competed with old ones, and dozens of contradictory explanations for the most common phenomena were advanced and debated. The skeptics concluded that nothing was known and nothing was knowable. Their position led inevitably to the most shocking of all possible views: atheism.

There was no necessary link between the new science and an attack upon established religion. So Galileo had argued all along. Few of the leading scientists ever saw a contradiction between their studies and their faith. Sir Robert Boyle endowed a lectureship for the advancement of Christian doctrine and contributed money for the translation of the New Testament into Turkish. Still by the middle of the century attacks upon the Church were increasing and some blamed the new science for them. Thus it was altogether fitting that one of the leading mathematicians of the day should also provide the method for harmonizing faith and reason.

René Descartes (1596–1650) was the son of a provincial lawyer and judge. He was trained in one of the best Jesuit schools in France before taking a law degree in 1616. While it was his father's intention that his son practice law, it was René's intention that he become educated in "the school of life." He entered military service in the Dutch Republic and after the outbreak of the Thirty Years' War, in the Duke of Bavaria's army. Descartes was keenly interested in mathematics, and during his military travels he met and was tutored by a leading Dutch mathematician. For the first time he learned of the new scientific discoveries and of the advances made in mathematics. In 1619 he dreamt of discovering the scientific principles of universal knowledge. After this dream, Descartes returned to Holland and began to develop his system. He was on the verge of publishing his views when he learned of Galileo's condemnation. Reading Galileo's *Dialogue Between the Two Great Systems of the World* (1632), Descartes discovered that he shared many of the same opinions and had worked out mathematical proofs for them. He refrained from publishing until 1637 when he brought out the *Discourse on Method*.

In the *Discourse on Method*, Descartes demonstrated how skepticism could be used to produce certainty. He began by declaring that he would reject everything that could not be clearly proven beyond doubt. Thus he rejected the material world, the testimony of his senses, all known or imagined opinions. He was left only with doubt. But what was doubt, if not thought, and what was thought, if not the workings of his mind. The only thing of which he could be certain, then, was that he had a mind. Thus, his famous formulation: "I think, therefore I am." From this first certainty came another, the knowledge of perfectibility. He knew that he was imperfect and that a perfect being had to have placed that knowledge within him. Therefore, a perfect being—God—existed.

Descartes' philosophy, known as Cartesianism, rested on the dual existence of matter and mind. Matter was the material world subject to the incontrovertible laws of mathematics. Mind was the spirit of the creator. Descartes was one of the leading mechanistic philosophers, believing that all objects operated in accord with natural laws. He invented analytic geometry and made important contributions to the sciences of optics and physics upon which Newton would later build. Yet it was in his proof that the new science could be harmonized with the old religion that Descartes made his greatest contribution to the advancement of learning. Despite the fact that his later work was condemned by the Catholic church and that he preferred the safety of Protestant Holland to the uncertainty of his Catholic homeland, Cartesianism became the basis for the unification of science and religion.

"I shall attempt to make myself intelligible to everyone," Descartes wrote. Like many of the new scientists, he preferred the use of vernacular languages to elite Latin, hoping that his work would reach beyond the narrow bounds of high culture. Descartes was one of many new scientists who saw the practical import of what they had learned and who hoped to bring that knowledge to the aid of the material well-being of their contemporaries. John Dee (1527–1608) translated the Greek geometrician Euclid into English so that ordinary people might "find out and devise new works, strange engines and instruments for sundry purposes in the commonwealth." Though many of the breakthrough discoveries of the new scientists would not find practical use for centuries, the spirit of discovery was to have great impact in an age of commerce and capital. The quest for mathematical certainty and prime movers led directly to improvements in agriculture, mining, navigation, and industrial activity. It also brought with it a sense of control over the material world, which provided a new optimism for generations of Europeans.

Empires of Goods

"The discovery of America and that of a passage to the East Indies by the Cape of Good Hope, are the two greatest and most important events in the history of mankind." So wrote the great Scottish economist Adam Smith (1723–90) in *The Wealth of Nations* (1776). For Smith and his generation the first great age of commerce was coming to an end. Under the watchful eye of the European states, a worldwide marketplace for the exchange of commodities had been created. First the Dutch and then the English had established monopoly companies to engage in exotic trades in the East. First the Spanish and Portuguese, then the English and French had established colonial dependencies in the Atlantic, which they carefully nurtured in hope of economic gain. Protected trade had flourished beyond the wildest dreams of its promoters. Luxury commodities became staples; new commodities became luxuries. Trade enhanced the material life of all European peoples, though it came at great cost to the Asians, Africans, and Latin Americans whose labor and raw materials were converted into the new crazes of consumption.

Though long-distance trade was never as important to the European economy as was inland and intracontinental trade, its development in the seventeenth and eighteenth centuries

The Geographer *by Jan Vermeer van Delft, 1669. A Dutch cartographer, holding dividers, is shown surrounded by charts, a globe, and other paraphernalia of his craft. Such cartographers combined the skills of artist and mathematician.*

had a profound impact upon life-styles, economic policy, and ultimately on warfare. It was the Dutch who became the first great commercial power. Their achievements were based on innovative techniques, rational management, and a social and cultural environment that supported mercantile activities. Dutch society was freer than any other, open to new capital, new ventures, and new ideas. The Dutch innovated in the organization of trade by developing the concept of the entrepôt, a place where goods were brought for storage before being exchanged. They pioneered in finance by establishing the Bank of Amsterdam. They led in shipbuilding by developing the flyboat, a long, flat-hulled vessel designed specifically to carry bulky cargoes like grain. They traded around the globe with the largest mercantile fleet yet known. It was not until the end of the seventeenth century that England and France surpassed the Dutch. This reversal owed less to new innovations than it did to restrictions on trade. Because the Dutch dominated the European economy, the French and English began to pass laws to eliminate Dutch competition. The English banned imports carried in Dutch ships; the French banned Dutch products. Both policies cut heavily into the Dutch superiority and both ultimately resulted in commercial warfare.

The Marketplace of the World

By the seventeenth century, long-distance trade had begun to integrate the regions of the world into a single marketplace. Slaves bought in Africa mined silver in South America. The bullion was shipped to Spain, where it was distributed across Europe. Most went to Amsterdam to settle Spanish debts, Dutch bankers having replaced the Italians as the paymasters of Europe. From Holland the silver traveled east to the Baltic Sea, the Dutch lifeline where vital stores of grain and timber were purchased for home consumption. By the 1630s over five hundred Dutch ships a year called at Gdansk, the largest of the Baltic ports. From there the silver was transported to the interior of Poland and Russia, the great storehouses of European raw materials. Even more of this African-mined Spanish silver, traded by the Dutch, was carried to Asia to buy spices in the South Sea Islands, cottons in India, or silk in China. Millions of ounces flowed from America to

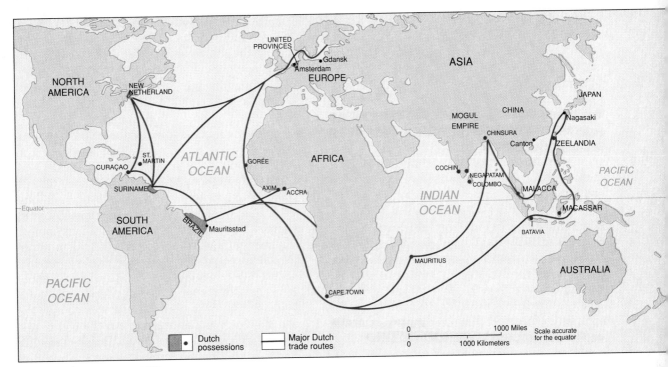

Dutch Trade Routes, ca. 1650

Asia via the European trading routes. On the return voyage, brightly colored Indian cottons were traded in Africa to purchase slaves for the South American silver mines.

The remarkable fact about the expansion of European trade in the seventeenth and eighteenth centuries is that it took place as a result of the ingenuity of traders rather than because of technological or geographical discoveries. By the sixteenth century all the major trading routes had already been opened. The Spanish moved back and forth across the Atlantic; the Dutch and Portuguese sailed around the tip of Africa to the Indian Ocean. The Baltic trade connected the eastern and western parts of Europe as Danes, Swedes, and Dutch exchanged Polish and Russian raw materials for English and French manufactured goods. The Mediterranean, which had dominated world trade for centuries, was still a vital artery of intercontinental trade, but its role was diminishing. In 1600 almost three-quarters of the Asian trade was still land based, much of it carried through the Middle East to the Mediterranean. A century later nearly all Asian trade was carried directly to western Europe by Dutch and English vessels. Commercial power was shifting

to the northern European states just as dramatically as was military and political power.

The technology associated with commerce achieved no breakthroughs to compare with the great transformations of the fifteenth century, when new techniques of navigation made transatlantic travel possible. It is certainly true that there continued to be improvements. The astronomical findings of the new science were a direct aid to navigation as were the recorded experiences of so many practiced sea travelers. The materials used to make and maintain ships improved with the importation of pitch and tar from the east and with the greater availability of iron and copper from Scandinavia. It was the Dutch who made the single most important innovation in shipbuilding. To gain maximum profit from their journeys to the Baltic, the Dutch designed the so-called flyboats. Flyboats sacrificed speed and maneuverability, but they were cheap to build and could be manned by small crews. They carried no heavy armaments and were thus well adapted to the serene Baltic trade.

It was unspectacular developments like the flyboat that had such an impact on seventeenth- and eighteenth-century transcontinental trade.

Innovation, organization, and efficient management were the principal elements of what historians have called the commercial revolution. Concerted efforts to maximize opportunities and advantages accounted for the phenomenal growth in the volume and value of commercial exchange. One of the least spectacular and most effective breakthroughs was the replacement of bilateral with triangular trade. In bilateral trade, the surplus commodities of one community were exchanged for those of another. This method, of course, restricted the range of trading partners to those with mutually desirable surplus production: England and Italy were unlikely to swap woolens or Sicily and Poland to trade grain. For those with few desirable commodities, bilateral trade meant the exchange of precious metals for goods, and throughout much of the sixteenth and early seventeenth centuries bullion was by far the most often traded commodity. Triangular trade created a larger pool of desirable goods. British manufactured goods could be traded to Africa for slaves, the slaves could be traded in the West Indies for sugar, and the sugar could be consumed in Britain. Moreover, the merchants involved in shifting these goods from place to place could achieve profits on each exchange. Indeed their motive in trading could now change from dumping surplus commodities to matching supply and demand.

Equally important were the changes made in the way trade was financed. As states, cities, and even individuals could stamp their own precious metal, there were hundreds of different European coins with different nominal and metallic values. The influx of American silver further destabilized an already unstable system of exchange. The Bank of Amsterdam was created in 1609 to establish a uniform rate of exchange for the various currencies traded in that city. From this useful function a second developed, transfer, or giro, banking, a system that had been invented in Italy. In giro banking, various merchant firms held money on account and issued bills of transfer from one to another. This transfer system meant that merchants in different cities did not have to transport their precious metals or endure long delays in having their accounts settled. Giro banking facilitated exchanges between merchants and allowed money to circulate more often simply by staying in the same place. The Bank of Amsterdam soon became the center of European transfer banking, the number of accounts grew from 700 to 2,700 during the course of the seventeenth century.

Giro banking also aided the development of bills of exchange, an early form of checking. Merchants could conclude trades by depositing money in a given bank or merchant house and then having a bill drawn for the sum they owed. Bills of exchange were especially important in international trade as they made large-scale shipments of precious metals to settle trade deficits unnecessary. By the end of the seventeenth century, bills of exchange had become negotiable, that is, they could pass from one merchant to another without being redeemed. Thus a Dutch merchant could buy French wines in Bordeaux with a bill of exchange drawn on an account in the Bank of Amsterdam. The Bordeaux merchant could then purchase Spanish oranges and use the same bill of exchange as payment. There were two disadvantages to this system: ultimately the bill had to return to Amsterdam for redemption, and when it did the account on which it was drawn might be empty. The establishment of the Bank of England in 1694 overcame these difficulties. The Bank of England was licensed to issue its own bills of exchange, or bank notes, which were backed by the revenue from specific English taxes. This security of payment was widely sought after, and the Bank of England soon became a clearing house for all kinds of bills of exchange. The Bank would buy in bills at a discount, paying less than their face value, and pay out precious metal or their own notes in exchange. Again, the discounting of bills allowed for the rapid turnover of money, while the security offered by the Bank lowered the risks of business.

The effects of these and many other small-scale changes in business practice helped fuel prolonged growth in European commerce. It was the European merchant who made this growth possible, accepting the risks of each individual transaction, building up small pools of capital from which successive transactions could take place. Most mercantile ventures were conducted by individuals or families and were based on the specialized trade of a single commodity. Trade offered high returns because it entailed high risks. The long delays in moving goods and their uncertain arrival; the unreliability of agents and the unscrupulousness of other traders; the inefficiencies in transport and communication all weighed heavily against success. Those who succeeded did so less by luck than by hard work. They used family members to receive shipments. They lowered shipping costs by careful packaging. They lowered protection costs by securing their trade routes. Financial publications lowered the costs of information. Ultimately, lower costs meant lower prices. For centuries luxury goods dominated intercontinental trade. But by the eighteenth century European merchants had created a world marketplace in which the luxuries of the past were the common fare of the present.

Consumption Choices

As long-distance trade became more sophisticated, merchants became more sensitive to consumer tastes. Low-volume, high-quality goods like spices and silks could not support the growing merchant communities in the European states. These goods were the preserve of the largest trading companies and, more importantly, they had reached saturation levels by the early seventeenth century. The price of pepper, the most used of all spices, fell nearly continuously after 1650. Moreover, triangular trade allowed merchants to provide a better match of supplies and demands. The result was the rise to prominence of a vast array of new commodities, which not only continued the expansion of trade but also reshaped diet, life-styles, and patterns of consumption. New products came from both east and west. Dutch and English incursions into the Asian trade provoked competition with the Portuguese and expanded the range of commodities that were shipped back to Europe. An aggressive Asian triangle was created in which European bullion bought Indonesian spices that were exchanged for Persian silk and Chinese and Japanese finished goods. In the Atlantic, the English were quick to develop both home and export markets for a variety of new or newly available products.

The European trade with Asia had always been designed to satisfy consumer demand rather than to exchange surplus goods. Europeans manufactured little that was desired in Asia, and neither merchants nor governments saw fit to attempt to influence Asian tastes in the way they did those of Europeans. The chief commodity

imported to the East was bullion, tons of South American silver, perhaps a third of all that was produced. In return came spices, silk, coffee, jewels, jade, porcelain, dyes, and a wide variety of other exotic goods. By the middle of the seventeenth century the Dutch dominated the spice trade, obtaining a virtual monopoly over cinnamon, cloves, nutmeg, and mace and carrying the largest share of pepper. Each year Europeans consumed perhaps a million pounds of the four great spices and 7 million pounds of pepper. Both Dutch and English competed for preeminence in the silk trade. The Dutch concentrated on Chinese silk, which they used mostly in trade with Japan. The English established an interest in lower-quality Indian silk spun in Bengal and even hired Italian silk masters to try to teach European techniques to the Indian spinners.

The most important manufactured articles imported from the East to Europe were the lightweight, brightly colored Indian cottons known as calicoes. It was the Dutch who first realized the potential of the cotton market. Until the middle of the seventeenth century cotton and cotton blended with silk were used in Europe only for wall hangings and table coverings. Colorful Asian chintz contained floral patterns that Europeans still considered exotic. But the material was also soft and smooth to the touch, and it soon replaced linen for use as underwear and close-fitting garments among the well-to-do. The fashion quickly caught on and the Dutch began exporting calicoes throughout the Continent. The English and French followed suit, establishing their own trading houses in India and bringing European patterns and designs with them for the Asians to copy. The calico trade was especially lucrative because the piece goods were easy to pack and ship and, unlike consumables, could be stored indefinitely. When the English finally came to dominate the trade in the middle of the eighteenth century, they were shipping over a million cloths a year into London. The craze for calicoes was so great that both the English and French governments attempted to ban their import to protect their own clothing industries.

Along with the new apparel from the East came new beverages. Coffee, which was first drunk in northern Europe in the early seventeenth century, became a fashionable drink by the end of the century. Coffeehouses sprang up in the

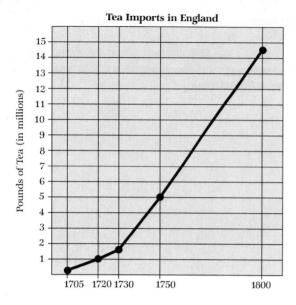

Tea Imports in England

major urban areas of northern Europe. There political and intellectual conversation was as heady as the strong Middle Eastern brew that was served. The Dutch and English both established themselves in the coffee trade, which was centered in the Middle Eastern seaport of Mocha. By the beginning of the eighteenth century the Dutch began to grow their own coffee for export from their island colony of Java and the two different types of coffee competed for favor.

As popular as coffee became among the European elites, it paled in comparison to the importance of tea as both an import commodity and a basic beverage. While coffee drinking remained the preserve of the wealthy, tea consumption spread throughout European society. It was probably most important in England, where the combination of China tea and West Indian sugar created a virtual revolution in nutrition. The growth in tea consumption was phenomenal. In 1706 England imported 100,000 pounds of tea. By the end of the century the number had risen to over 15 million pounds. The English imported most of this tea directly from China, where an open port had been established at Canton. Originally just one of a number of commodities that was carried on an Asian voyage, tea soon became the dominant cargo of the large English merchant

ships. Some manufactured goods would be brought to India on the outward voyage, to fill as much cargo space as possible, but once the ships had loaded the green and black teas, they sailed directly home. Almost all tea was purchased with bullion as the Chinese had even less use for European goods than did other Asians. It was not until the discovery that the Chinese consumed large quantities of opium, which was grown in India and Southeast Asia, that a triangular trade developed.

The success of tea was linked to the explosive growth in the development of sugar in Europe's Atlantic colonies. The Portuguese had attempted to cultivate sugar in the Azores at the end of the fifteenth century, but it was not until the settlement of Brazil, whose hot, humid climate was a natural habitat for the cane plants, that widespread cultivation began. The island of Barbados became the first English sugar colony. Barbados turned to sugar production accidentally when its first attempts to market tobacco failed. The planters modeled their development on Brazil, where African slaves were used to plant, tend, and cut the giant canes from which the sugar was extracted. For reasons that will never be fully understood, the English had an insatiable appetite for sugar's sweetness. It was taken plain, like candy, used in small quantities in almost all types of recipes, and diluted in ever increasing quantities of tea. Hot, sweet tea became a meal for the lower orders of English society, a meal which, unlike beer, provided a quick burst of energy. By 1700 the English were sending home over 50 million pounds of sugar besides what they were shipping directly to the North American colonies. This quantity doubled by 1730 and still there was no slackening of demand. What might have become a valuable raw material in English trade instead became a staple of consumption.

The triangular trade of manufactures—largely reexported calicoes—to Africa for slaves, who were exchanged in the West Indies for sugar, became the dominant form of English overseas trade. Colonial production depended upon the enforced labor of hundreds of thousands of Africans. Gold and silver, tobacco, sugar, rice, and indigo were all slave crops. Africans were enslaved by other Africans and then sold to Europeans to be used in the colonies. Over six million black slaves were imported into the Americas during the course of the eighteenth century. While rum and calicoes were the main commodities exchanged for slaves, the African tribes that dominated the slave trade organized a highly competitive market. Every colonial power participated in this lucrative trade. Over three million slaves were imported into the Portuguese colony of Brazil; by the end of the eighteenth century there were 500,000 slaves and only 35,000 French inhabitants of the sugar island of Saint Domingue. But it was the English with their sugar colonies of Barbados and Jamaica and their tobacco colonies of Virginia and Maryland who ultimately came to control the slave trade. The prosperity of Newport, Rhode Island, in North America and the port of Liverpool in Lancashire were built entirely upon the slave trade as were hundreds of plantation fortunes. The sweet tooth of Europe was fed by the sweat of black Africans.

Sugar was by far the dominant commodity of the colonial trade but it was not the only one. Furs and fish had first driven Europeans toward North America and both remained important commodities. Beaver and rabbit skins were the most common materials for making headgear in an age in which everyone wore a hat. The Canadian cod schools were among the richest in the world and the catch was shipped back either salted or dried. The English established what amounted to a manufacturing industry on the Newfoundland coast, where they dried the tons of fish that they caught. In the eighteenth century, rice was grown for export in the southern American colonies, particularly South Carolina. Rice never achieved great popularity in England, though it was in constant demand in the German states. Tobacco was the first new American product to come into widespread use in Europe, and its popularity—despite various official efforts to ban its use as dirty and unhealthy—grew steadily. American tobacco was grown principally in the colonies of Virginia and Maryland and shipped across the ocean, where it was frequently blended with European varieties. Although the English were the principal importers, it was the Dutch who dominated the European tobacco trade, making the most popular blends.

The new commodities flooded into Europe from all parts of the globe. By the middle of the eighteenth century tea, coffee, cocoa, gin, and rum were among the most popular beverages.

These were all products that had been largely unknown a century earlier. Among the wealthy, tea was served from porcelain pots imported from China; among all classes it was drunk with sugar imported from America. Beaver hats and Persian silks were fashionable in the upper reaches of society; rabbit caps and calico prints in the lower. New habits were created as new demands were satisfied. Tea and sugar passed from luxury to staple in little more than a generation and the demand for both products continued to increase. To meet it, the European trading powers needed to create and maintain a powerful and efficient mercantile system.

Dutch Masters

For the nearly eighty years between 1565 and 1648 that the Dutch were at war they grew ever more prosperous. While the economies of most other European nations were sapped by warfare, the Dutch seemed to draw strength from their interminable conflict with the Spanish empire. They did have the advantage of fighting defensively on land and offensively on sea. Land war was terribly costly to the aggressor, who had to raise large armies, transport them to the site of battles or sieges, and feed them while they were there. The defender simply had to fortify strong places, keep its water routes open to secure supplies, and wait for the weather to change. Sea war—or piracy, depending on one's viewpoint—required much smaller outlays for men and material and promised the rewards of captured prizes. The Dutch became expert at attacking the Spanish silver fleets, hunting like a lion against a herd by singling out the slower and smaller vessels for capture. The Dutch also benefited from the massive immigration into their provinces of Protestants who had lived and worked in the southern provinces. They brought with them vital skills in manufacturing and large reserves of capital for investment in Dutch commerce.

The Dutch grounded their prosperity on commerce. Excellent craftsmen, they took the lead in the skilled occupations necessary for finishing cloth, refining raw materials, and decorating consumer goods. They were also successful farmers, especially given the small amounts of land with which they had to work and the difficult ecological conditions in which they worked it. But their greatest abilities were in trade. Like the Venetians they were a water people and they proved to be skillful at moving goods from place to place and in developing the machinery and knowledge to move them efficiently.

Though the Dutch Republic comprised seven separate political entities, with a total population of about two million, the province of Holland was preeminent among them. Holland contained more than a quarter of this population and its trading port of Amsterdam was one of the great cities of Europe. The city had risen dramatically in the seventeenth century, growing from a mid-sized urban community of 65,000 in 1600 to a metropolis of 170,000 fifty years later. The port was one of the busiest in the world, for it was built to be an entrepôt. Vast warehouses and docks lined its canals. Visitors were impressed by the bustle, the cleanliness, and the businesslike appearance of Amsterdam. There were no great public squares and few recognizable monuments. The central buildings were the Bank and the Exchange, testimony to the dominant activities of the residents.

"The Dutch must be understood as they really are, the carriers of the world, the middle persons in trade, the factors and brokers of Europe," wrote the Englishman Daniel Defoe (1660–1731), who was much impressed by their prosperity. The Dutch dominated all types of European trade. They carried more English coal than England, more French wine than France, more Swedish iron than Sweden. Dutch ships outnumbered all others in every important port of Europe. Goods were brought to Amsterdam to be redistributed throughout the world. Dutch prosperity rested first upon the Baltic trade. Even after it ceased to expand in the middle of the seventeenth century, the Baltic trade composed over a quarter of all of Holland's commercial enterprise. The Dutch also were the leaders in the East Indian trade throughout the seventeenth century. They held a virtual monopoly on the sale of exotic spices and the largest share of the pepper trade. Their imports of cottons and especially of porcelain began new consumer fads that soon resulted in the development of European industries. Dutch potteries began to produce china, as lower-quality ceramic goods came to be known. Dutch trade in the Atlantic was of less importance, but the Dutch did have a colonial presence in the New World, controlling a number of small islands and the rapidly growing mainland settlement of New Netherland. Yet the Dutch still dominated the secondary market in tobacco and sugar, becoming the largest processor and refiner of these important commodities.

In all of these activities the Dutch acted as merchants rather than as consumers. Unlike most other Europeans they regarded precious metal as a commodity like any other and took no interest in accumulating it for its own sake. This attitude enabled them to pioneer triangular trading and develop the crucial financial institutions necessary to expand their overseas commerce. The Dutch were not so much innovators as improvers. They saw the practical value in Italian accounting and banking methods and raised them to new levels of efficiency. They made use of marine insurance to help diminish the risks of mercantile activity. Their legal system favored the creation of small trading companies by protecting individual investments. The European stock and commodity markets were centered in Amsterdam. Shares of the Dutch East India Company were traded with the same confidence as gold and silver, and by the 1670s over 500 commodities were traded on the Amsterdam exchange. Even a primitive futures market evolved for those who wished to speculate.

There were many explanations for the unparalleled growth of this small maritime state into one of the greatest of European trading empires. Geography and climate provided one impetus, the lack of sufficient foodstuffs another. Yet there were cultural characteristics as well. One was the openness of Dutch society. Even before the struggle with Spain, the northern provinces had shown a greater inclination toward religious toleration than had most parts of Europe. Amsterdam became a unique center for religious and intellectual exchange. European Jews flocked there, as did Catholic dissidents like Descartes. They brought with them a wide range of skills and knowledge along with capital that could be invested in trade. There was no real social nobility among the Dutch and certainly no set of values that prized investment in land over investment in trade. The French and Spanish nobility looked with scorn upon their mercantile classes and shunned any form of commercial investment, and the English, though more open to industry and trade, sank as much of their capital as possible into landed estates and country houses. The Dutch economic elite invested in trade. By the middle of the seventeenth century the Dutch Republic enjoyed a reputation for cultural creativity that was the envy of the Continent. A truly extraordinary school of Dutch artists led by Rembrandt celebrated this new state born of commerce with vivid portrayals of its people and its prosperity.

Mercantile Organization

Elsewhere in Europe, trade was the king's business. The wealth of the nation was part of the prestige of the monarch and its rise or fall part of the crown's power. Power and prestige were far more important to absolute rulers than was the profit of merchants. Indeed, in all European states except the Dutch Republic, the activities of merchants were scorned by both the landed elite and the salaried bureaucrats. Leisure was valued by the one and royal service by the other. The pursuit of wealth by buying and selling somehow lacked dignity. Yet the activities of the mercantile classes took on increasing importance for the state for two reasons. First, imported goods, especially luxuries, were a noncontroversial target for taxation. Customs duties and excise taxes grew all over Europe. Representative assemblies composed of landed elites were usually happy to grant them to the monarch, and merchants could pass them on to consumers in higher prices. Secondly, the competition for trade was seen as a competition between states rather than individual merchants. Trading privileges involved special arrangements with foreign powers, arrangements that recognized the sovereign power of European monarchs. In this way, trade could bring glory to the state.

The competition for power and glory derived from the theory of mercantilism, a set of assumptions about economic activity that were commonly held throughout Europe and that guided the policies of almost every government. There were two interrelated ideas. One was that the wealth of a nation resided in its stock of precious metal, and the other was that economic activity was a zero-sum game. There was thought to be a fixed amount of money, a fixed amount of commodities, and a fixed amount of consumption. Thus what one country gained, another lost. If

England bought wine from France and paid £100,000 in precious metal for it, then England was £100,000 poorer and France £100,000 richer. If one was to trade profitably, it was absolutely necessary to wind up with a surplus of precious metal. Therefore it was imperative that governments regulate trade so that the stocks of precious metal were protected from the greed of the merchants. The first and most obvious measure of protection, then, was to prohibit the export of coin except by license, a prohibition that was absolutely unenforceable and was violated more often by government officials than by merchants.

These ideas about economic activity led to a variety of forms of economic regulation. The most common was the monopoly, a grant of special privileges in return for both financial considerations and an agreement to abide by the rules set out by the state. In the context of the seventeenth-century economy, there were a number of advantages to monopolies. First, of course, were those that accrued to the crown. There were direct and indirect revenues: monopolists usually paid considerable fees for their rights, and their activities were easy to monitor for purposes of taxation. The crown could use the grant of monopoly to reward past favors or to purchase future support from powerful individuals. There were also advantages for the monopolists. They could make capital investments with the expectation of long-term gains. This advantage was especially important in attracting investors for risky and expensive ventures like long-distance trade. Indeed, there were even benefits for the economy as a whole, as monopolies increased productive investment at a time when most capital was being used to purchase land, luxury goods, or offices.

Two monopoly companies, the English and the Dutch East India companies, dominated the Asian trade. The English East India Company, founded in 1600 with a capital of £30,000, was given the exclusive right to the Asian trade and immediately established itself throughout the Indian Ocean. The Dutch East India Company was formed two years later with ten times the capital of its English counterpart. By the end of the century the Dutch company employed over twelve thousand people. Both companies were known as joint-stock companies, an innovation in the way in which businesses were organized. Subscribers owned a percentage of the total value of the company, based on the number of shares they bought, and were entitled to a distribution of profits on the same basis. Initially, the English company determined profits on single voyages and was to distribute all of its assets to its shareholders after a given period. But changes in legal practice gave the company an identity separate from the individuals that held the shares. Now shares could be exchanged without the breakup of the company as a whole. Both Amsterdam and London soon developed stock markets to trade the shares of monopoly companies.

Both East India companies were remarkably good investments. The Dutch East India Company paid an average dividend of 18 percent for over two hundred years. The value of English East India Company shares rose fivefold in the second half of the seventeenth century alone. Few other monopoly companies achieved a record comparable to that of the East India companies. The English Royal African Company, founded in 1672 to provide slaves for the Spanish colonies, barely recouped costs and was soon superseded by private trade. Even the French East Indian and African companies, which were modeled on the Dutch and English, were forced to abandon their monopolies. The Dutch and English companies were successful not because of their special privileges but because they were able to lower the costs of protecting their ships and cargoes.

Monopolies were not the only form of regulation in which seventeenth-century government engaged. For those states with Atlantic colonies, regulation took the form of restricting markets rather than traders. In the 1660s the English government, alarmed at the growth of Dutch mercantile activity in the New World, passed a series of Navigation Acts designed to protect English shipping. Colonial goods—primarily tobacco and sugar—could be shipped to and from England only in English boats. If the French wanted to purchase West Indian sugar, they could not simply send a ship to the English colony of Barbados loaded with French goods and exchange them for sugar. Rather, they had to make their purchases from an English import-export merchant and the goods had to be unloaded in an English port before they could be reloaded to be shipped to France. As a result, the English reexport trade skyrocketed. In the year 1700 reexports amounted to nearly 40 percent of all English commerce.

With such a dramatic increase in trading, all moved in English ships, shipbuilding boomed. English coastal towns enjoyed heightened prosperity as did the great colonial ports of Bristol and Liverpool. For a time, colonial protection proved effective.

French protectionism was as much internal as colonial. The French entered the intercontinental trade later than their north Atlantic rivals, and they were less dependent upon trade for their subsistence. Of all the states of Europe, only France could satisfy its needs from its own resources. But to achieve such self-sufficiency required coordination and leadership. In the 1670s Louis XIV's finance minister, Jean-Baptiste Colbert (1619–83) developed a plan to bolster the French economy by protecting it against European imports. First Colbert followed the English example of restricting the reexport trade by requiring that imports come to France either in French ships or in the ships of the country from which the goods originated. In addition, he used tariffs to make imported goods unattractive in France. He sponsored a drive to increase French manufacturing, especially of textiles, tapestries, linens, glass, and furniture. To protect the investments in French manufacturing, enormous duties were placed on the import of similar goods manufactured elsewhere. The Venetian glass industry, for example, suffered a serious blow from Colbert's tariffs. English woolen manufacturers were also damaged and the English sought retaliatory measures. But in fact, the English had already begun to imitate this form of protection. In the early eighteenth century England attempted to limit the importation of cotton goods from India to prevent the collapse of the domestic clothing industry.

The Navigation Acts and Colbert's program of protective tariffs were directed specifically against Dutch reexporters. The Dutch were the acknowledged leaders in all branches of commerce in the seventeenth century. There were many summers when there were more Dutch vessels in London Harbor than there were English ships. In the 1670s the Dutch merchant fleet was probably larger than the English, French, Spanish, Portuguese, and German fleets combined. Restrictive navigation practices were one way to combat an advantage that the Dutch had built through heavy capital investment and by breaking away from the prevailing theories about the relationship between wealth and precious metals. The English and French Navigation Acts cut heavily into the Dutch trade and ultimately both the English and French overtook them. But protectionism had its price. Just as the dynastic wars were succeeded by the wars of religion, so were the wars of religion succeeded by the wars of commerce.

The Wars of Commerce

It was not inevitable that economic competition would lead to warfare, only that restrictive competition would. This was the lesson that Adam Smith attempted to teach in 1776. He argued that in economic affairs, that government governs best that governs least. Monopolies, special trading privileges, tariffs—all were equally destructive of commerce, wealth, and political stability. Smith advocated a policy of laissez-faire toward all commercial enterprise. Governments should leave commerce to follow its natural path without any legislative interference. This freedom would allow nations to grow, wealth to accumulate, and goods to circulate freely. But Smith's ideas were built upon a century of commercial warfare, which had sapped the strength of even the strongest European states. Hindsight made it easy to see that restrictive economic policies led to political and military confrontations.

The view ahead was much cloudier. For one thing, the belief that there was a fixed amount of trade in the world was still strong in the late seventeenth century. One country's gains in trade were another's losses. Economic rivalry was just that. There was not more than enough to go around and it could not be easily understood how the expansion of one country's trade could benefit all countries. Moreover, trade, like wealth itself, was still viewed as part of the glory of a state and therefore of the glory of the monarch. It was another of the personal attributes of the absolute ruler. Thus competition for trade was the same as competition for territory or subjects, part of the struggle by which the state grew powerful. Louis XIV and his ministers compared Dutch trading superiority in the seventeenth century to Spanish military superiority in the sixteenth. Its very existence posed a national danger. From these ideas followed warfare. Much of the warfare of the century between 1660 and 1763 was explicitly commercial. Wars were fought over protective regulations, access to markets, smuggling, and colonies. Most took place on the high seas or in small colonial outposts. But some of the bloodiest fighting, especially the land wars of the late seventeenth century, demonstrated how commercial interests could become intertwined with dynastic and political concerns.

The Mercantile Wars

Commercial warfare in Europe began between the English and the Dutch in the middle of the seventeenth century. That these two states should find themselves enemies was surprising for they had much in common. Both were maritime peoples with strong seafaring traditions. They were also natural trading partners. For centuries English wool and woolen cloth had been imported into the Low Countries for processing. Both were Protestant states that had resisted the perils of the Counter-Reformation. The English had supported the Dutch in their struggle with Philip II, and Queen Elizabeth called them "our most ancient and familiar neighbors." For a time, when the English rebelled against their king and established a commonwealth, they were even both republics. But for all their natural affinities, the English and Dutch increasingly found themselves rivals for trade. Both had established aggressive overseas trading companies in the Atlantic and in Asia. In the early seventeenth century the Dutch were the undisputed leaders, their carrying capacity and trade monopolies the greatest in the world. But the English were rising quickly. Their Atlantic colonies began to produce valuable new commodities like tobacco and sugar and their Asian trade was expanding decade after decade. Conflict was inevitable.

It began in the east where competition for the establishment of trading outposts at vital geographical points led to small armed confrontations. In the early seventeenth century, the English were forcibly evicted from the Spice Islands and Indonesia, two of the most lucrative trading centers. Matters deteriorated considerably in 1651 when Cromwell's regime passed the first Naviga-

Painter Jan Peter depicts an incident in the naval warfare caused by trade rivalry between the Dutch and the English. The Dutch fleet sailed up the Medway River and destroyed many English vessals, towing away a battleship.

tion Ordinance, which barred the Dutch from transporting the goods of other states into England. This measure struck at the very heart of the Dutch entrepôt system. The result was a series of three naval wars in 1652–54, 1665–67, and 1672–74.

Though the Dutch had by far the larger fleet, few of their ships were fitted for naval warfare. The flyboats, which had given them such an overwhelming advantage in bulk trading, were easy prey for the armed English merchant vessels. It is estimated that in the three wars over 2,500 Dutch ships were captured and placed into English service. By 1675 perhaps as much as half of the English merchant fleet was foreign-built. The Dutch, of course, had their own successes in capturing English cargoes, and their privateers were especially active in the second and third naval wars with England. Naval warfare was by no means limited to battles between heavily armed men-of-war. Equally important was the seizing of richly laden trading vessels on their return voyages from the Atlantic or Asia. The Dutch had made a living from the Spanish treasure fleets during the Eighty Years' War (1568–1648). But the shoe was now on the other foot. There were many more Dutch vessels on the seas than English ones and Dutch cargoes were normally more valuable. There can be no doubt that on balance the wars

were disastrous for Dutch shipping and Dutch commerce.

The principle of restricted navigation ran like a thread through the Anglo-Dutch wars. The English had to protect their burgeoning colonial trade from the superior Dutch carrying capacity if English commerce was to grow. Restricting carrying to English ships provided incentive to merchants, work for the shipbuilding industry, and closer ties between the English and North American economies. The Navigation Act of 1660 not only restricted trade to English ships, it also enumerated certain goods that could not be imported from the Dutch Republic in any circumstances. For the Dutch the principle of "free ships, free goods" lay at the heart of the matter. Because they had few natural resources, they had developed a manufacturing and trading economy. Paying the excess freight charges and extra customs duties would make their finished products uncompetitive in the international marketplace. Closing the English market for certain commodities lowered their value by creating oversupply.

The Dutch had little choice but to strike out against English policy, but they also had little chance of overall success. Their spectacular naval victory in 1667, when the Dutch fleet surprised many English warships at port and burned both ships and docks at Chatham, obscured the fact that Dutch commercial superiority was slipping. In 1664 the English conquered New Netherland on the North American mainland and renamed it New York. With this defeat, the Dutch lost their largest colonial possession and became more dependent than ever on English reexports. Moreover, the wars intensified commercial rivalries between the states. Anti-Dutch sentiment in England and anti-English sentiment in the United Provinces, whipped up by official propaganda in both newspapers and pamphlets, grew during the periods of belligerence. The wars were costly to both states, nearly bankrupting the English crown in 1672. Anglo-Dutch rivalry was finally laid to rest after 1688, when William of Orange, stadtholder of Holland, became William III (1689–1702), king of England.

The Anglo-Dutch commercial wars were just one part of a larger European conflict. Dutch commerce was as threatening to France as it was to England, though in a different way. Under Colbert, France pursued a policy of economic independence. The state supported internal industrial activity through the financing of large workshops and the encouragement of new manufacturing techniques. Dutch imports constantly jeopardized the survival of these new (and inferior) French commodities. Not only could the Dutch buy raw materials cheaply, but the Dutch were also the most skilled artisans in the world. They could produce nearly any commodity of a higher quality and at a lower price than could the French. Colbert decided that only preventive tariffs would stop Dutch trading from ruining French industry. "As we have destroyed Spain on land, we must destroy Holland at sea. The Dutch have no right to seize all trade," Colbert declared. To achieve this aim, Colbert levied a series of punitive tariffs on Dutch imports, which severely depressed both trade and manufacture in Holland. Import of manufactured goods that directly competed with French production was prohibited, as was refined sugar, one of the most important commodities exported from Holland to France. Though the Dutch retaliated with restrictive tariffs of their own—in 1672 they banned the import of all French goods for an entire year—the Dutch economy depended upon free trade. The Dutch had much more to lose than did France in a battle of protective tariffs.

But the battle that Louis XIV had in mind was to be more deadly than one of tariffs. Greedily he eyed the Spanish Netherlands—to which he had a weak claim through his Habsburg wife—and believed that the Dutch stood in the way of his plans. Indeed, he had nothing but contempt for the merchant republic. The Dutch had entered into an alliance with the English and Swedes in 1668 to counter French policy, and Louis was determined to crush them in retaliation. He successfully bought off both of Holland's supposed allies, providing cash pensions to the kings of England and Sweden in return for England's active participation and Sweden's passive neutrality in the impending war. In 1672 Louis' army, over one hundred thousand strong, invaded the Low Countries and swept all before them. Only the opening of the dikes prevented the French from entering the province of Holland itself.

The French invasion coincided with the third Anglo-Dutch war, and the United Provinces found themselves besieged on land and sea. Their international trade was disrupted, their manufacturing industries were in ruins, and their military budget skyrocketed. Only able diplomacy and skillful military leadership prevented total Dutch demise. A separate peace was made with England, and Spain, whose sovereign territory had been invaded, entered the war on the side of the Dutch as did a number of German states. Louis' hope for a lightning victory faded and the war settled into a series of interminable sieges and reliefs of fortified towns. The Dutch finally persuaded France to come to terms in the Treaty of Nijmegen (1678–79). While Louis XIV retained a number of the territories he had taken from Spain, his armies withdrew from the United Provinces and he agreed to lift most of the commercial sanctions against Dutch goods. The first phase of mercantile warfare was over.

The Wars of Louis XIV

Mercantile competition added a new element to European warfare but it did not supplant the old causes of conflict. National security and dynastic ambition provided equally powerful motives for settling differences by might. So too did glory, the driving force behind the foreign policy of Louis XIV. Only on his deathbed did he confess to "having loved glory too much." It was

Louis' ambition to restore the ancient Burgundian territories to the French crown and to provide secure northern and eastern borders for his state. Pursuit of these aims involved him in conflicts with nearly every other European state. Spain had fought for eighty years to preserve the Burgundian inheritance in the Low Countries. By the Peace of Westphalia (1648), the northern portion of this territory became the United Provinces while the southern portion remained loyal to the crown and became the Spanish Netherlands. This territory provided a barrier between Holland and France that both states attempted to strengthen by establishing fortresses and bridgeheads at strategic places. French designs on the Spanish Netherlands were bound to lead to conflict with Spain and the Dutch Republic. In the east, Louis XIV eyed the duchies of Lorraine and Alsace and the large swath of territory further south known as Franche-Comté. The Peace of Westphalia had granted France control of a number of imperial cities in these duchies, and Louis aimed to link them together. All of these territories were ruled by Habsburgs: Alsace and Lorraine by the Austrian Holy Roman Emperor, Franche-Comté by the Spanish king.

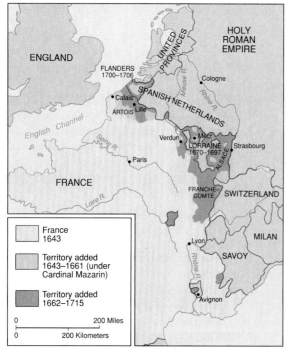

France under Louis XIV

French expansion in either direction not only threatened the other states directly involved but also posed a threat to European security in general. In the late seventeenth century, ambassadors and ministers of state began to develop the theory of a balance of power in Europe. This was a belief that no state or combination of states should be allowed to become so powerful that its existence threatened the peace of the others. Behind this purely political idea of the balance of power lay a theory of collective security that knit together the European state system. Balance of power politics demonstrated clearly that religious considerations had all but disappeared from diplomacy. In the last quarter of the seventeenth century the balance of power was easily practiced. France was as strong as all of the rest of the major states combined, and only their coalition could prevent Louis XIV from getting his way.

Louis showed his hand clearly enough in the Franco-Dutch war that had ended in 1679. Though he withdrew his forces from the United Provinces and evacuated most of the territories he had conquered, by the Treaty of Nijmegen France absorbed Franche-Comté as well as portions of the Spanish Netherlands. Louis began plotting his next adventure almost as soon as the treaty was signed. Over the next several years, French troops advanced steadily into Alsace, ultimately forcing the city of Strasbourg to recognize French sovereignty. A vital bridgehead on the Rhine, Strasbourg was ideal as either an offensive or a defensive position. Expansion into northern Italy was similarly calculated. Everywhere Louis looked, French engineers rushed to construct fortresses and magazines in preparation for another war.

It finally came in 1688 when French troops poured across the Rhine to seize Cologne. A united German empire led by Leopold I, Archduke of Austria, combined with the maritime powers of England and Holland, led by William III, to form the Grand Alliance, the first of the great balance of power coalitions. In fact, the two sides proved so evenly matched that the Nine Years' War (1688–97) settled very little. After his initial aggression, Louis XIV retreated to his fortress positions and withstood attacks in the Rhineland and the Spanish Netherlands. The real importance of the Nine Years' War was that it demonstrated that a successful European coalition could be formed against France. It also signified the permanent shift in alliances that resulted from the Revolution of 1688 in England. Although the English had allied with France against the Dutch in 1672, after William became king he persuaded the English Parliament that the real enemy was France. English naval power and finance were vital to the success of the Grand Alliance. England now aspired to a place as one of the great European powers, an aspiration that was quickly achieved.

The dreary details of these seemingly unending wars would be of little concern were it not for what happened next. The Franco-Dutch war had revealed Louis' appetite for the Spanish Netherlands, the Nine Years' War his hunger for the German Rhineland. Both ambitions were considered too dangerous to be tolerated by the other major European states. Even a conflict as inconclusive as the Nine Years' War might have convinced Louis XIV to be satisfied with his past gains. After all, he was no longer young—he was nearly sixty when the Peace of Ryswick ended the war in 1697—and the French economy suffered terribly from maintaining a standing army of over two hundred thousand soldiers. Louis could not successfully invade the empire, but neither could the combined might of the Grand Alliance successfully invade France. Louis' greatest objective, to secure the borders of his state, had withstood its greatest test. He might have rested satisfied but for the vagaries of births, marriages, and deaths. The great Habsburg dynasty had one last trick to play upon the peoples of Europe.

Like his father, Louis XIV had married a daughter of the king of Spain. Philip IV had married his eldest daughter to Louis XIV and a younger one to Leopold I of Austria, who subsequently became the Holy Roman Emperor (1658–1705). Before he died, Philip finally fathered a son, Charles II (1665–1700), who attained the Spanish crown at the age of four and was mentally and physically incapable of ruling his vast empire. For decades it was apparent that there would be no direct Habsburg successor to an empire which, despite its recent losses, still contained Spain, South America, the Spanish Netherlands, and most of Italy. Louis XIV and Leopold I both had legitimate claims to an inheritance that would have irreversibly tipped the European balance of power.

As Charles II grew increasingly feeble, efforts to find a suitable compromise to the problem of the Spanish succession were led by William III who, as stadtholder of Holland, was vitally interested in the fate of the Spanish Netherlands and, as king of England, in the fate of the Spanish American colonies. In the 1690s two treaties of partition were drawn up. The first achieved near universal agreement but was nullified by the death of the German prince who was to inherit the Spanish crown. The second, which would have given Italy to Louis' son and everything else to Leopold's son, was opposed by Leopold, who had neither naval nor commercial interests and who claimed most of the Italian territories as imperial fiefs. As one of Leopold's ministers proclaimed: "Milan, Naples, Sicily; the rest can be taken by whoever wants it."

All of these plans had been made without consulting the Spanish. If it was the aim of the European powers to partition the Spanish empire

THE SPANISH SUCCESSION

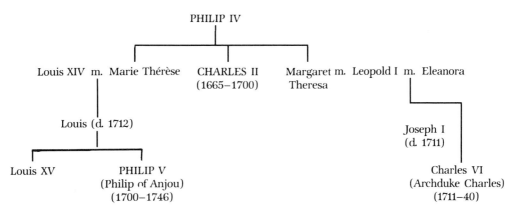

in order to prevent any one state from inheriting too much of it, it was the aim of the Spanish to maintain their empire intact. To this end, they devised a brilliant plan. Charles II bequeathed his entire empire to Philip of Anjou, the younger grandson of Louis XIV, with two stipulations. First that Philip renounce his claim to the French throne, and second that he accept the empire intact, without partition. If he—or more to the point, if his grandfather Louis XIV—did not accept these conditions then the empire would pass to Archduke Charles, the younger son of Leopold I. Such provisions virtually assured war between France and the empire unless compromise between the two powers could be reached. But before terms could even be suggested, Charles II died and Philip V (1700–1746) was proclaimed king of Spain and its empire.

Thus the eighteenth century opened with the War of the Spanish Succession (1702–14). Emperor Leopold rejected the provisions of Charles' will and sent his troops to occupy Italy. Louis XIV confirmed the worst fears of William III when he provided his grandson with French troops to "defend" the Spanish Netherlands. William III revived the Grand Alliance and initiated a massive land war against the combined might of France and Spain. The allied objectives were twofold: to prevent the unification of the French and Spanish thrones and to partition the Spanish empire so that both Italy and the Netherlands were ceded to Austria. The objective of Louis XIV was simply to preserve as much as possible of the Spanish inheritance for the house of Bourbon.

William III died in 1702 and was succeeded by Anne (1702–14). John Churchill (1650–1722), Duke of Marlborough and commander in chief of the army, continued William's policy. England and Holland again provided most of the finance and sea power, but in addition the English also provided a land army nearly seventy thousand strong. Prussia joined the Grand Alliance, and disciplined Prussian troops helped offset the addition of the Spanish army to Louis' forces. In 1704 Churchill defeated French forces at Blenheim in Germany and in 1706 at Ramillies in the Spanish Netherlands. France's military ascendancy was over.

Efforts to negotiate a peace settlement took longer than the war itself. The Austrians had taken control of Italy, the English and Dutch had secured the Spanish Netherlands, and the French had been driven back beyond the Rhine. The Allies believed that they could now enforce any treaty they pleased upon Louis XIV and along with concessions from France attempted to oust his grandson, Philip V, from the Spanish throne. This proved impossible to achieve though it took more than five years to learn the lesson. By then the European situation had taken another strange twist. Both the Emperor Leopold and his eldest son had died. Now Leopold's younger son, Archduke Charles, inherited the empire as Charles VI (1711–40) and raised the prospect of an equally dangerous combined Austrian-Spanish state. Between 1713 and 1714 a series of treaties at Utrecht settled the War of the Spanish Succession. Spanish possessions in Italy and the Netherlands were ceded to Austria; France abandoned all its territorial gains east of the Rhine and ceded its North American territories of Nova Scotia and Newfoundland to England. England also acquired from Spain Gibraltar on the southern coast of Spain and the island of Minorca in the Mediterranean. Both were strategically important to English commercial interests. English intervention in the Nine Years' War and the War of the Spanish Succession did not result in large ter-

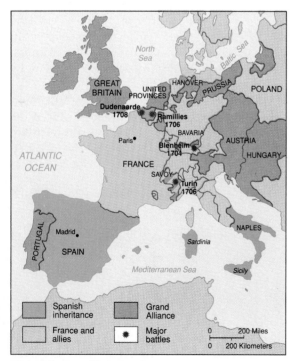

War of the Spanish Succession

ritorial gains but it did result in an enormous increase in English power and prestige. Over the next thirty years England would assert its own imperial claims.

The Colonial Wars

The Treaty of Utrecht (1713–14) ushered in almost a quarter-century of peace in western Europe. Austrian rule in the Netherlands and Italy remained a major irritant to the Spanish but Spain was too weak to do more than sulk and snarl. The death of Louis XIV in 1715 quelled French ambitions for a time and even led to an Anglo-French accord, which guaranteed the preservation of the settlement reached at Utrecht. Peace allowed Europe to rebuild its shattered economy and resume the international trade that had been so severely disrupted over the last forty years. The Treaty of Utrecht had resolved a number of important trading issues, all in favor of Great Britain, as England was known after its union with Scotland in 1707. In addition to receiving Gibraltar and Minorca from Spain, Britain was also granted the monopoly to provide slaves to the Spanish American colonies and the right to send one trading ship a year to them. In east and west, Britain was becoming the dominant commercial power in the world.

At least some of the reason for Britain's preeminence was the remarkable growth of the Atlantic colonies. By the middle of the eighteenth century tobacco and sugar were becoming staple commodities and control of their importation enriched merchants in Bristol and London as well as the British treasury. Moreover, the mainland colonies were finally beginning to show a profit, though less by production than by consumption. Over a million people now inhabited the thirteen colonies and they were awash in British goods. The colonial economy was booming and consumer goods that were in demand in London, Paris, and Amsterdam were also in demand in Boston, Philadelphia, and New York. Like every other colonial power, the British held a monopoly on their colonial trade. They were far less successful than were the Spanish and French in enforcing the notion that colonies existed only for the benefit of the parent country. But the English Parliament continued to pass legislation aimed at restricting colonial trade with other nations and

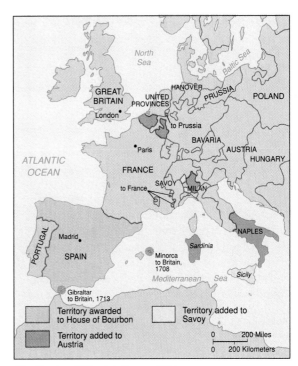

The Treaty of Utrecht, Europe 1714

other nations' colonies. Like almost all other mercantile restrictions, these efforts were stronger in theory than in practice. Tariffs on imports and customs duties on British goods provided a double incentive for smuggling—as if any incentive other than the massive profits to be made were needed.

The problem of smuggling—and its not so distant cousin, piracy—was endemic to long-distance trade. Almost every feature of the mercantile economy created conditions favorable to illegal commercial activities. Monopolies limited entry to products and markets, even though monopolists usually could not satisfy demand. Tariffs and duties raised prices. Restricted trading partnerships created artificial scarcities. Smugglers provided solutions to all of these problems. They increased the amount of commodities available, lowered the price of goods, and allowed for direct exchange between colonies controlled by different European states. Moreover, the European nations encouraged privateering—the polite term for official piracy—during times of war. Individual entrepreneurs were given license to prowl the trading lanes and to capture the ships of other nations. Cargoes were seized; the ships and crews held for ransom. Most of the goods taken found their way onto the black market despite official efforts to claim a portion for the state. Successful privateers were not always interested in the niceties of declared and undeclared wars, nor were the navies of the states themselves.

During wartime, goods that could be used directly for warfare were declared contraband, that is, articles that could not be traded at all. The ships of neutral nations could be searched and their contraband cargoes seized. The definition of what was, or was not, contraband led to much confusion. With so much unofficial interference with trade, official searches and seizures raised the political temperature among the various colonial powers. A confrontation was not long in coming, though it was perhaps surprising that it should take place first between Spain and England.

The seeds of the Anglo-Spanish conflict were sown at Utrecht. Philip V described the English occupation of Gibraltar as "a thorn in the foot of Spain." Moreover, the trading concessions that the English had received had become deeply resented. The Spanish claimed that the single English ship permitted to trade with the Spanish American colonies was constantly resupplied by a flotilla that made the journey with it. Goods smuggled from the West Indies and the mainland colonies were everywhere in Spanish America. This illicit trade grew dramatically with the establishment of English settlements in Georgia on the border of the Spanish colony of Florida. To combat what they saw as deliberate provocation, the Spanish ordered their naval vessels to stop English vessels entering Spanish colonial ports and to search their cargoes for illegal goods. The English complained that this measure turned the Spanish coast guard into officially authorized pirates. A Captain Robert Jenkins told a parliamentary committee how his ship had been ransacked and turned adrift without its navigational instruments and how he had been tied to the mast and his ear cut off. His story inflamed public opinion. In 1739 England declared war.

Though the War of Jenkins' Ear (1739–48), as it was known, settled little between Spain and Britain, it demonstrated for the first time that the English were prepared to go to war to defend their colonies and their colonial trade. During the war an invasion force landed in the Spanish West Indies, thus indicating that regular British troops would be committed to protect overseas possessions. Parliament had long resisted this policy and the change of direction was a result of the new mercantile block that was emerging as a force in British political life. Some, like Sir William Pitt the Elder (1708–78), who emerged as the leader of the House of Commons in the 1750s, saw colonial dominion as the path to national prosperity; others were protecting their own narrow interests as West Indian planters. But no matter what the motive, the new mercantile block helped shift British policy toward colonial rather than Continental affairs.

France emerged as Britain's true colonial rival. Dutch prosperity had withered as that of France and Britain had bloomed. The French established a thriving East India trade and were principally responsible for opening China to the west. In the Caribbean, the French had the largest and most profitable of the West Indian sugar

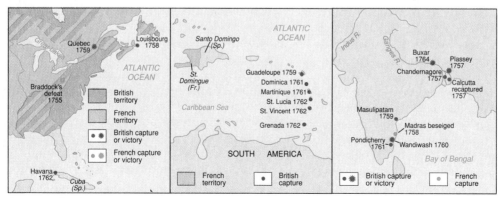

Seven Years' War

islands, Saint Domingue (modern-day Haiti), which outproduced all the British islands. In North America France held not only Canada, with its rich fishing and fur-trapping areas, but laid claim to the entire continent west of the Ohio River, a claim the English colonists hotly disputed. Nevertheless, French settlers occupied what towns there were on the Mississippi River and established an important trading port at New Orleans.

Anglo-French relations in North America had gone from bad to worse throughout the early eighteenth century. The French did not so much settle their colonial territory as occupy it. They surveyed the land, established trading relations with the Native Americans, and built forts at strategic locations. These outposts were designed to protect French commerce and to halt the westward expansion of the English settlers. The English, in contrast, had built a new society in the North American wilderness. They had developed fixed communities, which grew larger and more prosperous by the decade, and they had welcomed new immigrants from all over Europe. By 1750 there were nearly one and a quarter million settlers in British North America. There were little more than seventy-five thousand in the far larger French territories. In the face of such a disparity of numbers, France determined to defend its colonies by establishing an overseas military presence. Regular French troops were shipped to Canada and installed in Louisburg, Montreal, and Quebec. Their presence emboldened the French traders in their conflicts with the British. Ultimately, the British responded with troops of their own and sent an expeditionary force to clear the French from the Ohio River Valley. This action was the immediate cause of the Seven Years' War (1756–63).

Although the Seven Years' War had a bitter Continental phase, it was essentially a war for empire between the English and the French. There were three main theaters: the North American mainland, the West Indian sugar plantations, and the eastern coast of India. British forces also attacked French settlements in Africa in an attempt to disrupt the slave trade so essential to sugar production. All over the globe, the British won smashing victories. The British navy blockaded the water route to Canada, inflicting severe hardship on French settlers in Montreal and

War and Peace, 1648–1763

1648	Peace of Westphalia
1652–54	First Anglo-Dutch war
1665–67	Second Anglo-Dutch war
1672	Franco-Dutch war
1672–74	Third Anglo-Dutch war
1678–79	Treaty of Nijmegen
1688	Revolution of 1688; William of Orange becomes William III of England Grand Alliance formed
1688–97	Nine Years' War (France vs. Grand Alliance)
1697	Peace of Ryswick
1702–14	War of the Spanish Succession
1713–14	Treaty of Utrecht
1739–48	War of Jenkins' Ear
1756–63	Seven Years' War
1763	Peace of Paris

Quebec. British forces ultimately captured both towns. After some initial successes, the French were driven back west across the Mississippi River and their line of fortresses in the Ohio Valley fell into English hands. The English also succeeded in taking all the French sugar islands except Saint Domingue. British success in India was equally complete. The French were chased from their major trading zone and English dominance was secured.

By the end of the Seven Years' War, Britain had become a global imperial power. In the Peace of Paris (1763) France ceded all of Canada in exchange for the return of its West Indian islands. British dominion in the East Indian trade was recognized and led ultimately to British dominion of India itself. In less than a century the ascendancy of France was broken and Europe's first modern imperial power had been created.

European commercial expansion was the first step in a long process that would ultimately transform the material life of all human beings. The quest for new commodities led to the sophistication of transportation, marketing, and distribution, all vital developments for agricultural changes in the future. The ability to move large quantities of goods from place to place and to exchange them between different parts of the globe laid the foundation for organized manufacturing. The practical impact of scientific discovery, as yet only dimly glimpsed, would soon spur the transformation of handicrafts into industries. In the eighteenth century the material world was still being conquered and the most unattractive features of this conquest were all too plainly visible. Luxuries for the rich were won by the labors of the poor. The pleasures of sugar and tobacco were purchased at the price of slavery for millions of Africans. The greed of merchants and the glory of princes was an unholy alliance that resulted in warfare around the globe. But it was a shrinking globe, one whose peoples were becoming increasingly interdependent, tied together by the goods and services that they could provide to each other.

Suggestions for Further Reading

General Reading

* A. Rupert Hall, *The Revolution in Science 1500–1750* (London: Longman, 1983). The best introduction to the varieties of scientific thought in the early modern period. Detailed and complex.

* Jan de Vries, *The European Economy in an Age of Crisis* (Cambridge: Cambridge University Press, 1976). A comprehensive study of economic development, including long-distance trade and commercial change.

* K. H. D. Haley, *The Dutch in the Seventeenth Century* (London: Thames and Hudson, 1972). A well-written and illustrated history of the golden age of Holland.

* Derek McKay and H. M. Scott, *The Rise of the Great Powers 1648–1815* (London: Longman, 1983). An outstanding survey of diplomacy and warfare.

The New Science

* Margaret C. Jacob, *The Cultural Meaning of the Scientific Revolution* (New York: Knopf, 1988). Scientific thought portrayed in its social context.

* Stillman Drake, *Galileo* (New York: Hill and Wang, 1980). A short but engaging study of the great Italian scientist.

* Allen Debus, *Man and Nature in the Renaissance* (Cambridge: Cambridge University Press, 1978). An

* Indicates paperback edition available.

especially good account of the intellectual roots of scientific thought.

Charles Webster, *The Great Instauration: Science, Medicine, and Reform* (London: Duckworth, 1975). A complicated but rewarding analysis of experimental science and the origins of scientific medicine.

* Frank E. Manuel, *Sir Isaac Newton: A Portrait* (Cambridge, MA: Harvard University Press, 1968). A readable account of one of the most complex intellects in European history.

Empires of Goods

* Ralph Davis, *The Rise of the Atlantic Economies* (Ithaca, NY: Cornell University Press, 1973). A nation-by-nation survey of the colonial powers.

K. N. Chaudhuri, *The Trading World of Asia and the English East India Company* (Cambridge: Cambridge University Press, 1978). A brilliant account of the impact of the Indian trade on both Europeans and Asians.

* Sidney Mintz, *Sweetness and Power* (New York: Viking Press, 1985). An anthropological examination of the lure of sugar and its impact upon Western society.

* Philip Curtin, *The Atlantic Slave Trade* (Madison, WI: University of Wisconsin Press, 1969). A study of the importation of African slaves into the New World with the best estimates of the numbers of slaves and their destinations.

* Simon Schama, *The Embarrassment of Riches* (New York: Knopf, 1987). A social history of the Dutch Republic, which explores the meaning of commerce in Dutch society.

* Holden Furber, *Rival Empires of Trade in the Orient 1600–1800* (Minneapolis: University of Minnesota Press, 1976). A comprehensive survey of the battle for control of the Asian trade in the seventeenth and eighteenth centuries.

The Wars of Commerce

A. C. Carter, *Neutrality or Commitment: The Evolution of Dutch Foreign Policy 1667–1795* (London: Edward Arnold, 1975). A tightly written study of the objectives and course of Dutch diplomacy.

Charles Wilson, *Profit and Power* (London: Longman, 1957). Still the best study of the Anglo-Dutch wars of the mid-seventeenth century.

Paul Langford, *The Eighteenth Century 1688–1815* (New York: St. Martin's Press, 1976). A reliable guide to the growth of British power.

Ragnhild Hatton, ed., *Louis XIV and Europe* (London: Macmillan, 1976). An important collection of essays on French foreign policy in its most aggressive posture.

Richard Pares, *War and Trade in the West Indies 1739–63* (Oxford: Oxford University Press, 1936). A blow-by-blow account of the struggle for colonial supremacy in the sugar islands.

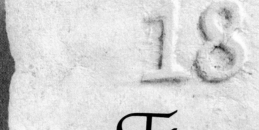

18

The New
European Powers

Calling the Tune

Frederick the Great loved music. During his youth it was one of his private passions that so infuriated his father. Mathematics, political economy, modern languages, even dreaded French, were the subjects that a future king of Prussia should learn. But music, never. Rather the boy should be at the hunt watching the dogs tear apart a stag, or on maneuvers with the Potsdam guards, a troop of soldiers all nearly seven feet tall. This was the regimen King Frederick William I prescribed for his son. But Frederick the Great loved music. He secretly collected all the books and manuscripts he could find on the subject, outspending his tiny allowance in the process. He had Johann Quantz (1697–1773), the great-

est flutist of the day, placed on his staff to teach him and to conspire with him against his father. At night, while the old king drank himself into a stupor—an activity he warmly recommended to his son— Frederick would powder his hair, put on a jacket of the latest French style, and regale his friends with his newest compositions. He and Quantz would take turns playing the flute, and the young spectators would do their best to imitate what they believed to be the essence of courtly manners. A lookout guarded the door in case the king wandered by unexpectedly. Once the musicians were almost discovered and Frederick's fine new jacket was tossed on the fire, but the flutes and

musical scores remained safely hidden.

After he became king, Frederick the Great could indulge his passion more openly. Yet he preferred to hold his concerts, usually small gatherings, at the Palace of San Souci, which he built in Potsdam. A special music room was designed for the king's use and he lavished attention on it. The great chandelier, lit by a circle of candles, illuminated the center of the room and highlighted the soloist. The entire palace reflected Frederick's personal taste. Unlike most great palaces of state, it was small, functional, and beautiful. Here Frederick could escape the mounting cares of governing one of the most powerful states

in Europe by reading, corresponding with eminent French intellectuals, and playing the flute. In this picture, *Das Flötenkonzert* (the Flute Concert), Frederick is portrayed performing in his great music room. Before a small audience of courtiers and intimates, he plays to the accompaniment of cello, violins, and piano.

Frederick's talent was real enough. A British visitor to Sans Souci, who had little reason to flatter the king, reported: "I was much pleased and surprised with the neatness of his execution. His performance surpassed anything I had ever heard among the dilettanti or even professors." This judgment is reinforced when one studies the expressions of the three men

in the left-hand corner of the painting. They are taking genuine pleasure in the music they are hearing, all the more genuine in that the king's back is to them. So, too, are the musicians who are accompanying the king. There is as much joy as concentration upon their faces.

Frederick's musical accomplishment was not unique among eighteenth-century monarchs. Joseph II of Austria was also a skilled flutist. But it was not so much music as accomplishment that was coming to be valued among the monarchs of the new European powers. Catherine the Great of Russia corresponded with philosophers; Frederick the Great brought the great French intellectual Voltaire (1698–1778) to

his court—though they quickly took a dislike to each other. The acquisition of culture seemed to matter more and more as the century wore on. Museums, opera houses, great art collections were established all over the Continent. The Hermitage in Saint Petersburg was stocked with the works of Dutch and English masters. The British Museum was founded in London with the support of King George II, who deposited his great library there. Whether this veneer of culture did anything to lessen the brutality of warfare and power politics is a matter of opinion. But as a veneer it was as highly polished as the flute that Frederick the Great is so delicately pressing to his mouth.

Europe in 1714

The Peace of Utrecht (1713–14) brought about a considerable reorganization of the political geography of Europe. Utrecht created a new Europe in the west, while the Treaty of Nystad (1721) created a new Europe in the east. Both agreements reflected the dynamics of change that had taken place over the previous century. The rise of France on the Continent and of Britain's colonial empire around the globe were facts that could no longer be ignored. The decline of Sweden and Poland and the emergence of Russia as a great power were the beginning of a long-term process that would continue to dominate European history.

All of this could be seen on a map of Europe in the early eighteenth century. The political divisions of the Continent in 1714 presaged the future. France's absorption of Alsace and encroachments into Lorraine would be a bone of contention between the French and Germans for two centuries and ultimately contributed to the outbreak of World Wars I and II. The political footballs of the Spanish Netherlands and Spanish Italy, now temporarily Austrian, continued to be kicked about until the nationalist movements of the nineteenth century gave birth to Belgium, Luxembourg, and a united Italy. The emergence of Brandenburg-Prussia on the north German coast and the gradual decline in the power of the Holy Roman Emperor were both vital to the process that created a unified Germany and a separate

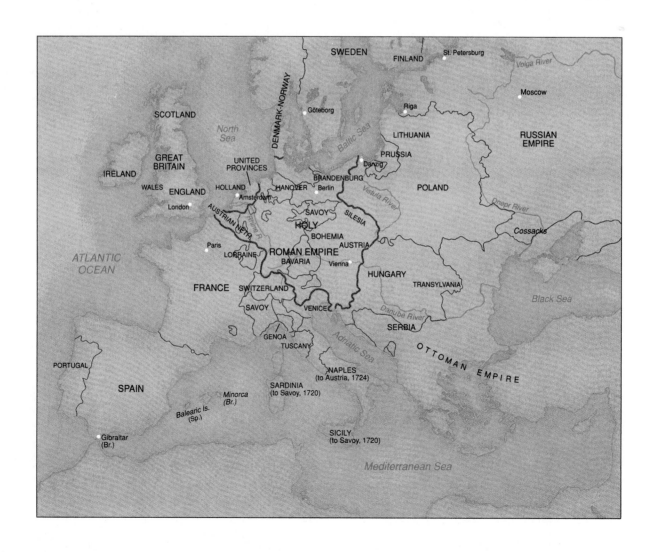

Austria. In the southeast, the slow but steady reconquest of the Balkans from Ottoman dominion restored the historic southern border of the Continent. The inexorable expansion of Russia was also already apparent.

The West

Perhaps the most obvious transformation in the political geography of western Europe was the expansion of European power around the globe. In the Atlantic, Spain remained the largest colonial power. Through its vice-royalty system it controlled all of central America, the largest and most numerous of the Caribbean islands, North America from Colorado to California (as well as Florida), and most of South America. The other major colonial power in the region was Portugal, which shared dominion over the South American continent. The Portuguese colony of Brazil, which began as a series of coastal settlements, was now expanding inland as missionaries and explorers carved a path through the jungles and millions of slaves were imported to work its fields. Brazilian production of sugar, dyestuffs, timbers, and exotic commodities amply repaid the meager investment the Portuguese had made.

In North America the French and British shared the eastern half of the continent. The French controlled most of it. They had landed first in Canada and then slowly made their way down the Saint Lawrence River. New France, as their colonial empire was called, was a trading territory and it expanded along the greatest of the waterways, the Great Lakes, and the Ohio, Missouri, and Mississippi rivers. Major settlements were on Lake Erie (near present-day Cleveland), at the base of Lake Michigan (near present-day Chicago), and at the juncture of the Missouri and Mississippi rivers (near present-day Saint Louis). French settlements had sprung up as far south as the Gulf of Mexico, where New Orleans was founded in 1718. France also claimed the territory of Louisiana, named for Louis XIV, which stretched from New Orleans to Montana, though it remained unsettled and unexplored. The British settlements were all coastal, stretching from Maine to Georgia on the Atlantic seaboard. Unlike the French, the British settled their territory and

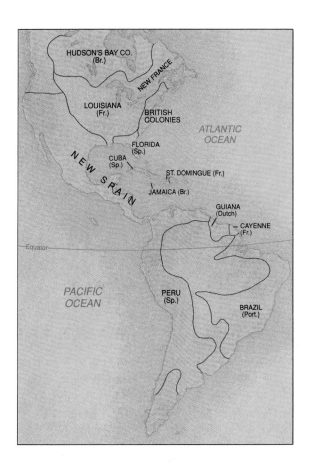

were only interested in expansion when their population, which was doubling every twenty-five years, outgrew its resources. By the early eighteenth century the ports of Boston, New York, Philadelphia, and Charleston were thriving commercial centers. Only in the British colonies had the old world been reestablished in the new.

Europeans managed their eastern colonial territories differently than they did those in the west. Initially the Portuguese and the Dutch had been satisfied with establishing trading factories—coastal fortresses that could be used as warehouses and defended against attack. But in the seventeenth century, the European states began to take control of vital ports and lucrative islands. Here the Dutch were the acknowledged leaders, replacing the Portuguese who had begun the process at the end of the sixteenth century. Holland held by force or in conjunction with local leaders all the Spice Islands in the Pacific. The Dutch also occupied both sides of the Malay Peninsula and nearly all the coastal areas of the

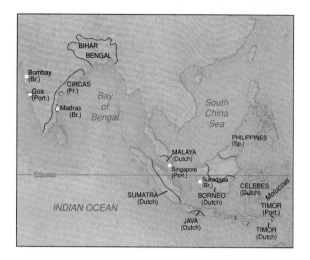

islands in the Java Sea. Dutch control of Ceylon was strategically important for its Indian trade. Compared to the Dutch Republic, all other European states had only a minor territorial presence in the East, with the exception of Spain, which still controlled the Philippines. The British had limited their eastern outposts to trading establishments. Through these they maintained a significant presence in India, especially in Bombay on the west coast, Madras on the east coast, and Calcutta in Bengal. During the eighteenth century the British began to colonize the Indian subcontinent directly.

Imperial expansion was the most obvious change in the geopolitical boundaries of Europe, but it was not the only one. A brief tour of the western states after the Treaty of Utrecht reveals some others. In 1707 England and Scotland formally joined together to form Great Britain, one of the newly emerging European powers. In addition to its eastern and western colonies, Britain had also gained control of Gibraltar at the foot of Spain, and Minorca, one of the Balearic Islands in the Mediterranean. Both territories were strategically important to British commerce. But the greatest changes in Britain's geopolitical makeup had to do with its sovereigns. After the Revolution of 1688, Britain had shared a ruler with Holland, but there had never been any attempt to integrate the two states. After William III died in 1702 the two countries went their separate ways. In 1714 Queen Anne died without a surviving heir and the British throne passed to George of Hanover, a German prince whose rich territories on the

North Sea brought Britain into Continental affairs in a new and unforeseen way.

Across the English Channel were the Low Countries, now permanently divided between the United Provinces in the north, led by Holland, and those provinces in the south that had remained loyal to the Spanish crown in the sixteenth century. By 1714 the golden age of the Dutch was over. Though the Dutch remained one of the most prosperous peoples in Europe and continued as a colonial and maritime power, their small numbers and meager natural resources eventually outweighed their abilities as innovators and managers. Gradually they lost their eastern empire to Britain, their predominance in European trade to France. What the Dutch gained at Utrecht was security, the right to maintain their forces in the towns along the border between France and the old Spanish Netherlands. The Spanish Netherlands, the original Burgundian inheritance, were now being slowly dismembered.

Since the accession of Louis XIV, France had plucked small pieces from the territories that had been contested between Habsburg and Valois since the fifteenth century. Between French aggression and the Dutch occupation of such important places as Ghent and Ypres, the ability of the southern provinces to maintain a separate identity suffered a grave blow. But not as grave as that formalized at Utrecht, when sovereignty over this territory was assigned to Austria, ostensibly because the emperor was a Habsburg, but really because the balance of power in western Europe demanded it.

To the south lay France, still the most powerful nation in Europe despite its losses in the War of the Spanish Succession. By 1714 Louis XIV had broken forever the danger of Spanish encirclement that had been the worry of every French king since Francis I in the early sixteenth century. Though Louis' Continental wars were the most spectacular aspect of his foreign policy, in fact it was his strategy of "creeping defense" that was more successful. Louis had methodically set out to occupy those territories that were strategically necessary to defend his state from invasion by the Dutch, the Spanish, the British, or the emperor. In the northeast he consolidated the imperial towns that France had acquired in 1648 by absorbing the Duchy of Bar. In the north he absorbed a healthy portion of Flanders including Dunkirk on the English Channel and the prosperous clothing town of Lille. He pushed the eastern boundary of his state to the Rhine by overrunning Alsace and parts of Lorraine. Strasbourg remained French under the settlement of 1714, testimony to the fact that it was possible to hold France only at the western banks of the Rhine. Finally, farther to the south Louis had won and held Franche-Comté, once the center of Burgundy. In 1714 France was larger, stronger, and better able to defend its borders than ever before. It was also exhausted from its efforts.

As France expanded, so Spain contracted. Less than two centuries earlier a Spanish king had

On this tapestry, Louis XIV is shown preparing for a triumphant entry into Dunkirk, which he had bought from the king of England. The city was one of Louis' first territorial acquisitions and one of the few that he obtained peacefully.

dreamed of being monarch over all of Europe. Now a Bourbon sat on the great Habsburg throne and Spain was slowly being sliced to pieces, losing an island here, a possession there. By 1714 the European territories of the Spanish empire had been reduced to Iberia itself. But the loss of its European empire was to prove a blessing in disguise for Spain, which now entered upon a new and unexpected phase of growth and influence. Under the Bourbon monarchy Spain revived.

The center of Europe remained occupied by the agglomeration of cities, bishoprics, principalities, and small states known collectively as the Holy Roman Empire, but now more accurately called the German empire. There were still over three hundred separate jurisdictions, most of them vulnerable to preying neighbors such as Louis XIV. Bavaria in the south, and Saxony, Brandenburg, and Hanover in the north were among the most important of the large states with the added twist that Hanover was now ruled by the king of Great Britain. The emperor, now officially prohibited from interference in the internal administration of the large states, was less dominant in German affairs than he had been before the Thirty Years' War. Each election of each successive Habsburg further diminished the emperor's power in the German empire.

Increasingly, Habsburg power centered on Austria, Bohemia, and Hungary. This was especially true during the reign of Leopold I (1655–1705). Withstanding threats on all sides, Leopold was able to expand his state both to the west and to the south and to bring Austria into the ranks of the great European powers. Such an outcome could hardly have been foreseen in the middle of the seventeenth century, when the Ottomans made their last great thrust into the interior of Europe. They captured more of Hungary and threatened Leopold's hereditary lands. In 1683 the Ottomans besieged Vienna itself, and only the arrival of seventy thousand Polish-led troops saved it from falling. But from that time forward, Austrian forces scored stunning victories. By 1699 almost all of Hungary had been retaken by Austria; at the Treaty of Passarowitz in 1718 Austria gained the rest of Hungary and Serbia. When the Treaty of Utrecht granted Austria control of the Netherlands, Lombardy, and Naples, the Austrian Habsburgs took the place of their Spanish cousins as rulers of a European empire.

Austria's Italian possessions included the vast southern territories of Naples (including Sicily after 1720) and the rich industrial area surrounding Milan in the north. Alongside the Austrian territories a number of independent city-states continued to flourish on the Italian peninsula. Venice on the Adriatic and Genoa on the Mediterranean were no longer the great commercial states that they had been in the sixteenth century. But both remained prosperous and independent. The Grand Duchy of Tuscany, with its great city of Florence, and the Papal States had expanded over the course of the seventeenth century, absorbing their smaller neighbors until both were large consolidated territories. To the west of the Italian states was the Duchy of Savoy, a state which had maintained control over the vital Alpine passes that joined western and central Europe. Savoy had pursued a flexible foreign policy, pleasing whichever of its powerful neighbors was most dangerous and accepting the patronage of whichever seemed most friendly. Client of the Spanish, French, and Austrians, Savoy grew and prospered. After the War of the Spanish Succession Savoy was counted one of the victors even though it had fought on both sides. Duke Victor Amadeus II became a king when he received the island of Sicily, which he exchanged with Austria for Sardinia in 1720.

The East

This was western Europe in 1714. In the east, it was the Treaty of Nystad (1721) ending the Great Northern War (1700–1721) that fixed the political geography. Here the emerging powers were Russia and Prussia, those in decline were Sweden and Poland. The critical factor in eastern European politics remained access to the sea. Outlets to the Baltic Sea in the north and the Black Sea in the south were the vital lifeline for this part of the Continent and control of these outlets was the central motivation for the long years of war fought among the eastern states. The expansion of Russia is one of the central events in European history, and the early eighteenth century is its pivotal period. During the long years of social and economic recovery after the death of Ivan the Terrible in 1584, Russia had been easy prey for its powerful neighbors Sweden and Poland. Through a series of wars and political pacts, Russia had ceded most of its Baltic territo-

its German territories: those on the North Sea went to Hanover, those on the Baltic to Prussia. Livonia, Estonia, and the eastern provinces were returned to Russia. Though Sweden could not maintain its position in the face of Russian and Prussian supremacy, it was able to hold on to its vital gains from the Danes. Sweden had built its own window to the west at Göteborg on the North Sea, and from there it could carry on a direct trade with Britain and the Netherlands.

The acquisition of Pomerania from Sweden was just one of the territorial gains made by Brandenburg-Prussia. Since the end of the Thirty Years' War, this strange configuration of a state had been steadily growing. Its geographical heart was in Brandenburg, one of the domains of the Holy Roman Empire. From the capital at Berlin the princes of Brandenburg directed the accumulation of small neighboring German lands: Magdeburg and Halle to the southwest, a piece of Pomerania to the northeast. But while Brandenburg expanded in every direction, it could do little to join itself to the kingdom of Prussia. A huge swath of Poland, cutting between the two, stood in the way. This division of Brandenburg-Prussia was its most important geopolitical feature. In the eighteenth century, the determination to expand to the east dominated Prussian history.

This aim meant, of course, eventual conflict with Poland. Despite its political weakness, Poland was one of the largest landmasses in Europe and one of the most pivotal. On its southern border it held back Ottoman expansion, on its eastern border it held back the Russians. Its great port of Gdansk on the Baltic dominated the grain and timber trade with northern Europe as well as local Baltic commerce between Scandinavia and the mainland. Sweden and Russia, the eastern powers, controlled Poland politically, helping nominate its elected kings and ensuring that its decentralized form of aristocratic government kept Poland weak. Poland served as a useful counterweight in the balance of power in eastern Europe. Except for its Baltic territories, Poland was not yet seen as a great prize to be fought over. But by the beginning of the eighteenth century it was already a helpless giant ready to be toppled. Not too many decades would pass before one state or another was ready to provide the push.

ries to Sweden while it had relinquished land and population in the west to Poland. Peter the Great (1682–1725) set out to reclaim what had been lost. As a result of the Great Northern War, Russia regained the eastern Baltic coastline from the southeastern end of Finland to Riga in the west. Russia now occupied both sides of Lake Ladoga and controlled all of the vital Baltic ports in the east. Peter built a new Russian capital on the Gulf of Finland to be a window to the west. In this new city, named Saint Petersburg, Peter laid the foundation for the Russian navy.

What Russia gained, Sweden lost. At the height of its power in the middle of the seventeenth century, Sweden had dominated the Baltic. It occupied all of Finland—though only the southern coastal areas were actually colonized—controlled the important eastern coast of Norway, and had gained a foothold in Germany. Most importantly, Sweden had captured the southern tip of its own peninsula from the Danes, making the mainland portion of its state whole. But Sweden's century-long rise to power was followed by a rapid period of decline. The small and relatively poor population could not long succeed in governing an empire. The Great Northern War ended whatever pretensions Sweden had left. It lost all of

The Rise of Russia

In 1721 Peter I, the Great, who had been tsar in Russia since 1682, assumed the title of Emperor of All Russias. The Treaty of Nystad had confirmed the magnitude of his victory over the Swedes in the Great Northern War, both in territory and prestige. The title *tsar*, or caesar, no longer seemed enough. Emperor was more fitting. The change created consternation in the courts of Europe. Just a quarter century before, no one had cared very much what the king of Russia called himself. The Russian tsar was just another of the exotic eastern rulers whose preposterous titles Europeans were willing to recognize in order to conduct their business. In fact, little was known for sure about the Russian ruler or his state. What little mercantile contact there was between Russia and the west was conducted entirely by westerners. Foreign merchants were allowed to live in Moscow in a separate ghetto called "Germantown." Their letters were the principal source of western knowledge about the vast Muscovite empire.

Peter the Great changed all of this. Twice he visited Europe to discover the secrets of western prosperity and might. He arranged marriages between the closest heirs to his throne, including his son Alexis, and the sons and daughters of German princes and dukes. By 1721 he had established twenty-one separate foreign embassies. The sons of the Russian gentry and nobility were sent west—sometimes forcibly—to further their education and to learn to adapt to western outlooks. Peter recruited Europeans to fill the most important skilled positions in the state: foreign engineers and gunners to serve in the army; foreign architects to build the new capital at Saint Petersburg; foreign scholars to head the new state schools; foreign administrators to oversee the new departments of state. Peter borrowed freely and adapted sensibly. If necessary, he would drag his countrymen kicking and screaming into the modern world.

By 1721 Russia was recognized all over Europe as an emerging power. The military defeat of the seemingly invincible Swedes had made monarchs from Louis XIV to William III sit up and take notice. And the great Russian victory at Poltava in 1709 was no fluke. Peter's forces followed it up

This portrait of Peter the Great by his court painter Louis Caravaque pays homage to Peter's intense interest in naval matters. Ships flying English, Dutch, Danish, and Russian flags prepare for maneuvers under his command.

with several strong campaigns which proved that Russia could organize, equip, finance, and train an up-to-date military force. Moreover, Peter's absorption of Sweden's Baltic territories made Russia a power in the north. A navy, built mostly by foreigners, was now capable of protecting Russian interests and defending important ports such as Riga and Saint Petersburg. Even the Dutch, who had long plotted the decline of Swedish might, now became nervous. Thus it was unsettling that Peter wished to be recognized as emperor. Russia was now a European power, but European powers were headed by kings. There was only one emperor in Europe—the Holy Roman Emperor—and those who aspired to that title did so in the traditional way, by attempting to bribe the German electors. No one simply declared himself emperor. Rather, no one ever had before Peter the Great.

Russia Turns West

Peter the Great was not the first Russian tsar to attempt to borrow from western developments. The process had been underway for decades. The opening of the northern port of Archangel led to direct contact with British and Dutch traders, who brought with them new ideas and useful products, which were adapted to Russian needs and conditions. Russia was a vast state and Europe was only one of its neighbors. Its religion had come from Byzantium rather than Rome, thus giving Russian Christianity an eastern flavor. Its Asian territories mixed the influence of Mongols and Ottomans; its southern borders met Tartars and Cossacks. While most European states were racially and ethnically homogeneous, Russia was a loose confederation of diverse peoples. Yet it was the western states that posed the greatest threat to Russia in the seventeenth century, and it was to the west that Tsar Alexis I (1645–76) and his son Peter turned their attention.

It would be wrong to see Peter's westernizing innovation as a systematic program. System implies an organization not to be associated with the chaotic, often contradictory, policies that Peter pursued. More to the point, nearly all of what he did was done to enhance military efficiency rather than civil progress. In his thirty years of active rule there was only one year—1724—during which he was not at war. Vital reforms like the poll tax (1724), which changed the basis of taxation from the household to the individual adult male, had enormous social consequences. The new policy of taxing individuals officially erased whole social classes. A strict census taken (and retaken) to inhibit tax evasion became the basis for further governmental encroachments on the tsar's subjects. Yet the poll tax was not designed for any of these purposes. It was instituted to increase tax revenue for war. Similarly, the establishment of compulsory, lifetime military service required of the land-owning classes (the nobility and gentry) was undertaken to provide officers and state servants for an expanding military machine.

Yet if Peter's reforms were not systematic and developed from little other than military necessity, nevertheless they constituted a fundamental transformation in the life of all Russian people. The creation of a gigantic standing army and an entirely new navy meant conscription of the Russian peasantry on a grand scale. As the wars continued, those liable for military service progressed from bachelors aged sixteen to thirty to any adult male under the age of fifty. In a ten-year period of the Great Northern War the army absorbed 330,000 conscripts, most of whom never returned to their homes. Military service was not confined to the peasantry. Traditionally, the rural gentry raised and equipped the local conscript forces and gave them what training they could. Most gentry lived on estates that had been granted to them along with the resident peasants as a reward for their military contributions. Peter the Great intensified the obligations of the gentry. Not only were they to serve the state for life, but they were to accompany their regiments to the field and lead them in battle. When too old for active military service, they were to perform administrative service in the new departments of state.

The expansion of military forces necessitated an expansion of military administration as well. Peter's first innovation was the creation of the Senate, a group of nine senior administrators who were to oversee all aspects of military and civil government. The Senate became a permanent institution of government led by an entirely new official, the Procurator-General, who presided over its sessions and could propose legislation as well as oversee administration. From the Senate emanated five hundred officials known as the fiscals, who traveled throughout the state looking for irregularities in the process of tax assessment and collection. The fiscals were to locate tax evaders and to identify corrupt tax collectors. They quickly developed into a hated and feared internal police force.

Peter's efforts to reorganize his government went a step further in 1722, when he promulgated the Table of Ranks. This was an official hierarchy of the state divided into three categories—military service, civil service, and those who owned landed estates. Each category contained fourteen ranks and it was decreed that every person who entered the hierarchy did so at the bottom and worked his way up. The creation of the Table of Ranks was significant in a number of ways. It demonstrated Peter's continued commitment to merit as a criterion for advancement. This standard had been shown in the military, where officers were promoted on the basis of service and experience rather than birth or background. Equally important was Peter's decision to make the military service the highest of the three categories. This reversed the centuries-old position of the landed aristocracy and the military service class. Though the old nobility also served in the military and continued to dominate state service, the Table of Ranks opened the way for the infusion of new elements into the Russian elite.

Many of those who were able to advance in the Table of Ranks did so through attendance at the new institutions of higher learning that Peter founded. His initial educational establishments were created to further the military might of the state. The colleges of Mathematics, Engineering, and Artillery, which became the training grounds for his army officers, were all founded during the Great Northern War. But Peter was interested in liberal education as well. He had scores of western books translated into Russian. He had a press established in Moscow to print original works, including the first Russian newspaper. For a time Peter actually edited the paper himself. He decreed that a new, more westernized alphabet replace that used by the Russian Orthodox Church and that books be written in the language that the people spoke rather than in the formal literary language of religious writers. He also introduced Arabic numerals into official accounting records. His agents bought artwork and manuscripts from all over Europe, which were displayed in the public library and museum that he established. Though he did not live to see it open officially, Peter was principally responsible for the creation of a Russian Academy of Sciences (1724).

Peter's reforms of government and society were matched by his efforts to energize the economy. No state in Europe had as many natural resources as did Russia, yet manufacturing barely existed there. As with everything else he did, Peter took a direct hand in establishing factories for the production of textiles, glass, leather, and most importantly, iron and copper. The state directly owned about half of these establishments, most of them on a larger scale than any known in the west. By 1726 more than half of all Russian exports were manufactured goods and Russia had become the largest producer of iron and copper in the world.

In all of these ways and more Peter the Great transformed Russia. But the changes Peter wrought did not come without cost. The traditions of centuries were not easily broken. Intrigue against Peter led first to confrontation with the old military elite and later to conflict with his only son, Alexis. It remains unclear if the plot with which Alexis was connected existed anywhere other than in Peter's mind, but it is abundantly clear that Alexis' death from torture plunged the state into a succession crisis in 1725. Finally, the great costs of westernization were paid by the masses of people who benefited little from the improvement in Russia's international standing or from the social and economic changes that affected the elites.

Peter the Great was a precocious child. He began his education at the age of two, using a book similar to the illustrated Russian speller whose "Z" page is seen below.

Life in Rural Russia

Nearly 97 percent of the Russian people lived on the land and practiced agriculture. Farming techniques and agrarian life-styles had changed little for centuries. Although the black earth, a belt of extremely rich land, ran through southern and central Russia, most of the country's soil was poor. Harsh climate and low yields characterized Russian agriculture. Thirty-four of the one hundred Russian harvests during the eighteenth century can be termed poor or disastrous, yet throughout the century state taxation was making larger and larger demands upon the peasantry. During Peter's reign alone, direct taxation increased by 500 percent, most of it in the form of consumption taxes that struck particularly hard at the bottom levels of society.

The theory of the Russian state was one of service, and the role of Russian peasants was to serve their master. Beginning in the mid-seventeenth century, the peasantry had undergone a change in status. The law code of 1649 formalized a process that had been underway for over a century whereby peasants were turned into the property of their landlords. During the next century laws curtailed the ability of peasants to move freely from one place to another, eliminated their right to hold private property, and abolished their freedom to petition the tsar against their masters. At the same time that landlords increased their hold over peasants, the state increased its hold over landlords. They were made responsible for the payment of taxes owed by their peasants and for the military service due from them. By the middle of the eighteenth century over half of all peasants—3.2 million adult males in 1727 and 6.7 million in 1782—had thus become serfs, the property of their masters, without any significant rights or legal protection.

Private landlords reckoned their wealth in the number of serfs they owned. But in fact most owned only a small number, fewer than fifty in the middle of the eighteenth century. This resulted from the common practice whereby a father divided his estate among all of his surviving sons. Most gentry were small landholders, constantly in debt and rarely able to meet their financial and service obligations to the state. This life of poverty at the top was, of course, magnified at the bottom. Although western visitors to Russia returned home with stories of noblemen with hundreds of household serfs, and of serf orchestras and serf poets, the reality for the vast majority of serfs was far less colorful. They lived in small villages where they divided up their meager surplus to pay their taxes and drew lots to see who would be sent for military service. When the debts of their lords became too heavy, it was the serfs who were foreclosed upon. Serf families or particularly desirable individuals would be sold at auction, some to be resettled in new villages with more prosperous landowners, others to be deployed at the whim of their purchasers.

If serfs made up the bottom half of the Russian peasantry, there were few advantages to being in the top half among the state peasants. State peasants lived on lands owned by the monarchy itself. Like the serfs, they were subject to the needs of the state for soldiers and workers. The use of forced labor was a feature of each of Peter's grandiose projects. Saint Petersburg was built on the backs of peasant conscripts. From 1709, when the project began, perhaps as many as 40,000 laborers a year were forced to work on the various sites. Even skilled workers were pressed into service. In 1713, one thousand carpenters were rounded up and brought to the new city. Over half had run away by the following year. The unhealthy conditions of the swampy environment from which the new capital rose claimed the lives of thousands of these workers, as did the appalling conditions of overwork and undernourishment in which they lived.

Many Russian peasants were resigned to their fate. They developed a philosophy of submission and a rich folk culture that valued a stubborn determination to endure. For those who would no longer bend to the knout—the heavy leather whip that was the omnipresent enforcer of obedience—there was only flight or rebellion. Each proved equally fruitless. Hundreds of thousands of serfs fled to state-owned lands in hope of escaping the cruelties of individual landlords. Although severe penalties were imposed for aiding runaway serfs, in fact most state overseers and many private landlords encouraged runaways to settle on their lands. Many who escaped to either Siberia or Poland eventually found themselves re-enserfed.

The Enlightened Empress

Of all the legacies of Peter the Great, perhaps the most important was that government could go on without him. During the next thirty-seven years six tsars ruled Russia, "three women, a boy of twelve, an infant, and a mental weakling," as one commentator acidly observed. More to the point, each succession was contested as there were no direct male heirs to the throne in this period. Peter's wife, his two grandsons, his daughter, and a niece all served a turn. Nevertheless, despite turmoil at the top, government continued to function smoothly and Peter's territorial conquests were largely maintained. Russia also experienced a remarkable increase in numbers during this period. Between 1725 and 1762 population increased from 13 to 19 million, a jump of nearly one-third in a single generation. This explosion of people dramatically increased the wealth of the landholding class, who reckoned their status by the number of serfs they owned. At the beginning of the seventeenth century, a nobleman with more than five hundred serfs was considered one of the wealthiest subjects in the state. By the end of the century an owner of five hundred serfs was considered moderately well-to-do.

The expansion of the economic resources of the nobility was matched by a rise in legal status and political power. This was the period sarcastically dubbed "the emancipation of the nobility," a phrase that captures not only the irony of the growing gap between rich and poor but also the contrast between the social structures of Russia and those of western Europe. In return for their privileges and status, Peter the Great extended the duties the land-owning classes owed to the state. By granting unique rights, like the ownership of serfs, to the descendants of the old military service class, Peter the Great had forged a Russian nobility. Lifetime service, however, was the price of nobility. Women were the true estate managers in Russia, since their husbands were constantly occupied in military or administrative service.

In order to gain and hold the throne, each succeeding tsar had to make concessions to the nobility. At first it was a few simple adjustments. The sons of wealthy landowners who completed a course of education at one of the state academies were allowed to enter the Table of Ranks in the middle of the hierarchy rather than at the bottom. Then life service was commuted to a term of twenty-five years, still a long time in a world of short lives and sudden deaths. But these concessions were not enough. Twenty-five years of service did not solve the problem of estate management, especially as the tasks of management grew along with the population of serfs. Thus the next capitulation was that a single son could remain on the estate and escape service altogether. This decree opened the door more than a crack. The births of younger sons were concealed; owners of multiple estates claimed the exemption of one son for each. Most decisively, the talented remained at home to serve the family while the wastrels were sent to serve the state. Finally in 1762, the obligation for state service by the nobility was abolished entirely. If nothing else, Russia had westernized its aristocracy.

The abolition of compulsory service was not the same as the abolition of service itself. In fact the end of compulsory service enabled Catherine II, the Great (1762–96), to enact some of the most important reforms of her reign. At first, Catherine's accession seemed nothing more than a continuation of monarchical instability. She came to the throne as a result of a coup against her husband, the feeble-minded Peter III (1762), and her first two acts were to have him murdered and to lower the salt tax. Each bought her a measure of security. Catherine was a dynamic personality who alternately captivated and terrified those with whom she came into contact. A British visitor to her court reported that her gaze was like that of "a small wild animal, so piercing and full of desire that it was difficult to endure." Her policies were as complex as her personality, influenced alike by the new French ideas of social justice and the nobility of the human race and the traditional Russian ones of absolute rule over an enserfed and subhuman population. As she observed to the French writer Denis Diderot (1713–84): "You philosophers are lucky men. You write on paper and paper is patient. Unfortunate Empress that I am, I write on the susceptible skins of living beings." Catherine handled these contrasting dimensions of her rule masterfully, which gained her abroad the reputation as the most enlightened of all European monarchs and at home the sincere love and devotion of her people. Thus it was said, "Peter created Russia's body, but Catherine endowed it with a soul." (See Special Feature, "Catherine Before She Was Great," pp. 560–561.)

The most important event in the early years of Catherine's reign was the establishment of a legislative commission to review the laws of Russia. Catherine herself wrote the *Instruction* (1767) by which the elected commissioners were to operate. She borrowed her theory of law from the French jurist Baron de Montesquieu (1689–1755) and her theory of punishment from the Italian reformer Cesare Beccaria (1738–94). Among other things, Catherine advocated the abolition of capital punishment, torture, serf auctions, and the breakup of serf families by sale. Few of these radical reforms were ever put into practice. But one of the most important aspects of the legislative commission was that it drew upon the service of elected noblemen, who came to Saint Petersburg with lists of local grievances. Catherine and her advisers were able to learn firsthand about the failures of rural administration and to take steps to correct them.

With this knowledge Catherine set about, in 1775, the restructuring of local government. Russia was divided into fifty provincial districts, each with a population of between 300,000 and 400,000 inhabitants. Each district was to be governed by both a central official and elected local noblemen. This reform was modeled upon the English system of justices of the peace. The failure of all previous local reforms had stemmed from the absence of a resident local nobility. The abolition of compulsory service finally made possible the establishment of local institutions. In 1785, Catherine issued the Charter of the Nobility, a formal statement of the rights and privileges of the noble class. The Charter incorporated all the gains the nobility had made since the death of Peter the Great, but it also instituted the requirements for local service that had been the basis of Catherine's reforms. District councils with the right to petition directly to the tsar became the centerpiece of Russian provincial government.

In order to train the local nobility for government service, Catherine introduced educational reforms. Peter had established military schools for the nobility and had staffed them with foreigners. The University of Moscow had been founded in 1755, and its faculty too was dominated by European emigrants. Catherine saw the need to broaden the educational system. Borrowing from the Austrian system, she established provincial elementary schools to train the sons and daughters of the local nobility. To staff these, Catherine created teachers' colleges so that the state would have its own educators. Hostility to formal education on the part of the nobility slowed the pace of these reforms. Though the program called for the equal education of women, except in Saint Petersburg and Moscow few women attended either elementary or high schools. Some provincial schools found students only by resorting to the tactics of factory owners—that is, by forced enrollment.

Catherine's reforms did little to enhance the lives of the vast majority of her people. Though she often spoke in the terms of the French philosophers who saw the enserfment of fellow humans as a blot on civilization, Catherine effectively took no action either to end serfdom or to soften its rigors. In fact, by grants of state land Catherine gave away 800,000 state peasants, who were immediately turned into serfs. So, too, were the millions of Poles who became her subjects after the partition of Poland in 1793 and 1795. The epitaph that she wrote for herself, "when she ascended the throne of Russia she wished to do good, and tried to bring happiness, freedom and prosperity to her subjects," bore little relation to the experience of the Russian peasants.

Indeed, the most significant uprising of the century, Pugachev's revolt (1773–75), took place during her reign. Emelyan Pugachev (1726–75) was a Cossack who in his youth had been a military adventurer. Disappointed in his career, he made his way to the Ural mountains, where he recruited Asian tribesmen and laborers forced to work in the mines. By promising freedom and land ownership, he drew peasants to his cause. Pugachev declared himself to be Tsar Peter III, the murdered husband of Catherine II. He began with small raiding parties against local landlords and military outposts and soon had gained the allegiance of tens of thousands of peasants. In 1774, with an army of nearly twenty thousand, Pugachev took the city of Kazan and threatened to advance on Moscow. It was another year before state forces could effectively control the rebellion. Finally, Pugachev was betrayed by his own followers and sent to Moscow to be executed. Thousands of the rebels met similar fates. The town in

Catherine Before She Was Great

Catherine the Great wasn't always called the Empress of all the Russias. In fact, she wasn't always called Catherine. Sophie of Anhalt-Zerbst was the daughter of a petty German prince whose estates were too poor to provide for his family. He hired himself out as a military officer to the kings of Prussia and became governor of the dreary Baltic port of Stettin. Here Sophie passed her childhood. The family lived comfortably enough and Sophie was provided with a French governess, Babette Cardel. From Babette she learned not only the language of the French but also their ways. Sophie was no easy child to handle. Her natural curiosity about nearly everything led to some narrow escapes, and she was nearly killed at the age of three when she pulled a cupboard down upon herself. To curiosity was added spirit, and the shouting matches in which she and Babette engaged were long remembered. Indeed, Babette took to bribing young Sophie with sweets, which in the long run did less to soften her temper than to ruin her teeth.

By far the most significant event of Sophie's childhood was the sudden sickness that overtook her at the age of seven. She was seized by coughing, fevers, and fits that incapacitated her for weeks. For a time her life was in danger. It was not unusual for unexplained illness to appear and disappear with bewildering suddenness, and this is what happened to Sophie. One morning she awoke without fever and without the racking cough that had seared through her body. But in its place had come a physical change. Weeks of lying on her side had deformed her physique: "I had assumed the shape of a letter Z. My right shoulder was much higher than the left, the backbone running in a zigzag and the left side falling in," she later recalled. Such a result was as mysterious as the illness that occasioned it. Doctors were sought for advice. None could help until at last a veterinarian who practiced on the limbs of horses and cows was found. He prescribed a useless concoction of medicines but also built a body frame for Sophie which was designed to reshape her deformity. She wore this for four years until she regained her former posture.

Sophie's father was a strict Lutheran who prescribed a regimen for the education of his children that was to be precisely followed. At the age of seven, just after her recovery, Sophie was told that she could no longer play with her toys but must begin to behave as an adult. Tutors were brought to teach her history and geography, and a Lutheran minister was deputed to train her in religion. Sophie took delight in confounding her religion instructor and in general showed the same high spirits as she entered adolescence that she had in childhood.

Though Sophie did not have a close relationship with her mother—in later years they quarreled incessantly—it was her mother who showed her the world outside Stettin. Joanna of Holstein-Gottorp had grown up surrounded by courtly pomp rather than military rigor. Though her family, too, came from the ranks of the minor princes of the Holy Roman Empire, marriages and inclination had brought them into the circle of German aristocratic life. This was a world for which Joanna longed, and every year she visited her relations in Brunswick. Sophie began to accompany her mother on these trips, and they became for her the principal means to escape the boredom of life in Stettin. On one visit to Berlin she was introduced to Frederick William I, king of Prussia. Her relatives included a future king of Sweden and a future queen of Britain. These trips to Brunswick and Berlin opened Sophie's eyes to the possibility of a life different than the one she had expected, the possibility of life with one of the crown princes of Europe.

As it happened, Sophie had little need to wish. By a strange twist of fate, another of her mother's innumerable cousins had recently been declared heir to the throne of Russia. This was Peter, soon to be duke of Holstein-Gottorp and ultimately to be Peter III of Russia. Empress Elizabeth of Russia was childless and Peter was her nearest relative. She determined to have him married to an eligible German princess, and after much casting about, the choice fell on Sophie. In 1744 Sophie was summoned to Russia. Joanna was thrilled with

the prospect, not only because of the possibility of a successful marriage for her daughter, but also because she was to have a role in the affair. Princely marriages were matters of international diplomacy. In the case of Russia, Frederick the Great of Prussia took more than a neighborly interest. It was he who pushed the claims of a daughter of one of his own military dependents and it was he who enlisted Joanna to become an agent of Prussia at the Russian court. No one asked Sophie what she thought, since her opinion hardly mattered.

The journey to Russia was a trip that Sophie would never forget. Though Stettin was no tropical paradise, the climate there had little prepared Sophie and her mother for the rigors of the east. Carriages gave way to sleighs, and her heavy cloth clothing to sable. Sophie and Joanna huddled together for warmth, covering their faces and hands from the bitter arctic winds. It took nearly four weeks to reach Saint Petersburg, and when they arrived they were informed that they must hurry to join the royal court at Moscow. There they were received with unusual warmth as it was the sixteenth birthday of the new heir to the throne and all of Russian society was eager to see his bride-to-be.

Sophie's earliest meetings with her fiancé were not entirely satisfactory. In a strange land she might have expected strange customs, but Peter was a German like herself. Thus she was unprepared for their first interview, in which Peter professed his passionate love for one of the ladies of the court. Sophie was only fifteen and, by her own account at least, innocent in sexual matters. Peter's frank confession, which was accompanied by assurances that he would marry Sophie anyhow, caused her as much confusion as it did anger and resentment. She resolved to keep her own counsel and to attempt to please the empress if not the heir. Sophie spent the days before her marriage learning both the Russian language and the Eastern Orthodox religion. She would have to convert to the old faith before she could be betrothed. As part of her conversion, she had to take a Russian name and thus she came to be called Catherine. Whether her change of religion was sincere or not, it was required. Sophie was shrewd enough to realize the importance of the Church, and she won many admirers at court when, after being taken suddenly ill, she asked for an Orthodox priest rather than a Lutheran minister or a doctor.

Sophie's marriage took place in 1745 in one of the most magnificent ceremonies anyone could recall. By then she knew that she was alone in the world. She had fought bitterly with her mother, who had became a political liability after she bungled her role as an agent for Frederick the Great. Sophie shared nothing with her new husband—including the marriage bed. The household set up for her was composed entirely of spies for the empress and even her correspondence was monitored. She spent the next fifteen years supplementing the education that she had received as a child. She read everything that she could get hold of. Her Russian improved dramatically as she read Russian and French or German versions of the same works. She devoured the classics, especially history and philosophy, and for the first time became acquainted with the works of the new European writers whose reputations had reached as far as Russia. Sophie indulged her enthusiasm for riding, an exercise not usually taken by women. She also developed a passion for the handsome guardsmen who inhabited the palace. Perhaps in revenge for her husband's conduct, perhaps in return for his neglect, she took the first of more than twenty lovers. When she became pregnant in 1754, it was almost certainly not Peter's child. Eight years later the private life of Sophie of Anhalt-Zerbst ended. Then Empress Elizabeth died, the half-mad Peter III acceded to the throne, and Sophie, now known to the world as Catherine, began her remarkable public career.

which the rebellion began was razed to the ground and the name of the river that adjoined it was changed. No official memory of the man or the event was to be preserved, and upon pain of death, no one was to utter the name Pugachev.

The Two Germanies

The Thirty Years' War initiated a profound transformation of the Holy Roman Empire. Warfare had devastated imperial territory. It was decades before the rich imperial lands recovered and then the political consequences of the war had taken effect. There were now two empires, a German and an Austrian, though both were ruled by the same person. In the German territories, whether Catholic or Protestant, the Holy Roman Emperor was more of a constitutional than an absolute ruler. The larger states like Saxony, Bavaria, and Hanover made their own political alliances despite the jurisdictional control that the emperor claimed to exercise. Most decisively, so did Brandenburg-Prussia. By the beginning of the eighteenth century, the electors of Brandenburg had become the kings of Prussia and Prussia's military power and efficient administrative structure became the envy of its German neighbors. Prussia was becoming a player in the European balance-of-power game and a potential leader of the other German states.

The Austrian empire was composed of Austria and Bohemia, the Habsburg hereditary lands, and as much of Hungary as could be controlled. In Austria, the Habsburgs clung tightly to their power. Victories over the Turks had expanded their control in Hungary. For decades Austria was the center of the still-flourishing Counter-Reformation, and the power and influence of the Jesuits was as strong here as it was in Spain. The War of the Spanish Succession, which gave the Habsburgs control of the southern Netherlands and parts of Italy, brought Austria an enhanced role in European affairs. Austria remained one of the great powers of Europe and the leading power in the Holy Roman Empire despite the rise of Prussia. Indeed from the middle of the eighteenth century the conflict between Prussia and Austria was the defining characteristic of central European politics.

Frederick the Great painted this picture of himself surrounded by servants and members of his beloved Potsdam Grenadiers, a regiment of very tall soldiers. Frederick is third from right.

The Prussian Miracle

The transformation of Brandenburg-Prussia from a petty German principality to a great European power was one of the least expected developments of the eighteenth century. Like many other German states, Brandenburg-Prussia was important to the great European powers as a recruiting ground for their wars. Frederick William, the Great Elector (1640–88), had begun the process of forging Brandenburg-Prussia into a power in its own right by building a large and efficient military machine. At the beginning of the eighteenth century Prussia was on the winning side in both the War of the Spanish Succession and the Great Northern War. When the battlefield dust had cleared, Prussia found itself in possession of Pomerania and the Baltic port of Stettin. It was now a recognized power in eastern Europe.

Frederick William I (1713–40) and his son Frederick II, the Great (1740–86), turned this promising beginning into an astounding success. Frederick William I was a stern, humorless ruler who implanted his personality upon his policies. A devout Calvinist, Frederick William I deplored waste and display as much on moral as on fiscal grounds. The reforms he initiated were intended to subordinate both aristocracy and peasantry to the needs of the state and to subordinate the needs of the state to the demands of the military.

Because of its geographical position, Prussia's major problem was to maintain an efficient and well-trained army during peacetime. Defense of its exposed territories required a constant state of military preparedness, yet the relaxation of military discipline and the desertion of troops to their homes inevitably followed the cessation of hostilities. Frederick William I solved this problem by integrating the economic and military structures of his state. First he appointed only German officers to command his troops, eliminating the mercenaries who sold their services to the highest bidders. Then he placed these noblemen at the head of locally recruited regiments. Each adult male in every district was required to register for military service in the regiment of the local landlord.

These reforms dramatically increased the effectiveness of the army by shifting the burden of recruitment and training to the localities. But the system also had a serious drawback. It threatened

Prussian infantry officers display their uniforms in this painting from the late eighteenth century. Distinctive colorful and elaborate uniforms, different for each regiment, were common in European armies before the field-gray and khaki era of the twentieth century.

to impoverish the nobles by forcing them to take their own laborers off the land for military service. Frederick William I overcame this problem by instituting the seasonal call-up. Except in times of actual warfare, troops were called up and trained for specific periods of time and then returned to their agricultural pursuits. Thus the soldiers had the benefit of cumulative training, the nobles the benefit of their agricultural workers, and the state the benefit of both a standing army and a reserve force.

Yet despite all the attention that Frederick William I lavished on the military—by the end of his reign nearly 70 percent of state expenditures went to the army—his foreign policy was largely pacific. In fact, his greatest achievements were in civil affairs, reforming the bureaucracy, establishing a sound economy, and raising state revenues. Through generous settlement schemes and by welcoming Protestant and Jewish refugees,

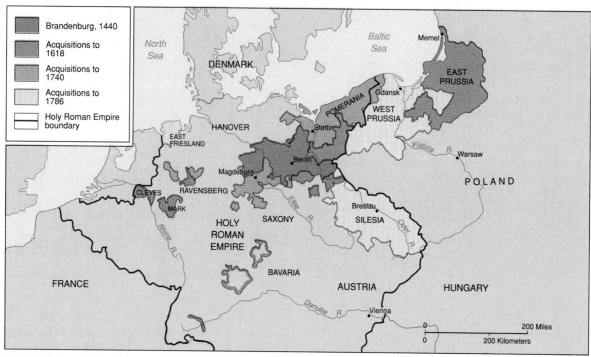

The Expansion of Prussia

Frederick William was able to expand the economic potential of these eastern territories. Unlike most other European monarchs, the king of Prussia was able to live from the rents of his own estates. Frederick William I pursued an aggressive policy of land purchase to expand the royal domain, and the addition of so many new inhabitants in Prussia further increased his wealth. While the major western European powers were discovering deficit financing and the national debt, Prussia was actually running a surplus.

Financial security was vital to the success of Frederick II, the Great (1740–86). Father and son had quarreled bitterly throughout Frederick's youth. Frederick William I treated his son as if he were a peasant on an estate rather than successor to the throne, and most observers expected that out of spite Frederick would tear down all that his father had built up. In fact father and son were cast in the same mold, with the unexpected difference that the son was the more ruthless and ambitious. With his throne, Frederick II inherited the fourth largest army in Europe and the richest treasury. He wasted no time in putting both to

use. His two objectives were to acquire the Polish corridor of West Prussia that separated his German and Prussian territories and the agriculturally and industrially rich Austrian province of Silesia to the southeast of Berlin. Just months after his coronation, Frederick invaded Silesia and by brilliant generalship, unflinching determination, and more than a little bit of luck, conquered it. The conquest of Silesia increased the size of Prussia by nearly a quarter and gave it an advanced capacity for mining and small industry. Within a decade the province dominated the Prussian economy, outproducing and outconsuming all other areas of Frederick's state.

It was Frederick's military prowess that earned him the title "the Great." But this was only a part of his achievement. More than his father, Frederick II forged an alliance with the Prussian nobility, integrating them into a unified state. A tightly organized central administration, which depended upon the cooperation of the local nobility, directed both military and bureaucratic affairs. At the center, Frederick worked tirelessly to oversee his government. Where Louis XIV had proclaimed, "I am the state," Frederick the Great announced "I am the first servant of the state." He put in place a superstructure for the training of future leaders of the state and for bettering the material lives of his subjects. He codified the laws of Prussia, abolished torture and capital punishment, and instituted agricultural techniques imported from the states of western Europe. By the end of Frederick's reign, Prussia had become a model for bureaucratic organization, military reform, and enlightened rule. Its place among the great powers was sure.

Austria Survives

Austria was the great territorial victor in the War of the Spanish Succession, acquiring both the Netherlands and parts of Italy. Austrian forces recaptured a large part of Hungary from the Turks, thereby expanding their territory to the south and the east. Hereditary ruler of Austria, Bohemia, King of Hungary, and Holy Roman Emperor of the German nation, Charles VI (1711–40) was recognized as one of Europe's most potent rulers. But appearances were deceptive. The apex of Austrian power and prestige had already passed. Austria had benefited from balance-of-power politics not so much from its own strength as from the leverage it could give to others. With the rise of Russia and Prussia there was now more than one fulcrum to power in eastern Europe.

The difficulties facing Austria ran deep. The Thirty Years' War had made the emperor more an Austrian monarch than an imperial German ruler. On the Austrian hereditary estates, the Catholic Counter-Reformation continued unabated, bringing with it the benefits of Jesuit education, cultural revival, and the religious unity necessary to motivate warfare against the Ottomans. But these benefits came at a price. Perhaps as many as two hundred thousand Protestants fled Austria and Bohemia, many resettling in Prussia and bringing with them their skills and capital. Religious intolerance was out of step with eighteenth-century political considerations, not to mention eighteenth-century ideas about freedom of thought and worship. Nor was uniformity easy to impose. For centuries the vision of empire had dominated Habsburg rule.

This meant that the Austrian monarchy was a multiethnic confederation of lands loosely tied together by loyalty to a single head. The components preserved a high degree of autonomy. As a Tyrolean nobleman wrote: "What does it concern the people of Tyrol what happens in Bohemia? They are flattered that they have a prince-protector who is a great monarch but they do not wish to pay for that honor by the loss of their fundamental laws." Such sentiments went double for Hungary, which elected the Habsburg emperor its king in a separate ceremony. Local autonomy continually restricted the imposition of central policy, and never were the localities more autonomous than in the matter of taxation.

A predominantly rural land, Austria was also predominantly agricultural. Less than 5 percent of the population lived in towns of ten thousand or more, less than 15 percent lived in towns at all. On the land the local aristocracy, whether nobility or gentry, exploited serfs to the maximum. Not only were serfs required to give labor service three days a week (and up to six during planting and harvest times), but the nobility maintained a full array of feudal privileges including the right to mill all grain and brew all beer. When they married, when they transferred property, even when they died, serfs paid taxes to their lord. As a result they had little left to give the state. In consequence, the Austrian army was among the smallest and the poorest of the major powers despite the fact that it had the most active enemies along its borders.

Lack of finance, lack of human resources, and lack of governmental control were the underlying problems of Austria, but they were not the most immediate difficulties facing Charles VI. With no sons to succeed him, Charles feared that his hereditary and elective states would go their separate ways after his death and that the great Habsburg monarchy would end. For twenty years his abiding ambition was to gain recognition for the principle that his empire would pass intact to his daughter, Maria Theresa. He expressed the principle in a document known as the Pragmatic Sanction, which stated that all Habsburg lands would pass intact to the eldest heir, male or female. Charles VI made concession after concession to gain acceptance of the Pragmatic Sanction, first from the semi-autonomous peoples of his own empire and then from the leaders of the other European powers. At every turn Austria demonstrated its inherent weakness, losing territory in Italy and Hungary during a series of bungled wars and failing to maintain a strong standing army in times of peace. Despite the Pragmatic Sanction, the leaders of Europe licked their lips at the prospect of a dismembered Austrian empire.

Maria Theresa (1740–80) quickly discovered what it was like to be a pregnant woman in a man's world. In 1740 Frederick of Prussia invaded the rich Austrian province of Silesia and attracted allies for an assault upon Vienna. Faced with Bavarian, Saxon, and Prussian armies, Maria Theresa might well have lost her inheritance had she not shown her remarkable capacities so early in her reign. She appeared before the Hungarian estates, accepted their crown, and persuaded them to provide her with an army capable of halting the allied advance. Though she was unable to reconquer Silesia, Hungarian aid helped her hold the line against her enemies, and five years of nearly continuous fighting demonstrated that Maria Theresa was every bit a Habsburg ruler.

The loss of Silesia, the most prosperous part of the Austrian domains, signaled the need for fundamental reform. The new eighteenth-century idea of building a state replaced the traditional Habsburg concern with maintaining an empire. Maria Theresa and her son Joseph II (1780–90) began the process of transformation. For Austria, state-building meant first the reorganization of the military and civil bureaucracy to clear the way for fiscal reform. As in Prussia, a central directory was created to oversee the collection of taxes and the disbursement of funds. This control was especially important in Austria, where local authorities traditionally withheld a significant portion of tax revenues for their own use. Maria Theresa personally persuaded her provincial estates both to increase taxation and to extend it to the nobles and the clergy. While her success was limited, she finally established royal control over the raising and collection of taxes. This concession was to be the basis of thoroughgoing reform in the reign of Joseph II.

The second element in Maria Theresa's reform program involved the condition of the

Maria Theresa and her family. Eleven of Maria Theresa's sixteen children are posed with the empress and her husband, Francis of Lorraine. Standing next to his mother is the future emperor Joseph II.

Austrian peasantry. Maria Theresa established the doctrine that the "peasant must be able to support himself and his family and pay his taxes in time of peace and war." She limited labor service to two days per week and abolished the most burdensome feudal dues. Joseph II ended serfdom altogether. The new Austrian law codes guaranteed peasants' legal rights and established their ability to seek redress through the law. Joseph II hoped to extend reform even further. In the last years of his life he abolished obligatory labor service and ensured that all peasants kept one-half of their income before paying local and state taxes. Such a radical reform met a storm of opposition and was ultimately abandoned at the end of the reign.

The reorganization of the bureaucracy, the increase in taxation, and the social reforms that created a more productive peasantry revitalized the Austrian state. The most ambitious plans for reorganizing the peasantry had to be abandoned, but much good came out of the reforms that were enacted, both for the peasants and for the state. The efforts of Maria Theresa and Joseph II to overcome provincial autonomy worked better in Austria and Bohemia than in Hungary. The Hungarians declined to contribute at all to state revenues, and Joseph II took the unusual step of refusing to be crowned king of Hungary so that he would not have to make any concessions to Hungarian autonomy. He even imposed a tariff on Hungarian goods sold in Austria. More seriously, parts of the empire already had been lost before the process of reform could begin. Prussia's seizure of Silesia was the hardest blow of all. Yet in 1740 when Frederick the Great and his allies swept down from the north few would have predicted that Austria would survive.

The Politics of Power

Frederick the Great's invasion of Silesia in 1740 was callous and cynical. Since the Pragmatic Sanction bound him to recognize Maria Theresa's succession, Frederick cynically offered her a defensive alliance in return for which she would simply hand over Silesia. It was an offer she should not have refused. Though Frederick's action initiated the War of the Austrian Succession, he was not alone in his desire to shake loose parts of Austria's territory. Soon nearly the entire continent became embroiled in the conflict.

The War of the Austrian Succession (1740–48) resembled nothing so much as a pack of wolves stalking its injured prey. Spain joined the fighting to recover its Italian possessions, Saxony claimed Moravia, France entered Bohemia, and the Bavarians moved into Austria from the south. With France and Prussia allied, it was vital that Britain join with Austria to maintain the balance of power. Initially the British did little more than subsidize Maria Theresa's forces, but once France renewed its efforts to conquer the Netherlands, both Britain and the Dutch Republic joined in the fray. That the British cared little about the fate of the Habsburg empire was clear from the terms of the treaty that they dictated at Aix-la-Chapelle in 1748. Austria was to recognize Frederick's conquest of Silesia, as well as the loss of parts of its Italian territories to Spain. France, which the British had always regarded as the real enemy, withdrew from the Netherlands in return for the restoration of a number of colonial possessions. The War of the Austrian Succession made Austria and Prussia permanent enemies and gave Maria Theresa a crash course in international diplomacy.

One of the things that she learned was that it was not always easy to distinguish friend from foe. This lesson was reinforced in 1756 when Britain and Prussia entered into a military accord at the beginning of the Seven Years' War (1756–63). Prussian expansion and duplicity had already alarmed both Russia and France, and Frederick II feared that he would be squeezed from east and west. He could hardly expect help from Maria Theresa, so he extended overtures to Britain, whose interests in protecting Hanover, the hereditary estates of their German-born king, outweighed their prior commitments to Austria. Frederick's actions drove France into the arms of both the Austrians and the Russians, and an alliance which included the German state of Saxony was formed in defense. Thus was initiated a diplomatic revolution in which France and Austria became allies after three hundred years as enemies.

Once again, Frederick the Great took the offensive and once again, he won his risk against the odds. His attack on Saxony and Austria in 1756 brought a vigorous response from the Russians, who interceded on Austria's behalf with a massive army. Three years later, at the battle of Kunersdorf, Frederick suffered the worst military defeat of his career when the Russians shattered his armies. "Of an army of 48,000 I have, as I write, less than 3,000 men left. This is a terrible mishap and I shall not survive it," he wrote after the battle. In 1760 his forces were barely a third of the size of those massed by his opponents, and it was only a matter of time before he was fighting defensively from within Prussia.

In 1762 Tsarina Elizabeth died. Her successor was the childlike Peter III, a German by birth who worshiped Frederick the Great. He had spent most of his youth marching soldiers back and forth in emulation of Frederick's innovative military maneuvers, much to the disgust of his wife, Catherine. When Peter came to the throne, he immediately negotiated peace with Frederick, abandoning not only his allies but also the substantial territorial gains that the Russian forces had made within Prussia. It was small wonder that the Russian military leadership joined in the coup d'état that brought Peter's wife, Catherine, to the throne in 1762. With Russia out of the war, Frederick was able to fend off further Austrian offensives and to emerge with his state, including Silesia, intact.

568 Chapter 18 The New European Powers

The Seven Years' War did little to change the boundaries of the German states, but it had two important political results. The first was to establish beyond doubt the status of Prussia as a major power and a counterbalance to Austria in central Europe. The existence of the dual Germanies, one led by Prussia and the other by Austria, was to have serious consequences for German unification in the nineteenth century and for the two world wars in the twentieth. The second result of the Seven Years' War was to initiate a long period of peace in eastern Europe. Both Prussia and Austria found themselves financially exhausted from two decades of fighting. Both states needed a breathing spell to initiate administrative and economic improvements, and the period following the Seven Years' War witnessed the sustained programs of internal reforms for which Frederick the Great, Maria Theresa, and Joseph II were famous.

This engraving by Le Mire is called The Cake of the Kings: First Partition of Poland, 1773. *The monarchs of Russia, Austria, and Prussia join in carving up Poland. The Polish king is clutching his tottering crown.*

Peace among the eastern European powers did not mean that they abandoned their territorial ambitions. Throughout the course of the eighteenth century one state had always swum against the tide. All over Europe absolute rulers reformed their bureaucracies, streamlined their administrations, increased their sources of revenues, and built enormous standing armies. All over Europe except in Poland. There the autonomous power of the nobility remained as strong as ever. No monarchical dynasty was ever established and each elected ruler not only confirmed the privileges of the nobility but usually was forced to extend them. In the Diet, the Polish representative assembly, small special-interest groups could bring legislative business to a halt by exercising their veto power, and rarely did the interests of one part of this vast kingdom coincide with the interests of the others. Given the size of Poland's borders its army was pathetically inadequate for the task it had to face. During the Seven Years' War Poland was used as a staging ground for Russian assaults on Prussia and for Prussian attacks on Austria. The Polish monarchy was helpless to defend its subjects from the destruction on all sides.

In 1764 Catherine the Great and Frederick the Great combined to place one of Catherine's former lovers on the Polish throne and to turn Poland into a weak dependent. Russia and Prussia had different interests in Poland's fate. For Russia, Poland represented a vast buffer state that kept the German powers at a distance from Russia's borders. It was more in Russia's interest to dominate Polish foreign policy than to conquer its territory. For Prussia, Poland looked like another helpless flower, "to be picked off leaf by leaf," as Frederick observed. Poland seemed especially appealing because Polish territory, including the Baltic port of Gdansk, separated the Prussian and Brandenburg portions of Frederick's state.

By the 1770s the idea of carving up Poland was being actively discussed in Berlin, Saint Petersburg, and Vienna. Austria, too, had an interest in a Polish partition, especially to maintain its power and status with the other two states, and perhaps to use Polish territory as a potential bargaining chip for the return of Silesia. None of the powers considered for a moment the interest of the Poles or their ability to resist. In fact, while their fate was being sealed abroad, the Poles were engaged in a series of destructive civil wars at home, wars actively encouraged by Catherine and Frederick. Finally, in 1772, the three great eastern powers struck a deal. Russia would take a large swath of the grain fields of northeast Poland, which included over one million people, while Frederick would unite his lands by seizing West Prussia. Austria gained both the largest territories, including Galicia, and the greatest number of people, nearly two million Polish subjects. Though Austrian ministers had been in on the plans from the beginning, it proved more difficult to convince Maria Theresa of the morality of the deal. After all, she knew what it was like to have her state dismembered and to be unable to do anything about it. How could she help but feel compassion for the Poles? As it was said, "she wept and wept and took and took."

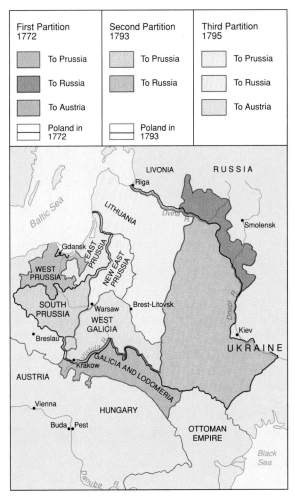

The Partition of Poland

The Greatness of Britain

By the middle of the eighteenth century, Great Britain had become the leading power of Europe. It had won its spurs in Continental and colonial wars. Britain was unsurpassed as a naval power, able to protect its far-flung trading empire and to make a show of force in almost any part of the world. Perhaps more impressively for a nation that did not support a large standing army, British soldiers had won decisive victories in the European land wars. British interests comprised one of the scales in the European balance of power and it was the one that was always favorably tipped. Until the American Revolution, Britain came up a winner in every military venture it undertook. But might was only one part of British success. Economic preeminence was every bit as important. British colonial possessions in the Atlantic and Indian oceans poured consumer products into Britain for export to the European marketplaces. Growth in overseas trade was matched by growth in home production. British advances in agricultural technique had transformed Britain from an importer to an exporter of grain. The manufacturing industries that other European states attempted to create with huge government subsidies flourished in Britain through private enterprise.

British military and economic power was supported by a unique system of government. In Britain the nobility served the state through government. The British constitutional system, devised in the seventeenth century and refined in the eighteenth, shared power between the monarchy and the ruling elite through the institution of Parliament. Central government integrated monarch and ministers with chosen representatives from the localities. Such integration not only provided the crown with the vital information necessary to formulate national policy, but it eased acceptance and enforcement of government decisions. Government was seen as the rule of law which, however imperfect, was believed to operate for the benefit of all.

The parliamentary system gave Britain some of its particular strengths, but they came at a cost. Politics was a national pastime rather than the business of an elite of administrators and state servants. Decentralization of decision making led to half-measures designed to placate competing interests. Appeals to public opinion, especially by candidates for Parliament, often played upon fears and prejudices that divided rather than united the nation. Moreover, the relative openness of the British system hindered diplomatic and colonial affairs, in which secrecy and rapid changes of direction were often the monarch's most potent weapons. These weaknesses came to light most dramatically during the struggle for independence waged by Britain's North American colonists. There the clash of principle and power was most extreme and the strengths and weaknesses of parliamentary rule were ruthlessly exposed.

The British Constitution

The British Constitution was a patchwork of laws and customs that was only gradually sewn together to form a workable system of government. Many of its greatest innovations came about through circumstance rather than design, and circumstance continued to play an essential role in its development in the eighteenth century. At the apex of the government stood the king, not an absolute monarch like his European counterparts, but not necessarily less powerful for having less arbitrary power. The British people revered monarchy and the monarch. The theory of mixed government depended upon the balance of interests represented by the monarchy in the crown, the aristocracy in the House of Lords, and the people in the House of Commons, "the most beautiful combination ever framed," as George III (1760–1820) declared. Less abstractly, the monarch was still regarded as divinely ordained and a special gift to the nation. The monarch was the actual and symbolic leader of the nation as well as the "Supreme Head" of the Church of England. Allegiance to the Anglican church, whether as a political creed among the elite or as a simple matter of devotion among the populace, intensified allegiance to the king.

The political power of the British monarch was limited by law. A series of statutes enacted after the Revolution of 1688 clearly defined the king's prerogatives and the subject's rights. The king could no longer suspend or dispense with the laws of the land, nor could he dismiss royal judges

at his pleasure. The Act of Succession (1701) established that only Protestants could wear the crown, thus bypassing the Catholic heirs of James II in favor of the princes of Hanover. More important than these general constraints were those designed to bring the crown into partnership with Parliament. No army could be raised without the consent of Parliament, just as no tax could be established or collected. At first, it was legislated that a new Parliament had to be called every three years, but the Septennial Act (1716) extended the period to seven. In reality, Parliament sat in continuous session, since most of the vital bills to fund the government and the military were passed for one year only.

The partnership between crown and representative body was best expressed in the idea that the British government was composed of King-in-Parliament. Parliament consisted of three separate organs: monarch, lords, and commons. Though each existed separately as a check upon the potential excesses of the others, it was only when the three functioned together that parliamentary government could operate. The king was charged with selecting ministers, initiating policy, and supervising administration. The two Houses of Parliament were charged with raising revenue, making laws, and presenting the grievances of subjects to the crown. Obviously there was much overlap between these responsibilities. The king could hardly initiate foreign or domestic policy without the necessary revenues, which only Parliament could grant him. Parliament's presentation of grievances was hardly practicable without the willingness of the king to redress them.

There were 558 members of the House of Commons after the union with Scotland in 1707. Most members of the lower House were nominated to their seats. The largest number of seats were located in small towns where a local oligarchy, or neighboring patron, had a customary right to make nominations that were invariably accepted by the electorate. Even in the largest cities influential citizens made arrangements for nominating members in order to avoid the cost and confusion of an actual election. Contests in which competing candidates appealed to the electorate, either on personal or political grounds, were the exception rather than the rule. Campaigns were ruinously expensive for the candidates—an election in 1754 cost the losing candidates £40,000—and potentially dangerous to the local community, where bitter social and political divisions boiled just below the surface.

The British gentry dominated the Commons, occupying over 80 percent of the seats in any session. Most of these members also served as unpaid local officials in the counties, as justices of the peace, captains of the local militias, or collectors of local taxes. They came to Parliament not only as representatives of the interests of their class, but as experienced local governors who understood the needs of both crown and subject. Most had direct connections with those who sat in the House of Lords, many through ties of blood, all through ties of service. The peerage and the gentry together formed the class that in most other European societies was labeled the nobility. Their division into the two houses of Parliament obscured similarities in background, outlook, and interest. Dozens of members of the House of Commons were the sons of members of the House of Lords. Such ties enabled the two houses of Parliament to work together in enacting legislation.

Nevertheless, the crown had to develop methods to coordinate the work of the two houses of Parliament and facilitate the passage of governmental programs. The king and his ministers began to use the deep royal pockets of offices and favors to bolster their friends in Parliament. Not only were those employed by the crown encouraged to find a place in the House of Commons, but those who had a place in Parliament were encouraged to take employment from the crown. Parliamentary patrons were eagerly solicited to nominate the king's servants, and many mutually beneficial arrangements resulted. Despite its potential for abuse, this was a political process that integrated center and locality, and at first it worked rather well. Those with local standing were brought into central offices. There they could influence central policymaking while protecting their local constituents. These officeholders, who came to be called *placemen*, never constituted a majority of the members of Parliament. They formed the core around which eighteenth-century governments operated but it was a core that needed direction and cohesion. It was such leadership and organization that was the essential contribution of eighteenth-century politics to the British Constitution.

Parties and Ministers

Though parliamentary management was vital to the crown, it was not the crown that developed the basic tools of management. Rather these techniques originated within the political community itself and their usefulness was only slowly grasped by the monarchy. The first and, in the long term, most important tool was the party system. Political parties initially developed in the late seventeenth century around the issue of the Protestant succession. Those who opposed James II because he was a Catholic attempted to exclude him from inheriting the crown. They came to be called by their opponents Whigs, which meant Scottish horse thieves. Those who supported James' hereditary rights but who also supported the Anglican church came to be called by their opponents Tories, which meant Irish cattle rustlers. The Tories cooperated in the Revolution of 1688 that placed William and Mary on the throne because James had threatened the Anglican church by tolerating Catholics and because Mary had a legitimate hereditary right to be queen. After the death of Queen Anne in 1714, the Tories supported the succession of James III, James II's Catholic son who had been raised in France, rather than of George I (1714–27), prince of Hanover and Protestant great-grandson of James I. An unsuccessful rebellion to place James III on the throne in 1715 discredited the leadership of the Tory party, but did not weaken its importance in both local and parliamentary politics.

The Whigs supported the Protestant succession and a broad-based Protestantism. They attracted the allegiance of large numbers of dissenters, those—heirs to the Puritans of the seventeenth century—who practiced forms of Protestantism different from the Anglican church. The Whigs' greatest strengths were in urban areas and among merchants, craftsmen, and shopkeepers. The Tories supported the Anglican church and the hereditary Stuart monarchy. They found their allies in the countryside and small villages, and among the landed elite. The struggle between Whigs and Tories was less a struggle for power than it was for loyalty to their opposing viewpoints. As the Tories opposed the Hanoverian succession and the Whigs supported it, it was no mystery which party would find favor with George I. Moreover, as long as there was a pretender to the British throne—another rebellion took place in Scotland in 1745 led by the grandson of James II—the Tories continued to be tarred with the brush of disloyalty.

The division of political sympathies between Whigs and Tories helped create a set of groupings to which parliamentary leadership could be applied. A national, rather than a local or regional outlook, could be used to organize support for royal policy as long as royal policy conformed to that national outlook. The ascendancy of the Whigs enabled George I and his son George II (1727–60) effectively to govern through Parliament, but at the price of dependence upon the Whig leaders. Though the monarch had the constitutional freedom to choose his ministers, realistically he could choose only Whigs, and practically none but the Whig leaders of the House of Commons. Happily for the first two Georges they found a man who was able to manage Parliament but desired only to serve the crown.

Sir Robert Walpole (1676–1745) came from a long-established gentry family in Norfolk. Walpole was an early supporter of the Hanoverian succession and an early victim of party warfare. When the Tories temporarily gained power, Walpole was impeached for financial mismanagement in 1712 and imprisoned for a time in the Tower of London. But once George I was securely on the throne, Walpole became an indispensable leader of the House of Commons. His success rested upon his extraordinary abilities: he was an excellent public speaker; he relished long working days and the details of government; and he understood better than anyone else the intricacies of state finance. Walpole became First Lord of the Treasury, a post that he transformed into first minister of state. From his treasury post, Walpole assiduously built a Whig parliamentary party. He carefully dispensed jobs and offices, using them as bait to lure parliamentary supporters. Walpole's organization paid off both in the passage of legislation desired by the crown and at the polls, where Whigs were returned to Parliament time and again.

From 1721 to 1742 Walpole was the most powerful man in the British government. He refused an offer of a peerage so that he could continue to lead the House of Commons. Wal-

pole's long tenure in office was as much a result of his policies as of his methods of governing. He brought a measure of fiscal responsibility to government by establishing a fund to pay off the national debt. In foreign policy he pursued peace with the same fervor that both his predecessors and successors pursued war. At one point he even went so far as to form an alliance with France to ensure European tranquillity. The long years of peace brought prosperity to both the landed and merchant classes, but they also brought criticism of Walpole's methods. The way in which he used government patronage to build his parliamentary party was attacked as corruption. So too were the ways in which the pockets of Whig officeholders were lined. During his last decade in office Walpole struggled to survive. His attempt to extend the excise tax on colonial goods nearly led to his loss of office in 1733. His refusal to respond to the clamor for continued war with Spain in 1741 finally led to his downfall.

Walpole's twenty-year rule established the pattern of parliamentary government. The crown needed a "prime" minister who was able to steer legislation through the House of Commons. It also needed a patronage broker who could take control of the treasury and dispense its largess in return for parliamentary backing. Walpole's personality and talents had combined these two roles. Hereafter they were divided. Those who had grown up under Walpole had learned their lessons well. The Whig monopoly of power continued unchallenged for nearly another twenty years. The patronage network Walpole had created was vastly extended by his Whig successors. Even minor posts in the customs or the excise offices were now exchanged for political favor, and only those approved by the Whig leadership could claim them. The cries of corruption grew louder: "He admits no person to any considerable post of trust and power under him who is not either a relation, a creature, or a thorough-paced tool." The cries of opposition were taken up not only in the country houses of the long disenfranchised Tories, but in the streets of London, where a popular radicalism developed in opposition to the Whig oligarchy. They were taken up as well in the North American colonies, where two million British subjects champed at the bit of imperial rule.

America Revolts

Britain's triumph in the Seven Years' War (1756–63) had come at great financial cost to the nation. At the beginning of the eighteenth century, the national debt stood at £14 million; in 1763 it had risen to £130 million despite the fact that Walpole's government had been paying off some of it. Then, as now, the cost of world domination was staggering. George III (1760–1820) came to the throne with a desire to break the Whig stranglehold on government and a taste for reform. He was to have limited success on both counts, though not for want of trying. In 1763 the king and his ministers agreed that reform of colonial administration was long overdue. Reform of colonial administration would have the twin benefit of shifting part of the burden of taxation from Britain to North America and of making the commercial side of colonization pay.

This was sound thinking all around, and in due course Parliament passed a series of duties on goods imported into the colonies, including glass, wine, coffee, tea, and most notably sugar. The so-called Sugar Act (1764) was followed by the Stamp Act (1765), a tax on printed papers such as newspapers, deeds, and court documents. Both acts imposed taxes in the colonies similar to those that already existed in Britain. Accompanying the acts were administrative orders designed to cut into the lucrative black market trade. In 1763 it was estimated that the quantity of goods smuggled into the colonies equaled the quantity legally imported. The government instituted new rules for searching ships and transferred authority over smuggling from the local colonial courts to Britain's Admiralty courts. Though British officials could only guess at the value of the new duties imposed, it was believed that with effective enforcement £150,000 would be raised. All this would go to pay the vastly greater costs of colonial administration and security.

British officials were more than perplexed when these mild measures met with a ferocious response. Assemblies of nearly every colony officially protested the Sugar Act. They sent petitions to Parliament begging for repeal and warning of

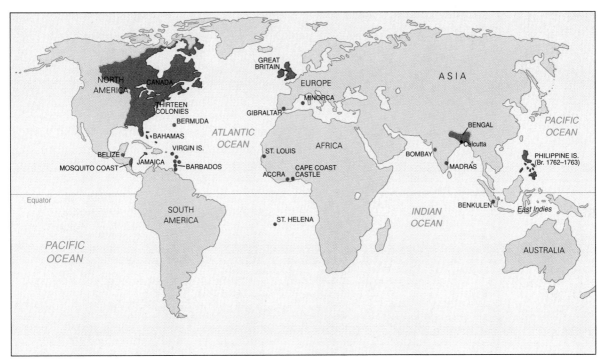

The British Empire, ca 1763

dire economic and political consequences. Riots followed passage of the Stamp Act. Tax collectors were hounded out of office, their resignations precipitated by threats and acts of physical violence. In Massachusetts mobs that included political leaders in the colony razed the homes of the collector and the lieutenant-governor. However much the colonists might have regretted the violence that was done, they believed that an essential political principle was at stake. It was a principle of the freedom of an Englishman.

At their core, the protests of the American colonists underscored the vitality of the British political system. The Americans argued that they could not be taxed without their consent and that their consent could come only through representation in Parliament. Since there were no colonists in Parliament, Parliament had no jurisdiction over the property of the colonists. Taxation without representation was tyranny. There were a number of subtleties to this argument that were quickly lost as political rhetoric and political action heated up. In the first place, the colonists did tax themselves through their own legislatures and much of that money paid the costs of administration and defense. Secondly, as a number of pamphleteers pointed out, no one in the colonies had asked the British government to send regiments of the army into North America. The colonists had little reason to put their faith in British protection. Hard-fought colonial victories were tossed away at European negotiating tables, while the British policy of defending Indian rights in the Ohio Valley ran counter to the interests of the settlers. When defense was necessary, the colonists had proven themselves both able and cooperative in providing it. A permanent tax meant a permanent army, and a standing army was as loathed in Britain as it was in the colonies.

Colonists also tried to draw a distinction between internal and external taxation in opposing the Stamp Act. They deemed regulation of overseas commerce a legitimate power of Parliament but argued that the regulation of internal exchange was not. But this distinction was lost once the issue of parliamentary representation was raised. If the colonists had not consented to British taxation, then it made no difference whether taxation was internal or external. The

passion generated in the colonies was probably no greater than that generated in Britain. The British government also saw the confrontation as a matter of principle, but for Britain the principle was parliamentary sovereignty. This, above all, was the rock upon which the British Constitution had been built over the last century. Parliament had entered into a partnership with the crown. The crown had surrendered—willingly or not—many of its prerogatives. In return, Parliament had bound the people to obedience. There were

The New European Powers

1707   England and Scotland unite to form Great Britain

1713–14   Peace of Utrecht ends War of the Spanish Succession (1702–14)

1714   British crown passes to House of Hanover

1721   Treaty of Nystad ends Great Northern War (1700–1721)

1721–42   Sir Robert Walpole leads British House of Commons

1722   Peter the Great of Russia creates Table of Ranks

1740   Frederick the Great of Prussia invades Austrian province of Silesia

1748   Treaty of Aix-la-Chapelle ends War of the Austrian Succession (1740–48)

1756–63   Seven Years' War pits Prussia and Britain against Austria, France, and Russia

1773–75   Pugachev's Revolt in Russia

1774   Boston Tea Party

1775   American Revolution begins

1785   Catherine the Great of Russia issues Charter of the Nobility

well-established means by which British subjects could petition Parliament for redress of grievances against the monarch, but there were no channels by which they could question the sovereignty of Parliament.

Once the terms of debate had been so defined, it was difficult for either side to find a middle ground. Parliamentary moderates managed repeal of the Stamp Act and most of the clauses of the Sugar Act, but they also joined in passing the Declaratory Act (1766), which stated unequivocally that Parliament held sovereign jurisdiction over the colonies "in all cases whatsoever." This was a claim that became more and more difficult to sustain as colonial leaders began to cite the elements of resistance theory that had justified the Revolution of 1688. Then the protest had been against the tyranny of the king, now it was against the tyranny of Parliament. American writers borrowed from the rich literature of opposition that had attacked Walpole and the Whig leaders to prove that Parliament was corrupt and no longer acted as representative of the people. Propagandists claimed that a conspiracy existed to deprive the colonists of their property and rights, to enslave them for the benefit of special interests and corrupt politicians. "I love Great Britain and revere the King," wrote one colonial pamphleteer. "But it is my duty to hand down freedom to my posterity compatible with the rights of Englishmen."

The techniques of London radicals who opposed parliamentary policy were imported into the colonies. Newspapers were used to whip up public support; boycotts brought ordinary people into the political arena; public demonstrations like the Boston Tea Party (1774) were carefully designed to intimidate; mobs were occasionally given free rein. Though the government had faced down these tactics when they were used in London to support John Wilkes (1725–97), an ardent critic of royal policy, they were less successful when the crisis lay an ocean away. When, in 1770, British troops fired upon a Boston mob, American propagandists were provided with empirical evidence that Britain intended to enslave the colonies. Violence was met by violence, passion by passion. In 1775 full-scale fighting was under way. Eight years later Britain withdrew from a war it could not win, and the American colonies were left to govern themselves.

By the end of the third quarter of the eighteenth century, Europe had a new political configuration. A continent once dominated by a single power—Spain in the sixteenth century and France in the seventeenth—was now dominated by a states system in which alliances among several great powers held the balance. Despite the loss of its American colonies, Great Britain had proved the most potent of the states. Its victories over the French in the Seven Years' War and over France and Prussia in the War of the Austrian Succession secured its position. But it was a position that could only be maintained through alliances with the German states, either with Prussia or Austria. The rise of Prussia provided a counterweight to French domination of the Continent. Though these two states found themselves allies in the middle of the century, the ambitions of their rulers made them natural enemies, and it would not be long before French and Prussian armies were again pitted against each other. France, still the wealthiest and most populous of European states, had slumbered through the eighteenth-century reorganization. The legacies of Louis XIV took a long time to reach fruition. He had claimed glory for his state, giving the French people a sense of national identity and national destiny, but making them pay an enormous price in social and economic dislocation. Thus the mid-eighteenth century was to be an age of the greatest literary and philosophical achievement for France, but the late eighteenth century was to be an age of the greatest social upheaval that Europe had ever known.

Suggestions for Further Reading

General Reading

* Olwen Hufton, *Europe: Privilege and Protest 1730–1789* (Ithaca, NY: Cornell University Press, 1980). An excellent survey of the political and social history of the mid-eighteenth century.

* Leonard Krieger, *Kings and Philosophers 1689–1789* (New York: Norton, 1970). A brilliant depiction of the personalities and ideas of eighteenth-century Europe.

* M. S. Anderson, *Europe in the Eighteenth Century 1713–1783* (London: Longman, 1976). A country-by-country survey of political developments.

Nicholas Riasanovsky, *A History of Russia* (New York: Oxford University Press, 1984). The best one-volume history of Russia.

Europe in 1714

* Derek McKay and H. M. Scott, *The Rise of the Great Powers* (London: Longman, 1983). An outstanding survey of diplomacy and warfare.

* H. C. Darby and H. Fullard, eds., *The New Cambridge Modern History*, Vol. 14, *Atlas* (Cambridge: Cambridge University Press, 1970). An invaluable collection of historical maps showing the changing boundaries of Europe over centuries.

The Rise of Russia

* Paul Dukes, *The Making of Russian Absolutism 1613–1801* (London: Longman, 1982). An extensive survey of the Russian monarchy in its greatest period.

* B. H. Sumner, *Peter the Great and the Emergence of Russia* (New York: Collier Books, 1962). A short and readable study; the best introduction.

* M. S. Anderson, *Peter the Great* (London: Thames and Hudson, 1978). A well-constructed, comprehensive biography.

* Jerome Blum, *Lord and Peasant in Russia* (New York: Columbia University Press, 1961). The best work on the social life of Russians.

John T. Alexander, *Catherine the Great: Life and Legend* (Oxford: Oxford University Press, 1989). The most up-to-date and enjoyable of many biographies.

* Dominique Maroger, ed., *The Memoirs of Catherine the Great* (New York: Collier Books, 1961). The empress' own reflections on her life.

The Two Germanies

* H. W. Koch, *A History of Prussia* (London: Longman, 1978). An up-to-date study of the factors that led to Prussian dominance of Germany.

Sidney Fay and Klaus Epstein, *The Rise of Brandenburg-Prussia to 1786* (New York: Holt, Rinehart, and Winston, 1964). The best introductory survey.

* Gerhard Ritter, *Frederick the Great* (Berkeley: University of California Press, 1974). A classic biography; short and readable.

* Walther Hubatsch, *Frederick the Great of Prussia* (London: Thames and Hudson, 1975). A full account of the reign of Prussia's greatest leader.

* Ernst Wangermann, *The Austrian Achievement* (New York: Harcourt Brace Jovanovich, 1973). The most readable study of Austrian politics, culture, and society in the eighteenth century.

* Paul Bernard, *Joseph II* (New York: Twayne, 1968). A reliable guide to the life and times of this reforming Austrian leader.

* T. C. W. Blanning, *Joseph II and Enlightened Despotism* (London: Longman, 1970). Displays the relationship between new ideas, reform policies, and the practical necessities of government.

C. A. Macartney, *Maria Theresa and the House of Austria* (Mystic, CT: Verry Inc., 1969). Still the best introductory study.

The Greatness of Britain

* J. C. D. Clark, *English Society 1688–1832* (Cambridge: Cambridge University Press, 1985). A bold reinterpretation of the most important features of English society.

* J. H. Plumb, *The Origins of Political Stability, England 1675–1725* (Boston: Houghton Mifflin, 1967). A comprehensive account of the contributions of Walpole to the establishment of the British Constitution.

Ragnhild Hatton, *George I Elector and King* (Cambridge, MA: Harvard University Press, 1978). An outstanding biography that shows the German side of a British monarch.

* John Brewer, *Party Ideology and Popular Politics at the Accession of George III* (Cambridge: Cambridge University Press, 1976). Examines the pressures on the political system in the late eighteenth century.

* Ian Christie and Benjamin W. Labaree, *Empire or Independence 1760–1777* (New York: Norton, 1977). Surveys the American troubles from the British point of view.

* Bernard Bailyn, *The Ideological Origins of the American Revolution* (Cambridge, MA: Harvard University Press, 1967). A brilliant interpretation of the underlying causes of the break between Britain and the North American colonies.

* Edward Countryman, *The American Revolution* (New York: Hill & Wang, 1985). A readable, up-to-date narrative of the events of the American Revolution.

* Indicates paperback edition available.

19

High and Low in the Eighteenth Century

Happy Families

"Happy families are all alike," wrote Lev Tolstoy in the nineteenth century when the idea of a happy family was already a cliché. Such an idea would never have occurred to his eighteenth-century forebears. For them the happy family was doubly new—new in the change in relationships within the family, new in the stress on happiness itself. Personal happiness was an invention of the Enlightenment, the result of novel attitudes about human aspirations and human capabilities. "Happiness is a new idea in Europe," wrote Louis de Saint-Just (1767–94). It emerged in response to the belief that what was good brought pleasure and what was evil brought pain. Happiness, both individual and collective, became the yardstick by which life was measured. This meant a reorientation in personal conduct and most of all a reorientation of family life. Especially for those with an economic cushion, a pleasurable family life was essential. Husbands and wives were to become companions, filled with romantic love for each other and devoted to domestic bliss. Children, the product of their affection, were to be doted upon, treated not as miniature adults to be lectured and beaten, but as unfilled vessels into which all that was good was to be poured.

Were ever a couple more in love than the husband and wife depicted in *A Visit to the Wet Nurse* by Jean-Honoré Fragonard (1732–1806)? The man clasps his wife's arm to his cheek, she lays her hand on his shoulder. Their sighs are almost audible! Together they admire the fruit of their love, the baby asleep in the cradle. It is hard to guess which parent dotes more, the mother with her rapturous expression or the father with his intensity. He kneels on a cushion in almost religious devotion, his hands folded as if in prayer. Who can doubt their companionship or their love for their babe? They have come together to see how the wet nurse is caring for their child. Doubtless it was they who provided the rather opulent bassinet, which makes such a contrast with the other furniture in the room, and the linens and pillows into which the baby has nestled.

At the beginning of the eighteenth century, the use of a wet nurse was still common among the families of the French bourgeoisie, the class to which this couple—judging from their clothes—undoubtedly belongs. As time moved on, however, more and more families began to keep their children at home, more and more mothers began to nurse their babies themselves. In part this change was a response to the higher mortality rate among infants sent out to wet nurses. The unsanitary environment of the towns ran a close race with the neglect that many wet nurses showed to their charges. But a wet nurse who could be supervised, that is, one who lived near enough to be visited, but far enough away from the town to enjoy wholesome air, might be the best of both worlds. This is just what the couple here has found, and today they come, with their other child (the boy in the hat), to see their baby sleeping peacefully, the wet nurse sitting attentively at the infant's side.

But there are two families in this picture, and they are hardly alike. At first glance, the wet nurse looks like an old woman, perhaps even an aging nanny. She sits with her distaff in her hand, for the arrival of her clients has interrupted her spinning. It is shocking to realize that she cannot be much older than thirty, an age beyond which wealthy families would not hire her for fear either that she would not have much milk or that it would be sour. The two younger children are undoubtedly hers, the youngest probably just weaned so that all of the milk would go to the baby. No adoring husband sits beside the wet nurse. Her husband, if he is still alive, is hard at work with no leisure time for visits to the country. Not only does the wet nurse have to sell her milk, but she also spins, to keep her family clothed and to earn a little extra to put away for hard times. The newest fads of the age have passed her family by. While the child in the cradle will be spoiled by toys manufactured especially for children—puzzles, games, rocking horses, and balls—the children of the wet nurse must make do with household objects and their own imagination. A ball of yarn thrown to the cat helps the elder child while away the hours. Like much else in the eighteenth century, the world of the family was divided between high and low.

The Nobility

At the apex of European society in the eighteenth century was the nobility. But it was far from a homogeneous group. Noble power and position differed widely from state to state. Perhaps more importantly, even within the same state there was an enormous range of wealth and power among members of the noble order. At the top, the greatest peers were also the richest of the king's subjects. Some of them were wealthy beyond description, like the Esterházy family of Hungary, who owned in excess of 10 million acres of land and controlled 700,000 peasants. But also considered part of the Hungarian nobility was the much larger number called the "sandaled nobility" because of their reputed inability to buy proper shoes. While Prince Miklós Esterházy (1714–90) built himself a palace modeled on Versailles, most of the sandaled nobility lived in houses of clay, roofed with reeds. Though the impoverished nobility were undoubtedly the more numerous of the order, it was the wealthy who set the tone of elite life in Europe.

The eighteenth-century nobility spawned a culture that was as rich as it was costly. Decorative architecture, especially interior design, reflected the increasing sociability of the aristocracy. Entertainment became a central part of aristocratic life, losing its previous formality. In this atmosphere music became one of the passions of noble culture. The string quartet made its first appearance in the eighteenth century and chamber music enjoyed unparalleled popularity. Only the wealthiest could afford to stage private operas, the other musical passion of the age. Again the Esterházys were in the forefront, employing 22 musicians and a conductor, who for most of the late eighteenth century was Joseph Haydn (1732–1809), the "father" of the modern symphony. Haydn's post was not an honorary one. In addition to hiring and managing the orchestra, he was expected to direct two operas and two concerts a week, as well as the music for Sunday services. An aristocratic patron was essential for the aspiring composer. If he could not find one or if, like Wolfgang Amadeus Mozart (1756–91), he could not bend his will to one, he could not flourish. While Haydn lived comfortably in a palace,

The seven-year-old musical prodigy Wolfgang Amadeus Mozart plays the harpsichord while his father Leopold plays the violin and his sister Nannerl sings. The boy won great ovations on concert tours throughout Europe.

Mozart, probably the greatest musical genius in Western history, lived impoverished in a garret and died at age 35 from lack of medical attention.

Musical entertainments in European country houses were matched by the literary and philosophical entertainments of the urban salons. There were to be found the most influential thinkers of the day presenting the ideas of the Enlightenment, a new European outlook on religion, society, and politics. The Enlightenment was not an aristocratic movement; indeed, many Enlightenment ideas were profoundly anti-aristocratic. But it was the nobility who had the leisure to read, write, and discuss, and many of the nobility were actively engaged in the intellectual and social changes that the Enlightenment brought in its wake. Though enlightened thinkers sought the improvement of life for the many, they pitched their appeal to the few. "Taste is thus like philosophy," Voltaire opined. "It belongs to a very small number of privileged souls."

All That Glitters

Eighteenth-century Europe was a society of orders gradually transforming itself into a society of classes. At the top, as vigorous as ever, was the nobility, the privileged order in every European state. Nobles were defined by their legal rights. They had the right to bear arms, the right to special judicial treatment, the right to tax exemptions. In Russia only nobles could own serfs; in Poland only nobles could hold government office. In France and Britain the highest court positions were always reserved for noblemen. Nobles dominated the Prussian army. In 1786 out of nearly 700 senior officers only 22 were not noblemen. The Spanish nobility claimed the right to live idly. Rich or poor, they shunned all labor as a right of their heritage. Swedish and Hungarian noblemen had their own legislative chambers, just as the British had the House of Lords. Noble privilege was as vibrant as ever.

Though all who enjoyed these special rights were noble, not all nobles were equal. In many states the noble order was subdivided into easily identifiable groups. The Spanish *grandees*, the upper nobility, were numbered in the thousands; the Spanish *hidalgos*, the lower nobility, in the hundreds of thousands. In Hungary out of 400,000 noblemen only about 15,000 belonged to the "landed" nobility who held titles and were exempt from taxes. The "landed" nobility were personally members of the upper chamber of the Hungarian Diet, while the lesser nobility sent representatives to the lower chamber. This was not unlike the situation in England where the elite class was divided between the peerage and the gentry. The peerage held titles, were members of the House of Lords, and had a limited range of judicial and fiscal privileges. In the mid-eighteenth century there were only 190 British peers. The gentry, which numbered over 20,000, dominated the House of Commons and local legal offices but were not strictly members of the nobility. The French nobility was informally distinguished among the small group of peers known as the *Grandes*, whose ancient lineage, wealth, and power set them apart from all others; a rather larger service nobility whose privileges derived in one way or another from municipal or judicial service; and what might be called the country nobility, whose small estates and local outlook made their fiscal immunities vital to their survival.

These distinctions among the nobilities of the European states masked a more important one: wealth. As the saying went, "all who were truly noble were not wealthy, but all who were truly wealthy were noble." In the eighteenth century, despite the phenomenal increase in mercantile activity, wealth was still calculated in profits from the ownership of land. In different parts of Europe the nobility used different methods to maintain their land-based wealth. In places like Britain, Spain, Austria, and Hungary forms of entail were the rule. Simply, an entail was a restriction prohibiting the breakup of a landed estate either through sale or inheritance. The owner of the estate was merely a caretaker for his heir and while he could add land he could not easily subtract any. Entailed estates grew larger and larger and, like magnets, attracted other entailed estates through marriage. In Britain, where primogeniture—inheritance by the eldest son—accompanied entail, four hundred families owned one-quarter of the entire country. Yet this concentration of landed wealth paled into insignificance when compared to the situation in Spain, where just four families owned one-third of all the cultivatable land. In the east, where land was plentiful, the Esterházys of Hungary and the Radziwills of Poland owned millions of acres.

The second method by which the European nobility ensured that the wealthy would be noble was by absorption. There were several avenues to upward mobility, but by the eighteenth century the holding of state offices was the most common. In France, for example, a large number of offices were reserved for the nobility. Many of these were owned by their holders and passed on to their children, but occasionally an office was sold on the market and the new holder was automatically ennobled. The office of royal secretary was one of the most common routes to noble status. The number of secretaries increased from 300 to 900 during the course of the eighteenth century, yet despite this dilution the value of the offices continued to skyrocket. An office that was worth 70,000 French pounds at the beginning of the century was worth 300,000 by the 1780s. In fact, in most European societies there was more room for new nobles than there were aspiring candidates. This was because of the costs that maintaining the new status imposed. In Britain anyone who could live like a gentleman was accounted one. But the practice of entail made it very difficult for a newcomer to purchase the requisite amount of land. Philip V increased the number of Spanish *grandees* in an effort to dilute their power, yet when he placed a tax upon entrance into the lower nobility, the number of *hidalgos* dropped precipitously.

For the wealthy, aristocracy was becoming an international status. The influence of Louis XIV and the court of Versailles lasted for well over a century and spread to town and country life. Most nobles maintained multiple residences. The new style of aristocratic entertainment required more public space on the first floor, while the increasing demand for personal and familial privacy necessitated more space in the upper stories. The result was larger and more opulent homes. Here the British elite led all others. Over one hundred fifty country houses were built in the early eighteenth century alone, including Blenheim Palace, which was built for John Churchill, Duke of Marlborough, at a cost of £300,000. To the expense of architecture was added the expense of decoration. New materials, like West Indian mahogany, occasioned new styles, and both drove up costs. The high-quality woodwork and plastering made fashionable by the English Adam brothers was quickly imitated on the Continent. Only the Spanish nobility shunned country estates, preferring to reside permanently in towns.

The building of country houses was only one part of the conspicuous consumption of the privileged orders. Improvements in travel, both in transport and roads, permitted increased contact between members of the national elites. The stagecoach linked towns, and canals linked waterways. Both made travel quicker and more enjoyable. The grand tour of historical sites continued to be used as a substitute for formal education. Young men would pass from country house to country house buying up antiquities, paintings, and books along the way. The grand tour was a means of introducing the European aristocracies to each other and also a means of communicating taste and fashion among them. Whether it was a Russian noble in Germany, a Swede in Italy, or a Briton in Prussia, all spoke French and shared a cultural outlook.

Much of this was cultivated in the salons, a social institution begun by French women in the seventeenth century that gradually spread throughout the Continent. The salons, especially in Paris, blended the aristocracy and bourgeoisie with the leading intellectuals of the age. Here wit and insight replaced polite conversation. At formal meetings, papers on scientific or philosophical topics were read and discussed. At informal gatherings new ideas were examined and exchanged. The British ambassador to Spain was appalled to discover that men and women were still kept separated in the salons of Madrid and that there was no serious conversation during evenings out. It was in the salons that the impact of the Enlightenment, the great European intellectual movement of the eighteenth century, first made itself felt.

The Enlightenment

In 1734 there appeared in France a small book entitled *Philosophical Letters Concerning the English Nation*. Its author, Voltaire (1694–1778) was a well-known poet who had made a name for himself as a wit in the Parisian salons. He had spent two years in Britain and while there he made it his business to study the differences between the peoples of the two nations. In a simple but forceful style Voltaire demonstrated time and again the superiority of the British. They practiced religious toleration and were not held under the sway of a venal clergy. They valued people for their merits rather than their birth. Their political constitution was a marvel—"The English nation is the only one on earth that has succeeded in controlling the power of kings by resisting them." They made national heroes of their scientists, their poets, and their philosophers. In all of this Voltaire contrasted British virtue with French vice. He attacked the French clergy and nobility directly, the French monarchy implicitly. Not only did he praise the genius and accomplishments of Sir Isaac Newton above those of René Descartes, but he also graphically contrasted the Catholic church's persecution of Descartes with the British state's celebration of

Newton. "England, where men think free and noble thoughts," Voltaire enthused.

It is difficult now to recapture the psychological impact that the *Philosophical Letters* had on the generation of educated Frenchmen who first read them. The book went through ten editions in a decade, five in the first year of its publication. It was officially banned and publicly burned, and a warrant was issued for Voltaire's arrest. The *Letters* dropped like a bombshell upon the moribund intellectual culture of the Church and the universities and burst open the complacent, self-satisfied Cartesian world view. The book ignited in France a movement that would soon be found in nearly every corner of Europe. Though the influence of French culture was already great, the influence of French counterculture was to be even greater. Nevertheless, the Enlightenment was by no means a strictly French phenomenon. Its greatest figures included the Scottish economist Adam Smith (1723–90), the Italian legal reformer Cesare Beccaria (1738–94), and the German philosopher Immanuel Kant (1724–1804). While in France it was first composed of anti-establishment critics, in Scotland and the German states it flourished in the universities, and in Prussia, Austria, and Russia it was propagated by the monarchy. The Enlightenment began in the 1730s and was still going strong a half-century later when its attitudes had been absorbed into the mainstream of European thought.

The Enlightenment was less a set of ideas than it was a set of attitudes. At its core was criticism, a questioning of traditional institutions, customs, and morals. Some enlightened thinkers based their critical outlook on skepticism, the belief that nothing could be known for certain. When the Scottish philosopher David Hume (1711–76) was accused of being an atheist, he countered the charge by saying he was too skeptical to be certain that God did not exist. Though Hume was a systematic philosopher, most of the great figures of the Enlightenment were not so much philosophers as savants, knowledgeable popularizers whose skills were in simplifying and publicizing a hodgepodge of new views. As one Briton put it, "I shall be ambitious to have it said of me that I have brought philosophy out of libraries and schools to dwell at tea tables and in coffeehouses." In France Enlightenment

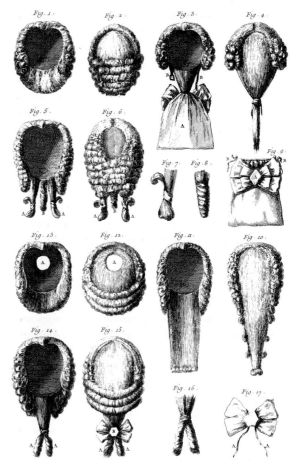

This illustration from Diderot's Encyclopedia *details the many types of wigs and tonsorial accessories worn by men in the eighteenth century. The tradition of wigwearing lingers on in British law courts.*

intellectuals were called *philosophes* and claimed all the arts and sciences as their purview. The *Encyclopedia* (35 volumes, 1751–80), edited by Denis Diderot (1713–84), was one of the greatest achievements of the age. Entitled the *Systematic Dictionary of the Sciences, Arts, and Crafts*, it attempted to summarize all acquired knowledge and to dispel all imposed superstitions. There was no better definition of a *philosophe* than that given them by one of their enemies. "Just what is a *philosophe*? A kind of monster in society who feels under no obligation towards its manners and morals, its proprieties, its politics, or its religion. One may expect anything from men of their ilk."

Enlightened thinkers attacked established institutions, above all the Church. Most enlightened thinkers were deists who believed in the existence of God on rational grounds only. Following the materialistic ideas of the new science, deists believed that nature conformed to its own material laws and operated without divine intervention. God, in a popular Enlightenment image, was like a clockmaker who constructed the elaborate mechanism, wound it, and gave the pendulum its first swing. After that the clock worked by itself. Deists were accused of being anti-Christian and they certainly opposed the ritual forms of both Catholic and Protestant worship. They also opposed the role of the Church in education, for education was the key to an enlightened view of the future. This meant, above all, conflict with the Jesuits. "Let's eat a Jesuit," was Voltaire's half-facetious comment.

Education was crucial because the Enlightenment was dominated by the idea of the British philosopher John Locke (1632–1704) that the mind was blank at birth, a *tabula rasa*—"white paper void of all characters"—and that it was filled up by experience. Contrary to the arguments of Descartes, Locke wrote in *An Essay Concerning Human Understanding* (1690) that there were no innate ideas and no good or evil that was not conditioned by experience. For Locke, as for a host of thinkers after him, good and evil were defined as pleasure and pain. We do good because it is pleasurable and we avoid evil because it is painful. Morality was a sense experience rather than a theological one. It was also relative rather than absolute. This was an observation that derived from increased interest in non-European cultures. The *Persian Letters* (1721) of Baron Montesquieu (1689–1755) was the most popular of a genre that described non-European societies that knew nothing of Christian morality.

By the middle of the eighteenth century the pleasure/pain principle enunciated by Locke had come to be applied to the foundations of social organization. If personal good was pleasure, then social good was happiness. The object of government, in the words of the Scottish moral philosopher Francis Hutcheson (1694–1746), "was the greatest happiness of the greatest number." This principle was at the core of *Crimes and Punishments* (1764), Cesare Beccaria's pioneering

work of legal reform. Laws were instituted to promote happiness within society. They had to be formulated equitably for both criminal and victim. Punishment was to act as a deterrent to crime rather than as retribution. Therefore Beccaria advocated the abolition of torture to gain confessions, the end of capital punishment, and the rehabilitation of criminals through the improvement of penal institutions. By 1776 happiness was established as one of the basic rights of man, enshrined in the American Declaration of Independence as "life, liberty, and the pursuit of happiness."

It was in refashioning the world through education and social reform that the Enlightenment revealed its orientation toward the future. *Optimism* was a word invented in the eighteenth century to express this feeling of liberation from the weight of centuries of traditions. "This is the best of all possible worlds and all things turn out for the best," was the satirical slogan of Voltaire's *Candide* (1759). But if Voltaire believed that enlightened thinkers had taken optimism too far, others believed that it had to be taken further still. At the end of *Candide* Voltaire opines that "everyone must cultivate their own garden," and it was that cultivation that ensured human progress. Progress, an idea that not all enlightened thinkers shared, was another invention of the age. It was expressed most cogently by the French philosopher the Marquis de Condorcet (1743–94) in *The Progress of the Human Mind* (1795) in which he developed an almost evolutionary view of human development from a savage state of nature to a future of harmony and international peace.

Three Enlightenment Figures

No brief summary can do justice to the diversity of enlightened thought in eighteenth-century Europe. Because it was an attitude of mind rather than a set of shared beliefs, there are many contradictory strains to follow. In his famous essay *What Is Enlightenment?* (1784) Immanuel Kant described it simply as freedom to use one's own intelligence. "I hear people clamor on all sides: Don't argue! The officer says: Don't argue, drill! The tax collector says: Don't argue, pay. The pastor says: Don't argue, believe." To all of them Kant replied: "Dare to know! Have the courage to use your own intelligence." From this point of view, the Enlightenment was as much a movement of people as of ideas. Its outstanding figures ran the gamut from aristocrats like Condorcet and Beccaria, to university professors like Smith and Kant, to those like Diderot and Jean-Jacques Rousseau (1712–78) who lived by their pens. Rousseau authored one of the most important Enlightenment tracts on education, disguised as the romantic novel *Émile* (1762) and one of the most important works on social theory, *The Social Contract* (1762), which opened with the gripping maxim "Man is born free and everywhere he is in chains." Rousseau's own life was one of loneliness and persecution and both his ideas and experiences were better suited for the period of revolution which he did not live to see than the period of Enlightenment in which he was always so uneasy. But allowing for the variety of ideas and personalities and the conscious individualism of an era discovering the importance of the self, an examination of the lives of David Hume, Baron Montesquieu, and Voltaire will capture much of the spirit of the age.

Jean-Jacques Rousseau

David Hume was born in Scotland in 1711. He came from a prosperous legal family, but as a younger son he had no prospect of living idly on the land. At the age of twelve he and his elder brother were sent to the University of Edinburgh for three years. Despite his devotion to his mother and her devotion to Calvinism, Hume early rejected Christianity. He spent the next several years reading and contemplating, having discovered a love of moral philosophy, which was then considered to be the study of human nature. At the age of twenty-seven Hume wrote his first major philosophical work, *A Treatise of Human Nature* (1739), which made absolutely no impression upon his contemporaries and did nothing to solve the financial difficulties in which he now

found himself. For a time he took a post as a merchant's clerk; then he served as a tutor; and finally he found a position as a private secretary. During the course of these various employments he continued to write, publishing a series of essays on the subject of morality and rewriting his treatise into *An Enquiry Concerning Human Understanding* (1748), his greatest philosophical work.

While his earliest writings were philosophical treatises, Hume considered himself a man of letters rather than a philosopher. Though he was extremely disappointed with the reception that his work had received—"it fell dead born from the press" was his own judgment—Hume did not engage in philosophical disputes. He twice applied for university posts and was twice rejected on the grounds of his writings against Christianity. Forced to fend for himself, Hume composed a history of England that was an immediate critical and popular success. He became the first Briton of letters to be able to live entirely on his income from writing. He visited the Continent, where he discovered that both his historical and philosophical works had achieved success. Hume's last years were occupied with his work on religion, for which he had already acquired the reputation as one of the leading skeptics and deists in Britain. He died in Edinburgh in 1776.

Hume made two seminal contributions to Enlightenment thought. In the first place, he argued that neither matter nor mind could be proved to exist with any certainty. Only perceptions existed, either as impressions of material objects or as ideas. This argument exploded the classic Cartesian synthesis of mind and matter, which dominated teaching in the schools. If human understanding was based on sensory perception rather than on reason, then there could be no certainty in the universe. Hume's second point launched a frontal attack upon established religion. If there

David Hume

could be no certainty, then the revealed truths of Christian religion could have no basis. In his historical analysis of the origins of religion Hume argued that "religion grows out of hope or fear." He attacked the core of Christian explanations based on either Providence or miracles by arguing that to anyone who understood the basis of human perception it would take a miracle to believe in miracles. Hume suppressed the publication of some of his more controversial writings on religion, which were not printed until after his death, when his work on moral philosophy and natural religion found a wide audience. He was the most penetrating of all Enlightenment thinkers and the greatest of all British philosophers.

In 1749 when Hume was in Italy and his genius was still largely unrecognized, he received in the mail a work from an admiring Frenchman, entitled *The Spirit of the Laws*. Charles-Louis de Secondat, Baron Montesquieu, was born in Bordeaux in 1689. His family were nobility of the robe, and he ultimately inherited both a large landed estate and the office of president of the Parlement of Bordeaux. He was educated first in an exclusive Catholic school and then studied law at the University of Bordeaux and in Paris. Though he was never very interested in the details of a legal career, he found the study of law intellectually challenging. After completing his education, Montesquieu settled into the routine of country life. He married a Calvinist of rather modest fortune, but a woman of unusual business skills, which were put to good effect during Montesquieu's frequent absences. The first sign of his intellectual abilities was his election to the Bordeaux Academy, a group dedicated to propagating the latest scientific and social ideas. As a member of the nobility, Montesquieu took a leading role in organizing the debates that the Academy held and even presented some of his own on topics as varied as the function of the kidneys and the causes of echoes. His satirical novel, *Persian Letters*, was published in 1721.

Persian Letters was a brilliant satire of Parisian morals, French society, and European religion all bound together by the story of a Persian despot who leaves his harem to learn about the ways of the world. The use of the Persian outsider allowed Montesquieu to comment on the absurdity of European customs in general and French practices in particular. The device of the harem allowed him to titillate his audience with exotic sexuality. The work was at once light and serious and it established Montesquieu as a new star in the literary firmament. His social standing allowed him into the very finest Parisian salons, where he cut a figure entirely different from that of the provincial magistrate of Bordeaux.

After this success, Montesquieu decided to sell his office and make the grand tour. He spent nearly two years in England for which, like Voltaire, he came to have the greatest admiration. Back in Bordeaux, Montesquieu began to assemble his thoughts for what he believed would be a great work of political theory. Though becoming progressively blind, he embarked upon a sustained program of reading in both classical and modern history. The two societies that he most admired were ancient Rome and present-day Britain, and he studied the forms of their government and the principles that animated them. *The Spirit of the Laws* was published in 1748, and despite its

The frontispiece from Montesquieu's The Spirit of the Laws *has a medallion of the author surrounded by allegorical figures, including the blind Justice. In the lower left corner are copies of the authors works.*

gargantuan size and densely packed examples, it was immediately recognized as a masterpiece. Catherine the Great of Russia kept it at her bedside, and it was the single most influential work for the framers of the United States Constitution.

In both the *Persian Letters* and *The Spirit of the Laws* Montesquieu explored how liberty could be achieved and despotism avoided. He divided all forms of government into republics, monarchies, and despotisms. Each form had its own peculiar spirit: virtue and moderation in republics, honor in monarchies, and fear in despotisms. Like each form, each spirit was prone to abuse and had to be restrained if republics were not to give way to vice and excess, monarchies to corruption, and despotisms to repression. Montesquieu classified regimes as either moderate or immoderate, and through the use of extensive historical examples attempted to demonstrate how moderation could be maintained through rules and restraints, through the spirit of the law.

For Montesquieu, a successful government was one in which powers were separated and checks and balances existed within the institutions of the state. As befit a provincial magistrate, he insisted upon the absolute separation of the judiciary from all other branches of government. The law needed to be independent and impartial and it needed to be just. Montesquieu advocated that law codes be reformed and reduced mainly to regulate crimes against persons and property. Punishment should fit the crime but should be humane. He was one of the first to advocate the abolition of torture. Like most Europeans of his age, he saw monarchy as the only realistic form of government, but he argued that for a monarchy to be successful, it needed a strong and independent aristocracy to restrain its tendency toward corruption and despotism. He based his arguments on what he believed was the case in Britain, which he praised as the only state in Europe in which liberty resided. This was one of the few points in which he was in total agreement with Voltaire, the most famous of all Enlightenment figures.

Voltaire was buried three times. It was a fitting end for a man whose career was so much larger than life. Born in Paris in 1694 into a bourgeois family with court office, François-Marie Arouet, who later took the pen name Voltaire, was educated by the Jesuits, who encouraged his

Voltaire

poetic talents and instilled in him an enduring love of literature. He was a difficult student, especially as he had already rejected the core of the Jesuits' religious doctrine. He was no less difficult as he grew and began a career as a poet and playwright. Despite his modest social background, he gained entry to the Parisian salons, where he entertained and scandalized with his irreverent wit. It was not long before he was imprisoned in the Bastille for penning verses that maligned the honor of the regent of France. Released from prison, he insulted a nobleman, who retaliated by having his servants publicly beat Voltaire. Voltaire issued a challenge for a duel, a greater insult than the first, given his low birth. Again he was sent to the Bastille and was only released on the promise that he would leave the country immediately.

Thus Voltaire found himself in Britain, where he spent two years learning English, writing plays, and enjoying his celebrity free from the dangers that celebrity entailed in France. Like Montesquieu, he identified the British with liberty, praising the ease with which the social classes met and the freedom of religion and ideas. When he returned to Paris in 1728, it was with the intention of popularizing Britain to Frenchmen.

He wrote and produced a number of plays and began writing the *Philosophical Letters* (1734), a work that not only secured his reputation but also forced him into exile, at the village of Cirey, where he moved in with the Marquise du Châtelet (1706–49). The Marquise du Châtelet, though only twenty-seven at the time of her liaison with Voltaire, was one of the leading advocates of Newtonian science in France. She built a laboratory in her home and introduced Voltaire to experimental science. While she undertook the immense challenge of translating Newton into French, Voltaire worked on innumerable projects: poems, plays, philosophical and anti-religious tracts (which she wisely kept him from publishing), and histories. It was one of the most productive periods of his life, and when the Marquise du Châtelet died in 1749, Voltaire was crushed.

Now past 50 years old, Voltaire began his travels. He was invited to Berlin by Frederick the Great, who admired him most of all the intellectuals of the age. The relationship between these two great egotists was predictably stormy and resulted in Voltaire's arrest in Frankfurt. Finally allowed to leave Prussia, Voltaire eventually settled in Geneva, where he quickly became embroiled in local politics and was none too politely asked to leave. He was tired of wandering and tired of being chased. His youthful gaiety and high spirits, which remained in Voltaire long past youth, were dealt a serious blow by the tragic earthquake in Lisbon in 1755, when thousands of people, attending church services, were killed. Optimism in the face of such a senseless tragedy was no longer possible. His black mood was revealed in *Candide* (1759), which was to become his enduring legacy. Voltaire was now a rich man and he purchased two adjacent estates on the French-Swiss border so that he could be safe from persecution on either side. In his last years, he became a social reformer, undertaking with his pen to undo the abominations of religious hatred. His motto became "abolish superstition" and his attacks upon the Church reinvigorated him for a time. He died in 1778 at the age of 84 and was buried first in Champagne.

Voltaire is remembered today for his savagely satirical *Candide*, which introduced the ivory-tower intellectual Dr. Pangloss, the overly optimistic Candide, and the very practical philosophy, "everyone must cultivate their own garden." Yet it was Voltaire's capacity to challenge all authority that was probably his greatest contribution to Enlightenment attitudes. He held nothing sacred. He questioned his own paternity and the morals of his mother; he lived openly with the Marquise du Châtelet and her husband; he once tore down a church because it obstructed his view; and he spoke as slightingly of kings and aristocrats as he did of his numerous critics. At the height of the French Revolution, Voltaire's body was removed from its resting place in Champagne and taken in great pomp to Paris, where it was interred in the Panthéon, where the heroes of the nation were put to rest. "Voltaire taught us to be free," was the slogan that the Parisian masses chanted during the funeral procession. It was an ending perhaps too solemn and conventional for one as irreverent as Voltaire. When the monarchy was restored after 1815, his bones were unceremoniously dumped in a lime pit.

The Impact of the Enlightenment

The Enlightenment was not as easily disposed of as the bones of Voltaire. A half-century of sustained critical thinking about humanity and society was bound to have its effect. As there was no single set of Enlightenment beliefs, so there was no single impact of the Enlightenment. Its general influence was felt everywhere, even seeping to the lowest strata of society. Its specific influence is harder to gauge. Paradoxically, enlightened political reform took firmer root in the east where the ideas were imported than in the west where they originated. It was absolute rulers who were most successful in borrowing Enlightenment reforms.

It is impossible to determine what part enlightened ideas and what part practical necessities played in the eastern European reform movement that began around mid-century. In at least three areas the coincidence between ideas and actions was especially strong: law, education, and the extension of religious toleration. Law was the basis of Enlightenment views of social interaction, and the influence of Montesquieu and Beccaria spread quickly. In Prussia and Russia the movement to codify and simplify the legal system did not reach fruition in the eighteenth century, but in both places it was well under way. The Prussian jurist Samuel von Cocceji (1679–1755) initiated the reform of Prussian law and legal administration. Cocceji's project was to make the enforcement of law uniform throughout the realm, to prevent judicial corruption, and to produce a single code of Prussian law. The code, finally completed in the 1790s, reflected the principles of criminal justice articulated by Beccaria. In Russia, the Law Commission summoned by Catherine the Great in 1767 never did complete its work. Nevertheless, profoundly influenced by Montesquieu, Catherine attempted to abolish tor-

Major Works of the Enlightenment

1690 *An Essay Concerning Human Understanding* (Locke)

1721 *Persian Letters* (Baron Montesquieu)

1734 *Philosophical Letters Concerning the English Nation* (Voltaire)

1739 *A Treatise of Human Nature* (Hume)

1740 *Pamela* (Richardson)

1748 *An Enquiry Concerning Human Understanding* (Hume)
The Spirit of the Laws (Baron Montesquieu)

1751–80 *Encyclopedia* (Diderot)

1759 *Candide* (Voltaire)

1762 *Émile; The Social Contract* (Rousseau)

1764 *Crimes and Punishments* (Beccaria)

1784 *What Is Enlightenment?* (Kant)

1795 *The Progress of the Human Mind* (Marquis de Condorcet)

1798 *An Essay on the Principles of Population* (Malthus)

ture and to introduce the Beccarian principle that the accused was innocent until proven guilty. In Austria, Joseph II presided over a wholesale reorganization of the legal system. Courts were centralized, laws codified, and torture and capital punishment abolished.

Enlightenment ideas also underlay the efforts to improve education in eastern Europe. The religious orders, especially the Jesuits, were the most influential educators of the age, and the Enlightenment attack upon them created a void that had to be filled by the state. Efforts at compulsory education were first undertaken in Russia under Peter the Great, but these were aimed at the compulsory education of the nobility. It was Catherine who extended the effort to the provinces, attempting to educate a generation of

Russian teachers. She was especially eager that women receive primary schooling, although the prejudice against educating women was too strong to overcome. Austrian and Prussian reforms were more successful in extending the reach of primary education, even if its content remained weak.

Religious toleration was the area in which the Enlightenment had its greatest impact in Europe, though again it was in the east that this was most visible. Freedom of worship for Catholics was barely whispered about in Britain, while neither France nor Spain were moved to tolerate Protestants. Nevertheless, within these parameters there were some important changes in the religious makeup of the western European states. In Britain, Protestant dissenters were no longer persecuted for their beliefs. By the end of the eighteenth century the number of Protestants outside the Church of England was growing, and by the early nineteenth century discrimination against Protestants was all but eliminated. In France and Spain relations between the national church and the papacy were undergoing a reorientation. Both states were asserting more independence—both theologically and financially—from Rome. The shift was symbolized by disputes over the role of the Jesuits, who were finally expelled from France in 1764 and from Spain in 1767.

In the east, enlightened ideas about religious toleration did take effect. Catherine the Great abandoned persecution of a Russian Orthodox sect known as the Old Believers. Frederick the Great was a deist himself. Prussia had always tolerated various Protestant groups, and with the conquest of Silesia it acquired a large Catholic population. Catholics were guaranteed freedom of worship, and Frederick even built a Catholic church in Berlin to symbolize this policy. Austria extended furthest enlightened ideas about toleration. Maria Theresa was a devout Catholic and actually increased religious persecution in her realm. But Joseph II rejected his mother's dogmatic position. In 1781 he issued a Patent of Toleration, which granted freedom of worship to Protestants and members of the eastern Orthodox church. The following year he extended this toleration to Jews.

Joseph's attitude toward toleration was as

practical as it was enlightened. He believed that the revocation of the Edict of Nantes at the end of the seventeenth century had been an economic disaster for France, and he encouraged religious toleration as a means to economic progress. A science of economics was first articulated during the Enlightenment. A group of French thinkers known as the *physiocrats* subscribed to the view that land was wealth and thus argued that agricultural activity, especially improved means of farming and livestock breeding, should take first priority in state reforms. As wealth came from land, taxation should be based only on land ownership, a principle that was coming into increased prominence, despite the opposition of the landowning class. Physiocratic ideas combined a belief in the sanctity of private property with the need for the state to increase agricultural output. In 1774, Louis XVI appointed the physiocrat Anne-Robert-Jacques Turgot (1727–81) minister of finance, but Turgot's radical schemes, especially for tax reform, doomed his career. Ultimately the physiocrats, like the great Scottish economic theorist Adam Smith, came to believe that government should cease to interfere with private economic activity. They articulated the doctrine *laissez faire, laissez passer*—"let it be, let it go." The ideas of Adam Smith and the physiocrats ultimately formed the basis for nineteenth-century economic reform.

If the Enlightenment did not initiate a new era, it did offer a new vision. The science of the material world opened the way for a science of the human world, whether in Hume's psychology, Montesquieu's political science, Rousseau's sociology, or Smith's economic theory. All of these subjects, which have such a powerful impact on contemporary life, had their modern origins in the Enlightenment. As the British poet Alexander Pope (1688–1744) put it: "Know then thyself, presume not God to scan/ The proper study of mankind is man." A new emphasis on self and on pleasure led to a new emphasis on happiness. All three fed into the distinctively Enlightenment idea of self-interest. Happiness and self-interest were values that would inevitably corrode the old social order, which was based upon principles of self-sacrifice and corporate identity. It was only a matter of time.

The Bourgeoisie

Bourgeois is a French word, and it carried the same tone of derision in the eighteenth century that it does today. The bourgeois was a man on the make, scrambling after money or office or title. He was neither well born nor well bred, or so said the nobility. Yet the bourgeoisie served vital functions in all European societies. They dominated trade, both nationally and internationally. They made their homes in cities and did much to improve the quality of urban life. They were the civilizing influence in urban culture, for unlike the nobility they were its permanent denizens. Perhaps most importantly, the bourgeoisie provided the safety valve between the nobility and those who were acquiring wealth and power but who lacked the advantages of birth and position. By developing their own culture and class identity, the bourgeoisie provided successful individuals with their own sense of pride and achievement and eased the explosive buildup of social resentments.

In the eighteenth century the bourgeoisie was growing in both numbers and importance. An active commercial and urban life gave many members of this group new social and political opportunities and many of them passed into the nobility through the purchase of land or office. But for those whose aspirations or abilities were different, this social group began to define its own values, which centered on the family and the home. A new interest in domestic affairs touched both men and women of the European bourgeoisie. Their homes became a social center for kin and neighbors and their outlook on family life reflected new personal relationships. Marriages were made for companionship as much as for economic advantage. Romantic love between husbands and wives was newly valued. So were children, whose futures came to dominate familial concern. Childhood was recognized as a separate stage of life and the education of children as one of the most important of all parental responsibilities. The image of the affectionate father replaced that of the hard-bitten businessman; the image of the doting mother replaced that of the domestic drudge.

Urban Elites

In the society of orders, nobility was the acid test. The world was divided into the small number of those who had it and the large number of those who did not. At the apex of the non-noble pyramid was the bourgeoisie, the elites of urban Europe whose place in the society of orders was ambiguous. Bourgeois, or burgher, simply meant town dweller, but as a social group it had come to mean wealthy town dweller. The bourgeoisie was strongest where towns were strongest: in western rather than in eastern Europe, in northern rather than southern Europe, with the notable exception of Italy. Holland was the exemplar of a bourgeois republic. More than half of the Dutch population lived in towns and there was no significant aristocratic class to compete for power. The Regents of Amsterdam were the equivalent of a European court nobility in wealth, power, and prestige, though not in the way in which they had accumulated their fortunes. The size of the bourgeoisie in various European states cannot be absolutely determined. At the end of the eighteenth century the British middle classes probably constituted around 15 percent of the population, the French bourgeoisie less than 10 percent. By contrast, the Russian or Hungarian urban elites were less than 2 percent of the population in those states.

Like the nobility, the bourgeoisie constituted a diverse group. At the top were great commercial families engaged in the expanding international marketplace and reaping the profits of trade. In wealth and power they were barely distinguishable from the nobility. At the bottom were the so-called petit-bourgeois; shopkeepers, craftsmen, and industrial employers. The solid core of the bourgeoisie was employed in trade, exchange, and service. Most were engaged in local or national commerce. Trade was the lifeblood of the city, for by itself the city could neither feed nor clothe its inhabitants. Most bourgeois fortunes were first acquired in trade. Finance was the natural outgrowth of commerce and another segment of the bourgeoisie accumulated or preserved their capital through the sophisticated financial instruments of the eighteenth century. While the very wealthy loaned directly to the central government or bought shares in overseas trading companies, most bourgeois participated in government credit markets. They purchased state bonds or lifetime annuities and lived on the interest. The costs of war flooded the urban credit markets with high-yielding and generally stable financial instruments. Finally, the bourgeoisie were members of the burgeoning professions that provided services for the rich. Medicine, law, education, and the bureaucracy were all bourgeois professions, for the cost of acquiring the necessary skills could be borne only by those already wealthy.

During the course of the eighteenth century, this combination of occupational groups was expanding both in numbers and in importance all over Europe. So was the bourgeois habitat. The urbanization of Europe continued steadily throughout the eighteenth century. A greater percentage of the European population were living in towns and a greater percentage were living in large towns of over 10,000 inhabitants which, of necessity, were developing complex socioeconomic structures. In France alone there were probably over a hundred such towns, each requiring the services of the bourgeoisie and providing opportunities for their expansion. And the larger the metropolis the greater the need. In 1600 only twenty European cities contained as many as 50,000 people; in 1700 that number had risen to thirty-two; and by 1800 to forty-eight. During the course of the eighteenth century the number of cities with 75,000 inhabitants doubled. London, the largest city, had grown to 865,000, a remarkable feat considering that in 1665 over a quarter of the London population died in the Great Plague. In such cities the demand for lawyers and doctors, for merchants and shopkeepers was almost insatiable.

Besides wealth, the urban bourgeoisie shared another characteristic: mobility. The aspiration of the bourgeoisie was to become noble, either through office or by acquiring rural estates. In Britain, a gentleman was still defined by life-style. "All are accounted gentlemen in England who maintain themselves without manual labor." Many trading families left their wharves and countinghouses to acquire rural estates, live off rents, and practice the openhanded hospitality of a gentleman. In France and Spain, nobility could still be purchased, though the price was constantly going up. For the greater bourgeoisie, the transition was easy; for the lesser, the failure to move up was all the more frustrating for being just beyond their grasp. The bourgeoisie did not only imagine their discomfort, they were made to feel it at every turn. They were the butt of jokes, of theater, and of popular songs. They were the first victims in the shady financial dealings of the crown and court, the first casualties in urban riots. Despised from above, envied from below, the bourgeoisie were uncomfortable with the present yet profoundly conservative about the future. The one consolation to their perpetual misery was that as a group they got richer and richer. And as a group they began to develop a distinctive culture that reflected their qualities and aspirations.

The Charm of the Bourgeoisie

Many bourgeoisie viewed their condition as temporary and accepted the pejorative connotations of the word itself. They had little desire to defend a social group out of which they fervently longed to pass. Others, whose aspirations were lower, were nevertheless uncomfortable with the status that they had already achieved. They had no ambition to wear the silks and furs reserved for the nobility or to attend the opening night at the opera decked in jewels and finery. In fact, such ostentation was alien to their existence and to the success that they had achieved. There was a real tension between the values of noble and bourgeois. The ideal noble was idle, wasteful, and ostentatious; the ideal bourgeois was industrious, frugal, and sober. Voltaire, who made his fortune as a financial speculator rather than a man of letters, aped the life-style of the nobility. But he could never allow himself to be cheated by a tradesman, a mark of his origins. When Louis XVI tried to make household economies in the wake of a financial crisis, critics said that "he acts like a bourgeois."

Even if the bourgeoisie did not constitute a class, they did share certain attitudes that constituted a culture. The wealthy among them participated in the new world of consumption, whether they did so lavishly or frugally. For those who aspired to more than their birth allowed, there was a loosening of the strict codes of dress that reserved certain fabrics, decorative materials, and styles to the nobility. Merchants and bankers could now be seen in colored suits or with pipings made of cloth of gold; their wives could be seen in furs and silks. They might acquire silverware, even if they did not go so far as the nobility and have a coat of arms engraved upon it. Coaches and carriages were also becoming common among the bourgeoisie, to take them on the Sunday rides through the town gardens or to their weekend retreats in the suburbs. Parisian merchants, even master craftsmen like clockmakers, were now acquiring suburban homes although they could not afford to retire to them for the summer months.

But more and more, the bourgeoisie was beginning to travel. In Britain whole towns were established to cater to leisure travelers. The southwestern town of Bath, which was rebuilt in the eighteenth century, was the most popular of all European resort towns, famous since Roman times for the soothing qualities of its waters. Bath was soon a social center as notable for its marriage market as for its recreations. Brighton, a seaside resort on the south coast, quadrupled in size in the second half of the eighteenth century. Bathing—what we would call swimming—either for health or recreation, became a middle-class fad, displacing traditional fears of the sea.

The leisure that wealth bestowed on the bourgeoisie quickly became, in good bourgeois fashion, commercialized. Theater and music halls for both light and serious productions proliferated. By the 1760s an actual theater district had arisen in London and was attracting audiences of over twenty thousand a week. London was unusual, both for its size and for the number of well-to-do visitors who patronized its cultural events. The size of the London audiences enabled the German-born composer Georg Friedrich Handel (1685–1759) to earn a handsome living by performing and directing concerts. He was one of the few musicians in the eighteenth century to live without noble patronage. But it was not only in Britain that theater and music flourished. Voltaire's plays were performed before packed houses in Paris, with the author himself frequently in attendance to bask in the adulation of the largely bourgeois audiences who attended them. In Venice it was estimated that over 1,200 operas were produced in the eighteenth century.

Rome and Milan were even better known, and Naples was the center for Italian opera. Public concerts were a mark of bourgeois culture, for the court nobility was entertained at the royal palaces or great country houses. Public concerts began in Hamburg in the 1720s and Frederick the Great helped establish the Berlin Opera House some decades later.

Theater and concert going were part of the new attitude toward socializing that was one of the greatest contributions of the Enlightenment. Enlightened thinkers spread their views in the salons, and the salons soon spawned the academies, local scientific societies which, though led and patronized by provincial nobles, included large numbers of bourgeois members. The academies sponsored essay competitions, built up libraries, and became the local center for intellectual interchange. A less structured form of sociability took place in the coffeehouses and tearooms that came to be a feature of even small provincial towns. In the early eighteenth century there were over two thousand London coffee shops where men—for the coffeehouse was largely a male preserve—could talk politics, read the latest newspapers and magazines, and indulge their taste for this still-exotic beverage. More exclusive clubs were also a form of middle-class sociability, some centering on political issues, some like the Chambers of Commerce centering on professional interests. Parisian clubs, called *sociétés*, covered a multitude of diverse interests. Literary *sociétés* were the most popular, maintaining their purpose by forbidding drinking, eating, and gambling on their premises.

Above all, bourgeois culture was literate culture. Wealth and leisure led to mental pursuits—if not always to intellectual ones. The proliferation of relatively cheap printed material had an enormous impact on the lives of those who were able to afford it. Holland and Britain were the most literate European societies and also, because of the absence of censorship, the centers of European printing. This was the first great period of the newspaper and the magazine. The first daily newspaper appeared in London in 1702; eighty years later, thirty-seven provincial towns had their own newspapers, while the London papers were read all over Britain. Then as now, the newspaper was as much a vehicle for advertise-

L'Amour au Théâtre Français (Love in the French Theatre) *(ca. 1716), by Antoine Watteau. The painting is thought to portray a scene from* Les Fêtes de l'Amour et de Bacchus, *a comic opera composed in 1672.*

ment as for news. News reports tended to be bland, avoiding controversy and concentrating on general national and international events. Advertising, on the other hand, tended to be lurid, promising cures for incurable ills, and the most exquisite commodities at the most reasonable prices. For entertainment and serious political commentary, the British reading public turned to magazines, of which there were over 150 separate titles by the 1780s. The most famous were *The Spectator*, which ran in the early part of the century and did much to set the tone for a cultured middle-class life, and the *Gentleman's Magazine*, which ran in the mid-century and was said to have had a circulation of nearly fifteen thousand. The longest-lived of all British magazines was *The Ladies Diary*, which continued in existence from 1704 to 1871 and doled out self-improvement, practical advice, and fictional romances in equal proportion.

The Ladies Diary was not the only literature aimed at the growing number of leisured and lettered bourgeois woman. Though enlightened thinkers could be ambivalent about the place of women in the new social order, they generally stressed the importance of female education and welcomed women's participation in intellectual pursuits. Whether it was new ideas about women or simply the fact that more women had leisure, a growing body of both domestic literature and light entertainment was available to them. This included a vast number of teach-yourself books aimed at instructing women how best to organize domestic life or how to navigate the perils of polite society. Moral instruction, particularly on the themes of obedience and sexual fidelity, was also popular. But the greatest output directed toward women was in the form of fanciful romances, from which a new genre emerged. The novel first appeared in its modern form in the 1740s. Samuel Richardson (1689–1761) wrote *Pamela* (1740), the story of a maid servant who successfully resisted the advances of her master until he finally married her. It was composed in long episodes, or chapters, that developed Pamela's character and told her story at the expense of the overt moral message that was Richardson's original intention. Richardson's novels were printed in installments and helped to drive up the circulation of national magazines.

Family Life

While the public life of the bourgeoisie can be measured in the sociability of the coffeehouse and the academy, private life must be measured in the home. There a remarkable transformation was under way, one that the bourgeoisie shared with the nobility. In the pursuit of happiness encouraged by the Enlightenment, one of the newest joys was domesticity. The image—and sometimes the reality—of the happy home, where love was the bond between husband and wife and care between parents and children, came to dominate both the literary and visual arts. Only those wealthy enough to afford to dispense with women's work could partake of the new domesticity, only those touched by Enlightenment ideas could attempt to make the change. But where it occurred, the transformation in the nature of family life was one of the most profound alterations in eighteenth-century culture.

The first step toward the transformation of family relationships was in centering the conjugal family in the home. In the past, the family was a less important structure for most people than the social groups to which they belonged or the neighborhood in which they lived. Marriage was an economic partnership at one end and a means to carry on lineage at the other. Individual fulfillment was not an object of marriage and this attitude could be seen among the elites in the high level of arranged marriages, the speed with which surviving spouses remarried, and the formal and often brutal personal relationships between husbands and wives.

Patriarchy was the dominant value within the family. Husbands ruled over wives and children, making all of the crucial decisions that affected both the quality of their lives and their futures. As late as the middle of the eighteenth century a British judge established the "rule of thumb," which asserted that a husband had a legal right to beat his wife with a stick, but the stick should be no thicker than a man's thumb. It was believed that children were stained with the sin of Adam at birth and that only the severest upbringing could clean some of it away. In nearly two hundred child-rearing advice books published in England before the middle of the eighteenth century, only three did not advise the beating of children. John Wesley (1703–91), the founder of Methodism, remembered his own mother's dictum that "children should learn to fear the rod and cry softly." Children were sent out first for wet-nursing, then at around the age of seven for boarding, either at school or in a trade, and finally into their own marriages.

There can be no doubt that this profile of family life began to change, especially in western Europe, during the second half of the eighteenth century. Though the economic elements of marriage remained strong—newspapers actually advertised the availability of partners and the dowries or annual income that they would bring to the marriage—other elements now appeared. Fed by an unending stream of stories and novels and a new desire for individual happiness, romantic and sexual attraction developed into a factor in marriage. Potential marriage partners were no longer kept away from each other or smothered by chaperons. The social season of polite society gave greater latitude to courtship in which prospective partners could dance, dine, and converse with each other in order to determine compatibility. Perhaps more importantly, the role of potential spouses in choosing a partner appears to have increased. This was a subtle matter, for even in earlier centuries parents did not simply assign a spouse to their children. But by the eighteenth century adolescents themselves searched for their own marriage partners and exercised a strong negative voice in identifying unsuitable ones.

The quest for compatibility, no less than the quest for romantic love, led to a change in personal relationships between spouses. The extreme formality of the past was gradually breaking down. Husbands and wives began spending more time with each other, developing common interests and pastimes. Their personal life began to change. For the first time houses were built to afford the couple privacy from their children, their servants, and their guests. Rooms were designed for specific functions and were set off by hallways. Corridors were an important innovation in creating privacy. In earlier architecture one walked through a room to the next one behind it. Now rooms were separated and doors could be closed. This new design allowed for an intimate life that earlier generations did not find necessary

The Snatched Kiss, *or* The Stolen Kiss *(1750s), by Jean-Honoré Fragonard, was one of the "series paintings" popular in the late eighteenth century. A later canvas entitled* The Marriage Contract *shows the next step in the lives of the lovers.*

and which they could not, in any case, put into practice.

Couples had more time for each other because they were beginning to limit the size of their families. There were a number of reasons for this development, which again pertained only to the upper classes. For one thing, child mortality rates were declining among wealthy social groups. Virulent epidemic diseases like the plague, which knew no class lines, were gradually disappearing. Moreover, though there were few medical breakthroughs in this period, sanitation was improving. Bearing fewer children had an enormous impact on the lives of women, reducing the danger of death and disablement in childbirth and giving them leisure time to pursue domestic tasks. This is not to say that the early part of a woman's marriage was not dominated by children; in fact, because of new attitudes toward child rearing it may have been so dominated more than ever. Many couples appear to have made a conscious decision to space births, though success was limited by the fact that the most common technique of birth control was *coitus interruptus*, or withdrawal.

The transformation in the quality of relationships between spouses was mirrored by an even greater transformation in attitudes toward children. There were many reasons why childhood now took on a new importance. Decline in mortality rates had a profound psychological impact. Parents could feel that their emotional investment in their children had a greater chance of fulfillment. But equally important were the new ideas about education, especially Locke's belief that the child enters into the world a blank slate whose personality is created through early education. This view not only placed a new responsibility upon parents but also gave them the concept of childhood as a stage through which individuals passed. This idea could be seen in the commercial sphere as well as in any other. In 1700 there was not a single shop in London that sold children's toys exclusively; by the 1780s there were toyshops everywhere, three of which sold nothing but rocking horses. Children's toys abounded: soldiers and forts; dolls and dollhouses. The jigsaw puzzle was invented in the 1760s as a way to teach children geography. There were also shops that sold nothing but clothes specifically designed for children, no longer simply adult clothes in miniature.

Most important of all was the development of materials for the education of children. This took place in two stages. At first so-called children's books were books whose purpose was to help adults teach children. Later came books directed at children themselves with large print, entertaining illustrations, and nonsensical characters, usually animals who taught moral lessons. In Britain the Little Pretty Pocket Book series, created by John Newbery (1713–67), not only encompassed educational primers but also included books for the entertainment of the child. Newbery published a Mother Goose book of nursery rhymes and created the immortal character of Miss Goody Two Shoes. Instruction and entertainment also lay behind the development of children's playing cards, in which the French specialized. Dice games, like one in which a child made a journey across Europe, combined geographical instruction with the amusement of competition.

The commercialization of childhood was, of course, directed at adults. The new books and games that were designed to enhance a child's education not only had to be purchased by parents but had to be used by them as well. More and more mothers were devoting their time to their children. Among the upper classes the practice of wet nursing began to decline. Mothers wanted to nurture their infants both literally by breast-feeding and figuratively by teaching them. Children became companions to be taken on outings to the increasing number of museums or shows of curiosities, which began to discount children's tickets by the middle of the century.

The preconditions of this transformation of family life could not be shared by the population at large. Working women could afford neither the cost of instructional materials for their children nor the time to use them. Ironically, they now began using wet nurses, once the privilege of the wealthy, for increasingly a working woman's labor was the margin of survival for her family. Working women enjoyed no privacy in the hovels in which they lived with large families in single rooms. Wives and children were still beaten by husbands and fathers and were unacquainted with enlightened ideas of the worth of the individual and the innocence of the child. By the end of the eighteenth century two distinct family cultures coexisted in Europe, one based on companionate marriage and the affective bonds of parents and children, the other based on patriarchal dominance and the family as an economic unit.

The Masses

The paradox of the eighteenth century was that for the masses life was getting better by getting worse. More Europeans were surviving than ever before, more food was available to feed them; there was more housing, better sanitation, even better charities. Yet for all of this, there was more misery. Those who would have succumbed to disease or starvation a century before now survived from day to day, beneficiaries—or victims—of increased farm production and improved agricultural marketing. The market economy organized a more effective use of land, but it created a widespread social problem. The landless agrarian laborer of the eighteenth century was the counterpart of the sixteenth-century sturdy beggar. In the cities, the plight of the poor was as desperate as ever. Men and women sold their labor or their bodies for a pittance while beggars slept at every doorway. Even the most openhearted charitable institutions were unable to cope with the massive increase in the poor. By the thousands, mothers abandoned their children to the foundling hospitals, where it was believed they would have a better chance of survival, even though hospital death rates were near 80 percent.

Not all members of the lower orders succumbed to poverty or despair. In fact, many were able to benefit from existing conditions to lead a more fulfilling life than ever before. The richness of popular culture, signified by a spread of literacy into the lower reaches of European society, was

Beggar Feeding a Child, *by Giacomo Ceruti. Every eighteenth-century European city had its legion of beggars. This man has done well enough to be able to feed himself and his little daughter for one more day.*

one indication of this change. So too were the reforms urged by enlightened thinkers to improve basic education and to improve the quality of life in the cities. For that segment of the lower orders that could keep its head above water, the eighteenth century offered new opportunities and new challenges.

Breaking the Cycle

Of all the legacies of the eighteenth century, none was more fundamental than the steady increase in European population that began around 1740. This was not the first time that Europe had experienced sustained population growth, but it was the first time that such growth was not checked by a demographic crisis. Breaking the cycle of population growth and crisis was a momentous event in European history despite the fact that it went unrecorded at the time and unappreciated for centuries after.

The figures tell one part of the story. In 1700 European population is estimated to have been 120 million. By 1800 it had grown 50 percent to over 180 million. And the aggregate hides significant regional variations. While France, Spain, and Italy expanded between 30 and 40 percent, Prussia doubled and Russia and Hungary may have tripled in number. Britain increased by 80 percent from about 5 to 9 million, but the rate of growth was accelerating. In 1695 the English population stood at 5 million. It took 62 years to add the next million and 24 years to add the million after that. In 1781 the population was 7 million, but it took only 13 years to reach 8 million and only 10 more years to reach 9 million. Steady population growth had continued without significant checks for well over half a century.

Ironically, the traditional pattern of European population found its theorist at the very moment that it was about to disappear. In 1798 Thomas Malthus (1766–1834) published *An Essay on the Principles of Population*. Reflecting on the history of European population, Malthus observed the cyclical pattern by which growth over one or two generations was checked by a crisis that significantly reduced population. From these lower levels new growth began until it was checked and the cycle repeated itself. Because people increased more quickly than did food supplies, the land could only sustain a certain level of population. When that level was near, population became prone to a demographic check. Malthus divided population checks into two categories, positive and preventive. Positive checks were war, disease, and famine, all of which Malthus believed were natural, although brutal, means of population control. Famine was the obvious result of the failure of food supplies to keep pace with demand; war was the competition for scarce resources; and disease often accompanied both. It was preventive checks that most interested Malthus. These were the means by which societies could limit their growth to avoid the devastating consequences of positive checks. Celibacy, late marriages, and sexual abstinence were among the choices of which Malthus approved, though abortion, infanticide, and contraception were also commonly practiced.

In the sixteenth and seventeenth centuries, the dominant pattern of the life cycle was high infant and child mortality, late marriages, and early death. All controlled population growth. Infant and child mortality rates were staggering: only half of all those born reached the age of ten. Late marriage was the only effective form of birth control—given the strong social taboos against sexual relations outside marriage—for a late marriage reduced a woman's childbearing years. Women in western Europe generally married between the ages of twenty-four and twenty-six; they normally ceased bearing children at the age of forty. But not all marriages lasted this fourteen- or sixteen-year span, as one or the other partner died. On average, the childbearing period for most women was between ten and twelve years, long enough to endure six pregnancies, which would result in three surviving children. (See Special Feature, "Giving Birth to the Eighteenth Century," pp. 600–601.)

Three surviving children for every two adults would, of course, have resulted in a 50 percent rise in population in every generation. Celibacy was one limiting factor, cities were another. Perhaps as much as 15 percent of the population in western Europe remained celibate either by entering religious orders that imposed celibacy or by lacking the personal or financial attributes necessary to make a match. Religious orders that enforced

celibacy were still central features of Catholic societies, and "spinsters," as unmarried women were labeled, were increasing everywhere. Cities were like sticky webs, trapping the surplus rural population for the spiders of disease, famine, and exposure to devour. Throughout the early modern period, urban areas grew through migration. Settled town dwellers might have been able to sustain their own numbers despite the unsanitary conditions of cities, but it was migrants who brought about the cities' explosive growth. Rural migrants accounted for the appallingly high urban death rates. When we remember that the largest European cities were continuously growing—London from 200,000 in 1600 to 675,000 in 1750; Paris from 220,000 to 576,000; Rome from 105,000 to 156,000; Madrid from 49,000 to 109,000; Vienna from 50,000 to 175,000—then we can appreciate how many countless thousands of immigrants perished before marriage. If urban perils were not enough, there were still the positive checks. Plagues carried away hundreds of thousands, wars halved populations of places in their path, and famine overwhelmed the weak and the poor. The worst famine in European history came as late as 1697, when one-third of the population of Finland starved to death.

The late seventeenth and early eighteenth centuries was a period of population stagnation if not actual decline. It was not until the third or fourth decade of the eighteenth century that another growth cycle began. It rapidly gained momentum throughout the Continent and showed no signs of abating after two full generations. More importantly, this upward cycle revealed unusual characteristics. In the first place fertility was increasing. This had several causes. In a few areas, most notably in Britain, women were marrying younger, thereby increasing their childbearing years. This pattern was also true in eastern Europe where women traditionally married younger. In the late eighteenth century the average age at marriage for Hungarian women had dropped to 18.6. Elsewhere, most notably in France, the practice of wet nursing was becoming more common among the masses. As working women increasingly took jobs outside the house, they were less able to nurse their own children. Finally, sexual activity outside marriage was rising. Illegitimacy rates, especially in the last decades of the century, were spurting everywhere. Over the course of the century they rose by 60 percent in France, more than doubled in England, and nearly quadrupled in Germany. So, too, were the rates of premarital pregnancy on the rise. The number of couples rushed to the altar in 1800 was nearly double that before 1750 in most of western Europe.

But increasing fertility was only part of the picture. More significant was decreasing mortality. The positive checks of the past were no longer as potent. European warfare not only diminished in scale after the middle of the century, it changed location as well. Rivalry for colonial empires removed the theater of conflict from European communities. So did the increase in naval warfare. The damage caused by war had always been more by aftershock than by actual fighting. The destruction and pillage of crops and the wholesale slaughter of livestock created food shortages that weakened local populations for the diseases that came in train with the armies. As the virulence of warfare abated, so did that of epidemic disease. The plague had all but disappeared from western Europe by the middle of the eighteenth century. The widespread practice of quarantine, especially in Hungary, which had been the crucial bridge between eastern and western epidemics, went far to eradicate the scourge of centuries.

Without severe demographic crises to maintain the cyclical pattern, the European population began a gentle but continuous rise. Urban sanitation, at least for permanent city dwellers, was becoming more effective. Clean water supplies, organized waste and sewage disposal, and strict quarantines were increasingly part of urban regulations. The use of doctors and trained midwives helped lower the incidence of stillbirth and decreased the number of women who died in childbirth. Almost everywhere levels of infant and child mortality were decreasing. More people were being born, more were surviving the first ten dangerous years, and thus more were marrying and reproducing. Increased fertility and decreased mortality could have only one result: renewed population growth. No wonder Malthus was worried.

Daily Bread

In the past, if warfare or epidemic diseases failed to check population growth, famine would have done the job. How the European economy conquered famine in the eighteenth century is a complicated story. There was no single breakthrough that accounts for the ability to feed the tens of millions of additional people who now inhabited the continent. Holland and Britain, at the cutting edge of agricultural improvement, employed dynamic new techniques that would ultimately provide the means to support continued growth, but most European agriculture was still mired in the time-honored practices that had endured for centuries. Still, not everyone could be fed or fed adequately. Widespread famine might have disappeared, but slow starvation and chronic undernourishment had not. It is certainly the case that hunger was more common at the end of the eighteenth century than at the beginning and that the nutritional content of a typical diet may have reached its lowest point in European history.

Nevertheless, the capacity to sustain rising levels of population can only be explained in terms of agricultural improvement. Quite simply, European farmers were now producing more food and marketing it better. In the most advanced societies this was a result of conscious efforts to make agriculture more efficient. In traditional open-field agriculture, communities quickly ran up against insurmountable obstacles to growth. The three-field crop rotation system left a significant proportion of land fallow each year, while the concentration on subsistence cereal crops progressively eroded the land that was in production. Common farming was only as strong as the weakest member of the community. There was little incentive for successful individuals to plow profits back into the land, either through the purchase of equipment or the increase of livestock. Livestock was a crucial variable in agricultural improvement. As long as there was only enough food for humans to eat, only essential livestock could be kept alive over the winter. Oxen, which were still the ordinary beasts of burden, and pigs and poultry, which required only minimal feed, were the most common. But

Giving Birth to the Eighteenth Century

"In sorrow thou shalt bring forth children." Such was Eve's punishment for eating of the forbidden tree, and that sorrow continued for numberless generations. Childbirth was painful, dangerous, and, all too often, deadly. Though successful childbirth needed no outside intervention whatsoever—there were no obstetricians in caves—without the accumulated wisdom of the ages, babies and mothers routinely perished. That wisdom was passed from mother to daughter and finally was accumulated by skilled women who practiced the craft of midwifery. Every village, no matter how small, had women who were capable of assisting others in childbirth. Midwives' skills ranged widely, from the use of herbal potions and strong drink to ease the pain of labor to a rudimentary understanding of how to assist a complicated delivery when the fetus was not in the proper position.

Midwives, who until the late seventeenth century were always women, were part of the support group that attended a woman during her labor. Typically, childbirth was a social occasion for women. Along with the midwife would be a wet nurse and female kin and neighbors, who would offer encouragement, bring refreshments, and tend to the ordinary chores that the pregnant woman would otherwise have performed herself. Without chemicals to induce contractions and without the ability to intervene in the delivery,

labor was usually a long-drawn-out affair. Ordinarily, it did not take place in bed, but rather in a room or a part of a room that had been set aside for the occasion. By the eighteenth century, at least in larger urban areas, poor women, who had no separate space for labor, could give birth in lying-in hospitals. Within the birthing room, the conclave of women was much like a social gathering. The pregnant woman was advised to adopt any positions that made her feel comfortable; standing and walking were favored in the belief that the effects of gravity helped the baby move downward. The woman might sit on a neighbor's lap or on a birthing stool, a chair open at the bottom, during contractions and delivery.

Most midwives subscribed to the philosophy of letting nature take its course. Because the difficulties and length of labor differed markedly from woman to woman, the midwife's most important contribution was to offer comfort and reassurance based on her long experience. By the seventeenth century manuals for midwives began to be published, some of them written by women, but most by male doctors whose surgical experiences provided them with ideas and information that were valuable to childbearing. Midwives and doctors were always at daggers drawn. Trained physicians increasingly saw childbirth as a process that could be improved by the application of

new medical knowledge, but as childbirth was a female experience, midwives jealously guarded their role in it. No matter how skilled they were, they were denied access to medical training that might have enabled them to develop lucrative practices on their own. Thus they had no intention of letting male doctors into their trade. For a time the compromise was the handbooks, which contained guides to anatomy, descriptions of the most common complications, and the direst warnings to call trained physicians when serious problems arose.

By the beginning of the eighteenth century the "man-midwife" had made his appearance in western Europe. Medically trained and usually experienced in other forms of surgery, the emergence of the man-midwife led to a number of breakthroughs in increasing the safety of childbirth. There can be no question that more mothers and children survived as a

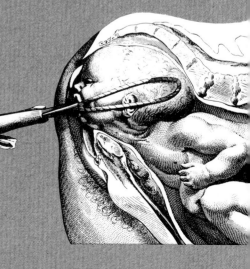

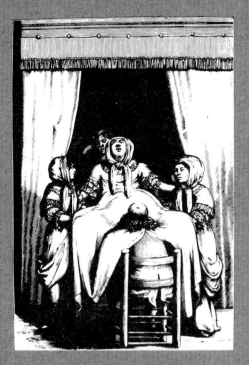

result of the man-midwives' knowledge and skills. But at the same time, the social experience of childbirth changed dramatically. What had been a female rite of passage, experienced by and with other women, now became a private event experienced by an individual woman and her male doctor. As female midwives were still excluded from medical training and licensing, their ability to practice their trade eroded in the face of new techniques and information to which they were denied access.

Though most man-midwives gained their training in hospitals where the poor came to give birth, they practiced mostly among the rich. New attitudes toward marriage and toward children made the pain and danger of childbirth less acceptable to husbands who sought every possible remedy they could afford. British and French man-midwives made large for-

tunes practicing their trade. Their first task was to ascertain that the fetus was in the proper position to descend. In order to do this, however, they had to make an examination that was socially objectionable. Though advanced thinkers could face their man-midwife with the attitude "I considered that through modesty I was not to give up my life"—as one English noblewoman reasoned—many women and more husbands were unprepared for the actual practice of a man. Thus students were taught as much about bedside manner as about medicine. They were not to examine the patient unless there was another person present in the room, they were not to ask direct questions, and they were not to face the patient during any of their procedures. They were taught to keep a linen on top of the woman's abdomen and to make the examination only by touch— incredulous students were reminded that the most famous French man-midwife was blind! If the fetus was in the correct position, nothing further would be done until the delivery itself. It was only when the fetus was in what was labeled an "unnatural" position that the skill of the physician came into play.

For the most part, a child that could not be delivered head first, face down was in serious risk of being stillborn and the mother in serious risk of dying in labor. This was the problem to which the physicians addressed themselves in the eighteenth century and for which they found remarkable solutions. Most answers came from better understanding of

female anatomy and a better visualization of the way in which the fetus moved during labor. The first advance was the realization that the fetus could be turned while still in the womb. Pressure applied on the outside of the stomach, especially in early stages of labor, could help the fetus drop down correctly. A baby who emerged feet first had to be turned face down before it was pulled through the birth canal.

For babies who could not be manually manipulated, the greatest advance of the eighteenth century was the invention of the forceps, or the *tire-tête* as the French called them. With forceps the physician could pull the baby by force when the mother was incapable of delivery. Forceps were used mostly in breech births but were also a vital tool when the baby was too large to pass through the cervix by contraction. The forceps were invented in Britain in the middle of the seventeenth century but were kept secret for more than fifty years. During that time they were used by three generations of a single family of man-midwives. In the eighteenth century they came into general use when the Scotsman William Smellie (1697–1765) developed a short, leather-covered instrument that enabled the physician to do as little damage as possible to either mother or child. Obstetrics now emerged as a specialized branch of medical practice. If neither the pain nor the sorrow of childbirth could be eliminated, its dangers could be lessened.

few animals meant little manure and without manure the soil could not easily be regenerated.

It was not until the middle of the seventeenth century that solutions to these problems began to appear. The first change was consolidation of landholdings so that traditional crop rotations could be abandoned. A second innovation was the introduction of fodder crops, some of which—like clover—added nutrients to the soil, while others—like turnips—were used to feed livestock. Better grazing and better winter feed increased the size of herds, while new techniques of animal husbandry, particularly crossbreeding, produced hardier strains. It was quite clear that the key to increased production lay in better fertilization, and by the eighteenth century some European farmers had broken through the "manure barrier." Larger herds, the introduction of clover crops, the use of human waste from towns, and even the first experiments with lime as an artificial fertilizer were all part of the new agricultural methods. The impact of new farming techniques was readily apparent. In Britain and Holland, where they were used most extensively, grain yields exceeded ten kernels harvested for

each one planted, while in eastern Europe, where they were hardly known, yields were less than five to one.

Along with the new crops that helped nourish both soil and animals came new crops that helped nourish people. Indian corn, or maize, was a staple crop for Native Americans and gradually came to be grown in most parts of western Europe. Maize not only had higher nutritional value than most other cereals, it also yielded more food per acre than traditional grains, reaching levels as high as forty to one. So, too, did the potato, which also entered the European diet from the New World. The potato grew in poor soil, required less labor, and yielded an abundant and nutritious harvest. It rapidly took hold in Ireland and parts of Prussia, from which it spread into eastern Europe. French and Spanish peasants reluctantly introduced it into their diet. Wherever it took root, the potato quickly established itself as survival food. It allowed families to subsist on smaller amounts of land and with less capital outlay. As a result, potato cultivation enabled people in some parts of Europe to marry younger and thus to produce more children.

It must be stressed, however, that these new developments involved only a very narrow range of producers. The new techniques were expensive and knowledge of the new crops spread slowly. Change had to overcome both inertia and intransigence. With more mouths to feed, profits from agriculture soared without landowners having to lift a finger. Only the most ambitious were interested in improvement. At the other end, peasant farmers were more concerned with failure than success. An experiment that did not work could devastate a community; one that did only meant higher taxes. Thus the most important improvements in agricultural production were more traditional ones. Basically, there was an increase in the amount of land that was utilized for growing. In most of western Europe there was little room for agricultural expansion, but in the east there remained great tracts of uncultivated land. In Russia, Prussia, and Hungary hundreds of thousands of new acres came under the plow, though it must be admitted that some of it simply went to replace land that had been wastefully exhausted in previous generations. In one German province, nearly 75 percent more land was in cultivation at

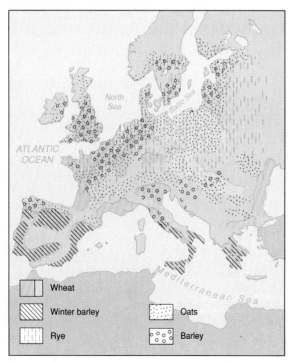

Cereal Crops

Agricultural techniques are illustrated in this plate from Diderot's Encyclopedia. *In the foreground, a man steers a high-wheeled, horse-drawn plow while a woman operates a hopper device to sow seeds.*

the end of the eighteenth century than had been at the beginning. Even in the west, drainage schemes and forest clearance expanded productive capacity.

There was also an upswing in the efficiency with which agricultural products were marketed. From the seventeenth century onward, market agriculture was gradually replacing subsistence agriculture in most parts of Europe. Market agriculture had the advantage of allowing specialization on farms. Single-crop farming enabled farmers to benefit from the peculiarities of their own soil and climate. They could then exchange their surplus for the range of crops they needed to subsist. Market exchange was facilitated by improved transportation and communication and above all by the increase in the population of towns, which provided demand. On a larger scale, market agriculture was able to respond to regional harvest failures in a way that subsistence agriculture could not. The most hated figure in the eighteenth century was the "grain engrosser,"

a middleman who bought up local surplus and shipped it away. Engrossers were accused of driving up prices—which they did—and of creating famines—which they did not. In fact, the national and international trade in large quantities of grain evened out regional variations in harvests and went a long way toward reducing local grain shortages. The upkeep of roads, the building of canals, and the clearing of waterways created a national lifeline for the movement of grain.

Finally, it is believed that the increase in agricultural productivity owed something to a change in climate that took place in the late eighteenth century. This is very difficult to substantiate and impossible to explain. It is thought that the annual ring of growth inside trees is an indicator of changes in climate. Hot years produce markedly different rings than cold ones; wet years are etched differently than dry ones. Examination of trees that are centuries old seems to indicate that the European climate was unusually cold and wet during the seventeenth century—some have even called it a little ice age—and that it gradually warmed during the eighteenth century. Even moderate climatic change, when combined with new techniques, new crops, expanded cultivation, and improved marketing, would go a long way toward explaining how so many more people were being fed at the end of the eighteenth century.

The Plight of the Poor

"Of every ten men one is a beggar, five are too poor to give him alms, three more are ill at ease, embarrassed by debts and lawsuits, and the tenth does not represent a hundred thousand families." So observed an eighteenth-century Frenchman about the distribution of wealth in his country. There can be no doubt that the most serious social problem of the eighteenth century centered on the explosion of poor people throughout Europe. There was grim irony in the fact that advances in the production and distribution of food and the retreat of war and plague allowed more people to survive from hand to mouth than ever before. Where their ancestors had succumbed to quick death from disease or starvation, they eked out a miserable existence of constant hunger and chronic pain with death at the end of a seemingly endless corridor.

It is impossible to gauge the number of European poor or to separate them into categories of greater and greatest misery. The truly indigent, the starving poor, probably composed 10 to 15 percent of most societies, perhaps as many as 20 million people throughout the Continent. They were most prevalent in towns but were an increasing burden on the countryside, where they wandered in search of agricultural employment. The wandering poor had no counterpart in the east, where serfdom kept everyone tied to the land, but the hungry and unsheltered certainly did. Yet the problem of poverty was not only to be seen among the destitute. In fact, the uniqueness of the poor in the eighteenth century is that they were drawn from social groups that even in the hungry times of the early seventeenth century had been successful subsistence producers. Perhaps another 40 percent of the population in western Europe was described by contemporaries as those without a fixed interest: in the country, those without land; in the towns, those without steady jobs.

It was easy to see why poverty was increasing. The relentless advance of population drove up the price of food and drove down the price of wages. In the second half of the eighteenth century, the cost of living in France rose by over 60 percent while wages rose only by 25 percent. In Spain the cost of living increased by 100 percent while wages rose only 20 percent. Only in Britain did wages nearly keep pace with prices. Rising prices made land more valuable. At the beginning of the eighteenth century, as the first wave of population expansion hit western Europe, smallholdings began to decrease in size. The custom of partible inheritance, by which each son received a share of land, shrank the average size of a peasant holding below that necessary to sustain an average-size family, let alone one that was growing larger. In one part of France it was estimated that thirty acres was a survival plot of land in good times. At the end of the seventeenth century 80 percent of the peasants there owned less than twenty-five acres.

As holdings contracted, the portion of the family income derived from wage labor expanded. In such circumstances males were more valuable than females, either as farmers or laborers, and there is incontrovertible evidence that European rural communities practiced female infanticide. In the end, however, it became increasingly difficult for the peasant family to remain on the land. Mediterranean sharecroppers fell further and further into debt until they finally lost their land entirely. Small freeholders were forced to borrow against future crops until a bad harvest led to foreclosure. Many were allowed to lease back their own lands, on short terms and at high rents, but most swelled the ranks of agricultural laborers, migrating during the planting and harvest seasons, suffering cruelly during winter and summer. In Britain the rural landless outnumbered the landed by two to one. In France there were as many as 8 million peasants who no longer owned their own land.

Emigration was the first logical consequence of poverty. In places where rural misery was greatest, like Ireland, whole communities pulled up stakes and moved to America. Frederick the Great attracted hundreds of thousands of emigrants to Prussia by offering them land. But most rural migrants did not move to new rural environments. Rather they followed the well-trodden paths to the cities. Many traditional domestic crafts were evolving into industrial activities. In the past, peasants supplemented their family income by processing raw materials in the home. Spinning, weaving, and sewing were common cottage industries in which the workers took in the work, supplied their own equipment, and were paid by the piece. Now, especially in the cloth trades, a new form of industrial activity was being organized. Factories, usually located in towns or larger villages, assembled workers together, set them at larger and more efficient machines, and paid them for their time rather than for their output. Families unable to support themselves from the land had no choice but to follow the movement of jobs.

Urban poverty seemed more extreme to observers because there were more poor to observe. They crowded into towns in search of work or charity, though they were unlikely to find much of either. It was certainly true that urban areas were better equipped to assist the poor than were the rural communities from which they came. But likelihood of finding aid only attracted more and more poor, straining and finally breaking the capacities of urban institutions. The death rate of these migrants and their children was staggering. It is perhaps best typified by the dramatic increase in the numbers of abandoned babies throughout western European cities. The existence of foundling hospitals in cities meant that unwed or poor mothers could leave their children in hopes that they would receive better care than the mother herself could provide. In fact, this was rarely the case. In the largest foundling hospital in Paris, only 15 percent of the children survived their first year of "care." But this did little to deter abandonment. In 1772, over 7,500 babies were left in this charnel house, representing 40 percent of all the children born in Paris that year. The normal rates of abandonment of between 10 and 15 percent of all children born in such diverse cities as Madrid and Brussels were little better.

Neither state nor private charities could cope with the flood of poor immigrants. Though the English pundit Samuel Johnson (1709–84) opined that "a decent provision for the poor is the true test of civilization," what he meant was provision for the deserving poor, those unfortunates who were physically or mentally unable to support themselves. The distinction between the worthy and unworthy poor was one involved with changing definitions of charity itself. In earlier times, charity was believed to benefit the soul of the giver as much as the body of the recipient. Thus the poor were socially useful, providing the rich with opportunity to do good works. But now the poor were coming to be viewed as a problem of social administration. Hospitals, workhouses, and more ominously, prisons were established or expanded to deal with them.

Hospitals were residential asylums rather than places for health care. They took in the old, the incapacitated, and increasingly, the orphaned young. Those in France were aptly named "Hotels of God," considering their staggering death rates. "There children dwell who know no parents' care/ Parents who know no children's care dwell there," one poet lamented. Workhouses existed for those who were capable of work but incapable of finding it. They were supposed to improve the values of the idle by keeping them busy, though in most places they served only to improve the profits of the industrialists, who rented out workhouse inmates at below-market wages. Prisons grew with crime. There were spectacular increases in crimes against property in all eighteenth-century cities and despite severe penalties that could include hanging for petty theft, more criminals were incarcerated than executed. Enlightened arguments for the reform of prisons and punishment tacitly acknowledged the social basis of most crime. As always, the victims of crime were mostly drawn from the same social backgrounds as the perpetrators. Along with all of their other troubles, it was the poor who were most commonly robbed, beaten, and abused.

Popular Culture

However depressing is this story of the unrelieved misery of the poor, we should not think of the masses of eighteenth-century society only as the downtrodden victims of social and economic forces beyond their control. For the peasant farmer about to lose his land or the urban artisan without a job, security was an overwhelming concern. While many were to endure such fates, many others lived comfortably by the standards of the age and almost everyone believed that things were better now than they had ever been before. Popular culture was a rich mixture of family and community activities that provided outlets from the pressures of work and the vagaries of fortune. It was no less sustaining to the population at large than was the purely literate culture of the elite, no less vital as a means of explanation for everyday events than the theories of the philosophers or the programs of the *philosophes*.

In fact, the line between elite and popular culture in the eighteenth century is a thin one. For one thing, there was still much mixing of social classes in both rural and urban environments. Occasions of display, like festivals, village fairs, or religious holidays, brought entire communities together and reinforced their collective identities. Moreover, there were many shared elements between the two cultures. All over Europe, literacy was increasing, the result of primary education, of new business techniques, and of the millions of books that were available in editions tailored to even the most modest purse. Nearly half of the inhabitants of France were literate by the end of the eighteenth century, perhaps 60 percent of those in Britain. Men were more likely to have learned to read than women, as were those who lived in urban areas. More than a quarter of French women could read, a number that had doubled over the century. As the rates of female literacy rose, so did overall rates, for women took the lead in teaching children.

Popular literacy spawned popular literature in remarkable variety. Religious works remained the most important, but they were followed by almanacs, romances, and, perhaps surprisingly, chivalric fiction. Religious tracts aimed at the populace were found throughout Europe. They contained stories of the saints in Catholic countries or of the martyrs in Protestant ones, proverbs intended to increase spirituality, and prayers to be offered for all occasions. Almanacs combined prophecies, home remedies, astrological tables, predictions about the weather, and advice on all varieties of agricultural and industrial activities. In the middle of the century just one of the dozens of British almanacs was selling over eighty thousand copies a year. Romances were the staple of lending libraries, which were also becoming a common feature of even small towns. These books were usually published in inexpensive installments spaced according to the time working families needed to save the pennies to purchase them. Written by middle-class authors, popular romances had a strong moral streak, promoting chastity for women and sobriety for men. Yet the best-selling popular fiction, at least in western Europe, was melodramatic tales of knights and ladies from the age of chivalry. These themes had seeped into popular consciousness after having fallen out of favor among the elites. But cultural tastes did not only trickle down. The masses kept the chivalric tradition alive during the eighteenth century; it would percolate up into elite culture in the nineteenth.

Nevertheless, literate culture was not the dominant form of popular culture. Traditional social activities continued to reflect the violent and even brutal nature of day-to-day existence. Village festivals were still the safety valve of youth gangs who enforced sexual morals by shaming husbands whose wives were unfaithful or women whose reputations were sullied. Many holidays were celebrated by sporting events that pitted inhabitants of one village against those of another. These almost always turned into free-for-alls in which broken bones were common and deaths not unknown. In fact, the frequent breakdown of sporting activities into gang wars was the principal cause for the development of rules for soccer as well as more esoteric games like cricket in Britain. Well-organized matches soon became forms of popular entertainment. Over twenty thousand spectators attended one eighteenth-century cricket match, and soccer and cricket soon became as popular for gambling as was horse racing among the wealthy.

Even more popular were the so-called blood sports, which continued to be the most common form of popular recreation. These were brutal competitions in which, in one way or another, animals were maimed or slaughtered. Dog- and cock-fighting were among those that still survive today. Less attractive to the modern mind were blood sports like bearbaiting or bullrunning, in which the object was the slaughter of a large beast over a prolonged period of time. Blood sports were certainly not confined to the masses—foxhunting and bullfighting were pastimes for the very rich—but they formed a significant part of local social activity.

So too did the tavern or alehouse, which in town or country was the site for local communication and recreation. There women and men gossiped and gambled to while away the hours between sundown and bedtime. Discussions and games became animated as the evening wore on, for staggering amounts of alcohol were consumed. "Drunk for a penny, dead drunk for two pennies, straw for nothing," advertised one of the thousands of British gin mills that dominated the poorer quarters of towns. The increased use of spirits—gin, brandy, rum, and vodka—changed the nature of alcohol consumption in Europe. Wine and beer had always been drunk in quantities that we would find astounding, but these beverages were also an important part of diet. The nutritional content of spirits was negligible. People drank spirits to get drunk. The British reformer Francis Place (1771–1854), who grew up in a working-class family, commented that the British masses had only two pleasures, "sex and drinking. And drunkenness is by far the most

The Cockpit (ca. 1759), by William Hogarth. The central figure is a blind nobleman who was said never to have missed an important cockfight. The steel spurs on the birds' legs enabled them to inflict serious damage in the heat of the battle.

desired." The level to which it rose in the eighteenth century speaks volumes about the changes in social and economic life that the masses of European society were now experiencing.

Eighteenth-century society was a hybrid of old and new. It remained highly stratified. Birth and occupation determined wealth, privilege, and quality of life as much as they had in the past, but there were now more paths toward the middle and upper classes, more wealth to be distributed among those above the level of subsistence. Opulence and poverty increased in step as the fruits of commerce and land enriched the upper orders while rising population impoverished the lower ones. Enlightenment ideas highlighted the contradictions. The attack on traditional authority, especially the Roman Catholic church, was an attack on a conservative, static world view. Enlightenment thinkers looked to the future, to a new world shaped by reason and knowledge, a world ruled benevolently for the benefit of all human beings. Government, society, the individual—all could be improved if only the rubble of the past was cleared away. They could hardly imagine how potent their vision would become.

Suggestions for Further Reading

General Reading

* Olwen Hufton, *Europe: Privilege and Protest 1730–1789* (Ithaca, NY: Cornell University Press, 1980). An excellent survey of the political and social history of the mid-eighteenth century.

* Leonard Krieger, *Kings and Philosophers 1689–1789* (New York: Norton, 1970). A brilliant depiction of the personalities and ideas of eighteenth-century Europe.

* Isser Woloch, *Eighteenth Century Europe, Tradition and Progress, 1715–89* (New York: Norton, 1982). Especially strong on social movements and popular culture.

* William Doyle, *The Old European Order 1660–1800* (Oxford: Oxford University Press, 1978). An important essay on the structure of European societies and the ways in which they held together.

* Raymond Birn, *Crisis, Absolutism, Revolution: Europe 1648–1789/91* (New York: Dryden Press, 1977). A reliable survey with especially good chapters on the Enlightenment.

The Nobility

Michael Bush, *Noble Privilege* (New York: Holmes & Meier, 1983). A good analytic survey of the rights of European nobles.

* J. V. Beckett, *The Aristocracy in England* (London: Basil Blackwell, 1986). A comprehensive study of a tightly knit national aristocracy.

* Albert Goodwin, ed., *The European Nobility in the Eighteenth Century* (New York: Harper & Row, 1967). Separate essays on national nobilities, including those of Sweden, Poland, and Spain.

* Norman Hampson, *The Enlightenment* (London: Penguin Books, 1982). The best one-volume survey.

* Peter Gay, *The Enlightenment: An Interpretation*, 2 vols. (New York: Knopf, 1966–69). A difficult but rewarding study by one of the leading historians of the subject.

Carolyn Lougee, *Le Paradis des Femmes: Women, Salons, and Social Stratification* (Princeton, NJ: Princeton University Press, 1976). A study of the foundation of the French salons and the role of women in it.

* Judith Sklar, *Montesquieu* (Oxford: Oxford University Press, 1987). A concise, readable study of the man and his work.

Theodore Besterman, *Voltaire* (Chicago: University of Chicago Press, 1976). The best of many biographies of an all-too-full life.

* John G. Gagliardo, *Enlightened Despotism* (New York: Thomas Y. Crowell, 1967). A sound exploration of the impact of Enlightenment ideas on the rulers of Europe, with most emphasis on the east.

The Bourgeoisie

Jan de Vries, *European Urbanization 1500–1800* (Cambridge, MA: Harvard University Press, 1984). An important, though difficult study of the transformation of towns into cities with the most reliable estimates of size and rates of growth.

* P. J. Corfield, *The Impact of English Towns 1700–1800* (Oxford: Oxford University Press, 1982). A thorough survey of the role of towns in English social and economic life.

* Elinor Barber, *The Bourgeoisie in Eighteenth Century France* (Princeton, NJ: Princeton University Press, 1955). Still the best study of the French bourgeoisie.

* Simon Shama, *The Embarrassment of Riches* (Berkeley: University of California Press, 1987). The social life of Dutch burghers richly portrayed.

* Ian Watt, *The Rise of the Novel* (Berkeley: University of California Press, 1957). An important essay on the relationship between literature and society in the eighteenth century.

David Garrioch, *Neighborhood and Community in Paris, 1740–90* (Cambridge: Cambridge University Press, 1986). A good microstudy of Parisian neighborhoods and of the people who inhabited them.

George Sussman, *Selling Mothers' Milk: The Wet-Nursing Business* (Bloomington: Indiana University Press, 1982). A study of buyers and sellers in this important social marketplace.

Samia Spencer, *French Women and the Age of Enlightenment* (Bloomington, IN: Indiana University Press, 1984). A survey of the role of women in French high culture.

* Lawrence Stone, *The Family, Sex and Marriage in England 1500–1800* (New York: Harper & Row, 1979). A controversial but extremely important argument about the changing nature of family life.

* Jean Louis Flandrin, *Families in Former Times* (Cambridge: Cambridge University Press, 1979). Strong on family and household organization.

The Masses

* Michael W. Flinn, *The European Demographic System* (Baltimore: Johns Hopkins University Press, 1981). The best single-volume study, especially for the nonspecialist reader.

E. A. Wrigley and R. S. Schofield, *The Population History of England* (Cambridge, MA: Harvard University Press, 1981). The most important reconstruction of a national population by a team of researchers.

Olwen Hufton, *The Poor in Eighteenth Century France* (Oxford: Oxford University Press, 1974). A compelling study of the life of the poor.

* Roy Porter, *English Society in the Eighteenth Century* (London: Penguin Books, 1982). A breezy, entertaining survey of English social life.

* J. M. Beattie, *Crime and the Courts in England* (Princeton, NJ: Princeton University Press, 1986). A difficult but sensitive analysis of crime and criminal justice.

* Peter Burke, *Popular Culture in Early Modern Europe* (New York: Harper & Row, 1978). A wide survey of practices throughout the Continent.

Robert Muchembled, *Popular Culture and Elite Culture in France, 1400–1750* (Baton Rouge, LA: Louisiana State University Press, 1985). A complex but richly textured argument about the relationship between two cultures.

* Robert Malcolmson, *Popular Recreation in English Society, 1700–1850* (Cambridge: Cambridge University Press, 1973). Sport and its role in society.

* Indicates paperback edition available.

The French Revolution and the Napoleonic Era, 1789–1815

"Let Them Eat Cake"

The Queen of France was bored. Try as she might, Marie Antoinette (1755–93) found insufficient diversion in her life at the great court of Versailles. When she was fourteen, she had married the heir to the French throne, the future Louis XVI. By the age of nineteen, she was queen of the most prosperous state in continental Europe. Still she was bored. Her life, she complained to her mother, Empress Maria Theresa of Austria, was futile and meaningless. Maria Theresa advised the unhappy queen to suffer in silence or risk unpleasant consequences.

Sometimes mothers know best. As head of the Habsburg Empire, Maria Theresa understood more about politics than her youngest child. She understood that people have little sympathy with the boredom of a monarch, especially a foreign-born queen. But Marie Antoinette chose to ignore maternal advice and pursued amusements and intrigues that had unpleasant consequences indeed.

Unpopular as a foreigner from the time she arrived in France, Marie Antoinette suffered a further decline in her reputation as gossip spread about her gambling and affairs

at court. The public heard exaggerated accounts of the fortunes she spent on clothing and jewelry. In 1785 she was linked to a cardinal in a nasty scandal over a gift of a diamond necklace. In spite of her innocence, rumors of corruption and infidelity surrounded her name. Dubbed "Madame Deficit," she came to represent all that was considered decadent in royal rule.

She continued to insist, "I am

afraid of being bored." To amuse herself, she ordered a life-size play village built on the grounds of Versailles, complete with cottages, a chapel, a mill, and a running stream. Then, dressed in the silks and muslins intended as the royal approximation of a milkmaid's garb, she whiled away whole days with her friends and children, all pretending they were inhabitants of this picturesque "Hamlet." Her romantic view of country life helped pass the time, but it did little to bring her closer to the struggling peasants who made up the majority of French subjects.

Marie Antoinette's problems need not have mattered much. Monarchs before her had been considered weak and extravagant. The difference was that her foibles became public in an age when the opinion of the people affected political life. Rulers, even those believed to be divinely appointed, were subjected to a public scrutiny all the more powerful because of the growth of the popular press. Kings, their ministers, and their spouses were held accountable—a dangerous phenomenon for an absolute monarchy.

This Austrian-born queen may not have been more shallow or spendthrift than other queens, but it mattered that people came to see her that way. The queen's reputation sank to its nadir when it was reported that she dismissed the suffering of her starving subjects with the haughty retort: "Let them eat cake." What better evidence could there be of the queen's insensitivity than this heartless remark?

Marie Antoinette never said, "Let them eat cake," but everyone thought she did. This was the kind of callousness that people expected from the monarchy in 1789. Marie Antoinette understood the plight of her starving subjects, as her correspondence indicates. Probably a courtier at Versailles was the real source of the brutal retort, but the truth didn't matter. Marie Antoinette and her husband were being indicted by the public for all the political, social, and fiscal crises that plagued France.

In October 1793, Marie Antoinette was put on trial by the Revolutionary Tribunal and found guilty of treason. She was stripped of all the trappings of monarchy and forced to don another costume. Dressed as a poor working woman, her hair shorn, the former queen mounted the guillotine, following in the footsteps of her hus-

band, who had been executed earlier that year. The monarchy did not fall because of a spendthrift queen with too much time on her hands. Nor did it fall because of the mistakes of the well-meaning but inept king. The monarchy had ceased to be responsive to the profound changes that shook France. It fell because of a new concern in the land for royal accountability in words and deeds. A rising democratic tide carried with it ideas about political representation, participation, and equality. If a queen could change places with a milkmaid, why should not a milkmaid be able to change places with a queen?

The Crisis of the Old Regime in France, 1715–48

France in the eighteenth century, the age of the Enlightenment, was a state invigorated by new ideas. It was also a world dominated by tradition. The traditional institutions of monarchy, Church, and aristocracy defined power and status. Talk of reform, progress, and perfectibility coexisted with the social realities of privileges and obligations determined by birth. The eighteenth century was a time when old ways prevailed even as a new view of the world was taking shape.

At the end of the eighteenth century, a number of foreign visitors to France commented on the disparities that characterized French social and political life. One English visitor in particular, Arthur Young (1741–1820), an agronomist writing on his travels in France in the 1780s, observed that although a prosperous land, France was pocked with extreme poverty; although a land of high culture and great art, it was riddled with ignorance, illiteracy, and superstition; although a land with a centralized bureaucracy, it was also saddled with local interests and obsolete practices. The French nation presented a great challenge to any observer attempting to make sense of its diversity.

Charles Dickens (1812–70), a British novelist of the next century, captured well the contradictions of the age:

It was the best of times, it was the worst of times, it was the age of wisdom, it was the age of foolishness, it was the epoch of belief, it was the epoch of incredulity, it was the season of Light, it was the season of Darkness, it was the spring of hope, it was the winter of despair, we had everything before us, we had nothing before us, we were all going direct to Heaven, we were all going direct the other way.

Dickens recognized that the tensions generated by the clash of continuity and change made this an exciting and complex period in both Britain and France. In France, reformers talked of progress while peasants still used wooden plows. The *philosophes* glorified reason in a world of violence, superstition, and fear. The great crisis of eighteenth-century France, the French Revolution,

destroyed what we now know as the old regime. But the Revolution was as much a product of continuities and traditions as it was a product of change and the challenge of new ideas.

Louis XV's France

When Louis XV (1715–74) died, he was a hated man. In his fifty-nine-year reign, he managed to turn the public against him. He was denounced as a tyrant who was trying to starve his people, a slave to the mistresses who ruled his court, and an indecisive sybarite dominated by evil ministers. Louis XV's apathy and ineptitude contributed to his poor image. The declining fortunes and the damaged prestige of the monarchy, however, reflected more than the personality traits of an ineffectual king: they reflected structural challenges to fiscal solvency and absolutist rule that the monarchy was unable to meet.

Louis XV, like his great-grandfather Louis XIV, laid claim to rule as an absolute monarch. He insisted that "the rights and interests of the nation...are of necessity one with my own, and lie in my hands only." Such claims failed to mask the weaknesses of royal rule. Louis XV lacked a sufficiently developed bureaucracy to administer and tax the nation in an evenhanded fashion. By the beginning of the eighteenth century, the absolute monarchy had extended royal influence into the new areas of policing, administration, lawmaking, and taxation. But none of this proved sufficient to meet the growing needs of the state.

The growing tensions between the monarch and the aristocracy found expression in various institutions, especially the *parlements*, the thirteen sovereign courts in the French judicial system with their seats in Paris and a dozen provincial centers. The magistrates of each parlement were members of the nobility, some of them nobles of recent origin and others of long standing, depending on the locale. The king needed the parlements to record royal decrees before they could become law. This recording process conferred real political power on the parlements, which could withhold approval for the king's policies by refusing to register his decrees. When the king attempted to make new laws, the magistrates could refuse to endorse them. When decrees involved taxation, they often did. Because magistrates purchased their offices in the parlements, the king found it difficult to control the courts. His fiscal difficulties prevented him from buying up the increasingly valuable offices in order to appoint his own men. Stripping magistrates of their positions was considered tantamount to the theft of property. By successfully challenging the king, the parlements became a battleground between the elite, who claimed that they represented the nation, and the king, who said the nation was himself.

The king repeatedly attempted to neutralize the power of the parlements by relying instead on his own state bureaucracy. His agents in the provinces, called *intendants*, were accountable directly to the central government. The intendants, as the king's men, and the magistrates who presided in the parlements represented contradictory claims to power. As the king's needs increased in the second half of the eighteenth century, the situation was becoming intolerable for those exercising power and those aspiring to rule in the name and for the good of the nation.

The nadir of Louis XV's reign came in 1763 with the French defeat in the Seven Years' War both on the Continent and in the colonies. In the Treaty of Paris, France ceded territory, including its Canadian holdings, to Great Britain. France lost more than lands; it lost its footing in the competition with its chief rival Great Britain, which had been pulling ahead of France in international affairs since the mid-eighteenth century. The war was also a financial debacle, paid for by loans secured against the guarantee of victory. The defeat not only left France barren of funds; it also promoted further expenditures for strengthening the French navy against the superior British fleet. New taxation was the way out of the financial trap in which the king now found himself.

Louis XV's revenue problem was not easily solved. In order to raise taxes, the king had to turn to the recording function of the parlements. Following the costly Seven Years' War, the parlements chose to exercise the power of refusal by blocking a proportional tax to be imposed on nobles and commoners alike. The magistrates resisted taxation with an argument that confused liberty with privilege: the king, the magistrates asserted, was attacking the liberty of his subjects by attempting to tax those who were exempt by virtue of their privileged status.

René Nicolas Charles Augustin de Maupeou

(1714–92), Louis XV's chancellor from 1768 to 1774, decided that the political power of the parlements had to be curbed. In 1770, in an attempt to coerce the magistrates into compliance with the king's wishes, he engineered the overthrow of the Parlement of Paris, the most important of the high courts. Those magistrates who remained obdurate were sent into exile. New courts whose membership was based on appointment instead of the sale of offices took their place amid much public criticism. Ultimately, Maupeou's attempt failed. His action did nothing to improve the monarch's image and it did less to solve the fiscal problems of the regime. The conflict between Louis XV and the parlements revealed the dependent nature of the monarchy that claimed to be absolute and accountable only to God.

The dignity and prestige of the monarchy were seriously damaged in the course of Louis XV's long reign. His legacy was well captured in the expression erroneously attributed to him, *aprés moi le déluge*—"after me, the flood." Continuing to live the good life at the court, he failed dismally to offset rising state expenditures—caused primarily by military needs—with new sources of revenue. In 1774 Louis XV died suddenly of smallpox. His unprepared twenty-year-old grandson, Louis XVI (1774–92), a young man who amused himself by hunting and pursuing his hobby as an amateur locksmith, was left to try to stanch the flood.

The End of the Old Regime

Louis XV left to his heir Louis XVI the legacy of a disastrous deficit. Deficits were not unknown to the monarchs of France, who had centuries of experience in spending more than they had, but this debt promised to be worse than most. From the beginning of his reign, Louis XVI was caught in the vicious circle of excessive state spending—above all, military spending—followed by bouts of heavy borrowing. Borrowing at high rates required the government to pay out huge sums in interest and service fees on the loans that were keeping it afloat. These outlays in turn piled the state's indebtedness ever higher, requiring more loans, and threatening to topple the whole financial structure and the regime itself.

In inheriting this trouble-ridden fiscal structure, Louis XVI made his own contribution to it.

Following in the footsteps of his grandfather, Louis XVI involved France in a costly war, the War of American Independence (1775–83), by supporting the thirteen colonies in their revolt against Great Britain. The involvement brought the French monarchy to the brink of bankruptcy. Contrary to public opinion, most of the state's expenditures did not go toward lavishing luxuries on the royal court and the royal family at Versailles. They went to pay off loans. More than half of the state budget in the 1780s represented interest on loans taken to pay for foreign military ventures.

The king needed money and he needed it fast. To those who could afford to purchase them, the king continued to sell offices that carried with them titles, revenues, and privileges. He also relied on the sale of annuities that paid high interest rates and that attracted speculators, large and small. The crown had leased out its rights to collect the salt tax in return for large lump-sum advances from the Royal General Farms, a syndicate of about one hundred wealthy financier families. The Royal General Farms reaped healthy profits on their annual transactions at the state's expense. The combined revenues collected by the king through these various stratagems were little more than a drop compared to the vast ocean of debt that threatened to engulf the state.

The existing tax structure proved hopelessly inadequate to meet the state's needs. The *taille*, a direct tax, was levied, either on persons or on land, according to region. Except for those locales where the *taille* was attached to land, the nobility was always exempt from direct taxation. Members of the bourgeoisie could also avoid the direct tax as citizens of towns enjoying exemption. That meant that the wealthy, those best able to pay, were often exempt. Indirect taxes, like those on salt (the *gabelle*) and on food and drink (the *aide*), and internal and external customs taxes were regressive taxes that hit hardest those least able to pay. The peasantry bore the brunt of the nation's tax burden, as the drawing of a simple farmer carrying on his back a noble and a priest conveyed. Louis XVI knew all too well that he could not squeeze blood from a stone by increasing indirect taxes. A peasantry too weighted down would collapse—or rebel.

The privileged elite persisted in rejecting the crown's attempts to tax them. As one of the first acts of his reign, in 1775 Louis XVI had restored the magistrates to their posts in the parlements, treating their offices as a form of property of which they had been deprived. In his conciliatory act, Louis XVI nevertheless stressed that the self-interest of the aristocracy was at odds with the common good of the nation and urged the approval of his programs. By 1776 the Parlement of Paris was again obstructing royal decrees.

Louis XVI appointed Anne Robert Jacques Turgot (1727–1781) as his first controller-general. Turgot's reformist economic ideas were influenced by Enlightenment *philosophes*. In order to generate revenues, Turgot reasoned, France needed to prosper economically. The government was in a position to stimulate economic growth by eliminating regulations, by economizing at court, and by improving the network of roads through a tax on landowners. Each of Turgot's reforms offended established interests, thereby ensuring his early defeat. Emphasis on a laissez-faire economy outraged the guilds; doing away with the forced labor of peasants on the roads (the *corvée*) threatened privileged groups who had never before been taxed. As the king was discovering, divine right did not bring with it absolute authority or fiscal solvency.

As he floundered about for a solution to his economic difficulties, the king turned to a new adviser, Jacques Necker (1732–1804), a Swiss-born Protestant banker. The king and the public expected great things from Necker, whose international business experience was counted on to save the day. Necker, a prudent man, applied his accounting skills to measuring—for the first time—the total income and expenditures of the French state. The budget he produced and widely circulated allayed everyone's fears of certain doom and assured the nation that no new taxes were necessary—an assurance based on disastrous miscalculations.

Instead of raising taxes, Necker committed his ministry to eliminating costly inefficiencies. He promised to abolish venal offices that drained revenues from the crown. He next set his sights on contracts of the farmers-general, collectors of the indirect salt taxes, whom he likened to weeds sprouting in a swamp. Necker's aim was to reduce ordinary expenses of the realm in order to be ready for the extraordinary ones associated with waging a war. Such policies made him enemies in high places and numbered his days in office.

Necker and those who preceded him in controlling and directing the finances of the state under Louis XV and Louis XVI were committed to reforming the system. All the advisers recognized that the state's fiscal problems were structural and required enlightened solutions, but no two of them agreed on the same program of reforms. Necker had somehow captivated popular opinion and there was widespread regret expressed over his forced resignation.

Charles Alexandre de Calonne (1734–1802), appointed controller-general in 1783, had his own ideas of how to bail out the ship of state. He authored a program of reforms that would have shifted the tax burden off those least able to pay and onto those best able to support the state. Such a move would have minimized the differences between nobles and commoners. He proposed a tax on land proportional to land values, a measure that would have most seriously affected the land-rich nobility. In addition, taxes that affected the peasantry were to be lightened or eliminated. Finally, Calonne proposed the sale of Church lands for revenues. In an attempt to bypass the recalcitrant parlements, Calonne advised the crown in 1787 to convene an Assembly of Notables made up of 150 individuals from the magistracy, the Church hierarchy, the titled nobility, and municipal bodies, for the purpose of enlisting their support for reforms. Louis listened to Calonne, who was denounced by the Assembly of Notables for attacking the rights of the privileged. He too was forced to resign.

All of Louis XVI's attempts to persuade the nobility to agree to tax reforms had failed. Considered by his courtiers to be well-meaning but weak and ineffectual, Louis was incapable of the effort required either to inspire or to manipulate the privileged classes to support his plans. Aristocratic magistrates insisted on a constitution, in which their own right to govern would be safeguarded and the accountability of the king would be defined. In opposing the royal reforms, nobles spoke of the "rights of man" and used the term *citizen*. They rebuffed the monarch with the cry, "No taxation without consent." The nobility had no sympathy for tax programs that would have

resulted in a loss of privilege and what some nobles were beginning to consider an attack on individual freedom. Louis XVI was met with passivity from the Assembly of Notables and resistance from the Parlement of Paris and the provincial parlements.

In the 1780s, almost 50 percent of annual expenditures went to servicing the accumulated national debt of 4 billion livres and paying interest. The new controller-general, Archbishop Loménie de Brienne (1727–94) recommended emergency loans. The crown once again disbanded the Paris Parlement, which was now threatening to block loans as well as taxes. The aristocracy seemed on the verge of its own revolt against royal authority.

Louis XVI was a desperate man in 1788, so desperate that he yielded to the condition placed on him by the Paris Parlement: he agreed to convene the Estates-General, a medieval body that had not met since 1614 and that had been considered obsolete with the rise of a centralized bureaucratic government. The Estates-General included representatives from the three "estates" of the clergy, nobility, and commoners. About two hundred thousand subjects belonged to the first two estates. The Third Estate was composed of all those members of the realm who enjoyed a common identity only in their lack of privilege—over 23 million French people. In the 1614 voting of the Estates-General, each of the three orders was equally weighted. This arrangement favored the nobility, who controlled the first two estates. The nobility was understandably not worried by the prospect of the Estates-General deciding the tax-reform program. Many were sure that a new age of liberty was at hand.

The Three Estates

French society, to which the king and the noble elite turned in 1788, was divided by law and custom into a pyramid of three tiers called orders or estates. At the top were those who prayed—the clergy, followed by those who fought—the nobility. The base of the pyramid was formed by the largest of the three orders, those who worked—the bourgeoisie, the peasantry, and urban and rural workers. In the second half of the eighteenth century, these traditional groups no

This cartoon depicts the plight of the French peasants. An old farmer is bowed down under the weight of the privileged aristocracy and clergy while birds and rabbits, protected by unfair game laws, eat his crops.

longer reflected social realities—a situation that proved to be a source of serious problems for the Estates-General. The piety of the first order had been called into doubt as religious leaders were criticized for using the vast wealth of the Church for personal benefit instead of public worship. The protective military function of the second order had ceased to exist with the rise of the state and the changing nature of war. The bourgeoisie, those who worked with their heads, not their hands, shared privileges with the nobility and aspired to a noble life-style, in spite of their legal and customary presence in the ranks of the Third Estate.

The vast majority of French subjects who constituted the Third Estate certainly were identified by work, but the vast array of mental and physical labor—and lack of work—splintered the estate into a myriad of occupations, aspirations, and identities. All power flowed upward in this arrangement, with the First and Second Estates dominating the social and political universe. Women and men accepted this hierarchy as the natural organization of society in eighteenth-

century France. But it was a hierarchy whose rationale was under attack.

The king continued to stand at the pinnacle of the eighteenth-century social pyramid. Traditionally revered as the "father" of his subjects, he claimed to be divinely appointed by God. Kingship in this era had a dual nature. The king was both supreme overlord from feudal times, and he was absolute monarch. As supreme overlord he stood dominant over the aristocracy and the court. As absolute monarch he stood at the head of the state and society. When the king equated himself with the state—"*L'état, c'est moi,*" as Louis XIV boasted—all problems—economic, social, and political—also came to be identified with the king. Absolutism required a weakened nobility and a bureaucracy strong enough to help the monarchy to adjust to changes. After the death of Louis XIV in 1715, Louis XV and Louis XVI faced a resurgent aristocracy without the support of a state bureaucracy capable of successfully challenging aristocratic privilege or of solving fiscal problems.

"To live nobly," that is, to live as a noble, was the social ideal to which one could aspire in the eighteenth century. While the system of orders set clear boundaries of social status, distinctions within estates created new hierarchies. The clergy, a privileged order, contained both commoners and nobles, but leadership in the Church depended on social rank. The aristocracy retained control of the bishoprics, even as an activist element among the lower clergy agitated for reforms and better salaries. In a state in which the king claimed to rule by God's will, Catholicism, virtually enshrined as the state religion, was important in legitimizing the divine claims of the monarchy.

The nobility experienced its own internal tensions, generated by two groups: the older nobility of the sword, who claimed descent from medieval times; and the more recent nobility of the robe, who had acquired their position through the purchase of offices that conferred noble status. By increasing the numbers of the nobility of the robe, Louis XIV hoped to undermine the power of the aristocracy as a whole and to decrease its political influence. But aristocrats rallied and closed ranks against the dilution of their power. As a result, both Louis XV and Louis XVI faced a reviving rather than a declining aristocracy. One in four nobles had moved from the bourgeoisie to the aristocratic ranks in the eighteenth century; two out of every three had been ennobled during the seventeenth and eighteenth centuries. Nobles had succeeded in restoring their economic and social power. A growing segment of the aristocracy, influenced by Enlightenment ideas and the example of English institutions, was intent on increasing the political dominance of the aristocracy too.

The nobility strengthened their powers in two ways. First, they monopolized high offices and closed access to nonnobles. They took over posts in ministries, the Church, and the army. Second, the nobility benefited greatly from the doubling in land values brought on by the increase in the value of crops. Nobles enjoyed privileges, the greatest being, in most cases, exemption from taxes. Seeking ever higher returns from the land, some members of the aristocracy adopted new agricultural techniques to achieve greater crop yields. There were certainly poor aristocrats who lacked the lands to benefit from this trend, but those who did control sizable holdings profited greatly from higher dues paid to them, as they reaped increased incomes from crops. In addition, many aristocrats revived their feudal claims to ancient seigneurial, or lordly, privileges. They hired lawyers to unearth old claims and hired agents to collect dues. This was merely good business.

A spirit of innovation characterized the values of certain members of the nobility. Although technically prevented from participating in trade by virtue of their titles and privileges, an active group among the nobility succeeded in making fortunes in metallurgy, glassmaking, and mining. Others participated in trade. These nobles were an economically dynamic and innovative segment of the aristocracy. In spite of the obsolete aspect of their privileges, aristocrats were often responsible for the introduction of modern ideas and techniques in the management of estates and in the bookkeeping involved with collection of rents. Capitalist techniques were not unknown to nobles adapting to the marketplace. These nobles formed an elite partnership with forward-looking members of the bourgeoisie.

Common people, that is, those who did not enjoy the privileges of the nobility, embraced a broad range of the French populace. The peasantry was by far the largest group, joined in the designation as "commoners" by the middle class, or bourgeoisie, and by workers in both cities and rural areas. Most French peasants were free, no longer attached to the soil as serfs were in a feudal system. Yet all peasants endured common obligations placed on them by the crown and the privileged classes. Peasants owed the tithe to the Church, land taxes to the state, and seigneurial dues and rents to the landlord. A bewildering array of taxes afflicted peasants. In some areas peasants repaired roads and drew lots for military service. Dues affected almost every aspect of rural life, including harvests and the sale of property. In addition, indirect taxes like that on salt (the hated *gabelle*) were a serious burden for the peasantry. As if all this were not enough, peasants who were forced to take loans to survive from one harvest to another paid exorbitant interest rates. No matter how bad conditions were, peasants had to be sure to save the seed for next year's crop.

The peasants who staggered and collapsed under all these obligations were forced to leave the land. The precariousness of rural life and the increase in population in the countryside contributed to the permanent displacement and destitution of a growing sector of rural society. Without savings and destroyed by poor harvests, impoverished rural inhabitants wandered the countryside looking for odd jobs and eventually begging to survive. Many peasants with small plots were able to work for wages. The labor of women was essential to the survival of the rural family. Peasant women sought employment in towns and cities as seamstresses and servants in order to send money back home to struggling relatives. Children, too, added their earnings to the family pot. In spite of various strategies for survival, more and more families were disrupted by the end of the eighteenth century.

The bourgeoisie—as the term was used in the eighteenth century—meant those members of the middle class who lived on income from investments. Yet the term really embraced within it a whole hierarchy of professions from bankers and financiers to businessmen, merchants, entrepreneurs, lawyers, shopkeepers, and craftsmen. Along with the nobility, wealthy bourgeois formed the urban elites that administered cities and towns. Prestigious service to the state or the purchase of offices that carried with them noble status enabled the wealthiest members of the bourgeoisie to move into the ranks of the nobility.

Many bourgeois served as middlemen for the nobility by running estates and collecting dues.

Like the rest of the social universe, the world of artisans and workers was shaded with various gradations of wealth and status. Those who owned their own shops and perhaps employed other workers stood as an elite among the working class. In spite of their physical proximity, there was a vast difference between those who owned their own shops and those who earned wages or were paid by the piece. Wage earners represented about 30 percent of the population of cities and towns. And their numbers were swelling, as craftsmen were pushed out of their guilds and peasants were pushed off their land.

In 1775, the king in an attempt to promote free trade temporarily abolished the guilds. Those who worked in crafts were a labor elite, and guilds were intended to protect the corporations of masters, journeymen, and apprentices through monopolistic measures. Guilds insisted that they were best able to ensure the quality of goods. But the emphasis on free trade and the expansion of markets in the eighteenth century weakened the hold of the guilds. Merchants often took them over and paid workers by the piece. The effect was a reduction in the wages of skilled workers. By the 1780s, most journeymen who hoped to be masters knew that their dream would never be realized. Frustration and discontent touched workers in towns and cities who may not have shared a common work experience. But they did share a common anger about the high cost of food—especially bread.

In August 1788 Louis XVI announced that the Estates-General would meet at Versailles in May 1789. He directed each of the three estates—clergy, nobility, and commoners—to elect their representatives, who would come together to discuss the fiscal and political problems plaguing the nation. Every social group, from the nobles to the poorest laborers, had its own grievances and concerns, but all greeted the news with fireworks, parades, and toasts to the best of all kings.

The French Revolution and the End of the Old Regime

Those who lived through it were sure that there had never been a time like it before. The French Revolution, or the Great Revolution, as it was known to contemporaries, was a time of creation and discovery. The ten years from 1789 to 1799 were punctuated by genuine euphoria and democratic transformations. The Revolution achieved most in the area of politics. Revolutionary slogans and songs reflected people's hopes and a new expectation for the future. From the privileged elites who initiated the overthrow of the existing order to peasants and workers, women and men, who united against tyranny, the Revolution touched every segment of society.

The overthrow of absolutist monarchy brought with it new social theories, new symbols, and new behavior. The excitement of anarchy was matched by the terror of repression. Revolutionary France had to contend with a Europe-wide

Revolutionary France

war. The Revolution had its dark side of violence and instability. In the Revolution's wake came internal discord, civil war, and violent repression. In the search for a new order, political forms followed one upon the other in rapid succession: constitutional monarchy, republic, oligarchy. The creation of Napoleon's dictatorship at the end of the century was the act that signified that the Revolution had come to an end.

Similar revolutionary incidents flared up throughout Europe in the second half of the eighteenth century—in the Netherlands, Belgium, and Ireland. Absolute authority was challenged and sometimes modified. Across the Atlantic, American colonists concerned with the principle of self-rule had thrown off the yoke of the British in the War of Independence. But none of these events, including the American Revolution, was so violent in breaking with the old order, so extensive in involving millions of men and women in political action, and so consequential for the political futures of other European states, as was the French Revolution.

Many people alive for these events were sure that they had crossed the threshold of a new era. Succeeding generations agreed. The triumphs and contradictions of the revolutionary experiment in democracy mark the end of the old order and the beginning of modern history. Politics would never be the same again.

Taking Politics to the People

Choosing representatives for the Estates-General in March and April 1789 stirred up hope and excitement in every corner of France. From the very beginning, there were warning signs that a more astute monarch might have noticed. The call for national elections set in motion a politicizing process the king could not control. Members of the Third Estate, traditionally excluded from political and social power, were presented with the opportunity of expressing their opinions on the state of government and society. In an increasingly literate age, pamphlets, broadsides, and political tracts representing every political persuasion blanketed France. Those who could not read stood in marketplaces and city squares or sat around evening fires and had the political literature read to them. Farmhands and urban laborers realized that they were participating in the same process as their social betters. And they believed they had a right to speak and be heard.

This was a time of great hope, especially for people who had been buffeted by the rise in prices, decline in real wages, and the hunger that followed crop failures and poor harvests. Although probably better able than their grandparents to endure periodic hardships, most Frenchmen and women were sure that things were getting worse. Now there was the promise of a respite and a solution. Taxes could be discussed and changed, the state bureaucracy could be reformed—or better, abolished.

Intellectuals discussed political alternatives in the salons of the wealthy. Nobles and bourgeois met in philosophical societies dedicated to enlightened thought. Commoners gathered in cafes to drink and debate. The poor fell outside of this network of communication, but they were not immune to the ideas that emerged. In the end, people of all classes had opinions and they were more certain than ever of their right to express their ideas. Absolutism was in trouble, although Louis XVI did not know it, as people began to forge a collectively shared idea of politics. People now had a forum—the Estates-General—and a focus—the politics of taxation. But most important, they had the elections. The message of the elections and the representative principle on which they were based was that one could compete for power.

In competing for power, some members of the Third Estate were well aware of their vast numerical superiority over the nobility. Because of it, they demanded greater representation than the three hundred members per estate defined according to the practices of 1614. At the very least, they argued, the number of representatives of the Third Estate should be doubled to six hundred members, giving commoners equality in numbers with nobles and priests together. Necker, recalled as director-general of finance in August 1788, agreed to the doubling in the size of the Third Estate as a compromise but left unresolved the additional demand of vote by head rather than by order. If voting was to be left as it was, in accordance with the procedures of 1614, the nobility who controlled the First and Second Estates would determine all outcomes. With a voting procedure by head instead of by order, however, the deputies of the Third Estate could easily dominate the Estates-General, confident that they could count on liberal nobles, like the Marquis de Lafayette, and parish priests to defect from voting with the First and Second Estates and join their cause.

In conjunction with this political activity and in scheduled meetings, members of all three estates drew up statements of their problems. This took place in a variety of forums, including guilds and village and town meetings. The people of France set down their grievances in note-books—known as *cahiers de doléances*—that were then carried to Versailles by the deputies elected to the Estates-General. This was the first national poll of opinion commissioned by the crown, and it involved every level of society. It was a tool of political education as the mass of French people were being given the impression for the first time that they were part of the policy-making process.

"If only the king knew!" In this phrase, French men and women expressed their belief in the inevitability of their fate and the benevolence of their king. They saw the king as a loving and wise father who would not tolerate the injustices visited upon his subjects, if only he knew what was really happening. In 1789 peasants and workers were questioning why their lives could not be better, but they continued to express their trust in the king. Combined with their old faith was a new hope. The peasants in the little town of Saintes recorded their expectations in their *cahier*:

> Our king, the best of kings and father of a great and wise family, will soon know everything. All vices will be destroyed. All the great virtues of industriousness, honesty, modesty, honor, patriotism, meekness, friendliness, equality, concord, pity, and thrift will prevail and wisdom will rule supreme.

The *cahiers* expressed the particular griev-ances of each estate. These notebooks contained a collective outpouring of problems and are impor-tant for two major reasons. First, they made clear the similarity of grievances shared throughout France. Second, they indicated the extent to which a common political culture, based on a concern with political reform, had permeated different levels of French society. Both the privileged and the nonprivileged identified a common enemy in the system of state bureaucracy to which the

monarch was so strongly tied. Although the king was still addressed with respect, new concerns with liberty, equality, property, and the rule of law were voiced.

Those who opposed the Revolution later alleged that these notebooks proved the existence of a highly coordinated plot on the part of secret societies out to destroy the regime. They were wrong. Similarities in complaints, similarities in demands, similarities in language proved, not a conspiracy, but the forging of a new political consciousness. Societies and clubs circulated "model" *cahiers* among themselves, resulting in the use of similar forms and vocabulary. People were questioning their traditional roles and now had elected deputies who would represent them before the king. In the spring of 1789 a severe economic crisis that heightened political uncer-tainty swept through France. For a king expected to save the situation, time was running out.

Convening the Estates-General

The elected deputies arrived at Versailles at the beginning of May 1789, carrying in their va-lises and trunks the grievances of their estates. The opening session of the Estates-General took place in a great hall especially constructed for the event. The 1,248 deputies presented a grand spectacle as they filed to their assigned places to hear speeches by the king and his ministers. Contrasts among the participants were immediately apparent. Seated on a raised throne under a canopy at one end of the hall, Louis XVI was vested in full kingly regalia. On his right sat the archbishops and car-dinals of the First Estate, dramatically clad in the pinks and purples of their offices. On his left were the richly and decorously attired nobility. Facing the stage sat the 648 deputies of the Third Estate, dressed in plain black suits, stark against the colorful and costly costumes of the privileged. It was clear, in the most visual terms, that "clothes make the man." Members of the Third Estate had announced beforehand that they would not fol-low the ancient custom for commoners of kneel-ing at the king's entrance. Fired by the hope of equal treatment and an equal share of power, they had come to Versailles to make a constitu-tion. The opening ceremony degenerated into a moment of confusion over whether members of the Third Estate should be able to don their hats

This painting of the Oath of the Tennis Court is by the Revolution's leading artist, Jacques Louis David. Sieyès sits at a table on which Bailly stands reading the oath. Robespierre is seen clutching his breast in the group behind Sieyès.

in the presence of the king. Many saw in the politics of clothing a tense beginning to their task.

The tension between commoners and privileged was further aggravated by the unresolved issue of how the voting was to proceed. The Third Estate was adamant in its demand for vote by head. The privileged orders were equally adamant in insisting on vote by order. Paralysis set in, as days dragged into weeks and the Estates were unable to act. The body that was to save France from fiscal collapse was hopelessly deadlocked.

Two men in particular whose backgrounds made them unlikely heroes emerged as leaders of the Third Estate. One, the Abbé Emmanuel Joseph Sieyès (1748–1836), was a member of the clergy who frequented Parisian salons. The other, the comte Honoré Gabriel Victor de Mirabeau (1749–91), a black sheep among the nobility, had spent time in prison because of his father's charges that he was a defiant son who led a misspent, debauched, and profligate youth. In spite of his nobility, Mirabeau appeared at Versailles as a deputy for Aix and Marseilles to the Third Estate. His oratory and presence commanded attention from the start. As a consummate politician, Mirabeau combined forces with Sieyès, who had already established his reputation as a firebrand reformer with his eloquent pamphlet, "What Is the Third Estate?" published in January 1789. To the question posed in the title, Sieyès answered, "What is the Third Estate? Everything! What has it been in the political order up to the present? Nothing!"

Sieyès and Mirabeau reminded members of the Third Estate of the reformist consensus that characterized their ranks. Under their influence, the Third Estate decided to proceed with its own meetings. On 17 June 1789, the Third Estate, joined by some sympathetic clergy, changed its name to the National Assembly as an assertion of its true representation of the French nation. Three days later, members of the new National Assembly found themselves locked out of their regular meeting room by the king's guard. Outraged by this insult, they moved to a nearby indoor tennis court, where they vowed to stay together for the purpose of writing a constitution. This event, known as the Oath of the Tennis Court, marked the end of the absolutist monarchy and the beginning of a new concept of the state that power resided in the people. The Revolution had begun.

The drama of Versailles, a staged play of gestures, manners, oaths, and attire, also marked the beginning of a far-reaching political revolution. Although it was a drama that took place behind closed doors, it was not one unknown to the general public. Throughout May and June 1789, Parisians trekked to Versailles to watch the deliberations. Then they brought news back to the capital. Deputies wrote home to their constituents to keep them abreast of events. Newspapers that reported daily on these wranglings and pamphleteers who analyzed them spread the news throughout the nation. Information, often conflicting, stirred up anxiety; news of conflict encouraged action.

The frustration and the stalemate of the Estates-General threatened to put the spark to the kindling of urban unrest. The people of Paris had suffered through a harsh winter and spring under the burdens of high prices (especially of bread), limited supplies, and relentless tax demands. The

This lively amateur painting of the fall of the Bastille is by Claude Cholat, one of the attackers. Tradition has it that Cholat is manning the cannon in the background. The inscription proclaims that the painting is by one of the "Conquerors of the Bastille."

rioting of the spring had for the moment ceased, as people waited for their problems to be solved by the deputies of the Estates-General. The suffering of the urban poor was not new, but their ability to connect economic hardships with the politics at Versailles and to blame the government was. As hopes began to dim with the news of political stalemate, news broke of the creation of the National Assembly. It was greeted with new anticipation.

The Storming of the Bastille

The king, who had temporarily withdrawn from sight following the death of his son at the beginning of June, reemerged to meet with the representatives of each of the three estates and propose reforms, including a constitutional monarchy. But Louis XVI refused to accept the now popularly supported National Assembly as a legitimate body, choosing instead to rely on the three estates for advice. He simply did not understand that the choice was no longer his to make. He summoned troops to Versailles and began concentrating soldiers in Paris. Civilians constantly clashed with members of the military, whom they jostled and jeered. The urban crowds recognized the threat of repression that the troops represented. People decided to meet force with force. To do so, they needed arms themselves and they knew where to get them.

On 14 July 1789, the irate citizens of Paris stormed the Bastille, a royal armory that also served as a prison for a handful of debtors. The storming of the Bastille has become the great

symbol in the revolutionary legend of the overthrow of the tyranny and oppression of the old regime. But it is significant for another reason. It was an expression of the power of the people to take politics into their own hands. Parisians were following the lead of their deputies in Versailles. They had formed a citizen militia, known as the National Guard, and were prepared to defend their concept of justice and law.

The people who stormed the Bastille were not the poor, the unemployed, the criminals, or the urban rabble, as they were portrayed by their detractors. They were bourgeois and petit bourgeois, shopkeepers, guild members, family men and women, who considered it their right to seize arms to protect their interests. The Marquis de Lafayette (1757–1834), a noble beloved of the people because of his participation in the American Revolution, helped organize the National Guard. Under his direction, the militia adopted the tricolor flag as their standard. The tricolor combined the red and blue colors of the city of Paris with the white of the Bourbon royal family. It became the flag of the Revolution, replacing the fleur-de-lis of the Bourbons. It is the national flag of France today.

The king could no longer dictate the terms of the constitution. By their actions, the people in arms had ratified the National Assembly. Louis XVI was forced to yield. The events in Paris set off similar uprisings in cities and towns throughout France. National guards in provincial cities modeled themselves after the Parisian militia. Government officials fled their posts and abandoned their responsibilities. Commoners stood ready to

622

fill the power vacuum that now existed. But the Revolution was not just an urban phenomenon. The peasantry had their own grievances and their own way of making a revolution.

The Revolution of the Peasantry

In the spring and early summer of 1789, food shortages drove bands of armed peasants to attack manor houses throughout France. In the areas surrounding Paris and Versailles, peasants destroyed game and devastated the forests where the king and his nobles hunted. The anger reflected in these seemingly isolated events was suspended as the hope grew that the proceedings at Versailles would produce results. Remote as peasant involvement in the drawing up of the *cahiers* might have been, peasants everywhere expected that aid was at hand.

News of the events of Versailles and then of the revolutionary action in Paris did not reassure rural inhabitants. By the end of June the hope of deliverance from crippling taxes and dues was rapidly fading. The news of the Oath of the Tennis Court and the storming of the Bastille terrified country folk, who saw the actions as evidence of an aristocratic plot that threatened sorely needed reforms. As information moved along postal routes in letters from delegates to their supporters, or news was repeated in the Sunday market gatherings, distortions and exaggerations crept in. It seemed to rural inhabitants that their world was falling apart. Some peasants believed that Paris was in the hands of brigands and that the king and the Estates-General were victims of an aristocratic plot. Rural vision, fueled by empty stomachs, was apocalyptic.

This state of affairs was aggravated as increasing numbers of peasants had been pushed off the land to seek employment as transient farm laborers, moving from one area to another with the cycles of sowing and harvesting. Throughout the 1780s the number of peasants without land was increasing steadily. Filthy, poorly dressed, and starving men, women, and children were frightening figures to villagers who feared that the same fate would befall them with the next bad harvest. As one landowner lamented, "We cannot lie down without fear, the nighttime paupers have tormented us greatly, to say nothing of the daytime ones, whose numbers are considerable."

Most peasants had lived in the same place for generations and knew only the confines of their own villages. They were uneasy about what existed beyond the horizon. Transients, often speaking strange dialects, disrupted and threatened the social universe of the village. In order to survive, wanderers often resorted to petty theft, stealing fruit from trees or food from unwatched hearths. Traveling often in groups, hordes of vagabonds struck fear into the hearts of farmworkers, trampling crops and sleeping in open fields. Peasants were sure that these unfortunate souls were brigands paid by the local aristocracy to persecute a peasantry already stretched to the breaking point.

Hope gave way to fear. Beginning on 20 July 1789, peasants in different areas of France reacted with a kind of collective hysteria, spreading false rumors of a great conspiracy. Fear gripped whole villages, and in some areas spawned revolt. Just as urban workers had connected their economic hardships to politics, so too did desperate peasants see their plight in political terms. They banded together and marched to the residences of the local nobility, breaking into the chateaus with

This engraving from the late eighteenth century shows French country houses ablaze while speeding carriages carry their frightened owners to safety. The peasants attacked and looted the houses of the gentry and burned the rolls of feudal duties.

a single mission in mind: to destroy all legal documents by which nobles claimed payments, dues, and services from local peasants. They drove out the lords and in some cases burned their chateaus, putting an end to the tyranny of the privileged over the countryside. The peasants had taken matters into their own hands. In the bonfires of aristocratic documents, peasants intended to consign the last vestiges of aristocratic privilege to the flames.

The overthrow of privileges rooted in a feudal past was not as easy as that. Members of the National Assembly were aghast at the eruption of rural violence. They knew that to stay in power they had to maintain peace. They also knew that to be credible they had to protect property. Peasant destruction of seigneurial claims posed a real dilemma for the bourgeois deputies directing the Revolution. If they gave in to peasant demands, they risked losing aristocratic support and undermining their own ability to control events. If they gave in to the aristocracy, they risked a social revolution in the countryside, which they could not police or repress. Liberal members of the aristocracy cooperated with the bourgeois leaders in finding a solution.

In a dramatic meeting that lasted through the night of 4–5 August 1789, the National Assembly agreed to abolish the principle of privilege. The peasants had won—or thought they had. In the weeks and months ahead, rural people learned they had lost their own prerogatives—the rights to common grazing and gathering—and were expected to buy their way out of their feudal services. In the meantime, parliamentary action had saved the day, as the deputies stabilized the situation through legislating compromise.

Women's Actions

Women participated with men in both urban and rural revolutionary actions. Acting on their own, women were responsible for the most dramatic event of the early years of the Revolution: in October 1789 they forced the king and the royal family to leave Versailles for Paris to deal in person with the problems of bread supply, high prices, and starvation. Women milling about in the marketplaces of Paris on the morning of 5 October were complaining bitterly about the high cost and shortages of bread. The National Assembly was in session and the National Guards were patrolling the streets of Paris. But these trappings of political change had no impact on the brutal realities of the marketplace.

Women were in charge of buying the food for their families. Every morning they stood in lines with their neighbors reenacting the familiar ritual. Some mornings they were turned away, told by the baker or his assistants that there was no

A contemporary print of the women of Paris advancing on Versailles. The determined marchers are shown waving pikes and dragging an artillery piece. The women were hailed as heroines of the Revolution.

bread. On other days they did not have enough coins in their purses to buy this staple of their diet. Women, who were responsible for managing the consumption of the household, were most directly in touch with the state of provisioning the capital. When they were unable to feed their families, the situation became intolerable.

So it was on the morning of 5 October 1789, that six thousand Parisian women marched out of the city and toward Versailles. They were taking their problem to the king with the demand that he solve it. Later in the day, Lafayette, sympathetic to the women's cause, led the Parisian National Guard to Versailles to mediate events. The women were armed with pikes, the simple weapon available to the poorest defender of the Revolution, and they were prepared to use them. The battle came early the next morning, when the women, tired and cold from waiting all night at the gates of the palace, invaded the royal apartments and chased Marie Antoinette from her bedroom. Several members of the royal guards, hated by the people of Paris for alleged insults against the tricolor cockade, were killed by the angry women, who decapitated them and mounted their heads on pikes. A shocked Louis XVI agreed to return with the crowd to Paris. The crowd cheered Louis' decision, which briefly reestablished his personal popularity. But as monarch, he had been humiliated at the hands of women of the capital. "The baker, the baker's wife, and the baker's son" were forced to return to Paris that very day. Louis XVI was now captive to the Revolution, whose efforts to form a constitutional monarchy he purported to support.

The Revolution Threatened

The disciplined deliberations of committees intent on fashioning a constitutional monarchy replaced the passion and fervor of revolutionary oratory. The National, or Constituent, Assembly divided France into new administrative units for the purpose of establishing better control over municipal governments. The administrative reformers intended that by the creation of *départements* the central government would have greater control over local interests and that anarchy would be avoided.

In addition to new administrative trappings, the government promoted its own rituals. On 14 July 1790, militias from each of the newly created eighty-three *départements* of France came together in Paris to celebrate the first anniversary of the storming of the Bastille. A new national holiday was born and with it a sense of devotion and patriotism for the new France liberated by the Revolution. In spite of these unifying elements, however, the newly achieved revolutionary consensus showed signs of breaking down.

In February 1790 legislation dissolved all monasteries and convents, except for those that provided aid to the poor or that served as educational institutions. As the French church was stripped of its lands, Pope Pius VI (1775–99) denounced the principles of the Revolution. In July 1790 the government approved the Civil Constitution of the Clergy: priests now became the equivalent of paid agents of the state. By requiring an oath of loyalty to the state from all practicing priests, the National Assembly created a new arena for dissent: Catholics were forced to choose to embrace or reject the Revolution. Many "nonjuring" priests who refused to take the oath went into hiding. The wedge driven between the Catholic church and revolutionary France allowed a mass-based counterrevolution to emerge. Aristocratic émigrés who had fled the country because of their opposition to the Revolution were languishing because of lack of a popular base. From his headquarters in Turin, the king's younger brother, the comte d'Artois, was attempting to incite a civil war in France. When the revolutionaries decided to attack the Church not just as a landed and privileged institution but also as a religious one, the counterrevolution rapidly expanded.

The Constitution of 1791, completed after over two years of deliberations, established a constitutional monarchy with a ministerial executive power answerable to a legislative assembly. Louis XVI, formerly the divinely anointed ruler of France, was now "Louis, by the grace of God and the constitutional law of the state, King of the French." In proclaiming his acceptance of the constitution, Louis expressed the sentiments of many when he said, "The end of the revolution is come. It is time that order be reestablished so that the constitution may receive the support now most necessary to it; it is time to settle the opinion of Europe concerning the destiny of France, and to show that French men are worthy of being free."

Louis, who had been wrong often enough in the past, could not have been more mistaken when he declared that the end of the Revolution was at hand.

The Constitution of 1791 marked the triumph of the principles of the Revolution. But it was at best a precarious political compromise. Months before the ink was dry on the final document, the actions of the king doomed the new constitution to failure. To be successful, constitutional monarchy required a king worthy of honor and respect. Louis XVI seemed to be giving the revolutionaries what they wanted by cooperating with the framers of the constitution. Yet late one night in June 1791, Louis XVI, Marie Antoinette, and their children disguised themselves as commoners, crept out of the royal apartments in the Tuileries Palace, and fled Paris. Louis intended to leave France to join foreign forces opposing the Revolution at Metz. He got as far as Varennes, where he was captured by soldiers of the National Guards and brought back to a shocked Paris. The king had abandoned the Revolution. Although he was not put to death for another year and a half, he was more than ever a prisoner of the Revolution. The monarchy was effectively finished as part of a political solution and with its demise went liberal hopes for a constitutional settlement.

The defection of the king was certainly serious, but it was not the only problem facing the revolutionaries. Other problems plagued the revolutionary government, notably the fiscal crisis coupled with inflation, and foreign war.

In order to establish its seriousness and legitimacy, the National Assembly had been willing in 1789 to absorb the debts of the old regime. The new government could not sell titles and offices, as the king had done to deal with financial problems, but it did confiscate Church property. In addition, it issued treasury bonds in the form of *assignats* in order to raise money. The assignats soon assumed the status of banknotes. By spring 1790, in spite of growing public suspicion, the assignats became compulsory legal tender. Initially they were to be backed by land confiscated from the Church and now being sold by the state. But the need for money soon outran the value of the land available and the government continued to print assignats according to its needs. De-

preciation of French currency in international markets and inflation at home resulted. The revolutionary government found itself in a situation which in certain respects was worse than that experienced by Louis XVI before the calling of the Estates-General. Assignat-induced inflation produced a sharp decline in fortunes of bourgeois investors living on fixed incomes. Rising prices meant increased misery for workers and peasants.

New counter revolutionary groups were becoming frustrated with revolutionary policies. Throughout the winter and spring of 1791–92 people rioted and demanded that prices be fixed, as the assignat dropped to less than half of its face value. Peasants refused to sell their crops for the worthless paper. Hoarding further drove up prices. The situation was becoming desperate, caused now not by crop failures or the weather but by government policy. Angry crowds turned to pillaging, rioting, and murders, which became more frequent as the value of the currency declined and prices rose.

Foreign war beginning in the fall of 1791 also challenged stability. Some moderate political leaders welcomed war as a blessing in disguise, since it could divert the attention of the masses away from problems at home and could promote loyalty to the Revolution. Others envisioned war as a great crusade to bring revolutionary principles to oppressed peoples throughout Europe. The king and queen, trapped by the Revolution, saw war as their only hope of liberation. Louis XVI could be rightfully restored as the leader of a France defeated by the sovereigns of Europe. Others opposed the war, believing it would destabilize the Revolution. France must solve its problems at home, they argued, before fighting a foreign enemy. Louis, however, encouraged those ministers and advisers eager for battle. In April 1792, France declared war against Austria.

Individuals, events, economic realities, and the nature of politics conspired against the success of the first constitutional experiment. The king's attempt to flee France and the Revolution in the summer of 1791 seriously wounded the attempt at compromise. Many feared that the goals of the Revolution could not be preserved in a country at war and with a king of dubious loyalties.

Experimenting with Democracy

A political universe populated by individual citizens replaced the eighteenth-century world of subjects loyal to their king. This new construction of politics in which all individuals were equal ran counter to prevailing ideas about collective identities defined in guilds and orders. Before the Revolution, public opinion was being voiced outside of traditional institutions—in cafes, salons, and philosophical societies. French provincial academies sponsored a dynamic intellectual life as centers for debate over capital punishment, civic virtue, and the best form of government. Nobles and bourgeois met in these provincial academies to talk about government, power, and the means of social improvement.

New forms of social intercourse fostered the growth of democratic ideas and the emergence of a new political culture that was both progressive and democratic, and that considered individuals as perfectible. Political documents, like the Constitution of 1791, reflected these changes to some extent. But the revolutionaries intended to do more than reallocate political power: they aimed to change the ways people thought, talked, and lived. People needed new symbols to replace those that had been repudiated. They needed new words to talk about new political realities. The Revolution created its own calendar, setting the beginning of accounted time in the revolutionary era. The first day of the first year of the rest of history was 22 September 1792—the beginning of the Year I. New patterns of speech that were developed during the Revolution fostered a new way of looking at the world. People now addressed each other familiarly as "tu" instead of the more formal "vous," as the vague concepts of liberty, equality, and fraternity took root in people's lives.

The French Revolution was a school for the French nation. People on all levels of society learned politics by doing it. In the beginning, experience helped. The elites, both noble and bourgeois, had served in government and administration. But the rules of the game under the old regime had been very different, with birth determining power. After 1789, all men were declared free and equal, in opportunity if not in rights. Men of ability and talent, who had served as middlemen for the privileged elite under the old regime, now claimed power as their due. Many of them were lawyers, educated in the rules and regulations of the society of orders. They experienced firsthand the problems of the exercise of power in the old regime and had their own ideas about reform. But the school of the Revolution did not remain the domain of a special class. Women demanded their places. Workers seized their rights. And because of the inherent contradictions of representation and participation, experimenting with democracy led to outcomes that did not look very democratic at all.

Declaring Political Rights

"Liberty consists in the ability to do whatever does not harm another." So wrote the revolutionary deputies of 1789. Sounding a refrain similar to that of the American Declaration of Independence, the *Declaration of the Rights of Man and Citizen* appeared on 26 August 1789. The document amalgamated a variety of Enlightenment ideas drawn from the works of political philosophy, including those of Locke and Montesquieu. "Men are born and remain free and equal in rights. Social distinctions may be based only on common utility." Perhaps most significant of all was the attention given to property, which was declared a "sacred and inviolable," "natural," and "imprescriptable" right of man.

In the year of tranquillity that followed the violent summer of 1789, the new politicians set themselves the task of creating institutions based on the principle of liberty and others embodied in the *Declaration of the Rights of Man and Citizen.* The result was the Constitution of 1791, a documentary monument to the belief in a progressive constitutional monarchy. A king accountable to an elected parliamentary body would lead France into a prosperous and just age. The constitution acknowledged the people's sovereignty as the source of political power. It also enshrined the principle of property by making voting rights dependent on property ownership. All men might be equal before the law, but by the Constitution of 1791 only wealthy men had the right to vote for

Slaves revolting against the French in Saint Domingue in 1791. Napoleon sent an army to restore colonial rule in 1799, but yellow fever decimated the French soldiers and the rebels defeated the weakened French army in 1803.

representatives and hold office. A new male elite, those who owned property and controlled wealth, was emerging within the Revolution.

All titles of nobility were abolished. In the early period of the Revolution, civil liberties were extended to Protestants and Jews, who had been persecuted under the old regime. Previously excluded groups were granted freedom of thought and worship and full civil liberties. More reluctantly, slavery in the colonies was outlawed in 1794. Slave unrest in Saint Domingue (modern-day Haiti) had coincided with the political conflicts of the Revolution and exploded in rebellion in 1791, driving the revolutionaries in Paris to support black independence although it was at odds with French colonial interests. Led by Toussaint L'Ouverture (1743–1803), black rebels worked to found an independent Haitian state, which was declared in 1804. But the concept of equality with regard to race remained incompletely integrated with revolutionary principles, and slavery was reestablished in the French colonies in 1802.

Men were the subject of these newly defined rights. No references to women or their rights appear in the constitutions or the official Declarations of Rights. Women's organizations agitated for an equitable divorce law, and divorce was legalized in September 1792. Women were critical

actors in the Revolution from its very inception and their presence shaped and directed the outcome of events, as the women's march to Versailles in 1789 made clear. The Marquis de Condorcet (1743–94), elected to the Legislative Assembly in 1791, was one of the first to chastise the revolutionaries for overlooking the political rights of women who, he pointedly observed, were half of the human race. "Either no individual of the human race has genuine rights, or else all have the same; and he who votes against the right of another, whatever the religion, color, or sex of that other, has henceforth abjured his own." Condorcet argued forcefully but unsuccessfully for the right of women to be educated and for state support of this right. Women's talents, he warned, were slumbering under the ignorance of neglect.

"Woman, wake up!" In such a manner did Olympe de Gouges (d. 1793), a self-educated playwright and the daughter of a butcher, address French women in 1791. Aware that women were being denied the new rights of liberty and property extended to all men by the *Declaration of the Rights of Man and Citizen*, Gouges composed a *Declaration of the Rights of Woman and Citizen*, modeled on the 1789 document. "Article One. Woman is born free and remains equal in rights to man." Women are equal to men before the law in citizenship, duties, and property rights. "The right of property is inviolable and sacred to both sexes, jointly or separately." Gouges spoke out for the freedom of slaves and for women's political rights. She foreshadowed her own demise for her political beliefs at the mercy of revolutionary justice when she wrote, "Woman has the right to mount the scaffold; she must equally have the right to mount the rostrum."

The Second Revolution: The Revolution of the People

The first revolution of 1789 through the beginning of 1792 was based on liberty—the liberty to compete, to own, and to succeed. The second revolution that began in 1792 took equality as its rallying cry. This was the revolution of the working people of French cities. The popular movement that spearheaded political action in 1792 was committed to equality of rights in a way not characteristic of the leaders of the Revolution of 1789. Urban workers were not benefiting from the Revolution, but they had come to believe in their own power as political beings. Organized on the local level into sections, craftsmen in cities identified themselves as *sans-culottes*, literally those who did not wear knee breeches, to distinguish themselves from the privileged elite.

On 10 August 1792, the people of Paris stormed the Tuileries, chanting their demands for "Equality!" and "Nation!" The people tramped across the silk sheets of the king's bed and broke his fine furniture, reveling in the private chambers of the royal family. Love and respect for the king had vanished. What the people of Paris demanded now was universal manhood suffrage and participation in a popular democracy. Working people were now acting independently of other factions, and the bourgeois political leadership became quickly aware of the need to scramble.

Who constituted the popular movement? The self-designated *sans-culottes* were the working men and women of Paris. Some were wealthier than others, some were wage earners, but all shared a common identity as consumers in the marketplace. They hated the privileged (*les gros*), who appeared to be profiting at the expense of the people. The *sans-culottes* wanted government power to be decentralized, with neighborhoods ruling themselves through sectional organizations. As the have-nots, they were increasingly intent on pulling down the haves, and they translated this sense of vengeance into a new revolutionary justice. When they invaded the Tuileries Palace on the morning of 10 August, the *sans-culottes* did so in the name of the people. They saw themselves as patriots whose duty it was to brush the monarchy aside. The people were now a force to be reckoned with and feared.

"Terror is the Order of the Day"

Political factions characterized revolutionary politics from the start. The terms *Left* and *Right*, which came to represent opposite ends of the political spectrum, originated in a description of where people sat in the Assembly in relation to the podium. The arrest and trial of Louis XVI for treason, followed by his execution on the guillotine in January 1793, irrevocably polarized politics. As the royalist Right was weakened and eliminated, political factions within the new legislative body, the National Convention, were described in terms borrowed from geography. The Mountain, sitting in the upper benches on the left, was made up of members of the Jacobin Club (named for its meeting place in an abandoned monastery). The Jacobins were the most radical element in the National Convention, supporting democratic solutions and speaking in favor of the cause of people in the streets. The Plain held the moderates, who were concerned with maintaining public order against popular unrest. Many members of the Plain came to be called Girondins in the mistaken belief that they originated in the Gironde *département* of France.

Both Girondins and Jacobins were from the middle ranks of the bourgeoisie and both groups were dedicated to the principles of the Revolution. At first the two groups were more similar than different. Although controlling the ministries, the Girondins began to lose their hold on the Revolution and the war. The renewed European war fragmented the democratic movement, and the Girondins, unable to control violence at home, saw political control slipping away. They became prisoners of the Revolution when eighty thousand armed Parisians surrounded the National Convention in June 1793.

Girondin power had been eroding in the critical months between August 1792 and June 1793. A new leader was working quietly and effectively behind the scenes to weld a partnership between the popular movement of *sans-culottes* and the Jacobins. He was Maximilien Robespierre (1758–94), leader of the Mountain and the Jacobin Club. Robespierre was typical of the new breed of revolutionary politician. Only 31 years old in 1789, he wrote mediocre poems and attended the local provincial academy to discuss the new ideas, when he was not practicing law in his hometown of Arras. Elected to the Estates-General, Robespierre began to make his mark as a bright young man with a promising political future. He joined the Jacobin Club and quickly rose to become its leader. He was willing to take controversial stands on issues: unlike most of his fellow members of the Mountain, he opposed the war in 1792. Although neither an original thinker nor a compelling orator, Robespierre discovered with the Revolution that he was a stunning political

The Guillotine and Revolutionary Justice

In the sultry summer days of 1792, Parisians found a new way to entertain themselves. They attended executions. French men, women, and children were long accustomed to watching criminals being tortured and put to death in public view. During the old regime, spectators could enjoy the variety of a number of methods: drawing and quartering, strangling, or hanging. Decapitation, reputedly a less painful death, was a privilege reserved for nobles sentenced for capital crimes. The Revolution extended this formerly aristocratic privilege to all criminals condemned to death. What especially attracted people into public squares in the third year of the Revolution was the introduction of a novel method of decapitation. In 1792 the new instrument of death, the guillotine, became the center of the spectacle of revolutionary justice.

The guillotine promised to eliminate the suffering of its victims. Axes, swords, and sabers—the traditional tools of decapitation and dismemberment—were messy and undependable, producing slow and bloody ordeals when inept and drunken executioners missed their mark or victims flinched at the fatal moment. The design of the guillotine took all of this into account. On its easel-like wooden structure, victims, lying on their stomachs, were held in place with straps and a kind of

pillory. Heavy pulleys guaranteed that the sharp blade would fall efficiently from its great height. A basket was placed at the base of the blade to catch the severed head, another was used to slide the headless body for removal through the base of the scaffolding. In place of unintended torture and gore, the guillotine was devised as a humanitarian instrument to guarantee swift and painless death.

It should have been called the Louisette, after its inventor, Dr. Antoine Louis. In what now seems a dubious honor, the new machine was named instead after its greatest supporter, Dr. Joseph Ignace Guillotin, a delegate to the National Assembly. Both Guillotin and Louis were medical doctors, men of science influenced by Enlightenment ideas and committed to the Revolution's elimination of the cruelty of older forms of punishment. In the spirit of scientific experimentation, Louis' invention was tested on sheep, cadavers, and then convicted thieves. In 1792 it was used for the first time against another class of offenders, political prisoners.

Early in the Revolution, the Marquis de Condorcet, *philosophe* and mathematician, had opposed capital punishment with the argument that the state did not have the right to take life. Ironically, Maximilien Robespierre, future

architect of the Reign of Terror, was one of the few revolutionaries who agreed with Condorcet. Those who favored justice by execution of the state's enemies prevailed. The revolutionary hero and associate of the radical Jacobins, Jean Paul Marat (1743–93), who was himself stabbed to death in his bathtub, advocated the state's use of violence against its enemies: "In order to ensure public tranquillity, 200,000 heads must be cut off." By the end of 1792, as revolution and civil war swept over France, eighty-three identical guillotines were constructed and installed in each of the *départements* of France. For the next two years, the guillotine's great blade was rhythmically raised and lowered daily in public squares all over France. In the name of the Revolution, the "axe of the people" dispatched over 50,000 victims.

Although intended as a humanitarian instrument, the guillotine became the symbol of all that was arbitrary and repressive about a revolution run amok. Day and night in Paris, the Revolutionary Tribunal delivered the death sentence to the "enemies of the people." Most of those executed were members of what had been the Third Estate: members of the bourgeoisie, workers, peasants. Only 15 percent of the condemned were nobles and priests. During the Terror, the

guillotine was sometimes used to settle old scores. *Sans-culottes* turned in their neighbors, sometimes over long-standing grievances that owed more to spite than politics. The most fanatical revolutionaries had fantasies that guillotines were about to be erected on every street corner to dispense with hoarders and traitors. Others suggested that guillotines be made portable so that by putting justice on wheels, it could be taken directly to the people.

As usual, Paris set the style. The most famous of the guillotines stood on the Place du Carrousel, deliberately placed in front of the royal palace of the Tuileries. It was eventually moved to the larger Place de la Révolution in order to accommodate the growing numbers of spectators. Famous victims drew especially large crowds. The revolutionary drama took on the trappings of a spectacle, as hawkers sold toy guillotines, miniature pikes, and liberty caps as souvenirs, along with the usual food and drink. Troops attended these events but not to control the crowd. Members of the National Guard in formation, their backs to the people, faced the stage of the scaffold. They, like the citizenry, were there to witness the birth of a new nation and, by their presence, to give legitimacy to the event. The crowd entered into the ritual, cheering the victim's last words and demanding that the executioner hold high the severed head. In the new political culture death was a festival.

For two centuries, Western societies have debated the legit-imacy of the death sentence and have periodically considered the relative merits of the guillotine, the gas chamber, and the electric chair. For the French, the controversy temporarily ceased in 1794, when people were convinced that justice had gotten out of hand and that they had had enough. For the time being, the government put an end to capital punishment. The guillotine would return. But at the height of its use between 1792 and 1794, it had played a unique role in forging a new system of justice: the guillotine had been the great leveler. In the ideology of democracy, people were equal—in death as well as in life. The guillotine came to be popularly known as the "scythe of equality." It killed king and commoner alike.

632 Chapter 20 The French Revolution and the Napoleonic Era, 1789–1815

tactician. He gained a following and learned how to manipulate it. It was he who engineered the Jacobins' replacement of the Girondins as leaders of the government.

Robespierre's chance for real power came when he assumed leadership of the Committee of Public Safety in July 1793. Due to the threat of internal anarchy and external war, the elected body, the National Convention, yielded political control to the twelve-man Committee of Public Safety that ruled dictatorially under Robespierre's direction. The Great Committee, as it was known at the time, orchestrated the Reign of Terror (1793–94), a period of systematic state repression that meted out justice in the people's name. Summary trials by specially created revolutionary tribunals were followed by the swift execution of the guilty under the blade of the guillotine.

Influenced by the *Social Contract* (1762) and other writings of Jean-Jacques Rousseau, Robespierre believed that sovereignty resided with the people. For him individual wills and even individual rights did not matter when faced with the will of the nation. The king was dead; the people were the new source of political power. Robespierre saw himself in the all-important role of interpreting and shaping the people's will. His own task was to guide the people "to the summit of its destinies." As he explained to his critics, "I am defending not my own cause but the public cause." As head of the Great Committee, Robespierre oversaw a revolutionary machinery dedicated to economic regulation, massive military mobilization, and a punitive system of revolutionary justice characterized by the slogan, "Terror is the Order of the Day." Militant revolutionary committees and revolutionary tribunals were established in the *départements* to identify traitors and to mete out the harsh justice that struck hardest against those members of the bourgeoisie who were perceived as opponents of the government.

The guillotine became the symbol of revolutionary justice, but it was not the only means of execution. In Lyon, officials of the Reign of Terror had prisoners tied to stakes in open fields and fired on them with cannon. In Nantes, a Parisian administrator of the new justice had enemies of the Revolution chained to barges and drowned in the estuary of the Loire. The civil war, which raged most violently in the Vendée in the west of France,

consisted often of primitive massacres that sent probably a quarter of a million people to their deaths. The bureaucratized Reign of Terror was responsible for about forty thousand executions in a nine-month period, resulting in the image of the republicans as "drinkers of blood." (See Special Feature, "The Guillotine and Revolutionary Justice," pp. 630–631.)

The Cult of the Supreme Being, a civic religion influenced by Rousseau's ideas about nature, followed dechristianization. The cathedral of Notre Dame de Paris was turned into the Temple of Reason, and the new religion established its own festivals to undermine the persistence of Catholicism. The cult was one indication of the Reign of Terror's attempt to create a new moral universe of revolutionary values.

Conspicuously absent from the summit of political power were women. After 1793 Jacobin revolutionaries, who were willing to empower the popular movement of workers, turned against women's participation and denounced it. Women's associations were outlawed and the Society of Revolutionary Republican Women was disbanded. Olympe de Gouges was guillotined. Women were made unfit for political participation, the Jacobins declared, by their biological functions of reproduction and child-rearing. Rousseau's ideas about family policy were probably more influential than his political doctrines. His best-selling books, *La Nouvelle Héloïse* (1761) and *Emile* (1762), which combined went into seventy-two editions before 1789, were moral works that transformed people's ideas about family life. Under his influence, the reading public came to value a separate and private sphere of domestic and conjugal values. Rousseau's own relations with women and the fact that he put his five illegitimate children in foundling hospitals contradicted his ideas about familial virtues. Following Rousseau's lead, Robespierre and the Jacobins insisted that the role of women as mothers was incompatible with women's participation in the political realm.

Robespierre attacked his critics to the Left and to the Right, thereby undermining the support he needed to stay in power. He abandoned the alliance with the popular movement that had been so important in bringing him to power. Robespierre's enemies—and he had many—were able to break the identification between political

The French Revolution

August 1788	Louis XVI announces meeting of Estates-General to be held May 1789
5 May 1789	Estates-General convenes
17 June 1789	Third Estate declares itself the National Assembly
20 June 1789	Oath of the Tennis Court
14 July 1789	Storming of the Bastille
20 July 1789	Revolution of peasantry begins
26 August 1789	*Declaration of the Rights of Man and Citizen*
5 October 1789	Parisian women march to Versailles; force Louis XVI to return to Paris
February 1790	Monasteries, convents dissolved
July 1790	Civil Constitution of the Clergy
June 1791	Louis XVI and family attempt to flee Paris; are captured and returned
April 1792	France declares war on Austria
10 August 1792	Storming of the Tuileries
22 September 1792	Revolutionary calendar implemented
January 1793	Louis XVI executed
July 1793	Robespierre assumes leadership of Committee of Public Safety
1793–94	Reign of Terror
1794	Robespierre guillotined
1799	Napoleon overthrows the Directory and seizes power

power and the will of the people that Robespierre had established. As a result, he was branded a traitor by the same process that he had enforced against many of his own enemies and friends. He saved France from foreign occupation and internal collapse but he could not save democracy through terror. If the will of the people legitimated new political forms, how could one be sure that the will of the people was being interpreted correctly? In the summer of 1794, Robespierre was guillotined. The Reign of Terror ceased with his death.

The Revolution did not end with the fall of Robespierre, but his execution initiated a new phase. For some, democracy lost its legitimacy. The popular movement was reviled and *sans-culotte* became a term of derision. Jacobins were forced underground. Price controls were abolished, resulting in extreme hardship for most urban residents. Out of desperation in April 1795, the Jacobins and the *sans-culottes* renewed their alliance, united in a dying revolutionary gasp to demand, "Bread and the Constitution of 1793." The politics of bread had never been more accurately captured in slogan. People saw the universal manhood suffrage of the unimplemented 1793 constitution as the way to solve their economic problems. But the popular revolution had failed. People had no bread and they had no power.

The End of the Revolution

The Revolution that had begun with a bang ended with a whimper. In the four years after Robespierre's fall, a new government by committee called the Directory appeared to offer mediocrity, caution, and opportunism, in place of the idealism and action of the early years of the Revolution. No successor to Robespierre stepped forward to command center stage; there were no heroes like Lafayette or the great Jacobin orator Georges-Jacques Danton (1759–94) to inspire patriotic fervor. Nor were there women like Olympe de Gouges to demand in the public arena equal rights for women. Most people, numbed after years of change, barely noticed that the Revolution was over. Ordinary men in parliamentary institutions effectively did the day-to-day job of running the government. They tried to steer a middle path between royalist resurgence and popular insurrection. Ironically, this nearly forgotten period in the history of the French Revolution was the fulfillment of the liberal hopes of 1789 for a stable, constitutional rule.

The Directory, however, continued to be dogged by European war. A mass army of conscripts and volunteers had successfully extended France's power and frontiers. France expelled foreign invaders and annexed territories, including

Belgium, while increasing its control in Holland, Switzerland, and Italy. But the expansion of revolutionary France was expensive and increasingly unpopular. Military defeats and the corruption of the Directory undermined government control. The Directory might have succeeded in the slow accretion of a parliamentary tradition. But reinstatement of conscription in 1798 met with widespread protest and resistance. No matter what their political leanings, people were weary. The people turned to those who promised stability and peace. Ironically, the savior that they found was a military man who plunged France into sixteen more years of intermittent war.

The Reign of Napoleon, 1799–1815

Napoleon is one of those individuals about whom one can say that if he had not lived, history would have been different. He left his mark on an age and on a continent. The great debate that rages to this day about Napoleon revolves around the question of whether he fulfilled the aims of the Revolution or perverted them. In his return to a monarchical model, Napoleon resembled the enlightened despots of eighteenth-century Europe. In a modern sense, he was also a dictator, manipulating the French people through a highly centralized administrative apparatus. He locked French society into a program of military expansionism that depleted its human and material resources. Yet, in spite of destruction and war, he dedicated his reign to building a French state according to the principles of the Revolution.

Bonaparte Seizes Power

In Paris in 1795 a young, penniless, and unknown military officer moved among the wealthy and the beautiful of Parisian society and longed for fame. Already nicknamed at school "the Little Corporal" on account of his short stature, he was snubbed because of his background and ridiculed for his foreign accent. His story is typical of all stories of thwarted ambition. Yet the outcome of this story is unique. Within four years this young man had become ruler of France. The

story of his ascent to power is also a story of both the demise and the legacy of the Revolution.

Napoleon Bonaparte (1769–1821) was a true child of the eighteenth century. He shared the *philosophes'* belief in a rational and progressive world. Born in Corsica, which until a few months before his birth was part of the Republic of Genoa, he received his training in French military schools. Even as a youth, he was arrogant and ambitious. But he could have never hoped to rise to a position of leadership in the army during the old regime because he lacked the noble birth necessary for advancement. The highest rank Napoleon could hope to achieve was that of captain or major.

The Revolution changed everything for him. First, it opened up careers previously restricted by birth, including those in the military, to talent. Second, the Revolution made new posts available when aristocratic generals defected and crossed over to the enemy side both before and after the execution of the king. Finally, the Revolution created great opportunities for military men to test their mettle. Foreign war and civil war required military leaders devoted to the Revolution.

Bonaparte's early career seemed a web of contradictions. Forced to flee Corsica because he had

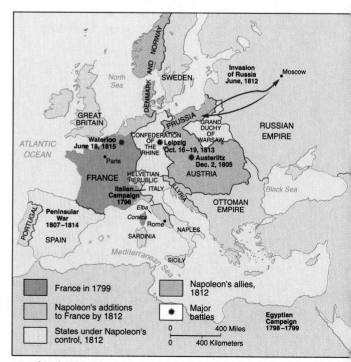

Napoleon's Empire

The 1804 coronation of Napoleon by Jacques Louis David. Pope Pius VII is seated behind the emperor, who is about to place a crown on the head of Josephine. Napoleon later ordered David to alter the painting to show the pope's hand raised in blessing.

sided with the Jacobins, he coolly crushed Parisian protesters who rioted against the Directory in 1795. His highly publicized campaigns in Egypt and Syria made him a hero at home as a defender of the government. Above all, his victories in the Italian campaign in 1796–97 launched his political career. As he extended French rule into central Italy, he became the embodiment of revolutionary values and energy. In 1799 he readily joined a conspiracy the pulled down the Directory, the government he had earlier preserved, and became the First Consul of a triumvirate of consuls.

Napoleon set out to secure his position of power by eliminating his enemies on the Left and weakening those on the Right. He guaranteed the security of property acquired in the Revolution, a move guaranteed to undercut royalists who wanted to return property to its original owners. Through policing forces and special criminal courts, law and order prevailed and civil war subsided. The First Consul promised a balanced budget and appeared to deliver it. Bonaparte spoke of healing the nation's wounds, especially those opened by religious grievances caused by dechristianization during the Revolution. Realizing the importance of religion in maintaining domestic peace, Napoleon reestablished relations with the pope in 1801 in the Concordat, which recognized Catholicism as the religion of the French and restored the Roman Catholic hierarchy.

Napoleon's popularity as First Consul flowed from his military and political successes and his religious reconciliation. He had come to power in 1799 by appealing for the support of the army. In 1802 Napoleon decided to extend his power by calling for a plebiscite in which he asked the electorate to vote him First Consul for life. Public support was overwhelming. An electoral landslide gave Napoleon greater political power than any of his Bourbon predecessors. Using revolutionary mechanisms, Napoleon laid the foundation for a new dynasty.

War and More War

Napoleon was at war or preparing for war during his entire reign. He certainly seemed up to the task of defeating the European powers. His military successes, real and apparent, before 1799 had been crucial in his bid for political power. By 1802, he had signed favorable treaties with both Austria and Great Britain. He appeared to deliver a lasting peace and to establish France as the dominant power in Europe. But the peace was

This engraving from the series Disasters of War by Francisco Goya depicts the horrors of war. The series was inspired by Napoleon's invasion and occupation of Spain from 1808 to 1813.

short-lived. In 1803 France embarked on an eleven-year period of continuous war. Under Napoleon's command, the French army delivered defeat after defeat to the European powers. Austria fell in 1805, Prussia in 1806, and the Russian armies of Alexander I were defeated at Friedland in 1807. In 1808 Napoleon invaded Spain in order to drive out British expeditionary forces intent on invading France. The great painter of the Spanish court, Francisco Goya (1746–1828), produced a series of etchings, *The Disasters of War*, that depicted the atrocities accompanying the Napoleonic invasion. Spain became a satellite kingdom in the French Empire, although the conflict continued.

Britain was the one exception to the string of Napoleonic victories. Napoleon initially considered sending a French fleet to invade the island nation. Lacking the strength necessary to achieve this, he turned to economic warfare and blockaded European ports against British trade. Beginning in 1806, the Continental System, as the blockade was known, erected a structure of protection for French manufactures in all continental European markets. The British responded to the tariff walls and boycotts with a naval blockade that succeeded in cutting French commerce off from its Atlantic markets. The Continental System did not prove to be the decisive policy that Napoleon had planned: the British economy was not broken and the French economy did not flourish when faced with restricted resources and the persistence of a black market in smuggled goods.

Still by 1810, the French leader was master of the Continent. French armies had extended revolutionary reforms and legal codes outside France and brought with them civil equality and religious toleration. They had also drained defeated countries of their resources and had inflicted the horrors of war with armies of occupation, forced billeting, and pillage. Napoleon's empire extended across Europe, with only a diminished Austria, Prussia, and Russia remaining independent. He placed his relatives and friends on the thrones of the new satellite kingdoms of Italy, Naples, Westphalia, Holland, and Spain. It was a fine empire, Napoleon later recalled in the loneliness of exile. Napoleon's empire did not endure, but at its acme, it seemed as though it would never fall.

Peace at Home

Napoleon measured domestic prosperity in terms of the stability of his reign. Through the

1802 plebiscite that voted him First Consul for life, he maintained the charade of constitutional rule, while he ruled as virtual dictator. In 1804, he abandoned all pretense and had himself proclaimed emperor of the French. Mimicking the rituals of kingship, he staged his own coronation and that of his wife Josephine at the cathedral of Notre Dame de Paris. Breaking the tradition set by Charlemagne, Napoleon took the crown from the hands of Pope Pius VII (1800–1823) and placed it on his own head.

Secure in his regime, surrounded by a new nobility that he created based on military achievement and talent, and that he rewarded with honors, Napoleon set about implementing sweeping reforms in every area of government. Like many of the men of the revolutionary assemblies who had received scientific educations in their youth, he recognized the importance of science for both industry and war. The Revolution had removed an impediment to the development of a national market by creating a uniform system of weights and measures. The metric system was established by 1799. But Napoleon felt the need to go further. France must be first in scientific research and application. To assure French predominance, Napoleon became a patron of science, supporting important work in the areas of physics and chemistry. Building for the future, Napoleon made science a pillar in the new structure of higher education.

The Directory had restored French prosperity through stabilization of the currency, fiscal reform, and support of industry. Napoleon's contribution to the French economy was the much needed reform of the tax system. He authorized the creation of a central banking system. French industries flourished under the protection of the state. The blockade forced the development of new domestic crops like beet-sugar and indigo, which became substitutes for colonial products. Napoleon extended the infrastructure of roads so necessary for the expansion of national and European markets.

Perhaps his greatest achievement was the codification of law, a task begun under the Revolution. Many of the new articles of the code were hammered out in Napoleon's presence, as he presided regularly over meetings with legal reformers. Combined with economic reforms, the code facilitated trade and the development of commerce by regularizing contractual relations and protecting property rights and equality before the law.

The civil laws of the new Napoleonic Code carved out a family policy characterized by hierarchy and subordination. Married women were neither independent nor equal to men in ownership of property, custody of children, and access to divorce. Women also lacked political rights. In the Napoleonic code, women, like children, were subjected to paternal authority. The Napoleonic philosophy of woman's place is well captured in an anecdote told by Madame Germaine de Staël (1766–1817), a leading intellectual of her day. As the daughter of Jacques Necker, the Swiss financier and adviser to Louis XVI at the time of the Revolution, she had been educated in Enlightenment ideas from an early age. On finding herself seated next to Napoleon at a dinner party, she asked him what was very likely a self-interested question: whom did he consider the greatest woman, alive or dead? Napoleon had no name to give her but he responded without pausing, "The one who has had the most children."

Napoleon turned his prodigious energies to every aspect of French life. He encouraged the arts, while creating a police force. He had monuments built but did not forget about sewers. He organized French administrative life in a fashion that has endured. In place of the popular democratic movement, he offered his own singular authority. In place of elections, clubs, and free associations, he gave France plebiscites and army service. To be sure, Napoleon believed in constitutions but he thought they should be "short and obscure." For Napoleon the great problem of democracy was its unpredictability. His regime solved that problem by eliminating choices.

Decline and Fall

Militarily, Napoleon went too far. The first cracks in the French facade began to show in the Peninsular War (1808–14) with Spain as Spanish guerrilla tactics proved costly for French troops. Napoleon's biggest mistake, the one that shattered the myth of his invincibility, occurred when he decided to invade Russia in June 1812. Having decisively defeated Russian forces in 1807, Napoleon entered into a peace treaty with Tsar Alexander I that guaranteed Russian allegiance to French policies. Alexander repudiated the Conti-

This 1835 painting by De Boisdenier depicts the suffering of Napoleon's Grand Army on the retreat from Moscow. The Germans were to meet a similar fate over one hundred years later when they invaded Russia without adequate winter clothing.

nental System in 1810 and appeared to be preparing for his own war against France. Napoleon seized the initiative, sure that he could defeat Russian forces once again. With an army of 500,000 men, Napoleon moved deep into Russia in the summer of 1812. The tsar's troops fell back in retreat. It was a strange war, one that pulled the French army to Moscow like a bird following breadcrumbs. When Napoleon and his men entered Moscow in September, they found a city in flames. The people of Moscow had destroyed their own city to deprive the French troops of winter quarters.

Winter comes early in Moscow, Napoleon's men discovered. They had left France basking in the warmth of summer and of certain and early victory. They now found themselves facing a severe Russian winter without overcoats, without supplies, and without food. The Russian strategy has become legendary. The Russians destroyed grain and shelter that might be of use to the French. Napoleon and his starving and frostbitten troops were forced into retreat. The horses of the French cavalry died because they were not properly shod for cold weather. The French army was

decimated. Fewer than 100,000 men made it back to France.

The empire began to crumble. Britain, unbowed by the Continental System, remained Napoleon's sworn enemy. Prussia joined Great Britain, Sweden, Russia, and Austria in opposing France anew. In the Battle of Nations at Leipzig in October 1813, France was forced to retreat. Napoleon refused a negotiated peace and fought on until the following March, when the victorious allies marched down the streets of Paris and occupied the French capital. Only then did Napoleon abdicate in favor of his young son, François, the titular king of Rome (1811–32).

Still it was not quite the end for Napoleon. While the European heads of state sat in Vienna trying to determine the future of Europe and France's place in it, Napoleon returned from his exile on the Mediterranean island of Elba. On 15 June 1815, Napoleon once again and for the final time confronted the European powers in one of the most famous military campaigns in history. With 125,000 loyal French forces, Napoleon seemed within hours of reestablishing the French Empire in Europe.

He had underestimated his opponents. The defeat of Napoleon's forces at Waterloo was decisive. Napoleon later explained, "Everything failed me just when everything had succeeded!" He had met his Waterloo, and with his defeat a new expression entered the language to describe devastating and permanent and irreversible downfall. Napoleon's return proved brief—it lasted only one hundred days. An era had come to an end. Napoleon was exiled to the less hospitable island of Saint Helena in the South Atlantic. For the next six years, Napoleon wrote his memoirs under the watchful eyes of his British jailors. He died a painful death from cancer on 5 May 1821.

The period of Revolution and Empire from 1789 to 1815 radically changed the face of France. A new, more cohesive elite of bourgeois and nobles emerged, sharing power based on wealth and status. Ownership of land remained a defining characteristic of both old and new elites. A new state bureaucracy, built on the foundations of the old, expanded and centralized state power.

The people as sovereign now legitimated political power. Napoleon at his most imperial never doubted that he owed his existence to the people. In this sense, Napoleon was the king of the Revolution—an apparently contradictory fusion of old forms and new ideology. Napoleon channeled democratic forces into enthusiasm for empire. He learned his lessons from the failure of the Bourbon monarchy and the politicians of the Revolution. For sixteen years Napoleon successfully reconciled the old regime with the new France. Yet he could not resolve the essential problem of democracy: the relationship between the will of the people and the exercise of political power. The picture in 1815 was not dramatically different from the situation in 1789. The Revolution might be over, but changes fueled by the revolutionary tradition were just beginning. The struggle for a workable democratic culture recurred in France for another century and elsewhere in Europe through the twentieth century.

The Reign of Napoleon

1799	Napoleon establishes consulate, becomes First Consul
1802	Plebiscite declares Napoleon First Consul for life
1801	Napoleon reestablishes relations with pope, restores Roman Catholic hierarchy
1804	Napoleon proclaims himself Emperor of the French
1806	Continental System implemented
1808–14	France engaged in Peninsular War with Spain
June 1812	Napoleon invades Russia
September 1812	French army reaches Moscow, is trapped by Russian winter
1813	Napoleon defeated at Battle of Nations at Leipzig
March 1814	Napoleon abdicates and goes into exile on island of Elba
March 1815	Napoleon escapes Elba and attempts to reclaim power
15 June 1815	Napoleon is defeated at Waterloo and exiled to island of Saint Helena

Suggestions for Further Reading

The Crisis of the Old Regime in France, 1715–48

C. B. A. Behrens, *Society, Government, and the Enlightenment* (New York: Harper & Row, 1985). A comparative study of eighteenth-century France and Prussia, focusing on the relationship between government and the ruling classes, that explains how pressures for change in both countries led to different outcomes, revolution in France, and reform in Prussia.

Olwen Hufton, *The Poor in Eighteenth-Century France, 1750–1789* (Oxford: Clarendon, 1974). Examines the lives of the poor before the Revolution and the institutions that attempted to deal with the problem of poverty.

Olwen Hufton, *Europe: Privilege and Protest, 1730–1789* (Sussex: The Harvester Press, 1980). An overview of the impact of rapid social, ideological, and economic changes on the concept and exercise of privilege.

Daniel Roche, *The People of Paris* (Berkeley, CA: University of California Press, 1987). An essay on popular culture in the eighteenth century, in which the author surveys the lives of the Parisian popular classes—servants, laborers, and artisans—and examines their housing, furnishing, dress, and leisure activities.

Isser Woloch, *Eighteenth-Century Europe: Tradition and Progress, 1715–1789* (New York: Norton, 1982). A discussion of eighteenth-century Europe, comparing social, economic, political, and intellectual developments elsewhere in Europe to the French experience, with special attention to cultural aspects, such as popular beliefs and religion.

The French Revolution and the End of the Old Regime

Georges Lefebvre, *The Great Fear of 1789* (New York: Pantheon Books, 1973). This classic study analyzes the rural panic that swept through parts of France in the summer of 1789. The Great Fear is presented as a distinct episode in the opening months of the Revolution, with its own internal logic.

François Furet and Denis Richet, *The French Revolution* (New York: Macmillan, 1970). Two experts on the French Revolution present a detailed overview of the period from 1789 to 1798 when Bonaparte returned to Paris.

Simon Schama, *Citizens* (New York: Knopf, 1989). A synthetic view that stresses the dynamic aspects of pre-revolutionary France, focussing on the nature of the social and cultural environment within which the Revolution occurred. The author argues that the violence of the Revolution was fueled by hostility to modernization.

D. M. G. Sutherland, *France, 1789–1815: Revolution and Counter-Revolution* (New York: Oxford University Press, 1986). An interpretation of the revolutionary period which stresses the struggle against counterrevolution and presents the Revolution as a complex and contradictory process of social and political conflict over incompatible rights and privileges enjoyed by significant portions of the population.

Michel Vovelle, *The Fall of the French Monarchy* (Cambridge: Cambridge University Press, 1984). A social history of the origins and early years of the Revolution beginning with a brief examination of the old regime and paying special attention to social and economic changes initiated by the Revolution, the role of the popular classes, and the creation of revolutionary culture.

Experimenting with Democracy

François Furet, *Interpreting the French Revolution* (Cambridge: Cambridge University Press, 1981). A series of essays challenging many of the assumptions concerning the causes and outcome of the Revolution and reviewing the historiography of the Revolution. The author argues that political crisis, not class conflict, was the Revolution's

primary cause and that revolutionary ideas concerning democracy are central to an understanding of the Terror.

Lynn Hunt, *Politics, Culture, and Class in the French Revolution* (Berkeley, CA: University of California Press, 1984). A study of the Revolution as the locus of the creation of modern political culture. The second half of the book examines the social composition and cultural experiences of the new political class that merged in the Revolution.

Joan B. Landes, *Women and the Public Sphere* (Ithaca, NY: Cornell University Press, 1988). Landes examines the genesis of the modern notion of the public sphere from a feminist perspective and argues that within the revolutionary process women were relegated to the private sphere of the domestic world.

Dorinda Outram, *The Body of the French Revolution: Sex, Class and Political Culture* (New Haven, CT: Yale University Press, 1989). Examines how images of the body in the late eighteenth century differed from class to class and how bourgeois attitudes toward physicality resulted in a gendered political discourse in which the hero replaced the king.

Albert Soboul, *The Sans-Culottes* (New York: Anchor, 1972). An exhaustive study of the artisans who composed the core of popular political activism in revolutionary Paris. The political demands and ideology of the *sans-culottes* are examined with the composition, culture, and actions of the popular movement during the Revolution.

The Reign of Napoleon, 1799–1815

Louis Bergeron, *France Under Napoleon* (Princeton, NJ: Princeton University Press, 1981). An analysis of the structure of Napoleon's regime, its social bases of support, and its opponents.

Felix Markham, *Napoleon* (New York: New American Library, 1963). This classic study treats both Napoleon's life and legend, while giving a balanced account of the social and intellectual life of the period and the impact of the Empire on Europe.

Jean Tulard, *Napoleon: The Myth of the Saviour* (London: Weidenfeld and Nicolson, 1984). This biography of Napoleon situates his rise to power within the crisis of legitimacy created by the destruction of the monarchy during the Revolution. The Empire is presented as a creation of the bourgeoisie who desired to end the Revolution and consolidate their gains and control over the lower classes.

Isser Woloch, *The French Veteran From the Revolution to the Restoration* (Chapel Hill, NC: University of North Carolina Press, 1979). Examines the social impact of revolutionary and Napoleonic policies by concentrating on the changing fortunes of war veterans.

21

Industrial Europe

Portrait of an Age

The Normandy train has reached Paris. The coast and the capital are once again connected. Passengers in their city finery disembark and are greeted by others who have awaited their scheduled arrival. Workmen stand ready to unload freight, porters to carry luggage. Steam billows forth from the resting engine, which is the object of all human activity. The engine stares at us as enigmatically as any character in a Renaissance portrait. We hardly think to ask what lies behind the round, black face with its headlight for an eye and chimney for a snout. Yet the train that has arrived in *La Gare Saint-Lazarre* by Claude Monet (1840–1926) is as much the central character in this portrait of the industrial age as was any individual in portraits of ages past.

The train's iron bulk dwarfs the people around it. Indeed, iron dominates our attention. Tons of it are in view. The rails, the lampposts, the massive frame of the station, no less than the train itself, are all formed from iron—pliable, durable, inexpensive iron, the miracle product of industrialization. The iron station with its glass panels became as central a feature of nineteenth-century cities as were stone cathedrals in the Middle Ages. Railway stations changed the shape of urban settings just as railway travel changed the lives of millions of people.

There had never been anything like it before. Ancient Romans had hitched four horses to their chariots; nineteenth-century Europeans hitched four horses to their stagecoaches. The technology of overland transportation had hardly changed in two thousand years. Coach journeys were long, uncomfortable, and expensive. They were governed by the elements and the muddy, rutted roads, which caused injuries to humans and horses with alarming regularity. First-class passengers rode inside, where they were jostled against one another and breathed the dust that the horses kicked up in front of them. Second-class passengers rode on top, braving the elements and risking life and limb in an accident.

Railway travel was a quantum leap forward. It was faster, cheaper, and safer. Overnight it changed conceptions of time, space, and, above all, of speed. People could journey to what once were distant places in a single day. Voyages became trips, and the travel holiday was born. Commerce was transformed, as was the way in which it was conducted. Large quantities of goods could be shipped quickly from place to place, orders could be instantly filled. The whole notion of locality changed, as salesmen could board a morning train for what only recently had been an unreachable market. Branch offices could be overseen by regional directors, services and products could be standardized, and the gap between great and small cities and between town and countryside could be narrowed. Wherever they went, the railroads created links that had never been forged before. In Britain, the railroad schedule became the source of the creation of official time. Trains that left London were scheduled to arrive at their destinations according to London time, which came to be kept at the royal observatory in Greenwich. Trains carried fresh fish inland from the coasts and fresh vegetables from rural farms to city tables. Mail moved farther and more quickly; news spread more evenly. Fashionable ideas from the capital cities of Europe circulated everywhere, as did new knowledge and discoveries. The railroads brought both diversity and uniformity.

They also brought wonderment. The engine seemed to propel itself with unimaginable power and at breathtaking speed. The English actress Fanny Kemble (1809–93) captured the sensation memorably: "You can't imagine how strange it seemed to be journeying on thus, without any visible cause of progress other than the magical machine, with its flying white breath and rhythmical, unvarying pace. I felt no fairy tale was ever half so wonderful as what I saw." For many the railroad symbolized the genius of the age in which they were living, an age in which invention, novelty, and progress were everywhere to be seen. It combined the great innovations of steam, coal, and iron that were transforming nearly every aspect of ordinary life. But for others, the railway was just as centrally a symbol of disquiet, of the passing of a way of life that was easier to understand and to control. "Seated in the old mail-coach we needed no evidence out of ourselves to indicate the velocity," wrote the English author Thomas De Quincey (1785–1859) in his obituary for the passing of horse travel. "We heard our speed, we saw it, we felt it. This speed was not the product of blind, insensate agencies, that had no sympathy to give, but was incarnated in the fiery eyeballs of the noblest among brutes."

The fruits of the railways, like the fruits of industrialization, were not all sweet. As the nineteenth century progressed, there could be no doubt that year by year one way of life was being replaced by another. More and more laborers were leaving the farms for the factories, and more and more products were being made by machines. Everywhere there was change, but it was not always or everywhere for the better. Millions of people poured into cities that mushroomed up without plan or intention. Population growth, factory labor, and ultimately the grinding poverty that they produced overwhelmed traditional means of social control. Families and communities split apart, the expectations of ordinary people were no longer predictable. Life was spinning out of control for individuals, for groups, for whole societies, an engine racing down a track that only occasionally ended as placidly as did the Normandy train at the Gare Saint-Lazarre.

The Traditional Economy

The curse of Adam and Eve was that they would earn their daily bread by the sweat of their brows. For generation after generation, age after age, economic life was dominated by toil. Man, woman, and child labored to secure their supply of food against the caprice of nature. There was nothing even vaguely romantic about the backbreaking exertion needed to crack open the hard ground, plant seeds beneath it, and protect the crops from the ravages of insects, birds, and animals long enough to be harvested. Every activity was labor intensive. Wood for shelter or fuel was chopped with thick, blunt axes. Water was drawn from deep wells by the long, slow turn of a crank or dragged in buckets from the nearest stream. Everything that was consumed was pulled or pushed or lifted. French women carried soil and water up steep terraces in journeys that could take as long as seven hours. "The women seemed from their persons and features to be harder worked than horses," Arthur Young (1741–1820), the English agricultural expert, observed with a combination of admiration and disgust. The capital that was invested in the traditional economy was human capital, and by the middle of the eighteenth century nearly eight out of every ten Europeans still tilled the soil, earning their bread by the sweat of their brow.

Though the traditional economy was dominated by agriculture, an increasing amount of labor was devoted to manufacture. The development of a secure and expanding overseas trade created a worldwide demand for consumer goods. In the countryside, small domestic textile industries grew up. Families would take in wool for spinning and weaving to supplement their income from agriculture. When times were good they would expend proportionately less effort in manufacturing; when times were bad, they would expend more. Their tasks were set by an entrepreneur who provided raw materials and paid the workers by the piece. Wages paid to rural workers were lower than those paid to urban laborers because they were not subject to guild restrictions and because they supplemented farm income. Thus entrepreneurs could profit from lower costs, although they had to bear the risk that the goods produced in this fashion would be of lesser quality or that markets would dry up in the interval. Though domestic industry increased the supply of manufactured commodities, it

Linen making, an engraving from Nuremberg by Franz Philipp Florin, 1705. The flax stems were soaked to soften the tough outer fibers, which were then removed by beating. The inner fibers were spun into linen on hand looms.

demanded even more labor from an already over-worked sector of the traditional economy.

Throughout the traditional economy, the limits on progress were set by nature. Good harvests brought prosperity, bad harvests despair. Over the long run the traditional economy ran in all too predictable cycles. Sadly, the old adage "eat, drink, and be merry for tomorrow we may be dead," was good advice. Prosperity was sure to bring misery in its train. The good fortune of one generation was the hard luck of the next, as more people competed for a relatively fixed quantity of food. No amount of sweat and muscle and, as yet, no amount of ingenuity could rescue the traditional economy from its pendulum swings of boom and bust.

By the eighteenth century the process that would ultimately transform the traditional economy was already under way. It began with the Agricultural Revolution, one of the great turning points in human history. Before it occurred, the life of every community and of every citizen was always held hostage to nature. The struggle to secure an adequate food supply was the dominant fact of life to which nearly all productive labor was dedicated. After the Agricultural Revolution, an inadequate food supply was a political rather than an economic fact of life. Fewer and fewer farmers were required to feed more and more people. In Britain, where nearly 70 percent of the population was engaged in agriculture at the end of the seventeenth century, less than 2 percent worked on farms at the end of the twentieth century. By the middle of the nineteenth century, the most advanced economies were capable of producing vast surpluses of basic commodities. The Agricultural Revolution was not an event, and it did not happen suddenly. It would not deserve the label *revolution* at all were it not for its momentous consequences: Europe's escape from the shackles of the traditional economy.

Farming Families

Over most of Europe, agricultural activity in the eighteenth century followed methods of crop rotation that had been in place for over a thousand years. Fields were divided into strips of land and each family "owned" a certain number of strips, which they cultivated for their livelihood.

Between one-half and one-third of village land lay fallow each year, so that its nutrients could be restored. Open-field farming, as this system was called, was communal rather than individual. Decisions on which crops to grow in the productive fields, where animals would be pastured, or how much wood could be cut from the common wastes affected everyone. Moreover, many activities, such as plowing, gleaning, and manuring, could not conveniently observe the distinctions of ownership of separate strips. Nor, given the realities of nature, could individual families be self-sustaining without the services of a village tanner or milkmaid or hog minder drawn from the closely intertwined group of kin and neighbors that constituted the community. Communal agriculture was effective, but it also limited the number of people that could survive on the produce from a given amount of land.

There were a number of reasons why this pattern of agricultural production remained immobile century after century. In the first place, there was little incentive for the peasantry to change it. Though they worked hard to ensure their subsistence, they had little desire to create a surplus. For one thing, almost every commodity produced in the village was perishable, and unless it could be consumed or converted at market into durable goods or cash it was largely worthless. For another thing, peasants owed much of their productivity—in one form or another—to their lords. In eastern Europe, serfdom tied the peasantry to the land, where they were used as laborers for the production of foodstuffs for export. Peasants in central Europe were still obligated to perform labor service for their lords, though in parts of Germany in the eighteenth century this obligation was being commuted to money rents. In France and in Scandinavia peasants "owned" much of their land in the sense that within the constraints imposed by the village, they could cultivate it as they saw fit and bequeath it to their heirs. But they paid dearly for these rights. Manorial taxes, in both money and kind, could take as much as half of each year's output, while demands from the state and the Church might absorb another quarter. The surplus wealth produced by the European peasantry, whether free or unfree, was extracted by their lords.

This is not to say that European peasants

were uninterested in bettering their immediate economic circumstances or that they obstructed agricultural change. Agriculture was a profoundly conservative occupation, for the risk of experimentation was nothing less than survival. Lords and peasants both practiced defensive innovation, introducing change only after its practical benefits were easily demonstrable. For example, in the mid-seventeenth century two French provincial parlements banned the cultivation of potatoes in the mistaken belief that they caused leprosy. Yet both potatoes and corn became peasant crops and spread rapidly throughout southern Europe, not least because as new commodities they were untaxed. Peasants bartered their surplus, hoarded their profits, and took what few advantages they could out of a system in which the deck was stacked against them.

As the European population entered a new cycle of growth in the second quarter of the eighteenth century, the traditional economy began to increase agricultural productivity in traditional ways. In the east new lands were colonized and slowly brought under cultivation. Frederick the Great welcomed immigrants to Prussia, where land was plentiful if not very fertile. In settled communities less productive land, which had provided fodder for animals at the end of the seventeenth century, now had to provide food for humans. Scrubland was cleared and hillsides terraced. Dry ground was irrigated by hand by women and children working in bucket brigades. As always, an increase in population initially meant an increase in productivity. For a time, more able-bodied workers produced more food. In the half-century that ended in the 1770s French peasants increased agricultural production by nearly 60 percent. The intensification of traditional methods rather than innovation accounted for the increase. The number of strips held by each family declined, but each strip was more carefully cultivated.

By the end of the eighteenth century the European population was reaching the point at which another check upon its growth might be expected. Between 1700 and 1800 total European population had increased by nearly 50 percent, and the rate of growth was continuing to accelerate. This vast expansion of rural population placed a grave strain upon agricultural produc-

tion. Decade by decade more families attempted to eke out an existence from the same amount of land. The gains made by intensive cultivation were now lost to overpopulation. In areas that practiced partible inheritance, farms were subdivided into units too small to provide subsistence. Competition for these "morsels" of land, as the French called them, was intense. Older sons bought out younger brothers; better-off families purchased whatever came on the market to prevent their children from slipping into poverty. Even in areas in which primogeniture was the rule, portions for younger sons and daughters ate into the meager inheritance of the eldest son. Over much of Europe it was becoming increasingly difficult to live by bread alone.

Rural Manufacture

The crisis of overpopulation meant that not only were there more mouths to feed, there were more bodies to clothe. This increased the need for spun and woven cloth, and thus for spinners and weavers. Traditionally, commercial cloth production was the work of urban artisans, but the

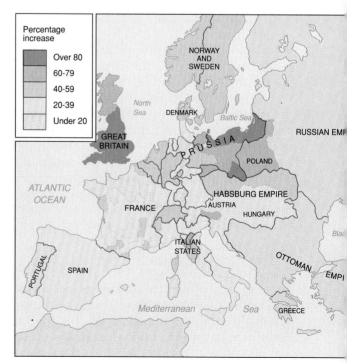

Population Growth in Europe, 1800–1850

*Eighteenth-century
cottage industry. The
entire family partici-
pates in the prepara-
tion of the flax.
Another cottager will
weave the thread into
cloth.*

expansion of the marketplace and the introduction of new fabrics, especially cotton and silk, had
eroded the monopoly of most of the clothing
guilds. Merchants could sell as much finished
product as they could find, and the teeming rural
population provided a tempting pool of inexpensive labor for anyone willing to risk the capital to
purchase raw materials. Initially, farming families took manufacturing work into their homes to
supplement their income. Spinning and weaving
were the most common occupations, and they
were treated as occasional work, reserved for the
slow times in the agricultural cycle. This was
known as cottage industry. It was by-employ-
ment, less important and less valuable than the
vital agricultural labor that all members of the
family undertook.

But by the middle of the eighteenth century,
cottage industry was developing in a new direction. As landholdings grew smaller, even good
harvests did not promise subsistence to many
families. This oversupply of labor was soon
organized into the putting-out system, which
mobilized the resources of the rural labor force
for commercial production of large quantities of
manufactured goods. The characteristics of the
putting-out system were similar throughout
Europe, whether it was undertaken by individual
entrepreneurs or lords of the manor, or even sponsored by the state. The process began with the
capital of the entrepreneur, which was used to
purchase raw materials. These materials were
"put out" to the homes of workers where the
manufacture took place, most commonly spinning or weaving. The finished goods were
returned to the entrepreneur, who sold them at a
profit, with which he bought raw materials to
begin the process anew.

The simplicity of the putting-out system was
one of its most valuable features. All of its essential elements were already present in rural communities. The small nest egg of a prosperous
farmer or small trader was all the money needed
to make the first purchase of raw materials. These
raw materials could be put out to his kin or closest
neighbors and the finished goods then delivered
to market along with surplus crops. Not only
could a small amount of cash begin the cycle of
putting-out, but that capital continued to circulate to keep the process in motion.

The small scale of the initial enterprise can be seen in the fact that many entrepreneurs had themselves begun as workers. In Bohemia, for example, some of the largest putting-out operations were run by serfs who paid their lords fees for the right to engage in trade. At the end of the eighteenth century there were over a quarter million spinners in the Bohemian linen industry alone, most of them organized into small groups around a single entrepreneur, though one monastery employed over 650 women spinners. Putting-out also required only a low level of skill and inexpensive, common tools. Rural families did their own spinning and rural villages their own weaving. Thus putting-out demanded little investment, either in plant, equipment, or education. Nor did it inevitably disrupt traditional gender-based tasks in the family economy. In most places spinning was women's work, weaving was done by men, and children helped at whichever task was under way. In fact, certain occupations, like lacemaking in France, were so gender-based that men would not even act as entrepreneurs. In Austria lacemaking was considered less honorable than other forms of clothmaking because of its association with women and household-based production. Performed at home, rural manufacture remained a traditional family-oriented occupation.

Because this form of manufacturing began as supplementary work, rural laborers were willing to accept low wages. In urban areas guild restrictions regulated the number of laborers and ensured that they were paid a living wage. Lower labor costs were probably a necessary condition for the success of domestic-based manufacturing. It was vital that the finished goods could be readily sold at market, for it was that sale that allowed the purchase of more raw material. If the entrepreneur could not dispose of his product, his network of workers collapsed. On the other hand, piecework provided farmers with the cushion they needed to survive too small harvests or too small plots of land. In the Swiss highlands during the late eighteenth century, farmers prospered on farms one-eighth the size of those tilled by their grandfathers. But more of their time was now occupied in cloth production than in agriculture. As long as rural manufacture supplemented agricultural income, it was seen as a benefit for every-

one involved—the entrepreneur, the individual worker, and the village community.

Gradually the putting-out system came to dominate the lives of many rural families. From small networks of isolated villages, domestic manufacture grew to cover entire regions. Perhaps as much as one-quarter of the inhabitants of the Irish province of Ulster were engaged in manufacturing linen by the end of the eighteenth century. Spinning and weaving became full-time occupations for families that kept no more than a small garden. But without agricultural earnings, piecework rates became starvation wages, and families unable to purchase their subsistence were forced to rely upon loans from the entrepreneurs who set them at work. Long hours in dank cottages performing endlessly repetitive tasks became the lot of millions of rural inhabitants. And their numbers increased annually. While the sons of farmers waited to inherit land before they formed their families, the sons of cottage weavers needed only a loom to begin theirs. They could afford to marry younger and to have more children, for children could contribute to manufacturing from an early age.

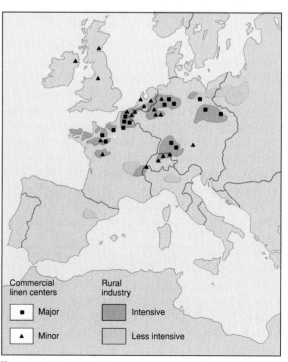

European Linen Industry

Consequently, the expansion of the putting-out system, like the expansion of traditional agriculture, fueled the continued growth of population. Like traditional agriculture, putting-out contained a number of structural inefficiencies. Both entrepreneur and worker were potential victims of unscrupulousness. Embezzlement of raw materials was a problem for the entrepreneur, arbitrary wage cuts for the laborers. Because the tasks were performed at home, the putter-out could not supervise the work. Most disputes in domestic manufacturing arose over specifications of quality. Workers would not receive full pay for poorly produced goods that could not be sold for full value. Inexperienced, aged, or infirm workers could easily spoil costly raw materials. One Bohemian nobleman created village spinning rooms on his estates so that young girls could be given four weeks of training before they set up on their own. Finally, the putting-out system was labor- rather than capital-intensive. As long as there were ready hands to employ, there was little incentive to seek better methods or more efficient techniques.

The Agricultural Revolution

The continued growth of Europe's population necessitated an expansion of agricultural output. In most places this was achieved by intensifying traditional practices, bringing more land into production and more labor to work the land. But in the most advanced European economies, first in Holland and then in England, traditional agriculture underwent a long but dynamic transformation, an agricultural revolution. It was a revolution of technique rather than technology. Humans were not replaced by machines nor were new forms of energy substituted for human and animal muscle. Indeed, many of the methods that were to increase crop yields had been known for centuries and practiced during periods of population pressure. But they had never been practiced as systematically as they came to be from the seventeenth century onward, and they were never combined with a commercial attitude toward farming. It was the willingness and ability of owners to invest capital in their land that transformed subsistence farming into commercial agriculture.

As long as farming was practiced in open fields, there was little incentive for individual landowners to invest in improvements to their scattered strips. While the community as a whole could enclose a small field or plant some fodder crops for the animals, its ability to change traditional practice was limited. In farming villages even the smallest landholder had rights in common lands, which were jealously guarded. Rights in commons meant a place in the community itself. Commercial agriculture was more suited to large rather than small estates and was more successful when the land could be utilized in response to market conditions rather than the necessities of subsistence.

The consolidation of estates and the enclosure of fields was thus the initial step toward change. This was a long-term process that took many forms. In England, where it was to become most advanced, enclosure was already under way in the sixteenth century. Prosperous families had long been consolidating their strips in the open fields, and at some point the lord of the manor and the members of the community agreed to carve up the common fields and make the necessary exchanges to consolidate everyone's lands. Perhaps as much as three-quarters of the arable land in England was enclosed by agreement before 1760. Enclosure by agreement did not mean that the breakup of the open-field community was necessarily a harmonious process. Riots preceding or following agreed enclosures were not uncommon.

Paradoxically, it was the middling rather than the poorest villagers who had the most to lose. The breakup of the commons initially gave the poor more arable land from which to eke out their subsistence, and few of them could afford to sacrifice present gain for future loss. These smallholders were quickly bought out. It was the middling-size holders who were squeezed hardest. Though prosperous in communal farming, these families did not have access to the capital necessary to make agricultural improvements such as converting grass to grain land or purchasing large amounts of fertilizer. They could not compete in producing for the market and gradually they, too, disappeared from the enclosed village. Their opposition to enclosure by agreement led, in the eighteenth century to enclosure by act of Parliament. Parliamentary enclosure was legislated by government, a government composed for the most part of large landowners. A commission would view the community's lands and divide them, usually by a prescribed formula. Between 1760 and 1815 over one and a half million acres of farmland were enclosed by act of Parliament. During the late eighteenth century the Prussian and French governments emulated this practice by ordering large tracts of land enclosed.

The enclosure of millions of acres of land was one of the largest expenses of the new commercial agriculture. Hedging or fencing off the land and plowing up the commons required extra labor beyond that necessary for basic agrarian activities. Thus many who sold the small estates that they received on the breakup of the commons remained in villages as agricultural laborers or leaseholders. But now they practiced a different form of farming. More and more agricultural activity became market-oriented. Single crops were sown in large enclosed fields and exchanged at market for the mixture of goods that previously had been grown in the village. Market production turned attention from producing a balance of commodities to increasing the yield of a single one.

The first innovation was the widespread cultivation of fodder crops such as clover and turnips. Crops like clover restore nutrients to the soil as they grow, shortening the period in which land has to lie fallow. Moreover, farm animals grazing on clover or feeding on turnips return more manure to the land, further increasing its productivity. Turnip cultivation had begun in Holland and was brought to England in the sixteenth century. But it was not until the late seventeenth century that Viscount Charles "Turnip" Townsend (1675–1738) made turnip cultivation popular. Townsend and other large Norfolk landowners developed a new system of planting known as the four-course rotation, in which wheat, turnips, barley, and clover succeeded one another. This method kept the land in productive use, and both the turnip and clover crops were used to feed larger herds of animals.

The ability of farmers to increase their livestock was as important as their ability to grow more grain. Not only were horses and oxen more productive than humans—a horse could perform seven times the labor of a man while consuming

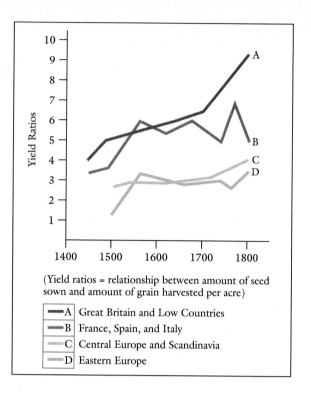

(Yield ratios = relationship between amount of seed sown and amount of grain harvested per acre)

A	Great Britain and Low Countries	
B	France, Spain, and Italy	
C	Central Europe and Scandinavia	
D	Eastern Europe	

only five times the food—but the animals also refertilized the land as they worked. Light fertilization of a single acre of arable land required an average of 25,000 pounds of manure. But animals competed with humans for food, especially during the winter months when little grazing was possible. To conserve grain for human consumption, lambs were led to the slaughter and the fatted calf was killed in the autumn. Thus the development of the technique of meadow floating was a remarkable breakthrough. By flooding low-lying land near streams in the winter, English and Dutch farmers could prevent the ground from freezing during their generally mild winters. When the water was drained, the land beneath it would produce an early grass crop on which the beasts could graze. This meant that more animals could be kept alive during the winter.

The relationship between animal husbandry and grain growing became another feature of commercial agriculture. In many areas farmers could choose between growing grain and pasturing animals. When prices for wool or meat were relatively higher than those for grain, fields could be left in grass for grazing. When grain prices rose, the same fields could be plowed. Consolidated enclosed estates made this convertible husbandry possible. The decision to hire field-workers or shepherds could be taken only by large agricultural employers. Whatever the relative price of grain, the open-field village continued to produce grain as its primary crop. Farmers who could convert their production in tune to the market could not only maximize their profits, they could also prevent shortages of raw materials for domestic manufacturers or of foodstuffs for urban and rural workers.

Convertible husbandry was but the first step in the development of a true system of regional specialization in agriculture. Different soils and climates favored different use of the land. In southern and eastern England the soil was thin and easily depleted by grain growing. Traditionally, these light soil areas had been used almost exclusively for sheep rearing. On the other hand, the clay soils of central England, though poorly drained and hard to work, were more suited to grain growing. The new agricultural techniques reversed the pattern. The introduction of fodder crops and increased fertilization rejuvenated thin soils, and southeastern England became the nation's breadbasket. Large enclosed estates provided a surplus of grain throughout the eighteenth century. By the 1760s England was exporting enough grain to feed over half a million people. Similarly, the midland clays became the location of great sheep runs and cattle herds. Experiments in herd management, crossbreeding, and fattening all resulted in increased production of wool, milk, meat, leather, soap, and tallow for candles.

There can be no doubt about the benefits of the transformation of agricultural practices that began in Holland and England in the seventeenth century and spread slowly to all corners of the Continent over the next two hundred years. Millions more mouths were fed at lower cost than

The Return of the Gleaners, *by Jules Breton, 1859. Gleaners were allowed one full day in the fields, at the end of which they were recalled by a shout or a bell lest they stray into the standing corn.*

ever before. In 1700 each person engaged in farming in England produced enough food for 1.7 people; in 1800 enough for 2.5. Cheaper food allowed more discretionary spending, which fueled the demand for consumer goods, which in turn employed more rural manufacturers. But there are no benefits without costs. The transformation of agriculture was also a transformation in a way of life. The open-field village was a community; the enclosed estate was a business. The plight of the rural poor was tragic enough in villages of kin and neighbors, where face-to-face charity might be returned from one generation to the next. With their scrap of land and their common rights, even the poorest villagers laid claim to a place of their own. But as landless laborers, either on farms or in rural manufacturing, they could no longer make that claim. They would soon be fodder for the factories, the "dark satanic mills" that came to disfigure the land once tilled in open-field villages. For the destitute, charity was now visited upon them in anonymous parish workhouses or in the good works of the comfortable middle class. In all of these ways the Agricultural Revolution changed the face of Europe.

The Industrial Revolution in Britain

Like the changes in agriculture, the changes in manufacturing that began in Britain during the eighteenth century were more revolutionary in consequence than in development. But their consequences were revolutionary indeed. A work force that was predominantly agricultural in 1750 had become predominantly industrial a century later. A population that for centuries had centered on the south and east was now concentrated in the north and west. Liverpool, Manchester, Glasgow, and Birmingham mushroomed into giant cities. While the population of England grew by 100 percent between 1801 and 1851, from about 8.5 million to over 17 million, the populations of Liverpool and Manchester grew by over 1,000 percent.

It was the replacement of animal muscle by hydraulic and mineral energy that made this continued population growth possible. Water and coal drove machinery that dramatically increased human productivity. In 1812 one woman could

The Colliery *by Leonard Defrance, 1778. Coal fueled the Industrial Revolution. The painting shows the pithead of a Belgian colliery in the late eighteenth century.*

spin as much thread as had two hundred women in 1770. What was most revolutionary about the Industrial Revolution was the wave after wave of technological innovation, a constant tinkering and improving of the ways in which things were made, which could have the simultaneous effects of cutting costs and improving quality. It was not just the great breakthrough inventions like the steam engine, the smelting of iron with coke, and the spinning jenny that were important, but also the hundreds of adjustments in technique that applied new ideas in one industry to another, that opened bottlenecks and solved problems. It was ingenuity rather than genius that was at the root of the Industrial Revolution in Britain.

The Industrial Revolution was a sustained period of economic growth and change brought about by the application of mineral energy and technological innovations to the process of manufacturing. It took place during the century between 1750 and 1850, though different industries moved at different paces, and sustained economic growth continued in Britain until the First World War. It is difficult to define the timing of the Industrial Revolution with any great precision because, unlike a political event, an economic transformation does not happen all at once. Nor are new systems and inventions ever really new. Coal miners had been using rails and wheeled carriages to move ore since the seventeenth century; in the sixteenth century "Jack of Newbury" had housed his cloth workers in a large shed. The one was the precursor of the railroad and the other the precursor of the factory, but each preceded the Industrial Revolution by more than a century. Before 1750 innovations made their way slowly into general use, and after 1850 the pace of growth slowed appreciably. By then, Britain had a manufacturing economy, less than a quarter of its labor force engaged in agriculture and nearly 60 percent involved in industry, trade, and transport.

Britain First

The Industrial Revolution occurred first in Britain, but even in Britain industrialization was a regional rather than a national phenomenon. There were many areas of Britain that remained untouched by innovations in manufacturing methods and agricultural techniques, though no one remained unaffected by the prosperity that industrialization brought. This was the result of both national conditions and historical developments. When industrialization spread to the Continent it took hold—as it had in Britain—in regions where mineral resources were abundant or where domestic manufacturing was a traditional activity. There was no single model for European industrialization, however much contemporaries looked toward Britain for the key to unlock the power of economic growth. There was as much technological innovation in France, as much capital for investment in Holland. Belgium was rich in coal, while eastern Europe enjoyed an agricultural surplus that sustained an increase in population. The finest cotton in the world was made in India, the best iron was made in Sweden. Each of these factors was in some way a precondition for industrialization, but none by itself proved sufficient. Only in Britain did these circumstances meld together.

Among Britain's blessings, water was foremost. Water was its best defense, protecting the island from foreign invasion and making it unnecessary to invest in a costly standing army. Rather Britain invested heavily in its navy to maintain its commercial preeminence around the globe. The navy protected British interests in times of war and transported British wares in times of peace. Britain's position in the Asian trade made it the leading importer of cottons, ceramics, and teas. Its colonies, especially in North America, not only provided sugar and tobacco, but also formed a rich market for British manufacturing.

But the commercial advantages that water brought were not confined to oceanic trade. Britain was favored by an internal water system that tied inland communities together. In the eighteenth century, no place in Britain was more than 70 miles from the sea or more than 30 miles from a navigable river. Water transport was far cheaper than hauling goods

Canals and Rivers

overland; a packhorse could carry 250 pounds of goods on its back or it could move 100,000 pounds by walking alongside a river pulling a barge. Small wonder that river transport was one of the principal interests of merchants and traders. Beginning in the 1760s private concerns began to invest in the construction of canals, first to move coal from inland locations to major arteries and then to connect the great rivers themselves. Over the next fifty years several hundred miles of canals were built by authority of Navigation Acts, which allowed for the sale of shares to raise capital. In 1760 the Duke of Bridgewater (1736–1803) lived up to his name by completing the first great canal. It brought coal to Manchester and ultimately to Liverpool. It cost more than £250,000 and took fourteen years of labor to build, but it repaid the duke and his investors many times over as an uneconomical coal field was brought into production. Not the least of the beneficiaries were the people of Manchester, where the price of coal was halved.

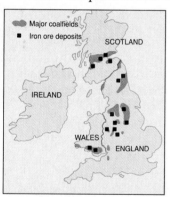

Coal and Iron Ore Deposits

Coal was the second of Britain's natural blessings on which it improved. Britain's reserves of wood were nearly depleted by the eighteenth century, especially those near centers of population. Coal had been in use as a fuel for several centuries, and the coal trade between London and the northern coal pits had been essential to the growth of the capital. Coal was abundant, much of it almost at surface level along the northeastern coast, and easily transported on water. The location of large coalfields along waterways was a vital condition of its early use. As canals and roadways improved, more inland coal was brought into production for domestic use. Yet it was in industry rather than in the home that coal was put to its greatest use. Here again Britain was favored, for large seams of coal were also located near large seams of iron. At first this coincidence was of little consequence since iron was smelted by charcoal made from wood and iron foundries were located deep in forests. But ultimately ironmakers learned to use coal for fuel, and then the natural economies of having mineral, fuel, and transport in the same vicinity were given full play.

The factors that contributed to Britain's early industrialization were not only those of natural advantage. Over the course of years, Britain had developed an infrastructure for economic advancement. The transformation of domestic handicrafts to industrial production depended as much upon the abilities of merchants as on those of manufacturers. The markets for domestic manufacturing had largely been overseas, where British merchants built up relationships over generations. Export markets were vital to the success of industrialization as production grew dynamically and most ventures needed a quick turnaround of sales to reinvest their profits in continued growth. The flexibility of English trading houses would be seen in their ability to shift from re-exporting eastern and North American goods to exporting British manufactures. Equally important, increased production meant increased demand for raw materials, Swedish bar iron for casting, Egyptian and American cotton for textiles, Oriental silk for luxuries. The expansion of shipping mirrored the expansion of the economy, tripling during the eighteenth century to over 1 million tons of cargo capacity.

The expansion of shipping, of agriculture, of investment in machines, plant, and raw material all required capital. Not only did capital have to exist, but it had to be made productive. Profits in agriculture, especially in the south and east, had somehow to be shifted to investment in industry in the north and west. The wealth of merchants, which flowed into London, had to be redistributed throughout the economy. More importantly, short-term investments had to give way to longterm financing. At the end of the seventeenth century, the creation of the Bank of England had begun the process of constructing a reliable banking system. The Bank of England dealt almost entirely with government securities, but it also served as a bill broker. It bought the debts of reputable merchants at a discount in exchange for Bank of England notes. Bank of England notes could then be exchanged between merchants, and this increased the liquidity of the English economy, especially in London. It also became the model for provincial banking by the middle of the eighteenth century.

Private family banks also grew in importance in London, handling the accounts of merchants and buying shares in profitable enterprises, of which the canals were a favorite. Regional banks, smaller and less well capitalized, began to use these private London banks as correspondents, that is as extensions of their own banks in the city. This allowed local manufacturers and city merchants to do business with one another. The connections between the regional banks and London facilitated the flow of capital from one section of the nation to the other. In 1700 there were just twelve provincial banks; by 1790 there were nearly three hundred. Banks remained reluctant to invest for the long term, preferring to discount bills for a few months, but after they developed a relationship with a particular firm, they were usually willing to continue to roll the debt over. Though the banking system was vital to large enterprises, in fact the capital for most industry was raised locally, from kin and neighbors, and grew by plowing back profits into the business. At least at the beginning, manufacturers were willing to take risks and to work for small returns to ensure the survival and growth of their business.

Minerals and Metals

There could have been no Industrial Revolution without coal. It was the black gold of the eighteenth century, the fuel that fed the furnaces and turned the engines of industrial expansion. The coal produced by one miner generated as much energy as twenty horses. Coal was the first capital-intensive industry in Britain, already well developed by the seventeenth century. Owners paid the costs of sinking shafts, building roads, and erecting winding machines. Miners were brought to a pit and paid piecework for their labor. Only the very wealthy could afford to invest in coal mining, and it was by chance that British law vested mineral rights in owners rather than users of the land, as was the case on the Continent. This meant that the largest English coalfields were owned by landed families of

means who were able to invest agricultural profits in mining. Britain's traditional elites thus played a crucial role in the industrial transformation of the agrarian economy from which their wealth and social standing had derived.

The technical problems of coal mining grew with demand. As surface seams were exhausted it became necessary to dig deeper shafts, to lower miners farther underground, and to raise the coal greater heights to the surface. Men loosened the coal from the seam, women and children hauled it to the shaft. They also cleared the tons of debris that came loose with the coal. Underground mining was extremely dangerous. Beyond all too frequent cave-ins, miners struggled against inadequate ventilation and light. Better ventilation was achieved by the expensive method of sinking second and third shafts into the same seam, allowing for cross breezes. Candles and sparks created by flintwheels addressed the problem of light, though both suffered from the disadvantage that most pits contained combustible gases. Even after a fireman walked through the mine, exploding gas with a long lighted stick, many miners preferred to work in total darkness, feeling the edges of the seam.

But by far the most difficult mining problem was water. As pits were sunk deeper they reached pools of groundwater, which enlarged as the coal

Women and children were the cheapest labor force during the English Industrial Revolution. They were sometimes employed in heavy work such as mining. Here, two children are shown being raised to ground level from the mine pit.

The pithead of a coal mine in the English Midlands in the 1790s. Old-fashioned horsepower is used side by side with the new steam technology. A Newcomen engine is in the center and a pumping engine is on the left.

was stripped away from the earth. Dripping water increased the difficulty of hewing, standing water the difficulty of hauling. The pit acted like a riverbed and was quickly filled. Water drainage presented the greatest obstacle to deep-shaft mining. Women and children could carry the water out in large skin-lined baskets, which were attached to a winding wheel and pulled up by horses. Primitive pumps, also horse powered, had been devised for the same purpose. Neither method was efficient or effective when shafts sank deeper. In 1709 Thomas Newcomen (1663–1729) introduced a steam-driven pump, which enabled water to be sucked through a pipe directly from the pit bottom to the surface. Though the engine was expensive to build and needed tons of coal to create the steam, it could raise the same amount of water in a day as 2,500 humans. Such economies of labor were enormous, and within twenty years of its introduction there were seventy-eight engines draining coal and metal mines in England.

Innovations like Newcomen's engine helped increase output of coal at just the time that it became needed as an industrial fuel. Between 1700 and 1830 coal production increased tenfold despite the fact that deeper and more difficult seams were being worked. Eventually, the largest demand for coal came from the iron industry. In 1793 just two ironworks consumed as much coal as the entire population of Edinburgh. Like mining coal, making iron was both capital- and labor-intensive, requiring expensive furnaces, water-powered bellows, and mills in which forged iron could be slit into rods or rolled into sheets. Ironmaking depended upon an abundance of wood, for it took the charcoal derived from ten acres of trees to refine one ton of iron ore. After the ore was mined, it was smelted into pig iron, a low-grade, brittle metal. Pig iron was converted to higher-quality bar iron in charcoal-powered forges that burned off some of its impurities. From bar iron came the rods and sheets used in casting household items like pots and nails or in making finer wrought-iron products like plows and armaments. Because each process in the making of iron was separate, furnaces, forges, and mills were located near their own supplies of wood. The shipping of the bulky ore, pig iron, and bar iron added substantially to its cost, and it was cheaper to import bars from Sweden than to carry them twenty miles overland.

The great innovations in the production of iron came with the development of techniques that allowed for the use of coal rather than wood charcoal in smelting and forging. As early as 1709 Abraham Darby (1678?–1717), a Quaker nail-maker, experimented with smelting iron ore with coke, coal from which most of the gas has been burned off. Iron coking greatly reduced the cost of fuel in the first stages of production, but because most ironworks were located in woodlands rather than near coal pits, the method was not widely adopted. Moreover, although coke made from coal was cheaper than charcoal made from wood, coke added its own impurities to the iron ore. Nor could it provide the intense heat needed for smelting without a large bellows. The cost of the bellows offset the savings from the coke until James

James Watt, painting by Carl von Breda. Watt was inaccurately given credit as the inventor of the steam engine after he developed a special condenser and air pump, which made possible the first practical cylindrical steam engine.

Watt (1736–1819) invented a new form of steam engine in 1775.

Like most innovations of the Industrial Revolution, Watt's steam engine was an adaptation of existing technology made possible by the sophistication of techniques in a variety of fields. Although James Watt is credited with the invention of the condensing steam engine, one of the seminal creations in human history, the success of his work depended upon the achievements of numerous others. Watt's introduction to the steam engine was accidental. An instrument maker in Glasgow, he was asked to repair a model of a Newcomen engine and immediately realized that it would work more efficiently if there were a separate chamber for the condensation of the steam. Though his idea was sound, Watt spent years attempting to implement it. He was continually frustrated that poor quality valves and cylinders never fit well enough together to prevent steam escaping from the engine.

Watt was unable to translate his idea into a practical invention until he became partners with the Birmingham ironmaker and manufacturer Matthew Boulton (1728–1809). At Boulton's works, Watt found craftsmen who could make precision engine valves, and at the foundries of John Wilkinson (1728–1808) he found workers who could bore the cylinders of his engine to exact specifications. Watt's partnership with Boulton and Wilkinson was vital to the success of the steam engine. But Watt himself possessed the qualities necessary to ensure that his ideas were transformed into reality. He persevered through years of unsuccessful experimentation and searched out partners to provide capital and expertise. He saw beyond bare mechanics, realizing the practical utility of his invention long before it was perfected. It was Watt who designed the mechanism to convert the traditional up-and-down motion of the pumping engine into rotary motion, which could be used for machines and ultimately for locomotion.

Watt's engine received its first practical application in the iron industry. Wilkinson became one of the largest customers for steam engines, using them for pumping, moving wheels, and ultimately increasing the power of the blast of air in the forge. Increasing the heat provided by coke in the smelting and forging of iron led to the transformation of the industry. In the 1780s

Henry Cort (1740–1800), a naval contractor, experimented with a technique for using coke as fuel in removing the impurities from pig iron. The iron was melted into puddles and stirred with rods. The gaseous carbon that was brought to the surface burned off, leaving a purer and more malleable iron than even charcoal could produce. Because the iron had been purified in a molten state, Cort reasoned that it could be rolled directly into sheets rather than first made into bars. He erected a rolling mill adjacent to his forge and combined two separate processes into one.

Puddling and rolling had an immediate impact upon iron production. There was no longer any need to use charcoal in the stages of forging and rolling. From mineral to workable sheets, iron could be made entirely with coke. Ironworks moved to the coalfields, where the economies of transporting fuel and finished product were great. Moreover, the distinct stages of production were eliminated. Rather than separate smelting, forging, and finishing industries, one consolidated manufacturing process had been created. Forges, furnaces, and rolling machines were brought together and powered by steam engines. Cort's rolling technique alone increased output 15 times. By 1808 output of pig iron had grown from 68,000 to 250,000 tons and of bar iron from 32,000 to 100,000 tons.

Cotton Is King

Traditionally British commerce was dominated by the woolen cloth trade, in which techniques of production had not changed for hundreds of years. Running water was used for cleaning and separating fleece; crude wooden wheels spun the thread; simple handlooms wove together the long warp threads and the short weft ones. It took nearly four female spinners to provide the materials for one male weaver, the tasks having long been gender-specific. During the course of the seventeenth century new fabrics appeared on the domestic market, particularly linen, silk, and cotton. It was cotton that captured the imagination of the eighteenth-century consumer, especially brightly colored, finely spun Indian cotton.

Spinning and weaving were organized as domestic industries. Work was done in the home

on small inexpensive machines to supplement the income from farming. Putters-out were especially frustrated by the difficulty in obtaining yarn for weaving in the autumn when female laborers were needed for the harvest. Even the widespread development of full-time domestic manufacturers did not satisfy the increased demand for cloth. Limited output and variable quality characterized British textile production throughout the early part of the eighteenth century. The breakthrough came with technological innovation. Beginning in the mid-eighteenth century a series of new machines dramatically increased output and, for the first time, allowed English textiles to compete with Indian imports.

The first innovation was the flying shuttle, invented by John Kay (1704–64) in the 1730s. A series of hammers drove the shuttle, which held the weft, through the stretched warp on the loom. The flying shuttle allowed weavers to work alone rather than in pairs, but it was adopted slowly for it increased the demand for spun thread, which was already in short supply. The spinning bottleneck was opened by James Hargreaves (17?–1778), who devised a machine known as the jenny. The jenny was a wooden frame containing a number of spindles around which thread was drawn by means of a hand-turned wheel. The first jennies allowed for the spinning of eight threads at once, and improvements brought the number to over a hundred. Jennies replaced spinning wheels by the tens of thousands. The jenny was a crucial breakthrough in redressing the balance between spinning and weaving, though it did not solve all problems. Jenny-spun thread was not strong enough to be used as warp, which continued to be wheel spun. But the jenny could spin cotton in unimaginable quantities.

As is often the case with technological change, one innovation followed another. The problem set by improvements in weaving gave rise to solutions for increasing the output of spinners. The need to provide stronger warp threads posed by the introduction of the jenny was ultimately solved by the development of the water frame. It was created in 1769 by Richard Arkwright (1732–92), whose name was also to be associated with the founding of the modern factory system. Arkwright's frame consisted of a series of water-power-driven rollers, which

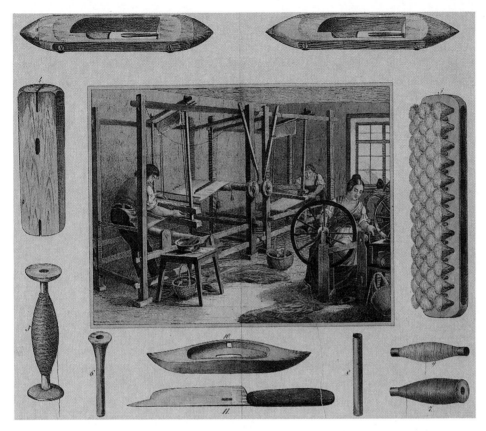

This hand-colored engraving shows the interior of a German weaver's shop around 1850. Two men are weaving at looms and two women are winding bobbins. The scene is bordered with details of tools such as shuttles and quills.

stretched the cotton before spinning. These stronger fibers could be spun into threads suitable for warp, and English manufacturers could finally produce an all-cotton fabric. It was not long before another innovator realized that the water frame and the jenny could be combined into a single machine, one that would produce an even finer cotton yarn than that made in India. The mule, so named because it was a cross between a frame and a jenny, was invented by Samuel Crompton (1753–1827), who sold its rights for only £60. It was the decisive innovation in cotton production. By 1811 ten times as many threads were being spun on mules than on water frames and jennies combined.

The original mules were small machines that, like the jennies, could be used for domestic manufactures. But increasingly, the mule followed the water frame into purposely built factories, where it became larger and more expensive. The need for large rooms to house the equipment and for a ready source of running water to power

it provided an incentive for the creation of factories, but secrecy provided a greater one. The original factories were called "safe-boxes," and whether they were established for the manufacture of silk or cotton, their purpose was to protect trade secrets. Innovators took out patents to prevent their inventions from being copied and fought long lawsuits to prevent their machines from being used. Workers were sworn to secrecy about the techniques they were taught. Imitators practiced industrial espionage as sophisticated as the age would allow: enticing knowledgeable workers; employing spies; copying inventions. Though the factory was designed to protect secrets, its other benefits were quickly realized. Manufacturers could maintain control over the quality of products through strict supervision of the work force. Moreover, workers in shifts could keep the costly machines in continuous use.

Richard Arkwright constructed the first cotton factories in Britain, all of which were designed to house water frames. The first was established in 1769 at Cromford near Nottingham, which was the center of stocking manufacture. The site was chosen for its isolation since stockings were an article of fashion in which secrecy was most important. The Cromford mill was a four-story building that ultimately employed over 800 workers. During the next quarter century Arkwright built over a dozen other mills, most in partnership with wealthy manufacturers. Arkwright's genius lay in industrial management rather than mechanical innovation. As others switched from frames to mules, Arkwright stubbornly stuck to his own invention. When steam power began to replace water, he failed to make the shift. But his methods of constructing and financing factories were undeniably successful. From a modest beginning as a traveling salesman of wigs, Sir Richard Arkwright died in possession of a fortune worth more than £500,000.

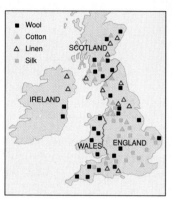

Textile Centers

The organization of the cotton industry into factories was one of the pivotal transformations in economic life. Domestic spinning and weaving took place in agricultural villages, factory production took place in mill towns. The location of the factory determined movements of population, and from the first quarter of the eighteenth century onward a great shift toward the northeast of England was under way. Moreover, the character of the work itself changed. The operation of heavy machinery reversed the traditional gender-based tasks. Mule spinning became men's work, while handloom weaving was taken over by women. The mechanization of weaving took longer than that of spinning, both because of difficulties in perfecting a power loom and because of opposition to its introduction by workers known as Luddites, who organized machine-breaking riots in the 1810s. The Luddites attempted to maintain the traditional organization of their industry and the independence of their labor. For a time, handloom weavers managed to survive by accepting lower and lower piece rates. But their competition was like that of a horse against an automobile. In 1820 there were over 250,000 handloom weavers in Britain; by 1850 the number was less than 50,000. Weaving as well as spinning became factory work.

The transformation of cotton manufacture had a profound effect upon the overall growth of the British economy. It increased shipping since the raw material had to be imported, first from the Mediterranean and then from America. American cotton, especially after 1794 when American inventor Eli Whitney (1765–1825) patented his cotton gin, fed a nearly insatiable demand. In 1750 Britain imported less than 5 million pounds of raw cotton; a century later the volume had grown to 588 million pounds. And to each pound of raw cotton, British manufacturers added the value of their technology and of their labor. By the mid-nineteenth century nearly half a million people earned their living from cotton, which alone accounted for over 40 percent of the value of all British exports. Cotton was undeniably the king of manufactured goods.

The Iron Horse

The first stage of the Industrial Revolution in Britain was driven by the production of consumer goods. Pottery, cast-iron tools, clocks, toys, and textiles, especially cottons, all were manufactured in quantities unknown in the early eighteenth century. These products fed a ravenous market at home and abroad. The greatest complaint of industrialists was that they could not get enough raw materials or fuel, nor could they ship their finished products fast enough to keep up with demand. Transportation was becoming a serious stumbling block to continued economic growth. Even with the completion of the canal network that linked the major rivers and improvement in highways and tollways, raw materials and finished goods moved slowly and uncertainly. It was said that it took as long to ship goods from Manchester to Liverpool on the Duke of Bridgewater's canal as it did to sail from New York to Liverpool on the Atlantic Ocean. Moreover, once the canals had a monopoly on bulk cargo, transportation costs began to rise.

The railroads changed the whole pattern of living during the Industrial Revolution. On this circular track, Richard Trevithick displayed his high-pressure steam locomotive, the "Catch-me-who-can," to a marvelling London public in 1808.

It was the need to ship increasing amounts of coal to foundries and factories that provided the spur for the development of a new form of transportation. Ever since the seventeenth century, coal had been moved from the seam to the pit on rails, first constructed of wood and later of iron. Broad-wheeled carts hitched to horses were as much dragged as rolled, but this still represented the most efficient form of hauling and these railways ultimately ran from the seam to the dock. By 1800 there was perhaps as much as three hundred miles of iron rail in British mines.

In the same year, Watt's patent on the steam engine expired, and inventors began to apply the engine to a variety of mechanical tasks. Richard Trevithick (1771–1833), whose father managed a tin mine in Cornwall, was the first to experiment with a steam-driven carriage. George Stephenson (1781–1848), who is generally recognized as the father of the modern railroad, made two crucial improvements. In mine railways the wheels of the cart were smooth and the rail was grooved. Stephenson reversed this construction to provide better traction and less wear. Perhaps more importantly, Stephenson made the vital improvement in engine power by increasing the steam pressure in the boiler and exhausting the smoke through a chimney. In 1829 he won a £500 prize with his engine "The Rocket," which pulled a load three times its own weight at a speed of 30 miles per hour and could actually outrun a horse.

In 1830 the first modern railway, the Manchester to Liverpool line, was opened. Like the Duke of Bridgewater's canal, it was designed to move coal and bulk goods, but surprisingly its most important function came to be moving people. In its first year the Manchester-Liverpool line carried over 400,000 passengers, which generated double the revenue derived from freight. The railway was quicker, more comfortable, and ultimately cheaper than the coach. Investors in the Manchester-Liverpool line, who pocketed a comfortable 9.5 percent when government securities were paying 3.5 percent, learned quickly that links between population centers were as important as those between industrial sites. The London to Birmingham and London to Bristol lines were both designed with passenger traffic in mind.

Railway building was one of the great boom activities of British industrialization. Since it came toward the end of the mechanization of factories, investors and industrialists were psychologically prepared for the benefits of technological innovation. By 1835 Parliament had passed 54 separate acts to establish over 750 miles of railways. Ten years later over 6,000 miles had been sanctioned and over 2,500 miles built; by 1852 over 7,500 miles of track were in use. The railways were built on the model of the canals. Private bills passed through Parliament, which allowed a company to raise money through the sale of stock. Most railways were trunk lines, con-necting one town to another or joining two longer lines together. They were run by small companies and few ultimately proved profitable. Only be-cause of the dominant influence of George Stephenson and his son Robert (1803–59) was there an attempt to establish a stan-dard gauge for tracks and engines. Britain was the only country in which the government did not take a leading role in building the railways. Hundreds of millions of pounds were raised pri-vately, and in the end it is calculated that the railroads cost £40,000 a mile to build, more than three times the cost per mile of railroads in the United States and on the Continent.

Railroads, ca. 1850

Nevertheless, the investment paid huge divi-dends. By the 1850s the original purpose of the railways was being realized as freight revenues finally surpassed passenger revenues. Coal was the dominant cargo shipped by rail and the speedy, efficient service continued to drive down prices. The iron and steel industries were mod-ernized on the back of demand for rails, engines, and cast-iron seats and fittings. In peak periods— and railway building was a boom-and-bust affair—as much as a quarter of the output of the rolling mills went into domestic railroads and much more into Continental systems. The rail-ways were also a massive consumer of bricks for beddings, sidings, and especially bridges, tunnels, and stations. Finally, the railways were a leading employer of labor, surpassing the textile mills in peak periods. Hundreds of thousands worked in tasks as varied as engineering and ditchdigging,

for even in this most advanced industry sophisti-cated, mechanized production went hand in hand with traditional drudgery. Over 60,000 workers were permanently engaged in the industry to run trains, mind stations, and repair track. Countless others were employed in manufacturing engines, carriages, boxcars, and the thousands of compo-nents that went into making them.

Most of all, the railroads changed the nature of people's lives. Whole new concepts of time, space, and speed emerged to govern daily activities. As Henry Booth, an early railroad official, observed, "notions which we have received from our ancestors and verified by our own experience are overthrown in a day. What was quick is now slow; what was distant is now near." Coach travel had ordinarily been limited to those with means, not only because it was expen-sive, but also because it was time-consuming. Ordinary people could not take off the days neces-sary to complete relatively short round-trip jour-neys. At the beginning of passenger rail service there was even a debate over whether provision should be made for third-class passengers, a class unknown on the coaches, where the only choices were riding inside for comfort or outside for sav-ings. Third-class passengers quickly became the staple of railroad service. The cheap excursion was born to provide short holidays or even daily returns. The career of Thomas Cook (1808–92), who became the world's first travel agent, began after he took a short excursion. Over 6 million people visited London by train to view the Crystal Palace exhibition in 1851, a number equivalent to a third of the population of England and Wales. The railways did more than link places; they brought people together and helped develop a sense of national identity by speeding all forms of communication.

Entrepreneurs and Managers

The Industrial Revolution in Britain was not simply invented. Too much credit is given to a few breakthroughs and too little to the ways in which they were improved and dispersed. The Industrial Revolution was an age of gadgets when people believed that new was better than old and that there was always room for improvement. "The age is running mad after innovation," the English moralist Dr. Johnson wrote. "All the business of the world is done in a new way; men are hanged in a new way." Societies for the advancement of knowledge sprang up all over Britain. Journals and magazines promoted new ideas and techniques. Competitions were held for the best invention of the year; prizes were awarded for agricultural achievements. Practical rather than pure science was the hallmark of industrial development.

Yet technological innovation was not the same as industrialization. A vital change in economic activity took place in the organization of industry. Putters-out with their circulating capital and hired laborers could never make the economies necessary to increase output and quality while simultaneously lowering costs. This was the achievement of industrialists, producers who owned workplace, machinery, and raw materials and who invested fixed capital by plowing back their profits. Industrial enterprises came in all sizes and shapes. A cotton mill could be started with as little as £300, or as much as £10,000. As late as 1840 less than 10 percent of the mills employed over 500 workers. Most were family concerns with under 100 employees, and many of them failed. For every story with a happy ending there was another with a sad one. When Major John Cartwright (1740–1824) erected a cotton mill, he was offered a Watt steam engine built for a distiller who had gone bankrupt. He acquired his machinery at the auction of another bankrupt. Cartwright's mill, engine, and machinery ended on the auction block less than three years later. There were over 30,000 bankruptcies in the eighteenth century, testimony both to the risks of business and the willingness of entrepreneurs to take them.

Manufacturing Centers

To survive against these odds, successful industrialists had to be both entrepreneur and manager. As entrepreneurs they raised capital, almost always locally from relatives, friends, or members of their church. Quakers were especially active in financing each other's enterprises. The industrial entrepreneur also had to understand the latest methods for building and powering machinery and the most up-to-date techniques for performing the work. One early manufacturer claimed "a practical knowledge of every process from the cotton-bag to the piece of cloth." Finally, entrepreneurs had to know how to market their goods. In these functions, industrial entrepreneurs developed logically from putters-out.

But industrialists also had to be managers. The most difficult task was organization of the workplace. Most gains in productivity were achieved through the specialization of function. The processes of production were divided and subdivided until workers performed a basic task over and over. The education of the work force was the industrial manager's greatest challenge. Workers had to be taught how to use and maintain their machines and disciplined to apply themselves continuously. At least at the beginning, it was difficult to staff the factories. Many employed children as young as seven from workhouses or orphanages who, though cheap to pay, were difficult to train and discipline. It was the task of the manager to break old habits of intermittent work, indifference to quality, and petty theft of materials. Families were preferred to individuals, for then parents could instruct and supervise their children. There is no reason to believe that industrial managers were more brutal masters than farmers or that children were treated better in workhouses than in mills. Labor was a business asset, what was sometimes called "living machinery," and its control with carrots and sticks was the chief concern of the industrial manager.

Who were the industrialists who transformed the traditional economy? Because British society was relatively open, they came from every conceivable background; dukes and orphans, merchants and salesmen, inventors and improvers.

Though some went from rags to riches, like Richard Arkwright, who was the thirteenth child of a poor barber, it was extremely difficult for a laborer to acquire the capital necessary to set up a business. Wealthy landowners were prominent in capital-intensive aspects of industries, for example, owning ironworks and mines, but few established factories. Most industrialists came from the middle classes, which while comprising a third of the British population, provided as much as two-thirds of the first generation of industrialists. These included lawyers, bankers, merchants, and those already engaged in manufacturing, as well as tradesmen, shopkeepers, and self-employed craftsmen. The career of every industrialist was different, as a look at two, Josiah Wedgwood and Robert Owen, will show.

Josiah Wedgwood (1730–95) was the thirteenth child of a long-established English potting family. He worked in the potteries from childhood but a deformed leg made it difficult for him to turn the wheel. Instead he studied the structure of the business. His head teemed with ideas for improving ceramic manufacturing, but it was not until he was thirty that he could set up on his own and introduce his innovations. These encompassed both technique and organization, the entrepreneurial and managerial sides of his business.

Wedgwood developed new mixtures of clays that took brilliant colors in the kiln and new glazes for both "useful" and "ornamental" ware. His technical innovations were all the more remarkable in that he had little education in mineral chemistry and made his discoveries by simple trial and error. But there was nothing of either luck or good fortune in Wedgwood's managerial innovations. He was repelled by the disorder of the traditional pottery with its waste of materials, uneven quality, and slow output. When he began his first works he divided the making of pottery into distinct tasks and separated his workers among them. One group did nothing but throw the pots on the wheel, another painted designs, a third glazed. To achieve this division of function, Wedgwood had to train his own workers almost from childhood. Traditional potters performed every task from molding to glazing and prized the fact that no two pieces were ever alike. Wedgwood wanted each piece to replicate another, and he stalked the works breaking defective wares on his wooden leg. He invested in

schools to help train young artists, in canals to transport his products, and in London shops to sell them. Wedgwood was a marketing genius. He named his famed cream-colored pottery Queen's ware and made special coffee and tea services for leading aristocratic families. He would then sell replicas by the thousands. In less than twenty years Wedgwood pottery was prized all over Europe, and Wedgwood's potting works were the standard of the industry.

Robert Owen (1771–1858) did not have a family business to develop. The son of a small tradesman, he was apprenticed to a clothier at the age of ten. As a teenager he worked as a shop assistant in Manchester, where he audaciously applied for a job as a manager of a cotton mill. At nineteen he was supervising five hundred workers and learning the cotton trade. Owen was immediately successful, increasing the output of his workers and introducing new materials to the mill. In 1816 he entered a partnership to purchase the New Lanark mill in Scotland. Owen found conditions in Scotland much worse than those in Manchester. Over five hundred workhouse children were employed at New Lanark, where drunkenness and theft were endemic. Owen believed that to

Jasperware copy of the Portland vase by Josiah Wedgwood. The Portland vase is one of the most famous ancient vases. It was found near Rome in the seventeenth century in a tomb believed to be that of Alexander Severus.

improve the quality of work one had to improve the quality of the workplace. He replaced old machinery with new, reduced working hours, and instituted a monitoring system to check theft. To enhance life outside the factory, he established a high-quality company-run store, which plowed its profits into a school for village children.

Owen was struck by the irony that in the mills machines were better cared for than were humans. He thought that with the same attention to detail that had so improved the quality of commodities he could make even greater improvements in the quality of life. He prohibited children under ten from mill work and instituted a ten-hour day for child labor. His local school took infants from a year old, freeing women to work and ensuring each child an education. Owen instituted old-age and disability pensions, funded by mandatory contributions from work-ers' wages. Taverns were closed and workers were fined for drunkenness and sexual offenses. In the factory and the village Owen established a princi-ple of communal regulation to improve both the work and the character of his employees. New Lanark became the model of the world of the future, and each year thousands made an indus-trial pilgrimage to visit it.

The Wages of Progress

Robert Owen ended his life as a social reformer. His efforts to improve the lot of his workers at New Lanark led to experiments to create ideal industrial communities throughout the world. He founded cooperative societies, in which all members shared in the profits of the business, and supported trade unions in which workers could better their lives. His followers planted colonies where goods were held in com-mon and the fruits of labor belonged to the laborers. Owen's agitation for social reform was part of a movement that produced results of last-ing consequence. The Factory Act (1833) pro-hibited factory work by children under nine, provided two hours of daily education, and effec-tively created a twelve-hour day in the mills until the Ten Hours Act (1847). The Mines Act (1842) prohibited women and children from working underground.

Nor was Owen alone in dedicating time and money to the improvement of workers' lives. The

A view of the New Lanark mills and village in Scotland in 1818, the time of Robert Owen's social experiments. The buildings included a school and a community center, which attracted many influential visitors from overseas.

rapid growth of unplanned cities exacerbated the plight of those too poor and overworked to help themselves. Conditions of housing and sanitation were appalling even by nineteenth-century stan-dards. *The Report on the Sanitary Condition of the Laboring Population in Britain* (1842), written by Edwin Chadwick (1800–1890) so shocked Parlia-ment and the nation that it helped to shift the burden of social reform to government. The Pub-lic Health Act (1848) established boards of health and the office of medical examiner while the Vaccination Act (1853) and the Contagious Dis-eases Act (1864) attempted to control epidemics. (See Special Feature, "Industry and the Environ-ment," pp. 666–667.)

The movement for social reform began almost as soon as industrialization. The Indus-trial Revolution initiated profound changes in the organization of British society. Cities sprang up from grain fields almost overnight. The lure of steady work and high wages prompted an exodus from rural Britain and spurred an unremitting boom in population. In the first half of the nine-teenth century the population of England dou-bled from 9 to 18 million, with growth most rapid in the newly urban north and west. In 1750 about 15 percent of the population lived in urban areas, by 1850 about 60 percent did. Industrial workers married younger and produced more children than their agricultural counterparts. For cen-

Industry and the Environment

The Industrial Revolution changed the landscape of Britain. Small villages grew into vast metropolises seemingly overnight. The rates of growth were absolutely staggering: in 1801 there were 75,000 people in Manchester; by 1851 the number had more than quadrupled. This unremitting boom in population did more than strain the resources of local authorities. It broke them apart. It was not that the new industrial cities were unplanned; they were beyond the capacity of planning. Every essential requirement for human survival became scarce and expensive. Shortages of food, water, and basic accommodation were commonplace.

Shantytowns sprang up wherever space would allow, making the flimsily built habitations of construction profiteers seem like palaces. There was loud complaint about these nineteenth-century rip-off artists, but in truth the need for housing was so desperate that people willingly lived anywhere that provided shelter. Houses were built back to back and side by side, with only narrow alleyways to provide sunlight and air. In Edinburgh one could step through the window of one house into the window of the adjoining one. Whole families occupied single rooms where members slept as they worked, in shifts. In Liverpool over 38,000 people were estimated to be living in cellars—windowless, underground accommodations that flooded with the rains and the tides.

Most cities lacked both running water and toilet facilities. Districts were provided with either pumps or capped pipes through which private companies ran water for a few hours each day. The water was collected in buckets and brought to the home, where it would stand for the rest of the day and serve indifferently for washing, drinking, and cooking. Outhouse toilets were an extravagant luxury; in one Manchester district 33 outhouses had to accommodate 7,095 people. They were a mixed blessing even in the middle-class districts where they were more plentiful, as there was no system of drainage to flush the waste away. It simply accumulated in cesspools, which were emptied manually about every two years. The thing that most impressed visitors as they approached an industrial city was the smoke; what impressed them most when they arrived was the smell.

The quality of life experienced by most of the urban poor who lived in these squalid conditions has been recorded by a number of contemporary observers. Friedrich Engels was a German socialist who was sent to England to learn the cotton trade. He lived in Manchester for two years and spent much of his time exploring the working-class areas of the city. "In this district I found a man, apparently about sixty years old, living in a cow stable," Engels recounted from one of his walking tours in *The Condition of the Working Class in England in 1844*. "He had constructed a sort of chimney for his square pen, which had neither windows, floor, nor ceiling, had obtained a bedstead and lived there, though the rain dripped through his rotten roof. This man was too old and weak for regular work, and supported himself by removing manure with a hand-cart; the dung-heaps lay next door to his palace!" From his own observations Engels concluded that "in such dwellings only a physically degenerate race, robbed of all humanity, degraded, reduced morally and physically to bestiality, could feel comfortable and at home." And as he was quick to point out, his own observations were no different from those of parliamentary commissioners, medical officers, or civic authorities who had seen conditions firsthand.

Among these observers, the most influential by far was Sir Edwin Chadwick (1800–1890), who began his government career as a commissioner for the poor law and ended it as the founder of a national system of public health. Chadwick wrote the report of a parliamentary commission, *The Sanitary Condition of the Laboring Population of Britain* (1842), which caused a sensation among the governing classes. Building on the work of physicians, overseers of the poor, and the most technical scholarship available, Chadwick not only painted the same grim picture of urban life as did Engels, he proposed a comprehensive solution to one of its greatest problems, waste management.

Chadwick was a civil servant and he believed that problems were solved by government on the basis of conclusions of experts. He had heard doctors argue their theories about the causes of disease, some believing in fluxes that resulted from combinations of foul air, water, and refuse; others believing disease was spread by the diseased, in this case Irish immigrants who settled in the poorest parts of English industrial towns. Though medical research had not yet detected the existence of germs, it was widely held that lack of ventilation, stagnant pools of water, and the accumulation of human and animal waste in proximity to people's dwellings all contributed to the increasing incidence of disease. Chadwick fixed upon this last element as crucial. Not even in middle-class districts was there any effective system for the removal of waste. Chamber pots and primitive toilets were emptied into ditches, which were used to drain rain off into local waterways. The few underground sewers that existed were square containers without outlets, which were simply emptied once filled. Chadwick's vision was for a sanitation system, one that would carry waste out of the city quickly and deposit it in outlying fields where it could be used as fertilizer.

Chadwick realized that the key to disposing of waste was a constant supply of running water piped through the system. Traditionally, only heavy rainstorms cleared the waste ditches in most cities, and these were too infrequent to be effective. The river had to be the beginning of the sewerage system as well as its end. River water had to be pumped through an underground construction of sewage pits that were built to facilitate the water's flow. Civil engineers had already demonstrated that pits with rounded rather than angular edges were far more effective, and Chadwick advocated the construction of a system of oval-shaped tunnels, built on an incline beneath the city. Water pumped from one part of the river would rush through the tunnels, which would empty into pipes that would carry the waste to nearby farms.

Chadwick's vision took years to implement. He had all of the zeal of a reformer and none of the tact of a politician. He offended nearly everyone with whom he came into contact, because he believed that his program was the only workable one and because he believed that it must be implemented whatever the price. He was uninterested in who was to pay the enormous costs of laying underground tunnel and building pumping stations and insisted only that the work begin immediately. In the end, he won his point. Sanitation systems became one of the first great public-works projects of the industrial age.

turies women had married in their middle twenties, but by 1800 age at first marriage had dropped to twenty-three for the female population as a whole and to nearly twenty in the industrial areas. This was in part because factory hands did not have to wait until they inherited land or money, and in part because they did not have to serve an apprenticeship. But early marriage and large families were also a bet on the future, a belief that things were better now and would be even better soon, that the new mouths would be fed and the new bodies clothed. This was an investment on the part of ordinary people similar to that made by bankers and entrepreneurs when they risked their capital in new businesses. Was it an investment that paid off?

It is difficult to calculate the benefits of the Industrial Revolution or to weigh them against the costs. What is certain is that there was a vast expansion of wealth as well as a vast expansion of people to share it. Agricultural and industrial change made it possible to support comfortably a population over three times that of the seventeenth century, when it was widely believed that England had reached the limits of expansion. Despite the fact that population doubled between 1801 and 1851, per capita income rose by 75 percent. That means that had the population remained stable, per capita income would have increased by a staggering 350 percent. At the same time, untold millions of pounds had been sunk into canals, roads, railways, factories, mines, and mills.

But the expansion of wealth is not the same as the improvement in the quality of life, for wealth is not equally distributed. An increase in the level of wealth may mean only that the rich are getting richer more quickly than the poor are getting poorer. Similarly, economic growth over a century involved the lives of several generations, which experienced different standards of living. One set of parents may have sacrificed for the future of their children, another may have mortgaged it. Moreover, economic activity is cyclical. Trade depressions, like those induced by the War of 1812 and the American Civil War, which interrupted cotton supplies, could have disastrous short-term effects. The "Great Hunger" of the 1840s was a time of agrarian crisis and industrial slump. The downturn of 1842 threw 60 percent of the factory workers in the town of Bolton out of work at a time when there was neither unemployment

insurance nor a welfare system. Finally, quality of life cannot simply be measured in economic terms. People with more money to spend may still be worse off than their ancestors, who may have preferred leisure to wealth or independence to the discipline of the clock.

Thus there are no easy answers to the quality-of-life question. In the first stages of industrialization it seems clear that only the wealthy benefited economically, though much of their increased wealth was reinvested in expansion. Under the impact of population growth, the Napoleonic wars, and regional harvest failure, real wages seem to have fallen from the levels reached in the 1730s. Industrial workers were not substantially better off than agricultural laborers when the high cost of food and rent is considered. But beginning around 1820 there is convincing evidence that the real wages of industrial workers were rising despite the fact that more and more work was semi- and unskilled machine-minding and more of it was being done by women, who were generally paid only two-thirds the wages of men. Though this increase in real wages was still subject to trade cycles, like the Great Hunger of the 1840s, it continued nearly unabated for the rest of the nineteenth century. Thus in the second half of the Industrial Revolution, both employers and workers saw a bettering of their economic situation. This was one reason why rural workers flocked to the cities and Irish peasants emigrated in the hundreds of thousands to work the lowest paid and least desirable jobs in the factories.

But economic gain had social costs. The first was the decline of the family as a labor unit. In both agricultural and early industrial activity families labored together. Workers would not move to mill towns without the guarantee of a job for all members of their family and initially they could drive a hard bargain. The early factories preferred family labor to workhouse conscripts and it was traditional for children to work beside their parents, cleaning, fetching, or assisting in minding the machines. Children provided an essential part of family income, and youngest children were the agency of care for infirm parents. Paradoxically, it was the agitation for improvement in the conditions of child labor that spelled the end of the family work unit. At first young children were barred from the factories and older ones allowed to work only a partial adult shift. Though reformers intended that schooling and leisure be substituted for work, the separation of children from parents in the workplace ultimately made possible the substitution of teenagers for adults, especially as machines replaced skilled human labor. The individual worker now became the unit of labor and during economic downturns it was adult males with their higher salaries who were laid off first.

The decline of the family as a labor unit was matched by other changes in living conditions when rural dwellers migrated to cities. Many rural habits were unsuited to both factory work and urban living. The tradition of "Saint Monday," for example, was one that was deeply rooted in the pattern of agricultural life. Little effort was expended at the beginning of the work week and progressively more at the end. Sunday leisure was followed by Monday recovery, a slow start to renewed labor. The factory demanded constant application six days a week. Strict rules were enforced to keep workers at their stations and their minds on their jobs. More than efficiency was at stake. Early machines were not only crude, they were dangerous, with no safety features to cover moving parts. Maiming accidents were common in the early factories and they were the fault of both workers and machines. Similarly, industrial workers entered a world of the cash economy. Most agricultural workers were used to being paid in kind and to barter exchange. Money was an unusual luxury that was associated with binges of food, drink, and frivolities. This made adjustment to the wage packet as difficult as adjustment to the clock. Cash had to be set aside for provisions, rent, and clothing. On the farm the time of a bountiful harvest was the time to buy durable goods; in the factory "harvest time" was always the same.

Such adjustments were not easy, and during the course of the nineteenth century a way of life passed forever from England. For some its departure caused profound sorrow; for others it was an occasion of good riddance. A vertically integrated society in which lord of the manor, village worthies, independent farmers, workers, and servants lived together interdependently was replaced by a society of segregated social classes. By the middle decades of the nineteenth century a class of capitalists and a class of workers had begun to form and had begun to clash. The middle classes aban-

doned the city centers, building exclusive suburban communities in which to raise their children and insulate their families. Conditions in the cities deteriorated under the pressure of overcrowding, lack of sanitation, and the absence of private investment. The loss of interaction between these different segments of society had profound consequences for the struggle to improve the quality of life for everyone. Leaders of labor saw themselves fighting against profits, greed, and apathy; leaders of capital against drunkenness, sloth, and ignorance. Between these two stereotypes there was little middle ground.

The Industrialization of the Continent

Though Britain took the first steps along the road to an industrial economy, it was not long before other European nations followed. There was intense interest in the British miracle, as it was dubbed by contemporaries. European ministers, entrepreneurs, even heads of state, visited British factories and mines in hope of learning the key industrial secrets that would unlock the prosperity of a new age. The Crystal Palace exhibition of manufacturing and industry held in London in 1851 was the occasion for a Continent-wide celebration of the benefits of technology and a chance for ambitious Europeans to measure themselves against the mighty British. By then many European nations had begun the transformation of their own economies and had entered a period of sustained growth.

There was no single model for the industrialization of the Continental states. Contemporaries continually made comparisons with Britain, but in truth the process of British industrialization was not well suited to any but the coal-rich regions in Belgium and the Rhineland. Nevertheless, all of Europe benefited from the British experience. No one else had to invent the jenny, the mule, or the steam engine. Although the British government banned the export of technology, none of these path-breaking inventions remained a secret for long. Britain had demonstrated a way to make cheap, durable goods in factories, and every other state in Europe was able to skip the long stages of discovery and improvement. Thus while industrialization began later on the Continent, it could progress more quickly. France and Germany were building a railroad system within years of Britain despite the fact that they had to import most of the technology, raw materials, and engineers.

Britain shaped European industrialization in another way. Its head start made it very difficult for follower nations to compete against British commodities in the world market. This meant that European industrialization would be directed first and foremost to home markets where tariffs and import quotas could protect fledgling industries. Though European states were willing to import vital British products, they placed high duties on British-made consumer goods and encouraged higher-cost domestic production. Britain's competitive advantage demanded that European governments become involved in the industrialization of their countries, financing capital-intensive industries, backing the railroads, and favoring the establishment of factories.

European industrialization was therefore not the thunderclap that occurred in Britain. In France it was a slow, accretive development that took advantage of traditional skills and occupations and gradually modernized the marketplace. In Germany industrialization had to overcome the political divisions of the empire, the economic isolation of the petty states, and the wide dispersion of vital resources. Regions rather than states industrialized in the early nineteenth century and parts of Austria, Italy, and Spain imported machinery and techniques and modernized their traditional crafts. But most of these states and most of the eastern part of Europe remained tied to a traditional agrarian-based economy that provided neither labor for industrial production nor purchasing power for industrial goods. These areas quickly became sources for raw materials and primary products for their industrial neighbors.

Industrialization Without Revolution

The experience of France in the nineteenth century demonstrates that there was no single path to industrialization. Each state blended together its natural resources, historical experiences, and forms of economic organization in unique combinations. While some mixtures resulted in explosive growth, as in Britain, others made for steady development, as in France.

French industrialization was keyed to domestic rather than export markets and to the application of new technology to a vast array of traditional crafts. The French profited, as did all of the Continental states, from British inventions, but they also benefited from the distinct features of their own economy. France possessed a pool of highly skilled and highly productive labor, a manufacturing tradition oriented toward the creation of high-quality goods, and consumers who valued taste and fashion over cost and function. Thus while the British dominated the new mass market for inexpensive cottons and cast-iron goods, a market with high sales but low profit margins, the French were producing luxury items whose very scarcity kept both prices and profits high.

Two decisive factors determined the nature of French industrialization: population growth and the French Revolution. From the early eighteenth to the mid-nineteenth centuries, France grew slowly. In 1700 French population stood at just under 20 million; in 1850 it was just under 36 million, a growth rate of 80 percent. In contrast, Germany grew 135 percent, from 15 to 34 million, and England 300 percent, from 5 to 20 million, during the same period. Nevertheless, France remained the most populous nation in western Europe, second on the Continent only to Russia. There is no simple explanation for France's relatively sluggish population growth. The French had been hit particularly hard by subsistence crises in the seventeenth century, and there is reliable evidence that the rural population consciously attempted to limit family size by methods of birth control as well as by delaying marriages. Moreover, France urbanized slowly at a time when city dwellers were marrying younger and producing larger families. As late as the 1860s a majority of French workers were farmers. Whatever the cause of this moderate population growth, its consequences were clear. France was not pressured by the force of numbers to abandon its traditional agricultural methods, nor did it face a shortage of traditional supplies of energy. Except during crop failures, French agriculture could produce to meet French needs, and there remained more than enough wood for domestic and industrial use.

A French steelworks, Manufacture Nationale, in Paris, 1800. At that time this was the only French steelworks that compared with those in Sheffield, England.

The consequences of the French Revolution are less clear. Throughout the eighteenth century, the French economy performed at least as well as had the British and in many areas better. French overseas trade had grown spectacularly until checked by military defeat in the Seven Years' War (1756–63). French agriculture steadily increased output while French rural manufactures flourished. A strong guild tradition still dominated urban industries, and although it restricted competition and limited growth, it also helped maintain the standards for the production of high-quality goods that made French commodities so highly prized throughout the world. The Revolution disrupted every aspect of economic life. Some of its outcomes were unforeseen and unwelcome. For example, Napoleon's Continental System, which attempted to close European markets to Britain, resulted in a shipping war, which the British won decisively and which eliminated France as a competitor for overseas trade in the mid-nineteenth century. But other outcomes were the result of direct policies, even if their impact could not have been entirely predicted. Urban guilds and corporations were abolished, opening trades to newcomers but destroying the close-knit

groups that trained skilled artisans and introduced innovative products. Similarly, the breakup of both feudal and common lands to satisfy the hunger of the peasantry had the effect of maintaining a large rural population for decades.

Despite the efforts of the central government, there had been little change in the techniques used by French farmers over the course of the eighteenth century. French peasants clung tenaciously to traditional rights that gave even the smallest landholder a vital say in community agriculture. Landlords were predominantly absentees, less interested in the organization of their estates than in the dues and taxes that could be extracted from them. Thus the policies of successive Revolutionary governments strengthened the hold of small peasants on the land. With the abolition of many feudal dues and with careful family planning, smallholders could survive and pass a meager inheritance on to their children. Even prosperous farmers could not grow into the large-scale proprietors that had enclosed English fields, for little land came on the market, and many parts of France practiced partible inheritance which, over time, tended to even out the size of holdings. French agriculture continued to be organized in its centuries-old patterns. While it was able to supply the nation's need for food, it could not release large numbers of workers for purely industrial activity.

Thus French industrial growth was constrained on the one hand by the relatively small numbers of workers who could engage in manufacturing and on the other by the fact that a large portion of the population remained subsistence producers, cash-poor and linked only to small rural markets. Throughout the eighteenth century the French economy continued to be regionally segregated rather than nationally integrated. The size of the state inhibited a highly organized internal trade, and there was little improvement of the infrastructure of transportation. Though some British-style canals were built, it must be remembered that canals in Britain were built to move coal rather than staple goods and France did not have much coal to move. Manufacturing concerns were still predominantly family businesses whose primary markets were regional rather than international. Roads that connected the short distances between producers and consumers were of greater importance to these producers than arterial routes that served the markets of others. Similarly, there was no national capital market until the mid-nineteenth century and precious few regional ones. Though French producers were as thrifty and profit-oriented as any others, they found it more difficult to raise the large amounts of capital necessary to purchase the most expensive new machinery and build the most up-to-date factories. Ironworks, coal mines, and railroads, the three capital-intensive ventures of industrialization, were financed either by government subsidy or by foreign investment.

All of these factors determined the slow, steady pace of French industrialization. Recovery after 1815 came in fits and starts. British inventors, manufacturers, and entrepreneurs were enticed to France to demonstrate new machinery and industrial techniques, but in most places the real engine of growth was skilled workers' steady application of traditional methods. By 1820 only sixty-five French factories were powered by steam engines, and even water-powered machinery was uncommon. Industrial firms remained small and were frequently a combination of putting-out and factory production. It was not until mid-

century that sustained industrial growth became evident. This was largely the result of the construction of railroads on a national plan, financed in large part by the central government. Whereas in Britain the railways took advantage of a national market, in France they created one. They also gave the essential stimulation to the modernization of the iron industry, in which much refining was still done with charcoal rather than coke; of machine making; and of the capital markets. Imported steel and foreign investment were vital ingredients in a process that took several decades to reach fruition.

The disadvantages of being on the trailing edge of economic change were mitigated for a time by conventional practices of protectionism. Except in specialty goods, agricultural produce, and luxury products, French manufactures could not compete with either British or German commodities. Had France maintained its position as a world trader, this comparative disadvantage would have been devastating. But defeat in the wars of commerce had led to a drawing inward of French economic effort. Marseilles and Bordeaux, once bustling centers of European trade, became provincial backwaters in the nineteenth century. But the internal market was still strong enough to support industrial growth, and domestic commodities could be protected by prohibitive tariffs, especially against British textiles, iron, and ironically, coal. Despite the fact that France had to import over 40 percent of its meager requirements of coal, it still insisted upon slapping high import duties upon British supplies. This was in part to protect French mine owners, who had never integrated their operations with iron production and therefore had no interest in keeping fuel costs low. Moreover, the slow pace of French industrialization allowed for the skipping of intermediate stages of development. France had hardly entered the canal age when it began to build its railways. Ultimately, industry moved from hand power to steam power in one long step.

While France achieved industrialization without an industrial revolution, it also achieved economic growth within the context of its traditional values. Agriculture may not have modernized, but the ancient village communities escaped the devastation modernization would bring. The orderly progression of generations of farming families characterized rural France until the shattering experiences of the Franco-Prussian War (1870) and the First World War (1914–18). Nor did France experience the mushroom growth of new cities with all of their problems of poverty, squalor, and homelessness. Slow population growth ameliorated the worst of the social diseases of industrialization while traditional rural manufacturing softened the transformation of a way of life. If France did not reap the windfall profits of the Industrial Revolution, neither did it harvest the bitter crop of social, economic, and spiritual impoverishment that was pulled in its train.

Industrialization and Union

The process of industrialization in Germany was dominated by the historic divisions of the empire of the German peoples. Before 1815 there were over three hundred separate jurisdictional units within the empire, and after 1815 there were still more than thirty. These included large advanced states like Prussia, Austria, and Saxony as well as small free cities and the personal enclaves of petty nobles who had guessed right during the Napoleonic wars. Political divisions had more than political impact. Each state clung tenaciously to its local laws and customs, which favored its citizens over outsiders. Merchants who lived near the intersection of separate jurisdictions could find themselves liable for several sets of tolls to move their goods and several sets of customs duties for importing and exporting them. These would have to be paid in different currencies at different rates of exchange according to the different regulations of each state. Small wonder that German merchants exhibited an intense localism, preferring to trade with members of their own state and supporting trade barriers against others. Such obstacles had a depressing effect on the economies of all German states, but pushed with greatest weight against the manufacturing regions of Saxony, Silesia, and the Rhineland.

Most of imperial Germany was agricultural land suited to a diversity of uses. The mountainous regions of Bavaria and the Austrian alpine communities practiced animal husbandry; there was a grain belt in Prussia, where the soil was poor but the land plentiful, and one in central Germany in which the soil was fertile and the land densely occupied. The Rhine Valley was one of the richest in all of Europe and was the center of German wine production. The introduction of the potato was the chief innovation of the eighteenth century. While English farmers were turning farms into commercial estates, German peasants were learning how to make do with less land.

Agricultural estates were organized differently in different parts of Germany. In the east, serfdom still prevailed. Peasants were tied to the land and its lord and were responsible for labor service during much of the week. Methods of cultivation were traditional, and neither peasants nor lords had much incentive to adopt new techniques. The vast agricultural domains of the Prussian Junkers, as these landlords were called, were built on the backs of cheap serf labor, and the harvest was destined for the Baltic export trade, where world grain prices rather than local production costs would determine profits. In central Germany, the long process of commuting labor service into rents was nearly completed by the end of the eighteenth century. The peasantry was not yet free, as a series of manorial relationships still tied them to the land, but they were no longer mere serfs. Finally, western Germany was dominated by free farmers who either owned or leased their lands and who had a purely economic relationship with their landlords. The restriction of peasant mobility in much of Germany posed difficulties for the creation of an industrial work force. As late as 1800 over 80 percent of the German population was engaged in agriculture, a proportion that would drop slowly over the next half-century.

Though Germany was well endowed with natural resources and skilled labor in a number of trades, it had not taken part in the expansion of world trade during the seventeenth century, and the once bustling Hanseatic ports had been far outdistanced by the rise of the Atlantic economies. The principal exported manufacture was linen, which was expertly spun and woven in Saxony and the Prussian province of Silesia. The linen industry was organized traditionally, with a mixture of domestic production managed on the putting-out system and some factory spinning, especially after the introduction of British mechanical innovations. But even the most advanced factories was still being powered by water, and thus they were located in mountainous regions where rapidly running streams could turn the wheels. In the 1840s there were only 22 steam-driven spinning mills in Germany, several of them established by the Prussian government, which imported British machines and technicians to run them. Neither linens nor traditional German metal crafts could compete on the international markets, but they could find a wider market within Germany if only the problems of political division could be resolved.

These were especially acute for Prussia after the reorganization of European boundaries in 1815 (see chapter 22). Prussian territory now included the coal- and iron-rich Rhineland provinces, but a number of smaller states separated these areas from Prussia's eastern domain. Each small state exacted its own tolls and customs duties whenever Prussian merchants wanted to move goods from one part of Prussia to the other. Such movement became more common in the nineteenth century as German manufacturing began to grow in step with its rising population. Between 1815 and 1865 the population of Germany grew by 60 percent to over 36 million. This was an enormous internal market, nearly as large as France, and the Prussians resolved to make it a unified trading zone by creating a series of alliances with smaller states known as the Zollverein (1834). The Zollverein was not a free-trade zone, as was the British empire, but rather a customs union in which member states adopted the liberal Prussian customs regulations. Every state was paid an annual portion of receipts based upon its population, and every state—except Prussia—increased its revenues as a result. The crucial advantage the Prussians received was the ability to move goods and materials from east to west, but Prussia reaped political profits as well. It forced Hanover and Saxony into the Zollverein and kept its powerful rival Austria out. Prussia's economic union soon proved to be the basis for the union of the German states.

The creation of the Zollverein was vital to German industrialization. It permitted the exploitation of natural advantages, like plentiful supplies of coal and iron, and it provided a basis for the building of railroads. Germany was a follower nation in the process of industrialization. It started late and it self-consciously modeled its success upon the British experience. British equipment and engineers were brought to Germany to attempt to plant the seeds of an industrial economy. German manufacturers sent their children to England to learn the latest techniques in industrial management. Friedrich Engels (1820–95) worked in a Manchester cotton factory, where he observed the appalling conditions of the industrial labor force and wrote *The Condition of the Working Class in England* (1845). Steam engines were installed in coal mines, if not in factories, and the process of puddling revolutionized iron making, though most iron was still smelted with charcoal rather than coke. Though coal was plentiful in Prussia, it was to be found at the eastern and western extremities of Germany. Even with the lowering of tolls and duties, it was still too expensive to move over rudimentary roads and an uncompleted system of canals.

Thus the railroads were the key to tapping the industrial potential of Germany. Here they were a cause rather than a result of industrialization. The agreements hammered out in the creation of the Zollverein made possible the planning necessary to build single lines across the boundaries of numerous states. Initially German railroads were financed privately, with much foreign investment. But ultimately governments saw the practical advantages of rail transport and took an active part in both planning and financing the system. Over a quarter of the track constructed in Prussia before 1870 was owned directly by the government, and most of the rest had been indirectly financed by the government, which purchased land and guaranteed interest on stock issues.

Germany imported most of its engines directly from Britain and thus adopted standard British gauge for its system. As early as 1850 there were over 3,500 miles of rail in Germany, with important roads linking the manufacturing districts of Saxony and the coal and iron deposits of the Ruhr. Twenty years later Germany was second only to Britain in the amount of track that had been laid and opened. By then it was no longer simply a follower. German engineers and machinists, trained in Europe's best schools of technology, were turning out engines and rolling stock second to none. And the railroads transported a host of high-quality manufactures, especially durable metal goods that came to carry the most prestigious trademark of the late nineteenth century: made in Germany.

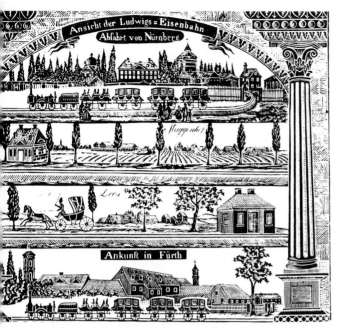

The train from Nuremberg to Fürth. This Bavarian train ran for the first time in 1835. Passengers rode the seven kilometers between Nuremburg and Fürth in coaches that closely resembled their horse-drawn predecessors.

The Lands That Time Forgot

Nothing better demonstrates the point that industrialization was a regional rather than a national process than a survey of those states that did not develop industrial economies by the middle of the nineteenth century. These states ranged from the Netherlands, which was still one of the richest areas in Europe, to Spain and Russia, which were the poorest. Also included were Austria-Hungary, the states of the Italian peninsula, and Poland. In all of these nations there was some industrial progress. The Bohemian lands of Austria contained a highly developed spinning industry; the Spanish province of Catalonia produced more cotton than did Belgium, and the Basque region was rich in iron and coal. Northern Italy mechanized its textile production, particularly silk spinning, while in the regions around both Moscow and Saint Petersburg factories were run on serf labor. Nevertheless, the economies of all these states remained nonindustrial and, with the exception of the Netherlands, dominated by subsistence agriculture.

There were many reasons why these states were unable to develop their industrial potential. Some, like Naples and Poland, were simply under-endowed with resources; others, like Austria-Hungary and Spain, faced difficulties of transport and communications that could not easily be overcome. Spain's modest resources were located on its northern and eastern edges while a vast, arid plain dominated the center. To move raw materials and finished products from one end of the country to the other was a daunting task, made more difficult by lack of waterways and the rudimentary condition of Spanish roads. Two-thirds of Austria-Hungary is either mountains or hills, a geographic feature that presented obstacles that not even the railroads could easily solve. But there was far more than natural disadvantage behind the failure of these parts of Europe to move in step with the industrializing states. Their social structure, agricultural organization, and commercial policies all hindered the adoption of new methods, machines, and modes of production.

Despite the fact that industrialization created new and largely unmanageable social problems, the follower states were eager for its benefits. All imported the latest products of technology, and the ruling elites in even the most traditional economies lived a material life similar to those in the most advanced. British entrepreneurs and craftsmen were courted by heads of state and their ministers and were offered riches in exchange for their precious knowledge. British industrialists set up textile factories in Moscow, built spinning machines in Bohemia, and taught Spanish miners how to puddle iron. Railroad pioneer George Stephenson himself surveyed the prospect of creating a passenger rail system in Spain, though he concluded pessimistically, "I have not seen enough people of the right sort to fill a single train." In the later part of the nineteenth century, French, Belgian, and German industrialists served similar roles. There were no traditional economies by choice. Industrialization was seen as a miracle and the latecomers worshiped avidly at its shrine.

It was work rather than faith that would produce economic salvation. The most common characteristic of the latecomers was a traditional agrarian structure that consumed the lion's share

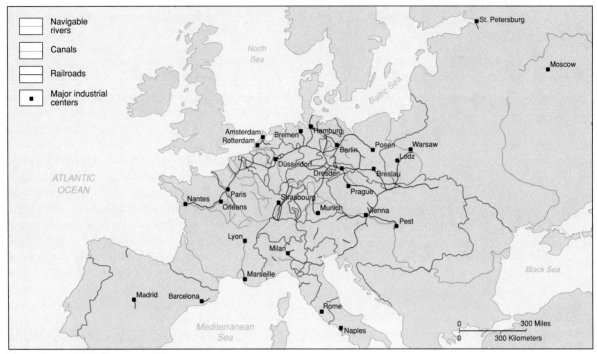

Legend:
- Navigable rivers
- Canals
- Railroads
- ■ Major industrial centers

The Industrial Revolution on the Continent

of labor and capital while producing little surplus for any but a small dominant class. In areas as dissimilar as Spain, Italy, and Russia, agriculture was organized in vast estates, which kept the mass of peasants perpetually poor. Sharecropping systems in the west and serfdom in the east differed only in formal organization. Both conditions made it impossible for peasants to accumulate the land necessary to invest in capital improvements or to send their children to towns to engage in industrial occupations. In Hungary, Poland, and Russia it was illegal for people to change occupations, and serfs who engaged in industrial activity paid their lords for the privilege. Though a number of serfs amassed considerable fortunes in organizing domestic or factory spinning, legal constraints restricted the efforts of potential entrepreneurs.

Similarly, the leaders of traditional economies maintained tariff systems that insulated their own producers from competition. Austrian tariffs were not only artificially high, they were accompanied by import quotas to keep all but the smallest fraction of foreign products from Austrian consumers. The Spanish government prohibited the importation of grain, forcing its

eastern provinces to pay huge transport costs for domestic grain despite the fact that cheaper Italian grain was readily available. Such policies sapped much-needed capital from industrial investment. There were many reasons for so-called protective tariffs, and it was not only the follower states that imposed them. France and the Zollverein protected domestic industry while Britain was converted to free trade only in the 1840s. But protection was sensible only when it protected rather than isolated. Inefficiently produced goods of inferior quality were the chief results of the protectionist policies of the follower nations. Failure to adopt steam-powered machines made traditionally produced linens and silks so expensive that smuggling occurred on an international scale. Though these goods might find buyers in domestic markets, they could not compete in international trade, and one by one the industries of the follower nations atrophied. Such nations became exporters of raw materials and foodstuffs. The export of Russian linen was replaced by the export of Russian flax. Spain, once the largest exporter of woolen cloth in Europe, now exported mainly wines and fruits. Those economies that remained traditionally organized came to be exploited for their resources by those that had industrialized.

This international situation was not all that different from the dual system that came into effect within the nonindustrialized states. In Austria-Hungary, for example, it was Hungary that was kept from industrializing, first by the continuation of serf-based agriculture, then by the high internal tariffs that favored Austrian over Hungarian manufactures. In Italy the division was between north and south. In Lombardy and Tuscany machine-based manufacturing took hold alongside mining and metallurgy. In 1860 northern Italy contained 98 percent of the railways and 87 percent of the roads that existed on the entire peninsula. In Naples and Sicily half-starved peasants eked out a miserable existence on once-rich soil that was now depleted from overuse. It was estimated that of the 400,000 people living in Naples, over 100,000 were destitute beggars. In Spain Catalonia modernized while Castile stagnated. Until the loss of its Latin American empire in the first half of the nineteenth century, Spain had a ready market for Catalonian textiles and handicrafts. But since Castile remained the cultural and administrative center of the state, it did little to encourage change and much government policy was actually counterproductive. The chief problem faced by these dual economies was that neither part could sustain the other. Traditional agriculture could not produce the necessary surplus of either labor or capital to support industry, and industry could not economize sufficiently to make manufactured goods cheap enough for a poor peasantry.

A Russian peasant tills a field with a primitive horse-drawn wooden plow. Russian fields produced low yields, partly because of the use of such crude farming methods.

Thus the advantages of being a follower were all missed. Technology could not be borrowed or stages skipped because the ground was not prepared for widespread industrial activity to be cultivated. Even by standing still they fell behind. While over the course of the nineteenth century male illiteracy dropped dramatically in the industrialized states—to 30 percent in Britain and France and 10 percent in Prussia—it remained at 75 to 80 percent in Spain and Italy and over 90 percent in Russia. There was more than irony in the fact that one of the first railroads built on the Continent was built in Austria but it was built to be powered by horses rather than engines. The first railways in Italy linked royal palaces to capital cities; those in Spain radiated from Madrid and bypassed most centers of natural resources. In these states the railroads were built to move the military rather than passengers or goods. They were state-financed, occasionally state-owned, and almost always lost money. They were symbols of the industrial age, but in these states they were symbols without substance.

The industrialization of Europe in the eighteenth century was an epochal event in human history. The constraints on daily life imposed by nature were loosened for the first time. No longer did population growth in one generation mean famine in the next; no longer was it necessary for the great majority of people to toil in the fields to earn their daily bread. Manufacture replaced agriculture as humanity's primary activity, though the change was longer and slower than the burst of industrialization that took place in the first half of the nineteenth century. For the leaders, Britain especially, industrialization brought international eminence. British achievements were envied, British inventors celebrated, Britain's constitutional and social organization lauded. A comparatively small island nation had become the greatest economic power in Europe. Industrialization had profound consequences for economic life, but its effects ran deeper than that. The search for new markets would result in the conquest of continents; the power of productivity unleashed by coal and iron would result in the first great arms race. Both would reach fruition in World War I, the first industrial war. For better or worse we still live in the industrial era that began in Britain in the middle of the eighteenth century.

Suggestions for Further Reading

General Reading

* Carlo Cipolla, ed., *The Fontana Economic History of Europe: The Emergence of Industrial Societies*, 2 vols. (London: Fontana Books, 1973). Country-by-country survey of Continental European industrialization.

* David Landes, *The Unbound Prometheus* (Cambridge: Cambridge University Press, 1969). Vigorously argued study of the impact of technology on British and European society from the eighteenth to the twentieth century.

* E. L. Jones, *The European Miracle*, 2d ed. (Cambridge: Cambridge University Press, 1987). A comparative study of the acquisition of technology in Europe and Asia and the impact that industrialization had upon the two continents.

* T. S. Ashton, *The Industrial Revolution* (Oxford: Oxford University Press, 1969). A brief, compelling account of the traditional view of industrialization.

The Traditional Economy

* E. A. Wrigley, *Continuity, Chance and Change* (Cambridge: Cambridge University Press, 1988). Explores the nature of the traditional economy and the way in which Britain escaped from it.

* L. A. Clarkson, *Proto-Industrialization: The First Phase of Industrialization?* (London: Macmillan, 1985). Study of domestic manufacturing and its connection to the process of industrialization.

J. D. Chambers and G. E. Mingay, *The Agricultural Revolution* (London: Batsford, 1966). The classic survey of the changes in British agriculture.

E. L. Jones, *Agriculture and the Industrial Revolution* (New York: John Wiley and Sons, 1974). Detailed study of the relationship between agricultural innovations and the coming of industrialization in Britain.

The Industrial Revolution in Britain

* Peter Mathias, *The First Industrial Nation*, 2d ed. (London: Methuen, 1983). Up-to-date general survey of British industrialization.

* Phyllis Deane, *The First Industrial Revolution*, 2d ed. (Cambridge: Cambridge University Press, 1979). The best introduction to the technological changes in Britain.

A. E. Musson, *The Growth of British Industry* (New York: Holmes & Meier, 1978). In-depth survey of British industrialization that is especially strong on technology.

* D. N. McCloskey and R. Floud, *The Economic History of Britain, Since 1700* (Cambridge: Cambridge University

* Indicates paperback edition available.

Press, 1981). Collection of essays by new economic historians. Quantitative in presentation and econometric in argument.

N. F. R. Crafts, *British Economic Growth During the Industrial Revolution* (Oxford: Oxford University Press, 1985). Study by a new economic historian arguing the case for slow economic growth in the early nineteenth century. Highly quantitative.

T. S. Ashton, *Iron and Steel in the Industrial Revolution* (Manchester: Manchester University Press, 1963). Lucid account of the transformation of iron making, including the story of James Watt.

Philip Bagwell, *The Transport Revolution from 1770* (London: Batsford, 1974). Thorough survey of the development of canals, highways, and railroads in Britain.

* Francois Crouzet, *The First Industrialists* (Cambridge: Cambridge University Press, 1985). Analysis of the social background of the first generation of British entrepreneurs.

* Harold Perkin, *The Origins of Modern English Society 1780–1880* (London: Routledge & Kegan Paul, 1969). Outstanding survey of British social history in the industrial era.

* E. P. Thompson, *The Making of the English Working Class* (New York: Random House, 1966). Brilliant and passionate study of the ways in which laborers responded to the changes brought about by the industrial economy.

Friedrich Engels, *The Condition of the Working Class in England in 1844* (London: Allen and Unwin, 1952). The classic eyewitness account of the horrors of the industrial city.

The Industrialization of the Continent

* Tom Kemp, *Industrialization in Nineteenth-Century Europe*, 2d ed. (London: Longman, 1985). Survey of the process of industrialization in the major European states.

* Clive Trebilcock, *The Industrialization of the Continental Powers 1780–1914* (London: Longman, 1981). Complex study of Germany, France, and Russia.

Sidney Pollard, *Peaceful Conquest* (Oxford: Oxford University Press, 1981). Argues for the regional nature of industrialization throughout western Europe.

Roger Price, *The Economic Transformation of France* (London: Croom Helm, 1975). Study of French society before and during the process of industrialization.

W. O. Henderson, *The Rise of German Industrial Power* (Berkeley, CA: University of California Press, 1975). Chronological study of German industrialization that centers on Prussia.

* Wolfgang Schivelbusch, *The Railway Journey* (Berkeley, CA: University of California Press, 1986). Social history of the impact of railways, drawn from French and German sources.

22

Social Transformations and Political Upheavals, 1815–1850

Potato Politics

Vegetables have histories too. But none has a more interesting history in the West than the humble potato. First introduced to northern Europe from the Andean highlands in South America at the end of the sixteenth century, it rapidly became a staple of peasant diets from Ireland to Russia. Frederick the Great encouraged its adoption in Prussia in the eighteenth century, well aware of its ability to contribute to the well-being of his people.

The potato's vitamins, minerals, and high carbohydrate content provided a rich source of energy to Europe's rural poor. By the nineteenth century attitudes toward the potato had been transformed from the seventeenth-century view that it caused leprosy to its canonization as "the miracle vegetable." It was simple to plant, it required little or no cultivation, and it did well in damp, cool climates. Best of all, it could be grown successfully on the smallest plots of land. One acre could support a peasant family of four for a year. Potato peelings helped sustain the family cow and pig, further supplementing family income.

The French painter Jean-François Millet (1814–75) provides a view of the peasant labor involved in *Planting Potatoes*. Millet, the son of a wealthy peasant family, understood well the importance of the potato crop in the peasant diet. The man and woman in this canvas plant their potatoes as a reverent act, bowing as field laborers might in prayer (as they do in Millet's more sentimental work, *The Angelus*). The primitive nature of the process is striking: the man uses a short hoe to scrape at what seems to be most unyielding soil. The peasants seem part of the nature that surrounds them, patient as the beast that waits in the shade, bent and gnarled and lovely as the tree that arches in the background.

French, Belgian, Scottish, German, and Polish peasants included the potato as a staple in their diets, but only Irish peasants relied on it exclusively. An all-potato diet may have been bland and dull but it was not a nutritional hardship. The cooked potato was a substitute for wheat. As the sole item of diet, it provided life-sustaining nutrients and a significant amount of the protein so necessary for heavy labor. The Irish adult male ate an average of twelve to fourteen pounds of potatoes a day—a figure that may seem preposterous to us today. The British economist Adam Smith, marveling at the strength, height, and health of the Irish at the end of the eighteenth century, attributed it all to the economy of the potato.

The fleshy root not only guaranteed health, it also affected social life. Peasants had traditionally delayed marriage and starting their families because of the unavailability of land. The potato changed that behavior. Now the potato allowed peasants with only a little land to marry and have children earlier. Millet's depiction of the man and woman working together in the field resonates with the simple fact that potato cultivation aided in the formation of the couple. Millet's couple are parents whose baby sleeps swaddled in a basket and shaded by the tree. In those peasant homes where family members did putting-out work for local entrepreneurs, potato cultivation drew little labor away from the spinning wheel and loom. It permitted prosperous farmers to devote more land to cash crops, since only a small portion of land was required to feed a family. Most commonly, however, the potato was the single crop grown by most Irish farmworkers.

Proverbs warned peasants against putting all their eggs in one basket, but no folk wisdom prepared the Irish for the potato disaster that struck them. In 1845 a fungus from America destroyed the new potato crop. Although they were certainly accustomed to bad harvests and crop failures, the peasants had no precedent for the years of blight that followed. From 1846 to 1850, famine and the diseases resulting from it—scurvy, dysentery, cholera, and typhus fever—killed over a million people in what became known as the Great Hunger. Another million people emigrated, many to the United States. Only the lucky survived the voyage across the ocean on the disease-infested death ships. Total dependence on the potato reaped its grim harvest, devastating all levels of Irish society. Within five years the Irish population was reduced by almost 25 percent.

The Irish potato famine has been called the "last great European *natural* disaster," to distinguish it from the man-made horrors of war and revolution. But it was as much a social disaster as a natural one. Food was the most political of issues. Many argued that the disaster could have been averted. The United Kingdom of Great Britain and Ireland had been created in 1801, and this political unit, which also included England, Scotland, and Wales, constituted one of the world's most prosperous states. The British government expected that the free market would solve the problems caused by famine once trade

barriers had been removed. The British Corn Laws, which had been enacted to protect domestic growers from foreign competition, were repealed in 1847. But the famine had hit the Irish so hard that they simply did not have the money to buy what grains might be available. Emergency work relief was established and soup kitchens were opened in the spring of 1847, but even this meager assistance was withdrawn because the famine coincided with a banking crisis in England. There is little to indicate that the continuation of work relief and soup kitchens could have reversed the death rates. In 1847 the problem was handed over to the Irish Poor Law system, a system Britain had imposed on Ireland in 1838. The workhouses created by the recent law were not intended to deal with disasters. Poor and starving Irish peasants were expected to support themselves. Mass deaths and mass graves were the inevitable result.

The Irish Great Hunger was the most striking example of the problem that plagued all Western societies in the first half of the nineteenth century: what to do with the poor. The Irish famine was an extreme case of crisis that Great Britain was unable to handle. In this context of poverty and the politics of food, Millet's melancholy painting of *Planting Potatoes* was a political statement. In its reverence for humble work, it presents the dignity and worthiness of the poor. It also confronts us with their isolation.

Europe in 1815

In his quest for empire, Napoleon had given Europe a geography lesson. Because no one state had been able to defeat him, Napoleon had made clear the territorial and political interdependence of the European powers. This lesson was not lost on the Great Powers as they sat down to redraw the map of Europe in 1815. The leaders of Russia, Austria, Prussia, and France shared with the British foreign secretary Lord Castlereagh (1769–1822) the vision of Europe as a machine that must be kept in running order. They looked on the whole of Europe as one entity and conceived of peace in terms of a general European security.

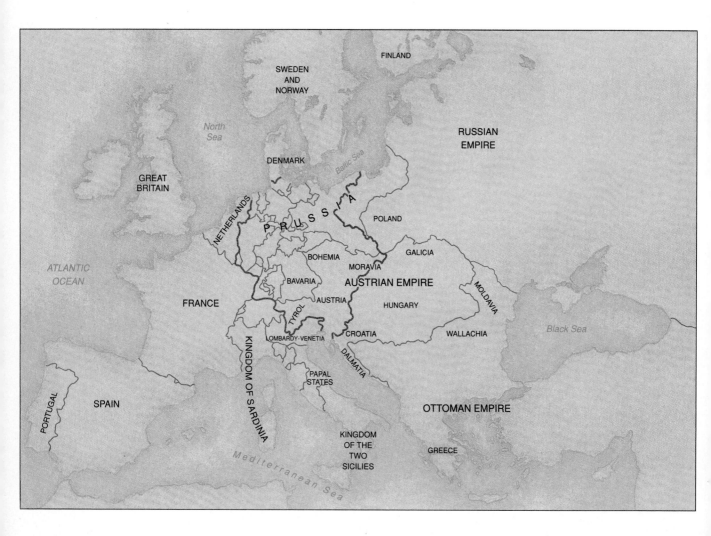

The primary goal of the European leaders who met in 1815 was to devise the most stable territorial arrangement possible. The settlement that emerged from their meeting was not simply a reaction to the ideological challenges of the French Revolution, nor was it a restoration of the European state system that had existed before Napoleon. During the negotiations traditional claims of the right to rule came head to head with new ideas about stabilization. The three principles of legitimacy, compensation, and balance of power dominated the 1815 settlement of negotiation and set the terms of international relations for succeeding generations. The equilibrium established in 1815 made possible a century-long European peace. Conflicts, to be sure, erupted, but they too took on the characteristics of the new system that was constructed at Vienna in 1815.

The Congress of Vienna

Because of the concern with establishing harmony at the time of Napoleon's defeat, the peace enforced against France was not a punitive one. After Napoleon's abdication in 1814, the Four Powers decided that leniency was the best way to support the restored Bourbon monarchy. After 1793 royalist émigrés referred to the young son of the executed Louis XVI as Louis XVII, although the child died in captivity and never reigned. In 1814 the Great Powers designated the elder of the two surviving brothers of Louis XVI as the appropriate candidate for the restored monarchy. Because of the circumstances of his restoration, the new king, Louis XVIII (1814–15; 1815–24), bore the ignominious image of returning "in the baggage car of the Allies." Every effort was made not to weigh Louis XVIII down with a harsh settlement. The First Peace of Paris, signed by the Allies with France in May 1814, had cut French frontiers back to the 1792 boundaries, which included Avignon, Venaissin, parts of Savoy, and German and Flemish territories, none of which had belonged to France in 1789. After the hundred-day return of Napoleon, the "usurper," the Second Peace of Paris of November 1815 somewhat less generously declared French frontiers restricted to the boundaries of 1790 and exacted from France an indemnity of 700 million francs.

An army of occupation consisting of 150,000 troops was also placed on French soil at French expense but was removed ahead of schedule in 1818. Contrary to the terms of the first treaty, the second treaty also required France to return plundered art treasures to their countries of origin.

As part of the first peace treaty, representatives of the victorious Allies agreed to convene in the Austrian capital of Vienna in September 1814 for the purposes of mopping up the mess created in Europe by French rule and restoring order to European monarchies. On the surface, the Congress of Vienna seemed to be no more than an excuse for endless partying among Europe's royalty. Glittering balls as financially costly as battles gave critics the impression that statesmen were waltzing their way through treaty arrangements. The survival of an old system of precedence and etiquette hobbled negotiations. Issues of who should sign a treaty first and who should have the preferred places at the dinner table were the subjects of endless debates and fatal duels. But the image of bewigged men arguing over which criterion should be used to determine who would enter a room first belied the reality of the diplomats' serious negotiations as they sought to fashion a lasting peace by redrawing the map of Europe.

The central actors whose personalities dominated the Congress were the Austrian minister of foreign affairs Prince Klemens von Metternich, British foreign secretary Viscount Castlereagh, French minister of foreign affairs Charles Maurice de Talleyrand, the Russian tsar Alexander I, and the Prussian king Frederick William III. In spite of personal eccentricities, animosities, and occasionally outright hostilities among Europe's leaders, all shared a common concern with reestablishing harmony in Europe.

The dominant partnership of Austria and Britain at the Congress of Vienna resulted in treaty arrangements that served to restrain the ambitions of Russia and Prussia. No country was to receive territory without giving up something in return, and no one country was to receive enough territory to make it a present or future threat to the peace of Europe. To contain France, some steps taken prior to the Congress were ratified or expanded. In June 1814 the Low Countries had been set up as a unitary state as a buffer against future French expansion on the Continent and a block to the revival of French sea power. The new Kingdom of the Netherlands had been created out of the former Dutch Republic and the Austrian Netherlands and placed under the rule of William I of Orange (1815–40). The Catholic southern provinces were thus uneasily reunited with the Protestant northern provinces, regions that had been separated since the Peace of Westphalia in 1648. Lest there be any doubt about the intended purpose of this new kingdom, Great Britain gave William I of the Netherlands 2 million pounds to fortify his frontier against France.

restored to Austria. The Italian duchies of Tuscany, Parma, and Modena were placed under the rule of Habsburg princes.

After the fall of Napoleon, the Allies made no attempt to restore the Holy Roman Empire. Napoleon's Confederation of the Rhine, which organized the majority of German territory under French auspices in 1806, was dissolved. In its place the German Confederation was created by reorganizing the three hundred petty states into thirty-eight. The German Confederation was intended as a bulwark against France and not to serve any nationalist or parliamentary function. The thirty-eight states, along with Austria as the thirty-ninth, were represented in a new Federal Diet at Frankfurt, dominated by Austrian influence.

All of these changes were the result of carefully discussed but fairly noncontroversial negotiations. The question of Poland was another matter indeed. Successive partitions by Russia,

The reestablishment of a monarchy that united the island kingdom of Sardinia with Piedmont and that included Savoy, Nice, and part of Genoa, contained France on its southeast border. To the east, Prussia was given control of the left bank of the Rhine. Switzerland was reestablished as an independent confederation of cantons. Finally, Bourbon rule was restored in Spain on France's southwestern border.

Austria's power was firmly established in Italy, either through outright territorial control or influence over independent states. The Papal States were returned to Pope Pius VII (1800–23), along with territories that had been Napoleon's Cisalpine Republic and the Kingdom of Italy. The Republic of Venice was absorbed into the Austrian empire. Lombardy and the Illyrian provinces on the Dalmatian coast were likewise

Austria, and Prussia in 1772, 1793, and 1795 had completely dismembered the land that had been Poland. Napoleon had reconstituted a small portion of Poland as the Grand Duchy of Warsaw. The dilemma of the Congress was what to do with this Napoleonic creation and with Polish territory in general. Fierce debate over Poland threatened to shatter congressional harmony.

Tsar Alexander I (1801–25) of Russia argued for a large Poland that he intended to be fully under his influence and that would extend Russian-controlled territories to the banks of the Oder. He also envisioned extending Russian dominance farther into central and eastern Europe. He based his claim on the significant contribution the Russian army had made to Napoleon's defeat. But such thinking conflicted with Austrian minister Metternich's pursuit of equilibrium.

Frederick William III (1797–1840) of Prussia contended that if a large Poland was to be created, Prussia would expect compensation by absorbing Saxony. Both Great Britain and France distrusted Russian and Prussian territorial aims. Talleyrand (1754–1838), the wily and brilliant French negotiator, was able to take advantage of his position of nothing to lose to work out a compromise. As a bishop under the old regime, a revolutionary who managed to keep his head, an exile in America during the Terror, Napoleon's chief minister, and now the representative of a Bourbon monarchy at the Congress, Talleyrand knew something about survival and taking advantage of opportunities. Talleyrand was also a shrewd and experienced diplomat who managed to convince the Allies to accept France, their defeated enemy, as an equal partner in negotiations. In the midst of the crisis over Poland, he persuaded Britain and Austria to sign a secret treaty with France to preserve an independent Polish territory. He then deliberately leaked news of the secret agreement of these powers to go to war, if necessary, to block Russian and

Prussian aims. Alexander I and Frederick William III immediately backed down. Talleyrand's private opinion of the other four powers was acidic: "Too frightened to fight each other, too stupid to agree."

But under Talleyrand's manipulation, agree they did. In the final arrangement, Prussia retained the Polish territory of Posen, and Austria kept the Polish province of Galicia. Kraków, with its population of 95,000, was declared a free city. Finally, a kingdom of Poland, nominally independent but in fact under the tutelage of Russia, emerged from what remained of the Grand Duchy of Warsaw. It was a solution that benefited no one in particular. Neither did it offend anyone too greatly, except, of course, the Poles.

In addition to receiving Polish territories, Prussia gained two-fifths of the kingdom of Saxony. Prussia also received territory on the left bank of the Rhine, the Duchy of Westphalia, and Swedish Pomerania. With these acquisitions Prussia doubled its population to around 11 million people. The Junkers,  the landed class of east Prussia, reversed many of the reforms of the Napoleonic period. The new territories that Prussia gained were rich in waterways and resources but geographically fragmented. The dispersal of holdings that was intended to contain Prussian power in central Europe spurred Prussia to find new ways of uniting its markets. In this endeavor, Prussia constituted a future threat to Austrian power over the German Confederation.

In Scandinavia, Russia's conquest of Finland was acknowledged by the members of the Congress and, in return, Sweden acquired Norway from Denmark. Unlike Austria, Prussia, and Russia, Great Britain made no claim to territories at the Congress. Having achieved its aim of containing France, its greatest rival for dominance on the seas, Britain returned the French colonies it had seized in war. For the time being, the redrawing of the territorial map of Europe had achieved its pragmatic aim of guaranteeing the peace. It was now left to a system of alliances to preserve that peace.

The Alliance System

Quadruple Alliance

Only by joining forces had the European powers been able to defeat Napoleon, and the necessity of a system of alliances was recognized even after the battles were over. Two alliance pacts dominated the post-Napoleonic era: the renewed Quadruple Alliance and the Holy Alliance. The Quadruple Alliance, signed by the victorious powers of Great Britain, Austria, Russia, and Prussia in November 1815, was intended to protect Europe against future French aggression and to preserve the status quo. In 1818 France, having completed its payment of war indemnities, joined the pact, which now became the Quintuple Alliance. The five powers promised to meet periodically over the next twenty years to discuss common problems and to ensure the peace.

The Holy Alliance, very different in tone and intent, was the brainchild of Alexander I and was heavily influenced by his mystical and romantic view of international politics. In this pact the monarchs of Prussia, Austria, and Russia agreed to renounce war and to protect the Christian religion. The Holy Alliance spoke of "the bonds of a true and indissoluble brotherhood . . . to protect religion, peace, and justice." Russia was able to give some credibility to the alliance with the sheer size of its army. While Castlereagh dismissed the Holy Alliance as nonsense, and career diplomats were aware of its hollowness as a treaty arrangement, it did indicate the willingness of Europe's three eastern autocracies to intervene in the affairs of other states.

The concept of Europe acting as a whole, through a system of periodic conferences, marked the emergence of a new diplomatic era. Conflict, however, was inherent in the commitment of parliamentary governments to open consultation and the need for secrecy in diplomacy. Dynastic

Holy Alliance

regimes sought to intervene in smaller states to buoy up despots. That certainly seemed to be the case in 1822, when European powers met to consider restoring the Bourbon monarchy in Spain. The British refused to cooperate and blocked united action by the Alliance. Great Britain acted as a counterbalance to interventionist tendencies. British Prime Minister George Canning did not agree with Metternich's policies and seemed to undermine Castlereagh's commitment to the alliance system as a whole when he declared, "Every nation for itself, and God for us all!" France took military action on its own in 1823, restored King Ferdinand VII, and abolished the Spanish constitution. Other opportunities for intervention arose in the fifteen years after the Congress of Vienna. The real test of the balance of power came in 1830, when many of the controversies that appeared to be settled in 1815 reemerged to challenge the system of alliances.

The New European Society

The peace that emerged from the Congress of Vienna did not restore the old order, although it did preserve principles of rule that a property-owning elite held dear. The search for stability, restoration, and the reaction to change characterized national and international affairs after 1815. Social structure and the world of production were undergoing dramatic transformations, and European states had to reckon with the fact that the daily lives of growing numbers of their subjects were transformed between 1815 and 1850. The demands of an international balance of power stood poised against the internal assaults on old social values in new arenas of conflict. Urbanization, industrialization, and economic uncertainties challenged Europeans in new ways in their search for stability.

Urban Life

In 1800, two out of every one hundred Europeans lived in a city. By 1850, the number of urban dwellers per hundred had jumped to five and was rising rapidly. In England, the shift was more concentrated than the general European pattern. With one out of every two people living in a city, England had become an urban society by mid-century. London was the fastest growing city in Europe, followed at some distance by Paris and Berlin. The numbers of smaller urban centers were also multiplying.

Massive internal migration caused most urban growth. People from the same rural areas often lived together in the same urban neighborhoods and even in the same boardinghouses. Irish emigrants crowded together in the "Little Dublin" section of London. Similarly, districts in other cities were set off by regional accents and native provincial dress. Workers from the same hometowns gravitated to their favorite cafes. These social networks helped make the transition from rural to urban life bearable for the tens of thousands of people who poured into Europe's cities in search of jobs and opportunity. Until mid-century, many migrants returned to their rural homes for the winter when work, especially in the building trades, was scarce in the city. Young migrant women who came to the city to work as servants sent money home to support rural relatives, or worked to save a nest egg—or dowry—in order to return to the village permanently. Before 1850 in London 20 percent of the workers were domestics and most of them were women.

Despite the support networks that migrants constructed for themselves, the city was not always a hospitable place. Workers were poorly paid and women workers were more poorly paid than men. When working women were cut free of the support of home and family, uncounted numbers were forced into part-time prostitution to supplement meager incomes. Growing numbers resorted to prostitution as a means of surviving in times of unemployment. It is conservatively estimated that there were 34,000 prostitutes in Paris in 1850 and 50,000 in London. The phenomenon of prostitution indicated changing mores about sexuality in the first half of the nineteenth century. The "angel" of middle-class households and the "whore" of the streets were subjects of fascination in fictional and nonfictional literature. Increased prostitution created a veritable epidemic of venereal diseases, especially syphilis, for which there was no known cure until the twentieth century.

This sketch of a lane in St. Giles, the notorious London slum, was made in the 1840s. Such squalor and overcrowding contributed to the miseries of the working class. Note the pig, which confronts a dog on its scavenging rounds.

Urban crime also grew astronomically, with thefts accounting for the greatest number of crimes. Social reformers identified poverty and urban crowding as causes of the increase in criminal behavior. In 1829 both Paris and London began to create modern urban police forces to deal with the challenges to law and order. Crime assumed the character of disease in the minds of middle-class reformers. Statisticians and social scientists, themselves a new urban phenomenon, produced massive theses on social hygiene, lower-class immorality, and the unworthiness of the poor. The pathology of the city was widely discussed. Always at the center of the issue was the "social question": the growing problem of what to do with the poor.

The Social Question

State-sponsored work relief expanded after 1830 for the deserving poor: the old, the sick, and children. Able-bodied workers who were idle were regarded as undeserving and dangerous, regardless of the causes of their unemployment. Performance of work became an indicator of moral worth, as urban and rural workers succumbed to downturns in the economic cycle. Those unable to work sought relief, as a last resort, from the state. What has been called "a revolution in government" took place in the 1830s and 1840s, as legislative bodies increased regulation of everything from factories and mines to prisons and schools. Poor relief was part of the general pattern of state involvement in social issues.

Poverty was not just an urban problem although it was both more conspicuous and more feared in urban areas. Politicians, social reformers, religious thinkers, and revolutionaries all had different solutions that followed one of two general orientations. There were those who argued, as in the case of the Irish famine, that the government must do nothing to intervene because the problem would correct itself, as Thomas Malthus had predicted forty years earlier, through the "natural" means of famine and death that would keep population from outgrowing available resources and food supplies. The Irish population, one of the poorest in Europe, had indeed doubled between 1781 and 1841, and for Malthusians, the Irish famine was the fulfillment of their vision that famine was the only way to correct overpopulation. Poverty was a social necessity; by interfering with it, this first group insisted, governments could only make matters worse.

A second group contended that poverty was society's problem, and perhaps society's creation, and not a law of nature. Thus, it was the social responsibility of the state to take care of its members. The question of how to treat poverty, or "the social question" as it came to be known among contemporaries, underlay many of the protests and reforms of the two decades before 1850 and fueled the revolutionary movements of 1848. Parliamentary legislation attempted to improve the situation of the poor and especially the working class in the 1830s and 1840s. In 1833 British reformers turned their attention to the question of child labor. Parliamentary investigations discovered horrifying abuses of young children. Against the opposition of those who argued for a free market for labor, Parliament passed the Factory Act of 1833, which prohibited the employment of children under nine years of age and restricted the work week of children aged nine to thirteen to forty-eight hours. No child in this age group could work more than nine hours a day. Teenagers between thirteen and eighteen years could work no more than sixty-nine hours a week. By modern standards, these "reformed" work loads present a shocking picture of the heavy reliance on child labor. The British Parliament commissioned investigations, compiled in the "Blue Books," that reported the abusive treatment of men, women, and children in factories. Similar studies existed for French and Belgian industry.

By the standards of 1833 the British legislation marked an initial step in state intervention in the workplace. Additional legislation over the next three decades further restricted children's and women's labor in factories and concerned itself with improvement of conditions in the workplace. At bottom the social question was the question of what was the state's role and responsibility in caring for its citizens.

This satiric cartoon is one of a series by Robert Cruikshank castigating the English factory system and its treatment of child labor.

Family Life

Industrialization profoundly altered the structure of daily life within the family during the first half of the nineteenth century. Changes affected both middle-class and working-class families, although to varying degrees. With the rise of the state and a growing emphasis on education, the socialization role of the family was gradually taken over by public institutions. By mid-century population growth was beginning to slow down throughout Europe, as people were choosing to restrict the size of their families. Europeans of earlier times had delayed marriage, practiced birth control, and engaged in abortion and infanticide to limit family size. But the nineteenth century marks the first time in history that the majority of Europeans recognized that having fewer children was a value and acted on it.

Why decisions about limiting family size were made and how they were implemented are among the most intimate and private of questions, whose answers can never really be known. But there is no doubt about the outcome of these decisions: people began having two or three children per family, instead of five or six. Economic motivation appears to have been primary. In the nineteenth century, children had little economic value as laborers. With the elimination of minors from the workplace, children were regarded in a different way. The hope of a better life for one's progeny required that existing resources be concentrated on fewer children. The middle-class pattern of small families became the dominant one in western Europe in the nineteenth century, as middle-class culture became more self-conscious.

Jane Austen (1775–1817), one of Europe's great novelists, created a picture of middle-class life in nineteenth-century England and of women's place in it. In *Pride and Prejudice* (1813) and *Emma* (1815), parents and guardians wait helplessly on the sidelines, hoping their charges will marry well. Young people, freed from the arranged marriages of the previous century, choose mates on the basis of affection and affinity. The couple is a locus for personal fulfillment. Yet the middle-class family exists in a network of value and status. In Austen's novels families are ranked according to their consumption of furniture, carriages, and pianofortes; the numbers of their servants; and the frequency of their trips to London. Austen chronicles the importance of income for marriage and status in a money-oriented society. The family is the primary arena of consumption.

The privacy of family life intensified with the transfer of paid work to a public workplace. Middle-class Europeans, whether French, German, or British, shared with Austen's families a taste for decorated interiors and material comforts in the home. In Germany, the Biedermeier style, named after a popular furniture-maker, appeared in 1815 and remained popular until mid-century. The Biedermeier style stressed coziness, intimacy, and domesticity, and was expressed in the furnishings, clothes, and paintings of the German middle class. To its critics the style was sentimental and vulgar. During this era middle-class consumers began collecting on a mass scale. They filled their homes with knickknacks, curios, and mass-produced art. By accumulating these objects, the middle class asserted its right as an arbiter of its own style. At the same time middle-class collecting reflected a curious aping of the great aristocratic collectors of a previous age.

A vast gulf separated working-class families from these middle-class consumers. Factory owner and social critic Friedrich Engels (1820–95) left a bleak but accurate account of working-class life in Manchester in *The Condition of the Working Class in England in 1844*. Working women, unsupervised children, and unemployed husbands figured prominently in his brutal tale of misery and immorality. Western culture redefined family life as the seat of solace, comfort, and consumption, but for the majority of the population that ideal remained out of reach.

Reformers confronted the disparities in family life and placed the blame squarely on women's absence from the home. Women had made industrialization possible, as they poured into the British and Continental textile factories and became the primary work force. Employers found women more adept and more dexterous than men in running the intricate new looms. Women worked for cheaper wages and were generally more docile than men in accepting the routinization of the factory. Men were considered more likely to organize, to riot, and to become rowdy. Women and children worked long hours under dire conditions. The number of women in factories was expanding rapidly in the 1830s and 1840s. The solution to the perceived decline in the working-class family was found in legislation to restrict women from the workplace and return them to

A bourgeois living room of pre-1848 Vienna. Such rooms were designed to promote the social life and cultural interests of the family unit. There was a musical corner and areas for conversation and reading.

the home to care for their husbands and children.

Children were an even cheaper work force than women. Some proponents of child labor argued that the choice was to have children running wild in the streets and unsupervised at home or in the disciplined environment of the factories. The situation at its worst was reflected in one eyewitness account of French silk manufacture. For eighteen hours a day six-year-old girls were harnessed to mechanical wheels to work.

Women's rights, little affected by industrialization, were increasingly disputed in public forums after 1815. In France, the equality of citizens before the law did not extend to women. Women's subservience in marriage was clearly defined: "A husband owes protection to his wife, a wife obedience to her husband." The law preserved a double standard for judging the behavior of women and men. In English law, men could terminate their marriages but their wives had no such access to divorce. Agitation for the right to divorce converging with notorious public scandals over abused married women achieved nothing before 1850. Critics blamed the decline in sexual mores on women's refusal to "know their place." By the mid-nineteenth century women were organizing to demand equal political rights, political representation, assistance in caring for children, and better living conditions. Through their own newspapers, journals, and pamphlets bourgeois women publicized their political demands for all women. John Stuart Mill, the leading liberal theorist, joined with women reformers in demanding full equality for British women. These movements achieved little in solid reforms before 1850, but they made clear the tensions within the family and within the law.

The growing emphasis on public education added its own special twist to the debate over family life and women's rights. Few agreed with French labor leader Flora Tristan (1801–44) and the utopian reformer Charles Fourier that women had the capacity and the right to receive an equal education with men. Most argued that women should be educated only to fulfill better their natural responsibilities as mothers. Napoleon's dictum, "The hand that rocks the cradle rules the nation," became the chief justification for educating girls as mothers.

In 1837 in Great Britain, an eighteen-year-old young woman became queen. Reigning until her death in 1901, Victoria gave her name to an age and its morals. Girls became queens of Portugal and Spain. But they, like the young Victoria, were little more than political figureheads, protecting the survival of dynastic claims and contributing little to the growing debate about women's proper place in society. Although the presence of women on European thrones may have provided inspiration for disenfranchised women, it did not affect the broader reality that everywhere women were deprived of the vote and equal protection before the law, that married women could not own property or claim custody of their own children. Victoria, ruler of one of the world's great nations, became the model for domestic bliss. The changing expectations about the emotional rewards of family life, reflected in the publicity of the queen's marriage to Prince Albert of Saxe-Coburg-Gotha in 1840, created a new image of proper womanhood that had little relation to the lives that most women led.

Family portrait of Queen Victoria, the Prince Consort, and their eldest children, painted by Franz Xavier Winterhalter in 1846. Their first daughter, Victoria, would become the mother of Kaiser Wilhelm II of Germany.

The New Ideologies

Early industrialization had been accomplished without a dramatically new technology. Wood, water, wind, and muscle—animal and human—the sources of energy in the preindustrial period, fueled the early stages of industrialization. Practices began to change slowly as crises in energy supply—deforestation and drought, for example—encouraged the use of coal as a more reliable and eventually more efficient fuel. After 1815, steam-driven mechanical power in production and transportation steadily replaced human and animal power. In deference to what it was replacing, the new mechanical force was measured in units of horsepower. The new technology challenged old values; new definitions of worth emerged from the changing world of work. The fixed, caste-like distinctions of the old aristocratic world were under attack or in disarray. Western intellectuals struggled with the changes of the new age as they sought to make sense of the way in which Europeans lived, looked at the world, and defined their place in it.

The political and economic upheavals of the first half of the nineteenth century encouraged a new breed of thinkers to search for ways to explain the transformations of the period. Before mid-century Europeans witnessed one of the most intellectually fertile periods in the history of the West. The search for understanding during this era gave birth to new ideologies—liberalism, nationalism, romanticism, conservatism, and socialism—that came to shape the ideas and institutions of the present day.

Liberalism

The term *liberal* was first used in a narrow, political sense to indicate the Spanish party of reform that supported the constitution modeled on the French document of 1791. But the term assumed much broader connotations in the first half of the nineteenth century as its appeal spread among the European middle classes. The two main tenets of belief that underlay liberalism were the freedom of the individual and the corruptibility of authority. As a political doctrine, liberalism built on Enlightenment rationalism and embraced the right to vote, civil liberties, legal equality, constitutional government, parliamentary sovereignty, and a free-market economy. Liberals firmly believed that less government was better government and that noninterference would produce a harmonious and well-ordered world. They also believed that human beings were basically good and reasonable and needed freedom in which to flourish. The sole end of government should be to promote that freedom.

No single representative thinker embodied all the tenets of liberal thought, but many shared similar ideas and beliefs. Liberal thinkers tried to make sense of the political conflicts of the revolutionary period and the economic disruptions brought on by industrialization. The Great Revolution at the end of the eighteenth century spawned a vast array of liberal thought in France. Republicans, Bonapartists, and constitutional monarchists cooperated as self-styled "liberals," who shared a desire to preserve the gains of the Revolution while ensuring orderly rule. By the mid-nineteenth century, liberal thinking constituted a dominant strain in British politics.

David Ricardo (1772–1823) was a stockbroker prodigy who by the age of twenty had made his fortune. In *Principles of Political Economy and Taxation* (1817), Ricardo outlined his opposition to government intervention in foreign trade and elaborated his "iron law of wages," which contended that wages would stabilize at the subsistence level. Increased wages would cause the working classes to increase, and the resulting competition in the labor market would drive wages down to the subsistence level. Other liberals, more concerned with social welfare than Ricardo, argued that state intervention was unavoidable but could be limited.

Jeremy Bentham (1748–1832), trained in British law, fashioned himself into a social philosopher. He founded utilitarianism, a fundamentally liberal doctrine that argued for human happiness through the "greatest happiness of the greatest number" in such works as *Introduction to the Principles of Morals and Legislation*. Bentham believed that government could achieve positive ends through limited and "scientific" intervention. Only the pursuit of social harmony justified interference with individual liberty. He found the best testing grounds for his theories in prisons among convicted criminals. By supporting the reform of penal codes and prison regulations in *Rationale of Punishments and Rewards* (1825), he hoped that rewards and punishments could be meted out to convicts in a measurable "geometry" of pain and pleasure. He was sure that behavior could be improved and that prisoners could be rehabilitated and returned as honest citizens to society.

The Scottish philosopher, economist, and historian James Mill (1773–1836) met Jeremy Bentham in 1808 and dedicated the rest of his life to promulgating Bentham's utilitarian philosophy. James Mill's son, John Stuart Mill (1806–73), reacted to his early and intense formation by his father in Benthamite ideas by rejecting tenets of utilitarianism. Forging his own brand of classical

liberalism in his treatise *On Liberty* (1859), the younger Mill became the greatest liberal thinker of the age. John Stuart Mill criticized Bentham for ignoring human emotions and for the mass tyranny implicit in his ideas. Mill went beyond existing political analyses to apply economic doctrines to social conditions in *Principles of Political Economy* (1848). With Harriet Taylor (d. 1858), who married him after years of intellectual collaboration, he espoused social reform for the poor and championed the equality of women and the necessity of birth control. By 1848, his writing on liberty and equality allowed him to question the sacredness of private property. Before his death, John Stuart Mill believed that a more equitable distribution of wealth was both necessary and possible.

Nationalism

In its most basic sense, nationalism before 1850 was the political doctrine that glorified the people united against the absolutism of kings and the tyranny of foreign oppressors. The success of the French Revolution and the spread of Napoleonic reforms boosted nationalist doctrines, which were most fully articulated on the Continent. In Germany, Johann Gottfried von Herder (1744–1803) rooted national identity in German folk culture. The *Fairy Tales* (1812–14) of the brothers Jacob Ludwig Grimm (1785–1863) and Wilhelm Carl Grimm (1786–1859) had a similar national purpose. The brothers painstakingly captured in print the German oral tradition of peasant folklore. The philosophers Johann Fichte (1762–1814) and Georg Wilhelm Friedrich Hegel (1770–1831) emphasized the importance of the state. Nationalism gave birth to a search for new symbols, just as the tricolor flag replaced the fleur-de-lis and the image of Marianne replaced the monarch as a result of the Great Revolution in France. There was a new concern with history, as nationalists sought to revive a common cultural past.

In the period between 1830 and 1850, many nationalists were liberals and many liberals were nationalists. The nationalist yearning for liberation meshed with the liberal political program of overthrowing tyrannical rule. Giuseppe Mazzini

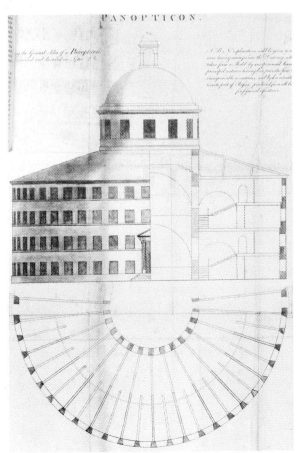

This model prison, called the Pantopicon, was designed by Jeremy Bentham. The circular arrangement allowed a centrally located guard to monitor all outside cells. The prison was never built, but the design influenced later prisons.

(1805–72) represented the new breed of liberal nationalist. An Italian patriot, he organized a secret revolutionary society called Young Italy in 1832 for the purpose of unifying Italy under a republican form of government. His goal was the betterment of all humanity through the establishment of national communities dedicated to peace and cooperation.

A less-than-liberal nationalist was political economist Georg Friedrich List (1789–1846), who formulated a statement of economic nationalism to counter the liberal doctrines of David Ricardo. Arguing that free trade worked only for the wealthy and powerful, List advocated a program of protective tariffs for developing German industries. British free trade, he perceived, was merely economic imperialism in disguise. List was one of the few nationalists who did not wholeheartedly embrace liberal economic doctrines. Beyond ideology and political practices, nationalism began to capture the imagination of groups who resented foreign domination. Expanding state bureaucracies did little to tame the centrifugal forces of nationalist feeling and probably exacerbated a desire for independence in eastern and central Europe, especially in the Habsburg-ruled lands.

Romanticism

Unlike liberalism and nationalism, which were fundamentally political ideologies, romanticism designated a variety of literary and artistic movements throughout Europe that spanned the period from the late eighteenth century to the mid-nineteenth century. One could be a nationalist and a romantic or a liberal and a romantic just as easily as one could hold opposite political views and be a follower of romanticism. Above all and in spite of variations, romantics shared similar beliefs and a common view of the world. Among the first romantics were the English poets William Wordsworth (1770–1850) and Samuel Taylor Coleridge (1772–1834), whose collaborative *Lyrical Ballads* (1798) exemplified the iconoclastic romantic idea that poetry was the result of "the spontaneous overflow of powerful feelings," rather than a formal and highly disciplined intellectual exercise. Romantics in general rebelled against the confinement of classical forms and refused to accept the supremacy of reason over emotions.

The English gardens designed at the end of the eighteenth century provide one of the best visual examples of the new romanticism. The formal gardens that surrounded the castles and manor houses of Europe's wealthy elite throughout the eighteenth century relied on carefully drawn geometric patterns, minutely trimmed hedges and lawns, and symmetrically arranged flowers planted in rows by size and by color to achieve the effect of total mastery of nature. The gardens at the great palace of Versailles are a good example of the formal landscaping chosen by France's kings and emulated by the wealthy everywhere in Europe. The romantic or English garden was, by contrast, a rebellious profusion of color in which the landscaper rejected the carefully drawn geometric patterns then in vogue and set out instead deliberately and somewhat paradoxically to imitate nature. The romantic aesthetic, whether in landscape gardening or in literature, recognized the beauty of untamed nature and the inspiration produced by the release of human emotions.

By rooting artistic vision in spontaneity, romantics endorsed a concept of creativity based on the supremacy of human freedom. The artist was valued in a new way as a genius through whose insight and intuition great art was created. Intuition, opposed to scientific learning, was endorsed as a valid means of knowing. Building on the work of the eighteenth-century philosopher Immanuel Kant (1724–1804), romanticism embraced subjective knowledge. Inspiration and intuition took the place of reason and science in the romantic pantheon of values.

Germaine de Staël (1766–1817), often hailed as the founder of French romanticism, was an extraordinary woman whose writings influenced French liberal political theory after 1815. Madame de Staël's mother followed the principles of education spelled out by Jean-Jacques Rousseau in *Emile* (1762), according to which the child was allowed to follow her own path of intellectual development. De Staël authored histories, novels, literary criticism, and political tracts that opposed what she judged to be the tyranny of Napoleonic rule. She, like many other romantics, was greatly influenced by the writings of Rousseau and through him she discovered that "the soul's elevation is born of self-consciousness." The recognition of the subjective meant for De Staël that women's vision was as essential as men's for the flowering of European culture.

"It is within oneself that one must look at what lies outside." Following De Staël's lead, Victor Hugo (1802–85), one of the great French novelists of the nineteenth century, identified another essential ingredient in romanticism. The turning inward "within oneself" so apparent in Hugo's poetry was profoundly influenced by the political events of the French Revolution and its principles of liberty and equality. His greatest novels, including *Notre-Dame de Paris* (1831) and *Les Misérables* (1862), offer bold panoramic sweeps of the social universe of Paris across the ages.

Nationalists in the first half of the nineteenth century were often romantics who valued the authenticity of the vernacular and folklore over the language and customs imposed by the foreign ruler. Herder and the brothers Grimm were German examples of the romantic appreciation of the roots of German culture. While French romantics emphasized the glories of their revolutionary heritage, German romantics stressed the importance of history as the source of one's identity. By searching for the self in a historic past, and especially in the Middle Ages, they glorified their collective cultural identity and national origins. Medievalism in Germany was at the heart of *Sturm und Drang* (Storm and Stress), a literary movement founded in the 1770s. A founder of the *Sturm und Drang* movement, Johann Wolfgang von Goethe (1749–1832), hailed as the greatest of modern German writers, inspired generations with his dramatic poem *Faust* (Part I: 1808; Part II: 1832). In the poem, Goethe recounts the traditional legend of a man who sells his soul to the devil in exchange for greater knowledge. Faust, who achieves mystical salvation in the poem's final scene, symbolizes for Goethe the spiritual crisis plaguing European civilization in the early nineteenth century.

Whether in words or in music or on canvas, romanticism conveyed a new way of understanding the world. The supremacy of the emotions over reason found its way into the works of the great romantic composers of the age. Liberation

Liberty Leading the People, *by Eugene Delacroix, 1831, captures the spirit of the French Romantics, who looked upon revolutionary action as a way to achieve union with the spirit of history.*

from the forms that dominated the classical era could be heard in the works of French composer Louis Hector Berlioz (1803–69), who set Faust's damnation to music, Polish virtuoso Frederic Chopin (1810–49) who created lyric compositions for the piano, and Hungarian concert pianist Franz Liszt (1811–86), who composed symphonic poems and Hungarian rhapsodies.

Canvases as different as those of J. M. W. Turner (1775–1851), the English landscape painter, and of Eugene Delacroix (1798–1863), the leader of the French romantic school in painting, shared an iconoclastic commitment in their art. Turner's intense and increasingly abstract vision of an often turbulent natural world and Delacroix's epic historical and political masterpieces shared a rebellious experimentation with color and a rejection of classical conventions and forms. Characteristic of a particular strain within romanticism was the political message of Delacroix's art. In the magnificent painting *Liberty Leading the People* (1831), for example, Delacroix immortalized the revolutionary events that swept Paris in 1830 in his moving portrayal of valiant revolutionaries of different social classes led into battle by a female Liberty.

In the postrevolutionary age of the years between 1815 and 1850 romanticism claimed to be no more than an aesthetic stance in art, letters, and music, a posture that had no particular political intent. Yet its validation of the individual as opposed to the caste or the estate was the most revolutionary of doctrines, just as its justification of subjective knowledge threatened to erode the authority of classical learning. Artists did not make revolutions but they supported them. Some stood by on the sidelines, others mounted the barricades, but all romantics no matter how political or apolitical helped shape a new way of looking at the world and helped define a new political consciousness.

Conservatism

Conservatism was not a rejection of political, economic, and social change. Like liberalism, conservatism represented a dynamic adaptation to a social system in transition. In place of individualism, conservatives stressed the corporate nature of European society; in place of reason and progress, conservatives saw organic growth and tradition. Liberty, argued British statesman Edmund Burke (1729–97) in *Reflections on the Revolution in France* (1790), must emerge out of the gradual development of the old order and not its destruction. On the Continent, conservatives Louis de Bonald (1754–1840) and Joseph de Maistre (1753–1821) defended the monarchical principle of authority against the onslaught of revolutionary events.

Conservatism took a reactionary turn in the hands of the Austrian statesman Prince Klemens von Metternich (1773–1859). The Carlsbad decrees of 1819 are a good example of the "Metternich system" of espionage, censorship, and university repression in central Europe, which sought to eliminate any constitutional or nationalist sentiments that had arisen during the Napoleonic period. The German Confederation approved the decrees against free speech and civil liberties and set up mechanisms to root out "subversive" university students. Students who had taken up arms in the Wars of Liberation (1813–15) against France had done so in hopes of instituting liberal and national reforms. Metternich's system aimed

at uprooting these goals. Student fraternities were closed and police became a regular fixture in the university. Political expression was driven underground for at least a decade. Metternich set out to crush liberalism, constitutionalism, and parliamentarianism in central Europe. His goals, although tolerated, were certainly not shared by more liberal regimes such as Great Britain's.

Socialism

Socialists and conservatives shared one point of view: both rejected the world as it was. Socialism, like other ideologies of the first half of the nineteenth century, grew out of the changes in the structure of daily life and the structure of power. There were as many stripes of socialists as there were liberals, nationalists, and conservatives. Socialists as a group shared a concern with "alienation," although they may not all have used the term.

Henri de Saint-Simon (1760–1825) rejected liberal individualism in favor of social organization and for this reason has been called the father of French socialism. To Saint-Simon the accomplishments and potential of industrial development represented the highest stage in history. In a perfect and just society, productive work would be the basis of all prestige and power. The elite of society would be organized according to the hierarchy of its productive members with industrial leaders at the top. Work was a social duty. The new industrial society that Saint-Simon foresaw would be both efficient and ethical, based on a religion similar to Christianity.

Like Saint-Simon, the French social theorist Pierre Joseph Proudhon (1809–65) recognized the social value of work. But unlike Saint-Simon, Proudhon refused to accept the dominance of industrial society. A self-educated typesetter of peasant origins, Proudhon gained national prominence with his ideas about a just society, free credit, and equitable exchange. In his famous pamphlet, *What Is Property?* (1840), Proudhon answered, "Property is theft." This statement was not, however, an argument for the abolition of private ownership. Proudhon reasoned that industrialization had destroyed workers' rights, which included the right to the profits of their own labor. In attacking "property" in its meaning of profits amassed from the labor of others, Proudhon was arguing for a socialist concept of limited possession: people had the right to own only what they had earned from their own labor. Proudhon, who did not himself participate in political agitation, held a profoundly anarchistic view of society, hated government, and favored instead small self-ruling communities of producers. Proudhon's world would be one of comfort but without great wealth.

At least one socialist believed in luxury. Charles Fourier (1772–1837), an unsuccessful traveling salesman, devoted himself to the study and improvement of society and formulated one of the most trenchant criticisms of industrial capitalism. In numerous writings between 1808 and his death, this eccentric, solitary man put forth his vision of a utopian world organized into units called phalansteries, that took into account the social, sexual, and economic needs of their members. With a proper mix of duties, everyone in the phalanstery would work only a few hours a day. In Fourier's scheme, work was not naturally abhorrent, but care had to be taken to match temperaments with tasks. Women and men fulfilled

Proudhon and His Children, *by Gustave Courbet, 1865. Proudon's literary and political activities often led to trouble with the authorities. He spent a number of years in prison or in exile.*

themselves and found pleasure and gratification through work. People would be paid according to their contributions in work, capital, and talent. In his visions of a better world, Fourier's phalansteries were always rural. Every aspect of life would be organized communally, although neither poverty nor property would be eliminated. Education would help eliminate discord and rich and poor would learn to live together in perfect harmony.

Charles Fourier's work, along with that of Saint-Simon and Proudhon, became part of the tradition of utopian thinking that can be traced back to Thomas More in the sixteenth century. Because he believed in the ability of individuals to shape themselves and their world, Fourier intended his critique of society to be a blueprint for living. Fourier's followers set up communities in his lifetime. Forty phalansteries were established in the United States alone; because of financial frustrations and petty squabbling, all of them failed.

The emancipation of women had been an issue acknowledged and then silenced by French revolutionary leaders at the end of the eighteenth century. The question of women's emancipation, tied as it often was to talk of freeing the slaves, reemerged again in the nineteenth century as a moral question. After 1815, it became a political question as well. Individual critiques coalesced into action by reform groups. Some social reformers and utopian thinkers put the issue of women's freedom at the center of their plans to redesign society. Saint-Simonians argued for woman's social elevation and searched for a female messiah. Other social reformers joined with conservative thinkers, who argued that women must be kept in their place and that place was in the home. Proudhon, for example, saw women's only choices to be working in the home as housewives or working in the streets as prostitutes. The socialist most committed to the emancipation of women as part of the liberation of humanity was Charles Fourier. He and his followers emphasized the material realities of the oppression of women by housework and child care, which needed to be shared as communal responsibilities. In his utopian schema, Fourier defended women's right to work and to control their own money.

Socialists, along with other ideologues in the decades before the middle of the nineteenth century, were aware of how rapidly their world was changing. Many felt that a revolution that would eliminate poverty and the sufferings of the working class was at hand. Followers of Saint-Simon, Fourier, and Proudhon all hoped that their proposals and ideas would change the world and prevent violent upheaval. Not all social critics were so sanguine. In January 1848, two young men, one a philosopher living in exile and the other a businessman working for his father, began a collaboration that would last a lifetime with the publication of a short tract entitled *The Communist Manifesto*. Karl Marx (1818–83) and Friedrich Engels (1820–95) described the dire situation of the European working classes throughout the 1840s. The growing poverty and alienation of the proletariat, the authors promised, would bring to industrialized Europe a class war against the capitalists. Exploited workers must prepare themselves for the moment of revolution by joining with each other across national boundaries: "Workers of the world, unite. You have nothing to lose but your chains." In light of subsequent events, the *Manifesto* appears to be a work of great predictive value. But neither Marx nor Engels realized that the hour of revolution was at hand.

Protest and Revolution

Few Europeans alive in 1830 remembered the age of revolution from 1789 to 1799. Yet the legends were kept alive from one generation to the next. Secret political organizations perpetuated Jacobin republicanism. Mutual-aid societies and artisan associations preserved the rituals of democratic culture. A revolutionary culture seemed to be budding in the student riots in Germany and in the revolutionary waves that swept across southern and central Europe in the early 1820s. Outside Manchester, England, in August 1819 a crowd of 80,000 people gathered in St. Peter's Field to hear speeches for parliamentary reform and universal male suffrage. The cavalry swept down on them in a bloody slaughter that came to be known as the "Peterloo" massacre, a bitter reference to the Waterloo victory four years before.

Massacre at St. Peter's or "BRITON'S STRIKE HOME"!!!

A savage satire of the Peterloo Massacre by cartoonist George Cruikshank, brother of caricaturist Robert Cruikshank (see photo, p. 689). One soldier urges the others on by telling them that the more poor people they kill, the less taxes they will have to pay for poor relief.

For most of the 1820s, Metternich, sitting comfortably in Vienna, was reassured that all was well. The diplomatic settlements of the Congress of Vienna and subsequent international conferences were working to maintain the status quo. Few understood—least of all Metternich—that the fabric of stability and order was beginning to unravel at the end of the decade.

The Revolutions of 1830

Poor harvests in 1829 followed by a harsh winter left people cold, hungry, and bitter. Misery fueled social protest and political issues of participation and representation commanded a new attention. The convergence of social unrest with long-standing political demands touched off revolutions apparently simultaneously all over Europe. Governmental failure to respond to local grievances sparked the revolutions of 1830. Highly diverse groups of workers, students, lawyers, professionals, and peasants rose up spontaneously to demand a voice in the affairs of government.

In France the late 1820s there was a period of increasing political friction. Charles X (1824–30), the former comte d'Artois, had never resigned himself to the constitutional monarchy accepted by his brother and predecessor, Louis XVIII. When Charles assumed the throne in 1824, he dedicated himself to a true restoration of kingship as it existed before the Revolution. To this end, he realigned the monarchy with the Catholic church and undertook several unpopular measures, including approval of the death penalty for those found guilty of sacrilege. The king's bourgeois critics, heavily influenced by liberal ideas about political economy and constitutional rights, sought increased political power through their activities in secret organizations and in public elections. The king responded to his critics by relying on his ultraroyalist supporters to run the government. In May 1830 the king dissolved the Chamber of Deputies and ordered new elections. The elections returned a liberal majority unfavorable to the king. Charles X retaliated with what proved to be his last political act, the Four Ordinances, in which he censored the press, changed the electoral law to favor his own candi-dates, dissolved the newly elected Chamber, and ordered new elections.

Opposition to Charles X might have remained at the level of political wrangling and journalistic protest, if it had not been for the problems plaguing the people of Paris. A severe winter in France had driven up food prices by 75 percent. Most urban dwellers were barely subsisting. The king had erred in hoping that France's recent conquest of Algeria in North Africa would keep the populace quiet. He underestimated the extent of hardship and the political volatility of the population. Throughout the spring of 1830 prices continued to rise and Charles continued to blunder. In a spontaneous uprising in the last days of July 1830, workers took to the streets of Paris. The revolution they initiated spread rapidly to towns and the countryside, as people throughout France protested the cost of living, hoarding by grain merchants, tax collection, and wage cuts. In "three glorious days" the restored Bourbon regime was pulled down and Charles X fled to England.

The people fighting in the streets demanded a republic, but they lacked organization and political experience. Liberal bourgeois politicians quickly filled the power vacuum. They presented Charles' cousin, the duc d'Orleans, as the savior of France and the new constitutional monarch. This July Monarchy, born of a revolution, put an end to the Bourbon Restoration. Louis-Philippe, the former duc d'Orleans, became "king of the French." The Charter that he brought with him was, like its predecessor, based on restricted suffrage, with property ownership a requisite for voting. The voting age was lowered from 30 to 25 and the tax requirement was also lowered. The electorate nearly doubled from 90,000 to 170,000, but nevertheless voting remained restricted to a small fraction of the population.

Popular disturbances did not always result in revolution. In Britain, rural and town riots erupted over grain prices and distribution, but no revolution followed. German workers broke their machines to protest low wages and loss of control of the workplace, but princes were not displaced. In Switzerland reformers found strength in the French revolutionary example. Ten Swiss cantons granted liberal constitutions and established universal manhood suffrage, freedom of expression, and legal equality.

In southern Europe, Greece had languished as a subjugated country for centuries. Turkish overlords ruled Greece as part of the Ottoman Empire. The longing for independence smoldered in Greece throughout the 1820s as public pressure to support the Greeks mounted in Europe. Greek insurrections were answered by Turkish retaliations throughout the Ottoman Empire. A Turkish fleet captured the island of Chios in the Aegean Sea off the west coast of Turkey in 1822 and massacred or enslaved the population. The atrocities committed by the Turks against Greeks in Constantinople provoked international support in the form of a Philhellenic (literally, "lover of Greece") movement supported by two of Britain's great romantic poets, Lord Byron (1788–1824) and Percy Bysshe Shelley (1792–1822). Byron sailed to the besieged Greek city of Missolonghi in 1824 to help coordinate the military effort, and there he contracted malaria and died. The sultan of Turkey had been able to call upon his vassal, the pasha of Egypt, to subdue Greece. In response Great Britain, France, and Russia signed the Treaty of London in 1827, pledging intervention on behalf of Greece. In a joint effort, the three powers defeated the Egyptian fleet. Russia declared war on Turkey the following year, seeking territorial concessions from the Ottoman Empire. Following the Russian victory, Great Britain and France joined Russia in declaring Greek independence.

The concerted action of the three powers in favor of Greek independence was neither an endorsement of liberal ideals nor a support of Greek nationalism. The British, French, and Russians were reasserting their commitment made at the Congress of Vienna to territorial stability. Yet beneath the veneer of their commitment, the Russians intervened, hoping for territorial gains in the Ottoman Empire. The British favored Ottoman stability, while distrusting Russian ambitions in the area. The Turks had been unable to maintain stability on their own. Finally, the three powers abandoned their policy of propping up the Ottoman Empire and supported instead the movement for Greek independence. But they did so on their own terms, as is evident in their decision to create a monarchy in Greece by placing a German-born prince on the new throne.

The overthrow of the Bourbon monarch in France served as a model for revolution in other parts of Europe. Following the French lead in the midst of the Greek crisis, the Belgian provinces revolted against the Netherlands. The Belgian uprising struck at the heart of the Vienna settlement. The Belgians wanted their own nation. Provoked by a food crisis similar to that in France, Belgian revolutionaries took to the streets in August 1830. As a symbol of their solidarity with the successful French Revolution, they flew the tricolor in defiance of their Dutch rulers. Belgians protested the deterioration of their economic situation and made demands for their own Catholic religion, their own language, and constitutional rights. Bitter fighting on the barricades in Brussels ensued and the movement for freedom and independence spread to the countryside.

The Great Powers disagreed on what to do. Russia, Austria, and Prussia were all eager to see the revolution crushed. France, having just established the new regime of the July Monarchy, and Great Britain, fearing the involvement of the central and eastern European powers in an area where Britain had traditionally had interests, were reluctant to intervene. A provisional government in Belgium set about the task of writing a constitution. All five great powers recognized Belgian independence, with the proviso that Belgium was to maintain the status of a neutral state.

Russia, Prussia, and Austria were convinced to accept Belgian independence because they were having their own problems in eastern and southern Europe. Revolution erupted to the east in Warsaw, Poland. Filled with a longing for national independence and driven by a desire for a true constitution, Polish army cadets and university students revolted in November 1830. Landed aristocrats and gentry helped establish a provisional government but soon split over how radical reforms should be. Polish peasants refused to support either landowning group. Within the year, Russia brought in 180,000 men to crush the revolution and reassert its rule over Poland. All pretext of constitutional rule ended. Thousands of Poles were executed; others fled to exile in western Europe, including the five thousand who settled in France. Inspired by the poetry of Adam Mickiewicz (1798–1855) and the music of Frederic Chopin (1810–49), many of them

'Gentlemen,' says Nicholas I, the bear, to the Polish revolutionaries of 1830, 'I know that you wish to address me; but to spare you from delivering a pack of lies, I desire that you hold your tongues.' The Polish rebellion of 1830–31 was brutally suppressed by the Russians. However, this brutality reinforced Polish national sentiment (the Poles rebelled again in 1863) and engaged the sympathy of the West for the Poles—as this English cartoon shows. (2)

This English cartoon of 1832 is titled "The clemency of the Russian monster." It shows Nicholas I in the guise of a bear with menacing teeth and claws addressing the Poles after crushing their rebellion against Imperial Russian rule.

dedicated themselves to the cause of Polish nationalism and to resurrecting an independent Polish kingdom. The Poles remained a captive people of the Habsburg, Hohenzollern, and Romanov empires until 1918–19.

In February 1831, the Italian states of Modena and Parma rose up to throw off Austrian domination of northern Italy. The revolutionaries were ineffective against Austrian troops. Revolution in the Papal States resulted in French occupation that lasted until 1838 without serious reforms. Nationalist and republican yearnings were driven underground, kept alive there in the Young Italy movement under the leadership of Guiseppe Mazzini.

Although the revolutions of 1830 are called "the forgotten revolutions" of the nineteenth century, they are important for several reasons. First, they made clear to European states their dependence on one another. The events of 1830 were a test of the Great Powers' commitment to stability and a balance of power in Europe. True to the principles of the Vienna settlements of 1815, European leaders preserved the status quo. Revolutions in Poland and Italy were contained by Russia and Austria without interference from the other powers. Where adaptation was necessary, as in

Greece and Belgium, the Great Powers were able to compromise on settlements, although the solutions ran counter to previous policies. Heads of state were willing to use the forces of repression to stamp out protest. Although each revolution followed its own pattern of development, all shared origins in domestic crises unsuccessfully addressed by those in power.

The international significance of the revolutions reveals a second important aspect of the events of 1830: the vulnerability of international politics to domestic instability. No state could practice diplomacy in a vacuum. Grain prices and demands for democratic participation had direct impact on the balance of power of European states. The five Great Powers broke down into two ideological camps. On the one hand were the liberal, constitutional states of Great Britain and France; on the other stood the autocratic monarchies of Russia, Austria, and Prussia. Yet ideological differences were always less important than the shared desire for internal stability as a prerequisite for international peace.

Finally, the 1830 revolutions exposed a growing awareness of politics at all levels of European society. If policies in 1830 revealed a shared consciousness of events and shared values among ruling elites, the revolutions disclosed a growing awareness among the lower classes of the importance of politics in their daily lives. The impact of the French revolution of 1830 throughout Europe demonstrated the degree to which peoples of different countries identified with international events. The cry for "liberty, equality, and fraternity" transcended national borders and the French language. The demands for constitutions, national identity, and civic equality resounded from the Atlantic to the Urals. Since the end of the eighteenth century, when the French Revolution attacked the foundations of the old order, statesmen had feared the possibility of a general European crisis based on political and social issues. The events of 1830 made such a crisis seem like a looming specter. In a dangerous combination, workers and the lower classes throughout Europe were politicized, yet they continued to be excluded from political power.

Reforming Great Britain

The right to vote had been an issue of contention in the revolutions of 1830 in western Europe. Only the Swiss cantons enforced the principle of one man, one vote. The July Revolution in France had doubled the electorate, but still only a tiny minority of the population (less than 1 percent) enjoyed the vote. Universal male suffrage had been mandated in 1793 during the Great Revolution but not implemented. This exclusion of the mass of the population from participation in electoral politics was no oversight. Those in power believed that the wealthiest property owners were best qualified to govern, in part because they had the greatest stake in politics and society. One also needed to own property in order to hold office. Because those who served in parliaments received no salary, only the wealthy had the resources and the leisure to represent the electorate. When confronted by his critics, Francois Guizot (1787–1874), French prime minister and chief spokesman for the July Monarchy, offered the glib advice to an aspiring electorate: "Get rich!"

The propertied ruled Britain too. There the dominance of a wealthy elite was strengthened by the geographic redistribution resulting from industrialization. Migration to cities had depleted the population of rural areas. Yet the electoral system did not adjust to these changes: large towns had no parliamentary representation, while dwindling county electorates maintained their parliamentary strength. Areas that continued to enjoy representation greater than that justified by their population were dubbed *rotten* or *pocket* boroughs to indicate a corrupt and antiquated electoral system. In general, urban areas were grossly underrepresented as the wealthy few controlled county seats. Liberal reformers attempted to rectify the electoral inequalities by reassigning parliamentary seats on the basis of density of population.

Vested interests balked at attempted reforms and members of Parliament wrangled bitterly. Popular agitation by the lower classes provoked the fear of civil war and helped break the parliamentary deadlock. The Great Reform Bill of 1832 proposed a compromise. Although the vast majority of the population still did not have the vote, the new legislation strengthened the industrial and commercial elite in the towns, enfranchised most of the middle class, opened the way to social reforms, and encouraged the formation of political parties.

Years of bad harvests, unemployment, and depression, coupled with growing dissatisfaction with the government's weak efforts to address social problems, put the spur to a new national reform movement in the 1830s. These new radical reformers, disillusioned with the 1832 Reform Bill because it strengthened the power of a wealthy capitalist class, argued that democracy was the only answer to the problems plaguing British society. In 1838 a small group of labor leaders, including representatives of the London Working Men's Association, an organization of craft workers, drew up a document known as the People's Charter. The single most important demand of the Charter was that all men must have the vote. In addition, Chartists petitioned for a secret ballot, salaries for parliamentary service, elimination of property qualifications in order to run for office, equal electoral districts, and annual elections. The proposal favored direct democracy, guaranteed by frequent elections that would ensure maximum accountability of officials to their constituents.

The Chartist movement was hated and feared by members of the British Establishment, who saw it as the thin end of a democratic wedge. Here the Chartists march to the House of Commons in 1842, carrying their Great Petition to the Commons.

Chartist appeal was greatest in periods of economic hardship. A violent mood swept through the movement in 1839. The Irish Chartist leader Feargus O'Connor (1794–1855) and the Irish journalist and orator James Bronterre O'Brien (1805–64) urged an unskilled and poorly organized working class to protest inequities through strikes that on occasion became violent. O'Brien thrilled his working-class listeners by haranguing "the big-bellied, little-brained, numbskull aristocracy." Chartism blossomed as a communal phenomenon in working-class towns and appeared to involve all members of the family: "Every kitchen is now a political meeting house; the little children are members of the unions and the good mother is the political teacher," one Chartist organizer boasted. Chartist babies were christened with the names of Chartist heroes. When Mrs. King of Manchester, England, attempted to register the birth of her son, James Feargus O'Connor King, her choice of names was challenged. The registrar demanded, "Is your husband a Chartist?" Mrs. King replied, "I don't know, but his wife is." Women organized Chartist schools and Sunday schools in radical defiance of local church organizations. Many middle-class observers were sure that the moment for class war and revolutionary upheaval had arrived. The government responded with force to the perceived threat of armed rebellion and imprisoned a number of Chartist leaders.

Throughout the 1840s bad harvests and economic hardships continued to fan the flames of discontent. National petitions signed by millions were submitted to the House of Commons, which stubbornly resisted the idea of universal manhood suffrage. Strikes and attacks on factories spread throughout England, Scotland, and Wales in 1842. Increased violence served to make the Parliament intransigent and caused the movement to splinter and weaken as moderates formed their own factions. The final moment for Chartism occurred in April 1848 when 25,000 Chartist workers, inspired by revolutionary events on the Continent, assembled in London to march on the House of Commons. They carried with them a newly signed petition demanding the enactment of the terms of the Charter. In response, the government deputized nearly 200,000 "special" constables in the streets. These deputized private citizens were London property owners and skilled workers intent on holding back a revolutionary rabble. Tired, cold, and rain-soaked, the Chartist demonstrators disbanded. No social revolution took place in Great Britain, and the dilemma of democratic representation was deferred. The vote proved to be an elusive goal.

Workers Unite

The word *proletariat* entered European languages before the mid-nineteenth century to describe those workers afloat in the labor pool who owned nothing, not even the tools of their labor, and who were becoming "appendages" to the new machines that dominated production. To workers, machines could mean the elimination of jobs or the deskilling of tasks; almost always machines meant a drop in wages. Mechanization deprived skilled craft workers of control of the workplace. In Great Britain, France, and Germany, groups of textile workers destroyed machines in protest. Workers demanding a fair wage smashed cotton power looms, knitting machines, and wool carding machines. Sometimes the machines were a bargaining point with employers for workers who used violence against them as a last resort. Machine-breakers tyrannized parts of Great Britain from 1811 to 1816 in an attempt to frighten masters. The movement was known as Luddism after its mythical leader, Ned Ludd. Workers damaged and destroyed property for more control over the work process, but such destruction met with severe repression. Over the next three decades sporadic but intense outbursts of machine-breaking occurred in continental Europe. Suffering weavers in Silesia and Bohemia resorted to destroying their looms in 1844.

Craft production continued to deteriorate with the rise in industrial competition. Skilled workers, fearing that they would be pulled down into the new proletariat because of mechanization and the increased scale of production, began organizing in new ways after 1830. Craft workers whose skills were threatened by industrialization, rather than unskilled proletarians, banded together in associations to assert their control over the workplace and to demand a voice in politics.

In Britain skilled craftsmen built on a tradition of citizenship. They resisted encroachments of factory production and some channeled their political fervor into the Chartist movement. Skilled workers in France also built on a cultural heritage of shared language and values to create a consciousness of themselves as an exploited class. Although the anticorporate legislation of the Great Revolution after 1789 had denied French workers the right to organize, worker organizations survived secretly and informally. Artisans reemerged as an important revolutionary force in the events of July 1830. Buffeted by the rise and fall in economic cycles and longing for a government responsive to their needs, skilled workers pulled down the Bourbon king. The success of the 1830 revolution served to legitimate the demands made by workers for political action. Workers now expected the government they helped create to ban machines and raise wages.

The new liberal government of the July Monarchy and the revolutionary workers were speaking different languages. When those in power talked of liberty, they meant free exchange of goods and unrestricted labor markets. For workers liberty meant their freedom in the workplace to control production and their right to associate with each other to gain their ends of improved working conditions. Skilled workers saw themselves as the true heirs of the Great Revolution of 1789 and felt that they could achieve "liberty, equality, and fraternity" only through the brotherhood and moral solidarity of the craft trades.

Uprisings and strikes in France increased dramatically from 1831 to 1834 and favored the destruction of the monarchy and the creation of a democratic republic. Many French craft workers grew conscious of themselves as a class and embraced a socialism heavily influenced by their own traditions and contemporary socialist writings. Republican socialism spread throughout France by means of a network of traveling journeymen and tapped into growing economic hardship and political discontent with the July Monarchy. Government repression drove worker organizations underground in the late 1830s, but secret societies proliferated. Increasingly, workers saw the validity of the slogan of the silk workers of Lyon: "Live Working or Die Fighting!"

Women were an important part of the work force in the industrializing societies. Nevertheless, the French historian and social observer Jules Michelet (1798–1874) exclaimed, "The working woman, what a blasphemous term!" Working men were keenly aware of the competition with cheaper female labor in the factories. Women formed a salaried work force in the home, too. In order to produce cheaply and in large quantities, some manufacturers turned to subcontractors for the simpler tasks in the work process. These new middlemen contracted out work like cutting and sewing to needy women, who were often responsible for caring for family members in their homes. This kind of subcontracting was called "sweated labor" because of the exertion and long hours involved in working in one's own home.

By dividing the work process and assigning unskilled and skilled tasks to female workers in the home, manufacturers deprived skilled workers in the shops of control over the production of an item from beginning to end. Cheap female labor paid by the piece allowed employers to profit by keeping overhead costs low and by driving down the wages of skilled workers. Trade unions opposed women's work both in the home and in the factories. Women's talents, union leaders explained, were more properly devoted to domestic chores; their accomplishments as paid workers were consistently regarded as inferior in skill and strength. Unions argued that their members should earn a family wage "sufficient to support a wife and children." Unions consistently excluded women workers from their ranks.

French labor leader Flora Tristan, herself a wife and mother, had a very different answer for those who wanted to remove women from the workplace and assign them to their "proper place" in the home. She recognized that working women needed to work in order to support themselves and their families. Tristan lectured to audiences in Europe and Latin America that the emancipation of women from their "slave status" was essential if the working class as a whole was to enjoy a better future. She deplored the economic competition between working men and women and denounced the degradation of women in both the home and the workplace. A working woman earned a third or less of the average working man's wages and women's working conditions were often deplorable. In the 1840s British parliamentary commissions heard the horrifying testimony of one young London dressmaker from the country who was forced to work grueling hours—often 20 hours a day—under unhealthy working conditions that had destroyed her health. She concluded that "no men could endure the work enforced from the dressmakers."

Working women's only hope, according to Tristan, lay in education and unionization. She urged working men and women to join together to lay claim to their natural and inalienable rights. In some cases, working women formed their own organizations like that of the Parisian seamstresses who joined together to demand improved working conditions. On the whole, however, domestic workers in the home remained isolated from other working women and many women in factories feared the loss of their jobs if they engaged in political activism. The wages of Europe's working women remained low, often below the level of subsistence. In the absence of a man's income, working women and their children were the poorest of the poor in European society at mid-nineteenth century. For some men and women of the working class, the 1840s was a time of mounting unrest, increased organization, and growing protest. Workers used their unity in associations, unions, and mutual-aid societies to press for full political participation and government action in times of economic distress. (See Special Feature, "Paris in 1840," pp. 706–707.)

The Revolutions of 1848

Europeans had never experienced a year like 1848. Beginning soon after the ringing in of the New Year, revolutionary fervor swept through nearly every European country. By year's end, regimes had been created and destroyed. France, Italy, the German states, Austria, Hungary, and Bohemia were shaken to their foundations. Switzerland, Denmark, and Romania experienced lesser upheavals. Great Britain had survived reformist agitation, and famine-crippled Ireland had endured a failed insurrection. No one was sure what had happened. Each country's conflict was based on a unique mix of issues, but all were connected in their conscious emulation of a revolutionary tradition.

Hindsight reveals warning signs in the two years before the 1848 cataclysm. Beginning in 1846 a severe famine—the last serious food crisis Europe would experience—racked Europe. Lack of grain drove up prices. An increasing percentage of disposable income was spent on food for survival. Lack of spending power severely damaged markets and forced thousands of industrial workers out of their jobs. The famine hurt everyone—

Paris in 1840

At the height of his power, in 1810, Napoleon envisioned Paris as the capital of Europe, a mecca of art, style, and learning, "the most beautiful city that could ever exist." He never achieved his dream. Paris in 1840 was certainly a center of fashion and culture, but it was far from the extravagant beauty Napoleon dreamed of. Dark, dirty, ugly, rat-infested slums dominated the "city of lights." It is reported that General Blücher, commander of the victorious Prussian forces that entered Paris in 1814, stood on the heights overlooking the city and predicted that Paris would achieve what invading armies could not: the destruction of France.

Early nineteenth-century Paris was a medieval city that housed a modern population. By 1840 Paris held one million people, twice as many as it had only forty years earlier. The fastest growth occurred between 1830 and 1850, when 350,000 new residents were recorded. One out of every two Parisians was not born in the city, but had migrated to it. The city acted like a magnet, attracting provincials in search of employment and opportunity. The craftsman Martin Nadaud was typical of many immigrants who came to the capital expecting to find its streets literally paved with gold. He found instead raw sewage, inadequate water supplies, overcrowded housing, disease, and poverty. Sixty-five percent of all Parisians were so poor that they paid no

taxes. Fifty percent officially qualified as "indigents" and were eligible for humiliating and inadequate poor relief. Eighty percent of the people who died in Paris were buried in paupers' graves.

A bad situation got worse when a cholera epidemic ravaged the city for 189 days in 1832, leaving 18,000 people dead and 30,000 others afflicted. The

vast majority of those stricken were from the lower classes. City dwellers knew nothing about the etiology of cholera, but they understood that the poor were dying and the rich were not. To explain their apparent immunity, the bourgeoisie decided that the cholera epidemic was the fault of the poor, whose decadent life-styles created the disease and caused it to spread. Moralists railed that godlessness and sexual excess were taking their toll. Outraged bourgeois demanded sanitation—but of the spiritual sort.

If the bourgeoisie blamed the epidemic on immorality, workers attributed it to a conspiracy. The wealthy, they argued, were poisoning the water supply of the poor in order to limit their numbers. Such collective delusions gave rise to fear and general panic. Wealthy bourgeois fled the city to sit out the disease in rural peace. Among the lower classes, vigilante groups proliferated for the purpose of eliminating bourgeois villains. Several well-dressed gentlemen who strayed into working-class neighborhoods were executed for no greater offense than carrying suspicious-looking bottles that might contain contaminated fluids.

Urban life was further polarized by a rising crime rate that many felt portended the end of civilization. Gangs of homeless youths roamed city streets, fanning bourgeois fears. Gavroche, a character in Victor Hugo's *Les Misérables*, was one such fictional child of the streets who participated in the uprising of 1832. Hugo was sympathetic to the child's plight; many of his bourgeois readers were not. The title of a minor police official's best-selling account of urban life, *On the Dangerous Classes*, said it all to a terrified bourgeoisie. Crime was everywhere. In his *Human Comedy*, a vast collection of novels and short stories appearing between 1830 and 1850, Honoré de Balzac (1799–1850) created gangsters and thieves who were not only part of the criminal underworld but who also ran the police, commerce, and finance.

During the July Monarchy social-scientific studies presented the city as a giant laboratory. Misery was measured. The hair color, height, and place of birth of prostitutes were recorded. Infanticides and suicides were tallied. The studies concluded that poverty caused demoralization, violence, and crime. Reformers argued for low-cost housing, mass sanitation, and lighting. Yet the regime did little to address urban problems. Instead, the government undertook what seemed to many a curious public-works project of building a ring of fortifications around the city of Paris.

As other European cities began dismantling fortifications, Paris was the only city in the nineteenth century to enclose itself behind a fortified wall. Fortifications aggravated urban problems as thousands of workers flocked to the city to compete for the new jobs. Police complained about crime on the work sites and the increase in prostitution that they were unable to control. Fortifying the city played on people's fears. Why, it was asked, were troops, supplies, and equipment pulled back from the French-German border and concentrated in the capital? If France feared a foreign war, why was it preparing for one at the expense of its national frontiers?

Public debate raged over the excessive costs of the program. When it was discovered that the gun turrets on the forts could swivel inward and be aimed at the city as well as outward at an invading enemy, critics were sure they knew what was happening. The government, they charged, was preparing itself for a defensive action against its own capital and against its own citizens. There was reason for suspicion. After 1840 the government relied increasingly on the military as a repressive police force, spurning the National Guard, a citizen militia, as unreliable, and its own municipal police as inefficient. Troops were the monarchy's solution to the problems of law and order. Paris in 1840 had been turned into an armed camp.

The fortifications were never used against Parisians. When the revolution came in February 1848, the troops refused to fire on the people. The problems of the city of Paris were so severe that people from all classes shared an apocalyptic vision. At the end of June 1848, thousands of Parisian bourgeois joined the army in pitched battle against the city's revolutionary workers. Fifteen hundred people died in the fighting. Three thousand more insurgents were ruthlessly put to death. Most of the 12,000 arrested were deported to Algeria. The worst fears of urban life had reached their climax.

the poor, workers, employers, and investors—as recession paralyzed the economy.

The food crisis took place in a heavily charged political atmosphere. Throughout Europe during the 1840s middle and lower classes had intensified their agitation for democracy. Chartists in Great Britain argued for a wider electorate. Bourgeois reformers in France campaigned for universal manhood suffrage. Known as the "banquet" campaign because its leaders attempted to raise money by giving speeches at subscribed dinners, the movement appeared to be developing a mass following by taking its cause directly to the people. In making demands for political participation, those agitating for the vote necessarily criticized those in power. Freedom of speech and freedom of assembly were demanded as inalienable rights. The food crisis combined with political activism were the ingredients of an incendiary situation.

In addition to a burgeoning democratic culture, growing demands for national autonomy based on linguistic and cultural claims spread through central, southern, and eastern Europe. The revolts in Poland in 1846, although failures, encouraged similar movements for national liberation among Italians and Germans. Even in the relatively homogeneous nation of France, concerns with national mission and national glory grew among the regime's critics. National unity was primarily a middle-class ideal. Liberal lawyers, teachers, and businessmen from Dublin to Budapest to Prague agitated for separation from foreign rule. Austria, with an empire formed of numerous ethnic minorities, had the most to lose. Since 1815, Metternich had been ruthless in stamping out nationalist dissent. By the 1840s national claims were assuming a cultural legitimacy that was difficult to dismiss or ignore.

The events in France in the cold February of 1848 ignited the conflagration that swept Europe. On 22 February bourgeois reformers had staged their largest banquet to date in Paris in support of extension of the vote. City officials became nervous at the prospect of thousands of workers assembling for political purposes and canceled the scheduled banquet. This was the spark that touched off the powder keg. In a spontaneous uprising Parisians demonstrated against the government's repressive measures. Skilled workers

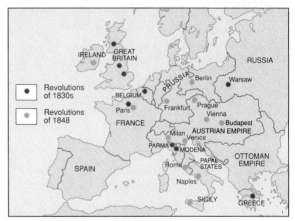

Revolutions of 1830–1848

took to the streets not only in favor of the banned banquet but also with the hope that the government would recognize the importance of labor to the social order. Shots were fired; a demonstrator was killed. The French Revolution of 1848 had begun.

Events moved quickly. The National Guard, a citizen militia of bourgeois Parisians, defected from Louis-Philippe. Many army troops garrisoned in Paris crossed the barricades to join revolutionary workers. The king attempted some reform, but it was too little and too late. Louis-Philippe fled. The Second Republic was proclaimed at the insistence of the revolutionary crowds on the barricades. The Provisional Government, led by the poet Alphonse de Lamartine (1790–1869), included members of both factions of political reformers of the July Monarchy: moderates who sought constitutional reforms and an extension of the suffrage; and radicals who favored universal manhood suffrage and social programs to deal with poverty and work. Only the threat of popular violence held together this uneasy alliance.

The people fighting in the streets had little in common with the bourgeois reformers who assumed power on 24 February. Workers made a social revolution out of a commitment to their "right to work," which would replace the right to property as the organizing principle of the new society. Only one member of the new Provisional Government was a worker and he was included as a token symbol of the intentions of the new government. He was known as "Albert, the worker," and was not addressed by his surname, Martin. The government acknowledged the demand of the "right to work" and set up two mechanisms to guarantee workers' relief. First, a commission of workers and employers was created to act as a grievance and bargaining board and settle questions of common concern in the workplace. Headed by the socialist Louis Blanc (1811–82) and known as the Luxembourg Commission, the worker-employer parliament was an important innovation but accomplished little other than deflecting workers' attention away from the problems of the Provisional Government. The second measure was the creation of "national workshops" to deal with the problems of unemployment in Paris. Although the name was taken from Blanc's plan for worker control of production, the national workshops were no more than an inefficient charity program that paid men minimal wages. The national workshops quickly proved disastrous. Workers from all over France poured into Paris with the hope of finding jobs. The workshops, however, had a residency requirement that even Parisians had difficulty meeting. As a result, unemployment skyrocketed. Furthermore, the government was going bankrupt trying to support the program. The need to raise taxes upset peasants in the provinces. National pressure mounted to repudiate the programs of the revolution.

French workers were too weak to dominate the revolution. In May the government dissolved the workshops, and recalled General Louis Cavaignac (1802–57) from service in Algeria to maintain order. In a wave of armed insurrection, Parisian workers rebelled in June. Using troops from the provinces who had no identification with the urban population and employing guerrilla techniques he had mastered in Algeria, Cavaignac put down the uprising. The June fighting was the bloodiest that Paris had ever seen. The Second Republic was placed under the military dictatorship of Cavaignac until December, when presidential elections were scheduled.

France was not alone in undergoing revolution in 1848. The overthrow of the July Monarchy at the end of February set off shock waves of protest in central and eastern Europe. Long-suppressed desires for civil liberties and constitutional reforms erupted in widespread popular disturbances in Prussia and the German states.

Fearing a war with France and unable to count on Austria or Russia for support, the princes who ruled Baden, Württemberg, Hesse-Darmstadt, Bavaria, Saxony, and Hanover followed the advice of moderate liberals and acceded quickly to revolutionary demands. In Prussia,. King Friedrich Wilhelm IV (1840–61) preferred to use military force to respond to popular demonstrations. Only in mid-March 1848 did the Prussian king yield to the force of the revolutionary crowds building barricades in Berlin by ordering his troops to leave the city and by promising to create a national Prussian assembly. The king was now a prisoner of the revolution.

Meanwhile, the collapse of absolute monarchy in Prussia gave further impetus to a constitutional movement among the liberal leaders of the German states. The governments of all the German states were invited to elect delegates to a national parliament in Frankfurt. The Frankfurt parliament, which was convened in May 1848, had as its dual charge the framing of a constitution and the unification of Germany. It was composed for the most part of members of the middle class, with civil servants, lawyers, and intellectuals predominating. In spite of the principle of universal manhood suffrage, there was not a single worker among the eight hundred men elected. To most parliamentarians, who were trained in universities and shared a social and cultural identity, nationalism and constitutionalism were inextricably related. Germans consistently linked national identity with political goals of independence and self-expression.

As straightforward as the desire for a German nation appeared to be, it was complicated by two important facts. First, there were non-German minorities living in German states. What was to be done with the Poles, Czechs, Slovenes, Italians, and Dutch in a newly constituted and autonomous German nation? Second, there were Germans living outside the German states under Habsburg rule in Austria, in Danish Schleswig and Holstein, in Posen (Poznan), in Russian Poland, and in European Russia. How were they to be included within the linguistically and ethnically constituted German nation? No matter how small the circle was drawn, it included non-Germans; no matter how wide, it excluded Germans. After much wrangling over a "small" Germany that excluded Austrian Germans and a "large" Germany that included them, the Frankfurt Parliament opted for the small-Germany solution in March 1849. The crown of the new nation was offered to the unpredictable Friedrich Wilhelm IV of Prussia, head of the largest and most powerful of the German states. Unhappy with his capitulation to the revolutionary crowd in March 1848, the Prussian king refused to accept a "crown from the gutter." He had his own plans to rule over a middle-European bloc but not at the behest of liberal parliamentary rule. The attempt to create a German nation crumbled with his unwillingness to lead.

Revolution in Austrian-dominated central Europe was concentrated in three places: Vienna, where German students, workers, and middle-class liberals were agitating for constitutional reform and political participation; Budapest, where the Magyars, the dominant ethnic group in Hungary, led a movement for national autonomy; and Prague, where Czechs were attempting self-rule. By April 1848, Metternich had fallen from power and the Viennese revolutionaries had set up a constituent assembly. In Budapest, the initial steps of the patriot Lajos Kossuth (1802–94) toward establishing a separate Hungarian state seemed equally solid, as the Magyars defeated Habsburg troops. Habsburg armies were more successful in Prague, where they crushed the revolution in June 1848.

The Habsburg empire was also under siege in Italy, where the Kingdom of the Two Sicilies, Tuscany, and Piedmont declared new constitutions in March 1848. Championed by Charles Albert of Piedmont, Venice and Lombardy rose up against Austria. Italian middle-class intellectuals and professionals championed the idea of national unification and the expulsion of the hated Austrian overlords. Nationalist sentiments had percolated underground in the Young Italy movement, founded in 1831 by Giuseppe Mazzini. Mazzini, a tireless and idealistic patriot, favored a democratic revolution. In spite of a reputation for liberal politics, Pope Pius IX (1846–78) lost control of Rome and was forced to flee the city. Mazzini became head of the Republic of Rome, created in February 1849.

The French government decided to intervene to protect the pope's interests and sent in troops to defeat the republicans. One of Mazzini's disciples, Giuseppe Garibaldi (1807–82), returned from exile in South America to undertake the defense of Rome. Garibaldi was a capable soldier who had learned the tactics of guerrilla warfare by joining independence struggles in Brazil and Argentina. Although his legion of poorly armed patriots and soldiers of fortune, known from their attire as the Red Shirts, waged a valiant effort to defend the city from April to June 1849, they were no match for the highly trained French army. French troops restored Pius IX as ruler of the Papal States.

Meanwhile, from August 1848 to the following spring, the Habsburg armies fought and finally defeated each of the revolutions. Austrian

In this incident from the revolutionary year of 1848, Imperial Austrian troops fire on a Viennese crowd assembled at the convening of the Estates General to petition for their right to a voice in the new social order.

success can be explained in part because the various Italian groups of Piedmontese, Tuscans, Venetians, Romans, and Neapolitans continued to identify with their local concerns and lacked coordination and central organization. Both Mazzini and Pius IX had failed to provide the focal point of leadership necessary for a successful national movement.

By the fall of 1849, Austria had solved the problems in its own capital and with Italy and Hungary by military dominance. Emperor Ferdinand I (1835–48), whose authority had been weakened irreparably by the overthrow of Metternich, abdicated in favor of his eighteen-year-old nephew, Franz Josef I (1848–1916). Austria understood that a Germany united under Freidrich Wilhelm IV of Prussia would undermine Austrian dominance in central Europe. In 1850 Austrians threatened the Prussians with war if they did not give up their plans for a unified Germany. In November of that year Prussian ministers signed an agreement with their Austrian counterparts in the Moravian city of Olmutz. The convention became known as "the humiliation of Olmutz" because Prussia was forced to accept Austrian dominance or go to war. In every case, military force and diplomatic measures prevailed to defeat the national and liberal movements within the German states and the Austrian Empire.

Europe in 1850

By 1850, a veneer of calm spread over central Europe. In Prussia, the peasantry were emancipated from feudal dues, and a constitution, albeit conservative and based on a three-class system, was established. Yet beneath the surface, there was the deeper reality of Austrian decline and Prussian challenge. The great Habsburg empire needed to call on outside help from Russia to defeat its enemies within. The imperial giant was again on its feet but for how long? In international relations, Austria's dominance in the German Confederation had diminished, as Prussia assumed greater political and economic power.

The 1848 revolutions spelled the end to the concert of Europe as it had been defined in the peace settlement of 1815. The European powers were incapable of united action to defend established territorial interests. Perhaps France would have provoked united action if it had attempted to extend its revolution throughout Europe as it had done in 1792. Instead, pragmatism prevailed. The British failed to support independence for Hungary, for example, because they feared the consequences for Russian ambitions that would be unchecked with a weaker Austria.

The revolutions of 1848 failed in part because of the irreconcilable split between moderate liberals and radical democrats. The participation of the masses had frightened members of the middle classes who were committed to moderate reforms that did not threaten property. In France, working-class revolutionaries had attempted to replace property with labor. Property triumphed. In the face of more extreme solutions, members of the middle class were willing to accept the increased authority of existing rule as a bulwark against anarchy. In December 1848 Prince Louis Napoleon, nephew of the former emperor, was elected president of the Second Republic by a wide margin. The first truly modern French politician, Louis Napoleon managed to appeal to everyone— workers, bourgeois, royalists, and peasants—by making promises that were vague or unkeepable. Severe repression forced radical protest into hiding. The new Bonaparte bided his time, apparently as an ineffectual ruler, until the moment in 1851 when he seized absolute power.

Similar patterns emerged elsewhere in Europe. In Germany, the bourgeoisie accepted the dominance of the old feudal aristocracy as a guarantee of law and order. Repressive government, businessmen were sure, would restore a strong economy. The attempts in 1848 to create new nations based on ethnic identities were in shambles by 1850.

Nearly everywhere throughout Europe constitutions had been systematically withdrawn with the recovery of the forces of reaction. With the French and Swiss exceptions, the bid for the extension of the franchise failed. The propertied classes remained in control of political institutions. Radicals willing to use violence to press electoral reforms were arrested, killed, or exiled. The leadership of the revolutionary movements had been decapitated, and there seemed no effective opposition to the rise and consolidation of state power.

The 1848 revolutions have been called a turning point at which modern history failed to turn. Contemporaries wondered how so much action could have produced so few lasting results. Yet the perception that nothing had changed was wrong. Conservatives and radicals alike turned toward a new realism in politics. Everywhere governments were forced to adapt to new social realities. No longer could the state ignore economic upheavals and social dislocations, if it wanted to survive. Revolutionaries also learned the lesson of repression. The state wielded powerful forces of violence against which nationalists, socialists, republicans, and liberals had all been proven helpless.

Suggestions for Further Reading

Europe in 1815

Robert Gildea, *Barricades and Borders, Europe 1800–1914* (Oxford: Oxford University Press, 1987). A synthetic overview of economic, demographic, political, and international trends in European society.

Harold Nicolson, *The Congress of Vienna: A Study in Allied Unity, 1812–1822* (New York: Viking Press, 1965). Dissects the maneuverings of the Allied diplomats and analyzes their cooperation in reconstructing Europe.

Alan Sked, *The Decline and Fall of the Habsburg Empire, 1815–1918* (London: Longman, 1989). A revisionist interpretation that demonstrates the strength and viability of Europe's greatest dynasty throughout the nineteenth century.

The New European Society

Joel Mokyr, *Why Ireland Starved: A Quantitative and Analytical History of the Irish Economy, 1800–1850* (London: George Allen & Unwin, 1983). An analysis of the structural factors that produced poverty in pre-famine Ireland and a thorough examination of the impact of the famine.

Redcliffe N. Salaman, *The History and Social Influence of the Potato*, revised impression edited by J. G. Hawkes (Cambridge: Cambridge University Press, 1985). The classic study of the potato. A major portion of the work is devoted to the potato famine.

Louise A. Tilly and Joan W. Scott, *Women, Work and Family* (New York: Holt, Rinehart and Winston, 1978). An overview of the impact of a wage economy on the family and on women's work.

The New Ideologies

Jonathan Beecher, *Charles Fourier: The Visionary and His World* (Berkeley: University of California Press, 1986). An intellectual biography, which traces the development of Fourier's theoretical perspective and roots it firmly in the social context of nineteenth-century France.

William H. Sewell, Jr., *Work and Revolution in France: The Language of Labor From the Old Regime to 1848* (Cambridge: Cambridge University Press, 1980). Traces nineteenth-century working-class socialism to the corporate culture of Old Regime guilds through traditional values, norms, language, and artisan organizations.

Gareth Stedman Jones, *Languages of Class: Studies in English Working Class History, 1832–1982* (Cambridge: Cambridge University Press, 1983). A series of essays, including topics on working-class culture and Chartism, that examine the development of class consciousness.

Edward P. Thompson, *The Making of the English Working Class* (New York: Pantheon Books, 1963). Spans the late eighteenth to mid-nineteenth centuries in examining the social, political, and cultural contexts in which workers created their own identity and put forward their own demands.

Protest and Revolution

Maurice Agulhon, *The Republican Experiment, 1848–1852* (Cambridge: Cambridge University Press, 1983). Traces the Revolution of 1848 from its roots to its ultimate failure in 1852 through an analysis of the ideologies of the republicanism of workers, peasants, and the bourgeoisie.

Clive Church, *Europe in 1830: Revolution and Political Change* (London: George Allen and Unwin, 1983). Considers the origins of the 1830 revolutions within a wider European crisis through a comparative analysis of European regions.

Peter N. Stearns, *1848: The Revolutionary Tide in Europe* (New York: Norton, 1974). Surveys the causes, impact, and legacy of the revolutions in France, Germany, the Habsburg Empire, and Italy, which shattered the diplomatic framework established at the Congress of Vienna and served as a transition to a new society.

Dorothy Thompson, *The Chartists: Popular Politics in the Industrial Revolution* (New York: Pantheon Books, 1984). Thompson demonstrates that Chartism was an extraordinary coalition of women, laborers, artisans, and alehouse keepers whose goals were transforming public life and forging a new political culture.

23

State-Building and Social Change In Europe, 1850–1871

The Birth of the German Empire

Secret fancies bubbled in Otto von Bismarck's brain. As he explained in long letters to his wife, he imagined that the Prussian king and German princes crowding round him were pregnant women seized by "strange cravings." He longed to be a "bomb and blow up, bringing the whole building down in ruins." In the next moment, he imagined himself a midwife assisting at a momentous birth. In spite of his remarkable train of thought, Otto von Bismarck (1815–98) was not a fanciful man. The birth in his daydream was the proclamation of the German Empire on 21 January 1871. The building was the Versailles Palace outside Paris. As the Prussian statesman stood in the great Hall of Mirrors on that fateful day, surrounded by German aristocrats, he could not forget the years of struggle and planning that preceded this event. His tension and anticipation provoked his strangely explosive fantasies.

The newly established Second Reich, successor to the Holy Roman Empire, united the German states into a single nation. The unification process had been a precarious pregnancy, with years of foreign wars and a herculean labor of diplomatic maneuverings. The placid, glossy scene painted by Anton von Werner (1843–1915) hardly suggests Bismarck's violent emotions on this momentous day. Bismarck saw his task in the female metaphor of birth. Yet this warrior group was the most masculine of gatherings. Look at the painting. The richly marbled and mirrored room, the site of the birth, figures as prominently in the tableau as the uniformed princes and aristocrats, who, with sabers, helmets, and standards raised, cheer the new emperor. The massive mirrors reflect more than this soldier society standing before the long windows of the opposite wall; they reflect a humiliation. This is, after all, the great hall built by Louis XIV at Versailles, one of Europe's greatest palaces, to reflect and glorify the power of absolutist France. Here the kings of France presided over lavish ceremonies and opulent receptions. Here Napoleon I honored his generals victorious in conquering central Europe. Here not long ago Napoleon III had danced on the parqueted floors with Queen Victoria of Britain. The choice of the Hall of Mirrors as the meeting place for the German princes, who had successfully combined forces to defeat the French Second Empire in only six weeks of war in the fall of 1870, was intended as an assertion of German superiority in Europe.

In less than a decade German unity had been achieved through military victories over Denmark, Austria, and France. The gilded moldings that commemorate the age of the Sun King are matched by the glitter of golden ribbons, medals, buttons, and cuffs of German uniforms, by the soft glow of burnished Prussian helmets. France was about to be stripped of its territories of Alsace and Lorraine; now the French were to be stripped of their dignity, as the Prussian king stands on luxuriant French carpeting to assert his claim. There is an arrogance here in the details on which Werner dwells. The French understood and promised to avenge it.

Look at the painting again. There on the dais is King Wilhelm I of Prussia, flanked by his son Crown Prince Friedrich Wilhelm and his son-in-law, Friedrich I, the Grand Duke of Baden, whose upraised hand signals the cheer for the new emperor. At the foot of the steps, like a loyal retainer, stands the self-described midwife, Otto von Bismarck. Yet there is something amiss here. The new German emperor, the person for whom the event has been orchestrated, stands to one side of the canvas. Bismarck commands its center. If most eyes of the cheering princes turn to the emperor, ours are pulled to the chancellor of the new Reich, who is singled out in his pure white uniform. Werner is telling us that this is the statesman's event, for it is he who has crafted a united Germany. Bismarck got what he wanted: a German Empire under the leadership of the Prussian king.

In both hands Bismarck clasps the proclamation of empire, the document wrested out of endless wrangling among the heads of the thirty-eight German states. The kings of Saxony, Bavaria, and Württemberg refused to attend the ceremony. Some who did attend were disgruntled and resentful. Even Bismarck's sovereign was not happy with the document, nor did he like the title assigned to him. He would have preferred to be "emperor of Germany" rather than "German emperor." Before the ceremony, Wilhelm I refused to speak to Bismarck. Yet the artist reveals none of this in the impassive faces and the sturdy stances of the two men.

Bismarck understood that symbols forge unity. The artist Werner, too, attends to symbol. Beneath the red-encased document, Bismarck firmly grasps his Prussian military helmet. Military victories had ensured Prussian predominance over a united Germany. To Bismarck's left, in profile facing the emperor, stands Count Helmuth von Moltke (1800–1891), head of the Prussian General Staff and the man responsible for reorganizing the Prussian army with Bismarck's support. Medals for bravery and service to his sovereign adorn Moltke's chest. With one foot forward, Moltke is a man of action, almost caught in mid-stride, a man ready to move into the future.

The unification of Germany was not achieved by democratic means. Bismarck understood the new age: as he explained in a speech to the Prussian Diet, "The great questions of the time are not decided by speeches and majority decisions—that was the error of 1848 and 1849—but by iron and blood." The new Reich was a "state of princes," an empire born of the union of force and military conquest. A century earlier, Voltaire, the French philosopher of the Enlightenment, had his own theory of creation: God gave the English the seas, the French the land, and the Germans the clouds. Fragmented and without a state, Germans could claim a rich, if ethereal, culture of philosophy, music, and literature in the previous century. In 1871, with the proclamation of the German Empire, Germans had put their feet on the ground. The struggle for land and sea, so easily assigned by Voltaire, lay ahead.

Building Nations: The Politics of Unification

The revolutions of 1848 had occurred in a period of experimentation from below. Radicals enlisting popular support had tried and failed to reshape European states for their own nationalist, liberal, and socialist ends. Governments in Paris, Vienna, Berlin, and a number of lesser states had been swept away. The revolutions had created a power vacuum but no durable solutions. To fill that vacuum, a new breed of politicians emerged in the 1850s and 1860s, men who did not speak of restorations or concerted European efforts. These were men who understood the importance of the centralized nation-state and saw the need of reforms from above. They also had a new appreciation of the importance of foreign policy successes as a means of furthering domestic programs. Cavour of Italy, Bismarck of Germany, and Louis Napoleon of France shared a new realism about means and ends.

Between 1815 and 1850, those who experimented with political power had worked from below or outside the traditional political system. In the 1850s and 1860s those committed to radical transformations worked from within the existing system. When revolutionary goals were achieved, direction came from above. National unification had escaped the grasp of liberals and radicals between 1848 and 1850. After 1850 liberal nationalism was subordinated to conservative state-building. Military force validated what intellectuals and revolutionaries had not been able to legitimate through ideological claims.

The Crimean War

After 1815, Russia had flexed its muscles as the greatest military power in Europe. With the containment of France in 1815, Russia was committed to preserving the status quo in the West. It had fulfilled its role as policeman of Europe by supporting Austria against Hungary and Prussia in 1849 and 1850. But Russia sought greater power to the south in the Balkans. The Bosporus, the narrow strait connecting the Black Sea with the Sea of Marmara, and the Dardanelles, connecting the Sea of Marmara with the Aegean Sea, were controlled by the Ottoman Empire. Russia hoped to benefit from Ottoman weakness caused by internal conflicts and gain control of the straits, which were the only outlet for the Russian fleet to the warm waters of the Mediterranean, Russia's southern outlet to the world.

At the center of the hope for Ottoman disintegration lay the "Eastern Question," the term used to designate the problems surrounding the European territories controlled by the Ottoman Empire. Each of the Great Powers—including Russia, Great Britain, Austria, Prussia, and France—hoped to benefit territorially from the collapse of Ottoman control. In 1853 Great Power rivalry over the Eastern Question created an international situation that led to war.

In 1853 the Russian government demanded that the Turkish government recognize Russia's right to protect Greek Orthodox believers in the Ottoman Empire. The Russian action was a response to measures taken by the French government during the previous year, which had gained from the Turkish government rights for Roman Catholic religious orders in certain sanctuaries in the Holy Land. In making its claims as protector, Russia demanded that the decision that responded to French pressure also be rescinded. The Turkish government refused Russian demands and the Russians, feeling that their prestige had been damaged, ordered troops to enter the Danubian Principalities held by the Turks. In October 1853, the Turkish government, counting on support from Great Britain and France, declared war on Russia.

Russia easily prevailed over its weaker neighbor to the south. In a four-hour battle, a Russian squadron destroyed the Turkish fleet off the coast

Lithograph of the Charge of the Light Brigade at the battle of Balaklava, 1854. The Charge was one of the most controversial events in military history. Public opinion blamed the commanders, Lord Lucan and Lord Raglan, but the confusion of battle caused their orders to be misinterpreted, leading to disaster.

of Sinope. Tsar Nicholas I (1825–55) drew up the terms of a settlement with the Ottoman Empire and submitted them to Great Britain and France for review. The two western European powers, fearing Russian aggrandizement at Turkish expense, responded by declaring war on Russia on 28 March 1854, the date which marked a new phase in the Crimean War. Both Great Britain and France, like Russia, had ambitions in the Balkans and the eastern Mediterranean. Great Britain feared Russian expansion as a threat to its trade and holdings in India and had a vested interest in an independent and weak Turkey presiding over the straits. The French hoped that by entering into a partnership with the British to defeat the Russians, they would be able to lay claim to greater power and status in European international pol-

itics. The Austrian Empire, frightened by Russia's seizure of the Danubian Principalities of Moldavia and Walachia, remained neutral but threatened to enter the war with Britain and France on the side of Turkey. The Italian kingdom of Piedmont-Sardinia joined the war on the side of the western European powers in January 1855, hoping to make its name militarily and win recognition for its aim to unite Italy into a single nation. Without explicit economic interests, the Great Powers and the lesser Italian state of Piedmont-Sardinia were motivated by ambition, prestige, and rivalry in the Balkans.

British and French troops landed in the Crimea, the Russian peninsula extending into the Black Sea, in September 1854, with the intention of capturing Sevastopol, Russia's heavily fortified chief naval base on the Black Sea. In March 1855, Nicholas I died and was succeeded by his son Alexander II (1855–81), who wanted to bring the war to a speedy end. His attempts to negotiate a peace in the spring of 1855 repeatedly failed. In battle, the Russians continued to resist as the allies laid siege to the fortress at Sevastopol, which fell only after 322 days of battle on 11 September 1855. The defeated Russians abandoned Sevastopol, blew up their forts, and sank their own ships.

Russia, now facing the threat of Austrian entry into the war, agreed to preliminary peace terms. In the Peace of Paris of 1856, Russia relinquished its claim as protector of Christians in Turkey. The British gained the neutralization of the Black Sea. The mouth of the Danube was returned to Turkish control, and an international commission was created to oversee safe navigation on the Danube. The Danubian Principalities were placed under joint guarantee of the powers, and Russia gave up a small portion of Bessarabia. In 1861 the Principalities were united in the independent nation of Romania.

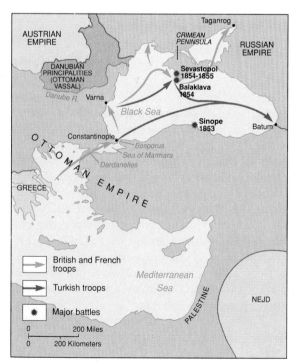

The Crimean War

The Crimean War had the highest casualty rate of any European war between 1815 and 1914. Three-quarters of a million soldiers—Russian, French, British, and Turkish—died. Because of nonexistent sanitary practices in caring for the wounded, four out of five succumbed to disease, especially typhus and cholera. The English nurse Florence Nightingale (1820–1910) brought medical reforms to the theater of war, introduced sanitation, and organized barracks hospitals, all of which saved the lives of countless British soldiers. (See Special Feature, "A Working Woman," pp. 720–721.) But 450,000 Russian soldiers died. Russians suffered disproportionately, claiming two-thirds of all dead and wounded. Of those who died in battle, many died needlessly under poorly prepared leaders. A typical example occurred during the battle of Balaklava. Alfred, Lord Tennyson (1809–92) described the bravery of the six hundred troops of the British Light Brigade ordered into battle by incompetent and confused commanders. British soldiers charged down a narrow valley flanked by Russian guns on the heights on both sides and into the teeth of yet another battery at the head of the valley. The battlefield became known as the Valley of Death.

> Theirs not to make reply,
> Theirs not to reason why,
> Theirs but to do and die.
> Into the Valley of Death
> Rode the six hundred.

When the dust of the fighting had settled, the battlefield lay strewn with the bodies of nearly two-thirds of the soldiers of the Light Brigade. Their horses, slain, too, lay beside them.

This was a war no one really won. A war over obscure disagreements in a faraway peninsula in the Black Sea nevertheless had dramatic and enduring consequences. Russia ceased playing an active role in European affairs and turned toward expansion in central Asia. Its withdrawal opened up the possibility for a move by Prussia in central Europe. The rules of the game had changed. The concert of Europe so carefully crafted by European statesmen in 1815 came to an end with the Crimean War. With the Peace of Paris of 1856, the hope that goals could be achieved by peaceful means also died. Piedmont-Sardinia, an empty-handed victor, realized that only the force of the cannon could achieve the unification of Italy.

Unifying Italy

Italy had not been a single political entity since the end of the Roman Empire in the West in the fifth century. The movement to reunite Italy culturally and politically was known as the *Risorgimento*, literally, "resurgence," and had its roots in the eighteenth century. Hopes for unification encouraged by reorganization during the Napoleonic era were repeatedly crushed throughout the first half of the nineteenth century. Revolutionary movements failed to cast out foreign domination by Austria in 1848.

Both Guiseppe Mazzini's Young Italy movement and Guiseppe Garibaldi's Redshirts had as their goal in 1848 a united republican Italy achieved through direct popular action. But they had failed. It took a politician of aristocratic birth to recognize that Mazzini's and Garibaldi's model of revolutionary action was doomed against the powerful Austrian military machine. Mazzini was a moralist. Garibaldi was a fighter. But Camillo Benso di Cavour (1810–61), the opportunistic politician, was a realist. He knew that only as a unified nation could Italy lay claim to status as a great power in Europe. And he saw that a united Italy could be achieved only through the manipulation of diplomacy and military victory. He understood that international events could be made to serve national ends.

As premier for Piedmont-Sardinia from 1852 to 1859 and again in 1860–61, Cavour was well placed to launch his campaign for Italian unity. The kingdom of Piedmont-Sardinia had made itself a focal point for unification efforts. Piedmont-Sardinia's king, Carlo-Alberto (1831–49) had stood alone among Italian rulers in opposing Austrian domination of the Italian peninsula in 1848 and 1849. Severely defeated by the Austrians, he was forced to abdicate. With his death in exile, Carlo-Alberto became a saint martyred for the cause of unification. He was succeeded by his son Victor Emmanuel II (1849–61), who had the good sense to appoint Cavour as his first minister. From the start, Cavour undertook liberal administrative reforms that included tax reform, stabilization of the currency, improvement of the railway system, the creation of a transatlantic steamship system, and the support of private enterprise. With these programs Cavour created

This Italian tricolor flag echoes the tricolor banner of the French Revolution. It had first been used in an uprising against the pope in 1794, and it soon became the standard of Italian unity.

for Piedmont-Sardinia the dynamic image of progressive change. He involved Piedmont-Sardinia in the Crimean War, thereby securing its status among the European powers.

Most important, however, was his successful pursuit of an alliance with France against Austria in 1858. Cavour shrewdly secured the French pledge of support, including military aid if necessary, against Austria in the Treaty of Plombières, signed by Napoleon III in 1858. The treaty was quickly followed by an arranged provocation against the Habsburg monarchy. Austria declared war in 1859 and was easily defeated by French forces in the battles of Magenta and Solferino. The peace, signed in November 1859 at Zurich, joined Lombardy to Piedmont-Sardinia. Cavour wielded the electoral weapon of the plebiscite, a method of direct voting that gives to electors the choice of voting for or against some important public question, in order to unite Tuscany, Parma, and Modena under Piedmont's king.

Cavour's approach was not without its costs. His partnership with a stronger power meant sometimes following France's lead. French bullying provoked fits of rage and forced Cavour to

A Working Woman

Women have always worked. But how society has valued women's work has changed over time. After 1850 women of all income levels, not just the wealthy, were expected to retire from the workplace upon marrying. Women's proper role was that of wife and mother in the home, caring for her husband and family, watching over her children. Young women worked before they married in order to help parents and to save dowries. There is no doubt that many women continued to work for wages because they had to; they were too poor to live by society's norms. But mid-nineteenth-century European culture reinforced the idea that woman's place was in the separate domestic sphere of private pleasures and unpaid labor. To be a "public" man was a valued attribution. The same adjective applied to a woman meant she was a harlot.

Yet it is this culture that immortalized Florence Nightingale, a woman who valued what she called "my work" above home and family. She was a single woman in an age when more and more women were making the choice to remain unmarried; but it was also an age in which *spinster* was a term of derision and a sign of failure. Miss Nightingale, as she was known, received the British Empire's Order of Merit for her life achievements. Queen Victoria, the most maternal and domestic of queens, hailed her as "an example to our sex." Nightingale was widely regarded as the greatest woman of her age, among the most eminent of Victorians. A highly visible and outspoken reformer, Nightingale deviated from woman's unpaid role as nurturer in the private sphere. How could she be an "example" to the women of her time?

Florence Nightingale was hailed as a national heroine because of her work during the Crimean War in organizing hospital care at Scutari, a suburb outside Constantinople (on the Asiatic side of the Bosporus). In the Crimea, she entered her own field of battle, attacking the mismanagement, corruption, and lack of organization characteristic of medical treatment for British soldiers. She campaigned for better sanitation, hygiene, ventilation, and diet, and in 1855 the death rate plummeted from 42 percent to 2 percent thanks to her efforts. The *London Times* declared, "There is not one of England's proudest and purest daughters who at the moment stands on as high a pinnacle as Florence Nightingale."

It was a pinnacle not easily scaled. Blocked by her family and publicly maligned, Nightingale struggled against prevailing norms to carve out her occupation. She was the daughter of a wealthy gentry family, and from her father she received a man's classical education. Women of her milieu were expected to be educated only in domestic arts. The fashion of the day emphasized woman's confinement to the home: crinolines, corsets, and trains restricted movement and suggested gentility. This was the life of Nightingale's older sister and one that "the Angel of the Crimea" fiercely resisted. Nightingale railed at the inequity of married life: "A man gains everything by marriage: he gains a 'helpmate,' but a woman does not." Her memoirs are filled with what she called her "complaints" against the plight of women.

Nightingale was not a typical working woman. She struck out on her career as a rebel. Because of her wealth, she did not need to work, yet she felt driven to be useful. Her choice of nursing much alarmed her family, who considered the occupation at best to be on the level with domestic service. For them, nursing was worse in fact, because nurses worked with the naked bodies of the sick. Thus, nurses were either shameless or promiscuous or both. Nightingale shattered these taboos. She visited nursing establishments throughout Europe, traveling alone— another feat unheard of for women in her day—and studied their methods and techniques. She conceived of her own mission to serve God through caring for others.

As with any exceptional individual, character and capabilities must figure in an explanation of achievements. Nightingale was a woman of drive and discipline who refused to accept the limited choices available to Victorian

women. She possessed, in her sovereign's words, "a wonderful, clear and comprehensive head." Yet her unique talents are not enough to explain her success. In many ways, Nightingale was not a rebel but an embodiment of the changing values of her age. In 1860, she established a school to train nurses, just as similar institutions were being created to train young women as teachers. These occupations were extensions of women's roles from the arena of the home into society. In keeping with their domestic roles, women remained nurturers in the classroom and at the sickbed.

These new female professions were also poorly paid. Significantly, Florence Nightingale, honored as she was in her lifetime, received no salary for her contributions to the British state. Her work was supported by donations from benefactors and administrative protectors she referred to as her "masters."

She and other women of her class, including Elizabeth Fry (1780–1845), who was a Quaker minister, prison reformer, banker's wife, and mother of ten, and the English writer and political reformer Harriet Martineau (1802–76), were regarded as philanthropists, women who donated their time and expertise to the public good. Theirs was the moral obligation of the wealthy toward the poor. It also sprang out of the nature of women, contemporary moralists asserted, to mother and to heal. The definition of women's proper role did not need to be dismantled to accommodate these activities. It needed merely to be stretched.

Florence Nightingale spent a good part of the last forty-five years of her life in a sickbed suffering from what she called "nervous fever." During this period she wrote incessantly and continued to lobby for her programs, benefiting, one of her biographers claimed, from the freedom to think and write provided by her illness. It may well be true that her invalidism protected her from the claims on her time made by her family and by society. It may also be true that she, like many of her middle-class female contemporaries, experienced debilitation or suffered from hypochondria in direct proportion to the limitations they experienced.

Mid-century Europe had witnessed a series of failed protests on behalf of women against social and political restrictions. In spite of reform movements,

women did not enjoy the franchise or equal property rights. Access to divorce was available only to women wealthy enough to afford it. Yet women did participate in new activities and enter new occupations justified by their role as nurturers. Nightingale herself believed that the right to vote was less important than financial independence for women. New occupations labeled as "women's work" were essential to the expansion of industrial society. A healthy and literate population guaranteed a strong citizenry, a strong army, and a strong work force. As helpmeets, women entered a new work sector identified by the adjective *service*. Women were accepted as clerical workers, performing the "housekeeping" of business firms and bureaucracies.

After mid-century, gender differences, socially defined virtues for men and women, hardened. Individualism, competition, and militarism were the values of the world of men. Familial support, nurturance, and healing were female virtues. These were the separate and unequal worlds created by the factory and the battlefield. The virtues of the private sphere were extended into the public world with the creation of new forms of poorly paid female labor. In this sense, Florence Nightingale was not a rebel. This "Lady with the Lamp," whom fever-ridden soldiers called their mother, was another working woman.

resign from office temporarily in 1859 over a war ended too early by Napoleon III. The need to cajole French support meant enriching France with territorial gain in the form of Nice and Savoy. Piedmont-Sardinia, however, got more than it gave up. In the summer of 1859 revolutionary assemblies in Tuscany, Modena, Parma, and the Romagna, wanting to eject their Austrian rulers, voted in favor of union with the Piedmontese. By April 1860 these four areas of central Italy were under Victor Emmanuel's rule. Piedmont-Sardinia had doubled in size to become the dominant power on the Italian peninsula.

Southern Italians took their lead from events in central Italy and in the spring of 1860 initiated disorders against the rule of King Francis II (1859–61) of Naples. Uprisings in Sicily inspired Guiseppe Garibaldi to return from his self-imposed exile to organize his own army of Red Shirts, known as the Thousand, who liberated Sicily, and then crossed to the Italian mainland to expel Francis II from Naples. Garibaldi next turned his attention to the liberation of the Holy City, where a French garrison protected the pope. After his defeat in Rome in 1849, Garibaldi had never lost sight of his mission to free all of Italy from foreign rule, even when in the 1850s he had lived on New York's Staten Island as a candlemaker and had become a naturalized citizen of the United States.

As Garibaldi's popularity as a national hero grew, Cavour became alarmed at the competition in uniting Italy and took secret steps to block the advance of the Red Shirts and their leader. To seize the initiative, Cavour directed the Piedmontese army into the Papal States. After defeating the pope's troops, Cavour's men crossed into the Neapolitan state and scored important victories against forces loyal to the king of Naples. Cavour proceeded to annex southern Italy for Victor Emmanuel, using plebiscites to seal the procedure. At this point, in 1860, Garibaldi yielded his own conquered territories to the Piedmontese ruler, making possible the declaration of a united Italy under Victor Emmanuel II, who reigned as king of Italy from 1861 to 1878.

The new king of Italy was now poised to acquire Venetia, still under Austrian rule, and Rome, still ruled by Pope Pius IX, and he devoted

Unification of Italy

much of his foreign policy in the 1860s to these ends. In 1866, when Austria lost a war with Prussia, Italy struck a deal with the victor and gained control of Venetia. When Prussia prevailed against France in 1870, Victor Emmanuel II took over Rome. The boot of Italy, from top to toe, was now a single nation. The pope remained in the Vatican, opposed to an Italy united under King Victor Emmanuel II. The new national government sought to impose centralization with a heavy hand and had little regard for preserving regional differences and regional cultures. Cavour's liberal constitutional principles, combined with moderately conservative stands on social issues, produced an alienation, especially in southern Italy, among both the peasantry and nobility.

Cavour did not live to see the united Italy that he had worked so hard to fashion. He had succeeded where poets and revolutionaries had failed in preparing the ground for a unification because he understood that the world had changed dramatically in the first half of the nineteenth century. He appreciated the relationship between national and international events and was able to manipulate it for his own ends. Both Cavour and his counterpart in Germany, Otto von Bismarck, considered themselves realists who shared a recognition of diplomacy as an instrument of domestic policy.

Unifying Germany

Seldom in modern history does an individual emerge as a chessmaster, overseeing international politics and domestic affairs as if the world were a great board game with movable pieces. Otto von Bismarck was aware that the game he was playing was one of high risks and high stakes. His vision was limited to the pragmatic pursuit of preserving the power of his beloved Prussia. For him the empire was not an end in itself but a means of guaranteeing Prussian strength. In an age of realistic politicians, he emerged as the supreme practitioner of *Realpolitik*, the ruthless pursuit by any means, including illegal and violent ones, to advance the interests of his country.

Bismarck was a Junker, an aristocratic estate-owner from east of the Elbe River, who entered politics in 1847. As a member of the United Diet of Prussia, he made his reputation as a reactionary when he rose to speak in favor of hunting privileges for the nobility: "I am a Junker and I want to have the advantages of it." In the 1850s, he became aware of Prussia's future in the center of Europe: he saw that the old elites must be allied with the national movement in order to survive. The problem was that nationalism was the property of the liberals, who had been defeated in 1848. Bismarck appropriated it. Liberals and Junkers shared an interest in unification but for different political ends. As a politician, Bismarck learned how to exploit their common ground.

In 1850 Prussia had been forced to accept Austrian dominance in central Europe or go to war. Throughout the following decade, however, Prussia systematically undermined Austrian power by wielding the trade agreements of the Zollverein as a tool to exclude Austria from German economic affairs. In 1862, at the moment of a crisis provoked by the king over military reorganization, Bismarck became minister-president of the Prussian cabinet and foreign minister. He overrode the parliamentary body, the Diet, by reorganizing the army without a formally approved budget. In 1864 he constructed an alliance between Austria and Prussia for the purpose of invading Schleswig, a predominantly German-speaking territory controlled by the king of Denmark, whose population hoped to become part of the German Confederation. Within five days of invasion, Denmark yielded the duchies of Schleswig and Holstein, now to be ruled jointly by Austria and Prussia.

Ascertaining that he had a free hand in central Europe, Bismarck skillfully promoted a crisis between Austria and Prussia over management of the territories. Counting on the neutrality of France and Great Britain, the support of Piedmont-Sardinia, and good relations with Russia, Bismarck led his country into war with Austria in June 1866. The war took its name from its short duration. In this Seven Weeks' War Austrian forces proved to be no match for the better-equipped and better-trained Prussian army. Bismarck dictated the terms of the peace, which demonstrated that he had no desire to cripple Austria, only to exclude it from a united Germany in which Prussia would be the dominant force. Austria's exclusion from Germany forced the Austrian government to deal with its own internal problems of imperial organization. In 1867, in response to pressures from the subject nationalities, the Habsburg Empire transformed itself into a dual monarchy of two independent and equal states under one ruler, who would be both the emperor of Austria and the king of Hungary. In spite of the reorganization, the nationalities problem persisted, and ethnic groups began to agitate for total independence from imperial rule.

Bismarck's biggest obstacle to German unification was laid to rest with Austria's defeat. The south German states, however, continued to resist the idea of Prussian dominance. Prussia's militarism, its Protestant religion, and its economic strength threatened antimilitarists, Catholics, and the ruling elites of the southern states. Liberals, democrats, and socialists from the south feared the political consequences of Prussian conservatism. But growing numbers of people in Baden, Württemberg, Bavaria, and the southern parts of Hesse-Darmstadt recognized the necessity of uniting under Prussian leadership.

Many French observers were troubled by the Prussian victory over Austria and were apprehensive over what a united Germany might portend for the future of French dominance in Europe. Napoleon III made clear his opposition to further Prussian growth and attempted unsuccessfully to contain Prussian ambitions through diplomatic maneuverings. Instead, France found itself stranded without important European allies. In the spring of 1870, Bismarck decided to seize the initiative and provoke a crisis with France.

Bismarck recognized that war with France could be the dramatic event needed to forge cooperation and unity among all German states. The issue of succession to the Spanish throne gave him the opportunity he sought. Bismarck skillfully created the impression that the French ambassador had insulted the Prussian king, then leaked news of the incident to the press in both countries. Enraged and inflamed French and Prussian publics both demanded war.

As a direct result of this misunderstanding deliberately manufactured by Bismarck, France declared war on Prussia in July 1870. The southern German princes, as Bismarck hoped, immediately sided with the Prussian king. For years before hostilities broke out, the Prussians had been preparing for war. They had been sending Prussian army officers disguised as landscape painters into France to study the terrain of battle. French troops carried maps of Germany but were ignorant of the geography of their own country

Im Etappenquartier vor Paris, 1871. *This 1894 painting by Anton von Werner shows Prussian troops making themselves at home in a French drawing room on their way to victory in Paris. The Prussians occupied the city for only forty-eight hours.*

Unification of Germany

the bureaucracy as a mainstay of the emperor. The new Reichstag—the national legislative assembly—was to be elected by means of universal male suffrage, a concession to the liberals. Yet the constitution was not a liberal one, since the Reichstag was not sovereign and the chancellor was accountable only to the emperor. Policy was made outside the domain of electoral politics. The federal structure of the constitution, especially with regard to taxation, also kept the central parliament weak. Most liberals supported the constitution, but a minority persisted in a tradition of radical dissent. Critics felt that true constitutional government had been sacrificed to the demands of empire. As one liberal remarked, "Unity without freedom is a unity of slaves." Bismarck spoke in confidence of his aim "to destroy parliamentarianism by parliamentarianism." According to this formula, Bismarck hoped that a weak Reichstag would undermine parliamentary institutions better than any dictatorial ruler.

In the 1860s another great crisis in statebuilding had been resolved across the Atlantic. The United States had cemented political unity through the use of force in its Civil War. Just as Bismarck had resolved his crisis through "blood and iron," so did the president of the United States, Abraham Lincoln (1809–65), mobilize the greater human and industrial resources of the North against the agrarian, slave-owning South. Republican democracy triumphed in the United States, while a neo-absolutism emerged in Germany. Yet there is a remarkable similarity between the two events. In both countries wars eventually resulted in a single national market without internal tariffs. The wars made possible a single financial system through which capital could be raised. In both countries unified national economies paved the way for the expansion of industrial power.

Nationalism and Force

It is commonplace in the Western historical tradition to speak of nations as if they were individuals possessing emotions, making choices, taking actions, having ideas. "Russia turned inward"; "Germany chose its enemies as well as its friends"; "France vowed revenge"; "Great Britain

where the battles were waged. Sent into battle against the Germans, French troops roamed around in search of their commanders and each other. The Germans had learned new deployment strategies from studying the use of railroads in the American Civil War of 1861–65. Unlike the Germans, the French had not coordinated deployment with the new technology of the railroad. Although French troops had the latest equipment, they were sent into battle without instructions on how to use it. Finally, the Prussian-led German army was superior, outnumbering French troops 450,000 to 260,000. All these factors combined to spell disaster for the French. Within a matter of weeks, it was clear that France had lost this Franco-Prussian War. The path was now clear for the declaration of the German Empire in January 1871.

Bismarck, always the pragmatist, understood clearly that Europe was not the same place that it had been a decade or two earlier. "Anyone who speaks of Europe is wrong—it is nothing but a set of national expressions." This understanding was the key to his success. In unifying Germany, Bismarck built on the constitution of the North German Confederation formed in 1867, which guaranteed Prussian dominance. Bismarck used

took pride in its achievements." On one level, to attribute volition, feeling, and insight to an abstract entity like the "nation" is nonsense. But on another level, the personification of nation-states was one of the great achievements of statesmen throughout Europe between 1850 and 1870. The language and symbols they put in place created the nation itself, a new political reality whose forms contain modern political consciousness. The nation-state became an all-knowing being whose rights had to be protected, whose destiny had to be assured. Before the nineteenth century the person of the king had embodied the nation. With the political upheavals of the mid-century revolutions, the use of force, and the creation of new states, symbols took the place of monarchs to communicate a single undivided entity. A female form, whether it was Britannia of Great Britain or Marianne of France, could be used to capture the purity, strength, and vulnerability of the new nationalist concept.

The nation was above all a creation that minimized or denied real differences in dialect and language, regional loyalties, local traditions, and village identities. The crises in state-building in Italy and Germany had been resolved finally by violence. No power was acknowledged to exist above the nation-state. No power could sanction the nation's actions but itself. Force was an acceptable alternative to diplomacy. War was a political act and a political instrument, a continuation of political relations. Violence and nationalism were inextricably linked in the unification of both Italy and Germany in the third quarter of the nineteenth century.

Reforming European Society

The revolutions of 1848 had failed to deal with social problems, just as they had failed to realize nationalist aspirations. After the revolutions, government repression silenced radical movements throughout Europe. But repression could not maintain social harmony and promote growth and prosperity. In the third quarter of the nineteenth century Europe's leaders recognized that reforms were needed to build dynamic and competitive states.

Three different models for social and political reform developed in Europe after 1850. One model is that of France, where the French emperor worked through a highly centralized administrative structure and with a highly valued elite of specialists in order to achieve social and economic transformation. The French model is a technocratic one that emphasized the importance of specialized knowledge to achieve material progress. Reform in France relied on both autocratic direction and liberal participation.

Great Britain provides another model, in which reform was fostered through liberal parliamentary democracy. In government by "amateurs," with local rather than a highly centralized administration, British legislation alternated between a philosophy of freedom and one of protection. But reforms were always hammered out by parliamentary means with the support of a gradually expanding electorate.

Finally, Russia offers a model for reform. Like Britain, Russia had avoided revolution at mid-century. Like Britain, it hoped to preserve social peace. Yet the Russian model for reform stands in dramatic contrast to Britain's. Russia was still a semifeudal society in 1850's. Beginning in the late 1850s, Russia embarked on a radical restructuring of society by autocratic means. Reforms in the three societies had little in common ideologically but all reflected a commitment to progress and an awareness of the state's role and responsibility in achieving it.

The Rise and Fall of the Second Empire in France, 1852–70

Napoleon III ruled France from mid-century until 1870. His apprenticeship for political leadership was an unusual one. Louis Napoleon (1808–73) was a nephew of the emperor Napoleon I. The child Louis, born at the peak of French glory, was old enough to remember the devastation of his uncle's defeat in 1815. He dedicated his exiled youth to preparing for his family's restoration as rulers of France. With the death of Napoleon's son, the duc de Reichstadt, in 1832, Louis was aware that the mantle of future power and the family destiny fell to him.

Karl Marx said of Louis Napoleon, in comparing him with his uncle, Napoleon I, that history happens the first time as tragedy and the second time as farce. There was much that passed as farcical before Louis Napoleon established France's Second Empire in 1852, as one attempt after another to seize power failed. Yet those who viewed Louis Napoleon as a figure of derision were misled: by 1848 he understood the importance of shaping public opinion to suit his own ends. He wielded the Napoleonic legend to play on the dissatisfaction of millions. He understood that in order to succeed in an electoral system, he had to promise something to everyone. That is exactly what he did in the fall of 1848 when he spoke of prosperity, order, and the end of poverty, slogans that sent different and incompatible messages to a bourgeoisie who wanted social peace, workers who wanted jobs and social justice, and peasants who wanted land and freedom from taxes. Universal manhood suffrage was for the first time employed in a French national election. Recognizing its legitimating power, Louis Napoleon swept the field, the only candidate supported by all social classes.

In spite of his awareness of his own importance, nobody took Louis Napoleon very seriously, even when as the dark-horse candidate he was elected president of the Second Republic in December 1848. The politicians were sure that he could be managed, so insignificant did he seem. They and the rest of France were literally caught sleeping before dawn on 2 December 1851 when the nephew of the great Napoleon seized power in a coup détat and became dictator of France. Exactly one year later, he proclaimed himself Emperor Napoleon III and set about the tasks of establishing his dynasty and reclaiming French imperial glory.

Napoleon III's regime has been condemned for its decadence and its spectacle. On the surface, the world of the Second Empire glittered like a fancy-dress ball, as men in sparkling uniforms and women in full-skirted, low-necked gowns waltzed to gay tunes. Courtesans in open carriages, parading through the newly landscaped Bois de Boulogne, became as famous as cabinet members. But to judge the empire on superficial criteria alone would be a mistake. The Second Empire achieved significant successes in a variety of areas. Napoleon III supported economic expansion and industrial development. During his reign the French economy prospered and flourished. The discovery of gold in California and Australia fueled a demand for French products in international markets and initiated a period of sustained economic growth that lasted beyond Napoleon III's reign into the 1880s. A new private banking system, founded in 1852 by financiers and key political figures, enabled the pooling of investors' resources, small and large, to finance industrial expansion. Stable, authoritarian government encouraged increased investment in state public works programs.

Napoleon III surrounded himself with advisers who saw in prosperity the answer to all social problems. Between 1852 and 1860 the government supported a massive program of railroad construction. Jobs multiplied and investment increased. Agriculture expanded as railroad lines opened new markets. The rich got richer but the extreme poverty of the first half of the nineteenth century was shrinking. Brutal misery in city and countryside did not disappear but, on the whole, the standard of living increased, as wages rose faster than prices.

The best single example of the energy and commitment of the imperial regime was the rebuilding of the French capital. As Sir Edwin Chadwick (1800–1890), Britain's leading public health reformer, put it, Napoleon III found Paris stinking and left it sweet. Before mid-century Paris was one of the most unsanitary, crime-ridden, and politically volatile capitals in Europe. Within fifteen years it had been transformed into a city of lights, wide boulevards and avenues, monumental vistas, parks, and gardens. Napoleon III was the architect of the idea for a new Paris, something his uncle never had the time or resources to accomplish. But the real credit for carrying through these municipal improvements goes to Baron Georges Haussmann (1809–91).

As Prefect of the Seine from 1853 to 1870, Baron Haussmann typified the technocrat in power. He was called the Attila of the straight line for the ruthless manner in which his protractor cut through city neighborhoods, destroying all that lay in his pencil's path. Poor districts were turned into rubble to make way for the elegant apartment buildings of the Parisian bourgeoisie. The new housing was too expensive for workers,

Workers demolish buildings to make way for the new Rue des Ecoles during the rebuilding of the city of Paris. By 1870, few traces of the medieval walled city could be found.

who were pushed out of Paris to the suburbs. The boundaries of the city expanded. As workers from all over France migrated to the capital in search of jobs, the population nearly doubled, increasing by just under a million in the 1850s and 1860s. A poor and volatile population encircled the city of monuments and museums. Paris as the radical capital of France was being physically dismantled and a new, more conservative political entity rose in its place, as the middle classes took over the heart of the city. This process was very different from the development of other urban areas like London, where the middle class fled to the suburbs, leaving behind the problems of urban life.

Much has been made of the policing benefits of rebuilding the city of Paris. Wider streets facilitated the movement of troops, which could more easily crush revolutionary disturbances. While the control aspect of urban reconstruction was not lost on Haussmann and Napoleon III, it was not the primary purpose of the vast public works project that lasted for the whole regime. Napoleon

wanted Paris to be the center of Western culture and the envy of the world. Its wide, straight avenues served as the model for other French cities. The new Paris became an international model copied in Mexico City, Brussels, Madrid, Rome, Stockholm, and Barcelona between 1870 and 1900. American city planners of the City Beautiful movement were also influenced by the "Haussmannization" of Paris. In spite of financial scandals that plagued the reconstruction near the end of the regime, few disputed that Napoleon III had transformed Paris into one of the world's most beautiful cities.

Just as a new Paris would make France the center of culture, Napoleon III intended his blueprint for foreign policy to restore France to its pre-1815 status as the greatest European power. French governments after 1815 had been forced to abandon adventurous foreign policies. By involving France in both the Crimean War and the war for Italian unification Napoleon III reversed this pattern. The emperor had undertaken both wars with the hope of further increasing French economic and diplomatic prominence on the Continent. Napoleon III supported Piedmont-Sardinia not out of any sense of altruism, in spite of his claim that he was "doing something for Italy." The accession of Nice and Savoy increased French territory— and reversed the settlements of 1815.

The Italian campaign complicated relations with Great Britain, which feared a resurgent French militarism. French construction of the Suez Canal between the Red Sea and the Mediterranean also created tensions with Great Britain, protective of its own dominance in the Mediterranean and the Near East. Nevertheless, the free-trade agreement between the British and the French in 1860—the Chevalier-Cobden Treaty— was a landmark in overseas policy and a commitment to liberal economic policies.

The Second Empire's involvement in Mexico was another matter. It was simply a fiasco. The Mexican government had been chronically unable to pay its foreign debts and France was Mexico's largest creditor. Napoleon III hoped that by intervening in Mexican affairs he could strengthen ties with Great Britain and Spain, to whom the Mexicans also owed money. The emperor planned to turn Mexico into a satellite empire that would be economically profitable to France. The United States, occupied with civil war, did not interfere in 1861 when Napoleon III sent in a military expedition to "pacify" the Mexican countryside. With the backing of Mexican conservatives who opposed Mexican president Benito Juaréz (1806–72), Napoleon III supported the Austrian archduke Maximilian (1832–67) as emperor of Mexico. The reasons for the choice of Maximilian are obscure, although the gesture was probably intended to win favor in the Viennese court. Max, as he was known, was well-meaning but inept. After he was crowned in 1863, the new Mexican emperor struggled to rule in an enlightened manner, but he was stymied from the beginning by the lack of popular support. Napoleon III recalled the 34,000 French troops that, at considerable expense, were keeping Maximilian's troubled regime in place. Abandoned, Maximilian was captured and executed by a firing squad in the summer of 1867. The Mexican disaster revealed the weaknesses of Napoleon III's regime and damaged French prestige in the international arena. Intensely aware of

public criticism, the emperor undertook the reorganization of the army and a series of liberal reforms, including increasing parliamentary participation in affairs of state, and granting to trade unions the right of assembly.

The Prussian victory over Austria in the Seven Weeks' War had dramatically changed the situation on the Continent. Pundits in Paris were fond of saying that the Austrian loss really marked the defeat of France. France's position within Europe was threatened and Napoleon III knew it. In 1870 the humiliatingly rapid defeat of French imperial forces in the Franco-Prussian War brought to an end the experiment in liberal empire.

In 1870 France remained a mixture of old and new. Although industrial production had doubled between 1852 and 1870, France was still an agricultural nation. Foreign trade expanded by 300 percent, growing faster than that of any other nation in Europe. Six times as many miles of railroad track crisscrossed France at the time Napoleon III went into exile as when he came into power. Napoleon III did not create the economic

The Execution of the Emperor Maximilian (1868), by Eduoard Manet. The United States pressured France to withdraw support for the Mexican imperial venture, which led to disaster for Maximilian and the reinstatement of Benito Juarez as president.

boom from which all of Europe benefited between 1850 and 1880, but he did build on it, using the state to stimulate and enhance prosperity. His policies favored business and initiated a financial revolution of enduring benefits. The technocratic model of rule by specialists was not applied, however, to the army in forcing it to modernize. Nor had foreign policy benefited from the careful calculations employed in domestic administration. The empire had become the victim of its own myth of invincibility.

The Victorian Compromise

Contemporaries were aware of two facts of life about Great Britain in 1850: first, that Britain had an enormously productive capitalist economy of sustained growth; and second, that Britain enjoyed apparent social harmony without revolution and without civil war. As revolutions ravaged continental Europe in 1848, the British took pride in a parliamentary system that valued a tradition of freedom. British statesmen were not reluctant to point out to the rest of the world that Great Britain had achieved industrial growth without rending the social fabric.

The political rhetoric of stability and calm was undoubtedly exaggerated. Great Britain at mid-century had its share of serious social problems. British slums rivaled any in Europe. Poverty, disease, and famine ravaged the kingdom. Many feared that British social protests of the 1840s would result in upheavals similar to those in continental Europe. Yet Great Britain avoided a revolution. One explanation for Britain's relative calm lay in the shared political tradition that emphasized liberty as the birthright of English citizens. Building on an established political culture, the British Parliament was able to adapt to the demands of an industrializing society. Adaptation was gradual, but as slow as it seemed, a compromise was achieved among competing social interests. The great compromise of Victorian society was the reconciliation of industrialists' commitment to unimpeded growth with workers' need for the protection of the state.

The British political system was democratized slowly after 1832. The Reform Bill of that year gave increased political power to the industrial and manufacturing bourgeoisie, who joined a landed aristocracy and merchant class. The property qualification meant that only 20 percent of the population was able to vote. The next step toward democracy was not taken for another thirty-five years. In 1867, under conservative leadership a second Reform Bill was introduced. Approval of this bill doubled the electorate, giving the vote to a new urban population of shopkeepers, clerks, and workers. In 1884, farm laborers were enfranchised. Women, however, remained disenfranchised; they were granted the vote only after World War I. Through parliamentary cooperation between Liberals and Conservatives, the male franchise was slowly implemented without a revolution.

The lives and careers of two men, William Ewart Gladstone (1809–98) and Benjamin Disraeli (1804–81) exemplify well the particular path the British government followed in maintaining social peace. Rivals and political opponents, both men served as prime ministers and both left their mark on the age. From different political perspectives, they contributed to British reform in the second half of the nineteenth century.

This painting by Alfred Morgan of Gladstone riding in an omnibus is titled One of the People. *This mode of transport was thought of as a social leveler because all classes of people could afford the fares.*

William Gladstone was an example of a British statesman with no counterpart elsewhere in Europe: he was a classical liberal who believed in free enterprise and was opposed to state intervention. Good government, according to Gladstone, should remove obstacles to talent, competition, and individual initiative but should interfere as little as possible in economy and society. Surprisingly, this leader of the Liberal party began his long parliamentary career at the other end of the political spectrum as a Tory. The son of a successful merchant and slave trader, Gladstone enjoyed the benefits of wealth and attended Eton and Oxford, where he studied classics and mathematics. Discouraged by his father from a career in the Church of England, Gladstone used his connections to launch a parliamentary career in 1832. He gradually left behind his conservative opposition to parliamentary reform and his support of protective tariffs. In 1846 as a member of the government, Gladstone broke with Tory principles and voted in favor of free trade. The best government, he affirmed in true liberal fashion, was the one that governed least.

Those who knew Gladstone in these early years were struck not by his brilliance but by his capacity for hard work and assiduous application to the task at hand. He chopped wood for relaxation. In his spare time he wrote a three-volume study on Homer and the Homeric age. He practiced an overt morality, and targeted prostitutes in the hope of convincing them to change their lives. Gladstone was not blind to social problems, but he considered private philanthropy the best way to correct them.

Many of the significant advances of the British liberal state were achieved during Gladstone's first term as prime minister (1868–74). Taking advantage of British prosperity, Gladstone abolished tariffs, cut defense expenditures, lowered taxes, and sponsored sound budgets. He furthered the liberal agenda by disestablishing the Anglican church in Ireland in 1869. The Church had been the source of great resentment to the vast majority of Irish Catholics, who had been forced to pay taxes to support the Protestant state church.

Gladstone reformed the army, in disrepute after its poor performance in the Crimea, so that one could no longer purchase a commission. Training and merit would justify all future advancements. Similarly, Gladstone reformed the civil service system by separating it from political influence and seniority. Merit and examinations were intended to ensure the most efficient and effective system of government administration. The secret ballot was introduced to prevent coercion in voting. Finally, the Liberals stressed the importance of education for an informed electorate and passed an Education Act that aimed to make elementary schooling available to everyone.

These reforms added up to a Liberal philosophy of government. Liberal government was, above all, an attack on privilege. It sought to remove restraints on individual freedom and to foster opportunity and talent. Liberal government sought to protect democracy through education. Voting men must be educated men. As one Liberal put it, "We must educate our masters." Liberals governed in the interests of the bourgeoisie and with the belief that what was good for capitalism was good for society. Tariffs were, therefore, kept low or eliminated to promote British commerce. At base, Gladstone believed that all political questions were moral questions and that fairness and justice could solve political problems. In spite of his moral claims, his programs made him enemies among special interests, including farmers and the Church of England, because his policies undermined their protection and privileges.

During these years another political philosophy also left its mark on British government. This was conservatism. Under the flamboyant leadership of Benjamin Disraeli, the Conservative party supported state intervention and regulation on behalf of the weak and disadvantaged. Disraeli sponsored the Factory Act of 1875, which set a maximum of fifty-six hours on the factory work week. The Public Health Act established a sanitary code. The Artisans Dwelling Act defined minimum housing standards. Probably the most important conservative legislation was the Trade Union Act, which permitted picketing and other peaceful labor tactics.

Disraeli's personal background and training were very different from Gladstone's and made him unique in British parliamentary politics. He was known primarily as a novelist, social critic, and failed financier before he entered the political arena in 1837. His father was a Jewish mer-

Benjamin Disraeli

chant descended from a family of Spanish refugees in Venice. Disraeli senior became a British subject in 1801, three years before Benjamin's birth. In embracing English culture, the senior Disraeli had his children baptized in the Anglican church.

The split between Disraeli and Gladstone was clearly apparent in 1846 when they, both Tories, disagreed over the issue of free trade versus tariffs. Disraeli moved on to champion protection and through the early 1860s consistently opposed Gladstone's financial system. Unlike the Liberals, Disraeli insisted on the importance of traditional institutions like the monarchy, the House of Lords, and the Church of England. Queen Victoria named him the First Earl of Beaconsfield for his strong foreign policy and social reforms. "Dizzy's" real cleverness and contribution to British politics was in an area that few contemporaries appreciated at the time. Disraeli's work in organizing a national party machinery facilitated the adaptation of the parliamentary system to mass politics. His methods of campaigning and building a mass base of support were used by successful politicians regardless of political persuasion.

The terms *liberal* and *conservative* hold none of the meaning today that they did for men and women in the nineteenth century. Classical liberalism has little in common with its twentieth-century counterpart, which favors an active, interventionist state. Disraeli is a far more likely candidate for the twentieth-century liberal label than is Britain's leading nineteenth-century liberal statesman. Disraeli placed value in the ability of the state to correct and protect. Because of his interventionist philosophy, he may be compared with Continental statesmen like Bismarck and Napoleon III.

In spite of Liberal hopes, Great Britain never had a purely laissez-faire economy. As the intersecting careers of Gladstone and Disraeli demonstrate, the British model combined free enterprise with intervention and regulation. The clear issues and the clear choices of the two great parties—Liberal and Conservative—dominated parliamentary life after mid-century. In polarizing parliamentary politics, they also invigorated it.

Reforming Russia

In 1850 Russia was an unreformed autocracy, a form of government in which the tsar held absolute power. Without a parliament, without a constitution, and without civil liberties for its subjects, the Russian ruler governed through a bureaucracy and a police force. Economically, Russia was a semifeudal agrarian state with a class of privileged aristocrats supported by serf labor on their estates.

For decades—since the reign of Alexander I (1801–25)—the tsars and their advisers realized that they were out of step with developments in western Europe. An awareness was growing that serfdom was uncivilized and morally wrong. The remnants of feudalism had been swept away in France in the Great Revolution at the end of the eighteenth century. Prussia had abolished hereditary serfdom beginning in 1806. Among the European powers, only Russia remained a serf-holding nation. Russian serfs were tied to the land and owed dues and labor services in return for the

This satiric engraving by Gustave Doré, made in 1854, points up the callousness of Russian landowners. Masters hard-pressed for cash are seen betting their serfs on the turn of a card at the gaming table.

lands they held. Peasant protests mounted, attracting public attention to the plight of the serfs. A Russian aristocrat, Baron N. Wrangel (1847–1920), recounted in his memoirs a story from his childhood in the 1850s, when he was about ten years old, that exemplifies the growing social awareness of the problem:

> One day we were sitting quietly on the terrace listening to the reading aloud of *Uncle Tom's Cabin*, a [recently translated] book that was then in fashion. My sisters could not get over the horrors of slavery and wept at the sad fate of poor Uncle Tom. "I cannot conceive," said one of them, "how such atrocities can be tolerated. Slavery is horrible." "But," said Bunny, in her shrill little voice, "we have slaves too."

In spite of growing moral concern, there were many reasons to resist the abolition of serfdom. Granting freedom to all serfs was a vastly complicated affair. How were serf-holders to be compensated for the loss of labor power? What was to be the freed serf's relationship to the land? Personal freedom would be worthless without a land allotment. Yet landowners opposed loss of land as strongly as loss of their work force. A landless work force would be a serious social threat, if western European experience could be taken as an example.

Hesitation about abolition evaporated with the Russian defeat in the Crimean War. The new tsar, Alexander II (1855–81), viewed Russia's inability to repel an invasion force on its own soil as proof of its backwardness. Russia had no railroads and was forced to transport military supplies by carts to the Crimea. It took Moscow three months to provision troops, while the enemy could do so in three weeks. Alexander II believed in taking matters into his own hands. Russia must be reformed. Abolition of serfdom would permit a well-trained reserve army to exist without fear of rebellion. Liberating the serfs would also create a system of free labor so necessary for industrial development. Alexander interpreted rumblings within his own country as the harbinger of future upheavals similar to those that had rocked France and the Austrian Empire. He explained to the Muscovite nobility, "It is better to abolish serfdom from above than to wait until the serfs begin to liberate themselves from below."

In March 1861 the tsar signed the emancipation edict that liberated the serfs. Serfdom was eliminated in Poland three years later. Alexander II, who came to be known as the "Tsar-Liberator," compromised between landlord and serf by allotting land to freed peasants, while requiring from the former serfs redemption payments that were spread out over a period of forty-nine years. The peasant paid the state in installments; the state reimbursed the landowner in lump sums. To guarantee repayment, the land was not granted directly to individual peasants but to the village commune (*mir*), which was responsible for collecting redemption payments.

Emancipation of the serfs, Alexander's greatest achievement, was a reform of unprecedented scale. It affected 52 million peasants, over 20 million of them enserfed to private landowners. By comparison, Abraham Lincoln's Emancipation Proclamation less than two years later freed 4 million American slaves. Beneath the surface of the Russian liberation, peasants soon realized, however, that the repayment schedule increased their burdens and responsibilities. The peasants resented being forced to pay for land they considered rightfully theirs. An old peasant saying reflected this belief: "We are yours"—they acknowledged to the landlords—"but the land is ours." It was not an accident that the *mir* arrangement prevented mobility; Alexander had no intention of creating a floating proletariat similar to that of western Europe. He wanted his people closely tied to the land—but freed of the servility of feudal obligations.

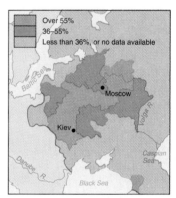

Russian Serfs

Over 55%
36–55%
Less than 36%, or no data available

The abolition of serfdom did not solve the problem of Russian backwardness. Farming methods and farming implements remained primitive. Russian agriculture did not become more productive. Nor did emancipation result in a contented and loyal peasantry. Frustrations festered. A large proportion of peasants received too little land to make their redemption payments.

Many peasants in the south received smaller plots of land than they had farmed under serfdom. The commune replaced the landowner in a system of peasant bondage. Redemption payments were finally abolished in 1907, but not before exacerbating social tensions in the countryside.

The real winner in the abolition of serfdom was not the landowners and certainly not the peasantry, but the state. A bureaucratic hierarchy and a financial infrastructure were expanded. Other reforms in the system of credit and banking contributed significantly to rapid economic growth. With the help of foreign—especially French—investment, railway construction increased dramatically from 660 miles of track in 1855 to 14,000 by 1880. Thanks in large part to the new transportation network, Russia became a world grain supplier during this period, with exports increasing threefold. But development was uneven and remained uncoordinated. The coexistence of the old alongside the new combined with the speed of change created friction and promised future unrest.

Alexander II, a man conservative by temperament but aware that Russia must move forward, did not stop here. In 1864 he introduced *zemstvos*, local elected assemblies, on the provincial and county levels, to govern local affairs. The three classes of landowners, townspeople, and peasants elected representatives who were responsible for implementing educational, health, and other social welfare reforms. Similar statutes governing towns were passed in 1870. In the spirit of modernization the state also undertook judicial reforms. New provincial courts were opened in 1866. Corporal punishment was to be eliminated. Separate courts for peasants still endured, however, preserving the impression that peasants were a lower class of citizens subject to special jurisdiction.

With the military triumph of Prussia over France in 1870–71, the tsar found the excuse he had been looking for in the 1860s to push through fundamental military reforms. Alexander II had admired the Prussian military model since his childhood. In 1874 he used that model to require that all young men on reaching the age of twenty be eligible for conscription in "defense of the fatherland." Fifteen years of service were specified but only six were served in active duty. This was a

significant reduction from the twenty-five years of active service that peasant and lower-class conscripts had formerly served. Although length of service was reduced according to educational level, the military reforms were, on the whole, democratizing because they eliminated an important privilege of the wealthy.

In spite of this vast array of "Great Reforms"—emancipating the serfs, creating local parliamentary bodies, reorganizing the judiciary, modernizing the army—Russia was not sufficiently liberalized or democratized to satisfy the critics of autocracy. Between 1860 and 1870 a young generation of intelligentsia, radical intellectuals who benefited from the democratization in education and were influenced by the rhetoric of revolution in the West, assumed a critical stance in protest against the existing order. Although not itself a class, many members of the intelligentsia shared a similar background as the student sons and daughters of petty officials or priests. Young women, who often sought the education in Switzerland that was denied to them at home, were especially active in supporting ideas of emancipation.

In 1873 the imperial government considered the Western liberal and socialist ideas of the intelligentsia so threatening that it ordered Russian students studying in Switzerland to return home. Many returning students combined forces with radical intellectuals in Russia and decided to "go to the people." About 2,500 educated young men and women traveled from village to village to educate, to help, and in some cases to attempt to radicalize the peasants. These populist crusaders sought to learn from what they considered to be the source of all morality and justice, the Russian peasantry. They paid dearly for what proved to be a fruitless commitment to populism in the mass trials and repression of the late 1870s.

Some of the tsarist regime's critics fled into exile to reemerge as revolutionaries in western Europe, where they continued to oppose the tsarist regime and helped shape the tradition of revolution and dissent in Western countries. Other educated men and women who remained in Russia chose violence as the only effective weapon against absolute rule. Terrorists who called themselves "Will of the People" decided on assassination as the best strategy and condemned the tsar to death. In the "emperor hunt" which followed, numerous attempts were made on the tsar's life. Miraculously Alexander II escaped even the bombing of his own living quarters in the Winter Palace. The tsarist state responded with stricter controls, but repression only fanned the flames of discontent.

In response to attempts on his life and the assassination of public officials intended to cripple the central regime, Alexander II put the brakes on reform in the second half of his reign. The Great Reforms could not be undone, however, and had set in motion sweeping economic and social changes. The state encouraged capitalist growth and witnessed the rise of a professional middle class and the formation of an embryonic factory proletariat. Serfdom was dead forever. Yet reforms had increased expectations for an equally dramatic political transformation that failed to materialize. In the end, the "Will of the People" movement succeeded in its mission. A terrorist bomb killed Alexander II, the "Tsar-Liberator," in St. Petersburg in 1881.

The Politics of Leadership

Modern politics emerged in Europe only after 1850. Until that time traditional political categories prevailed. When faced with revolutionary upheavals, regimes aimed for stability and permanence. Only after 1850 did a new breed of political leaders appear who understood the world of politics and directed it to their own ends. Three statesmen typify the new approach to the public world of power: Camillo di Cavour, Otto von Bismarck, and Louis Napoleon.

In old regime Europe, power flowed downward from the monarch perched atop a hierarchically organized social system that was often depicted as a pyramid. The source of royal power was both timeless and historic. As God's appointed agents, the sovereigns of Europe reinforced their right to rule with the continuity of their dynasties. Men of great political acumen ministered to their royal masters and were legitimated by royal power. In the years between 1789 and 1850 this system was challenged, as kings were displaced, sometimes restored to power,

sometimes executed. In the Austrian Empire, Spain, France, the Low Countries, Italy, and the German states, kingship, even when accepted, no longer went unquestioned. Divine authority was an archaic idea to the growing numbers of those who spoke of democratic principles and rallied to banners that represented new concepts of liberty and equality.

In the first half of the nineteenth century, men and women had learned that those in power could be questioned. The good of the people was the primary justification for government. Power now flowed upward from the citizenry to their appointed and elected representatives. The new power brokers were those who could control and direct the flow, not merely be carried along or swept away by it. These new political men were realists in the same tradition as Machiavelli and reflected the new political culture of the nineteenth century.

Political realists like Cavour, Bismarck, and Louis Napoleon understood the importance of public opinion. Public opinion had been a central fact of political life from the eighteenth century, but as revolutionary events in France demonstrated, public opinion proved unreliable building material for a stable government. The new political leaders appreciated public opinion for what it was—an unreliable guide for policymaking, often a dangerous beast that must be controlled and tamed. But above all, it was a tool in the shaping of consensus, the molding of support. The new political realists understood also the power of the press. Cavour achieved first prominence and then power by founding his own newspaper, *Il Risorgimento.* Louis Napoleon ran Europe's first modern political campaign, manipulating the printed word to shape his image and tailor his message to different audiences. Bismarck used public opinion and fashioned an image of German power that served his political ends.

The new political men also shared, to varying degrees, a disregard for traditional morality in decision-making. They were often politically amoral, willing to use whatever methods guaranteed success. As Bismarck succinctly put it, at the end of his long career in public life, "Politics ruins the character." Machiavelli, too, shared this dis-

This cartoon from the London News, 1848, *shows newsboys selling election broadsides for Louis Napoleon and his opponent, General Cavignac. The boys are fighting over the merits of their respective candidates.*

leaned toward liberal ideas, while Bismarck was unquestionably conservative, and Louis Napoleon held a blend of liberal and conservative views. Yet they willingly enacted similar policies and sponsored similar legislation, not from any shared political commitment, but because of their desire to strengthen and promote their national entities. In order to maintain power, they adapted to circumstance; they did not insist on principle. As Bismarck explained it, he always had more than one arrow in his quiver.

Finally, the new political men were risk takers. They acted without the safety net of tradition or political legitimacy under them. Bismarck saw himself on a tightrope but one he felt prepared to walk. Just as Jeremy Bentham earlier in the century had figured the relationship between actions and outcomes in terms of profits and losses, the new statesmen were calculators; they weighed levels of risk appropriate for the ends they sought to achieve. *Realpolitik* was less the invention of a particular statesman and more a characteristic of the new age of gamesmanship in statecraft.

regard for traditional morality. The new political men forged their own standards by which they judged the correctness of decisions and policies. The nation-state was the supreme justification for all actions. Cavour, Bismarck, and Louis Napoleon saw struggle as the central fact of life. Nation-states were inherently competitive, with conflicting objectives. *Realpolitik* meant that statesmen had to think in terms of military capability, technological dominance, and the acceptable use of force. Without a traditional morality of right and wrong, these leaders recognized that there could be no arbiter outside the interests of the nation-state. From exile in England following his military defeat and his abdication, Napoleon III placed the welfare of France above his failed ambitions. At the former emperor's funeral, his son led a cheer not for the empire but for France.

Modern European statesmen did not, however, share a common ideological outlook. Cavour

Changing Values and the Force of New Ideas

Like the political world, the material world was changing rapidly after 1850. The world of ideas that explained the place of women and men in this new universe was rapidly changing as well. The railroad journey became the metaphor for the new age. The locomotive hurtling forward signified the strength, power, and progress of materialism. Yet the passenger was strangely dislocated, the intervening landscape between one point and another a blur seen through a carriage window. New points of reference must be found; new roots must be put down. In the period between 1850 and 1870 a materialist system of values emerged, as behaviors changed. This was as true for the private world of the home as it was for the public world of high politics.

In any age, changes in material life find their way into literature, philosophy, science, and art.

Changes in the environment affect the way people look at the world. In turn, intellectuals can have a profound effect on values and behavior. Truly great thinkers not only reflect their times; they also shape them. The third quarter of the nineteenth century was especially rich in both the creativity and critical stance that shaped modern consciousness. Amid the tumult of new ideas in the period after 1850, two titans stand out. Not artists, but scientists—one of biology, the other of society—they sought regularity and predictability in the world they observed and measured. The ideas of Charles Darwin and Karl Marx both reflected and changed the world they lived in.

People alive during the third quarter of the nineteenth century called themselves "modern." They were, indeed, "modern," since in their values and view of the world they were closer to their twentieth-century progeny than they were to their eighteenth-century grandparents.

The Politics of Homemaking

At the Great Exhibition of 1851 in London the achievements of modern industry were proudly displayed for all the world to see. Engineering marvels and mechanistic wonders dwarfed the thousands of visitors who came to the Crystal Palace to view civilization at its most advanced. In the midst of the machinery of the factory, household items took their place. "Modern" kitchens with coal-burning stoves were showcased, and the artifacts of the ideal home were carefully displayed. Predictably, mechanical looms, symbols of the new age, were exhibited; but inkstands, artificial flowers, thermostats, and cooking utensils were also enshrined. Visitors did not find strange this juxtaposition of the public world of production with the private world of the home in an exhibition celebrating British superiority.

The world of the home, not immune from changes in society and the economy, was invested with new power and meaning in mid-nineteenth-century Europe. Home was glorified as the locus of shelter and comfort where the harsh outside world could be forgotten. In 1870 an article in a popular Victorian magazine explained that the home functioned as a haven: "Home is emphatically [man's] place of rest, where his wife is his friend who knows his mind, where he may be himself without fear of offending, and relax the strain that must be kept out of doors: where he may feel himself safe, understood, and at ease."

Throughout Europe, the home served another function as a symbol of status and achievement. Objects of a proper sort indicated wealth, upward mobility, and taste. In the belief that the more objects that could be displayed the better, the middle-class home of the third quarter of the nineteenth century was most often overdecorated. Drapes hung over doors and windows, pictures and prints covered the walls, and overstuffed furniture filled the rooms. All were intended to convey gentility and comfort.

Industrialization had separated the workplace from the home. Protective legislation before mid-century attempted to ease women out of the work force. Middle-class women were expected to assume primary responsibility for the domestic goals of escape and status. Just as the workplace was man's world, the private world of the home was woman's domain. After 1850 magazines, handbooks, and guidebooks that instructed women on how to fulfill their domestic duties proliferated. The most famous of the instruction manuals in Britain was Mrs. Beeton's *Book of Household Management* (1861). The title is instructive. The business concept of management could now be applied to the home. Mrs. Beeton told her readers, "The functions of the mistress of the house resemble those of the general of an army or the manager of a great business concern." "Home economics" was invented during this period. As the marketplace had its own rules and regulations that could be studied in the "dismal science" of economics, the domestic sphere too, women were told, could benefit from the application of rational principles of organization.

Women were also well informed by popular literature on how to get a man and keep him. Manuals cautioned women not to be too clever, since women with opinions were not popular with men. Mrs. Beeton's advice centered on food as the way to a man's heart. A wife's duty, she explained, was above all to provide her man with a hot meal, prepared well and served punctually. Meals became elaborate occasions of several

Sir W. S. Gilbert, the comic-opera librettist, indulged his sense of irony to debunk Victorian pretense and opulence with this cluttered rococo interior. The room was designed by Norman Shaw for Grimes Dyke, Gilbert's house at Busey in Hertfordshire.

courses requiring hours of work. Women's magazines bombarded a growing readership with menus and recipes for the careful housewife. Status was communicated not by expensive foods but by extravagant preparation. Meal-planning was an art, women learned, one whose practice required and assumed the assistance of household servants.

Before this time, women had produced in the home products they could now buy in the marketplace. Purchases of bread, beer, soap, and candles saved housewives hours of labor every week. But with rising expectations about the quality of life in the home, women had more rather than less to do each day. Handbooks prescribed rules on etiquette and proper manners. The rituals of domestic life from letter-writing to afternoon visits to serving tea were minutely detailed for middle-class audiences. The woman of the house was instructed in the care and education of her children, health, cleanliness, nutrition, and the management of resources. Thrift, industry, and orderliness, the virtues of the business world, had their own particular meaning in the domestic sphere.

To the Victorian mind, gentility and morality were inextricably interwoven. A woman who failed in her duty to maintain a clean and comfortable hearth threatened the safety of her family. An 1867 English tract warned: "The man who goes home on a Saturday only to find his house in disorder, with every article of furniture out of its place, the floor unwashed or sloppy from uncompleted washing, his wife slovenly, his children untidy, his dinner not yet ready, or spoilt in the cooking, is much more likely 'to go on a spree' than the man who finds his house in order, the furniture glistening from the recent polishing, the burnished steel fire-irons looking doubly resplendent from the bright glow of the cheerful fire, his well-cooked dinner laid on a snowy cloth, and his wife and children tidy and cheerful."

The ideal was very far from the experiences of most families throughout Europe after mid-century. The "science" of homemaking presupposed a cushion of affluence out of reach to the men, women, and children who made up the vast majority of the population. Working-class wives and mothers often had to earn wages if their families were to survive. One Englishwoman, Lucy Luck (1848–1922), began her working career in a silk mill at the age of eight. By law allowed to work only half a day, the child Lucy returned to

This female aboveground coal-mine worker was photographed in 1864 by Arthur J. Munby. Such women, who sorted the coal, had low status and no prospects. They were regarded as "unsexed, immoral Amazons."

her foster home at the end of her shift to labor late into the night plaiting straw for baskets. In her reminiscences, she looked back over her life: "I have been at work for forty-seven years, and have never missed one season, although I have a large family [of seven surviving children]." Lucy, who married at the age of eighteen, learned that on her own she could not survive with a man's income or without resorting to the "bad life" of crime and prostitution. In the marriage, the couple could not survive without Lucy's wages.

Like Lucy Luck, many women held jobs outside the home or did piecework to supplement the meager family incomes. In 1866 women constituted a significant percentage of the French labor force, including 45 percent of all textile workers. At the height of the rhetoric about the virtues of domesticity, as many as two married Englishwomen in five worked in the mills in industrial areas like Lancashire. Working women often chose the "sweated labor" that they could perform in their home because it allowed them to care for their children while being paid by the piece. Home workers labored in the needle trades, shoemaking, and furniture making in their cramped living quarters under miserable conditions; and they worked for a third or less of what men earned.

The "haven" of the home was not insulated from the perils of the outside world. Nor was every home a happy one. Venereal diseases rose dramatically in Western nations, belying the image of the devoted couple. By the end of the nineteenth century 14 to 17 percent of all deaths in France were attributable to sexually transmitted diseases. These diseases were blind to class distinctions. Illegitimacy rates rose in the first half of the nineteenth century and remained high after 1850 among the working classes, defying middle-class standards of propriety. Illegitimate births were highest in urban areas, where household life assumed its own distinctive pattern among working-class families, with couples often choosing free union instead of legal marriage.

Because virtue was defined in terms of woman's roles as wife and mother, working women were regarded as immoral. Social evils were, according to this reasoning, easily attributed to the "unnatural" phenomenon of women leaving the home to work in a man's world. Women continued to work and, in some cases, to organize to demand their rights. Women like Lucy Luck did not and could not accept the prescription that good mothers did not work, since her wages fed her children. The politics of homemaking defined women as mothers and hence legitimated the poor treatment and poor pay of women as workers. Yet the labor of women outside as well as inside the home remained the norm.

Nor did all middle-class women accept approved social roles. Increasing numbers of middle-class women in western Europe protested their circumscribed sphere. Critics argued that designating the home as woman's proper domain stifled individual development. Earlier in the century, Jane Austen (1775–1817), one of Britain's greatest novelists, had to keep a piece of muslin work on her writing table in the family drawing room to cover her papers lest visitors detect evidence of literary activity. In the next generation, Florence Nightingale (1820–1910) refused to accept the embroidery and knitting to which she was relegated at home. This period in Western society witnessed both the creation of the cult of domesticity and the stirrings of feminism among middle-class women, whose demand for equal treatment for women was to become more important after 1870. Patterns of behavior changed within the family, and they were not fixed immutably in social practice. Woman's place and woman's role proved to be much disputed questions in the new politics of homemaking.

The New World of Realism in the Arts

The term *realism* was first used in 1850 to describe the paintings of Gustave Courbet (1819–77), but the spirit of realism characterized a wide array of artistic endeavors. Realism in the arts and literature was a rejection of Romantic idealism and subjectivity. Realists responded to the disillusionment with the political failures of mid-century by withdrawing from politics. And they

The Stone Breakers, *by Gustave Courbet, 1849. This realistic painting of common laborers at their toil stirred violent protests at the Paris Salon of 1850. The subject matter was considered unworthy of the heroic size (more than five by seven feet) of the canvas. Proudhon, who wrote about it at length, saw the painting as an indictment of capitalism.*

responded directly to the challenges of urban and industrial growth by confronting the alienation of modern existence. In *The Artist's Studio* (1855) Courbet portrayed himself surrounded by the intellectuals and political figures of his day. He may have been painting a landscape but contemporary political life crowded in; a starving Irish peasant and her child crouch beneath his easel. Of his unrelenting canvases, none more fittingly portrays the harsh realism of bourgeois life than the funeral ceremony depicted in *Burial at Ornans* (1849–50) or the brutality of workers' lives than *Stone Breakers* (1849).

Idealization in Romantic literature yielded to novels depicting the objective and unforgiving social world after mid-century. Through serialization in journals and newspapers, fiction reached out to mass audiences, who got their "facts" about modern life through stories that often cynically portrayed the monotony and boredom of daily existence. In *Hard Times* (1854), set in the imaginary city of Coketown, Charles Dickens (1812–70) creates an allegory that exposes the sterility and soullessness of industrial society through "fact, fact, fact everywhere in the material aspect of the town; fact, fact, fact everywhere in the immaterial."

Gustave Flaubert (1821–80), the great French Realist novelist, critiqued the Western intellectual tradition in his unfinished *Dictionary of Accepted Ideas* (1881). In the novel *Bouvard et Pécuchet* (1881) Flaubert satirized modern man's applications of Enlightenment ideas about the environment and progress by showing that they are foolish and often at odds with common sense. The main characters of the novel know everything there is to know about theories and applied sciences but they know nothing about life. His best known work, *Madame Bovary* (1856), recounts the story of a young country doctor's wife whose desire to escape from the boredom of her provincial existence leads her into adultery and results eventually in her destruction. Flaubert was put on trial for obscenity and violating public morality with his tale of the unrepentant Emma Bovary. This beautifully crafted novel is marked by an ironic detachment from the hypocrisy of bourgeois life. Mary Ann Evans (1819–80), writing under the pseudonymn George Eliot, was also concerned with moral choices and responsibilities in novels like *Middlemarch* (1871–72), a tale of provincial English life considered to be her greatest work.

The problem of morality in the Realist novel is nowhere more apparent than in the works of the Russian writer Fyodor Dostoyevsky (1821–81). Dostoyevsky's protagonists wrestle with a universe where God no longer exists and where they must shape their own morality. The impoverished student Raskolnikov in *Crime and Punishment* (1866) justifies his brutal murder of an old woman that occurs in the opening pages of the novel. Realist art and literature addressed an educated and elite public but did not flinch before the unrelenting poverty and harshness of contemporary life. The morality of the Realist vision lay not in condemning the evils of modern life and seeking their political solutions, as an earlier generation of Romantics did, but in depicting social evils for what they were, failures of a smug and progressive middle class.

Charles Darwin and the New Science

Science had a special appeal to a generation of Europeans disillusioned with the political failures of idealism in the revolutions of 1848. This was not an age of great scientific discovery but one of synthesis of previous findings and their technological applications. Science was, above all, to be useful in promoting material progress.

Charles Darwin (1809–82), the preeminent scientist of the age, was a great synthesizer. Darwin began his scientific career as a naturalist with a background in geology. As a young man, he sailed around the world on the *Beagle* (1831–36). He collected specimens and fossils as the ship's naturalist, with his greatest finds in South America and especially the Galapagos Islands. He spent the next twenty years of his life taking notes of his observations of the natural world. In chronically poor health, Darwin produced five hundred pages of what he called "one long argument." *On the Origin of Species by Means of Natural Selection* (1859) was a book that changed the world.

Darwin's argument was a simple one: life forms originated in and perpetuated themselves through struggle. The outcome of this struggle was determined by "natural selection," or what came to be known as "survival of the fittest." Better adapted individuals survived, while others died out. Competition between species and within species produced a dynamic model of organic evolution. Darwin did not use the word *evolution* in the original edition, but a positivist belief in an evolutionary process permeated the 1859 text.

Evolutionary theory was not new. Nor was materialism a new concept in organic biology. In the 1850s, others were coming forward with similar ideas about natural selection, including most notably A. R. Wallace (1823–1913), who stressed geographic factors in biological evolution. Darwin's work was a product of discoveries in a variety of fields—philosophy, history, and science. He derived his idea of struggle from Malthus' *Essay on Population* and borrowed across disciplines to construct a theory of "the preservation of favored races in the struggle for life" (part of the book's subtitle). The publication of *Origin of Species* made Darwin immediately famous. Scientific theory was the stuff of front-page headlines. Like Samuel Smiles, a businessman who published the best-seller *Self-Help* in 1860, Darwin spoke of struggle and discipline, although in nature, not in the marketplace. In the world of biology, Darwin's ideas embodied a new Realist belief in progress based on struggle. Force explained the past and would guarantee the future, as the fittest survived. These were ideas that a general public found applicable to a whole range of human endeavors and to theories of social organization.

Karl Marx and the Science of Society

"Just as Darwin discovered the law of development of organic nature, Marx discovered the law of development of human history." So spoke Friedrich Engels (1820–95), longtime friend of and collaborator with Karl Marx (1818–83), over Marx' grave. Marx would have been pleased with Engels' eulogy: he called himself the Darwin of

Kit's Writing Lesson, *by Robert Martineau, was inspired by the mid-Victorian self-help movement. The major proponent of self-help was Samuel Smiles, whose writings emphasized the moral and economic advantages of self-improvement and self-reliance as opposed to dependence on others.*

sociology. Marx footnoted as corroborating evidence Darwin's "epoch-making work on the origin of the species" in his own masterwork, *Das Kapital*, the first volume of which appeared in 1867. As the theorist of the socialism which he called "scientific," Marx viewed himself as an evolutionist who demonstrated that history is the dialectical struggle of classes.

Engels first encountered Marx in Paris. It was a meeting of kindred spirits. One German author was seeking out the other. Engels had just written *The Condition of the Working Classes in England in 1844*. Marx was an iconoclast. The son of a Prussian lawyer who had converted from Judaism

to Christianity, Marx rejected the study of the law and belief in a deity. In exile because of his political writings, Marx was the most brilliant of the German young Hegelians, philosophers heavily influenced by the ideas of Georg Friedrich Hegel (1770–1831), which held sway over the German intellectual world of the 1830s and 40s. By the mid-1840s, Marx was in rebellion against Hegel's idealism and was developing his own materially grounded view of society. When Engels and Marx first met, they talked daily for two weeks about their common concern with social injustice and the struggles of the poor. Their momentous encounter was the beginning of a lifelong collaboration.

Engels was a wealthy German businessman whose father owned factories in Manchester, England. When Marx was expelled from France in 1847 on the request of the Prussian government, Engels financed his move to London, where he eventually took up permanent residence in 1849. While Karl Marx studied in the main reading room of the British Museum, Engels paid for the Marx family's expenses, bailed them out in hard times, and even assumed responsibility for Marx' illegitimate son, whose mother was the family maid. Karl Marx, who was to become the foremost critic of the capitalist system, joked self-disparagingly that he could not survive without Engels, since he did not know how to manage money.

The philosophy that evolved in these years of collaboration with Engels was built on a materialist view of society. Human beings were not defined by their souls but by their labor. Labor was a struggle to transform nature by producing commodities useful for survival. Their ability to transform nature by work differentiated men and women from animals. Building on this fundamental concept of labor, Marx and Engels saw society as divided into two camps: those who own property and those who do not. Nineteenth-century capitalist society was divided into two classes: the bourgeoisie, those who owned the means of production as its private property, and the proletariat, the propertyless working class.

This materialist perspective on society was the engine driving Marx' theory of history. For Marx, every social system based on a division into classes carries within it the seeds of its own destruction. Marx and Engels used a biological metaphor to explain this destruction. The growth of a plant from a seed is a dialectical process in

This illustration by Gustave Doré appeared in The Condition of the Working Class in England *by Friedrich Engels. Small and cramped industrial working-class houses with their tiny, walled back yards are framed by railway lines.*

which the germ is destroyed by its opposite, the plant. The mature plant produces seed while continuing its form. The different stages of history are determined by different forms of the ownership of production. In a feudal-agrarian society, the aristocracy controlled and exploited the unfree labor of serfs. In a world of commerce and manufacturing, the capitalist bourgeoisie are the new aristocracy exploiting free labor for wages.

Marx was more than an observer: he was a critic of capitalism. His labor theory of value was the wedge he drove into the self-congratulatory rhetoric of the capitalist age. Labor is the source of all value, he argued, and yet the bourgeois employer denies workers the profit of their work by refusing to pay them a decent wage. Instead, he pockets the profits. Workers are separated or *alienated* from the product of their labor. But more profoundly, in a capitalist system all workers are alienated from the creation that makes them human, they are alienated from their labor.

Marx predicted that capitalism would produce more and more goods but would continue to pay workers the lowest wages possible. By driving out smaller producers, the bourgeoisie will increase the size of the proletariat. Yet Marx was optimistic. As workers are slowly pauperized, they will become conscious of their exploitation and they will revolt. The force of these ideas mobilized thousands of contemporaries aware of the injustices of capitalism. Few thinkers in the history of the West have left a more lasting legacy than Karl Marx. The legacy survived the fact that much of his analysis rested on incorrect predictions about the increasing misery of workers and the inflexibility of the capitalist system.

Karl Marx was a synthesizer who combined economics, philosophy, politics, and history in a wide-ranging critique of industrial society. Marxism spread across Europe as workers responded to its message. Marx did not cause the increase in the organization of workers that took place in the 1860s, but his theories did give shape and focus to a growing critique of labor relations in the second half of the nineteenth century. Political parties throughout Europe coalesced around Marxist beliefs and programs. Marxists were beginning to be heard in associations of workers, and they helped found the International Working Men's Association in London in 1864, an organization of French, German, and Italian workers dedicated to "the end of all class rule." The promise of a common association of workers transcending national boundaries became a compelling idea to those who envisioned the end of capitalism. The importance of the international exchange of ideas and information cannot be underestimated as a means of promoting labor organization in western Europe. In 1871 Marx and his followers turned to Paris for proof that the revolution was at hand.

A New Revolution? The Siege of Paris and the Commune

Soundly defeated on 2 September 1870, Napoleon III and his fighting force of 100,000 men became Prussia's prisoners of war. With the emperor's defeat, the Second Empire collapsed. But even with the capture of Napoleon III, the French capital city of Paris refused to capitulate. The dedication of Parisians to the ongoing war with the Prussians was evident from the first. The regime's liberal critics in Paris seized the initiative to proclaim France a republic. If a corrupt and decadent empire could not save the nation, then France's Third Republic could.

In mid-September 1870 two German armies surrounded Paris and began a siege that lasted for over four months. Only carrier pigeons and balloon-transported passengers linked Paris with the rest of France. In the beginning Parisian heroism, unchallenged by battle, seemed festive and unreal. Bismarck's troops were intent on bringing the city to its knees not by fighting but by cutting off its vital supply lines. By November, food and fuel were dwindling and Parisians were facing starvation. Undaunted, they began to eat dogs, cats, and rats. By December, famine threatened to become a reality. Most people had no vegetables and no meat. Rationing was ineffective and a black market prevailed in which the wealthy could buy whatever was available. Horses disappeared from the streets and the zoo was emptied as antelope, camel, donkey, mule, and elephant became desirable table fare. The Bois de Boulogne, the city's largest park, was leveled for timber to build barricades and for fuel. But the wood was too green and would not burn. The

Interior of a meat market in Paris during the siege of 1870–71. Food shortages were taking their toll, as the sign advertising dog and cat meat attests.

bitter cold of one of the century's most severe winters heightened the horror.

Yet the population was committed to fighting on. Men and women became part of the city's citizen militia, the National Guard, and trained for combat against the Germans. "Siege fever" swept the city. In spite of dire conditions, there were moments of euphoria. Collective delusions, perhaps intensified by empty stomachs, convinced Parisians they were invincible against the enemy. Citizens joined clubs to discuss politics and preparedness and probably to keep warm. Patents on inventions to defeat the Germans proliferated. Most of them were useless and silly, like the musical machine gun that was intended to lure its victims within firing range. The enemy at their gates absorbed the total attention of the urban population. There was no life other than the war.

Apparently with the goal of terrorizing the population, the Germans began a steady bombardment of the city at the beginning of January 1871. The shells fell for three weeks but Parisian resistance prevailed. But the rest of France wanted an end to the war. The Germans agreed to an armistice at the end of January 1871 in order that French national elections could be held to elect representatives to the new government. In the elections, French citizens outside Paris repudiated the war and returned an overwhelmingly conservative majority to seek peace.

Thus, the siege came to an end. Yet it left deep wounds that still festered. Parisians felt they had been betrayed by the rest of France. Through four months as a besieged city, they had sacrificed, suffered, and died. Parisians believed that they were defenders of the true republic, the true patriots. Among Parisians, disparities of wealth were more obvious than ever before. Some wealthy citizens had abandoned the city during the siege. The wealthy who stayed ate and kept warm. Poor women who stood in food lines from before dawn every day to provision their families knew that there was food—but not for them.

The war was over but Paris was not at peace. The new national government, safely installed outside Paris at Versailles, attempted to reestablish normal life. The volatility of the city motivated the government's attempt in March 1871 to disarm the Parisian citizenry by using army troops. In the hilly neighborhood of northern Paris, men, women, and children poured into the streets to protect their cannons and to defend their right to bear arms. In the fighting that followed the Versailles troops were driven from the city. Paris was in a state of siege once again.

The spontaneity of the March uprising was soon succeeded by organization. Citizens rallied to the idea of the city's self-government and established the Paris Commune, as other French cities followed the capital's lead. Karl Marx hailed this event as the beginning of the revolution that would overthrow the capitalist system and saw in it the beginning of the dictatorship of the proletariat. But what occurred between March and May 1871 was not a proletarian revolution. It was rather a continuation of the state of siege that had held Paris through the fall and early winter months. Parisians were still at war. It was not war against a foreign enemy, nor was it a class war. It was a civil war against the rest of France.

The social experiment of self-defense in the Commune lasted for seventy-two days, as armed women formed their own fighting units, the city council regulated labor relations, and neighborhoods ruled themselves. In May 1871, government troops reentered the city and brutally crushed the Paris Commune. In one "Bloody Week" 25,000 Parisians were massacred and 40,000 others were arrested and tried. Of the 10,000 rebels convicted, 5,000 were sent to a penal colony in the southwestern Pacific Ocean. Such reprisals inflamed radicals and workers all over Europe. The myth of the Commune became a rallying cry for revolutionary movements throughout the world and inspired the future leaders of the Russian revolutionary state.

The Commune was important at the time but not as a revolution. It offered two lessons to men and women at the end of the third quarter of the nineteenth century. First, it demonstrated the power of patriotism. Competing images of the nation were at stake, one Parisian, the other French, but no one could deny the power of national identity to mobilize a whole city to suffer and to sacrifice. Second, the Commune made clear the power of the state. No revolutionary movement could succeed without controlling the

massive forces of repression at the state's command. The Commune had tried to recapture a local, federal view of the world but failed to take sufficient account of the power of the state that it opposed. In writing of this lesson two decades later, Friedrich Engels wondered if revolution would ever again be possible in the West.

Western societies had crossed the threshold into the modern age in the third quarter of the nineteenth century. Strong states from Great Britain to Russia were committed to creating and preserving the conditions of industrial expansion. The machine age, railroads, and metallurgy were spreading industrial development much more widely through western and central Europe than had been possible before 1850. Italians and Prussians, in attempting to join the ranks of nation-states, realized that the road to a strong nation could only be achieved with industrial development and social reforms.

State-building in Western societies went hand in hand with the growth in the social responsibilities of government. The national powers that would dominate world politics and economy in

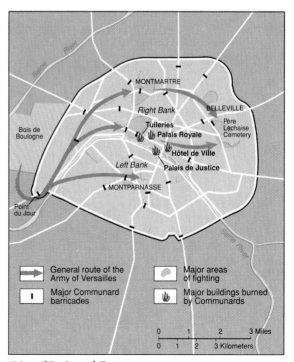

Seige of Paris and Commune

the twentieth century all underwent modernizing transitions in the 1860s. These included the United States, France, Great Britain, and Germany. The Austrian Empire, too, undertook programs to modernize its government and economy; and the Russian Empire established social reforms of unparalleled dimensions. New nations came into existence in this period through the limited use of armed force. With the establishment of the German Empire, Otto von Bismarck, the most realistic of politicians, was intent on preserving the peace in Europe by balancing the power of the great European states. Europeans prided themselves on being both modern and realistic in the third quarter of the nineteenth century. Peace was possible if it was armed and vigilant. Reform, not revolution, many were sure, was the key to the future progress of European societies.

Suggestions for Further Reading

Building Nations: The Politics of Unification

Derek Beales, *The Risorgimento and the Unification of Italy* (London: George Allen & Unwin Ltd., 1982). Drawing a distinction between unification and national revival, Beales situates the period of unification within the larger process of the cultural and political revival.

Gordon A. Craig, *Germany, 1866–1945* (New York: Oxford University Press, 1978). This synthetic view of German history provides a thorough examination of German unification. Craig analyzes all aspects of imperial development with special attention to the institutional framework, its politics, economy, and diplomacy.

Denis Mack Smith, *Cavour* (London: Weidenfeld and Nicolson, 1985). Smith contrasts Cavour and his policies to Garibaldi and Mazzini and attends to the challenge of regionalism in the unification process.

James J. Sheehan, *German Liberalism in the Nineteenth Century* (Chicago: University of Chicago Press, 1978). Explores the problems of transferring Western liberalism to Germany by examining the origins of German liberalism, the revolutions of 1848, and the politics of the Bismarckian state.

Reforming European Society

David Pinkney, *Napoleon III and the Rebuilding of Paris* (Princeton: Princeton University Press, 1972). Describes how Paris was transformed into the monumental city that became not only a manifestation of French culture, but also a symbol of European culture as a whole. The planning, financing, and building of Napoleon III's Paris are analyzed, as is the impact of the rebuilding on the city's residents.

Alain Plessis, *The Rise and Fall of the Second Empire, 1852–1871*, translated by Jonathan Mandelbaum (Cambridge: Cambridge University Press, 1985). Discusses the Second Empire as an important transitional period in French history, when the conflict was between traditional and modern values in political, economic, and social transformations.

W. H. C. Smith, *Second Empire and Commune: France, 1848–1871* (London: Longman, 1985). Places the reign of Louis Napoleon in its domestic and international context and argues that the Empire was destroyed by external forces.

H. Seton Watson, *The Russian Empire, 1801–1917* (Oxford: The Clarendon Press, 1967). This narrative history describes the social and economic background of late imperial Russia with attention to intellectual trends and political ideologies.

Changing Values and the Force of New Ideas

Jacques Barzun, *Darwin, Marx, Wagner: Critique of a Heritage* (Garden City, NY: Doubleday Anchor, 1958). A classic study of mid-nineteenth century intellectual and cultural trends situates the roots of the modern heritage in the science and art of this period.

Jenni Calder, *The Victorian Home* (London: B. T. Batsford, 1977). A cultural and social history of Victorian domestic life in which the author describes both bourgeois and working-class domestic environments.

Bonnie G. Smith, *Ladies of the Leisure Class: The Bourgeoises of Northern France in the Nineteenth Century* (Princeton, NJ: Princeton University Press, 1981). Explores the impact of industrialization on the lives of bourgeois women in northern France and demonstrates how the cult of domesticity emerged in a particular community.

Edith Thomas, *The Women Incendiaries*, translated by James and Starr Atkinson (New York: George Braziller, 1966). One of the few studies that examines the prominent role played by women in the Paris Commune, the study considers how instrumental women were in the burning of Paris and more generally considers contemporary feminists debates.

Martha Vicinus, *Independent Women: Work and Community for Single Women, 1850–1920* (Chicago: The University of Chicago Press, 1985). Chronicles the choice that Victorian women made to live outside the norms of marriage and domesticity in various communities of women, including sisterhoods, nursing communities, colleges, boarding schools, and settlement houses.

24

The Crisis of
European Culture,
1871–1914

Speeding to the Future

"We want to demolish museums and libraries." These are not the words of an anarchist or a terrorist but of a poet. The Italian writer Emilio Marinetti (1876–1944) endeavored, symbolically at least through the power of his pen, to destroy the citadels of Western culture at the beginning of the twentieth century. Marinetti was not alone in wanting to pull down all that preserved art and learning in the West. Joined by other artists and writers who called themselves futurists, Marinetti represented a desire to break free of the past. By shocking complacent bourgeois society with their art, futurists hoped to fashion a new and dynamic civilization. Although they were a small group with limited influence, their concerns were shared by a growing number of intellectuals who judged European culture to be in the throes of a serious moral and cultural crisis. Futurist ideas also reflected the growing preoccupation among European men and women who spurned the value of tradition for dealing with the challenges of the future.

The futurist painter Umberto Boccioni (1882–1916) captures an aspect of the dynamic intensity of this changing world in his *Riot in the Galleria* (1910). Look at the painting. The setting is a galleria, the equivalent of a modern shopping mall, in front of a respectable *caffè*, an Italian coffee shop, this one frequented by well-dressed men and women, clearly members of the middle class. Here is a modern urban scene, a public space in every way characteristic of the new age of enjoyment and consumption.

There is a story here. In a flurry of light and shadow, a rush of figures moves toward the middle ground of the canvas. At the center of this movement are two women engaged in a brawl that seems to pull the figures of shoppers and strollers toward it. The fact that the brawlers are female is intended to underscore the irrationality of the incident. Yet the brawl itself is not compelling our attention. It is rather the movement of the crowd, like moths to a flame, that Boccioni intends us to see. This is a painting about movement. These objects in motion are little more than vibrations in space, faceless and indistinguishable as individuals. The crowd does not walk or run. It appears instead to be in flight. In his studies for the canvas Boccioni reduces movement to a series of lines both swirling and directed.

The riot Boccioni depicts here is an irrational event. This is no ordinary rabble: it is a well-dressed mob, as the blurred but sumptuously flowered hats and the occasional yellow straw boaters make clear. Movement is taking place without forethought, fueled by the attraction of violence and the possibility of participating in it. There are those on the periphery who have not joined the frenzy, but we as spectators are confident they will be swept up in the action as the energy of the brawl sucks everything to its center like the vortex of a tornado. European society seemed to many contemporaries to be moving into an abyss, a world of tumultuous change but one without values.

In the violence of the riot we are shown beauty of movement that surpasses that of an orderly waltz. Boccioni uses the warm glow of the electric lights, symbol of the modern age, to illuminate a "new reality." Golden tones, warm oranges and rosy hues, shadowed in delicate purples, create a mosaic whose beauty in the play of color is strangely at odds with the theme of the two brawling figures who activate the crowd. There is no meaning beyond the movement.

Riot in the Galleria reflects the preoccupation with change in the early twentieth century. Life was moving so fast that European society seemed to have outrun its own heritage by 1900. Technology was transforming Europe with a breakneck speed unmatched in human history. Science undermined the way people thought about themselves by challenging moral and religious values as hollow and meaningless. The natural sciences threw into doubt the existence of a creator. New forms of communication and transportation— the telephone, the wireless telegraph, the bicycle, the automobile, the airplane—were obliterating traditional understandings of time and space. The cinema and the X ray altered visual perception and redefined the ways people saw the world around them. This was a period of intense excitement and vitality in the history of the West, one which traditional values did not always explain.

Like the political revolutionaries of an earlier age, futurist artists issued "manifestoes." They sought the liberation of the human spirit from a world that could no longer be understood or controlled. Liberation could only be achieved through immersion in mass society and rapid change. Boccioni's goal was a revolutionary one: "Let's turn everything upside down . . . . Let's split open our figures and place the environment inside them."

Not all contemporary artists went as far in embracing the new age as Marinetti, Boccioni, and the other futurists. Many of Europe's intellectuals understood the attempt to break free of the stranglehold of Western tradition. In the arts, French impressionists, including Edouard Manet (1832–83), Claude Monet (1840–1926), Edgar Degas (1834–1917), and Pierre-Auguste Renoir (1841–1919) experimented with capturing the nature of light on canvas. They painted scenes from modern life, including urban subjects, that broke with traditional forms by emphasizing the private, individual lives of the middle class.

The moral dimensions of the cultural crisis

affecting the West were grasped early by the German philosophers Arthur Schopenhauer (1788–1860), who made pessimism into a philosophical category, and Friedrich Nietzsche (1844–1900), who argued against all religion and glorified the superman. Georges Sorel (1847–1922) in France reflected on the importance of violence, and his countryman Alfred Jarry (1873–1907) used the stage to show that nonsense and irrationality ruled everywhere.

The futurists went beyond the radical cultural critique of European intellectuals when they proclaimed, "A speeding automobile is more beautiful than *The Victory of Samothrace.*" By declaring that modern mechanical invention surpassed the beautiful ancient Greek statue enshrined in the Louvre museum in Paris, Boccioni intended to establish the supremacy of contemporary achievement.

Boccioni has been recognized as one of the great artists of the twentieth century. In his sculpture and painting, he aimed to capture the vitality and excitement of the new age. The desire to destroy all traditional values led Boccioni and the futurists to embrace violence and war as "hygienic." Futurism glorified the masses and rejected traditional elites as sterile. The individual was no longer at the center of the new culture. Change, technology, and, above all, violence were exalted. As the First Futurist Manifesto urged, "Let us leave Wisdom behind . . . Let us throw ourselves to be devoured by the Unknown." With the figures in his canvas swept up into an irrational mass, Boccioni emphasizes the rush and unpredictability of daily life. Beauty was a speeding car swallowing up the landscape and it was a crowd sucked into the whirlwind of collective irrationality. Boccioni met his own death in 1916 as a soldier in the war that he welcomed as a purifying event.

The "whirling life of steel, of pride, of fever and of speed" identified by the futurists in their 1910 Manifesto suggested a new universe of continuous upheaval. Futurists were not alone in their confusion over what to keep and what to reject in Western culture or in their inability to break entirely with the past. But they were single-minded in their rebellion against constraints. Before 1914 a new generation of Europeans rushing forward abandoned the lessons of the past for the promise of the future.

European Economy and the Politics of Mass Society

Between 1871 and 1914, the scale of European life was radically altered. Industrial society had promoted largeness as the norm, as growing numbers of people worked under the same roof. Large-scale heavy industries fueled by new energy sources dominated the economic landscape. Great Britain, the leader of the first industrial revolution of the eighteenth century, slipped in prominence as an industrial power at the end of the nineteenth century, as Germany and the United States devised successful competitive strategies of investment, protection, and control.

The organization of factory production throughout Europe and the proximity of productive centers to distribution networks meant ever greater concentration of populations in urban areas. Like factories, cities were getting bigger at a rapid rate and were proliferating in numbers. Berlin, capital of the new German nation, mushroomed in size in the last quarter of the nineteenth century. In the less industrialized parts of eastern Europe, cities also underwent record growth. Warsaw, St. Petersburg, and Moscow all expanded by at least 400,000 inhabitants each. Budapest, the city created by uniting the towns of Buda and Pest in 1872, tripled in size between 1867 and 1914 and was typical of the booming growth of provincial cities throughout Europe. With every passing year proportionately fewer people remained on the land. Those who did stay in the agricultural sector were linked to cities and tied into national cultures by new transportation and communications networks.

Changes in the scale of political life paralleled the rise of heavy industry and the increasing urbanization of European populations. Great Britain experienced the transformation in political organization and social structure before other European nations. But after 1870 changes in politics influenced by the scale of the new industrial society spread to every European country. Mass democracy was on the rise and was pushing aside the liberal emphasis on individual rights valued by parliamentary governments everywhere.

In spite of dramatic changes in politics and society, the old order still persisted. Throughout

Europe monarchy remained the dominant form of government, whether in the small German dynasties or the great Habsburg holdings. The progeny of Britain's Queen Victoria married the sons and daughters of Europe's other royal houses, seeming to make Europe's aristocrats one extended family network. But the age of royal influence was in twilight. In 1901 Victoria, Britain's longest reigning monarch, died; her son and successor Edward VII (1901–11) died ten years later. Their obsequies symbolized the end of an era. New industrial and financial leaders assumed positions of power among Europe's ruling elite. A new style of politics brought new political actors into the public arena at the beginning of the twentieth century.

Women were excluded from national political participation, although the right to vote was gradually being extended to all men in western Europe, regardless of property or social rank. Paradoxically, the extension of the suffrage worked to undermine the significance of parliaments. Political parties developed as interest groups with single issues that were at odds with the liberal policies of the nineteenth century. Demagogues appealing to anti-Semitic, antiliberal, and antilabor voters attracted mass followings. Extra-parliamentary groups—lobbies, trade unions, and cartels—grew in influence and power and came to exert pressure on the political process. The politics of mass society made clear the contradictions inherent in democracy. Propaganda, the ability to control information, became the avenue to success.

Great Britain, Germany, France, and Austria-Hungary, all with very different political traditions, had to adapt to the new realities of mass politics. The challenges of trade unions in England, socialism in Germany, political scandals in France, and anti-Semitic politics in Austria provide strikingly different vantage points on a common phenomenon, the crisis in European liberalism and the new politics of mass society.

Regulating Boom and Bust

Between 1873 and 1895 an epidemic of slumps battered the economies of European nations. These slumps, characterized by falling prices, downturns in productivity, and declining profits, have been called the "Great Depression" of the nineteenth century. In reality, the economic downturn of this period was not a great depression like the one that followed the crash of 1929. It did not strike European nations simultaneously, nor did it affect all countries with the same degree of severity. But the so-called Great Depression of the late nineteenth century and the boom period of intense economic expansion from 1895 to 1914 did teach industrialists, financiers, and politicians one important lesson: alternative booms and busts in the business cycle were dangerous and had to be regulated.

Too much of a good thing brought on the steady deflation of the last quarter of the nineteenth century. In the world economy, there was an overproduction of agricultural products—a sharp contrast to the famines that had ravaged Europe only fifty years earlier. Overproduction resulted from two new factors in the world economy: technological advances in crop cultivation, and the low cost of shipping and transport, which had opened up European markets to cheap agricultural goods from the United States, Canada, and Argentina. The absolute numbers of those employed in agriculture remained more or less constant, as world output soared. Cheap foreign grains, especially wheat, flooded European markets and drastically drove down agricultural prices. The drop in prices affected purchasing power in other sectors and resulted in long-term deflation and unemployment.

Financiers, politicians, and businessmen dedicated themselves to eliminating the boom-and-bust phenomenon, which they considered dangerous. Why were cyclic downturns considered so dangerous at the end of the nineteenth century when they had not been before? Earlier in the century, manufacturers of textiles could endure "bust" periods of depressed prices and declining profits without great hardship. Small family firms requiring little capital could move in and out of production to meet demand. But by the last quarter of the nineteenth century that situation had changed dramatically. The application of science and technology to industrial production required huge amounts of capital. The two new sources of power after 1880, petroleum and electricity, could only be developed with heavy capital investment. Large, mechanized steel plants were costly and out of reach for small family firms of the scale that had industrialized so successfully earlier in the century in textiles. Heavy machinery, smelting furnaces, buildings, and transport were all beyond the abilities of the small entrepreneur. In order to raise the capital necessary for the new heavy industry at the end of the nineteenth century, firms had to look outside themselves to the stock market, banks, or the state to find adequate capital resources.

But investors and especially banks refused to invest without guarantees on their capital. Bankers all over Europe were intent on minimizing risks and they certainly wanted to avoid the uncertainties of the business cycle. Because investment in heavy industry meant tying up capital for extended periods of time, banks insisted on safeguards against falling prices. The solution they demanded was the elimination of uncertainty through the regulation of markets.

Regulation was achieved through the establishment of *cartels*, combinations of firms in a given industry united to fix prices and to establish production quotas. Not as extreme as the monopolies that appeared in the United States in the same period and for the same purpose, cartels were agreements among big firms intent on controlling markets and guaranteeing profits. *Trusts* were another form of collaboration that resulted

in the elimination of unprofitable businesses. Firms joined together horizontally within the same industry—for example all steel producers agreed to fix prices and set quotas. Or they combined vertically by controlling all levels of the production process from raw materials to the finished product and all other ancillary products necessary to or resulting from the production process. This type of cartel was exemplified by a single firm that controlled everything to produce and market a single product from raw materials and fuel through sales and distribution.

Firms in Great Britain, falling behind in heavy industry, failed to form cartels and for the most part remained in private hands. But heavy industry in Germany, France, and Austria, to varying degrees, sought regulation of markets through cartels. International cartels appeared that regulated markets and prices across national borders within Europe. Firms producing steel, chemicals, coke, and pig iron all minimized the effects of competition through the regulation of prices and output.

Banks, which had been the initial impetus behind the transformation to a regulated economy, in turn formed consortia to meet the need for greater amounts of capital. A *consortium*, paralleling a cartel, was a partnership among

Foundry of the Firm of Friedrich Krupp at Essen, 1875. *The Krupp foundry in Germany was one of the wonders of the industrial age. The Krupp firm manufactured the first steel artillery and was the first in Europe to use the Bessemer process for steelmaking.*

A cartoon from a pamphlet published in Britain by the Tariff Reform League in 1903. The tree represents Britain's free-trade policy. The other nations of the world are harvesting the benefits of the British policy.

banks, often international in character, in which interest rates and the movement of capital were regulated by mutual agreement. The state, too, played an important role in directing the economy. In capital-poor Russia, the state used indirect taxes on the peasantry to finance industrialization and railway construction at the end of the nineteenth century. Russia industrialized with the sweat of its peasants. Russia also needed to import capital, primarily from France after 1887. The state had to guarantee foreign loans and regulate the economy to pay interest on foreign capital investment. Foreign investors were not willing to leave the export of capital to chance or the vagaries of the business cycle. The state must intervene.

Throughout Europe nation-states protected domestic industries by erecting tariff barriers that made foreign goods noncompetitive in domestic markets. Only Great Britain among the major powers stood by a policy of free trade. Europe was split into two tiers—the haves and have-nots: those countries with a solid industrial core and those that had remained unindustrialized. This division had a geographic character, with the north and west of Europe heavily developed and capitalized and the southern and eastern parts of Europe remaining heavily agricultural. For both the haves and have-nots, tariff policies were an attractive form of regula-

tion by the state to protect established industries and to nurture those industries struggling for existence.

Economic regulation was not a twentieth-century creation, as critics of the welfare state contend. Intervention and control began in the late nineteenth century, very much under the impetus of bankers, financiers, and industrialists. Capitalists looked on state intervention not as an intrusion but as a welcome corrective to the ups and downs of the business cycle. Regulation did not emerge from any philosophical or ideological assumption about government but came about as a result of the very real need for capital to enable heavy industry to expand and the equally compelling need to protect profits in order to encourage financiers to invest.

Challenging Liberal England

Great Britain had avoided revolution and social upheaval in the nineteenth century. It prided itself on the progress achieved by a strong parliamentary tradition. One writer caught the self-congratulatory spirit of the age in an 1885 book on popular government: "We Englishmen pass on the Continent as masters of the art of government." Parliamentary government was based on a homogeneous ruling elite. Aristocrats and businessmen and financial leaders shared a common educational background in England's elitist educational system of the public schools and the universities of Oxford or Cambridge. Schooling produced a common outlook and common attitudes toward parliamentary rule, whether in Conservative or Liberal parties, and guaranteed a certain stability in policies and legislation.

In the 1880s, issues of unemployment, public health, housing, and education challenged the attitudes of Britain's ruling elite and fostered the advent of an independent working-class politics. Between 1867 and 1885 extension of the suffrage increased the electorate fourfold. Protected by the markets of its empire, the British economy did not experience the roller-coaster effect of recurrent booms and busts after 1873. Nor did Britain experience severe economic crisis between 1890 and 1914, a period of growing labor unrest. But after 1900 wages stagnated, as prices continued to rise.

VOTE FOR

Home Rule.

Democratic Government.

Justice to Labour

No Monopoly.

No Landlordism

Temperance Reform.

Healthy Homes.

Fair Rents.

Eight-Hour Day.

Work for the Unemployed.

KEIR HARDIE.

Printed and Published by F. W. Scr se & Co. [L.S.C.], 151, Barking Road, Canning Town, London, E.

An election poster of 1895 exhorts voters to send Keir Hardie to Parliament. His positions on labor issues are succinctly stated.

Traditional parliamentary politics had little to offer those workers whose standard of living suffered a real decline. The quality of urban housing deteriorated, exemplified by the severe overcrowding of London's East End.

Workers responded to their distress by supporting militant trade unions. Trade unions, drawing on a long tradition of working-class associations, were all that stood between workers and the economic dislocation caused by unemployment, sickness, or old age. In addition, new unions of unskilled and semiskilled workers flourished, beginning in the 1880s and 1890s. A Scottish miner, James Keir Hardie (1856–1915), attracted national attention as the spokesman for a new political movement, the Labour party, whose goal was to represent workers in Parliament. In 1892 Hardie was the first independent working man to sit in the House of Commons. Hardie and his party convinced trade unions that it was in their best interests to support Labour candidates instead of Liberals in parliamentary elections after 1900. Unions, as extraparliamentary groups, worked successfully toward achieving a parlia-

mentary voice. By 1906, the new Labour party had 29 seats in Parliament.

Yet Parliament seemed to be failing the poor. So argued a group of intellectuals concerned with social welfare who called themselves Fabians. They named themselves after the Roman dictator Fabius, who was noted for his delaying tactics, which enabled him to avoid decisive battle with Hannibal in the Punic Wars; Fabius believed in cutting off the supplies of his enemies and engaging in skirmishes. Following his lead, the Fabians were socialists, not in a Marxist sense of ultimate revolutionary confrontation, but socialist in a gradualist sense of a reformist commitment to social justice. Led by Beatrice Webb (1858–1943) and Sidney Webb (1859–1947), and including in their number playwright and critic George Bernard Shaw (1856–1950), theosophist Annie Besant (1847–1943), and novelist H. G. Wells (1866–1946), the Fabians proved to be successful propagandists who were able to keep issues of social reform in the public eye. They advocated collective ownership and state direction of production through gradual reforms. At the turn of the century, the Fabian Society threw its support and the power of its tracts on social issues behind Labour party candidates. Intellectuals now joined with trade unionists in demanding public housing, better public sanitation, municipal reforms, and improved pay and benefits for working people.

The existence of the new Labour party pressured Conservatives and Liberals to develop more enlightened social policies and programs. After 1906, under threat of losing votes to the Labour party, the Liberal party heeded the pressures for reform. The "new" Liberals supported legislation to strengthen the right of unions to picket peacefully. Led by David Lloyd George (1863–1945), who was chancellor of the exchequer, Liberals sponsored the National Insurance Act of 1911. Modeled after Bismarck's social welfare policies, the act provided compulsory payments to workers for sickness and unemployment benefits. In order to gain approval to pay for this new legislation, Lloyd George recognized that Parliament itself had to be renovated. The Parliament Bill of 1911 reduced the House of Lords, dominated by Conservatives resistant to proposed welfare reforms, from its status as equal partner with the House of Commons. Commons could and now did raise taxes without the consent of the House of Lords to pay for new programs that benefited workers and the poor.

Social legislation did not silence unions and worker organizations. To the contrary, protest increased in the period up to the beginning of World War I in 1914. There was little doubt about the ability of militant trade unions to mobilize workers. In 1910 three of every ten manual workers belonged to a union, and this figure doubled to 60 percent of the work force between 1910 and 1914. In these years, strike waves broke over England. Unions threatened to paralyze the economy. Coal miners, seamen, railroad workers, and dockers protested against stagnant wages and rising prices.

The high incidence of strikes was a consequence of growing distrust of Parliament and distrust, too, of a regulatory state bureaucracy responsible for the social welfare reforms. Workers felt manipulated by a system unresponsive to their needs. Labour's voice grew more strident. The Trade Unions Act of 1913 granted unions legal rights to settle their grievances with management directly. In the summer of 1914, a railway worker boasted, "We are big and powerful enough to fight our own battle without the aid of Parliament or any other agency. There could be no affection between the robber and the robbed." Only the outbreak of war in 1914 ended the possibility of a general strike by miners, railwaymen, and transport workers. The question of Irish Home Rule also plagued Parliament. In Ulster in northern Ireland army officers of Protestant Irish background threatened to mutiny. In addition, women agitating for the vote shattered parliamentary complacence. The most advanced industrial nation with its tradition of peaceful parliamentary rule had entered the age of mass politics.

A union leader addresses striking British coal miners in 1912. Labor unions became increasingly militant after the turn of the century, as rising unemployment and declining real wages cut into the gains of the working class.

Political Struggles in Germany

During his reign as chancellor of the German Empire (1871–90), Otto von Bismarck formed shrewd alliances that hampered the development of effective parliamentary government. He repeatedly and successfully blocked the emergence of fully democratic participation. In Germany, all males had the right to vote, but the German parliament, the Reichstag, enjoyed only restricted powers in comparison to the British Parliament. Bismarck's objective remained always the successful unification of Germany, and he promoted cooperation with democratic institutions and parties only so long as that goal was enhanced.

Throughout the 1870s the German chancellor collaborated with the German liberal parties in constructing the legal codes, the monetary and banking system, the judicial apparatus, and the railroad network that pulled the new Germany together. Bismarck backed German liberals in their antipapal campaign in which the Catholic church was declared the enemy of the German state. He suspected the identification of Catholics with Rome, which the liberals depicted as an authority in competition with the nation-state. The anti-Church campaign, launched in 1872, was dubbed *Kulturkampf*, "struggle for civilization," because its supporters contended that it was a battle waged in the interests of humanity.

The legislation of the *Kulturkampf* expelled Jesuits from Germany, removed priests from state service, attacked religious education, and instituted civil marriage. Bishops and priests who followed the instructions of Pope Pius IX (1846–78) not to obey the new laws were arrested and expelled from Germany. Many Germans grew concerned over the social costs of such widespread religious repression and the Catholic Center party increased its parliamentary representation by rallying Catholics as a voting block in the face of state repression. With the succession of a new pontiff, Leo XIII (1878–1903), Bismarck took the opportunity of negotiating a settlement with the Catholic church, cutting his losses, and bringing the *Kulturkampf* to a halt. Bismarck had grown wary of the demands of the National Liberal party for an increasing share of political power.

Bismarck's repressive policies also targeted the Social Democratic party. The Social Democrats were committed to a Marxist critique of capitalism and to international cooperation with other socialist parties. Seeing them as a threat to stability in Germany and in Europe as a whole, he set out to smash them. In 1878, using the opportunity for repression presented by two attempts on the emperor's life, Bismarck outlawed the fledgling Socialist party. The Anti-Socialist Law forbade meetings among socialists, fund-raising, and distribution of printed matter. The law relied on expanded police powers and was a fundamental attack on civil liberties and freedom of choice within a democratic electoral system. Nevertheless, individual Social Democratic candidates stood for election in this period and learned quickly how to work with middle-class parties in order to achieve electoral successes. By 1890 Social Democrats had captured 20 percent of the electorate and controlled 35 Reichstag seats, in spite of Bismarck's anti-Socialist legislation.

Throughout the 1880s as his ability to manage Reichstag majorities declined and as Socialist strength steadily mounted, Bismarck grew disenchanted with universal manhood suffrage. Beginning in 1888 the chancellor found himself at odds with the new emperor Wilhelm II (1888–1918) over his foreign and domestic policies. The young emperor dismissed Bismarck in March 1890 and abandoned the chancellor's anti-Socialist legislation. The Social Democratic party became the largest Marxist party in the world and by 1914, the largest single party in Germany.

The socialism of the German Social Democrats was modified in the 1890s. Although it had never been violent or insurrectionary, social democracy moved away from a theory of revolution and toward a democratic "revisionism" that favored gradual reform through parliamentary participation. Those who continued to maintain a more orthodox Marxist position, such as August Bebel (1840–1913) and Karl Kautsky (1854–1938), believed capitalism would destroy itself, as Karl Marx had predicted, without any violent action by German Social Democrats. Bebel confided to Friedrich Engels in 1885 that he went to bed every night with the confidence that "the last hour of bourgeois society strikes soon."

The struggle between Bismarck and the pope is symbolized in this cartoon. Bismarck's chessmen include "Germania," the press, and antimonastic legislation. The pope marshals encyclicals, interdicts, and the Syllabus of Errors.

Revisionism was both practical and democratic. Its leader, Eduard Bernstein (1850–1932), introduced aspects of Fabian state socialism into the German movement. This grass-roots transformation favored evolutionary rather than revolutionary political action. Workers were the primary force behind the shift away from the catastrophe theory of Bebel and Kautsky. Their standard of living had been improving in Germany and the prospect of the imminent collapse of capitalism seemed slight to workers intent on achieving further gains. Union membership grew dramatically among unskilled workers after 1895. Working-class organizations, tolerated earlier by Social Democrats for their future potential, now became centers of power and pressed for practical benefits for their members.

During the period when the Social Democratic movement had been outlawed, Bismarck had employed carrot-and-stick methods to woo the working class away from the Marxists. The stick with which Bismarck beat back the political opposition had been the Anti-Socialist laws. The carrot that he and then Wilhelm II used to win mass support was social welfare legislation, including accident insurance, sick benefits, and old age and disability benefits introduced by the state. But such legislation did not undermine the popularity of socialism nor did it attract workers away from Marxist political programs, as the mounting electoral returns demonstrated. Social Democracy built its rank-and-file union membership by employing sophisticated organizational techniques to expand its mass base of support.

The success and popularity of the Social Democratic party cemented a stronger alliance on the Right among Conservatives. Realizing that they could not beat the Left, right-wing groups decided to copy them. Unable to defeat social democracy by force or by state-sponsored welfare policies, Bismarck's successors set out to organize mass support. Agrarian and industrial interests united strongly behind state policies. An aggressive foreign policy was judged as the surest way to win over the masses. Leagues were formed to exploit nationalism and patriotism among the electorate over issues of naval and military expansion and colonial development.

In the end the Reichstag failed to defy the absolute authority of Emperor Wilhelm II, who was served after 1890 by a string of ineffectual chancellors. Despite its constitutional forms, Germany was ruled by a state authoritarianism in which the bureaucracy, the military, and various interest groups exercised influence over the emperor. A high-risk foreign policy that had a mass appeal was one way to circumvent a parliamentary system incapable of decision-making. Constitutional solutions had been short-circuited in favor of authoritarian rule.

Political Scandals and Mass Politics in France

The Third Republic in France had an aura of the accidental about its origins and of the precarious about its existence. Founded in 1870 with the defeat of Napoleon III's empire by the Germans, the Third Republic claimed legitimacy by placing itself squarely within the revolutionary democratic tradition. Yet its early days were marked by bloody social conflict and its existence was plagued by ongoing struggles among contenders for power both on the Right and Left who sought to control it.

In spite of surface indications of political conflict, the Third Republic successfully worked toward the creation of a national community based on a common identity of citizens. Compulsory schooling, one of the great institutional transformations of French government in 1885, socialized French children in common values,

patriotism, and identification with the nation-state. Old ways, local dialects, superstitious practices, and peasant insularity dropped away or were modified under the persistent pressure of a centralized curriculum of reading, writing, arithmetic, and civics. Compulsory service in the army for the generation of young men of draft age served the same ends of communicating national values to a predominantly peasant population.

Technology also accelerated the process of shaping a national citizenry, as railroad lines tied people together and the infrastructure of roads made distances shrink. People could now travel back and forth between village and city, town and countryside with ease and frequency. Common expectations for a better life and upward mobility moved through rural populations that for most of the nineteenth century had not looked beyond the horizon of the village. Young working women were particularly influential in the transfer of values from urban to rural areas as they moved from the village to the town in search of domestic and industrial jobs, and then returned to their villages with new outlooks and new goals for their families.

Information was controlled at the center—Paris—and distributed on a national scale. Villagers in southern France read Parisian newspapers over their morning bowls of coffee and learned—with a previously unimaginable immediacy—about French foreign exploits and parliamentary wrangles. A truly national and mass culture emerged in the period between 1880 and 1914. Common symbols, like the bust of "Marianne," appeared in every city hall all over France, and a common vocabulary of patriotism spread across the land. French people were not necessarily more political, but they were political in a new way that enabled them to identify their own local interests with national issues.

Two events, in particular, that occurred in the three decades before World War I indicate the extent of the transformation of French political life. The first, the Boulanger Affair, involved the attempt of a French general to seize power. The second, the Dreyfus Affair, involved all of French society in the treason conviction of a Jewish army captain.

General Georges Boulanger (1837–91) was a popular and romantic figure who captured the imagination of the French press. As minister of war, Boulanger became a hero to French soldiers when he undertook needed reforms of army life. He won over businessmen by leading troops against strikers. Above all, he cultivated the image of a patriot ready to defend France's honor at any cost. Known as "the Man on Horseback" because of his ability to look dashing in public appearances astride his black horse, Boulanger was a shallow man whose success and national popularity were created by a carefully orchestrated publicity campaign that made him the most popular man in France by 1886.

Boulanger's potential in the political arena attracted the attention of right-wing backers, including monarchists who hoped eventually to restore kingship to France. Supported by big-money interests who favored a strengthened executive and a weaker parliamentary system, Boulanger undertook a nationwide political campaign, hoping to appeal to those unhappy with the Third Republic and promising vague constitutional reforms. General Boulanger's 1889 campaign managers successfully manipulated images that were recognizable to a rural electorate. Religious lithographs carried likenesses of the modern "messiah," the blond-bearded general, in place of Jesus. Campaign workers were recruited

at the local level. Boulangists hoped that through universal suffrage an authoritarian government could be established. By 1889 Boulanger was able to amass enough national support to frighten the defenders of parliamentary institutions. The charismatic general ultimately failed in his bid for power and fled the country because of allegations of treason. But he left in his wake an embryonic mass movement on the Right that operated outside the channels of parliamentary institutions. Boulanger's success was due to a new nationalism that flexed its muscles after 1880. Cultural symbols like the flag and the nation-in-arms moved from the revolutionary tradition of the Left to become part of the appeal of the new right-wing groups that were growing in importance.

A very different type of crisis began to take shape in 1894 with the controversy surrounding the trial of Captain Alfred Dreyfus (1859–1935) that came to be known simply as "the Affair." Dreyfus was an Alsatian Jewish army officer accused of selling military secrets to the Germans. His trial for treason served as a lightning rod for xenophobia—the hatred of foreigners, especially Germans—and anti-Semitism, the hatred of Jews. Dreyfus was stripped of his commission and

Captain Dreyfus, accused of treason, marches with a "guard of dishonor." After Dreyfus was declared innocent, he became a lieutenant colonel in the French army and was enrolled in the Legion of Honor.

honors and sentenced to solitary confinement for life on Devil's Island, a convict colony off French Guiana in South America.

Illegal activities and outright falsifications by Dreyfus' superiors in order to secure a conviction came to light in the mass press. The nation was soon divided. Those who supported Dreyfus' innocence, the pro-Dreyfusards, were for the most part on the Left of the political spectrum and spoke of the Republic's duty to uphold justice and freedom. The anti-Dreyfusards were associated with the traditional institutions of the Catholic church and the army and considered themselves to be defending the honor of France. Among those who upheld the conviction were right-wing groups, monarchists, and virulent anti-Semites.

Dreyfus was eventually exonerated of treason and granted a full pardon in 1905. On the personal level, the Affair represented the ability of an individual to seek redress against injustice. On the national level, the Affair represented an important transformation in the nature of French political life. Existing parliamentary institutions had been found wanting and unable to cope with the mass politics stirred up by Dreyfus' conviction. New groups entered public life after 1894, coalescing around the question of the guilt or innocence of an individual man. The newspaper press vied with parliament and the courts as a forum for investigation and decision-making. Intellectuals, too, organized. Leagues on the Left and on the Right took shape; unions, cooperatives, and professional societies all raised their voices. These organizations manipulated propaganda around issues of national defense and republican justice.

The crises provoked by Boulanger's attempt at power and the Dreyfus Affair demonstrated the major role of the press and the importance of public opinion in exerting pressure on the system of government. The press emerged as a myth-maker in shaping and channeling public opinion. Émile Zola (1840–1902), the great French novelist, spearheaded the pro-Dreyfusard movement with his damning article "I Accuse!" in which he pointed to the military and the judiciary as the "spirits of social evil" for persecuting an innocent man. The article appeared in a leading French newspaper and was influential in securing Dreyfus' eventual exoneration and the discovery of the real culprit, one of Dreyfus' colleagues in the General Staff. The Third Republic was never in danger of collapsing but it was transformed. The locus of power in parliament was challenged by pressure groups outside of it.

Defeating Liberalism in Austria

In the 1870s the liberal values of the bourgeoisie dominated the Austro-Hungarian Empire. The Habsburg monarchy had adjusted to constitutional government, which was introduced throughout Austria in 1860. Faith in parliamentary government based on a restricted suffrage had established a tenuous foothold. After the setbacks of 1848 and the troublesome decade of the 1860s, when Prussia had trounced Austria and Bismarck had routed the hope of an Austrian-dominated German Empire, the Austrian bourgeoisie counted on a peaceful future with a centralized, multinational state dedicated to order and progress.

There is no better symbol of middle-class political and cultural aspirations in this period than the monumental rebuilding of the city of Vienna that took place after 1860. The belt of public and private buildings on the *Ringstrasse*, "Ring Street," girding the old central city and separating it from its suburbs was dramatic testimony to bourgeois self-confidence. Grandiose buildings, likened to "cakes on platters," glorified constitutional government, economic vitality, the fine arts, and educational values. Monumental architecture was intended to legitimize bourgeois claims to power and to link Austrian institutions with the great cultural heritage of the West. The buildings were blatant copies of past architectural styles—massive Gothic for the city hall, Renaissance for the university, and early baroque for the theater. Yet this was more than a self-confident statement of Austria's inheritance of a rich cultural tradition. Vienna's ruling class was fortifying itself behind the edifices of Western politics and culture against the onslaught of the new age.

In reality, the Austrian bourgeoisie was weaker than its French or British counterparts. The Austrian ruling class was heavily dependent on the Habsburg emperor and identified itself

A view of the city of Vienna in the second half of the nineteenth century. In the left foreground is the Schwartzenberg Palace. Behind it are the gardens and mansions of the Ringstrasse. In the distance can be seen the Danube River and the Vienna hills.

with the values of the aristocracy. Rapid economic growth had strengthened bourgeois status between 1840 and 1870, but it had also unleashed new social forces that existing institutions were unable to control. Liberal values of constitutional monarchy, centralization, restricted suffrage, and multinational government came up against new and threatening forces of anti-Semitism, socialism, nationalism, and mass politics.

By 1900 liberal politicians were being eliminated as a directing force in national politics. The new politicians who replaced them rejected the liberal-rational values of progress and order and moved into a realm colored by charisma, fantasy, and demagoguery. A new Right wielded mass political strategies that embraced the irrational and the violent.

The new groups laying claim to political power and displacing a weak Austrian bourgeoisie were peasants, workers, urban artisans and shopkeepers, and the colonized Slavic peoples of the empire. Bourgeois politics and laissez-faire economics had offered little or nothing to these varied groups, who were now claiming the right of participation. Mass parties were formed based on radical pan-Germanic feeling, anticapitalism that appealed to peasants and artisans, hatred of

the Jews shared by students and artisans, and nationalist aspirations that attracted the lower middle classes. In 1895 Karl Lueger (1844–1910) used anti-Semitism in his successful campaign for the office of mayor of Vienna. Lueger's election was the first serious sign of the collapse of Austrian liberalism. Jews were identified with capitalists and the irrational hatred directed at them unified different groups and helped to sweep Lueger into office.

Austrian poet and playwright Hugo von Hofmannsthal (1874–1929) understood the rejection of bourgeois politics in the age of expanded suffrage: "Politics is magic. He who knows how to summon the forces from the deep, him will they follow." The creation of a scapegoat by means of anti-Semitism and racism became the means of uniting the masses against a common foe and in favor of a common nationalist program. In Austria antiliberal politics grew stronger in the years before 1914. The great buildings on the Ringstrasse that had attempted to connect Austrian political life with the glories of the European past were mocked as relics of a dead age. Centrifugal forces of pan-Germanism and nationalism were pulling the parliamentary system apart. An urban and capitalist middle class that ruled Austria by virtue of a limited suffrage based on property had lost ground to new groups that were essentially anticapitalist and antiliberal in their outlook and for whom parliamentary deliberations held no promise. The rejection of liberalism was a "revolt against the fathers." A new style of leader had emerged in Vienna at the end of the century, charismatic in style and violent in appeal. The "politics of fantasy" based on a new electorate was fast becoming the nightmare of parliamentary disintegration.

The political experiences of Great Britain, Germany, France, and Austria between 1871 and 1914 make clear the common challenges confronting Western parliamentary systems in a changing era of democratic politics. In spite of variations, each nation experienced its own challenge to liberal parliamentary institutions and each shaped its own variety of responses to a new international phenomenon—the rise of the masses as a political force.

Outsiders in Mass Politics

By the end of the nineteenth century the masses were replacing the individual in political culture. A faceless, nameless electorate became the basis of new political strategies and a new political rhetoric. A concept of class identification of workers was devalued in favor of interest-group politics in which lobbies formed around single issues to pressure European governments. But the apparently all-inclusive concept of mass society continued to exclude some groups. Women, ethnic minorities, and Jews were pushed to the margins. Outsiders in mass politics had little in common with one another except for the common experience of repression by the state. But they did not remain quietly on the periphery. Women and ethnic minorities learned to incorporate strategies and techniques of politics and organization that permitted them to challenge the existing political system. Others, including anarchists, rejected both the organizational techniques of mass society and the values of the nation-state. Outsiders, then, were both those intent on being integrated into mass politics and those who sought its destruction.

Feminists and the State

Women's emancipation had been a recurrent motif of European political culture throughout the nineteenth century. In the areas of civil liberties, legal equality with men, and economic autonomy, only the most limited reforms had been enacted. The cult of domesticity, important throughout the nineteenth century, assigned women to a separate sphere, that of the home. Glorifying domesticity was a recognition of women's unique contribution to society in the home, but it may itself have been a means of controlling women who protested the separation between public and private space.

European women were paid at best one-third to one-half of what men earned for the same work. In Great Britain, women did not enjoy equal divorce rights until the twentieth century. In France, married women had no control over their own incomes: all their earnings were considered their husbands' private property. From the Atlantic to the Urals, women were excluded from economic and educational opportunities. Serfs had been liberated. Working-class men gained the right to vote. But the new electoral politics that emerged in the last quarter of the nineteenth century explicitly excluded women.

Growing numbers of women, primarily from the middle classes, began calling themselves *feminist*, a term coined in France in the 1830s. The new feminists throughout western Europe differed from earlier generations in their willingness to organize mass movements and to appropriate the techniques of interest-group politics. The first international congress of women's rights, held in Paris in 1878, initiated an era of international cooperation and exchange among women's organizations. Women's groups now positioned themselves for sustained political action.

Feminism as a historic term is worth pondering. Like liberalism, which had pulled down kings and destroyed privilege, feminism aimed at eliminating social inequalities. Like socialism, feminism was a set of principles for action whose purpose was to build a better world. At base, feminism recognized the equality of the sexes, without denying difference. As John Stuart Mill in Great Britain and Ernest Legouvé (1807–1903), the French dramatist and leading proponent of women's rights, had demonstrated, one need not be female to be a feminist. Most feminists, however, were women and the leadership of the movement for equal rights was in women's hands. The converse—that most women were feminists—was not true. Contemporary critics often dismissed feminism on the grounds that it represented no more than a tiny minority of women. The same minority status characterized the trade union movement which in France, for example, had a smaller membership at the end of the nineteenth century than did feminist organizations.

European feminist organizations did not share a common agenda but grouped themselves around a series of related issues for legal, educational, economic, and political emancipation. Rather than speaking of a single feminism, it is more appropriate to speak of different *feminisms*. The General German Women's Association agitated for educational opportunities and democratic participation for women. In France, women working for the vote were a minority of the women's organizations. Many French feminists defended a "maternal politics" by which they sought protection for women's responsibilities in the home. Other feminists were involved in abortion reform, birth control issues, and repeal of state control of prostitution. The French League for the Rights of Women stood steadfastly against the vote as an end in itself and worked instead for legal and economic reforms. On the whole, however, feminist organizations were divided into two camps. In the first group were those who agitated for the vote; the second included those who thought that the vote was beside the point and that the central issues were economic, social, and legal reforms of women's status. Constituting the left wing of the second group were socialist women who were dedicated to needs of women of the working class.

The lessons of the new electoral politics were not lost on feminists seeking women's emancipation through the vote. Leaders like Hubertine Auclert (1848–1914) in France and Emmeline Pankhurst (1858–1928) in Great Britain recognized the need for a mass base of support. If women's organizations were to survive as competing interest groups, they needed to form political alliances, control their own newspapers and magazines, and keep their cause before the public eye.

Just as cartels, trade unions, and political parties had learned the game of influence and leverage so important for survival in the modern political milieu, so too did feminists rely on organization to achieve their ends. There was a growing willingness to use mass demonstrations, rallies, and violent tactics by a variety of women's organizations.

No movement operated more effectively in this regard than the British suffrage movement. In 1903, the Women's Social and Political Union (WSPU) was formed by a group of eminently respectable middle-class and aristocratic British women. At the center of the movement was Emmeline Pankhurst, a middle-aged woman of frail and attractive appearance, with a will of iron and a gift for oratory. Joined by her two daughters Christabel (1880–1958), a lawyer by training, and Sylvia (1882–1960), an artist, these three women succeeded in keeping women's suffrage before the British public and brought the plight of British women to international attention. Over the next seven years, the WSPU made considerable progress, attracting a growing number of followers, and successfully aligning itself with parliamentary supporters.

Women's demands for political power were the basis of an unheralded revolution in Western culture. In Great Britain the decade before the Great War of 1914 was a period of profound political education for women seeking the vote. An unprecedented 250,000 women gathered in Hyde Park in 1908 to hear more about female suffrage. Laughed at by men, ridiculed in the press, taunted in public demonstrations, women activists refused to be quiet and to know their place. If respectable women would never demonstrate for their rights, then the suffragists were willing to cease being respectable. Because they spoke out for voting rights, feminists were demeaned and humiliated and accused of not being *real* women by their detractors. One of the best examples of the rebellion of women against the limitations of their social roles took place on 18 November 1910, a day that came to be known among feminists as Black Friday. On that day, suffragists marched on Parliament, which had failed to support the vote for women. In a confrontation that lasted six hours, unarmed women battled with police to hold their ground. Rather than returning home as they were ordered, the women relentlessly pushed forward, meeting the blows and the wrath of London's bobbies. Many women were injured and many arrested.

The year 1910 marked the beginning of an era of increased militancy among women who were derisively called "suffragettes" in the press in order to distinguish them from the nonmilitant suffragists. A basic element in the new militancy was the willingness to use violence to achieve political emancipation. As Emmeline Pankhurst explained it, "The argument of the broken window pane is the most valuable argument in modern politics." Militant women set mailboxes on fire or poured glue and jam over their contents, threw bombs into country houses, and slashed paintings in the National Gallery. All over London the tinkling of thousands of shattered windowpanes ushered in a new age of women's political action. Mrs. Pankhurst was not naive about what her followers were doing: "There is something which governments care for more than human life and that is the security of property, and so it is through property that we shall strike the enemy." Suffragettes set fires in public buildings, churches, and hotels. As frustration grew, some assaulted members of the cabinet. One suffragette, Emily Wilding Davison (1872–1913), probably intent on suicide as an act of protest, was trampled to death when she threw herself under the king's horse on Derby Day at Epsom Downs in 1913. Mrs. Pankhurst and others advocated violence against personal property to highlight the violence done to women by denying them their rights. These tactics seemed to accomplish little before the war, although they certainly kept the issue of woman suffrage in the public eye until the outbreak of war in 1914. It was not until 1918 that British women were granted limited suffrage and not until 1928 that women gained voting rights equal to those of men.

Women suffered for their militancy, as civil disobedience evoked harsh repressive measures from the British government. Previous benevolence toward middle-class female prisoners arrested for attacks on property gave way to a new harshness that included the force-feeding of convicted suffragettes. Using tubes, hoses, and metal jaw clamps, prison guards and doctors poured gruel down the throats of imprisoned women who, as a form of protest, refused to eat. Such repressive measures only increased the solidarity within the women's movement and won the suffragettes international sympathy and support. Stymied, the government passed The Cat and Mouse Act in 1913. Imprisoned women who refused to eat were released, then reincarcerated once they had resumed eating and regained their strength. This "cat-and-mouse" pattern of release

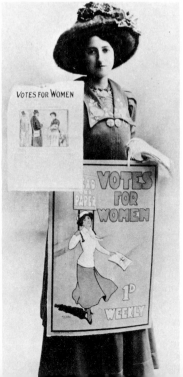

Emmeline Pankhurst (below, third from right) at a rally to turn out the vote against a government that was unresponsive to women's issues. Right: A young member of the National Women's Social and Political Union sells copies of the paper Votes for Women.

and reimprisonment could double or extend indefinitely a three-year sentence served in three-day segments. Many of the more dramatic tactics of the suffragettes, including getting arrested, were not available to working-class activists, who could not put aside their family responsibilities to serve jail sentences.

European women did not gain the right to vote easily. In France and Germany moderate and left-wing politicians opposed extension of the vote to women because they feared that women would strengthen conservative candidates. Many politicians felt that women were not "ready" for the vote and that they should receive it only as a reward—an unusual concept in democratic societies. Queen Victoria condemned women's agitation for the vote as a "mad, wicked folly." Only after war and revolution was the vote extended to women in the West; Germany in 1918, the United States in 1920, and France at the end of World War II.

Not all activist women saw the right to vote as the solution to women's oppression. Those who agitated for social reforms for poor and working-class women parted ways with the militant suffragettes. Sylvia Pankhurst, for example, left her mother and sister to their political battles in order to work for social reform in London's poverty-stricken East End. Differing from those who focused on woman's right to vote as a primary goal, women socialists were concerned with working-class women's "double oppression" in the home and in the workplace. The largest women's socialist movement existed in Germany, with 175,000 members by 1914. With its own newspaper, it operated independently of the men's socialist movement. German socialist women were opposed to suffrage on the grounds that giving middle-class women the vote did not address social issues.

Socialist women's lot was not an easy one, since union members often denied women's right to work and saw women's employment as a threat to men in the workplace. In Germany, socialist men opposed women industrial workers. Unions supported the concept of separate spheres for men and women and based their demands for a family wage on the need to maintain a separate private domain of the home. Socialist men argued that women's work often resulted in the neglect of children and could lead to the physical degenera-

tion of the family. Working women, socialist men argued, undermined existing wage scales and aided the exploitation of workers by their willingness to work for lower wages. Class oppression, countered German socialist leader and theorist Clara Zetkin (1857–1933), was the basis of women's oppression. For militants like Zetkin, socialism offered the only means to eliminate sexual inequalities.

The women's movements of the period from 1871 to 1914 differed socially and culturally from nation to nation. Yet there is a sense in which the women's movements constituted an international phenomenon. The rise in the level of political consciousness of women occurred in the most advanced Western countries almost simultaneously and had a predominantly middle-class character. Working-class women, most notably in Germany, united feminism with socialism in search of a better life. In spite of concerted efforts, women remained on the outside of societies that excluded them from political participation, access to education, and social and economic equality.

The Jewish Question and the Zionist Solution

The word *anti-Semitism*, meaning hostility to the Jews, was first used in 1879 to give a pseudo-scientific legitimacy to bigotry and hatred. Persecution was a harsh reality for Jews in eastern Europe at the end of the nineteenth century. In Russia, Jews could not own property and were restricted to living in certain territories. Organized massacres, or pogroms, in Kiev, Odessa, and Warsaw followed the assassination of Tsar Alexander II in 1881 and occurred again after the failed Russian revolution of 1905. Russian authorities blamed the Jews, perceived as perennial outsiders, for the assassination and the revolution and the social instability that followed them. Pogroms resulted in the death and displacement of tens of thousands of Russian and eastern European Jews.

Two million eastern European Jews migrated westward between 1868 and 1914 in search of peace and refuge. Seventy thousand settled in Germany. Others continued westward, stopping in the United States. Another kind of Jewish migration took place in the nineteenth century—the movement of Jews from rural to urban areas within nations. In eastern Europe Jewish migrations coincided with downturns in the economic cycle, and Jews became scapegoats for the high rates of unemployment and high prices that seemed to follow in their wake. Most migrants were peddlers, artisans, or small shopkeepers who were seen as threatening to small businesses. Differing in language, culture, and dress, they were viewed as alien in every way.

In western Europe Jews considered themselves as "assimilated" into their national cultures, identifying with their nationality as much as with their religion. Austrian and German Jews were granted full civil rights in 1867 on the principle that citizens of all religions enjoyed full equality. In France, Jews had been legally emancipated since the end of the eighteenth century. But the western and central European politics of the 1890s had a strong dose of anti-Semitism. Demagogues like Georg von Schönerer (1842–1921) of Austria were capable of whipping up a frenzy of riots and violence against Jews. They did not distinguish between assimilated and immigrant Jewish populations in their irrational denunciations.

Western and central European anti-Semitism assumed a new level of virulence at the end of the nineteenth century. Fear of an economic depression united aristocrat and worker alike in blaming a Jewish conspiracy. German anti-Semitism proliferated in the 1880s. "It is like a horrible epidemic," the scholar Theodor Mommsen (1817–1903) observed. "It can neither be explained nor cured."

Fear of the Jews was connected with hatred of capitalism. In France and Germany, Jews controlled powerful banking and commercial firms that became the targets of blame in hard times. Upwardly mobile sons of Jewish immigrants entered the professions of banking, trading, and journalism. They were also growing in numbers as teachers and academics. In the 1880s more than half of Vienna's physicians (61 percent in 1881) and lawyers (58 percent of barristers in 1888) were Jewish. Their professional success only heightened tensions and condemnations of Jews as an "alien race." Anti-Semitism served as a violent means of mobilizing mass support,

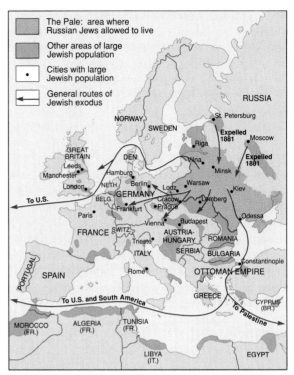

Jewish Migration

especially among those groups who felt threatened by capitalist concentration and large-scale industrialization. For anti-Semitic Europeans, Jews embodied the democratic, liberal, and cosmopolitan tendencies of the culture that they were consciously rejecting in their new political affiliations.

A Jewish leadership emerged in central and western Europe that treated anti-Semitism as a problem that could be solved by political means. For their generation at the end of the nineteenth century, the assimilation of their fathers and mothers was not the answer. Jews needed their own nation, it was argued, since they were a people without a nation. Zionism was the solution to what Jewish intellectuals called "the Jewish problem." Zion, the ancient homeland of Biblical times, would provide a national territory, and a choice, to persecuted Jews. Zionism became a Jewish nationalist movement dedicated to the establishment of a Jewish state. Although Zionism did not develop mass support in western Europe among assimilated Jews, its program for national identity and social reforms appealed to a large following of eastern European Jews in Galicia

(Poland), Russia, and the eastern lands of the Habsburg Empire, those directly subjected to the extremes of persecution.

Theodor Herzl (1860–1904), an Austrian Jew born in Budapest, was the founder of Zionism in its political form. As a student in Vienna, he encountered discrimination, but his commitment to Zionism developed as a result of his years as a journalist in Paris. Observing the anti-Semitic attacks in republican France provoked by the scandals surrounding the misappropriation of funds by leading French politicians and businessmen during the construction of the Panama Canal and the divisive conflict over the Dreyfus Affair in the 1890s, Herzl came to appreciate how deeply imbedded anti-Semitism was in European society. He despaired of the ability of corrupt parliamentary governments to solve the problem of anti-Semitism. In *The Jewish State* (1896), Herzl concluded that Jews must have a state of their own. Under his direction, Zionism developed a world organization and its own newspaper with the aim of establishing a Jewish homeland in Palestine.

Jews began emigrating to Palestine. With the financial backing of Jewish donors like the French banker Baron de Rothschild, nearly 90,000 Jews had established settlements there by 1914. Calculated to tap a common Jewish identification with an ancient heritage, from the beginning the choice of Palestine as a homeland was controversial. The problems arising from the choice have persisted through the twentieth century.

The promised land of the Old Testament, Zion is a holy place in Judaism. The Austrian psychoanalyst Sigmund Freud (1815–1939), who described himself as "a Jew from Moravia," was sympathetic to the Zionist cause but critical of the idea of Palestine as a Jewish state. He considered the idea unworkable and one bound to arouse Christian and Islamic opposition. Freud feared that Palestine would arouse the suspicions of the Arab world and challenge "the feelings of the local natives." He would have preferred a "new, historically unencumbered soil."

Some Jewish critics of Zionism felt that a separate Jewish state would prove that Jews were not good citizens of their respective nation-states and would exacerbate hostilities toward Jews as outsiders. Yet Zionism had much in common with the European liberal tradition because it sought in the creation of a nation-state for Jews the solution to social injustice. Zion, the Jewish nation in the Middle East, was a liberal utopia for the Jewish people. Zionism learned from other mass movements of the period the importance of a broad base of support. By the time of the First Zionist Congress, held in Basel, Switzerland, in 1897, it had become a truly international movement. Herzl was also well aware of the necessity for a charismatic leader and cast himself in the role of messiah for his people.

Zionism did not achieve its goals before World War I, and the Jewish state of Israel was not recognized by the world community until 1948. Before World War I anti-Semitism and anti-feminism were strongly linked in nationalist political programs, which insisted that the place for Jews was on the periphery and the place for women was in the home. Through the Zionist movement, Jews victimized by nationalism planned for their own nation-state as a solution.

Workers and Minorities on the Margins

In 1892 the Parisian trial of a bomb-throwing anarchist named Ravachol attracted great public attention. He and other French anarchists had captured the popular imagination with their threats to destroy bourgeois society by bombing private residences, public buildings, and restaurants. Ravachol's terrorist deeds represented the extreme rejection of participation in electoral politics. The public was frightened—but also fascinated. Ravachol opposed the state and the capitalist economy as the dual enemy that could only be destroyed through individual acts of random physical violence. For his crimes he was condemned to death and publicly executed.

The best-known anarchists of the late nineteenth century were those, like Ravachol, who engaged in terrorist assassinations and bombings. Although not all anarchists were terrorists intent on destruction, all shared a desire for a revolutionary restructuring of society. Most anarchists were loners. They dreamed of the collapse of the capitalist system with its exploitation and inequality and of the emergence of a society based on personal freedom, autonomy, and justice. Anarchists spurned the Marxist willingness to organize and participate in parliamentary politics. They disdained the tyranny of new organizations and bureaucracies that worked for gradual reforms at the expense of principles of justice.

There was no single anarchist doctrine, but the varieties of anarchism all shared a hope in a future free from constraints. Mikhail Bakunin (1814–76), a member of the Russian nobility, absorbed the works and the message of the French social critic Pierre-Joseph Proudhon. Bakunin became Europe's leading anarchist spokesman. Unlike Proudhon, Bakunin was a man of revolutionary action who espoused the use of violence to achieve individual liberation. All existing institutions must be swept away before ownership of production could be collectivized. Bakunin broke with Marx, whom he considered a "scientific bourgeois socialist" out of touch with the mass of workers.

Bakunin

Bakunin's successor in international anarchist doctrine was also a Russian of aristocratic lineage—Prince Petr Kropotkin (1842–1921). Kropotkin joined together communism and anarchism, arguing that goods should be communally distributed, "from each according to his ability, to each according to his needs." Based on his own empirical observations, Kropotkin opposed competition and dominance as laws of nature and stressed human interdependence.

It is difficult to measure the extent of Bakunin's or Kropotkin's influence, since whatever followers they might have inspired were not overtly or formally organized. Anarchism's greatest appeal was in the less industrialized countries of southern Europe: Spain, Italy, and southern France. In these countries, a grass-roots anarchism germinated in working-class communities. Russia, too, had developed a strong populist tradition in the second half of the nineteenth century similar to anarchism in its opposition to state tyranny. But anarchism was primarily a western European phenomenon.

Anarchism had special appeal to workers in trades staggering under the blows of industrial capitalism. Calling themselves anarcho-syndicalists, artisans, especially in France, were able to combine local trade union organization with anarchist principles. Alienation from the political process was strong among the French working class, who had the recent, bitter memories of repression during the Paris Commune in 1871 and the sterility and corruption of the party politics of the Third Republic. Most of these workers were in skilled trades that suffered from high rates of unemployment and chronically depressed wages.

Unlike union movements in the industrialized countries of Great Britain and Germany, French trade unions remained small and weak and local without the resources to undertake sustained action. French unions had gained legal recognition in 1884, eight years after Great Britain, but six years before Germany. Unlike the trade unions of other western European states, anarcho-syndicalist unions were militantly opposed to issues of improved wages and better working conditions. Workers who combined trade unionism with anarchism shared an apocalyptic vision of social transformation. The contrast between the Labour party in Great Britain and the German Social Democrats on the one hand and the French anarcho-syndicalists on the other highlighted the split between advanced industrial countries and less-developed areas of Europe, where an artisanal class was attempting to preserve autonomy and control.

The journalist and social thinker Georges Sorel (1847–1922) captured the philosophy of anarcho-syndicalism in his book *Reflections on Violence* (1908). Sorel described the "myth," or shared belief, in the "general strike," a kind of final judgment day when justice would prevail. In order to be ready for the collapse of bourgeois society, anarcho-syndicalists must not collaborate with the existing system by accepting benefits and improvements from it. Instead, workers were to hold themselves ready by employing a technique of "direct action" to maintain worker solidarity. "Direct action" was a symbolic gesture, which did not advance the revolution but helped workers remain aware of their exploitation. A typical example of "direct action" was the agreement among the militantly revolutionary barbers' union to nick their customers periodically with the razor while shaving them. Acts such as this were meaningless in themselves—except perhaps to those who experienced them—but were intended to raise the level of commitment to a common cause.

The problems of disaffected groups in general intensified before 1914. Anarchists and anarcho-syndicalist workers deplored the centralization and organization of mass society. Yet anarchism posed no serious threat to social stability because of the effectiveness of policing in most European states. As Friedrich Engels observed at the turn of the century, random violence directed against politics and the economy was no match for the repressive forces at the command of the nation-state. The politics of mass society excluded diverse groups, including women, Jews, and ethnic minorities from participation. Yet the techniques, values, and organization of the world of politics remained available to all these groups. It was the outbreak of war in 1914 that silenced, temporarily at least, the challenge of these outsiders.

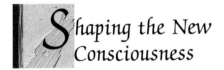

Shaping the New Consciousness

Imagine a world that discovered how to eliminate the difference between night and day. Imagine further a civilization that could obliterate distance or shrink it. Imagine a people who could see for the first time into solid mass, into their own bodies, and send images through space. These are the imaginings of fable and fantasy that can be traced back to prehistory. But what had always been the stuff of magic became reality between 1880 and 1914. The people of the West used science and technology to reshape the world and their understanding of it.

The discoveries of science had ramifications that extended beyond the laboratory, the hospital, and the classroom. Science changed the way people thought and the way they lived. It improved the quality of life by defeating diseases, improving nutrition, and lengthening life span. But scientific knowledge was not without its negative costs. Scientific discoveries led to new forces of destruc-

tion. Scientific ideas challenged morals and religious beliefs. Science was invoked to justify racial and sexual discrimination. Traditional values and religious belief also did combat with the new god of science, as philosophers proclaimed that God was dead. New disciplines claimed to study society scientifically with methods similar to those applied to the study of bacilli and the atom. A traditional world of order and hierarchy gave way to a new reality in which the center was no longer holding and the limits were constantly expanding.

The Authority of Science

What may seem commonplace at the end of the twentieth century was no less than spectacular at the end of the nineteenth. Scientific discoveries in the last quarter of the century pushed out the frontiers of knowledge. In physics, James Clerk Maxwell (1831–79) discovered the relation between electricity and magnetism. Maxwell showed mathematically that an oscillating electric charge produces an electromagnetic field and that such a field radiates outward from its source at a constant speed—the speed of light. His theories led to the discovery of the electromagnetic spectrum, comprising radiation of different wavelengths, including X rays, visible light, and radio waves. This discovery had important practical applications for the development of the electrical industry and led to the invention of radio and television. Within a generation, the names of Edison, Westinghouse, Marconi, Siemens, and Bell entered the public realm.

Discoveries in the physical sciences succeeded one another with great rapidity. The periodic table of chemical elements was formulated in 1869. Radioactivity was discovered in 1896. Two years later Marie Curie (1867–1934) and her husband Pierre (1859–1906) discovered the elements radium and polonium. At the end of the century, Ernest Rutherford (1871–1937) identified alpha and beta rays in radioactive atoms. Building on the new discoveries, Max Planck (1858–1947), Albert Einstein (1879–1955), and Niels Bohr (1885–1962) dismantled the classical physics of absolute and determined principles and left in its place modern physics based on relativity and uncertainty. In 1900 Planck propounded a theory that renounced the emphasis in classical physics on energy as a wave phenomenon in favor of a new "quantum theory" of energy as emitted and absorbed in minute, discrete amounts.

The name *Einstein* has become synonymous with genius in the twentieth century. In 1905 Albert Einstein formulated his special theory of relativity in which he established the relationship of mass and energy in the famous equation $E = mc^2$. In 1916 he published his general theory of relativity, a mathematical formulation that created new concepts of space and time. Einstein disproved the Newtonian view of gravitation as a force and instead saw it as a curved field in the time-space continuum created by the presence of mass. No one at the time foresaw that application of Einstein's theory that a particle of matter could be converted into a great quantity of energy would unleash the greatest destructive power in history—the atomic and hydrogen bombs—something that Einstein, a pacifist, lived to see developed in his lifetime.

Although there were no more dramatic discoveries than those in the physical sciences, the biological sciences too witnessed great breakthroughs. Research biologists dedicated themselves to the study of disease-causing microbes and to the chemical bases of physiology. French chemist Louis Pasteur (1822–95) studied microorganisms to find methods of preventing the spread of diseases in humans, animals, and plants. He developed methods of inoculation to provide protection against anthrax in sheep, cholera in chickens, and rabies in animals and humans.

The pace of breakthroughs in biological knowledge and medical treatment was staggering. The malaria parasite was isolated in 1880. The control of diseases such as yellow fever contributed toward improvement in the quality of life. Knowledge burst the bounds of disciplines and new fields developed to accommodate new concerns. Research in human genetics, a field that was only beginning to be understood, was begun in the first decade of the twentieth century. The studies of Austrian botanist Gregor Mendel (1822–84) in the crossbreeding of peas in the 1860s led to the Mendelian laws of inheritance. Scientists at the time ignored Mendel, but after the turn of the century Mendel's discoveries were

used in pursuing the problem of the transmission of hereditary characteristics.

Biological discoveries resulted in new state policies. Public health benefited from new methods of prevention and detection of diseases caused by germs. A professor at the University of Berlin, Rudolf Virchow (1821–1902) discovered the relationship between microbes, sewage, and disease that led to the development of modern sewer systems and pure water for urban populations. Biochemistry, bacteriology, and physiology promoted a belief in social progress through state programs. After 1900 health programs to educate the general public spread throughout Europe.

Discoveries that changed the face of the twentieth century proliferated in a variety of fields. This was a time of firsts in all directions: airplane flights and deep-sea expeditions, based on technological applications of new discoveries, pushed out boundaries of exploration above the land and below the sea. In 1909, the same year that work began in human genetics, American explorer Robert E. Peary (1856–1920) reached the North Pole. In that year, too, plastic was first manufactured, under the trade name Bakelite. Irish-born

Robert E. Peary. His claim to the discovery of the North Pole was questioned when Frederick Cook announced that he had reached the North pole before Peary. After an investigation, the U.S. Congress upheld Peary's claim.

British astronomer Agnes Mary Clerke (1842–1907) did pioneering work in the new field of astrophysics. Rutherford proposed a new spatial reality in his theory of the nuclear structure of the atom, which stated that the atom can be divided and that it consists of a nucleus surrounded by electrons revolving in orbits.

The values of an age are often revealed in the accomplishments it chooses to honor. In 1896 Swedish industrialist Alfred Nobel (1833–96), who had invented dynamite and amassed a fortune through the manufacture of explosives, established the Nobel Prizes. To be drawn from a bequest of $9.2 million, the prizes were to recognize achievement internationally in five areas: physics, physiology or medicine, chemistry, literature, and peace. Literary figures and peacemakers, poets and philosophers had long been recognized as shapers of Western culture. At the end of the nineteenth century scientists assumed a pride of place in their company.

Establishing the Social Sciences

Innovations in the social sciences paralleled the drama of discovery in the biological and physical sciences. The "scientific" study of society purported to apply the same methods of observation and experimentation to human interactions. After 1870, sociology, economics, history, psychology, anthropology, and archaeology took shape at the core of new social scientific endeavors. They, like the "hard" sciences, had benefits to offer Western women and men that improved the quality of life. But just as scientific advances could be applied to destructive ends, so, too, did the social sciences promote inequities and prejudices in the Western world.

Archaeology uncovered lost civilizations. Heinrich Schliemann (1822–90) discovered Troy. Schliemann, a German businessman, captured the imagination of Europeans when he used his own fortune to open up what he believed to be the ruins of the sites mentioned in Homeric verse. Sir Arthur Evans (1851–1941) began excavations in Crete in 1900 and over the next eight years unearthed the remains of Minoan culture. Both men used scientific procedures to reconstruct ancient cultures. Historians, too, applied new

techniques to the study of the past. German historian Leopold von Ranke (1795–1886) eschewed a literary form of historical writing that relied on legend and tradition in favor of objective, "scientific" history based on documentation and other forms of material evidence. Ranke produced influential multivolume histories of Prussia, England, France, and the world.

The social scientific study of economics came to the aid of businessmen. Influenced by the quantum theory of physics, economists posited a new view of the economy that revised the classical models of Adam Smith and David Ricardo. The neoclassical economic theory of Alfred Marshall (1842–1924) and others recognized the centrality of individual choice in the marketplace, while dealing with the problem of overproduction: how can businesses know they have produced enough to maximize profits? Economists concerned with how individuals responded to prices devised a theory of marginal utility, by which producers could calculate costs and project profits in a reliable fashion based on a pattern of response of consumers to price changes.

"Scientific" psychology developed in a variety of directions. Wilhelm Wundt (1832–1920) established the first laboratory devoted to psychological research in Leipzig in 1879. From his experiments he concluded that thought is grounded in physical reality. The Russian physiologist Ivan Pavlov (1849–1936) had already received the Nobel Prize for physiology or medicine for his study of the dog's digestive system when he began his famous series of experiments demonstrating the conditioned reflex in dogs. Other psychological models competed for theoretical primacy. With his theory of personality development and the creation of psychoanalysis, the science of the unconscious, Sigmund Freud (1859–1939) greatly influenced the direction of psychology. (See Special Feature, "Sigmund Freud, Explorer of Dreams," pp. 776–777.) Freudian probing of the unconscious was a model greatly at odds with the behavioral perspective of conditioned responses based on Pavlov's work.

The new social science of criminology claimed scientific veracity after 1880. In 1885, Sir Francis Galton (1822–1911), a cousin of Charles Darwin, proved the individuality of fingerprints through scientific study and thereby initiated an important method of identifying criminals. Criminologists joined psychiatrists as expert witnesses in criminal trials for the first time at the end of the nineteenth century. Galton also propagated pseudoscientific ideas about eugenics, the improvement of the human race through selective breeding. Anthropological studies of primitive cultures influenced eugenic assumptions about racial inferiority.

The new specialties of forensic medicine and criminal anthropology came into being at the end of the century. *The Criminal Man* (1876), written by Italian criminologist Cesare Lombroso (1836–1909), claimed to be a scientific study of the physical attributes of convicted criminals. Through observation and statistical compilation, Lombroso discovered the "born criminals," individuals whose physical characteristics determined their deviance. Criminals, he claimed, could be identified by their looks. With statistics Lombroso demonstrated, for example, that left-handed, red-headed people with low foreheads were naturally disposed to a life of crime. Even during his lifetime, Lombroso's ideas were widely disputed and subsequently discredited but their temporary dominance was a good indication of how scientific claims justified prejudicial assumptions. Against Lombroso the French school of criminology stressed the social determinants of crime and saw poverty and malnutrition as explanations for the different physical appearance of criminals.

The psychology of crowd behavior originated in the work of the French physician Gustave Le Bon (1841–1931). In *Psychology of Crowds* (1895), Le Bon argued that the masses were instinctively irrational. Through his "science" he arrived at the political judgment that democracy was a despicable and dangerous form of government. Émile Durkheim (1858–1917) is regarded as the founder of modern sociology. In his famous study of suicide as a social phenomenon, Durkheim pitted sociological theory against psychology and argued that deviance was the result not of psychic disturbances but of environmental factors and hereditary forces.

Heredity became a general explanation for behavior of all sorts. The novels of Émile Zola (1840–1902) presented a popular view of biological determinism. Zola's protagonists were doomed by self-destructive characteristics they inherited from their parents. Everything from poverty, drunkenness, crime, and a declining birth rate could be attributed to biologically determined causes. For some theorists, this reasoning teetered on the edge of racism and ideas about "better blood." Intelligence was now measured for the first time "scientifically" with IQ tests developed at the Sorbonne by the psychologist Alfred Binet (1857–1911) in the 1890s. The tests did not acknowledge the importance of cultural factors in the development of intelligence and scientifically legitimated a belief in natural elites. Not least of all, science was also invoked in support of a particular system of gender relations, one that itself was undergoing assault and upheaval between 1871 and 1914.

The "New Woman" and the New Consciousness

New scientific ideas had a formative impact on prevailing views of gender relations and female sexuality. The natural sciences were employed to prove the inferiority of women in the species. In *The Descent of Man* (1871), Charles Darwin, the giant of evolutionary theory, concluded that the mental power of man was higher than that of woman. The female's need for male protection, the father of evolution reasoned, had increased her dependence over time while at the same time increasing the competition of natural selection among men. The result, Darwin argued, was inequality between the sexes. Darwin went on to reject women's emancipation as out of step with biological realities. What Darwin presented was a vicious and closed circle in which women's dependence had made them inferior and their inferiority kept them dependent. These attitudes toward gender and race marked the advent of biological "proofs" to justify social policies. Darwin and his disciples who applied biological principles to society came to be known as "social Darwinists," specialists who claimed that "survival of the fittest" was a concept that could be applied to all social interactions between races and between the sexes.

Darwin was not the only man of science who had ideas about woman's proper place. Others made a dubious case for brain size as an index of superiority. The French physiologist Paul Broca (1824–80), a contemporary of Darwin's, countered in 1873 that the skull capacity of the two sexes was very similar and that a case for inferiority could not be based on measurement. But Broca was atypical. Most scientific opinion argued in favor of female frailty and outright inferiority. Social Darwinists adapted evolutionary biology to the debate over inequality between the sexes. They complemented their race theories with evolutionary theories of sexual division: "What was decided among the prehistoric Protozoa cannot be annulled by an Act of Parliament." Sexless prehistoric protozoa held the message for social Darwinists that women should not enjoy the right to vote.

In general, the natural sciences worked to reinforce the idea of women as reproducers whose proper role was nurturing and whose proper domain was the home. The social sciences, in particular sociology, echoed these findings by asserting that the male-dominated household was a proof of social progress.

These "scientific" arguments justified the exclusion of women from educational opportunities and from professions like medicine and law. Biology became destiny as women's attempts at equal education came up against closed doors. Stalwarts broke the prohibitions, but women who gained higher education in these decades were the exception that proved the rule. Those women who were able to get an education were blocked from using it. There was a generalized fear in Western societies that women who attempted to exceed their "natural" abilities would damage their reproductive functions and neglect their nurturing roles. The specter of sickly children and female nervous disorders was invoked to oppose demands for co-education. Women's education was assigned to the church and was intended to meet the needs of the family. The creation of the first separate women's colleges in the late 1860s marked the beginning of the pioneering era of higher education for women.

In this age of scientific justification of female inferiority, the "new woman" emerged. All over Europe the feminist movement had demanded social, economic, and political progress for women. But the "new woman" phenomenon exceeded the bounds of the feminist movement and can be described as a general cultural phenomenon. The search for independence was overwhelmingly a middle-class phenomenon that had

a psychological as well as a political significance in the years between 1880 and 1914. Victorian stereotypes of the angel at the hearth were crumbling. The "new woman" was a woman characterized by intelligence, strength, and sexual desire, in every way man's equal. The Norwegian playwright Henrik Ibsen (1828–1906) created a fictional embodiment of the phenomenon in Nora, the hero of *A Doll's House* (1879), who was typical of the restive spirit for independence among wives and mothers confined to suffocating households and relegated to the status of children. Contemporary opinion condemned Nora as immoral for abandoning her home, her husband, and her children.

The "new woman's" pursuit of independence included control over her own body. The term *birth control* was first used by the American, Margaret Sanger (1879–1966), although the reality itself was not new. Women had always known of and employed contraceptive and abortive techniques to limit family size. What was different in the period before 1914 was the militant public discussion of means of preventing conception and of the death and debilitation that resulted from primitive methods. The development of a process of vulcanizing rubber in the mid-nineteenth century had made condoms available to a mass market, but they were little employed. A growing number of women, among whom were medical doctors, decided to take information to the public. A common result was state repression of their activities. A birth-control advocate in Great Britain, Annie Besant (1847–1933), was charged with corrupting youth for distributing books that dealt with contraception. Aletta Jacobs (1849–1929), the first woman to practice medicine in Holland, opened a contraceptive clinic in 1882. Leagues for distributing contraceptive information were formed elsewhere in Europe. Birth-control advocates aimed to preserve women's health and to give them some control over their reproductive lives.

Discussions of con-

Annie Besant

Sigmund Freud, Explorer of Dreams

Sigmund Freud was a disciplined man, precise and punctual in his habits. In many ways, his life was typical of a Viennese bourgeois professional at the end of the nineteenth century. His day was like a railway timetable, scheduled to the minute whether in seeing patients, dining with his family, or taking his daily constitutional. He even calculated his pleasures, counting as his only indulgence the twenty cigars he smoked every day.

The order in Freud's life seemed curiously at odds with his dedication to the study of disorder. He was a man of science, a medical doctor specializing in the organic diseases of the nervous system. Early in his career he began to question physiological explanations for certain nervous disorders and to search for another reason for the disorders of the mind. His exploration took him to Paris in 1885 to study with the leading French neurologist Jean Martin Charcot (1825–1893), whose work on hysteria had won him an international reputation. Surrounded by hysterics in Charcot's clinic, Freud wondered whether organic physical illnesses could be traced to psychological problems. Freud explored the value of hypnosis as a technique for uncovering the secret workings of the mind. He learned that emotions alone could produce physical symptoms like blindness and paralysis. By hypnotizing patients, Freud caught glimpses of the world of the unconscious as a vast and hidden terrain. He approached this new territory as an explorer.

Freud created a new science of the unconscious, psychoanalysis, when he rejected physiological causes for nervous disorders in favor of psychological ones. He intended psychoanalysis as a theory of personality and a method of treatment, or therapy. This was a dramatic break with existing theories of madness and mental disorder. On his seventieth birthday, Freud looked back over his own career and described his achievement: "The poets and philosophers before me discovered the unconscious; what I discovered was the scientific method by which the unconscious can be studied."

The hostile reaction to Freud's break with existing ideas about mental disorders was further aggravated by the importance he attributed to sexuality. Colleagues in Vienna were shocked by the direction that his work was taking. Freud began by hypothesizing that disturbed patients developed neurotic symptoms because of the repression of memories of actual sexual abuse as children. He moved away from this recognition of sexual abuse to a theory in which the subject had *fantasied* about sex as a child and then had repressed it. In searching for the root of psychological disorders, Freud argued that sexual conflicts originating in early childhood were the cause of adult neuroses. Repressed sexual desire thereby became the key to understanding human behavior.

Freud's self-described scientific method, which allowed him to probe the unconscious, was *free association*. Patients were encouraged to talk, or "associate," in a relaxed atmosphere. The couch in the doctor's office has become the enduring symbol of the psychoanalytic method. Patients were particularly encouraged to talk about their dreams. The unconscious, Freud argued, manifests itself in dreams. The role of the psychoanalyst is to examine the content of the dream and interpret it, facilitating recognition and hence a cure in the patient.

Freud's first major work and probably the most important study of his career, *The Interpretation of Dreams* (1900), heralded the new century. Working with his own dreams and those of his patients, Freud posited that a dream is the fulfillment of a wish. Dreams are not literal in their meaning; their symbols and context must always be interpreted. The experiences of our conscious lives are rearranged in dreams. For Freud, nothing was accidental. Jokes, obsessions, and even slips of the tongue ("Freudian slips") as well as dreams were indicators of unconscious desires. In later life Freud was supposed to have said that "sometimes a cigar is just a cigar." But in his dream theory every object had meaning in the context of the

fictitious names. In subsequent works, Freud went on to detail the uncharted land of the unconscious discovered in his work on dreams with his designations for the components of personality—the "ego," the "superego," and the "id."

Sigmund Freud gave to Western culture a new vocabulary. His lexicon has survived throughout the twentieth century and has entered common parlance as a way of explaining our daily lives in psychological terms that range from the "anal retentive stage" to "sublimation." He bequeathed to Western men and women a new way of looking at the world. Freud's work sounded the death knell for the nineteenth century's blind faith in reason. For Freud human beings were driven by subterranean instincts and desires. The horrors of war and destruction in the twentieth century confirmed for Freud his belief of the irrationality of Western civilization.

Freud died in exile in London in 1939, having fled from the Nazi occupation of his beloved Vienna. During his lifetime and ever since, his theories have been refuted as explaining nothing more than the psychic world in which he lived—the world of European middle-class men at the beginning of the twentieth century. But there can be no denying that his exploration of the land of dreams in the world of the unconscious was a revolutionary event in the history of Western thought.

patient's associations, whether cigar, banana, flight of stairs, or broken candle. Freud used his own dreams and his relationship with his parents to describe the neurotic personality and to suggest the *Oedipus complex* so important to his later work on childhood sexuality. Here the child's unresolved desire for the parent of the opposite sex formed the basis for all ego development. In famous case studies such as "Dora," "The Wolf Man," and "The Rat Man," Freud described the symptoms and histories of patients to whom he assigned

traception brought into the public arena the premise that women, like men, were sexual beings. This was reinforced by the frank discussions of sexuality in the works of Sigmund Freud. The first English translation of Freud's *The Interpretation of Dreams* appeared in 1913 with a warning note from the publisher that its sale should be limited to doctors, lawyers, and clerics. Richard von Krafft-Ebing (1840–1902) and Havelock Ellis (1859–1939) also contributed to the public discussion of sex in their works on sexuality and sexual deviance. By 1900 sexuality and reproduction were openly connected to discussions of women's rights.

The new sciences had worked to change the world. At the same time, those intent on preserving traditional values invoked scientific authority. But as the uncertainty over gender roles at the beginning of the twentieth century makes clear, science was a way of thinking as well as a body of doctrine. Traditional ideas might be scientifically justified but they would not go unchallenged.

The New Consumption

The great Russian novelist Lev Tolstoy (1828–1910) was an astute observer of the world in which he lived. In 1877 he condemned the materialism that characterized European society: "Money is a new form of slavery, and distinguishable from the old simply by the fact that it is impersonal—that there is no human relation between master and slave." Although he was speaking as a moral philosopher, Tolstoy had put his finger on something that economists were just beginning to understand—the extension of a money economy. Tolstoy was aware of how peasants freed from the land became entangled in a web of financial obligations that constituted a new form of serfdom.

At the end of the nineteenth century the role of money changed in ways affecting all of Western society. Workers were beginning to share in the benefits of industrial prosperity. This prosperity differed dramatically by geographic region and by occupation. But the expansion in the ranks of a salaried working class augured a shift in patterns of behavior. Lagging behind the industrial revolutions but no less important was a revolution in consumption patterns among European popula-

tions. The new consumer age is best illustrated by the creation of the big department stores of the last quarter of the nineteenth century. The Bon Marché Department Store in Paris occupied over 52,000 square feet and contained a vast selection of goods. Everything from initialed toilet paper to household furniture was now located under a single roof. The department store was intended to satisfy every need. Advertising and the art of display became industries in themselves, whose goal was to encourage people to buy things they did not need. The promise of the good life, epitomized in the department store and preached by advertising, now seemed accessible to everyone.

Leisure time also became a consumer item in the late nineteenth century. In 1899, the American economist Thorstein Veblen (1857–1929) published a pathbreaking work that was little appreciated at the time. *The Theory of the Leisure Class* argued that leisure was a form of *conspicuous consumption*, a term Veblen coined. More than a theory, his work constituted a critique of the values of Western culture. Women and the family were, for Veblen, the primary vehicles for conspicuous consumption. Elegant dress, for example, conveyed status and served as a sign of leisure just as it had done in aristocratic society. Expensive clothing was designed to demonstrate abstinence from productive employment. For this purpose, women were actually "mutilated," in Veblen's term, by the corset that constricted their vitality and rendered them unfit for work. Women immobilized by their clothes and shoes became the ultimate symbols of social status.

The middle and upper classes controlled sufficient disposable income to allow them to "spend" time in such leisure pursuits as flocking to seaside resorts in Great Britain and on the Continent. Leisure-time activities, however, remained out of the financial reach of most working-class people, who could not afford the forms of entertainment pursued by the wealthy. Instead, working-class men congregated in cafes and pubs. Vaudeville and music halls rose in popularity from the 1880s, their low admission price attracting ever larger crowds. Scantily clad women's bodies became the center of a new mass entertainment with at least thirty "strip-tease" shows in Paris in the 1890s. These activities fostered fear among the middle classes that working-class leisure was degenerate. The newly inven-

This street scene, Outside the Théâtre Du Vaudeville, Paris, *was painted in about 1890 by Jean Beraud.*

ted cinema also exercised a growing appeal to European men and women of all ages and classes.

Not least important in the new leisure was the rise of organized sports. Strict organization of work life in mature industrial society may have made sports an attractive way of organizing leisure. Men—there were few organized sports for women—worked by the clock and now played by the clock as well. Sports also promoted national and regional identifications. Beginning in the 1860s men began playing the games they had learned as boys in English public schools. Rugby, football (soccer), and cricket soon developed national followings. Golf originated in Scotland in this period and spread throughout Europe and to the United States. Spectator sports grew in importance, with over 100,000 people attending British soccer matches at the beginning of the twentieth century. Victorians saw the necessity of "recreation," and endorsed the renewing, relaxing, and entertaining aspects of organized play.

Scouting also originated at the end of the nineteenth century as another form of organized leisure. Uniformed boys were taught "manly" virtues of self-reliance and teamwork. Team spirit was tied to patriotism. Scouting organizations for girls emphasized domestic virtues and household tasks. Amateur athletics and track-and-field events grew in popularity, especially after the establishment of an international Olympics competition modeled on the ancient Greek games. The first modern Olympiad was held in Athens in 1896, and except for the upheavals caused by war, the Olympic Games have been held at four-year intervals throughout the twentieth century.

Cycling became a popular competitive sport on the Continent with the establishment of the Tour de France at the beginning of the twentieth century. Some saw in the new pastime of bicycling a threat to the social order. Women, attracted by the exercise and mobility afforded by this new means of transportation, altered their costumes in favor of freedom of movement. For eminently practical reasons, they discarded their corsets and bustles and shortened their skirts. As women gained greater mobility, some observers saw in the "new woman" on the bicycle seat the decline of true womanhood and Western values.

The engineering marvel of the Eiffel Tower, built in 1889 for the World Exposition held in Paris, became a symbol not only of the French capital but of the values of the new age. New artifacts of European culture proliferated. Photography, motorcars, bicycles, motion-picture cameras, and X rays all created sensations when they appeared. London's Inner Circle underground railway was completed in 1884, and other lines soon followed, forming a vast urban subterranean network. In 1898, the miracle of underground transportation became a reality in Paris with the opening of the *métro,* or subway. Yet some observers saw in this new age only disruption and upheaval in traditional liberal values. The Eiffel Tower was criticized more than it was praised. It was a building, yet it was not. Its inside and its outside were confused. The admirers of classic architecture lamented the ugliness of this girdered monument whose main function was to demonstrate structural innovation for its own sake. The Eiffel Tower, like the values of the new age, critics warned, was hollow and would not endure.

Suggestions For Further Reading

European Economy and the Politics of Mass Society

Michael Burns, *Rural Society and French Politics: Boulangism and the Dreyfus Affair, 1886–1900* (Princeton, NJ: Princeton University Press, 1984). Examines the impact on rural France of two political watersheds of the Third Republic in order to gauge the importance of national politics in nonurban settings.

Albert S. Lindemann, *A History of European Socialism* (New Haven, CT: Yale University Press, 1983). Surveys socialist thought in the nineteenth and twentieth centuries and examines the relationship among ideology, institutions, and workers in their historical context.

Carl E. Schorske, *Fin-de-Siecle Vienna: Politics and Culture* (New York: Alfred A. Knopf, 1980). A series of essays describing the break with nineteenth-century liberal culture in one of Europe's great cities, as artists, intellectuals, and politicians responded to the disintegration of the Habsburg Empire.

Eugen Weber, *Peasants into Frenchmen: The Modernization of Rural France* (Stanford, CA: Stanford University Press, 1976). Views the integration of the French peasantry into national political life through agents of change, including the railroads, schools, and the army. The author contends that a national political culture took the place of traditional beliefs and practices between 1870 and 1914 in France.

Hans-Ulrich Wehler, *The German Empire, 1871–1918* (Leamington Spa: Berg Publishers, 1985). Stresses the institutional continuities of German society and links pre-World War I Germany to the rise of Nazism.

Outsiders In Mass Politics

Richard J. Evans, *The Feminist Movement in Germany, 1894–1933* (London: Sage Publications, 1976). Considers two conflicting approaches to bourgeois feminism: one radical and the other conservative and authoritarian, and discusses the role of social Darwinism in the women's movement and the place of feminism in political life.

Steven C. Hause and Anne R. Kenney, *Women's Suffrage and Social Politics in the French Third Republic* (Princeton, NJ: Princeton University Press, 1984). Examines the women's suffrage movement from its origins through its defeat after World War I in the Senate. Aims, tactics, and leadership of the women's movement receive special attention.

Richard Stites, *The Women's Liberation Movement in Russia: Feminism, Nihilism, and Bolshevism, 1860–1930* (Princeton, NJ: Princeton University Press, 1978). Situates the Russian women's movement within the contexts of both nineteenth-century European feminism and twentieth-century Communist ideology and traces its development from the early feminists through the rise of the Bolsheviks to power. Includes a discussion of the Russian Revolution's impact on the status of women.

William M. Reddy, *The Rise of Market Culture: The Textile Trade and French Society, 1750–1900* (Cambridge: Cambridge University Press, 1984). A cultural interpretation of the textile trade in the era of industrialization. Reddy examines the creation of market culture and workers' resistance to it through a study of collective action, workers' songs, bourgeois attitudes, and factory organization.

Shaping the New Consciousness

Stephen Kern, *The Culture of Time and Space, 1880–1918* (Cambridge, MA: Harvard University Press, 1983). Describes how late-nineteenth-century technological advances created new modes of thinking about and experiencing time and space.

Michael B. Miller, *The Bon Marché: Bourgeois Culture and the Department Store, 1869–1920* (Princeton, NJ: Princeton University Press, 1981). A social and cultural history of the department store as the creation and reflection of bourgeois culture.

Robert A. Nye, *Crime, Madness, and Politics in Modern France: The Medical Concept of National Decline* (Princeton, NJ: Princeton University Press, 1984). Nye shows how the medical concept of deviance was linked to a general cultural crisis in fin-de-siècle France.

William M. Reddy, *Money and Liberty in Modern Europe: A Critique of Historical Understanding* (Cambridge: Cambridge University Press, 1987). This essay on the role of money in modern Europe contends that its widespread use in exchange influenced social structure. Arguing that monetary exchange intensified existing social inequities, Reddy examines the expansion of commerce in France, Germany, and England.

Martin Wiener, *English Culture and the Decline of the Industrial Spirit, 1850–1980* (Cambridge: Cambridge University Press, 1981). A cultural history of growth and decline from Victoria to Thatcher. By drawing on literature, art, architecture, politics, and economics, the author describes the ambiguous attitude of the elite toward industry and argues that English culture was never conducive to sustained industrial growth.

Rosalind H. Williams, *Dream Worlds: Mass Consumption in Late Nineteenth-Century France* (Berkeley, CA: University of California Press, 1982). A historical overview of attitudes toward consumption and an examination of the creation of the consumer mentality in terms of the consumer revolution and its consequences.

25

Europe
and the World,
1870–1914

Mapping the World and Measuring Time

People drew maps before they knew how to write. Yet in 1885 only one-ninth of the land surface of the earth had been surveyed. Within the next decade, however, centuries-old ignorance diminished as cartographers, surveyors, and compilers fanned out around the globe to probe peninsulas and chart continents. By 1900, every continent, including Antarctica, had been explored and its measure taken.

This great leap forward in knowledge did not produce a standardized and uniform map of the world. State officials argued for the primacy of their own national traditions, symbols, colors, and units for measurement and blocked attempts at standardization. Mapmakers from Europe and the United States began to gather regularly in international conventions with the goal of devising a uniform map of the world that would satisfy everyone. Their attempts repeatedly failed.

One particular meeting in Paris in 1875 chose the meter, the unit of measurement whose practical application originated in the French Revolution, as the standard measurement for the world map. Supporters argued that it would provide mapmakers with a common language, easily understood and easily divisible. The British countered with yards and miles, unscientifically developed units of measurement to which they had been committed for centuries.

Mapmakers who acknowledged the logic of the meter could not agree on which prototype meter should be taken as standard. Should the meter be measured according to the common method of the movement of a pendulum? If so, gravitation varying from one place to another on the earth's surface would result in different meter lengths. Most agreed that the meter should be measured in reference to the arc of the meridian.

The prime meridian, the place on a map that indicates zero longitude, was itself not a fixed phenomenon. The debate over where the prime meridian should be located is a perfect example of the politics of mapmaking. Unlike the equator, which is midway between the North and South poles, zero longitude can be drawn anywhere. As a result maps of different national origins located the prime meridian to enhance their own claims to importance. Paris, Philadelphia, and Beijing were just three of the sites for zero longitude on nineteenth-century maps.

Uniformity, the cartographers insisted, would have advantages for everyone. Not least of all, a standardized map would make standardized timekeeping easier. Standard time could be calculated according to zones of longitude. Germany had five different time zones in 1891. In France every city had its own time taken from solar readings. The United States had over two hundred time zones from one coast to the other. In industrial societies with

FREEDOM · FRATERNITY · FEDERATION

MAP OF THE WORLD
SHOWING THE EXTENT OF THE BRITISH TERRITORIES IN 1786.

WORLD

IMPERIAL FEDERATION.—MAP OF THE WORLD SHOWING THE EXTENT OF THE BRITISH EMPIRE IN 1886.
STATISTICAL INFORMATION FURNISHED BY CAPTAIN J.C.R.COLOMB. M.P. FORMERLY R.M.A. ____ BRITISH TERRITORIES COLOURED RED.

railroad timetables and legal contracts, time had to be controlled and it had to be exact. Time had to be standardized. Specialists proposed that the Royal Observatory in Greenwich, England, was the best place to locate the prime meridian in order to calculate a standard time system. The French balked, insisting on Paris as the only candidate for the designation. In the end, there was compromise. The metric system prevailed as the standard for measurement, and the prime meridian passed through the Royal Greenwich Observatory, where standard time was calculated for most of the globe. All of this was possible for the first time only at the end of the nineteenth century.

In 1891 a young Viennese geographer named Albrecht Penck proposed an international map of the world. Penck's idea was a simple one: to produce a map using standard symbols and colors and omitting political boundaries. Original place names would be used out of respect for local usage. He did not live to see his international map of the world completed, and the disruptions of the twentieth century have slowed its progress. Penck's proposal came up against the harsh realities of mapmaking. Technology had made more-accurate knowledge possible. Political wranglings and national pride prevented knowledge from being standardized. A global vision remained subordinate to the limits of national boundaries.

The New Imperialism

The concept of empire was certainly not invented by Europeans in the last third of the nineteenth century. Before 1870 European states had controlled empires. The influence of Great Britain stretched beyond the limits of its formal holdings in India and South Africa. Russia held Siberia and central Asia, and France ruled Algeria and Indochina. Older empires, Spain for example, had survived from the sixteenth century but as hollow shells. What, then, was new about the "new imperialism" practiced by England, France, and Germany after 1870? In part, the new imperialism was the acquisition of territories on an intense and unprecedented scale. Industrialization created the tools of transportation, communication, and domination that permitted the rapid pace of global empire-building. Above all, what distinguished the new imperialism was the domination by the industrial powers over the nonindustrial world. The United States also participated in the new imperialism, less by territorial acquisition and more by developing an "invisible" empire of trade and influence in the Pacific. The forms of imperialism may have varied from nation to nation, but the basically unequal relationship between an industrial power and an undeveloped territory did not.

Only nation-states commanded the technology and resources necessary for the new scale of imperialist expansion. Rivalry among a few European nation-states—notably, Great Britain, France, and Germany—was a common denominator that set the standards by which these nations and other European states gained control of the globe by 1900. Why did the Europeans create vast empires? Were empires built for economic gain, military protection, or national glory? Questions about motives may obscure common features of the new imperialism. Industrial powers sought to take over nonindustrial regions, not in isolated areas but all over the globe. In the attempt they necessarily competed with one another, successfully adapting the resources of industrialism to the needs of conquest.

The Technology of Empire

For Europeans at the end of the nineteenth century, the world had definitely become a smaller place. Steam, iron, and electricity—the great forces of Western industrialization—were responsible for shrinking the globe. Technology

This postcard was issued by Kaiser Wilhelm II — whose cameo is seen in the inset — to celebrate the launching of the S.S. Imperator, *a German warship. The grandiose name, which means "emperor" in Latin, was typical of the superpatriotic propaganda of an imperialistic age.*

The Suez canel was opened with appropriate ceremony in 1869 by the Egyptian ruler, Ismā'īl Pasha. He sold his canal shares to Great Britain in 1875.

not only allowed Europeans to accomplish tasks and to mass-produce goods efficiently, but it also altered previous understandings of time and space.

Steam, which powered factories, proved equally efficient as an energy source in transportation. Great iron steamships fueled by coal replaced the smaller, slower, wind-powered, wooden sailing vessels that had ruled the sea for centuries. Steam-powered vessels transported large cargoes of people and goods more quickly and more reliably. Iron ships were superior to wood in their durability, lightness, water-tightness, cargo space, speed, and fuel economy. For most of the nineteenth century British trading ships and the British navy dominated the seas, but after 1880 other nations, especially Germany, challenged England by building versatile and efficient iron steamers. In a society in which time was money, steamships were important because, for the first time, ocean-going vessels could meet schedules as precisely and as predictably as could railroads. Just as the imperial Romans had used their network of roads to link far-flung territories to the capital, Europeans used sea lanes to join their colonies to the home country.

Until 1850 Europeans ventured no farther on the African continent than its coastal areas. Now the installation of coal-burning boilers on smaller boats permitted navigation of previously uncharted rivers. Steam power made exploration and migration possible and greatly contributed to knowledge of terrain, natural wealth, and resources. Smaller, steam-powered vessels also increased European inland trade with China, Burma, and India.

While technology improved European mobility on water, it also literally moved the land. Harbors were deepened to accommodate the new iron- and then steel-hulled ships. One of the greatest engineering feats of the century was the construction of a hundred-mile-long canal across the Isthmus of Suez in Egypt. Completed in 1869, the Suez Canal joined the Mediterranean and Red seas and created a new, safer trade route to the East. No longer did trading vessels have to make the long voyage around Africa's Cape of Good Hope. The Suez Canal was built by the French under the supervision of Ferdinand de Lesseps (1805–94), a diplomat with no technical or financial background who was able to promote construction because of concessions he received from the Said Pasha of Egypt. The canal could accommodate ships of all sizes. Great Britain purchased a controlling interest in the Suez Canal in 1875 to benefit its trade with India.

De Lesseps later presided over the initial construction of the Panama Canal in the Western Hemisphere. The combination of French mismanagement, bankruptcy, and the high incidence of disease among work crews enabled the United States to acquire rights to the Panama project and complete it by 1914. Fifty-one miles long, the Panama Canal connected the world's two largest bodies of water, the Atlantic and Pacific oceans, across the Isthmus of Panama by a waterway containing a series of locks. Now the passage from the Atlantic to the Pacific took less than eight hours—much less time than the various overland routes or the voyage around the tip of South America. Both the Suez and Panama canals were built in pursuit of speed. Shorter distances meant quicker travel, which in turn meant higher profits.

Technology also altered time by increasing the speed with which Westerners communicated with other parts of the world. In 1830, for example, it took about two years for a person sending a letter from Great Britain to India to receive a reply. In 1850, steam-powered mail boats shortened the time required for the same round-trip correspondence to about two or three months. But the real revolution in communication came through electricity. Thousands of miles of copper telegraph wire laced countries together; insulated underwater cables linked continents to each other. By the late nineteenth century a vast telegraph network connected Europe to every area of the world. In 1870 a telegram from London to Bombay arrived in a matter of hours, instead of months, and a response could be received back in London on the same day. Faster communications extended power and control throughout empires. Now Europeans could communicate immediately with their distant colonies, dispatching troops, orders, and supplies. This communication network eliminated the problem of overextension that had plagued Roman imperial organization in the third century. For the first time continents discovered by Europeans five centuries earlier were brought into daily contact with the West.

Technological advances in other areas helped foster European imperialism in the nineteenth century. Advances in medicine permitted European men and women to penetrate disease-laden swamps and jungles. After 1850, European explorers, traders, missionaries, and adventurers carried quinine pills. The bitter-tasting derivative of cinchona-tree bark, quinine was discovered to be an effective treatment for malaria. This treatment got its first important test during the

The transatlantic telegraph cable was the first intercontinental communications link of the electric age. This illustration shows the Great Eastern, the largest ship afloat, which finally succeeded in laying the cable in 1866.

French invasion of Algeria in 1830, and it allowed the French to stay healthy enough to conquer that North African country between 1830 and 1847. David Livingstone (1813–73) and Henry M. Stanley (1841–1904) were just two of the many explorers who crossed vast terrains and explored the waterways of Africa, after malaria, the number one killer of Europeans, had been controlled.

Europeans carried the technologies of destruction as well as survival with them into less-developed areas of the world. New types of firearms produced in the second half of the nineteenth century included breechloading rifles, repeating rifles, and machine guns. The new weapons gave the advantages of both accurate aim and rapid fire. The spears of African warriors and the primitive weaponry of Chinese rebels were no match for sophisticated European arms, which permitted their bearers to lie down while firing and to remain undetected at distances of up to half a mile.

The new technology did not cause the new imperialism. The Western powers used technological advances as a tool for establishing their control of the world. Viewed as a tool, however, the new technology does explain how vast areas of land and millions of people were conquered so rapidly.

Motives for Empire

If technology was not the cause but only a tool, what explains the new imperialism of the late nineteenth century? Were wealthy financiers, searching for high-yielding opportunities for investments, the driving force? Was profit the main motive? Were politicians and heads of state in the game for the prestige and glory that territorial expansion could bring them at home?

There are no easy or simple explanations for the new imperialism. Individuals made their fortunes overseas, and heavy industries like the Krupp firm in Germany prospered with the expansion of state-protected colonies. Yet many colonies were economically worthless. Tunisia and Morocco, acquired for their strategic and political importance, constituted an economic loss for the French, who poured more funds into their administration than they were able to extract. Each imperial power held one or more colonies whose costs outweighed the return. Yet this does not mean that some Europeans were simply irrational in their pursuit of empire or that they were driven by an atavistic desire to recapture the glories of a precapitalist past and willing to incur financial losses to do so.

Economics. The test for economic motivation cannot simply be reduced to a balance sheet of debits and credits because, in the end, an account of state revenues and state expenditures provides only a static picture of the business of empire. Even losses cannot be counted as proof against the profit motive in expansion. In modern capitalism, profits, especially great profits, are often predicated on risks. Portugal and Italy took great risks and failed as players in the game in which the great industrial powers called the shots. Prestige through the acquisition of empire was one way of keeping alive in the game. Imperialism was influenced by business interests, market considerations, and the pursuit of individual and national fortunes. Not by accident did the great industrial powers control the scramble and dictate the terms of expansion. Nor was it merely fortuitous that Great Britain, the nation that provided the model for European expansion, dedicated itself to the establishment of a profitable worldwide network of trade and investment. Above all, the search for investment opportunities, whether railroads in China or diamond mines in South Africa, lured Europeans into a world system that challenged capitalist ingenuity and imagination. Acquiring territory was only one means of protecting investments. But there were other benefits associated with the acquisition of territory that cannot be reduced to economic terms, and those too must be considered.

Geopolitics. Geopolitics, or the politics of geography, is based on the recognition that certain areas of the world are valuable for political reasons. The term, first used at the end of the nineteenth century, described a process well under way in international relations. Statesmen influenced by geopolitical concerns recognized the strategic value of land. Some territory was considered important because of its proximity to acquired colonies or to territory targeted for takeover. France, for example, occupied thousands of square miles of the Sahara Desert to protect its interests in Algeria.

Other territory was important because of its proximity to sea routes. Egypt had significance for Great Britain not because of its inherent economic potential but because it permitted the British to protect access to lucrative markets in India through the Suez Canal. Beginning in 1875, the British purchased shares in the canal. By 1879 Egypt was under the informal dual rule of France and Great Britain. The British used the deterioration of internal Egyptian politics to justify their occupation of the country in 1882. Protected access to India also accounted for Great Britain's maintenance of Mediterranean outposts, its acquisition of territory on the east coast of Africa, and its occupation of territory in southern Asia.

A third geopolitical motive for annexation was the necessity of fueling bases throughout the world. Faster and more reliable than wind-powered vessels, coal-powered ships were, nonetheless, dependent on guaranteed fueling bases in friendly ports of call. Islands in the South Pacific and the Indian Ocean were acquired primarily to serve as coaling stations for the great steamers carrying manufactured goods to colonial ports and returning with foodstuffs and raw materials. Ports along the southern rim of Asia served the same purpose. The need for protection of colonies, fueling ports, and sea-lanes led to the creation of naval bases like those on the Red Sea at Djibouti by the French, in Southeast Asia at Singapore by the British, and in the Hawaiian Islands at Honolulu by the Americans.

In turn, the acquisition of territories justified the increase in naval budgets and the size of fleets. Britain still had the world's largest navy, but by the beginning of the twentieth century, the United States and Germany had entered the competition for dominance of sea-lanes. Japan joined the contest by expanding its navy as a vehicle for its own claims to empire in the Pacific.

The politics of geography was land- as well as sea-based. As navies grew to protect sea-lanes, armies expanded to police new lands. Between 1890 and 1914, military expenditures of Western governments grew phenomenally, with war machines doubling in size. In both its impact on domestic budgets and its protection of markets and trading routes, geopolitics had a strong economic component. Governments became consumers of heavy industry; their predictable participation in markets for armaments and military supplies helped control fluctuations in the business cycle and reduce unemployment at home. A side effect of the growing importance of geopolitics was the increased influence of military and naval leaders in foreign and domestic policy-making.

Nationalism.   Many European statesmen in the last quarter of the nineteenth century gave stirring speeches about the importance of empire as a means of enhancing national prestige. In his Crystal Palace speech of 1872, Benjamin Disraeli, British Prime Minister in 1868 and 1874–80, put the challenge boldly to the British:

> I appeal to the sublime instinct of an ancient people ... The issue is not a mean one. It is whether you will be content to be a comfortable England, modelled and moulded upon Continental principles and meeting in due course an inevitable fate, or whether you will be a great country, an imperial country, a country where your sons, when they rise, rise to paramount positions and obtain not merely the esteem of their countrymen but command the respect of the world.

National prestige was not an absolute value but one weighed relatively. Possessing an empire may have meant "keeping up with the Joneses," as it did for smaller countries like Italy. Imperial status was important to a country like Portugal, which was willing to go bankrupt to maintain its territories. But prestige without economic power was the form of imperialism without its substance. Nation-states could, through the acquisition of overseas territories, gain bargaining chips to be played at the international conference table. In this way, smaller nations hoped to be taken seriously in the system of alliances that preserved "the balance of power" in Europe.

Western newspapers deliberately fostered the desire for the advancement of national interests. Newspapers competed for readers, and their circulations often depended on the passions they aroused. Filled with tales calculated to titillate and entertain, and with advertisements promising miracle cures, newspapers wrested foreign policy from the realm of the specialist and transformed politics into another form of entertainment. The drama and vocabulary of sporting events, whose mass appeal as a leisure activity also dates from this era, were now applied to imperialist politics. Whether it was a rugby match or a territorial conquest, readers backed the "home" team, disdained the opposition, and competed for the thrill of victory. This marked quite a change for urban dwellers whose grandparents worked the land and did not look beyond the horizon of their home villages. Newspapers forged a national consciousness whereby individuals identified with collective causes they did not fully comprehend. Some observed what was happening with a critical eye, identifying a deep-seated need in modern men and women for excitement in their otherwise dull and dreary lives.

Information conveyed in newspapers shaped opinion, and opinion, in turn, could influence policy. Leaders had to reckon with this new creation of "public opinion." In a typical instance, French newspaper editors promoted feverish public outcry for conquest of the Congo by pointing out the need to revenge British advances in Egypt. "Colonial fever" in France was so high in the summer of 1882 that French policymakers were pressured to pursue claims in the Congo Basin without adequate assessment or reflection. As a result, the French government evicted Belgians and Portuguese from the northern Congo territory and enforced questionable treaty claims rather than risk public censure for appearing weak and irresolute.

Public opinion was certainly influential— but it could be manipulated. In Germany, the government often promoted colonial hysteria through the press in order to advance its own political ends. Chancellor Otto von Bismarck used his power over the press to support imperialism and to influence electoral outcomes in 1884. His successors were deft at promoting the "bread and circuses" atmosphere that surrounded colonial expansion in order to direct attention away from social problems at home and to maintain domestic stability.

The printed word was also manipulated in Britain, critics asserted, by business interests during the Boer War (1899–1902) to keep public enthusiasm for the war effort high. J. A. Hobson (1858–1940), himself a journalist and theorist of imperialism, denounced the "abuse of the press" in his hard-hitting *Psychology of Jingoism* (1901), which appeared while the war was still being waged. Hobson recognized jingoism as the appropriate term for the "inverted patriotism whereby the love of one's own nation is transformed into hatred of another nation, and [into] the fierce craving to destroy the individual members of that other nation."

Certainly jingoism was not a new phenomenon in 1900, nor was it confined to Britain. Throughout Europe a mass public appeared increasingly willing to support conflict to defend national honor. Xenophobia, hatred of foreigners, melded with nationalism, both nurtured by the mass press, to put new pressures on the determination of foreign policy. Government elites, who formerly operated behind closed doors far removed from public scrutiny, were now accountable in new ways to faceless masses. Even in autocratic states like Austria-Hungary, the opinion of the masses was a powerful political force that could destroy individual careers and dissolve governments.

Every nation in Europe had its jingoes, those willing to risk war for national glory. Significantly, the term *jingo* was coined in 1878 during a British showdown with the Russians over Turkey. The sentiment was so strong that "The Russians shall not have Constantinople," that the acceptability of war was set to music:

> We don't want to fight,
> But, by Jingo, if we do,
> We've got the men,
> We've got the ships,
> We've got the money too.

This was the most popular music-hall song in Britain that year, and long after the crisis had faded the tune and its lyrics lingered.

To varying degrees, all of these factors—economics, geopolitics, and nationalism—motivated the actions of the three great imperialist powers—Britain, France, and Germany—and their less-powerful European neighbors. The same reasons account for the global aspirations of non-European nations like the United States and Japan. None of these powers acted independently—each was aware of what the others were doing and tailored its actions accordingly. Imperialism followed a variety of patterns but always with a built-in component of emulation and acceleration. It was both a cause and a proof of a world system of states in which the actions of one nation affected the others.

The European Search for Territory and Markets

Most western Europeans who read about the distant regions that their armies and statesmen were bringing under their national flags tended to regard these new territories as no more than entries on a great tally sheet or as colors on a map. The daily press recorded the numbers of square miles gained and the captive populations taken. But few Europeans looked on imperialism as a relationship of power between two parties and, like all relationships, one influenced by both partners. Fewer still understood or appreciated the distinctive qualities of the conquered peoples.

Among the nonindustrialized regions of the world that were the targets of western imperialism, societies were organized in two vastly different ways. Tribal societies predominated in sub-Saharan Africa. Built on the concept of community, tribal societies had no provision for the individual. In China, India, and other parts of Asia, hierarchies were the rule. Hierarchies, based on social divisions like the caste system in India, had individual leaders and mechanisms to regulate the inheritance of power and land. Though they were more difficult to conquer, hierarchical societies were also more likely to cooperate with Western powers because clearly identifiable ruling elites were willing to work with Westerners for their own ends.

For these reasons, European empire builders favored informal empires (as in China) or formal

A contemporary cartoon characterizes King Leopold of the Belgians as a monstrous snake crushing the life out of the black population of the Congo Free State. The territory was under the personal rule of the Belgian king from 1885 to 1908.

but indirect rule over hierarchical societies (as in India). Tribes, in contrast, had to be conquered outright and ruled both directly and formally. Formal empires required occupation of territory and the introduction of European institutions and European administrators, as was the case, for example, in the Belgian Congo. Influence over local dignitaries played an important role in informal empires. Western nations recognized the clear advantages of informal arrangements that incurred low administrative costs and guaranteed rights to exclusive control. Both tribal and hierarchical societies resisted attempted takeovers by European powers, but only hierarchical societies had any success.

Scrambling for Africa

European involvement in Africa in the last two decades of the nineteenth century is the clearest example of how Europeans established formal empires among widely dispersed tribal societies. Europeans were not new in Africa. For most of the nineteenth century Europeans controlled about 10 percent of the African continent. The situation changed at the end of the century: by 1914 nine European states had taken over 90 percent of the continent. Only Ethiopia, ruled by a strong emperor, and Liberia, under the protection of the United States, maintained their independence.

The abolition of the slave trade by Great Britain in 1807 sparked the first burst of colonization. The abolitionists provided passage to missionaries to set up hospitals and way stations in order to care for freed slaves, who were separated from their tribes, weak, and often sick, in the coastal towns of Africa. These temporary facilities became permanent when missionaries recognized that the freed slaves presented opportunities for conversion and Christianization.

Missionaries introduced Western ideas and values to newly baptized "noble savages." To educate and to convert became the tasks of Christian missionaries of every denomination. In the process of carrying out their mission, they sent accounts back home of Africa's natural wealth. The information they recorded about tribes and indigenous languages and customs provided invaluable tools for later explorers. Religious and philanthropic societies needed permanent bases

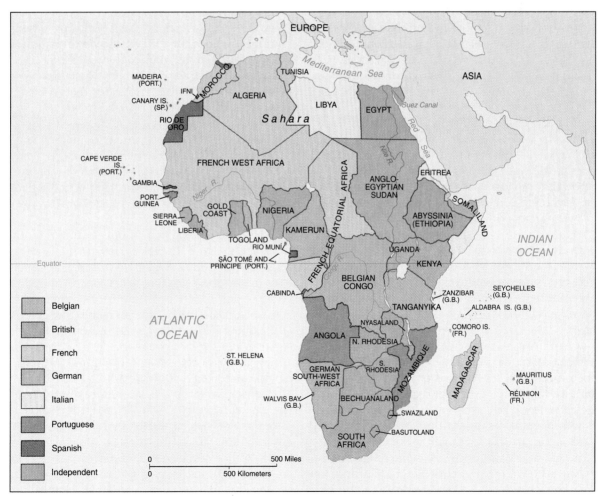

Africa, 1914

for their activities and so they began to acquire land. Their means of establishing ownership were not always popular among native populations. As one African proverb put it, "When you came here, we owned the land and you had the Bible; now we have the Bible and you own the land."

As Europeans began to acquire land, they began to need protection. Missions needed to be safeguarded against natives as well as from competing Europeans. Policing European holdings could be most efficiently achieved by converting territories into colonies. The British acted first, setting up a colony in West Africa. Mission stations, now fortified with a military presence, became the point of departure for a new generation of Europeans in Africa who were eager to explore the interior of the vast continent, to chart its geography, and to search for promised riches of gold, diamonds, and other minerals. Stories of the adventures of explorers of the 1850s and 1860s reported in the mass press lured thousands of speculators to South Africa to seek their fortunes in the newly discovered diamond mines or in the expanding trade in other commodities valuable to Western industrial society.

Until the 1870s, individual efforts defined the new European presence in Africa. Private backing financed the efforts of missionaries, explorers, adventurers, and merchants, and their holdings dotted the African landscape. In the last quarter of the nineteenth century, imperialism took on a new character with the large-scale involvement of European states and their representatives in the formal acquisition of land occupied and claimed by their citizens. Rather than creating the scramble, state intervention brought new features to the intense competition already under way: national rivalries, military conflict, and opportunities for war.

In the case of Great Britain, the reasons for territorial acquisition can be found in its nineteenth-century trading history. With a world empire that by the mid-1850s included holdings in India, Hong Kong, the South Pacific, Mauritius, Seychelles, Malta, Gibraltar, and the Cape of Good Hope, the British confidently ruled the seas. Through free trade, British manufacturers dominated European markets. Britain had nothing to fear from free trade and continually sought new markets for its exports. Seeing the British

accumulate both wealth and power, merchants and bankers from other Western nations began to develop their own world markets. They eventually sought state protection for their actions and promoted resistance against further British incursions in European, Asian, and African markets. They demanded that their governments impose tariffs to protect these new markets. Britain responded by rapidly developing new markets in areas not yet strangled by European protectionism.

German and French traders could circumvent British industrial advantage only by operating in areas free of the British presence. German merchants from Hamburg and Bremen, for example, sought overseas markets in West Africa in the first half of the nineteenth century. In exchange for German manufactured goods and schnapps, a cheap liquor distilled from Prussian potatoes, they brought back precious woods, skins, ivory, and palm oil (which was initially used in soap and candle manufacture and later as an industrial lubricant). German trade prospered and expanded in West Africa after 1850, and German interests became firmly entrenched in key trading ports and surrounding territories. By the mid-1880s, the German state had annexed Togo, Cameroons, South-West Africa, and the territory of German East Africa. The pattern of economic interests demanding state protection and forcing intervention proved a general one for European annexation in Africa.

Not every colony was built on trade, profitable or otherwise. The British held much territory where profitability was not of immediate importance. But often the flag was expected to follow trade—not the reverse—and was expected to protect private interests from competing claims. Parliamentary bodies, whether they were French, British, or German, were drawn into providing financial support for overseas ventures and assisting firms through state subsidies.

The formal seizure of territories accelerated in the early 1880s. State-supported colonizers stampeded for territory, often with no better motive than the fear that others would beat them to it. In the competition for land, the three great imperial nations, France, Germany, and Britain, began butting into one another in central and western Africa. In 1879 France decided to use military force to expand into the sub-Sahara, nurturing the dream of a trans-Saharan railway to connect its holdings in North and West Africa. The British Foreign Office judged such activity as "antagonistic" to British interests in Egypt and the Sudan. In 1881 France annexed Tunisia, and the following year Britain occupied Egypt. The French also antagonized the Belgians in the Congo. Hoping to protect their trade interests in Africa, the British negotiated with the Portuguese for control of the mouth of the Congo River. Both the French and the Germans opposed British and Portuguese claims as threatening to their own interests. The chaotic situation was becoming dangerous.

Conflict over the Congo made clear the necessity of drawing up the rules of the imperialist game. European statesmen recognized that jealousy and fear were promoting colonization and that these same motives were capable of promoting war. At the instigation of German chancellor Otto von Bismarck and French president Jules Ferry, representatives of fourteen nations, including the United States, met at Berlin in late fall 1884 to establish procedures for fair and orderly annexations in Africa. The conference acknowledged that the scramble for territory was well under way and sought to control it. The Berlin Act of 1885 set new rules for the game of empire building. Control of an area was to be the prerequisite for its annexation. Planting a flag was simply not enough.

Although regulation was the goal, intensified competition was the result. Particularly fierce rivalry centered on the headwaters of the Nile. The British felt that their control of the area was crucial to the prosperity of their endeavors in Egypt. The French had their own plans for controlling a swath of territory connecting Africa's east and west coasts and had speculated about damming the upper Nile, with the idea of linking French Somaliland in the east with Algeria in the north and Senegal in the west. By 1890, Britain had protected its exclusive claims through a series of treaties with Italy and Germany, whose interests in neighboring territories were acknowledged. Conflicting British and French claims to the Nile Valley threatened to escalate into armed conflict and war in 1898. A French expedition led by Captain J. P. Marchand (1863–1934) set up camp near the banks of the Nile and planted a French flag at Fashoda in southeastern Sudan. British General Horatio H. Kitchener (1850–1916), leading an Anglo-Egyptian army through the Sudan, met Marchand on 18 September 1898 at Fashoda and demanded his withdrawal. Marchand refused. Each evening, while both officers waited for further instructions from their home countries, they met each other in their jungle camps for evening cocktails. Back home the press whipped up war fever and hysteria over the confrontation that was little justified by Kitchener's and Marchand's genteel behavior. Factions and public opinion in London and Paris demanded war. This volatile situation endured until 3 November 1898, when the French government, crippled by serious problems at home and unwilling to risk war with Britain, ordered Marchand to withdraw.

The incident at Fashoda marked the end of one era and the beginning of another. The scramble for Africa was drawing to a close, as the vast majority of the continent had been partitioned. Among the European states the incident at Fashoda seemed to usher in a spirit of cooperation as France and Britain settled their differences amicably. Yet this veneer of accord masked real and harsher conflicts, especially regarding German claims in North Africa. What Fashoda really initiated was an era of friction, war hysteria, and the readiness to accept armed conflict as an appropriate response to colonial disagreements. It opened a new era of posturing and showdowns based on the concept of self-aggrandizement at the expense of one's enemies.

When the scramble was over, the French had carved out the largest African empire, mainly in the north and west, consisting of 4 million of Africa's 11.7 million square miles. In actual square miles taken, the British placed second, but they were arguably superior in the strategic and economic value of their territories in western, southern, and eastern Africa. Germany came to the scramble late, but by 1884 it stood as the third competitor for domination of Africa. As the German emperor explained it, Germany was looking for its place in the sun as a great world power.

Many of the territories acquired, which were useless for the export of capital, for the development of markets, and for their productive capacity, brought no economic advantage. Yet in ways not always direct, the acquisition of foreign territories was connected to economic concerns, the development of trade, and the maintenance of power. Italy's "collection of deserts" was no more than an empire of sand, but even sand empires were an example of how complicated the motivation to create a world empire could be.

Imperialism in Asia

The British Parliament proclaimed that on New Year's Day, 1877, Queen Victoria (1837–1901) would add the title of Empress of India to her many honors. India, the great jewel in the imperial crown, was a land Victoria had never seen. The queen's new title, not universally popular in Britain and unnoticed by most famine-stricken Indian peasants, in fact changed nothing about the way the British ruled India. Yet it was more than merely a symbolic assertion of dominance over a country long controlled by the British.

India was the starting point of all British expansion and it stood at the center of British

India, 1858–1914

foreign policy. To protect its sea routes to India and to secure its Indian markets, Britain acquired territories and carved out concessions all over the world. Devised by Prime Minister Benjamin Disraeli to flatter an aging monarch, the new title of empress was really a calculated warning to Russia, operating on India's northern frontier in Afghanistan, and to France, busily pursuing its own interests in Egypt.

Formal British rule in India began in 1861 with the appointment of a viceroy, who was assisted by legislative and executive councils. Both of these bodies included some Indian representatives. British rule encountered the four main divisions of the highly stratified Hindu society. At the top were Brahmans, the learned and priestly class, followed by the warriors and rulers, then by farmers and merchants, and finally by the peasants and laborers. On the outside existed the "untouchables," a fifth division intended to perform society's most menial tasks. Rather than disrupt this divisive caste system, the British found it to their advantage to maintain the status quo.

The special imperial relationship, rung in with the new year in 1877, originated in the seven-

Queen Victoria was proclaimed Empress of India in 1877, after most of the subcontinent became part of the British Empire. Here the Queen is seen at her writing table, attended by an Indian servant in national dress.

teenth century, when the British East India Company, a joint-stock venture free of government control, began limited trading in Indian markets. The need for regulation and protection firmly established British rule by the end of the eighteenth century. Conquest of the Punjab in 1849 brought the last independent areas under British control. Throughout this period Britain invested considerable overseas capital in India, and in turn India absorbed one-fifth of total British exports. The market for Indian cotton, for centuries exported to markets in Asia and Europe, collapsed under British tariffs and India became a ready market for cheap Lancashire cotton. The British also exploited India's agriculture, salt, and opium production for profit.

At the end of the eighteenth century, the British traded English wool and Indian cotton for Chinese tea and textiles. But Britain's thirst for Chinese tea grew, while Chinese demand for English and Indian textiles slackened. Britain discovered that Indian opium could be used to balance the trade deficit created by tea. British merchants and local Chinese officials, especially in the entry port of Canton, began to expand their profitable involvement in a contraband trade in opium. The East India Company held a monopoly over opium cultivation in Bengal. Opium exports to China mounted phenomenally: from 200 chests in 1729 to 40,000 chests in 1838. By the 1830s opium was probably Britain's most important crop in world markets. The British prospered as opium was pumped into China at rates faster than tea was flowing out. Chinese buyers began paying for the drug with silver.

Concerned with the sharp rise in addiction, the accompanying social problems, and the massive outflow of silver, the Chinese government reacted. As Chinese officials saw it, they were exchanging their precious metal for British poison. Addicts were threatened with the death penalty. In 1839, the Chinese government destroyed British opium in the port of Canton, touching off the so-called Opium War (1839–42). British expeditionary forces blockaded Chinese ports, besieged Canton, and occupied Shanghai. In protecting the rights of British merchants engaged in illegal trading, Great Britain became

A British gunboat, the Nemesis, *fires on Chinese junks during the Opium War. The* Nemesis *was one of the first ironclad warships ever built.*

the first Western nation to use force to impose its economic interests on China. The Treaty of Nanking (1842) initiated a series of unequal treaties between Europeans and the Chinese and set the pattern for exacting large indemnities.

Between 1842 and 1895, China fought five wars with foreigners and lost all of them. Defeat was expensive as China had to pay costs to the winners. Before the end of the century, Britain, France, Germany, and Japan had managed to establish major territorial advantages in their "spheres of influence," sometimes through negotiation and sometimes through force. By 1912, over fifty major Chinese ports had been handed over to foreign control as "treaty ports." British spheres included Shanghai, the lower Yangtze, and Hong Kong. France maintained special interests in South China. Germany controlled the Shantung peninsula. Japan laid claim to the northeast.

Spheres of influence grew in importance at the beginning of the twentieth century, when foreign investors poured capital into railway lines, which needed treaty protection from competing companies. Railways necessarily furthered foreign encroachment and opened up new territories to the claims of foreigners. As one Chinese official explained it, the railroads were like scissors that threatened to cut China into many pieces. As a result, China lost control of its trade and was totally unable to protect its infant industries. Foreigners established no formal empires in China, but the treaty ports certainly signaled both informal rule and indisputable foreign dominance.

Treaty ports were centers of foreign residence and trade, where rules of extraterritoriality applied. This meant that foreigners were exempt from Chinese law enforcement and that, although present on Chinese territory, they could be judged only by officials of their own countries. Extraterritoriality, a privilege not just for diplomats but one shared by every foreign national, implied both a distrust of Chinese legal procedures and a cultural arrogance about the superiority of Western institutions. These arrangements stirred Chinese resentment and contributed considerably to growing antiforeignism.

In order to preserve extraterritoriality and maintain informal empires, the Western powers appointed civilian representatives known as con-

suls. Often merchants themselves and, in the beginning, unpaid in their posts, consuls acted as the chieftains of resident merchant communities, judges in all civil and criminal cases, and spokesmen for the commercial interests of the home country. They clearly embodied the commercial intentions of Western governments. Initially they stood outside the diplomatic corps; later they were consigned to its lower ranks. Consuls were brokers for commerce and interpreted the international commercial law being forged. Consulates spread beyond China as Western nations used consuls to protect their own interests. In Africa consuls represented the trading concerns of European governments and were instrumental in the transition to formal rule.

The rise of Western influence in China coincided with and benefited from Chinese domestic problems, including dynastic decline, famine, and successive rebellions. The European powers were willing, however, to prop up the crumbling structure for their own ends. The Boxer Rebellion of 1900 made clear to the Western powers their limited ability to control social unrest in China. The Boxers, peasants so named by Westerners because of the martial rites practiced by their secret society, the Harmonious Fists, rose up against the foreign and Christian exploitation in north China. At the beginning of the summer of 1900, the Boxers—with the concealed encouragement of the Chinese government—killed Europeans and seized the foreign legations in Beijing. An international expeditionary force of 16,000 well-armed Japanese, Russian, British, American, German, French, Austrian, and Italian troops entered Beijing in August to defend the treaty interests of their respective countries. Led by a German general, the international force followed Kaiser Wilhelm II's urgings to remember the Huns: "Show no mercy! Take no prisoners!" Systematic plunder and slaughter followed. Beijing was sacked.

Abandoning earlier discussions of partitioning China, the international powers accepted the need for a central Chinese government—even one that had betrayed their interests—that would police a populace plagued by demographic pressures, famine, discrimination against minorities, excessive taxation, exorbitant land rents, and social and economic dislocations created by for-

European nations pursued imperialist endeavors elsewhere in Asia, acquired territories on China's frontiers, and took over states that had formerly paid tribute to the Chinese empire. The British acquired Hong Kong (1842), Burma (1886), and Kowloon (1898). The Russians took over the Maritime Provinces in 1858. The French made gains in Indochina (Annam and Tonkin) in 1884 and in 1893 and extended control over Laos and Cambodia.

Conflicts in Empires

Colonies easy to acquire were often difficult to maintain. Few understood the demands of colonial rule when the new imperialism began to intensify in the 1870s. German chancellor Otto von Bismarck, for example, looked on the pursuit of empire as a useful diversion that preserved peace in continental Europe by keeping France and Britain busy overseas and draining their resources. By 1885 Germany had entered into the race for empire, and the race no longer promised to be diversionary. Imperial rivalry intensified the competition among Western powers and created another arena for conflict. Disturbances thousands of miles away from Europe's great capitals did not dampen the hope at home that the pursuit of empire would cure Europe's ills. South Africa, North Africa, and eastern Asia, however, were three trouble spots that brought the Western powers not only up against native populations but also up against one another.

South Africa. The British took the Cape of Good Hope from the Dutch in 1795. The south African region had been settled by the Boers, descendants of Dutch farmers, who spoke only Afrikaans, a Dutch dialect, and lived apart in a culture that was Calvinist, traditional, and patriarchal. The Boer farming economy relied heavily on African slave labor. When the British outlawed slavery in the colonies in 1834, the Boers refused to continue to live in Cape Colony under British rule, packed up their belongings, and headed eastward into Natal on what has become known as the Great Trek (1837–44). Overcoming fierce Zulu resistance, they established the Natal Republic, which the British took over in 1843. Trekking northward,

The claims of the Boxer troops to invulnerability were believed by millions of Chinese. In this Chinese print, the Boxer forces use cannon, bayonets, dynamite, and sabers to drive the Western "barbarians" from the Middle Kingdom.

eign trade. During the previous year (1899), the United States had asserted its claims in China in the "Open Door" Policy. This policy, formulated by U.S. Secretary of State John Hay, was as much concerned with preserving Chinese sovereignty as it was with establishing equal economic opportunity for foreign competition in Chinese markets. Europeans and Americans wanted to send bankers to China, not gunboats. A stable central government facilitated their preferences. By operating within delineated spheres of influence and using established elites to further their own programs, Westerners protected their financial interests without incurring the costs and responsibilities of direct rule.

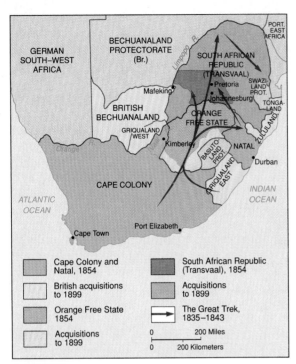

South Africa

the Boers established the Transvaal Republic and the Orange Free State. These two independent states, built by enslaving native Africans, became especially attractive to the British when diamonds and gold were discovered in South Africa in the 1870s and 1880s.

Thousands of Englishmen streamed into the region in search of their fortunes. Among them was a seventeen-year-old named Cecil Rhodes (1853–1902), who used money given to him by his aunt to book passage to South Africa in 1870. Rhodes was no adventurer or explorer in the tradition of Columbus or Magellan. Vaguely planning a career in the ministry or in law at the time of his departure, he was a sick young man in search of a cure for his tubercular lungs and weak heart. Rhodes first worked as a cotton planter. Within a year he had saved enough from his earnings to become an investor in a local railway. He moved from the cotton plantations to the newly discovered South African diamond fields, and from there to the gold mines, using shrewd investments, political maneuvering, unscrupulous business practices, and exploitation of cheap African labor to build a fortune from Africa's fabulous

natural wealth. By the time he was thirty-five, Rhodes controlled the entire diamond industry and his company, De Beers Consolidated Mining, produced 90 percent of the world's diamonds.

Rhodes viewed the Boer states as impediments to British control of the continent. He aimed to harness the long tradition of conflict between the Boers and the British for British aggrandizement. In 1896, Rhodes backed a raid into the Transvaal led by his friend Dr. Jameson. Working behind the scenes with other South African millionaires, known popularly as the "gold bugs," Rhodes hoped in vain that the thousands of British, who had rushed into the Boer state when gold was discovered, would rise up and pull down the government in Johannesburg, the capital. The Jameson Raid failed, but it did draw the British further into hostilities with the Boers.

Disputes provoked over the denial of voting rights to Uitlanders (British immigrants in Boer states) led to the Boers' declaration of war on Great Britain in 1899. The advantages of guerrilla tactics and knowledge of the terrain accounted for initial Boer successes. But superior numbers proved to be the deciding factor. Under the brutal command of General Kitchener, the British threw 350,000 troops against 60,000 Boer farmers. The international press condemned the British for their ruthless tactics of burning the farms in their path and interning Boer women and children in concentration camps. Thousands of those interned died. By the time the peace treaty was signed in 1902, 22,000 British, 25,000 Boers, and 12,000 Africans had died. Following the war, the British annexed the Boer states, which eventually became part of the newly formed Union of South Africa, established in 1910.

Thirty-three months of war cost the British the equivalent of half a billion dollars and made them the objects of international condemnation. The Boer War indicated to the world the extent to which Britain would go to protect and increase its holdings. It also made Britain vulnerable to widespread criticism for its naked aggrandizement. Kaiser Wilhelm's expression of sympathy for the beleaguered Boers brought into the open the rivalry between Germany and Britain. The war not only foreshadowed other African conflicts but it also dramatically illustrated the potential for hostility in European empires throughout the world.

At the time of his death in 1902, Rhodes was recognized as one of the great British empire builders. He had dedicated himself to the mission of British dominance of the vast African continent. While amassing his fortune, Rhodes argued for territorial acquisition as a necessary complement to a flourishing British economy. Trade and the flag must go forward together. He would annex the planets if he could, Rhodes explained, to ensure the strength of Great Britain's position in the world. In public speeches, Rhodes repeatedly lectured British statesmen, including British prime minister William Gladstone, on their duties to increase territorial holdings not just in Africa but also in Asia and throughout the world. Just as he used ruthless tactics in business, Rhodes considered war and rebellion as acceptable tools for furthering the aims of empire.

Other European nations had their empire builders, counterparts to Cecil Rhodes. Like him, these traders, businessmen, and soldiers of for-

tune, saw land acquisition as proof and guarantee of a nation's power and influence. Under the protection of national flags, they too sought their fortunes in Africa and Asia. Rhodes was unique only in the degree of his success: at the time of his death he was one of the world's wealthiest and most powerful men. One of his great schemes was to build a rail system that would run from north to south through a corridor of British holdings in Africa and thus, by connecting the Cape to Cairo, give Great Britain virtual control over the African continent. Although this rail system was never built, Rhodes' dream for his country was realized in his lifetime. By 1900 Great Britain had gained millions of square miles of African territory in Nigeria, Kenya, Uganda, Egypt, the Sudan, and Rhodesia. It was in Rhodesia, the country named for him in 1890 and now called Zimbabwe, that Rhodes was buried. By the beginning of the twentieth century, Great Britain ruled the world's greatest landed empire, the largest empire in history, one on which, as it was popularly claimed, the sun never set.

Crises in Morocco. In 1904, after two years of negotiations, Britain and France struck a series of colonial bargains over North Africa. The French agreed to cease obstructing British administration in Egypt, and the British accepted French influence in Morocco. This cooperation between Britain and France advanced further in 1905 when the Germans challenged French interests in Morocco. Under pressure, the French agreed to an international conference to deal with German complaints.

At the international conference held in the Spanish city of Algeciras in 1906, Russia, Great Britain, Italy, and the United States stood with France against Germany. Austria alone sided with Germany. The resulting Act of Algeciras affirmed an "open door" in Morocco, although France was granted control over Moroccan finances and de facto dominance over the North African country. This first Moroccan crisis marked the polarization of European states into two antagonistic and irreconcilable camps struggling over world hegemony.

Five years later internal struggles in Morocco precipitated a second Moroccan crisis. When the French responded to Moroccan instability by

The North African state of Morocco was a pawn in the imperial rivalries of Europe. A French cartoon of 1903 shows Morocco as a helpless rabbit being torn apart by the soldiery of several European countries.

The Sino-Japanese war of 1894 had its roots in disputes over territorial rights in Korea that dated from the seventh century. This Japanese print depicts one of a series of clashes between Chinese and Japanese troops that led to a treaty declaring Korea's "independence." Japan formally annexed Korea fifteen years later.

occupying the country, Germans, regarding this action as a violation of the 1906 agreement, sent a gunboat to Agadir, a harbor on Morocco's Atlantic coast. The British supported the French action and guaranteed French claims to Morocco, which became a French protectorate the following year. Germany received some territory in the Congo as poor compensation. Divisions between Germany and Austria-Hungary, supported now by Italy on the one side and France, Great Britain, and Russia on the other side had become more rigid. Although the conflict was peaceably settled, Germany's apparent willingness to use armed force to assert its claims marked a turning point in international relations.

Wars in Asia. The Sino-Japanese War of 1894–95 revealed Japan's intentions to compete as an imperialist power in Asia. The modernized and westernized Japanese army easily defeated the ill-equipped and poorly led Chinese forces. As a result, Japan gained the island of Taiwan. Pressing its ambitions on the continent, Japan locked

The New Imperialism in Africa and Asia

1834	Great Britain abolishes slavery in all its colonies
1837–44	Great Trek
1839–44	Opium War
1869	Suez Canal completed
1885	Berlin Act attempts to regulate imperialism in Africa
1894–95	Sino-Japanese War
1898	Fashoda incident
1899–1902	Boer War
1900	Boxer Rebellion
1904–05	Russo-Japanese War
1905	First Moroccan crisis
1911	Second Moroccan crisis

horns with Russia over claims to the Liaotung peninsula, Korea, and South Manchuria. Following its victory in the Russo-Japanese War of 1904 –05, Japan expanded into all of these areas, annexing Korea outright in 1910. The war sent a strong message to the West about the ease with which the small Asian nation had defeated the Russian giant and contributed to the heightening of anti-imperialist sentiments in China.

Results of a European-Dominated World

The nineteenth-century liberal belief in progress encouraged Europeans to impose their beliefs and institutions on captive millions. After all, industrial society had given the West the technology, the wealth, and the power to tame nature and dominate the world. Imperialists moralized that they had not only the right but also the duty to develop the nonindustrialized world for their own purposes. (See Special Feature, "The Power of Words," pp. 804–805.)

Europeans fashioned the world in their own image, but in doing so, Western values and Western institutions underwent profound and unintended transformations. Family values were articulated in an imperialist context, and race emerged as a key factor in culture. The discovery of new lands, new cultures, and new peoples altered the ways in which European women and men regarded themselves and viewed their place in the world. With the rise of new contenders for power, the United States and Japan, and growing criticism about the morality of capitalism, the Western world was not as predictable in 1914 as it had appeared in 1870.

A World Economy

Imperialism produced an interdependent world economic system with Europe at its center. Industrial and commercial capitalism linked together the world's continents in a communications and transportation network unimaginable in earlier ages. As a result, foreign trade increased from 3 percent of world output in 1800 to 33 percent by 1913. The greatest growth in trade occurred in the period from 1870 to 1914, as raw materials, manufactured products, capital, and men and women were transported across seas and continents by those seeking profits.

Most trading in the age of imperialism still took place among European nations and North America. But entrepreneurs in search of new markets and new resources saw in Africa and Asia opportunities for protected exploitation. Opportunities were not seized but created in nonindustrialized areas of the world, as new markets were shaped to meet the needs of Western producers and consumers. European landlords and managers trained Kenyan farmers to put aside their traditional agricultural methods and to grow more "useful" crops like coffee, tea, and sugar. The availability of cheaper British textiles of inferior quality drove Indian weavers away from their handlooms. Chinese silk producers changed centuries-old techniques to produce silk thread and cloth that was suited to the machinery and mass-production requirements of the French. Non-European producers undoubtedly derived benefits from this new international trading partnership, but those benefits were often scarce. Trade permitted specialization but at the choice of the colonizer, not the colonized. World production and consumption were being shaped to suit the needs of the West.

Capital in search of profits flowed out of the wealthier areas of Europe into the nonindustrialized regions of Russia, the Balkans, and the Ottoman Empire, where capital-intensive expenditures (on railways for instance) promised high returns. Capital investment in overseas territories also increased phenomenally as railroads were built to gain access to primary products. Great Britain maintained its overwhelming dominance in overseas investment with loans abroad greater than those of its five major competitors— France, Germany, Holland, the United States, and Belgium—combined.

The City of London had become the world's banker, serving as the clearinghouse for foreign investment on a global scale. The adoption of gold as the standard for exchange for most European currencies by 1874 further facilitated the operation of a single, interdependent trading and

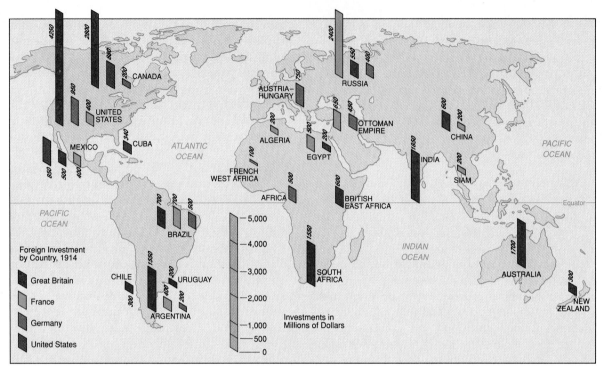

European Foreign Investment ca. 1878

investment system. Britain remained the world's biggest trading nation with half of its exports going to Asia, Africa, and South America, and the other half to Europe and the United States. But Germany was Britain's fastest-growing competitor with twice as many exports to Europe and expanding overseas trade by 1914. The United States had recently joined the league of the world's great trading nations and was running a strong third in shares of total trade.

Foreign investments often took the form of loans to governments or to enterprises guaranteed by governments. Investors might be willing to take risks, but they also expected protection, no less so than merchants and industrialists trading in overseas territories. Together trade and investment interests exerted considerable pressure on European states for control through acquisition and concessions. The vast amounts of money involved help explain the expectations of state involvement and the reasons why international competition, rivalry, and instability threatened to lead to conflict and to war.

Race and Culture

The West's ability to kill and conquer as well as to cure was, as one Victorian social observer argued, proof of its cultural superiority. Every colonizing nation had its spokesmen for the "civilizing mission" to educate and to convert African and Asian "heathens." Cultural superiority was only a short step from arguments for racial superiority. Prompted by the United States' involvement in the Philippines, the British poet, Rudyard Kipling (1865–1936), characterized the responsibilities of the advanced West as "the white man's burden." The smug and arrogant attitude of his poem about the white man's mission revealed a deep-seated and unacknowledged racism toward peoples considered "half devil and half child."

Views of cultural superiority received support from evolutionary theories, based on the scientific work of Herbert Spencer (1820–1903) and Charles Darwin (1809–82). In the 1880s, popularizers applied evolutionary ideas about animal and plant life to the development of human society. Just as animals could be hierarchically organized according to observable differences, so too, it was argued, could the different races of human beings. Race and culture were collapsed into each other. If Westerners were culturally superior, as they claimed, they must be racially superior as well. The "survival of the fittest" came to justify conquest and subjugation as "laws" of human interaction and, by extension, of relations among nations.

Women and Imperialism

Ideas about racial and cultural superiority were not confined to books by pseudoscientists and to discussions among policymakers. Public discussions about marriage, reproduction, motherhood, and childrearing reflected new concerns about furthering "the imperial race," the racial identity of white Westerners. Women throughout Western societies were encouraged by reformers,

politicians, and doctors to have more children and instructed to take better care of them. "Children [are] the most valuable of imperial assets," one British doctor instructed his readers. Healthy young men were needed in the colonies, they were told, to defend Western values. State officials paid greater attention to infant mortality at the end of the nineteenth century, set up health programs for children, and provided young women with training in home management, nutrition, and child care. These programs were no coincidence in an age of imperialism. Their rhetoric was explicitly imperialist and often racist in urging women to preserve the quality of the white race.

In the "White Man's Burden," Kipling advised, "Send forth the best ye breed." All over Europe newly formed associations and clubs stressed the need for careful mate selection. In Britain, Francis Galton (1822–1911) founded eugenics, the study of genetics for the purpose of improving inherited characteristics of the race. Imperialism, the propagandists proclaimed, depended on mothers,

The Red Dog (1892), by French artist Paul Gauguin. A growing disenchantment with Western civilization combined with the lure of the myth of the noble savage to lead Gauguin to Tahiti, where he painted the native people in a bold and bright "primitive" style.

The Power of Words

Conquest of African territories often involved sizable military expeditions and resulted in high death tolls among native populations. But imperial domination often took forms other than those reflected in battles and conquest. Language was an important tool of domination often overlooked in favor of more tangible indicators of control. Imperialist powers were able to extract natural wealth, employ native labor, and administer and control millions of Africans, not with bullets but with the power of words.

For certain kinds of profit, words were not necessary—terror and repression were enough. In the Congo rubber trade, for example, early Belgian adventurers could simply steal from or blackmail whole villages until they were stopped by the force of international opinion. But for other enterprises, like mining, that required organization, technology, and discipline, communication between the colonized and the colonizer was essential. Hierarchies of power and authority had to be established on the basis of orders given and orders understood. A shared language was the only means of moving beyond a state of siege to ongoing economic activity and, ideally, efficiency and profitability.

Europeans did not always choose simply to impose their own languages on colonized populations. Nor did they take the time and trouble to learn the numerous languages and countless dialects of the tribes with whom they came into contact. The politics of language was more complicated than either of these alternatives and varied from region to region.

Particularly instructive is the use of Swahili in eastern Africa and its adoption as a *lingua franca*, common language, in the Congo Free State, later the Belgian Congo, and now Zaire. Nineteenth-century missionaries identified Swahili, a Bantu language heavily influenced by Arab traders on the eastern coast of Africa in the seventeenth century, as the easiest language for Europeans to learn.

Belgians widely believed that Congolese natives were incapable of learning French, which they considered to be a superior language. In an area stretching 1,300 miles along the Congo River from the west coast of Africa to Stanley Falls, missionaries and explorers encountered at least eight principal languages. Both Catholic priests and various Protestant missionaries intent on converting natives recognized the utility of Swahili and set about codifying vocabularies and training manuals for their own missionaries. Priests were sent home if they were not properly trained in Swahili. In the same manner the Belgian government required basic language instruction in Swahili for administrators before they left the home country.

Trade with agricultural areas populated by Swahili-speaking natives contributed to the spread of Swahili among African workers moving into newly created urban areas like Elizabethville and into the towns around the Belgian-owned copper mines of the Katanga area of the Congo Free State. Unlike European settlers, Africans showed a willingness to learn new languages quickly. Through the influence of urban migration and the encouragement of Belgian overseers, Swahili became the common tongue of growing numbers of workers and urban dwellers.

While Belgians and other Westerners used Swahili to control native workers, they did not speak the language. This is an important distinction. Many Europeans had access to vocabularies—they used words rather than explained ideas or expressed feelings. In their pidgin Swahili, Europeans knew only how to give orders. Nouns were limited to concrete objects. True signs of language mastery—concern for syntax and grammar—were absent from Belgian training manuals. Verbs were listed only in their imperative forms—including the verb for love, *penda*. Most verbs referred to movements connected with employer-employee relations and domestic and agricultural work. In much the same way that modern-day tourists learn enough of a foreign language to order a meal or request the location of the restroom, Belgian managers and work bosses often learned how to channel labor and increase output with pidgin language skills that excluded the possibility of discussion and exchange of ideas. This was true

of the British in east Africa as well, in what became Tanzania, Uganda, Kenya, and Zanzibar. Natives identified the limited dialect the British spoke as *kisetla* Swahili—the dialect of the settlers.

This situation reinforced stereotypes and prevented communication between Europeans and Africans. Europeans concluded from their limited exchanges that natives were childlike and simple. And what did Africans think of the Europeans? The novelist George Orwell, the pseudonym of Eric Arthur Blair (1903–50), experienced the reverse of the stereotyping phenomenon in his early career as a British police officer in Burma. Forced against his better judgment to kill an elephant, Orwell concluded, "[The imperialist] wears a mask and his face grows to fit it." In the mask of authority, Orwell became the violent and destructive imperialist that the natives saw. This was a process without words in what Orwell described as "the utter silence" experienced by every European in the colonies.

The hierarchy of languages reinforced the silence. In 1908 the Charter of the Belgian Congo specified that French was the official language to be used at all state ceremonies. Native Africans, however, had no advanced training in French. Elementary French taught in the mission schools was intended to help the Congolese serve their Belgian masters as servants and low-level clerks. Furthermore, all decrees and regulations were to be published in French and Flemish, but not Swahili. As a result, Africans could not read the laws that governed them. But they could hear the laws translated for them into their regional languages by their own people.

Swahili, promoted by the state as the common language of work, expanded from a few hundred speakers in what is now central Zaire to become the first language of millions, including entire urban populations and a great majority of rural dwellers. Just as the French language was an effective barrier to Congolese participation in public life, Swahili in its variety of dialects effectively excluded Europeans from the private lives and popular customs of the Congolese. Within two generations, the Congolese were also able to use Swahili, encouraged as a language of deference and labor, as a bond of common identity and political resistance against their imperial rulers. Such was the power of words that the language imposed by the conqueror became the language of liberation.

women who would nurture healthy workers, strong soldiers and sailors, intelligent and capable leaders. High infant mortality and poor health of chlidren were attributed directly to maternal failings and not to environmental factors or poverty. Kaiser Wilhelm II stressed that German women's attention to the "three Ks"—Kinder, Kuche, Kirche (children, kitchen, church)— would guarantee a race of Germans who would rule the world. British generals and French statesmen publicly applied similar sentiments to their own countries and stressed that the future depended on the devotion of women to their family obligations.

Some European women participated directly in the colonizing experience. As missionaries and nurses, they supported the civilizing mission. As wives of officials and managers, they were expected to embody the gentility and values of Western culture. Most men who traded and served overseas did so unaccompanied by women. But when women were present in any numbers, as they were in India before 1914, they were expected to preserve the exclusivity of Western communities and to maintain class and status differentiations as a proof of cultural superiority.

Ecology and Imperialism

Ecology, the relationship and adjustment of human groups to their environment, was affected by imperial expansion, which dislocated the societies that it touched. Early explorers had disrupted little as they arrived, observed, and then moved on. The missionaries, merchants, soldiers, and businessmen who came later required that those with whom they came into contact must change their thought and behavior. In some cases, dislocation resulted in material improvements, better medical care, and the introduction of modern technology. For the most part, however, the initial ecological impact of the imperialist was negative. Western men and women carried diseases to people who did not share their immunity. Traditional village life was destroyed in rural India, and African tribal societies disintegrated under the European onslaught. Resistance existed everywhere, but only the Ethiopians, defeating the Italians at Adowa in 1896, managed to have any success in keeping out foreigners.

Education of native populations had as its primary goal the improvement of administration and productivity in the colonies. When foreigners

An Ethiopian painting depicting the battle of Adowa. The army of the Ethiopian emperor Menelik II was victorious over the invading Italians. This was the first major victory of an African country over a European power. Ethiopia never became a colony of any European imperial power.

A Foreign Merchant's Building in Yokohama (1861), *a woodblock print by the Japanese artist Sadahide. The women shown at the right exemplify the meeting of East and West. One wears the traditional Japanese kimono, while the other is dressed in typical Victorian Western clothing.*

ruled indirectly through existing indigeneous hierarchies, they often created corrupt and tyrannical bureaucracies that exploited natives. The indirect rule of the British in India was based on a pragmatic desire to keep British costs low.

When Asian and African laborers started producing for the Western market, they became dependent on its fluctuations. Victimized for centuries by the vagaries of weather, they now had to contend with the instability and cutthroat competition of cash crops in world markets. Individuals migrated from place to place in the countryside and from the countryside to newly formed cities. The fabric of tribal life unraveled. Such migrations necessarily affected family life, with individuals marrying later because they lacked the resources to set up households. The situation paralleled similar disruptions in English society at the beginning of the Industrial Revolution. Women as well as men migrated to find jobs. Many women, cut free of their tribes (as was the case in Nairobi), turned to prostitution, literally for pennies, as a means of survival.

In the most extreme example of the colonizer's disdain for the colonized, some European countries used their overseas territories as dumping grounds for hardened and incorrigible convicted criminals. Imitating the earlier example of the British in Australia, the French developed Guiana and New Caledonia as prison colonies in the hope that they could solve their social problems at home by exporting them.

New Imperial Contenders

The new imperialism was a European phenomenon, with two important exceptions: Japan and the United States. In the mid-nineteenth century, Japan was a rural and feudal island kingdom isolated from the rest of the world. It seemed destined for the same fate of Western control that was befalling China. Yet within two generations, Japan had become an industrial and imperial power with global aspirations. The spark for the change was lit in 1854 when Commodore Matthew C. Perry (1794–1858) sailed a U.S. squadron to Japan for the purpose of opening up Japanese ports to U.S. trading. Japan, like China, was forced to accept a series of unequal treaties, prompting Japanese attacks on foreigners and the collapse of the ruling shogunate.

The Meiji restoration that followed in 1868

The Imperial Russian Far Eastern Fleet at the Tsushima, Japan, in May 1905. Shortly after this picture was taken, the majority of the Russian fleet, under Admiral Rozhdestvenski, was captured or destroyed by the Japanese fleet under Admiral Togo in the battle of Tsushima Strait.

responded to the foreign threat neither by resistance nor by collaboration but by emulation. Meiji rulers sent young men to Europe to learn Western administration, technology, and military strategy. Feudalism was abolished and a Prussian-like constitution was adopted. Preserving traditional values of family life and paternal authority and employing the new knowledge from the West, by the 1880s Japan had industrialized in textiles and ten years later had moved into heavy industry. Japan telescoped into two decades changes that had taken western Europe centuries to accomplish. Foreign trade increased steadily with Japanese silk eventually surpassing its Chinese counterpart in world markets. The transformation, although breathtaking, was not without its costs: the pressures of population growth and the threat of exhaustion of resources.

Japan, once again taking its lead from the West, saw overseas expansion as the solution to its problems. In the Sino-Japanese war of 1894–95 and the Russo-Japanese War of 1904–05, Japan established an empire on the Asian mainland and extended its holding to the north and the south in the Pacific. The wars also gave notice to the world that, although small, Japan intended to take its place among the great imperial powers.

The United States provided another variation on imperial expansion. Its westward drive across the North American continent, beginning at the end of the eighteenth century, established the United States as an imperial power in the Western Hemisphere. By 1848, the relatively young American nation stretched over three thousand miles from one ocean to the other. It had met the opposition and resistance of the Native Americans with armed force, decimated them, and "concentrated" the survivors in assigned territories and, later, on reservations.

At the end of the nineteenth century, the United States, possessing both the people and the resources for rapid industrial development, turned to the Caribbean and the Pacific in pursuit of markets and investment opportunities. By acquiring stepping stones of islands across the Pacific in the Hawaiian Islands and Samoa, it secured fueling bases and access to lucrative east Asian ports. And by intervening repeatedly in Central America and building the Panama Canal, the United States established its hegemony in the Caribbean by 1914. Growing in economic power and hegemonic influence, both Japan and the United States had joined the club of imperial powers and were making serious claims against European expansion.

Critiquing Capitalism

Not least significant of the consequences of imperialism was the critique of capitalism it produced. Those who condemned it as exploitative and racist saw imperialism as an expression of problems inherent in capitalism. In 1902, J. A. Hobson (1858–1940) published *Imperialism, A Study*, a work that has remained in print ever since. In the book Hobson argued that underconsumption and surplus capital at home drove Western industrial countries overseas in search of a cure for these economic ills. Rather than solving the problems by raising workers' wages and thereby increasing their consumption power and creating new opportunities for investment in home markets, manufacturers, entrepreneurs, and industrialists sought higher profits abroad. Hobson considered these business interests "economic parasites," making large fortunes at the expense of national interests.

In the midst of world war, the future leader of the Russian Revolution, Vladimir Ilich Ulyanov (1870–1924), or to use his revolutionary name, Lenin, added his own critique of capitalism. He did not share Hobson's belief that capitalism was merely malfunctioning in its imperialist endeavors. Instead, Lenin argued in *Imperialism the Highest Stage of Capitalism* (1916) that capitalism is inherently and inevitably imperialistic. Because he was sure that Western capitalism was in the process of effecting its own destruction, Lenin called World War I the final "imperialist war."

Critics, historians, and economists have since pointed out that both works are marred by errors and omissions. Yet they stand at the beginning of almost a century of debate over the morality and economic feasibility of imperialism. Hobson as a liberal and Lenin as a Marxist highlighted the connections between social problems at home, whether in late Victorian England or in prerevolutionary Russia, and economic exploitation abroad.

Yet if electoral results and the popular press are any indication, Europeans not only accepted but warmly embraced the responsibilities of empire. Criticism of the backwardness of captive peoples prevailed. Victorian social scientist Walter Bagehot (1826–77) told the story of an aged savage who, upon returning to his tribe, informed them that he had "tried civilization for forty years and it was not worth the trouble." No matter how intelligent the judgment of this African might seem with hindsight, the possibility of returning to areas of the world not influenced by the civilization of the West was rapidly disappearing before 1914.

Conflict at Home: The European Balance of Power

In addition to mounting conflicts in colonized areas, European states were locked in a competition within Europe for dominance and control. The politics of geography combined with rising nationalist movements in southern Europe and the Ottoman Empire to create a mood of increasing confrontation among Europe's great powers. The European balance of power so carefully crafted by Bismarck began to disintegrate with his departure from office in 1890. By 1914 a Europe divided into two camps was no longer the sure guarantee of peace that it had a generation earlier.

The Geopolitics of Europe

The map of Europe had been redrawn in the two decades after 1850. By 1871 Europe consisted of five great powers, known as the Big Five—Britain, France, Germany, Austria-Hungary, and Russia—and a handful of lesser states. The declaration of a German Empire in 1871 and the emergence of Italy with Rome as its capital in 1870 unified numerous disparate states. Although not always corresponding to linguistic and cultural differences among Europe's peoples, national boundaries appeared fixed, with no country aspiring to territorial expansion at the expense of its neighbors. But the creation of the two new national units of Germany and Italy had legitimized nationalist aspirations and the militarism necessary to enforce them.

Under the chancellorship of Otto von Bismarck, Germany led the way in forging a new alliance system based on the realistic assessment of power politics within Europe. In 1873 Bismarck joined together the three most conservative powers of the Big Five—Germany, Austria-Hungary, and Russia—into the Three Emperors' League. Consultation over mutual interests and friendly neutrality were the cornerstones of this alliance. Identifying one's enemies and choosing one's friends in this new configuration of power came in large part to depend on geographic weaknesses. The Three Emperors' League was one example of the geographic imperatives driving diplomacy. Bismarck was determined to banish the specter of a two-front war by isolating France on the Continent.

Each of the Great Powers had a vulnerability, a geographic Achilles' heel. Germany's vulnerability lay in its North Sea ports. German shipping along its only coast could be easily bottlenecked by a powerful naval force. Such an event, the Germans knew, could destroy their rapidly growing international trade. What was worse, powerful land forces could "encircle" Germany. As Britain's century-old factories slowly became obsolete under peeling coats of paint, Germany enjoyed the advantages of a latecomer to industrialization forced to start from scratch by investing in the most advanced machinery and technology. The German Reich was willing to support industrial expansion, scientific and technological training, and social programs for its workers. Yet as Germany surged forward to seize its share of world markets, it was acutely aware that it was hemmed in on the Continent. Germany could not extend its frontiers the way Russia had to the east. German gains in the Franco-Prussian war in Alsace and Lorraine could not be repeated without risking greater enmity. German leaders saw the threat of encirclement as a second geographic weakness. Bismarck's awareness of these geographic facts of life prompted his engineering of the Three Emperors' League in 1873, two years after the founding of the German Empire.

Austria-Hungary was Europe's second largest landed nation and the third largest in population. The same factors that had made it a great European power—its size and its diversity—now threatened to destroy it. The ramshackle empire of Europe, it had no geographical unity. Its vulnerability came from within, from the centrifugal forces of linguistic and cultural diversity. Weakened by nationalities clamoring for independence and self-rule and by an unresponsive political system, Austria-Hungary remained backward agriculturally and unable to respond to the Western industrial challenge. It seemed most likely to collapse from social and political pressures.

Another feature must be added to the picture of Europe in the late nineteenth century. To the southeast on the map stood the Ottoman Empire, a great decaying conglomeration that bridged Europe and Asia. Politically feeble and on the verge of bankruptcy, the Ottoman Empire with Turkey at its core comprised a vast array of ethnically, linguistically, and culturally diverse peoples. In the hundred years before 1914, increasing social unrest and nationalist bids for independence had plagued the Ottoman Empire. As was the case with the Habsburgs in Austria-Hungary, the Ottomans maintained power with increasing difficulty over these myriad ethnic groups struggling to be free. The Ottoman Empire, called "the sick man of Europe" by contemporaries, found two kinds of relations sitting at its bedside: those who would do anything to ensure its survival, no matter how weak; and those who longed for and sought to hasten its demise. Fortunately for the Ottoman Empire, its enemies were willing to preserve it in its weakened state rather than see one of the other rival European powers benefit from its collapse.

The Ottomans had already seen parts of their holdings lopped off in the nineteenth century. Britain, ever conscious of its interests in India, had acquired Cyprus, Egypt, Aden, and Sudan from the Ottomans. Germany insinuated itself into Turkish internal affairs and financed the Baghdad Railway in the attempt to link the Mediterranean to the Persian Gulf. Russia acquired territories on the banks of the Caspian Sea and had plans to take Constantinople. But it was the volatile Balkan Peninsula that threatened to upset the European power balance. The Balkans appeared to be a territory that begged for dismemberment. Internally, the Slavs sought independence from their Habsburg and Turkish oppressors. External pressures were equally great with each of the major powers following its own geopolitical agenda.

The Instability of the Alliance System

The system of alliances formed between and among European states was guided by two realities of geopolitics. The first was the recognition of tension between France and Germany. France had lost its dominance on the Continent in 1870–71, when it was easily defeated by Prussia at the head of a nascent German Empire. With its back to the

Atlantic, France faced the smaller states of Belgium, Luxembourg, Switzerland, and Italy, and the industrially and militarily powerful Germany. It had suffered the humiliation of losing territory to Germany—Alsace and Lorraine in 1871—and was well aware of its continued vulnerability. Geopolitically France felt trapped and isolated and in need of powerful friends as a counterweight to German power.

The second reality guiding alliances was Russia's preoccupation with maintaining free access to the Mediterranean Sea. Russia, clearly Europe's greatest landed power, was vulnerable because it could be landlocked by frozen or blockaded ports. The ice that crippled its naval and commercial vessels in the Baltic Sea drove Russia east through Asia to secure another ice-blocked port on the Sea of Japan at Vladivostok in 1860 and to seek ice-free Chinese ports. Russia was equally obsessed with protecting its warm-water ports on the Black Sea. Whoever controlled the strait of the Bosporus controlled Russia's grain export trade, on which its economic prosperity depended. All diplomatic arrangements, especially after the turn of the century, took into account these two geopolitical realities.

Ostensibly, Russia had the most to gain from the extension of its frontiers and the creation of pro-Russian satellites. It saw that by championing Pan-Slavic nationalist groups in southeastern Europe, it could greatly strengthen its own position at the expense of the two great declining empires, Ottoman Turkey and Austria-Hungary. Russia hoped to draw the Slavs into its orbit by fostering the creation of independent states in the Balkans. A Serbian revolt began in two Ottoman provinces, Bosnia and Herzegovina, in 1874. International opinion pressured Turkey to initiate reforms. Serbia declared war on Turkey on 30 June 1876; Montenegro did the same the next day. Britain, supporting the Ottoman Empire because of its trading interests in the Mediterranean, found itself in a delicate position of perhaps condemning an ally when it received news of Turkish atrocities against Christians in Bulgaria. Prime Minister Disraeli insisted that Britain was bound to defend Constantinople because of British interests in the Suez Canal and India. While Britain stood on the sidelines, Russia, with Romania as an ally, declared war against the Ottoman Empire.

The war was quickly over, with Russia capturing all of Armenia, forcing the Ottoman sultan, Abdul Hamid II (1842–1918) to sue for peace on 31 January 1878.

Bismarck, a seemingly disinterested party acting as an "honest broker," hosted the peace conference that met at Berlin. The British succeeded in blocking Russia's intentions for a Bulgarian satellite and keeping the Russians from taking Constantinople. Russia abandoned its support of Serbian nationalism, and Austria-Hungary occupied Bosnia and Herzegovina. The peace concluded at the 1878 Congress of Berlin disregarded Serbian claims, thereby promising continuing conflict over the nationalities question.

The Berlin Congress also marked the emergence of a new estrangement among the Great Powers. Russia felt betrayed by Bismarck and abandoned in its alliance with Germany. Bismarck in turn cemented a Dual Alliance between Austria-Hungary and Germany in 1879 that survived until the collapse of the two imperial regimes in 1918. The Three Emperors' League was renewed in 1881, now with stipulations regarding the division of the spoils in case of a war against Turkey.

In 1882, Italy was asked to join the Dual Alliance with Germany and Austria-Hungary, thus converting it into the Triple Alliance, which prevailed until the Great War of 1914. Germany, under Bismarck's tutelage, signed treaties with Italy, Russia, and Austria-Hungary, and established friendly terms with Great Britain. A new Balkan crisis in 1885, however, shattered the illusion of stable relations.

Hostilities erupted between Bulgaria and Serbia. Russia threatened to occupy Bulgaria, but Austria stepped in to prevent Russian domination of the Balkans, thus threatening the alliance of the Three Emperors' League. Russia was further angered by German unwillingness to support its interests against Austrian actions in the Balkans. Germany maintained relations with Russia in a new Reinsurance Treaty drawn up in 1887, which stipulated that each power would maintain neutrality should the other find itself at war. Bismarck now walked a fine line, balancing off alliances and selectively disclosing the terms of secret treaties to nonsignatory countries with the goal of preserving the peace. He was described by

Linguistic Groups in the Balkans

his successor as the only man who could keep five glass balls in the air at the same time.

After Bismarck's resignation in 1890, Germany found itself unable to juggle all the glass balls. Germany allowed the arrangement with Russia to lapse. Russia, in turn, allied itself in 1894 with France. Also allied with Great Britain, France had broken out of the isolation that Bismarck had intended for it two decades earlier. The Triple Entente came into existence following the Anglo-Russian understanding of 1907. Now it was the Triple Entente of Great Britain, France, and Russia against the Triple Alliance of Germany, Austria-Hungary, and Italy.

There was still every confidence that these two camps could balance each other and preserve the peace. But in 1908–09 the unresolved Balkan problem threatened to topple Europe's precarious peace. Against Russia's objections, Austria-Hungary annexed Bosnia and Herzegovina, the provinces it had occupied since 1878. Russia supported Serbia's discontent over Austrian

acquisition of these predominantly Slavic territories that Serbia felt should be united with its own lands. Unwilling to risk a European war at this point, Russia was ultimately forced to back down under German pressure. Germany had to contend with its great geopolitical fear—hostile neighbors, France and Russia, on its western and eastern frontiers.

A third Balkan crisis erupted in 1912 when Italy and Turkey fought over the possession of Tripoli in North Africa. The Balkan states took advantage of this opportunity to increase their holdings at Turkey's expense. This action quickly involved great power interests once again. A second war broke out in 1913 over Serbian interests in Bulgaria. Russia backed Serbia against Austro-Hungarian support of Bulgaria. The Russians and Austrians prepared for war while the British and Germans urged peaceful resolution. Although hostilities ceased, Serbian resentment toward Austria-Hungary over its frustrated nationalism was greater than ever. Britain, in its backing of Russia, and Germany, in its support of Austria-Hungary, were enmeshed in alliances that could involve them in a military confrontation.

Great Britain did not share Germany's and Russia's fears of strangulation by blockade. And although the question of Irish home rule was a nationalities problem for Britain, it paled in comparison with Austria-Hungary's internal challenge. As an island kingdom, however, Great Britain relied on imports for its survival. The first of the European nations to become an urban and industrial power, Britain was forced to do so at the expense of its agricultural sector. It could not feed its own people without importing foodstuffs. Britain's geographic vulnerability was its dependence on access to its empire and the maintenance of open sea lanes. Britain saw its greatest menace coming from the rise of other sea powers—notably Germany.

From the very beginning of the competition for territories and concessions, no European state could act in Africa or Asia without affecting the interests and actions of its rivals at home. The African scramble made clear how interlocking the system of European states was after 1870. The development of spheres of influence in China underlined the value of world markets and international trade for the survival and expansion of western nations.

A "balance of power" among states guaranteed national security and independence until the end of the nineteenth century. But between 1870 and 1914, industrialization, technology, and accompanying capital formation created vast economic disparities. Conflict and disequilibrium challenged European stability and balance. Ultimately, it was the politics of geography on the European continent, not confrontations in distant colonies, that polarized the European states into two camps. Despite the unresolved conflicts pervading all of these crisis, European statesmen prided themselves on their ability to settle disputes through reason and negotiation. That was not to prove the case with the last and final Balkan crisis that exploded in the summer of 1914.

Suggestions for Further Reading

The New Imperialism

Michael W. Doyle, *Empires* (Ithaca, NY: Cornell University Press, 1986). Nineteenth-century imperialism is placed in a broad historical context, which emphasizes a comparative perspective of the European imperial experience.

Daniel R. Headrick, *The Tools of Empire: Technology and European Imperialism in the Nineteenth Century* (New York: Oxford University Press, 1981). By focusing on technological innovations in the nineteenth century, the author demonstrates how Europeans were able to establish control over Asia, Africa, and Oceania rapidly at little cost.

Daniel R. Headrick, *The Tentacles of Progress: Technology Transfer in the Age of Imperialism, 1850–1940* (New York: Oxford University Press, 1988). Argues that the transfer of technology to Africa and Asia by the Western imperial powers produced colonial underdevelopment.

The European Search for Territory and Markets

Winfried Baumgart, *Imperialism: The Idea and Reality of British and French Colonial Expansion, 1880–1914* (New York: Oxford University Press, 1982). Principally concerned with the motives that led to imperial expan-

---

European Crises and the Balance of Power

1871	German Empire created
1873	Three Emperors' League: Germany, Austria-Hungary, Russia
1874	First Balkan crisis; Serbian revolt in Bosnia and Herzegovina
1875	Russo-Turkish War
1876	Serbia declares war on Turkey; Montenegro declares war on Turkey
1878	Congress of Berlin
1879	Dual Alliance: Germany and Austria-Hungary
1881	Three Emperors' League renewed
1882	Triple Alliance: Germany, Austria-Hungary, and Italy
1885	Second Balkan crisis; Bulgaria vs. Serbia
1887	Reinsurance Treaty between Germany and Russia
1894	Russia concludes alliance with France
1907	Triple Entente: Great Britain, France, Russia
1908	Austria-Hungary annexes Bosnia and Herzegovina
1912	Third Balkan crisis; Italy vs. Turkey
1913	War erupts between Serbia and Bulgaria

---

sion, the author argues that motives were numerous and each action must be studied within its specific social, political, and economic context.

Raymond F. Betts, *The False Dawn: European Imperialism in the Nineteenth Century* (Oxford: Oxford University Press, 1976). Explores the ideology of the empire, as well as the process of cultural transmission through colonial institutions.

Eric Hobsbawm, *The Age of Empire, 1875–1914* (New York: Pantheon, 1987). A wide-ranging interpetive history of the late nineteenth century, which spans economic, social, political, and cultural developments.

Consequences of a European-Dominated World

Anna Davin, "Imperialism and Motherhood," *History Workshop* (Spring 1978) No 5: 9–65. Davin's article links imperialism and economic expansion with the increasing intervention of the state into family life. The author offers an analysis of an ideology that focused on the need to increase population in support of imperial aims and that led to the social construction of motherhood, domesticity, and individualism.

Johannes Fabian, *Language and Colonial Power: The Appropriation of Swahili in the Former Belgian Congo* (Cambridge: Cambridge University Press, 1986). Demonstrates how colonial power was exercised in the Belgian Congo through the study of the growth of Swahili as a *lingua franca.* The author pays particular attention to the uses of Swahili in industrial and other work situations.

Paul B. Rich, *Race and Empire in British Politics* (Cambridge: Cambridge University Press, 1986). An intellectual history of ideas about race in the imperial tradition. Focusing on the years between 1890 and 1970, the author examines the political dimensions of race and race ideology in British society.

Conflict at Home: The European Balance of Power

George F. Kennan, *The Decline of Bismarck's European Order: Franco-Russian Relations, 1875–1890* (Princeton, NJ: Princeton University Press, 1979). A diplomatic history of the origins of the 1894 military alliance between Russia and France, which views the alliance as a critical factor in the breakdown of the European balance of power established by Bismarck's diplomacy.

Alan Sked, *The Decline and Fall of the Habsburg Empire, 1815–1918* (London: Longman, 1989). An overview of the Habsburg Empire's history from Metternich to World War I. The author interprets the various historiographical debates over the collapse of Habsburg rule. Rather than treating the late empire as a case of inevitable decline, the book examines the monarchy as a viable institution within a multinational state.

26

War and Revolution, 1914–1920

Selling the Great War

Advertising is a powerful influence in modern life. Some feel that it makes us buy goods we do not need. Others insist that advertising is an efficient way of conveying information on the basis of which people make choices. The leaders of Western nations discovered the power of advertising in the years of world war from 1914 to 1918. Advertising did not create the Europe-wide conflict that became known as the Great War. Nor did it produce the enthusiasm that excited millions of Europeans when war was declared in 1914. But when death counts mounted, prices skyrocketed, and food supplies dwindled, the frenzy and fervor for the war flagged. Then governments came to rely more heavily on the art of persuasion. Survival and victory required the support and coordination of the whole society. For the first time in history, war had to advertise.

By the early decades of the twentieth century businessmen had learned that it was not enough to develop efficient technologies and to mass-produce everything from hair oil to corsets—they had to sell their goods to the public. People would not buy goods they did not know about and whose merits they did not understand. Modern advertising pioneered sales techniques that convinced people to buy. Now political

TAKE UP THE SWORD OF JUSTICE

leaders came to realize that the advertising techniques of the marketplace could be useful. Governments took up the "science" of selling—not products but the idea of war. It was not enough to have a well-trained and well-equipped army to ensure victory. Citizens had to be persuaded to join, to fight, to work, to save, and to

believe in the national war effort. Warring nations learned how to organize enthusiasm and how to mobilize the masses in support of what proved to be a long and bloody conflict.

Look at the poster on the facing page. Here is a dramatic appeal to German women to support war work. A stern soldier whose visage and bearing

816

communicate strength and sin-
gleness of purpose is backed up
by an equally determined young
woman. She is in the act of
handing him a grenade, as she
stands with him, her arm on
his shoulder in support, facing
the unseen enemy. Grenades
hang from his belt and from his
left hand, giving us the sense
that he is able to enter battle
properly armed thanks to this
dedicated woman's efforts. The
poster is a good representation
of the centrality of women's
work to the waging of a new
kind of war in the twentieth
century. The battlefront had to
be backed up by a "home
front"—the term used for the
first time in the Great War—of
working men, women, and even
children. The poster communi-
cates the dignity and worth that
lay in the concerted partnership
of soldiers and civilians to
defeat the enemy.

Early war posters stressed
justice and national glory. Later,
as weariness with the war
spread, the need for personal
sacrifice became the dominant
theme. Look at the sad female
figure rising from a sea of
suffering and death on the facing page. The woman, both
goddesslike and vulnerable,
symbolizes Great Britain. She is
making a strong visual plea for
action, seeking soldiers for her
cause. This appeal for volunteers for the armed forces was
unique to Great Britain, where
conscription was not established until 1916. Yet the image
is typical of every nation's
reliance on a noble female symbol to emphasize the justice of
its cause. The dark suffering
and death in the waters lapping

at her robes are reflected in her
eyes. She evinces a fierce determination as she exhorts, "Take
up the sword of justice." In
February 1915 Germany
declared the waters around the
British Isles to be a war zone.
All British shipping was subject
to attack as well as neutral
merchant vessels, which were
attacked without warning. In
May 1915 the *Lusitania* was
sunk, taking with it over 1,000
lives, including 128 Americans.
The poster frames an illuminated horizon where the ship
that is probably the *Lusitania*
steams ahead. We need not read
a word to understand the call to
arms against the perfidy of an
enemy who has killed innocent
civilians. The female figure's
determined jaw, clenched fist,
and outstretched arms communicate the nobility of the cause
and the certainty of success.

Civilians had to be mobilized
for two reasons. First, it became
evident early in the fighting that
the costs of the war were high
in human lives. Soldiers at the
front had to be constantly
replenished from civilian
reserves. Second, the costs of the
war in food, equipment, and
productive materials were so
high that civilian populations
had to be willing to endure
great hardships and to sacrifice
their own well-being to produce
supplies for soldiers at the
front. Advertising was used by
nations at war to coordinate
civilian and military contributions to a common cause. More
than communicating information, advertising inspired belief
in the justice of the national
cause in every warring country
and a commitment to total
victory, no matter how high the
price.

The War Europe Expected

In 1914 Europe stood confidently at the center of the world. Covering only 7 percent of the earth's surface, it dominated the world's trade and was actively exporting both European goods and European culture all over the globe. Proud of the progress and prosperity of urban industrial society, Europeans had harnessed nature to transform their environment. They extended their influence beyond the confines of their continent, sure that their achievements marked the pinnacle of civilization.

The values of nineteenth-century liberalism permeated the self-confident worldview of European men and women in 1914. Liberalism assured the middle classes that the world was at peace, governed by rules that could be known. Europeans assumed that they could discover these rules and fashion a better world. Science and industry were their tools for controlling nature and shaping institutions. If life was not yet perfect, it could become so.

Westerners took stability and harmony for granted as preconditions for progress. Yet they also recognized the utility of war. Local confrontations between European states in Africa had been successfully contained in recent times in bids for increased territory. While warfare was accepted as an instrument of policy, no one expected or wanted a general war. Liberal values served the goals of limited war, just as they had justified imperial conquest. Statesmen decided there were rules to the game of war that could be employed in the interests of statecraft. Science and technology also served war makers. Modern weapons, statesmen and generals were sure, would prevent a long war. Superiority in armed force became a priority for European states seeking to protect the peace.

"Armed peace" was the result of the beginning of the modern arms race as a defense against war. Leaders nevertheless expected and planned for a war, short and limited, in which the fittest and most advanced nation would win. Planners believed that their rivals could not triumph. War was acceptable because it would be quick and decisive. Previous confrontations among European states had been limited in duration and

European Alliances on the Eve of World War I

destruction, as in the case of Prussia and France in 1870, or confined to peripheries, as squabbles among the Great Powers in Africa indicated. The alliance system was expected to defend the peace.

As international tensions mounted, the hot summer days of 1914 were a time of hope and glory. The hope was that war, when it came, would be "over by Christmas." The glory was the promise of ultimate victory in the "crusade for civilization" that each nation's leaders held out to their people. Declarations of war were greeted with songs, flowers, wild enthusiasm, and dancing in the streets. Crowds welcomed the battles to come with the delirium of cheering a favorite team in a sports match. Some embraced war as a test of greatness, a purification of a society that had become lazy and complacent. When war did come in 1914, it was not an accident, it was a choice. Yet it was a choice that Europeans did not understand, one whose limits they could not control. Their unquestioned pride in reason and progress that had ironically led them to this war did not survive the four years of barbaric slaughter that followed.

The Alliance System

At the end of the nineteenth century, the world appeared to be coming together in a vast international network linked by commerce and finance. A system of alliances based on shared interests also connected states to one another. After 1905, the intricate defensive alliances between and among the European states maintained the balance of power between two blocs of nations and helped prevent one bloc from dominating the other. On the eve of the war, France, Great Britain, and Russia stood together in the Triple Entente. Since 1882, Germany, Austria-Hungary, and Italy had joined forces in the Triple Alliance. Other states allied with one or the other of these blocs in pacts of mutual interest and protection. Throughout the world, whether in North Africa, the Balkans, or Asia, the power of some states was intended to balance off the power of others. Yet the balance of power did not exist simply to preserve the peace. It existed to preserve a system of independent national societies—nation-states—in a precarious equilibrium. Gains in one area by one bloc had to be offset by compromises in another to maintain the balance. Limited conflict was a legitimate means of preserving equilibrium.

The alliance system of blocs reflected the growing impact of public opinion on international relations. Statesmen had the ability to manipulate the newspaper images of allies as good and rivals as evil. But controlling public opinion served to lock policymakers into permanent partnerships and "blank checks" of support for their allies. Western leaders understood that swings in public opinion in periods of crisis could hobble their efforts in the national interest. Permanent military alliances with clearly identified "friends," therefore, took the place of more fluid arrangements.

Although alliances that guaranteed military support did not cause war, they did permit weak nations to act irresponsibly, with the certainty that they would be defended by their more powerful partners. France and Germany were publicly committed to their weaker allies, Russia and Austria-Hungary respectively, in supporting imperialist ambitions in the Balkans from which they themselves derived little direct benefit. Because of

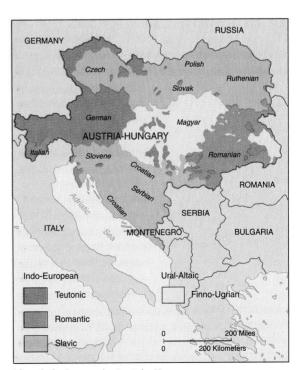

Linguistic Groups in Austria-Hungary

treaty commitments, no country expected to face war alone. The interlocking system of defensive alliances was structured to match strength against strength—France against Germany, for example—thereby making a prolonged war more likely than would be the case if a weak nation confronted a strong enemy.

Military Timetables

As with the alliance system, military timetables restricted the choices of leaders at times of conflict. The crisis of the summer of 1914 revealed the extent to which politicians and statesmen had come to rely on military expertise and strategic considerations for decisions. Military general staffs assumed increasing importance in state policymaking. War planners became powerful, as war was accepted as an alternative to the negotiation of differences.

Germany's military preparations are a good example of how war strategy exacerbated crises and prevented peaceful solutions. Alfred von Schlieffen (1833–1913), the Prussian general and chief of the German General Staff from 1891 to 1905, who developed the war plan, understood little about politics but spent his life studying the strategic challenges of warfare. His war plan was designed to make Germany the greatest power on the Continent. The Schlieffen Plan, which he set before his fellow officers in 1905, was a bold and daring one: in the likely event of war with Russia, Germany would launch a devastating offensive against France. Schlieffen reasoned that France was a strong military presence that would come to the aid of its ally, Russia. Russia, lacking a modern transportation system, could not mobilize as rapidly as France. Russia also had the inestimable advantage of the ability to retreat into its vast interior. If Germany were pulled into a war with Russia, its

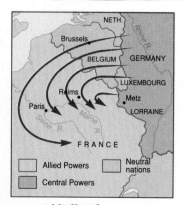

Schlieffen Plan

western frontier would be vulnerable to France, Russia's powerful ally. The Schlieffen Plan recognized that France must first be defeated in the west before Germany could turn its forces to the task of defeating Russia. As Schlieffen continued to insist until his death in 1913: "The *whole* of Germany must throw itself on *one* enemy—the strongest, most powerful, most dangerous enemy." For Schlieffen, France was that enemy.

The Schlieffen Plan thus committed Germany to a war with France regardless of particular circumstances. Furthermore, the plan, with its strategy of invading the neutral countries of Belgium, Holland, and Luxembourg in order to defeat France in six weeks and become the greatest power in Europe, ignored the rights of the neutral countries. Kaiser Wilhelm II of Germany explained, "Whoever, in the case of a European war, was not for me, was against me."

Germany was not alone in being driven by military timetables when conflicts arose. Russian military strategists planned full mobilization if war broke out with Austria-Hungary, which was menacing the interests of Russia's ally Serbia. Russia foresaw the likelihood that Germany would come to the aid of Austria-Hungary. Russia knew, too, that because of its primitive railway network it would be unable to mobilize troops rapidly. In order to compensate for this weakness, Russian leaders planned to mobilize *before* war was declared. German military leaders had no choice in the event of full Russian mobilization but to mobilize their own troops immediately and to urge the declaration of war. There was no chance of containing the conflict once a general mobilization on both sides was under way. Mobilization would mean war.

Like the Schlieffen Plan, the French Plan XVII called for the concentration of troops in a single area with the intention of decisively defeating the enemy. The French command, not well informed about German strengths and strategies, designated Alsace and Lorraine for the immediate offensive against Germany in the event of war. Plan XVII left Paris exposed to the German drive through Belgium called for in the Schlieffen Plan.

Military leaders throughout Europe argued that if their plans were to succeed, speed was essential. Delays to consider peaceful solutions would cripple military responses. Diplomacy bowed to military strategy. When orders to mobilize went out, armies would be set on the march. Like a row of dominoes falling with the initial push, the two great alliance systems would be at war.

Assassination at Sarajevo

A teenager with a handgun started the First World War. On 28 June 1914, Gavrilo Princip (1895–1918), a nineteen-year-old Bosnian Serb, pulled the trigger of his Browning revolver repeatedly, killing Archduke Franz Ferdinand and his wife, Sophie, in Sarajevo, the sleepy capital of the Austro-Hungarian province of Bosnia. Today, tourists visiting Sarajevo, in what is now Yugoslavia, can plant their feet in the cement prints where Princip stood on that fateful June day. These footprints, of either a murderer, as the Austrians contended, or a freedom-fighter, as Slav nationalists insisted, designate an important crossroads in the history of Western civilization. They mark the place where an individual act of terrorism catapulted the Western world into a long, violent, and bloody struggle for survival.

Neither the killer nor his victim seems important enough to justify such an outcome. It is true that Franz Ferdinand was the designated heir of the Habsburg throne. But the Archduke was not much loved by his uncle, Austrian emperor Franz Josef, who, it is alleged, expressed relief that his nephew's death meant one less worry. The assassination of a head of state was certainly not a novelty in Europe. Anarchist bombs and bullets had felled leaders all over Europe in the preceding three decades. Nations paused for a moment to mourn slain leaders, then resumed business as usual. A Habsburg noble, window-dressing for a decaying monarchy, assassinated while he was performing the useless function of reviewing military exercises in a backwater province, hardly seemed a likely candidate to shatter the peace of Europe.

Nor did young Princip seem any better suited for his role as precipitator of the Great War. He belonged to the Young Bosnian Society, a group of students, workers, a few peasants, Croats, Muslims, and intellectuals, who wanted to free Slavic populations from Habsburg control. Princip was part of a growing movement of South Slavs struggling for national liberation, who considered

Austrian archduke Franz Ferdinand and his wife Sophie leave the Senate House in Sarajevo on 28 June 1914. Five minutes later, Serbian terrorist Gavrilo Princip assassinated the couple.

themselves to be held in colonial servitude by Austria-Hungary. Other groups like the Unification or Death Society (known to its enemies as the Black Hand), headed by a high Serbian official, shared similar goals and hopes of uniting with an independent Serbia. To this end, South Slav liberation groups had made six attempts on Archduke Franz Ferdinand's life over the previous four years. Standing on a Sarajevo street corner as the Austrian noble paraded past in an open motor car, Princip succeeded where his compatriots had failed.

Struggle over control of the Balkans had been a long-standing issue that had involved all the major European powers for decades. As Austria-Hungary's ally since 1879, Germany was willing to support Vienna's showdown in the Balkans as a way of stopping Russian advances in the area. The alliance with Germany gave Austria-Hungary a sense of security and confidence to pursue its Balkan aims. Germany had its own plans for domination of the Continent and feared a weakened Austria-Hungary would undermine its own position in central Europe. Independent Balkan states to the south and east were also a threat to Germany's plans. German leaders hoped that an Austro-Serbian war would remain localized and would strengthen their ally, Austria-Hungary.

While Austria-Hungary had Germany's support, Serbia was backed by a sympathetic Russia that favored nationalist movements in the Balkans. Russia had, in turn, been encouraged by France, its ally by military pact since 1894, to take a firm stand in its struggle with Austria-Hungary for dominance among Balkan nationalities.

The five weeks between the assassination of the Archduke Ferdinand and the outbreak of the war were a period of intense diplomatic activity. The assassin's act was the stone dropped in the pond of Great Power politics that sent shock waves through every European nation. The assassination gave Austria-Hungary the excuse it needed to bring a troublesome Serbia into line. Austria-Hungary held Serbia responsible for the shootings. Leaders in Vienna had no evidence at the time to justify their allegations of a Serbian conspiracy, but they saw in this event the perfect pretext for military action. On 23 July 1914, Austria-Hungary issued an ultimatum to the small Balkan nation and secretly decided to declare war regardless of Serbia's response. The demands were so severe that, if met, they would have stripped Serbia of its independence. Austria's aim was to destroy Serbia. In spite of a conciliatory, although not capitulatory, reply from Serbia to its ultimatum, Austria-Hungary declared war on the Balkan nation on 28 July 1914. Russia mobilized two days after the Austro-Hungarian declaration of war against Serbia. Germany mobilized in response to the Russian action and declared war on Russia on 1 August and on France on 3 August. France had begun mobilizing on 30 July, when its ally, Russia, entered the war.

Great Britain stood briefly outside the fray in the futile attempt to mediate a settlement in the Austro-Serbian conflict. Britain's dependence on its alliance with France as a means of protecting British sea routes in the Mediterranean meant that Great Britain could not remain neutral once France declared war. On 4 August, after Germany had violated Belgian neutrality in its march to France, Great Britain honored its treaty obligations and declared war on Germany. Great Britain entered the war because it judged that a powerful Germany could use ports on the English Channel to invade the British Isles. Italy alone of the major powers remained for the moment outside the conflict. Although allied with Germany and Austria-Hungary, its own aspirations in the Balkans prevented it from fighting for the Austrian cause in 1914.

Self-interest, fear, and ambition motivated the Great Powers in different ways in the pursuit of war. The international diplomatic system that had worked so well to prevent war in the preceding decades now enmeshed European states in interlocking alliances and created a chain reaction. The Austro-Serbian war of July 1914 became a Europe-wide war within a month.

Sir Edward Grey (1862–1933), head of the British Foreign Office, understood clearly—as most of his contemporaries did not—what the war would mean for civilization in the West. Looking out his window at dusk on the eve of Great Britain's entry into the war, he prophesied, "The lamps are going out all over Europe. We shall not see them lit again in our lifetime." Because of the alliance system and the military timetables of the Great Powers, a darkness descended on Europe.

The War Europe Got

Early in the war, the best-laid plans of political and military leaders collapsed. First, Europe got a war that was not limited but one that quickly spread throughout Europe and became global. Switzerland, Spain, the Netherlands, and all of Scandinavia remained neutral, but every other European nation was pulled into the war. The conflict burst the limits of western Europe. In August 1914 Japan cast its lot with the Allies, as the Entente came to be known, and in November the Ottoman Empire joined the Central Powers of Germany and Austria-Hungary. In the following year Italy joined the war, not on the side of its long-term treaty partners, Germany and Austria-Hungary, but on the side of the Allies, with the expectation of benefiting in the Balkans from Austrian defeat. Bulgaria joined Germany and Austria-Hungary in 1915, seeking territory at Serbia's expense. By the time of the United States' entry in 1917, the war had become a world war.

The second surprise for the European powers was that they did not get a preventive war of movement, nor one of short duration. Within weeks, that pattern had given way to what promised to be a long and costly war of attrition. All started as Schlieffen's successors had planned, with German victory in battle after battle. The end seemed near. But in the space of less than a month the war changed in ways that no one had predicted. Technology was the key to understanding the change and to explaining the surprises.

Technology and the Trenches

In the history of nineteenth-century European warfare, armies had relied on mobile cavalry and infantry units whose greatest asset was speed. Rapid advance had been decisive in the Prussian victory over the French in 1870, which had resulted in the formation of the German Empire. Soldiers of the twentieth century were also trained for a moving war, high maneuverability, and maximum territorial conquest. Yet after the first six weeks of battle, soldiers were ordered to do something unimaginable to strategists of European warfare: they were ordered to dig ditches and fight from fixed positions. Soldiers on both sides shoveled out trenches four feet

Over the Top *by John Nash. The painting was inspired by the artist's own experiences in the trenches of World War I. The title and content reflect one of the major themes of trench warfare — soldiers ordered to advance from the relative safety of the trench into withering enemy fire.*

A typical World War I trench. Millions of soldiers lived amid mud, disease, and vermin, awaiting death from enemy shells. After the French army mutiny in 1916, the troops wrung this concession from their commanders: They did not have to charge German machine guns while armed only with rifles.

deep, piled up sandbags, mounted their machine guns, and began to fight an unplanned, defensive war.

The front lines of Europe's armies in the west wallowed within the 400 miles of trenches that ran from the English Channel to the Swiss frontier. The British and French on one side and the Germans on the other fought each other with machine guns and mortars, backed up by heavy artillery to the rear. Strategists on both sides believed they could break through enemy lines. As a result, the monotony of trench warfare was punctuated periodically by infantry offensives in which immense concentrations of artillery caused great bloodshed. Ten million men were

killed in this bizarre and deadly combination of old and new warfare.

Eyewitness accounts describe the horrors of the new trench warfare. In his fictionalized account, *All Quiet on the Western Front*, based on his own wartime experiences and published in 1928, German novelist Erich Maria Remarque (1898–1970) described life at the front: "When a shell lands in the trench we note how the hollow, furious blast is like a blow from the paw of a raging beast of prey. Already by morning a few of the recruits are green and vomiting. They are too inexperienced." He told of soldiers dying like flies, plastered on the walls of the trenches: "you could scrape them off with a spoon and bury them in a mess tin." The glamour of battle that attracted many young men disappeared quickly in the daily reality of living in mud with rats and constantly facing death. The British poet Wilfred Owen (1893–1918) wrote shortly before his own death in battle about how the soldier next to him had been shot in the head, soaking Owen in blood: "I shall feel again as soon as I dare, but now I must not."

The invention of new weaponry and heavy equipment had transformed war into an industry of increasing complexity. Military and naval staffs expanded to meet new needs of warfare. Old ways persisted. In their bright blue coats and red trousers, French and Belgian infantrymen made easy targets. Outmoded calvary units survived despite more efficient mechanization. The railroad made the mobilization, organization, and deployment of mass armies possible. Specialists were needed to control the new war machines that heavy industry had created.

It has been observed that the spade and the machine gun transformed war. The machine gun was not new in 1914, but its strategic value was not fully appreciated before then. The Maxim machine gun had been used by the British in the Matabele War in 1893 against African warriors. Fifty infantrymen with only four machine guns killed three thousand charging natives in less than ninety minutes. Strategists regarded this carnage as a stunning achievement but failed to ask how a weapon of such phenomenal destructive power would work against an enemy equally armed with machine guns instead of spears. Military strategists drew all the wrong conclusions. They continued to plan an offensive strategy when the weaponry developed for massive destruction had pushed them into fighting a defensive war from the trenches. Both sides resorted to concentration of artillery, increased use of poison gas, and unrestricted submarine warfare, in desperate attempts to break the deadlock caused by meeting armed force with force.

The necessity of total victory drove the Central Powers and the Allies to grisly new inventions. Late in the war, the need to break the deadlock of trench warfare ushered in the airplane and the tank. Neither was decisive in altering the course of

The British invented the tank, which made its combat debut in 1916. The new weapon terrified the German troops when first used on the Western Front. The British had developed it in heavy secrecy, under the pretext of constructing water tanks; hence the name.

Gassed, *by the American painter John Singer Sargent. A line of walking wounded, blinded by a German poison-gas attack, threads it way past fallen comrades, hanging onto each other behind a sighted leader. Poison gas was later thought to be self-defeating, and it was not used in World War II.*

the war, although the airplane was useful for reconnaissance and for limited bombing and the tank promised the means of breaking through defensive lines. Their success in isolated battles foreshadowed future warfare and new potential for destruction. Chlorine gas was first used in warfare by the Germans in 1915. "Mustard" gas, which was named for its distinctive smell and which caused severe blistering, was introduced two years later. The Germans were the first to use flamethrowers, especially effective against mechanized vehicles with vulnerable fuel tanks. Barbed wire, invented in the U.S. Midwest to contain farm animals, became an essential aspect of trench warfare as it marked off the no-man's-land between combatants and prevented surprise attacks. There were grim tales of advancing infantry possessing only a few pair of wire cutters being impaled by enemy fire on these fences of death.

The technology that had been viewed as a proof of progress was now channeled toward engineering new instruments of death. Yet technology itself produced a stalemate. New weapons sometimes produced their antidotes, for example, the invention of deadly gas was followed soon

after by gas masks. Each side was capable of matching the other's ability to devise new armaments. Deadlocks caused by technological parity forced both sides to resort to desperate concentrations of men and weaponry that resulted not in decisive battles but in ever escalating casualty rates. Improving their efficiency at killing, the European powers were not finding a way to end the war.

The Battle of the Marne

German forces seized the offensive in the west and invaded neutral Belgium at the beginning of August 1914. The Belgians resisted stubbornly but unsuccessfully. Belgian forts were systematically captured and the capital of Brussels fell under the German advance on August 20. After the fall of Belgium, German military might swept into northern France with the intention of inflicting a swift defeat on the French in six weeks.

In the years preceding the war, the German General Staff, unwilling to concentrate all of their troops in the west, had modified the Schlieffen Plan by committing divisions to its eastern frontier. The absence of the full German fighting force in the west did not appreciably slow the German advance through Belgium. Yet the Germans had underestimated both the cost of holding back the French in Alsace-Lorraine and the difficulty of maneuvering German forces and transporting supplies in an offensive war. Eventually, unexpected Russian advances in the east also siphoned off troops from the west. German forces in the west were so weakened by the offensive that they were unable to swing west of Paris, as planned, and instead chose to enter the French capital from the northeast by crossing the Marne River. This shift exposed the German First Army on its western flank and opened up a gap on its eastern flank.

Despite an initial pattern of retreat and a lack of coordination of forces, Allied French and British troops were ready to take advantage of the vulnerabilities in the German advance. In a series of battles between 6 and 10 September 1914 that came to be known as the First Battle of the Marne, the Allies counterattacked and advanced into the gap. The German army was forced to drop back. In the following months each army tried to outflank the other in what has been called "the race to the sea." By late fall it was clear that the battles from the Marne north to the border town of Ypres in northwest Belgium near the English Channel ended an open war of movement on the western front. Soldiers now dug in along a line of battle that changed little in the long three and a half years that followed until March 1918.

The Allies gained a strategic victory in the First Battle of the Marne by resisting the German advance in the fighting that quickly became known as the "miracle" of the Marne. The legend was further enhanced by true stories of French troops being rushed from Paris to the front in taxicabs. Yet the real significance of the Marne lay in the severe miscalculations of military leaders and statesmen on both sides, who had expected a different kind of war. They did not understand the new technology that made a short war unlikely. Nor did they understand the demands that this new kind of warfare would make on civilian populations. Those Parisian taxi-drivers foreshadowed how other European civilians would be called upon again and again to support the war in the next four years. The Schlieffen Plan was dead.

But it was no more a failure than any of the other military timetables of the Great Powers. The Battle of the Marne held the legacy of a long and bloody war that no one was prepared to fight.

"I don't know what is to be done—this isn't war." So spoke Lord Horatio Kitchener (1850–1916), one of the most decorated British generals of his time. He was not alone in his bafflement over the stalemate of trench warfare at the end of 1914. By that time, Germany's greatest fear, a simultaneous war on two fronts, had become a grim reality. The Central Powers were under a state of siege, cut off from the world by the great battlefront in the west and by the Allied blockade at sea. The rules of the game had been redefined, and the European powers settled in for a long war. Possessing more soldiers, more armaments, greater productive capacity, and access to overseas trade, the Allies appeared to have the staying power to win a protracted war against the Central Powers. The suspense of the four years that followed was that Germany and its partners verged on winning a war that they should have been doomed to lose.

•

War on the Eastern Front

War on Germany's eastern front was a mobile war, unlike its western counterpart, because there were relatively fewer men and guns in relation to the vast distances. The Russian army was the largest in the world. Yet it was crippled from the outbreak of the war by inadequate supplies and poor leadership. Having mobilized more rapidly than German planners thought possible, Russia was able to take advantage of Germany's commitment to the western front in the opening weeks of the war. Russia's transportation network was inadequate, however, to the needs of mobilization, and its railroads ran on tracks of a different gauge from those of the rest of Europe. The tsar's troops advanced into East Prussia and Austrian Galicia on foot. At the end of August 1914 the smaller German army, supported by divisions drawn from the west, delivered a devastating defeat to the Russians in the one great battle on the eastern front. At Tannenberg, the entire Russian Second Army was destroyed, and about 100,000 Russian soldiers were taken prisoner.

Faced with this humiliation, General Aleksandr Vasilievich Samsonov (1859–1914), head of the Russian forces, committed suicide on the field of battle. The German General Paul von Hindenburg (1847–1934), a veteran of the Franco-Prussian war of 1870, had been recalled from retirement to direct the campaign against the Russians because of his intimate knowledge of the area. Assisted by Quartermaster General Erich Ludendorff (1865–1937), Hindenburg followed the stunning victory of Tannenberg two weeks later with another devastating blow to Russian forces at the Masurian Lakes.

The Russians were holding up their end of the bargain in the Allied war effort, but at great cost. They kept the Germans busy and forced them to divert troops to the eastern front, weakening the German effort to knock France out of the war. In the south the tsar's troops defeated the Austro-Hungarian army at Lemberg in Galicia in September. This Russian victory gave Serbia a temporary reprieve. But by mid-1915 Germany had thrown the Russians back and was keeping Austria-Hungary propped up in the war. By fall Russia had lost most of Galicia, the Polish lands of the Russian empire, Lithuania, and parts of Latvia and Belorussia to the advancing enemy. These losses amounted to 15 percent of its territory and 20 percent of its population. The Russian army staggered, with over one million soldiers taken as prisoners of war and at least as many killed and wounded.

The Russian army, as one of its own officers described it, was being bled to death. Russian

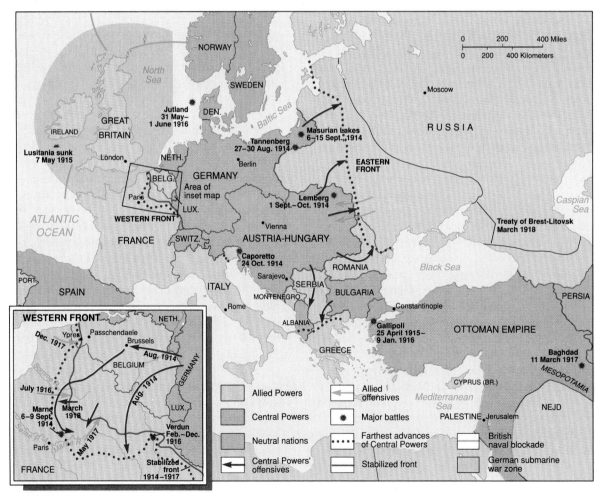

World War I

soldiers were poorly led into battle or not led at all because of the shortage of officers. Munitions shortages meant that soldiers often went into battle without rifles, armed only with the hope of scavenging arms from their fallen comrades. Poor planning and lack of any kind of intelligence system compounded deployment problems. High casualties were now rivaled by high numbers of desertions.

Despite these difficulties the Russians, under the direction of General Aleksei Brusilov (1853–1926), commander of the Russian armies in the southern part of the eastern front, remarkably managed to throw back the Austro-Hungarian forces in 1916 and almost eliminated Austria as a military power. But this was the last great campaign on the eastern front and Russia's last show of strength in the Great War. Problems of support and deployment undermined Brusilov's herculean efforts. In the end, as a British observer commented, "As so often happened in Russia, the Supreme Command ordered but the railways decided."

Russia's near destruction of the Austrian army tremendously benefited Russia's allies. In order to protect its partner, Germany was forced to withdraw eight divisions from Italy, alleviating the Allied situation in the Tyrol, and twelve divisions from the western front, providing relief for the French at Verdun and the British at the Somme. In addition, Russia sent troops to the aid of a new member of the Allied camp, Romania, an act which probably further weakened Brusilov's efforts. In response to Brusilov's challenge, the Germans established control over the Austrian army, assigning military command of the coalition to General Ludendorff.

By the summer of 1917, the tsardom had been overthrown and a provisional government ruled Russia. Tens of thousands of Russian soldiers were walking away from the war. Russia withdrew from the war and in March 1918 signed a separate peace by which Germany gained extensive territorial advantages and important supply bases for carrying on the war in the west. To protect these territories and their resources, the Germans had to maintain an army on this front. No longer fighting an enemy in the east, however, Germany could release the bulk of its forces to fight in the west.

War on the Western Front

Along hundreds of miles of trenches, the French and British tried repeatedly to expel the Germans from Belgium. Long periods of inactivity were punctuated by orgies of heavy bloodletting. A German prisoner of war described these events as "the suicide of nations." The enthusiasm of the first days of battle gave way to a weary resignation for soldiers at the front who could see no end to the massacre. Repeated German and Allied reassurances—"Morale is holding out"—suggested to the contrary that morale was low. The German phrase, "All quiet on the western front," used in military communiques to describe those periods of silence between massive shellings and infantry attacks, reported only the uneasy calm before the next violent storm.

Military leaders on both sides cherished the dream of a decisive offensive, the breakthrough that would win the war. In 1916 the Allies planned a joint strike at the Somme, a river in northern France flowing west into the English Channel, but the Germans struck first at Verdun, a small fortress city in northeast France. By concentrating great numbers of troops, the Germans outnumbered the French five to two. As General Erich von Falkenhayn (1861–1922), chief of the General Staff of the German army from 1914 to 1916, explained it, the German purpose in attacking Verdun was "to bleed the French white by virtue of our superiority in guns."

On the first day of battle one million shells were fired. Henri Barbusse (1873–1935) in his novel Le Feu (1916) brutally conveyed the terrible effects of shell-fire: "... Men squashed, cut in two, or divided from top to bottom, blown into showers by an ordinary shell, bellies turned inside out and scattered anyhow, skulls forced bodily into the chest as if by a blow with a club." The battlefield was a living hell as soldiers stumbled across corpse after corpse. Against the German onslaught, French troops were instructed to hold out though they lacked adequate artillery and reinforcements. General Joseph Joffre (1852–1931), commander-in-chief of the French army, was unwilling to divert reinforcements to Verdun.

The German troops advanced easily through the first lines of defense. But the French held their position for ten long, horrifying months of contin-

Painting by François Flameng of Verdun in flames. This city on the Meuse River in northern France has played an important part in resisting enemy invasion since the time of Attila the Hun in the fifth century.

uous mass slaughter from February to December 1916. General Henri Philippe Pétain (1856–1951), a local commander planning an early retirement before the war, bolstered morale by constantly rotating his troops to the point that most of the French army—259 of 330 infantry battalions—saw action at Verdun. Nearly starving and poorly armed, the French stood alone in the bloodiest offensive of the war. Attack strategy backfired on the Germans as their own death tolls mounted.

Pétain and his flamboyant general Robert Georges Nivelle (1856–1924) were both hailed as heroes for fulfilling the instruction to their troops: "They shall not pass." Falkenhayn fared less well and was dismissed from his post. Yet no real winners emerged from the scorched earth of Verdun, where observers could see the nearest thing to desert created in Europe. Verdun was a disaster. The French and the Germans each suffered about 600,000 casualties. A few square miles of territory had changed hands back and forth. In the end, no military advantage was gained. Almost 700,000 lives were lost. The legends of brilliant leadership of Pétain and Nivelle, who both went on to greater positions of authority, and the failed command of Falkenhayn, who retired in disgrace, obscured the real lesson of the battle: an offensive war under these conditions was impossible.

Still, new offensives were devised. The British went ahead with their planned offensive on the Somme in July 1916. For an advance of seven miles, 400,000 British and 200,000 French soldiers were killed or wounded. The American writer F. Scott Fitzgerald (1896–1940), who had served as an army officer in World War I, wrote of the battle of the Somme in his novel *Tender Is the Night* (1934). One of his characters is describing a visit to the Somme Valley after the war: "See that little stream. We could walk to it in two minutes. It took the British a whole month to walk to it—a whole empire walking very slowly, dying in front and pushing forward behind. And another empire walked very slowly backward a few inches a day, leaving the dead like a million bloody rugs." German losses brought the total casualties of this offensive to one million men. Despite his experience at Verdun, French general Robert Nivelle planned his own offensive in the Champagne region in spring 1917, sure that he could succeed where others had failed in "breaking the crust." The Nivelle offensive resulted in 40,000 deaths. Nivelle was dismissed. The French army was falling apart, with mutiny and insubordination everywhere.

The British believed they could succeed where the French had fallen. Under General Douglas Haig (1861–1928), the commander-in-chief of British expeditionary forces on the Continent, the British launched an attack in Flanders through the summer and fall of 1917. Known as the Passchendaele offensive, named for the village and ridge in whose "porridge of mud" much of the fighting took place, this campaign resulted in almost 400,000 British soldiers slaughtered for insignificant territorial gain. The Allies and the Germans finally recognized that "going over the top" in offensives was not working and could not work. The war must be won by other means. On the western front at the end of 1917, there was stalemate but there was still no solution.

War on the Periphery

Recognizing the stalemate in the west, the Allies attempted to open up other fronts where the Central Powers might be vulnerable. In the spring of 1915 the Allies were successful in convincing Italy to enter the war on their side by promising that it would receive at the time of the peace the South Tyrol and the southern part of Dalmatia and key Dalmatian islands, which would assure Italy's dominance over the Adriatic Sea. By thus capitalizing on Italian antagonism toward Austria-Hungary over control of this territory, the Allies gained 875,000 Italian soldiers for their cause. Although these Italian troops were in no way decisive in the fighting that followed, Great Britain, France, and Russia saw the need to build up Allied support in southern Europe in order to reinforce Serbian attempts to keep Austrian troops beyond its borders. The Allies also hoped that by pulling Germans into this southern front, some relief might be provided for British and French soldiers on the western front.

Germany, in turn, was well aware of the need to expand its alliances beyond Austria-Hungary if it was to compete successfully against superior Allied forces. Trapped as they were to the east and west, the Central Powers established control over a broad corridor stretching from the North Sea through central Europe and down through the Ottoman Empire to the Suez Canal so vital to British interests. In the Balkans, where the war had begun, the Serbs were consistently bested by the Austrians. By late 1915 the Serbs had been knocked out of the war, in spite of Allied attempts to assist them. Serbia paid a heavy price in the Great War: it lost one-sixth of its population through war, famine, and disease. The promise of booty persuaded Bulgaria to join Germany and Austria-Hungary. Over the next year and a half,

the Allies responded by convincing Romania and then Greece to join them.

The theater of war continued to expand. Although the Ottoman Empire had joined the war in late 1914 on the side of the Central Powers, its own internal difficulties attenuated its fighting ability. As a multinational empire consisting of Turks, Arabs, Armenians, Greeks, Kurds, and other ethnic minorities, it was plagued by Turkish misrule and Arab nationalism. Hence the Ottoman Empire was the weakest link in the chain of German alliances. Yet it held a crucial position. The Turks could block shipping of vital supplies to Russia through the Mediterranean and the Black seas. Coming to the aid of their Russian ally, a combined British and French fleet attacked Turkish forces at the Straits of the Dardanelles in April 1915. In the face of political and military opposition, First Lord of the Admiralty Winston Churchill (1874–1965) supported the idea of opening a new front by sea. Poorly planned and mismanaged, the expedition was a disaster. When the naval effort in the German-mined Straits failed, the British foolishly decided to land troops on the Gallipoli Peninsula, which extends from the southern coast of European Turkey. There British soldiers were trapped on the rocky terrain, unable to advance against the Turks, unable to fall back. Gallipoli was the first large-scale attempt at amphibious warfare. The Australian and New Zealand forces (ANZACS) showed great bravery in some of the most brutal fighting of the war. Critics in Britain argued that the only success of the nine-month campaign was its evacuation.

Britain sought to protect its interests in the Suez Canal. Turkish troops menaced the Canal effectively enough to terrify the British into maintaining an elaborate system of defense in the area and concentrating large troop reinforcements in Egypt. War with the Ottoman Empire also extended battle into the oil fields of Mesopotamia and Persia. This attempt at a new front was initially a fiasco for the British and Russian forces that threatened Baghdad. The Allies proceeded not only without plans but also without maps. They literally did not know where they were going. Eventually, British forces recovered and took Baghdad in 1917, while Australian and New Zealand troops captured Jerusalem. The tentacles of war spread out, following the path of Western economic and imperial interests throughout the world.

Most surprising of all was the indecisive nature of the war at sea. The great battleships of the British and German navies avoided confrontation on the high seas. The only major naval battle of the Great War took place in early 1916 at the Battle of Jutland in the North Sea. Each side inflicted damage on the other but, through careful maneuvering, avoided a decisive outcome to the battle. Probably the enormous cost of replacing battleships deterred both the British and the Germans from risking their fleets in engagements on the high seas. With the demands for munitions

and equipment on the two great land fronts of the war, neither side could afford to lose a traditional war at sea. Instead, the British used their seapower as a policing force to blockade German trade and strangle the German economy.

The German navy, much weaker than the British, relied on a new weapon, the submarine, which threatened to become decisive in the war at sea. Submarines were initially used in the first months of the war for reconnaissance. Their potential for inflicting heavy losses on commercial shipping became apparent in 1915. Undergoing technological improvements throughout the war, U-boats, or *Unterseeboots* as German submarines were called, torpedoed 6 million tons of Allied shipping in 1917. With cruising ranges as high as 3,600 miles, German submarines attacked Allied and neutral shipping as far away as off the shore of the United States and the Arctic supply line to Russia. German insistence on unrestricted use outraged neutral powers, who considered the Germans in violation of international law. The Germans rejected the requirements of warning an enemy ship and boarding it for investigation as too dangerous for submarines, which were no match for battleships above water. The Allies invented depth charges and mines that were capable of blowing German submarines out of the water. These weapons, combined with the use of the convoy system in the Atlantic and the Mediterranean, produced a successful blockade and antisubmarine campaign that put an end to the German advantage.

A German submarine takes on supplies at a harbor. The U-boats became widespread military weapons because of their effectiveness in surprise attack. These "iron coffins" were to take a terrible toll on Allied shipping in World War II.

Adjusting to the Unexpected: Total War

War devoured human and material resources at a rate unknown in the history of the West. The period from 1914 to 1918 marked the first time in history that the productive activities of entire populations were directed toward a single goal: military victory. The Great War became a war of peoples, not just of armies. Wars throughout history have involved noncombatants caught in the cross fire or standing in the wrong place at the wrong time. But this unexpected war of attrition required civilian populations to adjust to a situation in which what went on at the battlefront transformed life on the home front. Barbed wire and trenches defined the lines of battle but did not delimit the theater of war. For this reason, the Great War has become known as history's first *total* war.

Adjusting to the unexpected war of 1914, governments intervened to centralize and control every aspect of economic life. Technology and industrial capacity made possible a war of unimaginable destruction. The scale of production and distribution of war-related materials required for victory was unprecedented. To persuade civilians to suffer at home for the sake of the war, leaders pictured the enemy as an evil villain who must be defeated at any cost. The sacrifice required for a total war made total victory necessary. And total victory required an economy totally geared to fighting the war. Manufacture of consumer goods could not be justified if the resources required to produce them could be better used to sustain the war effort. Free labor choices and free markets disappeared. In the end, the ability to maintain and organize productive capacity on the home front proved decisive in winning the First World War.

Mobilizing the Home Front

While soldiers were fighting on the eastern and western fronts, businessmen and politicians at home were creating bureaucratic administrations to control wages and prices, distribute supplies, establish production quotas, and, in general, mobilize human and material resources. Just as governments had conscripted the active male population for military service, the Allies and the Central Powers now mobilized civilians of all ages and both sexes to work for the war. Even the very young were expected to "do their bit."

Women played an essential role in the mobilization of the home front. They had never been isolated from the experiences and hardships of war, but they now found new ways to support the war effort. In cities women went to work in munitions factories and war-related industries that had previously employed only men. Women filled service jobs, from fire fighters to trolley-car con-

During World War I, women workers flocked to the munitions plants to take the place of men who had marched off to war. The women above are operating cranes in a shell-filling factory.

ductors, jobs that were essential to the smooth running of industrial society and that had been left vacant by men. On farms women literally took up the plow, as both men and horses were requisitioned for the war effort. "If the women in war factories stopped for twenty minutes, we should lose the war." Thus did General Joffre recognize the contribution of women workers to the Allied war effort.

By 1918, 650,000 French women were working in war-related industries and in clerical positions in the army. And they had counterparts all over Europe. In Germany, two out of every five munitions workers were women. Women became more prominent in the work force as a whole, as the case of Great Britain makes clear: there the number of women workers jumped from 250,000 at the beginning of the war to 5,000,000 by the war's end. Women also served in the auxiliary units of the armed services in the clerical and medical corps in order to free men for fighting at the front. In eastern European nations, women entered combat as soldiers. Although most women were displaced from their wartime jobs with the return of men after the armistice, they were as important to the war effort as men fighting at the front.

In the first months of the war the private sector had been left to its own devices with nearly disastrous results. Shortages, especially of shells, and bottlenecks in production threatened military efforts. Governments were forced to establish controls and to set up state monopolies in order to guarantee the supplies necessary to wage war. Numbers were what mattered. According to the estimate of a specialist on war, a minimally trained regiment with field guns in 1914 could deliver more destructive power in one hour on a small area, a few hundred yards square, than had been fired by all the guns on both sides for the entire course of the Napoleonic wars. Waste on such a scale required careful organization.

Government agencies to control production and fuel distribution proliferated. In Germany, industrialists Walter Rathenau (1867–1922) and Alfred Hugenberg (1865–1951) worked with the government to impose controls and create state monopolies. By the spring of 1915, they had eliminated the German problem of munitions scarcity. France was in trouble six weeks after the outbreak of the war: it had used up half of its accumulated munitions supplies in the First Battle of the Marne. Compounding the problem was the fact that the government had pulled workers out of armaments factories to send them to the front. German occupation of France's northern industrial basin further crippled munitions production. Through government intervention, France improvised and relocated its war industries. The British government got involved in production, too, by establishing in 1915 the first Ministry of Munitions under the direction of David Lloyd George (1863–1945). Distinct from the Ministry of War, the Ministry of Munitions was to coordinate military needs with the armaments industry.

Soldiers do not live by munitions alone. An army proverbially travels on its stomach. In a war that leaders soon realized would be a long one, food supplies assumed paramount importance. Germany, dependent on food imports to feed its people and isolated from the world market by the Allied blockade, introduced rationing five months after the outbreak of the war. Other Continental nations followed suit. Government agents set quotas for agricultural producers. Armies were fed and supplied at the expense of domestic populations. Great Britain, which enjoyed a more reliable food supply by virtue of its sea power, did not impose food rationing until 1917.

Strict controls over scarce resources did not always solve problems of shortages. Civilian populations, especially in Germany and Russia, suffered severe hardships, with their diets falling below subsistence levels. The German war effort was badly weakened by shortages of labor, fuel, and food. Over 11,000 food substitutes with little or no nutritional value were created in Germany to give people at least the illusion of eating. Some of these synthetic foods were licensed and patented after the war and marketed throughout Western societies. The exceptionally harsh winter of 1916–17 came to be known in Germany as the "turnip winter," because this easy-to-grow root vegetable was all that kept people from starving. "For breakfast, turnip bread—lunch, turnip-stew—supper, turnip-cutlets and turnip salad," complained a soldier in *All Quiet on the Western Front.* Yet this soldier was fortunate enough to be enjoying something different from the usual fare of sawdust bread. Those who lived through the period swore they would never touch turnips again.

Three factors put food supplies at risk. First, the need for large numbers of soldiers at the front pulled farmers and peasants off the land. The resultant drop in the agricultural work force meant that land was taken out of production and what remained was less efficiently cultivated. Productivity declined. A second factor was fear of requisitioning and the general uncertainties of war that caused agricultural producers to hoard supplies. What little was available was traded on black markets. Finally, because all European countries depended to some extent on imports of food and fertilizers, enemies successfully targeted trade routes for attack.

War Governments

The strains of total war were becoming apparent. Two years of sacrificing, scrimping, and, in some areas, starving began to take their toll among soldiers and civilians on both sides. With the lack of decisive victories, war weariness was spreading. Work stoppages and strikes, which had virtually ceased with the outbreak of war in 1914, began to climb rapidly in 1916. Between 1915 and 1916 in France, the number of strikes by dissatisfied workers increased by 400 percent. Underpaid and tired workers went on strike, staged demonstrations, and protested exploitation. Labor militancy also intensified in the British Isles and Germany. Women, breadwinners for their families, were often in the forefront of these protests throughout Europe. Social peace between unions and governments was no longer held together by patriotic enthusiasm for war.

Politicians, too, began to rethink their suspension of opposition to government policies as the war dragged on. Dissidents among European socialist parties regained their prewar commitment to peace. Socialists everywhere had enthusiastically supported the declarations of war in 1914. By 1916, the united front that political opponents had presented against the enemy was crumbling under growing demands for peace. Organized opposition criticizing the war sometimes assumed a revolutionary direction, but most critics sought cooperation with socialists in other countries in a bid for international peace. Not all opposition was peaceful. In the fall of 1916, the Austrian prime minister was assassinated by a socialist attempting to bring an end to the war.

In a total war unrest at home guaranteed defeat. Governments knew that all opposition to war policies had to be eliminated. In a dramatic extension of the police powers of the state, whether among the Allies or the Central Powers, criticism of the government became treason. Censorship was enforced. Propaganda became more virulent. Those who spoke for peace were no better than the enemy. The governments of every warring nation resorted to harsh measures. Politicians who advocated a compromise peace, like former Prime Minister Joseph Caillaux (1863–1944) in France, were charged with treason and imprisoned without trial for two years. Others were executed. Parliamentary bodies were stripped of power, civil liberties were suspended, democratic procedures were ignored. The civilian governments of Premier Georges Clemenceau (1841–1929) in France and Prime Minister Lloyd George in Great Britain resorted to rule by emergency police power to repress criticism. Under Generals von Hindenburg and Ludendorff in Germany, military rule became the order of the day. Nowhere was government as usual possible in total war.

Every warring nation sought to promote dissension from within the societies of its enemies. Germany provided some aid for the Easter Rebellion in Ireland in 1916 in the hope that the Irish demand for independence that predated the war would deflect British attention and undermine fighting strength and morale. The British responded brutally to the Irish bid for independence, with bloody reprisals and the execution of Irish leaders. Germany also supported separatist movements among minority nationalities in the Russian empire and was responsible for returning Lenin under escort to Russia in April 1917. The British engaged in similar tactics. The British foreign secretary Arthur Balfour (1848–1930) worked with Zionist leaders in 1917 in drawing up the Balfour Declaration, which promised to "look with favor" on the creation of a Jewish homeland in Palestine. The British thereby encouraged Zionist hopes among central European Jews, with the intent of creating difficulties for German and Austrian rulers. Similarly, the British encouraged Arabs to rebel against Turks with the same promise of Palestine. Undermining the loyalties of colonized peoples and minorities would be at minimum a nuisance to the enemy. Beyond that, it could erode war efforts from within.

The Turning Point and Victory, 1917–18

For the Allies, 1917 began with a series of crises. Under the hammering of one costly offensive after another, French morale had collapsed and army military discipline was deteriorating. A combined German-Austrian force had eliminated the Allied states of Serbia and Romania. The Italians experienced a military debacle at Caporetto and were effectively out of the war.

The year 1917 was "the blackest year of the war" for the Allies. At the beginning of the year, the peril on the sea had increased with the opening of unrestricted U-boat warfare against Allied and neutral shipping. The greatest blow came when Russia, now in the throes of domestic revolution, withdrew. Germany was able to concentrate more of its resources in the west and fight a one-front war. Perhaps more significantly, it was able to utilize the foodstuffs and raw materials of its newly acquired Russian territories to buoy its home front.

Yet in spite of Allied reversals, it was not at all the case that the war was turning in favor of the Central Powers. Both Austria-Hungary and the Ottoman Empire teetered on the verge of collapse, with internal difficulties increasing as the war dragged on. Germany suffered from labor and supply shortages and economic hardship, resulting from the blockade and an economy totally dedicated to waging war.

The war had gone from a stalemate to a state of crisis for both sides. Every belligerent state was experiencing war weariness that undermined civilian and military morale. Pressures to end the war increased everywhere. Attrition was not working. Attacks were not working. Every country suffered on the home front and battlefront from strikes, food riots, military desertions, and mutinies. Defeatism was everywhere on the rise.

The Allies longed for the entry of the United States into the war. Although the United States was a neutral country, it had become an important supplier to the Allies from early in the war. Trade with the Allies had jumped from $825 million in 1914 to $3.2 billion in 1916. American bankers also made loans and extended credit to the Allies to the amount of $2.2 billion. By any financial measure, the United States had made a sizable investment in the Allied war effort and its economy was prospering.

Beginning with the sinking of the *Lusitania* in 1915, German policy on the high seas had incensed the American public. Increased U-boat activity in 1916 led U.S. President Woodrow Wilson (1856–1924) to issue a severe warning to the Germans to cease submarine warfare. The Germans, however, were driven to desperate measures. The great advantage of submarines was in sneak attacks, a procedure against the international rules that required warning. Germany initiated a new phase of unrestricted submarine warfare on 1 February 1917, when the German ambassador informed the U.S. government that U-boats would sink on sight all ships, including passenger ships, even those neutral and unarmed.

German machinations in Mexico were also revealed on 25 February 1917, with the interception of a telegram from Arthur Zimmermann (1864–1940), the German foreign minister. The telegram communicated Germany's willingness to support Mexico's recovery of "lost territory" in New Mexico, Arizona, and Texas in return for Mexican support of Germany in the event of U.S. entry into the war. U.S. citizens were outraged. On 2 April 1917, Wilson, who had won the presidential election of 1916 on the promise of peace, asked the U.S. Congress for a declaration of war against Germany: "It is a fearful thing to lead this great peaceful people into war, into the most terrible and disastrous of all wars, civilization itself seems to be in the balance. But the right is more precious than peace." Wilson led his country with idealism and resolution into a war that he described as "a People's War" for freedom and democracy for all nations of the world.

U.S. entry was the turning point in the war, tipping the scales dramatically in favor of the Allies. The United States contributed its naval power to the large Allied convoys formed to protect shipping against German attacks. In a total war, control and shipment of resources had become crucial issues, and it was in these areas that the U.S. entry gave the Allies indisputable superiority. The United States was also able to send "over there" tens of thousands of conscripts fighting with the American Expeditionary Forces under the leadership of General John "Black Jack" Pershing (1860–1948). They reinforced British and French troops and gave a vital boost to morale.

For such a rich nation, however, the help that the United States was able to give was at first very little. The U.S. government was new to the business of coordinating a war effort, but it displayed great ingenuity in creating a wartime bureaucracy that increased a small military establishment of 210,000 soldiers to 9,500,000 young men registered before the beginning of summer 1917. By July 1918, the Americans were sending a phenomenal 300,000 soldiers a month to Europe. By the end of the war 2,000,000 young American men had traveled to Europe—most for the first and only time in their lives—to fight in the war.

The U.S. entry is significant not just because it provided reinforcements, fresh troops, and fresh supplies to the beleaguered Allies. From a broader perspective, it marked a shift in the nature of international politics: Europe was no longer able to handle its own affairs and settle its own differences without outside help.

U.S. troops, although numerous, were not well trained and they relied on France and Great Britain for their arms and equipment. But the Germans correctly understood that they could not hold out indefinitely against this superior Allied force. Austria-Hungary was effectively out of the war. Germany had no replacements for its fallen soldiers, but it was able to transfer troops from Russia, Romania, and Macedonia to the west. It realized its only chance of victory lay in swift action. The German high command decided on a bold measure: one great, final offensive that would knock the combined forces of Great Britain, France, and the United States out of the war once and for all by striking at a weak point and smashing through enemy lines. The great surprise was that it almost worked.

Known as the Ludendorff offensive, after the general who devised it, the final German push began in March 1918. Secretly amassing tired troops from the eastern front pulled back after the Russian withdrawal, the Germans counted on the element of surprise to enable them to break through a weak sector in the west. On the first day of spring Ludendorff struck. The larger German force gained initial success against weakened British and French forces. Yet in spite of breaches in defense, the Allied line held. Allied Supreme Commander, General Ferdinand Foch (1851–1929), coordinated the war effort that withstood German offensives throughout the spring and early summer of 1918.

The final drive came in mid-July. More than one million German soldiers had already been killed, wounded, or captured in the months between March and July. German prisoners of war gave the French details of Ludendorff's plan. The Germans, now exposed and vulnerable, were placed on the defensive. The German army was rapidly disintegrating. On the other side, tanks, plentiful munitions, and U.S. reinforcements fueled an Allied offensive that began in late September. The German army retreated, destroying property and equipment as it went. With weak political leadership and indecision in Berlin, the Germans held on until early November. The end came finally after four years of war. On 11 November 1918, an armistice signed by representatives of the German and Allied forces took effect.

The terms of the armistice boded a harsh peace. As the victors danced in the streets, and the defeated allowed themselves to feel relief, the task of settling the peace loomed. More in pride than in prophecy, a member of the German armistice delegation cried out, "A nation of seventy millions of people suffers, but it does not die." It was a prophecy nonetheless.

Allied flags are paraded on Armistice Day in Vincennes, France. The long ordeal was over, but the relief and joy soon faded as the bitterness of the peace terms corroded postwar Europe.

Reshaping Europe: After War and Revolution

In the aftermath of war, the task of the victors was to define the terms of a settlement that would guarantee peace and stabilize Europe. Russia was the ghost at the conference table, excluded from the negotiations because of its withdrawal from the Allied camp in 1917 and its separate peace with Germany in March 1918. The Bolsheviks were dealing with problems of their own following the revolution, including a great civil war lasting through 1920. Much of what happened in the peace settlements reflected the unspoken concern with the challenge of revolution that the new Soviet Russia represented. Meanwhile, the new Russian leaders carefully watched events in the west, looking for opportunities that might permit them to extend their revolution to central Europe.

Settling the Peace

From January to June 1919, an assembly of nations convened in Paris to draw up the new European peace. Although the primary task of settling the peace fell to the Council of Four—Premier Georges Clemenceau of France, Prime Minister David Lloyd George of Great Britain, Prime Minister Vittorio Emanuele Orlando of Italy, and President Woodrow Wilson of the United States—small states, newly formed states, and non-European states, Japan in particular, joined in the task of forging the peace. The states of Germany, Austria-Hungary, and Soviet Russia were excluded from the negotiating tables where the future of Europe was to be determined.

President Wilson, who captured international attention with his liberal views on the peace, was the central figure of the conference. He was firmly committed to the task of shaping a better world: before the end of the war he had proclaimed the "Fourteen Points" as a guideline to the future peace and as an appeal to the people of Europe to support his policies. Believing that secret diplomacy and the alliance system were responsible for the events leading up to the decla-ration of war in 1914, he put forward as a basic principle, "open covenants of peace, openly arrived at." Other points included the reduction of armaments, freedom of commerce and trade, self-determination of peoples, and a general association of nations to guarantee the peace that became the League of Nations. The Fourteen Points were, above all, an idealistic statement of the principles for a good and lasting peace. The points that dealt with the evacuation of Belgium, the restoration of Alsace-Lorraine to France, and the establishment of an independent Poland were fulfilled to the letter. Wilson was required to com-

The Steam Roller of the West. *This satiric cartoon shows a French officer at the wheel and Uncle Sam as a passenger on a steamroller. With the flags of the "Big Four" flying, the machine relentlessly bears down on hapless German women and children.*

promise on or to relinquish other points. But Point 14, which stipulated "mutual guarantees of independence and territorial integrity" through the establishment of the League of Nations, was endorsed by the Peace Conference. The League, which the United States refused to join in spite of Wilson's advocacy, was intended to arbitrate all future disputes among states and to keep the peace.

Georges Clemenceau of France represented a different approach to the challenge of the peace, one motivated primarily by a concern for his nation's security. France had suffered the greatest losses of the war in both human lives and property destroyed, and no one was more aware than Clemenceau of the threat from the more populous and more highly industrialized Germany. In order to prevent a resurgent Germany, Clemenceau supported a variety of measures to cripple it as a military force on the Continent. Germany was disarmed. The territory west of the Rhine River was demilitarized, with occupation by Allied troops to last for a period of fifteen years. With Russia unavailable as a partner to contain Germany, France supported the creation of a series of states in eastern Europe carved out of former Russian, Austrian, and German territory. Wilson supported these new states out of a concern for self-determination of peoples. Clemenceau's main concern was self-defense.

Much time and energy were devoted to redrawing the map of Europe. In the West, few territorial changes took place, with the exception of the return of Alsace and Lorraine to France from Germany. In eastern Europe territorial changes were extensive. New states were created out of the lands of three failed empires. Based on self-determination, Finland, Latvia, Estonia, Lithuania, Poland, Czechoslovakia, Austria, Hungary, and Yugoslavia were all granted status as nation-states. However, the rights of ethnic and cultural minorities were violated in some cases because of the impossibility of redrawing the map of Europe strictly according to the principle of self-determination. In spite of good intentions, every new nation had its own national minority, a situation that held the promise of future troubles.

The Peace Conference produced five separate treaties with each of the defeated nations: Austria, Hungary, Turkey, Bulgaria, and Germany.

Europe After World War I

The treaty signed with Germany on 28 June 1919, known as the Treaty of Versailles because it was signed in the great Bourbon palace, preceded the others in timing and importance. In that treaty, the Allies imposed blame for the war on Germany and its expansionist aims in the famous War Guilt Clause. If the war was Germany's fault, then Germany must be made to pay. Reparations, once the price of defeat, were now exacted as compensation for damages inflicted by a guilty aggressor.

The principle of punitive reparations was included in the German settlement. But the total amount was not fixed. The Council of Four deliberately avoided setting a figure, as Lloyd George explained, out of fear of its effect on public opinion in Germany, where it would be considered too high, and in Britain and France, where it was likely to be considered too low. By 1920 the German people knew that Germany had to make a down payment of $5 billion against a future bill; had to hand over a significant portion of merchant ships, including all vessels of more than 1600 tons and, lose all German colonies; and had to deliver coal to neighboring countries. These harsh clauses, more than any other aspect of the peace settlement, came to haunt the Allies in the succeeding two decades. The German people learned in 1921 that they were expected to pay a staggering $32 billion to their former enemies, a figure double that of what was anticipated, because of Britain's request that service pensions and allowances be included in Germany's bill.

In the end, no nation got what it wanted from the peace settlement. The defeated nations felt that they had been badly abused. The victorious nations were aware of the compromises they had reluctantly accepted. Cooperation among nations was essential if the treaty was to work successfully. It had taken the combined resources of not only France and the British Empire but also Russia with its vast population and the United States with its great industrial and financial might to defeat the power of Germany and the militarily ineffective Austro-Hungarian Empire. A new and stable balance of power depended on the participation of Russia, the United States, and the British Empire. But Russia was excluded from and hostile to the peace settlement, the United States was uncommitted to it, and the British Empire declined to guarantee it. All three Great Powers backed off their European responsibilities at the end of the war. By 1920 all aspects of the treaty, but especially the reparations clause, had been questioned and criticized by the very governments that had written them and had accepted them. The search for a lasting peace had just begun.

Revolution in Russia, 1917–20

Every country has its prophets. So too did Russia in 1914 when a now-forgotten former government minister advised Tsar Nicholas II (1894–1917) to avoid war or else face a social revolution. Other advisers prevailed: they said that Russia must go to war because it was a Great Power with interests beyond its borders. But within its empire, the process of modernization was widening social divisions. Nicholas preferred to listen to those who promised that a short, successful war would strengthen his monarchy against the domestic forces of change.

The Last Tsar. The Romanov dynasty surely needed strengthening. In 1914 Russia was considered backward by the standards of Western industrial society. Russia still recalled a recent feudal past. The serfs had been freed in the 1860s, but the nature of the emancipation exacerbated tensions in the countryside and peasant hunger for land. Russia's limited, rapid industrialization in the 1880s and 1890s was an attempt to catch up with Great Britain, France, and Germany as a world industrial power. But the speed of such change brought with it severe dislocations, especially in the industrial city of Moscow and the capital of St. Petersburg.

Twelve years earlier in 1905 the workers of St. Petersburg (the Germanic name was changed to its Russian equivalent, Petrograd, in 1914 with the outbreak of hostilities with the Central Powers) protested hardships due to cyclical downturns in the economy. Urban workers appealed to the tsar as "little father" for relief from their hardships. On a Sunday in January 1905 the tsar's troops fired on a peaceful mass demonstration in front of the Winter Palace. A thousand people were killed, including many women and children, who were appealing to the tsar for relief.

The event, which came to be known as Bloody Sunday, set off a revolution that spread to Moscow and the countryside. In October 1905 the regime responded to the disruptions with a series of reforms that legalized political parties and established the Duma, or national parliament. Peasants, oppressed with their own burdens of taxation and endemic poverty, launched mass attacks on big landowners throughout 1905 and 1906. The government met workers' and peasants' demands with a return to repression in 1907. In the half-decade before the Great War, the Russian state stood as an autocracy of parliamentary concessions blended with severe police controls.

What workers had learned in 1905 was the power and the means of independent organization. Factory committees, trade unions, and "soviets," or workers' councils, proliferated. Despite winning a grant of legal status after 1906, unions gained little in terms of ability to act on behalf of their members. The peculiar relations between unions and the government only heightened worker radicalism: unions had the right to exist but little power. Rising expectations of organized workers were continually frustrated, driving workers to extreme solutions.

Unrest among factory workers revived on the eve of the Great War, a period of rapid economic

Russian imperial troops fire on demonstrators outside the Winter Palace in St. Petersburg. The people were asking for better working conditions and a more responsive government. This day, 22 January 1905, is known in Russian history as Bloody Sunday.

growth and renewed trade-union activity. Between January and July 1914, Russia experienced 3,500 strikes in a six-month period. Although economic strikes were considered legal, strikes deemed political were not. With the outbreak of war, all collective action was banned. Protest stopped, but only momentarily. The tsar certainly weighed the workers' actions in his decision to view war as a possible diversion from domestic problems.

Russia was less prepared for war than any of the other belligerents. Undoubtedly, it had more soldiers than other countries but it lacked arms and equipment. Problems of provisioning such a huge fighting force placed great strains on the domestic economy and on the work force. Under government coercion to meet the needs of war, industrial output doubled between 1914 and 1917, while agricultural production plummeted. The tsar, who unwisely insisted on commanding his own troops, left the government in the hands of his wife, the Tsarina Alexandra, a German princess by birth, and her eccentric peasant adviser, Rasputin. Scandal, sexual innuendo, and charges of treason surrounded the royal court. The incompetence of a series of unpopular ministers further eroded confidence in the regime. (See Special Feature, "The Women Who Started the Russian Revolution," pp. 842–843.)

In the end, the war sharpened long-standing divisions within Russian society. Led by women, poorly paid and underfed workers toppled the regime in the bitter winter of March 1917. This event was the beginning of a violent process of revolution and civil war. The tsar abdicated, and all public symbols of the tsardom were destroyed. The banner bearing the Romanov two-headed eagle was torn down and in its place the Red Flag flew over the Winter Palace. The tsar himself and the royal family were executed by the revolutionaries in July 1918.

Dual Power.   With the tsar's abdication, two centers of authority replaced autocracy. One was the Provisional Government, appointed by the Duma and made up of bourgeois liberals attempting to rule from the center; the other was the "soviets," committees or councils elected by workers and soldiers, who were supported by radical lawyers, journalists, and intellectuals in favor of socialist self-rule. The Petrograd Soviet was the most prominent among the councils. This duality of power was matched by duality in policies and objectives and guaranteed a short-lived and unstable regime.

The Women Who Started The Russian Revolution

Women in Russia, like their counterparts all over Europe in 1914, took over new jobs in the workplace as men marched off to war. Four out of every ten Russian workers were women, up from three of ten on the eve of the war. The situation was more dramatic in Petrograd, Russia's capital and principal industrial center, where, by 1917, women constituted 55 percent of the labor force. Russian working women faced greater hardships than their sisters in the West. Most women workers in Petrograd held unskilled, poorly paid jobs in the textile industries and worked grueling twelve- and thirteen-hour days. They left work only to stand for hours in long breadlines and then returned home to care for their elderly relatives and often sick children. Infant mortality was alarmingly high, with as many as half of all children dying before the age of three. Factory owners reported that nothing could be done. "The worker mother drudges and knows only need, only worry and grief," one commentator observed. "Her life passes in gloom, without light."

Russia was suffering badly in the war, with over two million soldiers killed by the beginning of 1917. News of disasters at the front reached mothers, wives, and sisters at home in spite of the government's efforts to hide the defeats. In the less than three years since the war had begun, prices had increased 400 percent and transport lines for food and coal had broken down. Bread was the main staple of meager diets. Supplies of flour and grain were not reaching towns and cities. People were starving and freezing to death. Young children were now working eleven-and-a-half hour days in the factories. The situation was dire, and working women knew that something must be done if their families were to survive.

The working women of Petrograd correctly understood that the intolerable state of affairs had come about because the government was unable to control distribution and to ration limited supplies. Carrying a double burden of supporting those at home unable to work and of producing in the factory the armaments essential for the war effort, women workers began demanding that labor organizations take action to alleviate the situation. In the winter of 1916–17, labor leaders advised exhausted and starving workers to be cautious and patient: workers must wait to strike until the time was ripe. Women workers did not agree. On 8 March 1917 (February 23 by the Russian calendar), over 7,000 women went on strike in acknowledgement of International Women's Day, an event initiated in the United States in 1909 to recognize the rights of working women. These striking women were angry, frustrated, hungry, and tired of watching their families starve while their husbands, brothers, and sons were away at the battlefront. The week before, the city had been placed on severe rationing because Petrograd was down to its last few days' supply of flour. Although the principal concern of the striking women was bread, their protest was more than just a food riot. Women left their posts in the textile mills to demand an end to the war and an end to the reign of Tsar Nicholas II. They were responding not to revolutionary propaganda but to the politics of hunger. Singing songs of protest, they marched through the streets to take their cause to the better-paid and more radical male metalworkers. Women appealed to working men to join the strike. By the end of the day, 100,000 workers had left their jobs to join demonstrations against the government.

The women did not stop there. They took justice into their own hands and looted bakeries and grocery shops in search of food. In the street demonstrations of the next several days, women and men marched by the thousands, attracting growing support from workers throughout the city and the suburbs. Forty demonstrators were killed when government troops fired into a crowd. Still the women were not deterred. Bolshevik leader Leon Trotsky recalled women's bravery in going up to detachments of soldiers: "More boldly than men, they take hold of the rifles and beseech, almost command: 'Put down your bayonets—join us!'" Stories abound of how poor working women persuaded officers and soldiers of the Cossacks, the tsar's privileged fighting force, to lay down their arms. It was rumored that soldiers abandoned the tsar because they would not fire on the crowds of women. A participant in one confrontation reported how women workers stood without flinching as a detachment of Cossacks bore down upon them. Someone in the crowd shouted out that these were the wives and sisters of soldiers at the front. The Cossacks lowered their rifles and turned their horses around. Troops like these, tired of the war, mutinied all over Petrograd. Within four days of the first action taken by women textile operatives, the government had lost the support of Petrograd workers, women and men, and its soldiers, who had joined the demonstrators. The tsar was forced to abdicate. From this point on the Romanov monarchy and the Russian war effort were doomed.

In those first days of protest, the women of Petrograd took action into their own hands, pouring into the streets to call for bread, peace, and the end of tsardom. They rejected autocracy and war in defense of their communities and their families. The eighth of March 1917 was women's day. The Russian Revolution had begun.

The problems facing the new regime soon became apparent as revolution spread to the provinces and to the battlefront. Peasants, who made up 80 percent of the Russian population, accepted the revolution and demanded land and peace. Without waiting for government directives peasants began seizing the land. Living by the imperatives of weather and short growing seasons, they wasted no time in establishing their claims to the land long denied to them. Peasants tried to alleviate some of their suffering by hoarding what little they had. The food crisis of winter persisted throughout the spring and summer, as breadlines lengthened and prices rose. Workers in cities gained better working conditions and higher wages. But wage increases were invariably followed by higher prices that robbed workers of all they gained. Real wages declined.

In addition to the problems of land and bread, the war itself presented the new government with other insurmountable difficulties. Hundreds of thousands of Russian soldiers at the front deserted the war, having heard news from home of peasant land grabs and rumors of a new offensive planned for July. The Provisional Government, concerned with Russia's territorial integrity and its position in the international system, continued to honor the tsar's commitments to the Allies by participating in the war. By spring 1917 six to eight million Russian soldiers had been killed, wounded, or captured. The Russian army was incapable of fighting.

The Provisional Government tried everything to convince its people to carry on with the war. In the summer of 1917, the Women's Battalion of Death, composed exclusively of female recruits, was enlisted into the army. Its real purpose, officials admitted, was to "shame the men" into fighting. The all-female unit, like its male counterparts, experienced high losses: 80 percent of the force suffered casualties. The Provisional Government was caught in an impossible situation: it could not withdraw from the war but neither could it fight. Continued involvement in the lost cause of the war blocked any consideration of social reforms.

While the Provisional Government was trying to deal with the calamities, many members of the intelligentsia, Russia's educated class, who had been exiled by the tsar for their political beliefs, now rushed back from western Europe to take part in the great revolutionary experiment. The-

Revolution and Civil War in Russia, 1914–20

orists of all stripes put their cases before the people. Those in favor of gradual reform debated with those who favored violent revolution the relative merits of various government policies. The months between February and July 1917 were a period of great intellectual ferment. It was the Marxists, or Social Democrats, who had the greatest impact on the direction of the revolution.

The Social Democrats believed that there were objective laws of historical development that could be discovered. Russia's future could only be understood in terms of the present situation in western Europe. Like Marxists in the West, the Russian Social Democrats split over how best to achieve a socialist state. The more moderate Mensheviks (the term means "minority") wanted to work through parliamentary institutions and were willing to cooperate with the Provisional Government. A *smaller* faction—despite its name—calling themselves Bolsheviks (meaning "majority") dedicated themselves to preparation for a revolutionary upheaval. After April 1917, the Bolsheviks refused to work with the Provisional Government and organized themselves to take control of the Petrograd Soviet.

The leader of the Bolsheviks was Vladimir Ilich Ulyanov (1870–1924), best known by his revolutionary name, Lenin. Forty-seven years old at the time of the revolution, Lenin had spent most of his life in exile or in prison. More a pragmatist than a theoretician, he argued for a disciplined party of professional revolutionaries, a vanguard who would lead the peasants and workers in a socialist revolution against capitalism. In contrast to the Mensheviks, he argued that the time was now ripe for a successful revolution, and that it could be achieved through the soviets.

Immediately upon arrival in Petrograd from Switzerland, Lenin threw down the gauntlet to the Provisional Government. In his April Theses, he promised the Russian people peace, land, and bread. The war must be ended immediately, he argued, because it represented an imperialist struggle that was benefiting capitalists. Russia's duty was to withdraw and wait for a world revolution. This was more than rhetoric on Lenin's part. His years in exile in the West and news of mutinies and worker protests convinced him that revolution was imminent. His revolutionary policies on land were little more than endorsements of the seizures already taking place all over Rus-

In this Communist poster of 1922 Lenin points to a utopian future as he proclaims, "Let the ruling class tremble before the Communist revolution." The rising sun in the background symbolizes the dawn of the socialist era.

sia. Even his promises of bread had little substance. But on the whole, the April Theses constituted a clear critique of the policies of the Provisional Government.

Dissatisfaction with the Provisional Government increased as the war dragged hopelessly on and bread lines lengthened. In the midst of these calamities, a massive popular demonstration erupted in July 1917 against the Provisional Government and in favor of the soviets, which excluded the upper classes from voting. The chants of workers and antiwar soldiers resounded in the streets of the capital: "Peace for the peasant huts, war for the palaces!" and "All power to the soviets!" The Provisional Government responded with repressive force reminiscent of the tsardom. The July Days were proof of the growing influence of the Bolsheviks among the Russian people. Although the Bolshevik leadership had withdrawn support for the demonstrations at the last moment, Bolshevik rank-and-file party members strongly endorsed the protest. Indisputably, Bolshevik influence was growing in the soviets despite repression and persecution of its leaders. Lenin was forced to flee to Finland.

As a result of the July Days, a socialist, Aleksandr Kerenski (1881–1970), was named prime minister and continued the Provisional Government's moderate policies. In order to protect the government from a coup on the right, Kerenski permitted the arming of the Red Guards, the workers' militia units of the Petrograd Soviet. The traditional chasm between the upper and the lower classes was now widening: the days of dual power were numbered.

Lenin and the Bolsheviks Seize Power. The second revolution came in November (October in the Russian calendar). This time it was not a spontaneous street demonstration by thousands of working women that triggered the revolution but rather the seizure of the Russian capital by the Red Guards of the Petrograd Soviet. The revolution was carefully planned and orchestrated by Lenin and his vanguard of Bolsheviks, who now possessed majorities in the soviets in Moscow and Petrograd and other industrial centers. Returning surreptitiously from Finland, Lenin moved through the streets of Petrograd disguised in a curly wig and head bandages, watching the Red Guard seize centers of communication and public buildings. The military action was directed by Lev Bronstein, better known by his revolutionary name, Leon Trotsky (1879–1940). The Bolshevik chairman of the Petrograd Soviet, Trotsky used the Red Guard to seize political control and arrest the members of the Provisional Government, trapped in their headquarters at the Winter Palace "like mice in cages." Kerenski escaped and fled the city.

The takeover was achieved with almost no bloodshed and was immediately endorsed by an All-Russian Congress of Soviets, which consisted of representatives of local soviets from throughout the nation who were in session amid the takeover of the capital. A Bolshevik regime under Lenin now ruled Russia.

The Russian Civil War, 1917–20. Lenin immediately set to work to end the war for Russia. After months of negotiation, Russia signed a separate peace with the Germans in March 1918 in the Treaty of Brest-Litovsk. By every measure, the treaty was a bitter humiliation for the new Soviet regime. The territorial losses were phenomenal. In a vast amputation, Russia was reduced to the size of its Muscovite period: it recognized the independence of the Ukraine, Georgia, and Finland; it relinquished its Polish territories, the Baltic States, and part of Belorussia to Germany and Austria-Hungary; and it handed over other territories on the Black Sea to Turkey. Lenin felt he had no choice: he needed to buy time to consolidate the revolution at home.

The Treaty of Brest-Litovsk was judged a betrayal not only outside Russia among the Allied powers but also inside Russia among some army officers who had sacrificed much for the tsar's war. To these military men, the Bolsheviks were no more than German agents who held the country in their sway. Combining forces with Cossacks, who feared the loss of their lands and privileges under a Bolshevik state, army officers formed the White Armies to engage in war against Trotsky's Red fighting force. Lacking sufficient organization, unable to coordinate their movements because the Bolsheviks dominated the country's center, and torn apart by different political goals, the White Armies ultimately failed to challenge successfully the Bolshevik hold on the reins of state. But in the three years of civil war between Whites and Reds, the Whites posed a serious threat to Bolshevik policies.

Anti-Bolshevik forces were assisted with materials by the Allies, who intended to keep the eastern front viable. The Allies sent over 100,000 troops and supplies for the purpose of overthrowing the Bolshevik regime by supporting its enemies. Allied support for the White Armies came primarily from the United States, Great Britain, France, and Japan and continued beyond the armistice that ended the Great War in 1918. Although Allied support was not crucial to the outcome of the civil war, it played a significant role in shaping Soviet perceptions of the outside world. For generations of Soviet citizens, anti-Bolshevik assistance has been viewed as the indication of a hostile and predatory capitalist world intent on destroying the fledgling Soviet state for its own ends. On the basis of Allied intervention, Bolsheviks not unreasonably expected a future encirclement by capitalist forces.

The civil war had another legacy for the future of the Soviet state. To deal with the anarchy caused by the fratricidal struggle, Lenin had to strengthen the government's dictatorial elements at the expense of its democratic ones. The new

Soviet state used state police to suppress all opposition. The dictatorship of the proletariat yielded to the dictatorship of the repressive forces.

In the course of the civil war, Lenin was no more successful than Kerenski and the Provisional Government in solving the problems of food supplies. Human costs of the civil war were high, with over 800,000 soldiers dead on both sides, and 2 million civilian deaths from dysentery and diseases caused by poor nutrition. Industrial production ceased and people fled towns to return to the countryside. In 1920 it seemed Russia could drop no lower. Millions had been killed in war or died from famine. Stripped of territories and sapped of its industrial strength, Russia was a defeated nation. Yet Bolshevik idealism about the success of the proletarian revolution prevailed. No longer sure that a world socialist revolution would come to their aid, Bolshevik leaders set out to build the future.

By every measure, the Great War was disastrously expensive. Some European nations suffered more than others, but all endured significant losses of life, property, and productive capacity. The costs of modern warfare had been foreseen in the years prior to the war. In 1910, the British economist Norman Angell published *The Great Illusion*. In this best-seller he argued that because war was so costly, no nation would engage in it. Angell enjoyed the dubious honor of being half-right. His assumption that war would destroy or cripple European economies was correct; his conclusion that this would be a deterrent to war was sadly mistaken.

The cost in human lives was enormous. In western Europe 8.5 million were dead; total casualties amounted to 37.5 million. France lost 20 percent of its men between the ages of 20 and 44, Germany lost 15 percent, and Great Britain 10 percent. But body counts cannot approximate the horror of death and bloodshed. Those who survived the devastation were often crippled in mind, if not in body.

The war also resulted in huge losses in productive capacity. National economies buckled under the weight of foreign debts and resorted to a variety of methods to bail themselves out, including taxes, loans, and inflations. The British debt ballooned from £650 million in 1914 to £7.4

billion in 1918. In France, the growth in the national debt was also dramatic: from 33 billion francs to 150 billion francs. Depreciation of the currency in both France and Germany victimized most severely those living on fixed incomes. The people of Europe continued to pay for the war long after the fighting had ended.

In spite of the tremendous losses in human life and in productive capacity, the size of populations and even prosperity were not permanently affected. Europe recovered in these areas. Yet the center of world markets and finance had shifted. The big winner in the war was the United States, now a creditor nation holding billions of dollars of loans to the Allies and operating in new markets established during the war. The shift was not a temporary move but a structural change. The United States now took its place as a Great Power in the international system.

The belief in a rational world order was irreparably damaged. The word *peace* is inadequate to describe the condition of Western society by 1920. The war had certainly ended. At Versailles and elsewhere in separate treaties, the protagonists had agreed to the settlement of differences. But the world of 1914 was gone. What was to replace it was still very much in flux. To the east, Russia was engaged in a vast experiment of building a new society. In the west, the absence of war was not peace.

British economist John Maynard Keynes warned that the peace settlement contained the seeds of a new destruction. Few listened. Those who did began referring to the Great War as World War One, a term coined in 1920 by a British army officer. Buried in that term was the cynicism that another great war would take place. The only uncertainty was when.

Suggestions for Further Reading

The War Europe Expected

Marc Ferro, *The Great War, 1914–1918* (London: Routledge & Kegan Paul, 1973). The origins of World War I within a broad social and cultural context. Stressing the importance of an imagined war and patriotism as two factors which precipitated actual conflict, Ferro shows how the gulf between imagination and reality led to domestic conflict and social unrest once war broke out.

James Joll, *The Origins of the First World War* (New York: Longman, 1984). In an examination of the decisions that brought about war in 1914, importance is placed on the limited options available to decision-makers. The July crisis, the international system, the arms race, domestic politics, the international economy, imperial rivalries, and cultural and psychological factors are considered in terms of their contributions to the outbreak of war.

Keith Robbins, *The First World War* (Oxford: Oxford University Press, 1984). The major cultural, political, military, and social developments between 1914 and 1918. Includes discussion of the course of the land war and modes of warfare.

The War Europe Got

Paul Fussell, *The Great War and Modern Memory* (New York: Oxford University Press, 1975). A cultural history of World War I, which treats the patterns and tendencies in war literature within the framework of a literary tradition. The author argues that the irony that dominates modern consciousness originated in the perception of the war by contemporary artists.

Gerd Hardach, *The First World War, 1914–1918* (Berkeley: University of California Press, 1977). Describes the changes in the world economy leading up to the war, the war's impact on trade, wartime monetary and fiscal policies, and the war's impact on labor. Each major power is included in an analysis of wartime economic history.

John Keegan, *The Face of Battle* (New York: Vintage Books, 1976). Soldiers' experiences are placed within the context of earlier forms of warfare at Agincourt and Waterloo. Emphasizes the impact of battlefield tactics and changing military technology on the average combatant.

B. E. Schmitt and H. C. Vedeler, *The World in a Crucible, 1914–1919* (New York: Harper & Row, 1984). A broad survey of the military and political history of World War I; the war is viewed here as a period of revolution in both warfare and politics. Includes considerable discussion of the Russian Revolution and a section on the entry of the United States into European affairs.

Denis Winter, *Death's Men: Soldiers of the Great War* (London: Penguin, 1979). Not an account of military strategy and battlefield tactics, *Death's Men* goes inside the infantrymen's war to convey the experience of war in the trenches.

Adjusting to the Unexpected: Total War

Raymond Aron, *The Century of Total War* (Boston: The Beacon Press, 1954). A classic work that places World War I within the larger political and military contexts of the twentieth century. World War I is described as the first example of total war, a type of warfare created by the use of new technology, which upset the planners' schemes and led to the geographical extension of war. The length and cost of the war are also discussed as factors that led to a reliance on ideology rather than strictly military aims in order to maintain support for the war effort.

Temma Kaplan, "Women and Communal Strikes in the Crisis of 1917–1922," in *Becoming Visible: Women in European History* edited by Renate Bridenthal, Claudia Koonz, and Susan Stuard (Boston: Houghton Mifflin, 1987). Analyzes the nature of female consciousness in the urban working class, focusing on Russian women's activities in February 1917, and women's responses to crises in Italy, Spain, and Mexico in the same period.

John Williams, *The Homefronts: Britain, France and Germany, 1914–1918* (London: Constable, 1972). A comparative study of the home fronts, their impact on the course of the war, and the war's impact on civilian life.

Reshaping Europe: After War and Revolution

Sheila Fitzpatrick, *The Russian Revolution, 1917–1932* (Oxford: Oxford University Press, 1982). An analysis of the October Revolution of 1917 from the perspective of Stalinist society. The February and October revolutions of 1917, the Civil War, and the economic policies of the 1920s are treated as various aspects of a unitary revolutionary movement.

Tsuyoshi Hasegawa, *The February Revolution: Petrograd, 1917* (Seattle: University of Washington Press, 1981). A thorough examination of the effects of World War I on Russian workers, liberals, and revolutionary parties leads to an interpretation of the February Revolution as the outcome of a conflict between the state and civil society. Particular attention is given to events leading to the abdication of the tsar, the establishment of the Provisional Government, and the early stages of the Russian Revolution.

Arno J. Mayer, *The Politics and Diplomacy of Peacemaking* (New York: Knopf, 1967). A comprehensive examination of the role of internal political concerns and the foreign policy of the warring nations as well as a thorough analysis of the struggle between Bolshevism, Wilsonian liberalism, and counterrevolution.

David Stevenson, *The First World War and International Politics* (Oxford: Oxford University Press, 1988). A study of the global ramifications of World War I, this work traces the development of war aims on both sides, the reasons peace negotiations failed, and why compromise proved elusive.

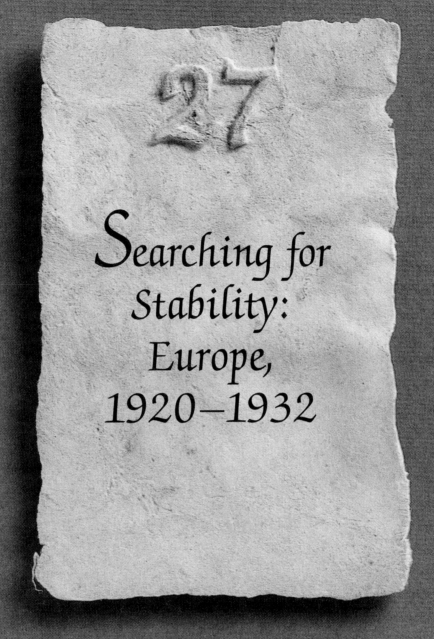

27

Searching for Stability: Europe, 1920–1932

Buildings for the Future

Buildings tell tales. Archaeologists trying to understand other civilizations excavate ancient dwellings in order to reconstruct past lives. Family life, social values, the nature of work, technology, and progress are all embodied in the structures in which people live and work. If future generations had only traces of the buildings of the twentieth century, they would nevertheless hold a key to understanding our civilization and values.

The twentieth-century architecture that we call "modern" was the child born from the union of technology and art in the aftermath of the Great War of 1914–18. In reaction to the horrors of the battlefront, a new generation of architects, many of them ex-soldiers, committed themselves to the creation of buildings as works of art that answered the needs of modern society. Those who followed the lead of the prewar avant-garde disdained imitating past masters. They saw their task as "starting from zero"—that is, striking out in a new direction unencumbered by the cultural baggage of a past that had proven itself to be morally bankrupt. In building for the future, the postwar generation felt that the present must create a new style of its own.

The battle cry for a new architectural style arose from defeated Germany and in particular from a single man, Walter Gropius (1883–1969). In 1919, only a few months after the Treaty of Versailles ended World War I, Gropius, a recent veteran of the front, founded the Bauhaus, a school based on the collaborative efforts of architects, sculptors, artists, and craftworkers. The untranslatable term *Bauhaus*, resulting from joining the German words "building" and "house," soon characterized a new movement in the arts and architecture. As director of the Bauhaus until 1928, Gropius attracted some of Europe's leading artists to the school, including the architects Marcel Breuer (1902–1981) and Ludwig Mies van der Rohe (1886–1969). Russian abstract artist Vasili Kandinski (1866–1944) and his Swiss colleague Paul Klee (1879–1940) were also members

Project for Glass Skyscraper *(1921), by Mies van der Rohe.*

of the teaching staff at the Bauhaus. Characterized by intense activity, exciting experimentation, and enthusiastic collaboration, the men and women who assembled at the Bauhaus pioneered new designs in everything from kitchen utensils and furniture to lighting fixtures and skyscrapers.

Gropius was a utopian dreamer who saw in buildings and in the humble objects of daily life the means of creating human happiness. Beauty in design was defined by the fit between form and function. Rather than rejecting industrial society, Gropius sought a new way of uniting art with it. Unlike other arts and crafts movements, the Bauhaus was willing to make use of the machine to produce for the masses, whether the production was of prefabricated houses or teacups. Gropius knew well that architecture does not move faster than the society it seeks to serve. But he also knew that it must keep pace with the world around it. The school's motto, one that Gropius considered realistic and responsible, proclaimed: "Art and technology—a new unity!"

Pictured here is one of the first Bauhaus models of a skyscraper. Modest by subsequent standards, its thirty-two stories dwarf the traditional buildings at its base. Steel and glass were expressly used to liberate the structure from supporting walls. With new engineering knowledge about support, loads, stress, and mass, sheer facades of glass opened up inside space to the outside world. Interior walls were eliminated. Gropius admired the new functional factory structures and early skyscrapers in the United States and Canada for their starkness and simplicity and sought to introduce their "majesty" to residential architecture.

The architects of the Bauhaus were in the right place at the right time. Germany needed new buildings, and in the period from 1924 to 1929 the return of economic prosperity allowed them to be built. Under Gropius' direction, working-class apartment blocks with open floor plans, unadorned facades, clean lines, and a stark

simplicity spread across the German landscape. Office buildings of reinforced concrete with little to distinguish them from the new residential housing also mushroomed. By the end of the decade Bauhaus architects had left their mark on German towns and cities. Then, seeking refuge from Hitler (eventually in the United States), Gropius and some of his associates transformed the skylines of America's great cities within a decade. In the second half of the twentieth century, the Bauhaus style of architecture spread throughout the world.

The architects of the Bauhaus changed the appearance of the modern world and with it the twentieth-century experience. Critics who longed for a traditional architecture of decoration and classical emulation judged the Bauhaus style to be barren and ugly. Yet its emphasis on design and function prevailed. The skyscrapers of the twentieth century are products of the lessons of war and technology and the idealistic pursuit of a better world that took shape very visibly in the 1920s.

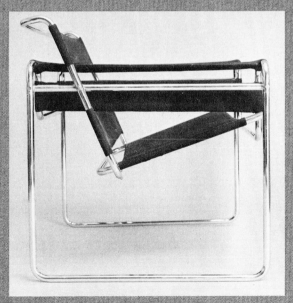

Armchair (B3) (1928), by Marcel Breuer.

Mapping International Politics In 1920s Europe

Europe in 1918 differed vastly from the prewar world of 1914. The changes that took place between 1918 and 1921 in the three years after the armistice made the European world different yet again. In 1918 parts of war-torn Europe faced the possibility of revolution. Russia, where revolution had destroyed tsardom, expectantly watched revolutionary developments in countries from the British Isles to eastern Europe. The Bolshevik leaders of Russia's revolution counted on the capitalist system to destroy itself. That did not happen. By 1921, revolutions had been brutally crushed in Berlin, Munich, and Budapest. The Soviets, meanwhile, had won the Civil War against

the Whites and survived the intervention of the British, French, Japanese, and Americans and the blockade with which they had surrounded Russia. But the new Russian regime was diplomatically isolated and in a state of almost total economic collapse.

In 1917–18, the United States had played a significant and central role in the waging of war and in the pursuit of peace. Under U.S. president Woodrow Wilson, who urged his country to guarantee European security and guide Europe's future, the American nation seemed promising as an active and positive force in international politics. By 1921, however, the United States had retreated to a position, not of isolation, but of selective involvement. For America, the period of wartime sacrifice was over; its participation in European international affairs would be uni-

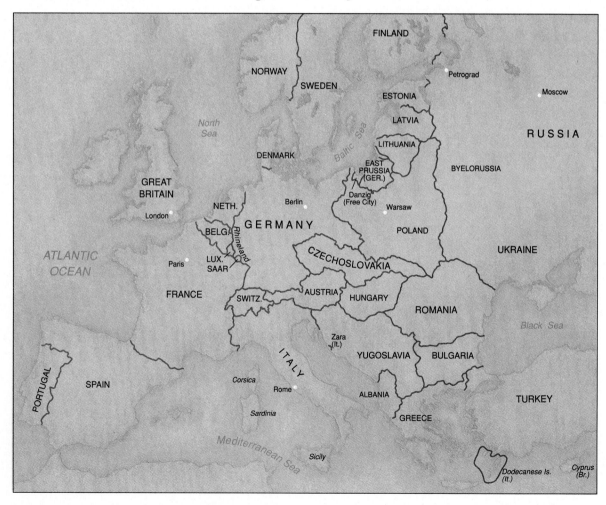

lateral, ad hoc, and based on America's own self-interest. With one giant, Russia, devastated and isolated, and the other, the United States, reluctant, Europeans faced an uncertain future. Power was no longer theirs to command and the exercise of power by others offered no assurances.

Anyone who could read a map held a key to forecasting what Europe's national and international problems would be in the 1920s. The future of Europe was embedded in its geography. Germany, despite some territorial losses after World War I, continued to sit as a large, landed nation at the center of the European continent. It exceeded all western European states in territory and population. A picket fence of newly created states separated Germany from Russia, the only country in Europe with greater land, population, and natural resources. On its western frontier, Germany shared a stretch of border with France. France considered itself unprotected in western Europe, with weak neighbors and with former allies uncommitted to France's security. Across the English Channel, the island nation of Great Britain maintained its detachment. But there was one major fact of international power that a map of Europe could not show. The United States, not a European power at all, was in a position to dominate and determine the future of the West.

East Central Europe

Before World War I, east central Europe was a region divided among four great empires—the Ottoman, the Habsburg, the Russian, and the German. Under the pressure of defeat those empires collapsed into their component national parts, and when the dust of the peace treaties had settled, the region had been molded into a dozen sovereign states. The victorious Allies were confident that they were pursuing the right course in shaping this area in their own democratic image according to the principles of nationalism and self-determination. But they had ulterior motives as well. They hoped that independent states newly created from fragments of empire would buffer Europe from the spread of communism westward and the expansion of German power eastward.

Beginning in the north and moving south, a swath of new independent states cut through the center of Europe. Finland had acquired its inde-

pendence from Russia in 1917. Estonia, Latvia, and Lithuania, also formerly under Russian rule, comprised the now independent Baltic states. After more than a century of dismemberment among three empires, Poland became a single nation again. Czechoslovakia was carved out of former Habsburg lands. Austria and Hungary shriveled to small independent states, no longer part of the once great Habsburg empire. Yugoslavia was pieced together from a patchwork of territories. Romania swelled, fed on a diet of settlement concessions. These new nations assured the victorious powers and especially France that the new political geography of east central Europe, wedged between Russian and German ambitions, would guarantee the peace.

World War I victor nations hoped that these new states would stabilize European affairs; they could not have been more wrong. They erred in three important ways in their calculations. First, many of the new states were internally unstable precisely because of the principle of national self-determination, the idea that nationalities had the right to rule themselves. Honoring the rights of nationalities was simple in the abstract, but application of the principle proved complicated and at times impossible. Religious, linguistic, and ethnic diversity abounded, and recognizing nationality often meant ignoring the rights of minorities. In Czechoslovakia, for example, the Czechs dominated the Slovaks and the Germans even though the Czechs were fewer in number. In Yugoslavia the Serbs prevailed against the Croats, the Slovenes, and other nationalities. Ethnic unrest plagued all of eastern Europe. Minority tensions weakened and destabilized the fragile governments.

Second, the struggle for economic prosperity further destabilized the new governments. East central Europe was primarily agricultural and the existence of the great empires had created guaranteed markets. The war disrupted the economy and generated social unrest. The peace settlements only compounded the economic problems of the region. When the Habsburg Empire disintegrated, the Danube River basin ceased to be a cohesive economic unit. New governments were saddled with borders that made little economic sense.

Creating cohesive economic units proved an insurmountable task for newly formed governments and administrations that lacked both resources and experience. Low productivity, unemployment, and overpopulation characterized most of east central Europe. Attempts to industrialize and to develop new markets confronted many obstacles. Much of the land was farmed on a subsistence basis. What agricultural surplus was created was difficult to sell abroad. East central Europeans, including Poles, Czechs, Yugoslavs, and Romanians, all tied to France through military and political commitments, were excluded from western European markets and were isolated economically from their treaty allies. Economic ties with Germany endured in ways that perpetuated economic dependence and threatened future survival.

Finally, common borders produced tensions over territories. The peace settlements made no one happy. Poland quarreled with Lithuania, and Czechoslovakia vied with Poland over territorial claims. Poland actually went to war with Russia for six months in 1920 in an effort to reclaim the Ukraine and expand its borders to what they had been over a century earlier. The Bolsheviks counterattacked and tried to turn the conflict into a revolutionary war to spread communism to central Europe. French military advisers came to the aid of the Poles and turned the Russians back. The Treaty of Riga, signed in March 1921, gave Poland much but not all of the territory it claimed.

Hungary, having lost the most territory in World War I, held the distinction of having the greatest number of territorial grievances against its neighbors—Czechoslovakia, Romania, and Yugoslavia. Yugoslavia made claims against Austria. Bulgaria sought territories controlled by Greece and Romania. Ethnicity, strategic considerations, and economic needs motivated claims for territory. Disputes festered, fed by the intense nationalism that prevented the cooperation necessary for survival.

Germany, the Soviet Union, and Italy had their own territorial claims against their east central European neighbors. The Weimar Republic refused to accept the loss of the "corridor" controlled by Poland that severed East Prussia from the rest of Germany. Nor was Germany resigned to the loss of part of Silesia to Poland. Russia refused to forget its losses to Romania, Poland, Finland, and the Baltic states. Italy, too weak to act on its own, nevertheless dreamed of expansion into Yugoslavia, Austria, and Albania. Despite the old saying that good fences make good neighbors, the redefined borders of eastern and central Europe produced only animosity.

Germany

From defeat, the German nation emerged strong. Its population of 60 million exceeded France's 40 million. If Germany was a wounded giant after its defeat in World War I, many—especially the French—felt that its injuries were only superficial. Because World War I had not been fought in Germany, German transportation networks and industrial plant had escaped serious damage. Its industry was fed by raw materials and energy resources unsurpassed anywhere in Europe outside Russia. In east central Europe, Germany had actually benefited from the dismantling of the Habsburg Empire and the removal of Poland and the Baltic states from Russian control. Replacing its formerly large neighbor to the east were weak states potentially susceptible to Germany's influence. Because the governments of east central Europe feared communism, they were not likely to ally with the Soviet state. The existence of the small buffer states left open the possibility of German collaboration with Russia, since the two large nations might be able to negotiate their interests in the area. Germany stood as the dominant nation in central Europe. It had the potential to strive once again for the European hegemony and world power it had failed to win through world war.

On its western frontier, Germany's prospects were not so bright. Alsace and Lorraine had been returned to France. From German territory, a demilitarized zone had been created in the Rhineland. Allied troops were settled there for fifteen years, a period of occupation that could be extended—at Germany's expense. The Saar district was under the protection of League of Nations commissioners, and the Saar coal mines were transferred to French ownership. A plebiscite in 1935 finally returned the region to Germany. Humiliated and betrayed by the geographic consequences of its defeat, Germany looked to recover its status.

Germany's primary foreign policy goal was revision of the treaty settlements of World War I. German politicians and military leaders perceived disarmament, loss of territory, and payment of reparations as serious obstacles in restoring Germany's position as a great power. In the mid-1920s statesmen spelled out the territorial aims of Germany's foreign policy: liberation of the Rhineland from foreign military occupation; return of the Saar basin; and recovery of the Corridor and Upper Silesia from Poland. These aims were recognized as clear territorial imperatives necessary if Germany hoped to reclaim its position as a great power in Europe.

German leaders set economic recovery as the basis of their new foreign policy. In 1922, Germany signed the Treaty of Rapallo with Russia, a peacetime agreement that shocked the western powers. Economics motivated the new Russo-Ger-

man partnership: German industry needed markets and the Russians needed loans to reconstruct their economy. Both states wanted to break out of the isolation imposed on them by the victors of World War I. However, Germany quickly learned that markets in Russia were limited and that hopes for recovery depended on financial cooperation with western Europe and the United States. At the end of 1923, Gustav Stresemann (1878–1929) assumed direction of the German Foreign Ministry and began to implement a conciliatory policy toward France and Britain. By displaying peaceful intentions he hoped to secure American capital for German industry and win the support of the West for the revision of the peace settlement.

Stresemann joined his French and British counterparts, Aristide Briand (1862–1932) and Austen Chamberlain (1863–1937), in fashioning a series of treaties at Locarno, Switzerland, in 1925. In a spirit of cooperation, Germany, France, and Belgium promised never again to go to war against each other and to respect the demilitarized zone that separated them. Britain and Italy "guaranteed" the borders of all three countries and assured the integrity of the demilitarized zone. The treaties initiated an atmosphere of goodwill, a "spirit of Locarno," that heralded a new age of security and nonaggression.

Under Stresemann's direction, Germany did not renounce its ambitions in eastern Europe.

This hopeful cartoon was inspired by the "spirit of Locarno." The artist saw the 1925 Locarno treaties as the long-awaited millennium of European peace. Fourteen years later, the German panzers rolled into Poland.

Stresemann expected Germany to recover the territory lost to Poland. He also knew that Germany must rearm and expand to the east. From the early 1920s until 1933, Germany secretly rearmed in violation of Versailles. Undercover, it rebuilt its army and trained its soldiers and airmen on Russian territory. Germany did not accept its place in the new Europe created by the Treaty of Versailles. It planned to be once again a sovereign great power with the same rights as other European countries.

Western Europe

Having learned the harsh lessons of 1870–71 and 1914–18, France understood well the threat posed by a united, industrialized, and well-armed Germany. During the years immediately following World War I, France deeply distrusted Germany. Neither the security of France nor the independence and autonomy of the smaller nations of Europe were safe from this powerful Germany. How was France to defend itself and Europe? France had a smaller population than Germany. French industrial production was not as great. France was devastated by the war and Germany was not. France did have certain advantages in 1921. It had the best-manned and best-equipped army in the world. Germany was disarmed. The Rhineland was demilitarized and occupied. But these military advantages would last only as long as the Treaty of Versailles was enforced. France knew that alone it could not enforce the treaty and keep Germany militarily weak. The wartime alliance of France, Britain, and the United States against Germany must be carried over into peacetime.

The Americans and the British refused to conclude a long-term peacetime alliance with the French. In place of an alliance in the west with Britain and the United States, therefore, France committed itself to an alliance in the east with Poland, and the Little Entente nations of Czechoslovakia, Romania, and Yugoslavia. Treaties with these four states of east central Europe gave France some security in the event of an attack. But the treaties were also liabilities because France would have to fight to defend east central Europe.

To keep Germany militarily and economically weak, the French attempted to enforce the Treaty of Versailles fully and completely in 1921–23. They were willing to do so alone if necessary. In 1923 the French army invaded the Ruhr district of Germany and occupied it with the intention of collecting reparations payments. This action showed the lengths to which France would go to enforce the treaty and control Germany. The Ruhr invasion only served to isolate France further from its wartime allies. The French government depended on loans from American banks to keep its budget balanced, and the Americans disapproved of the French use of military force to enforce the treaty.

In 1924–25, France had to reverse the direction of its foreign policy. It decided to cooperate with the United States and Great Britain rather than continue a policy of enforcing the treaty alone and keeping Germany weak. France withdrew its army from the Ruhr and some troops from the Rhineland. It agreed to lower German

reparations payments. In addition, by signing the Locarno treaties, France went along with the Anglo-American policy that rejected the use of military force against Germany and promoted German economic recovery.

French anxiety about security continued. Nothing indicated the nature of this anxiety more clearly than the construction, beginning in the late 1920s, of the Maginot Line, a system of defensive fortifications between Germany and France. Behind this wall France hoped to repel what many of its military leaders considered the inevitable German advance.

Throughout the 1920s French political leaders tried to engage Great Britain in guaranteeing the security of France and Europe. The British agreed to defend France and Belgium against possible German aggression. They stopped short, however, of promising to defend Poland and Czechoslovakia. After settling this matter at Locarno, Britain largely reverted to its prewar pattern of withdrawing from continental Europe and concentrating its attention on the demands of its global empire. In their policy toward Germany, British statesmen came to agree with the Americans in opposition to the French: a Germany that was satisfied because it was allowed to recover its economic strength was a better assurance of peace than a weakened but resentful and hostile Germany.

The United States in Europe

The Treaty of Versailles in 1919 was in many ways like the treaties drawn up in Westphalia in 1648 and in Vienna in 1815. All three treaties ratified in international law the changes brought about by the preceding wars—the realignment of states, the readjustment of power, and the redrawing of borders. More dramatically than its predecessors, the Versailles Treaty was a departure from what had gone before. The peace settlement of 1919 spelled the end to the system of independent European great powers that managed their international relations by themselves. The Treaty of Versailles marked the demise of European autonomy.

In World War I, Germany had conquered large areas of eastern Europe, defeated Russia, dominated the Balkans, brought the French army to the point of mutiny, and threatened Great Britain with submarine strangulation. It had done so with only a little help from the other Central Powers. In the end, the defeat of Germany required the combined forces of France, Russia, the British Empire, and the United States. American intervention had boosted French and British morale during the crucial months of 1917. In providing financial help, ships, troops, and supplies, the United States had rescued the Allied powers. A balance of power in Europe could no longer be maintained without outside help. Germany had been defeated, but if it recovered, France and Britain alone would probably not be able to protect Europe again. Security and peace now depended on the presence of an outside force to guarantee a stable balance of power in Europe and to defend western hegemony in the world. That outside force was the United States.

The United States was, however, unwilling to assume a new role as political leader of Europe and mediator of European conflict. It refused to sign a joint peace, arranging instead a separate peace with Germany. It also refused to join the League of Nations. Following the war, the League had been devised as an international body of nations committed, according to Article 10 of its Covenant, to "respect and preserve as against external aggression the territorial integrity and existing political independence" of others. Germany was excluded from membership until 1926; and the USSR (for Union of Soviet Socialist Republics,) was denied entry until 1934. Otherwise, the League of Nations claimed a global membership. The League's two governing bodies, the Council and the Assembly, sought to keep the peace through the cooperation of its member nations. The absence of U.S. support and the lack of any machinery to enforce its decisions undermined the possibility of the League's long-term effectiveness. The hopes that the international body could serve as a peacekeeper collapsed in 1931 with the League's failure to deal with the crisis of Japanese aggression against Manchuria.

The United States persisted in avoiding political and military obligations in Europe with the idea of protecting its own freedom and autonomy. Instead it sought to promote German economic recovery and reasoned that a peaceful and stable Europe would be reestablished without a real balance of power in Europe and without a commitment from the United States. But peaceful stability in Europe was like Humpty-Dumpty. Smashed in the war, it could not be put back together again—not without the glue and the props that only the United States could provide.

World War I should have taught the peoples and the leaders of Europe and the United States the dangers of a system of states based on national sovereignties, nationalist aims, and national rivalries. Instead of alleviating the grievances of 1914,

the peace settlement with its new territorial arrangements created new nations and new grievances based on national differences. The concern of each European state, old and new, to protect its borders and its markets testified to the enduring nationalism. Many feared that territorial settlements of the peace held the promise of another war. Even efforts at comprehensive international cooperation like the League of Nations did not overcome the problem of competitive nations. Nor did the Kellogg-Briand Pact signed by twenty-three nations in 1928. Named for U.S. Secretary of State Frank B. Kellogg (1856–1937) and French foreign minister Aristide Briand, who devised the plan, the pact renounced war. In the atmosphere of the 1920s, a time of hope and caution, the agreement carried all the weight of an empty gesture.

Economic Nationalism in the 1920s

When the Great War ended in 1918, the European nations set out to rebuild their shattered economies. Except in northeastern France, Belgium, and parts of Russia, productive capacity had not been significantly destroyed, but former markets and trade patterns had been devastated. Restoration of trade became a primary goal for nations trying to reestablish economic prosperity in the 1920s.

Belligerent nations had paid for the war not with taxes but through selling bonds at home and borrowing capital from abroad. Taxing domestic populations who were just beginning to recover after four years of war was not a political solution designed to win votes. Higher taxes would in fact have hampered economic recovery. For France the surest road to economic recovery was the collection of reparations from Germany. Britain saw recovery through the restoration of international trade. Reparations would draw wealth out of Germany. International trade, however, depended on Germany's recovery to the position of a prosperous trading partner. There was thus a fundamental tension between the goals of trade and those of reparations.

Economic recovery proved illusory for the

MARRIED AGAIN

IRELAND, *THE COLUMBUS DISPATCH*

Married Again. *This 1928 cartoon shows the wicked world once again pledging eternal fidelity to peace with the signing of the Kellogg-Briand pact. The cynical attitude of the artist was vindicated by the events of the later twentieth century.*

first years of the postwar decade. During the war, no European nation had been able to survive on its own, through its own productive capacity. In the postwar world, European leaders learned new and harsh lessons about economic self-sufficiency. A spirit of economic nationalism swept the Continent. Domestic markets were closed to foreign goods. The United States created special problems by imposing high tariffs that restricted the American market for European goods. In an international economy, when everyone wants to sell and nobody wants to buy, trade is impossible. A sluggish world trade, especially in conjunction with the U.S. policy of commercial protectionism, retarded the recovery of European nations, which hoped foreign exchange would be a means of paying off war debts. When prosperity and trade returned in the second half of the 1920s, economic restoration proved to be as illusory as recovery, built as it was on a precarious network of markets and investment that masked serious weaknesses.

Reparations and Debts

In 1918 the belligerent nations—winners and losers alike—had big bills on their hands. Although nations at war had borrowed from their own populations through the sale of war bonds, private citizens could not provide all the money needed to finance four years of war. France borrowed from Great Britain. Both Great Britain and France took loans from the United States. When all else failed, belligerent nations could and did print money not backed by productive wealth. Because more money had claims on the same amount of national wealth, the money in circulation was worth less. When the people who had purchased war bonds were then paid off with depreciated currency, they lost real wealth. Inflation had the same effect as taxation. The people had less wealth and the government had less debt. In the end, those who had purchased war bonds absorbed the costs of war through payoffs in depreciated currency. (See Special Feature, "The School of Hard Knocks and Inflation," pp. 862-863.)

Not surprisingly, those countries that had loaned out money during the war wanted to be repaid. The United States, for the first time in history the leading creditor nation in the world,

had no intention of forgiving war debts. Nor did it intend to accept repayment in less-valuable postwar currencies: loans were tied to gold. There is a saying that the lender is the prisoner of the borrower. If the borrower owes the lender five dollars, then the problem is the borrower's in paying back the five dollars. If the borrower, on the other hand, owes the lender a vast sum—say 5 million dollars—it is the lender who has a very big problem in being sure of repayment. The second example, the problem of the lender, was the problem facing the United States after the war. In a very real sense, the United States in the 1920s was imprisoned in its role as principal lender to Europe.

Britain, France, and Belgium counted on reparations from Germany to pay their war debts and to rebuild their economies. As for Germany, the postwar Reparations Commission determined that Germany owed the victors 132 billion gold marks ($33 billion) to be paid in annual installments of 2 billion gold marks ($500 million) plus 26 percent of the value of German exports. Reparations were calculated on the basis of the damages Germany had inflicted on the Allies.

The Allies never really expected Germany to pay the full amount, and most Germans believed it could not be paid. Germany, too, wanted to recover from the years of privation of the war. Substantial reparations payments would have transferred real wealth from Germany to the Allies. Transferring wealth would have cut into any increase in the German standard of living in the 1920s, and it would have diminished the investment needed to make the German economy grow. For the German people and for German leaders, reparations were an unacceptable, punitive levy that mortgaged the prosperity of future generations. International indebtedness and the assumptions about who was paying whom proved to be one of the great weaknesses of the international economy of the 1920s.

France was caught in the middle. Germany was not paying reparations and America was demanding from France war debt payment. Britain was taking a lenient attitude toward Germany. Raymond Poincaré (1860–1934), who had served as president of the Third Republic throughout the war and was prime minister of

French soldiers and engineers guard a German railroad locomotive during the French occupation of the Ruhr industrial district in 1923.

France from 1922 to 1924, insisted that Germany must pay reparations to enable France to recover and pay the United States. In January 1923, French and Belgian troops entered the Ruhr district of Germany, an area rich in coal and the center of the most important industrial complex in Europe. Their purpose was to collect reparations directly—by digging up coal and shipping it back to France. They intended to remain in the Ruhr until Germany was able and willing to pay reparations on its own.

The German government recommended that German miners, trainmen, and civic officials respond to the military presence with passive resistance. To pay idle employees and employers, the German government printed huge amounts of currency. The mark collapsed, and world currencies were endangered. The French occupation of the Ruhr, called an invasion by France's critics, was denounced throughout the world. With financial disaster looming, the British and Americans decided to intervene. A plan must be devised that would permit the German economy to prosper while funneling payments to France, so dependent on reparations for its own recovery and for its war debt payments to the United States.

In 1924, the American banker Charles G. Dawes (1865–1951), along with a group of international financial experts appointed by the Allied governments, sought a solution to the reparations problem. Politicians, most people believed, had put Europe into the reparations mess. Bankers, using sound business principles, could now reestablish prosperity. The priority of the Dawes Plan was to end inflation and restore economic prosperity in Germany. Germany was given a more modest and realistic schedule of payments and a loan from American banks to get payments started.

The protection of the German economy rather than the defense of French treaty rights commanded the attention and the concern of the United States. American bankers threatened not to renew their loan unless France agreed never again to enforce the Treaty of Versailles by military means without the consent of the British and Americans. Because the French treasury depended on the American loan to balance its national budget, France accepted the Dawes Plan and promised to undertake no more Ruhr invasions. France lost its independence in foreign policy and its status as a great power was permanently undermined.

Trade and Reparations

As important as reparations and war debts are in any understanding of the Western world in the 1920s, they cannot be considered in isolation. Debtor nations, whether Allies paying back loans to the United States or defeated nations paying reparations to the victors, needed to be able to sell their goods in world markets. They saw trade as the principal way to accumulate enough national income to pay back what they owed and to prosper domestically without burying their citizens under a mountain of new taxes. Restoration of international trade was, therefore, a central issue in resolving the problems of international indebtedness. Germany, for example, needed to regain markets lost during the war in order to rebuild foreign exchange. Profits from exports would both fuel domestic recovery and generate the capital necessary to pay reparations and repay loans.

If trade was to be the stepladder out of the financial hole of indebtedness, open markets and stable currencies were absolutely necessary. The United States recognized that its own best interests lay in promoting economic recovery in Europe. A stable Europe would give the United States a market for its own agricultural and industrial products and provide a guarantee for recovery of its loans and investments.

The proverbial monkey wrench in a smoothly functioning international economy was the trade policy of the United States. Republican political leaders in the United States insisted on high tariffs to protect domestic goods against imports. But high tariffs prevented Europeans from selling in the United States and earning the dollars they needed to repay war debts. They also hampered the recovery of European markets. Germany's hopes of establishing favorable trade balances in order to make capital payments to the United States were dashed, as American markets were walled off to German goods and American long-term capital investments in Germany remained low.

While blocking imports, the United States planned to expand its own exports to world markets, especially in Europe. American government officials, businessmen, farmers, and bankers all agreed on the importance of European markets for a prosperous American economy. The prob-

lem for American exporters, however, was the instability of European currencies in the first half of the 1920s. All over Europe governments allowed inflation to rise with the expectation that depreciating currencies would make their goods cheaper in world markets.

Depreciating European currencies on the one hand meant an appreciating dollar on the other. For the "grand design" of U.S. trade expansion, a strong dollar was no virtue. More and more German marks, British pounds, and French francs had to be spent to purchase American goods. The result was that fewer American exports were sold in European markets. After a certain point, selling European goods at lowered prices in American markets wiped out not only profits for European producers but even the possibility of covering costs. Instead of changing a tariff policy that seriously hampered the chances for recovery of European economies, and instead of canceling or forgiving war debts that threatened to soak up Europe's meager capital, the United States subscribed to another policy, one based on what was considered to be in the best interests of Europe and the United States. American banks were authorized to extend private loans to European governments.

New private loans to Germany were possible only after 1924 when the Dawes Plan redesigned reparations payments and inflation was controlled. Germany's capacity to pay was a central feature of the Dawes Plan, and thus for the first few years German payments were to be lowered and Germany was to be assisted by loans from the United States. The need to maintain a stable German currency received special attention. The Dawes Plan was based on the combined lessons of the hyperinflation of the preceding two years and the international disaster of the French occupation of the Ruhr. German leaders reminded the world that both these crippling events were consequences of reparations.

As a result of the Dawes Plan and the American loans, Germany was linked directly to the international economy after 1924. Germany's economic fate could now be determined by events occurring elsewhere. Two-thirds of Germany's long-term credits came from the United States. Conversely, the soundness of American banks depended on a solvent Germany, which now

The School of Hard Knocks and Inflation

For many who survived the horrors of the Great War, worse disruptions lay ahead. Inflation, like combat, wreaked havoc with people's lives. During the war prices had doubled in Great Britain, the United States, Germany, Canada, and Japan. Prices had trebled in France and Sweden. In Italy they had quadrupled. But all of that was nothing compared to what happened after the war in Germany, Austria, Hungary, Poland, and Russia. Inflation was so great, with prices increasing astronomically—by the tens of thousands—that a new term had to be created: *hyperinflation.* As prices reached staggering heights, currencies collapsed. In Germany in 1918 one prewar gold mark was worth two paper marks. By 1923 it took one billion paper marks to match a single gold mark in value. German people's hopes and their futures disappeared into the abyss of the nine zeroes that it took to write a numerical billion.

Twentieth-century women and men do not have to be schooled in basic facts about money. There is a world of education in buying food, clothing, and shelter. People learn on a daily basis how the price of eggs and the price of gasoline fluctuate in relation to factors that range far beyond their control. But there was no harsher school in the realities of modern economy than the

school of experience in Germany in the 1920s.

Inflation began in Germany during the war. Then the government printed money instead of levying taxes as the easiest way to pay off its war debts. After the war, inflation continued because big business in need of new capital and organized labor in search of jobs benefited from it. The inflation was further aggravated by depreciation of currencies in central and eastern European countries. Depreciation was prompted by the hollow hope that by making currencies worth less, exports would be more attractive and would earn the foreign exchange so necessary for prosperity. The Allied demands for reparations payments further undermined confidence in the mark. The result was that double-digit inflation became hyperinflation in the spring of 1922. When the French army occupied the Ruhr, and the German government printed money to subsidize the miners and trainmen who were conducting passive resistance, inflation became astronomical. German passive resistance to French occupation was a strategy with a very high price tag.

More and more paper money came into circulation without any corresponding increase in the amount of goods and services. Almost two thousand printing presses ran around the

clock, spewing out billions of bank notes that fueled the inflation. As the value of money plummeted, prices soared. A handful of apples cost cartloads of paper currency—hundreds of billions of marks—at the height of the inflation in the summer of 1923. The situation grew worse by the hour. People were paid twice a day so that they could rush to stores during their breaks and spend their earnings before their money became worth even less. Working people were malnourished, the unemployed starved. Only one in three German workers was fully employed by the end of 1923. Death rates rose as sicknesses related to poor diets spread. Few people could afford hospital care or doctors' fees. The middle classes, from upper to lower ranks, suffered most from hyperinflation. Their savings were wiped out, their investments destroyed, their property stripped from them. Widows and the aged living on pensions were reduced to poverty, and civil servants and teachers became paupers overnight, as previously comfortable salaries dwindled. Hyperinflation gave meaning to the saying that money wasn't worth the paper it was printed on.

Money stands as a symbol of value that permits exchange in the marketplace based on both expectation and trust. In hyperinflation, the magic of money became a nightmare. The value

rated. The German people learned that the economy was neither stable nor self-correcting. They learned in the harshest way possible that it responded to political choices and international events. Social groups accused one another. Small businesses blamed big capitalists. Civil servants saw unionized workers as the problem. Retailers blamed wholesalers.

The long finger of blame pointed beyond national borders. The Germans blamed the French with their reparations demands and their invading troops for the plight of Germany. Hyperinflation had negative repercussions for democracy, as extremist political groups on both right and left attracted growing numbers of followers by blaming the liberal and democratic Weimar Republic. Because of the horrors of inflation, German governments thereafter were committed to balanced budgets. When the Depression hit the German economy in 1929, the fear of a new inflation prevented the government from using deficit spending to bring back prosperity. The Depression in turn contributed to the burgeoning appeal of Hitler and the National Socialists. People grew cynical and defiant through suffering and sought security in extraordinary and extrademocratic solutions. Economic discontent bred a new politics in the school of hard knocks and inflation.

of commodities was destroyed, and with it, moral verities vanished, too. The world was turned upside down. Spending became a virtue; saving was a vice. To be thrifty was stupid, to plan for the future impossible. With soaring prices people lost security and stability as surely as if they had been in a military upheaval.

As in a war it is important to identify the enemy, so too in hyperinflation did people seek out the adversary. Many felt that the republican government of Weimar was to blame because it had accepted the peace treaty and made reparations payments. Socialists and Communists were singled out for special opprobrium. Jewish politicians, bankers, and financiers became scapegoats for Germany's economic problems. Confidence in the state evapo-

absorbed 18 percent of U.S. capital exports. This may well be regarded as the U.S. payment of "reverse" reparations to Germany with the hope of promoting its own interests. Wages and salaries in Germany increased significantly and German state welfare programs expanded. The United States recognized in German economic recovery the necessary prerequisite for stable European markets. By 1932 government leaders in Washington also supported revision of the Versailles Treaty with German interests in mind. Republican leaders minimized French concerns for security and ignored British channels for moving funds and resources. They supported instead increased and direct contact with Germany.

Growing U.S. involvement in European affairs flowed from its recently assumed role as a creditor nation. The international economy did not exist in isolation from political realities. To the contrary, economic and financial imperatives drove American foreign policy in Europe. Economic decisions were in turn influenced by strategic considerations. The motives and values of American business and politics converged in forging links between Europe and the United States that would promote stable markets and avoid revolutions. Germany was recognized and supported as a bulwark against Bolshevism, and for that reason Germany had to be prosperous. France's cry for protection against a strong Germany was silenced by the American need to export and by America's fear of communism.

Despite the scaled-down schedule of the Dawes Plan, reparations remained a bitter pill for German leaders and the German public to swallow. In 1929, American bankers devised a new plan under the leadership of the American businessman Owen D. Young (1874–1962), chairman of the board of General Electric. Although the Young Plan initially transferred $100 million to Germany, Germans saw the twentieth century stretching before them as year after year of nothing but humiliating reparations payments. To make matters worse, after 1928 American private loans shriveled in Germany, as American investors sought the higher yields of a booming stock market at home. In this atmosphere, reparations continued to undermine Weimar politics. During the summer of 1929, the National Socialist party under Adolf Hitler used the general resent-

ment over reparations to fan the flames of extremist politics.

Until the economic collapse of 1929, problems over reparations, trade, stable currencies, and international security had seemed on the way to being settled. The Locarno treaties augured well for French and German relations, and the Dawes Plan had scaled down and rescheduled reparations. With high employment, high profits, and high consumption, the United States set the pace for other industrial producers. Europe as a whole made rapid progress in manufacturing production during the second half of the decade, and by 1929 had surpassed its prewar (1913) per capita income. France experienced a faster rate of growth in the 1920s than the United States, increasing its output by 300 percent over the level in 1919. Not every country experienced the same high rates of growth—eastern Europe, for example, struggled mightily with attempts to industrialize. Nor were income gains distributed evenly to the rich and the poor. Nevertheless, Europe's economic future appeared rosy, and recovery seemed the order of the day.

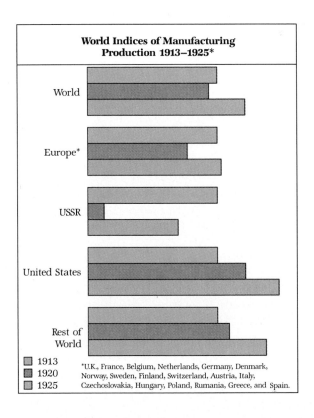

World Indices of Manufacturing Production 1913–1925*

World

Europe*

USSR

United States

Rest of World

■ 1913
■ 1920
■ 1925

*U.K., France, Belgium, Netherlands, Germany, Denmark, Norway, Sweden, Finland, Switzerland, Austria, Italy, Czechoslovakia, Hungary, Poland, Rumania, Greece, and Spain.

Yet structural weaknesses were present, although they went almost unnoticed. The false security of a new gold standard masked the instability and interdependence of currencies. Low prices prevailed in the agricultural sector, keeping incomes of a significant segment of the population low. The low rate of long-term capital investment was obscured in the flurry of short-term loans, whose disappearance in 1928 spelled the beginning of the end for European recovery. The protectionist trade policy of the United States conflicted with its insistence on repayment of war debts. Germany's resentment over reparations was in no way alleviated by the Dawes and Young repayment plans. The irresponsibility of American speculation in the stock market pricked the bubble of prosperity. No single factor caused the collapse that began in 1929. None of these factors operated in isolation. Taken together, however, they spelled a collapse of previously unimagined severity of the international economic system.

The Soviet Union's Separate Path

In the industrial era progress had often been pictured as a locomotive hurtling into the future. This sleek and powerful "iron horse" symbolized the process of industrialization in western Europe that had been in the making for over 150 years. In the West industrial power had been achieved at the cost of considerable social dislocation. In Russia in the 1920s, industrialization had barely begun.

In the decade following war, revolution, and civil war, the Soviet state committed its people to a program of rapid industrial growth in order to ensure its survival as a great power. Communism, Lenin was fond of saying, equaled socialism plus electrification. Russia, too, would have its hurtling locomotive, but one that had to be set in motion before the track was properly laid. The costs of Russia's rapid industrialization were wasted resources, enormous human suffering, and millions of lost lives. Laying track in the path of a moving train is neither easy nor efficient, and much is risked in the prospect of derailment.

Lenin's successor, Joseph Stalin (1879–1953), committed the Soviet people to the achievement in a single generation of what it had taken the West a century and a half to accomplish.

The Soviet Regime at the End of the Civil War

The revolution had been made and the civil war had been won in the name of "the dictatorship of the proletariat," as Lenin echoed Marx. The people were in control—or they were supposed to be. Representing the united rule of workers and peasants, the hammer and sickle on the Soviet flag were symbolic reminders of the commitment to rule from below. But at the end of the civil war in 1921, the Bolsheviks, not the people, were in charge. Having come to power in November 1917, the revolutionaries had struggled for survival for over three years against internal and external opposition. Although the revolutionaries had succeeded, serious problems remained.

The industrial sector, small as it was, was in total disarray by 1921. Famine and epidemics in 1921–22 killed and weakened more people than the Great War and the civil war combined. The countryside had been plundered to feed the Red and White armies. The combination of empty promises and a declining standard of living left workers and peasants frustrated and discontented. Urban strikes and rural uprisings defied short-term solutions. In March 1921 sailors at Kronstadt joined striking workers at nearby Petrograd to protest arbitrary Soviet rule. The proletarian revolutionary heroes of 1917 were rejecting the new Soviet regime. The Bolshevik party now faced the task of restoring a country exhausted by war and revolution, its resources depleted, its economy destroyed.

At the head of the Soviet state was Lenin, the first among equals in the seven-man Politburo. The Central Committee of the Communist party decided "fundamental questions of policy, international and domestic," but in reality the Politburo, the inner committee of the Central Committee, held the reins of power. The men of the Politburo were relatively young and extremely ambitious. United in ideology and outlook as Bolsheviks, the members of the Politburo differed over policies in everything from education to industrial production. In the early 1920s, the greatest challenges facing the Bolshevik leaders, now calling themselves Communists, were to stabilize the new government and restore the economy.

Among the Politburo seven, three men in particular attempted to leave their mark on the direction of Soviet policy: Leon Trotsky (1879–1940), Nikolai Bukharin (1888–1938), and Joseph Stalin (1879–1953). The great drama of Soviet leadership in the 1920s revolved around how the most brilliant (Trotsky) and the most popular (Bukharin) failed at the hands of the most shrewdly political (Stalin).

The two poles in the debate over the direction of economic development were on one end a planned economy totally directed from above, and on the other an economy controlled from below. In 1920–21 Leon Trotsky, at that time people's commissar of war, favored a planned economy based on the militarization of labor. The discipline and organization of the Red Army,

which he headed, could be applied to the masses to whip them into shape. Trade unions opposed such a proposal and argued for a share of control over production. Trotsky would have happily done away with trade unions as unnecessary in the new Bolshevik state. Lenin, however, favored a proletarian democracy and supported unions organized independently of state control.

The controversy was resolved in the short run at the Tenth Party Congress in 1921, when Lenin chose to steer a middle course between trade-union autonomy and militarization by preserving the unions and at the same time insisting on the state's responsibility for economic development. His primary goal was to stabilize Bolshevik rule in its progress toward socialism. He recognized that nothing could be achieved without the peasants. As a result, Lenin found himself embracing a new economic policy that he termed a "temporary retreat" from Communist goals.

The New Economic Policy

In 1921 Lenin ended the forced requisitioning of peasant produce, which had been in effect during the civil war. In its place, peasants were to pay a tax in kind, that is, a fixed portion of their yield, to the state. Peasants in turn were permitted to reinstate private trade on their own terms. Party leaders accepted this dramatic shift in economic policy because it held the promise of prosperity, so necessary for political stability. The actions of Lenin to return the benefits of productivity to the economy, combined with those of the peasants to reestablish markets, created the New Economic Policy, or NEP, that emerged in the spring and summer of 1921.

It remained for Nikolai Bukharin to give shape and substance to the economic policy that permitted Russian producers to engage in some capitalist practices. Along with Lenin and Trotsky, Bukharin was one of the founding fathers of the Soviet state and the youngest of the top Bolshevik leaders. By the age of seventeen, he had established his credentials as a professional revolutionary. Like Lenin he had been imprisoned under the tsarist regime and had been exiled for his beliefs. With the success of the Bolshevik revolution, Bukharin took his place on the Central Committee of the Communist party and on the

Leon Trotsky, a loser in the Soviet power struggle that followed the death of Lenin. Trotsky was exiled from Russia in 1929 and in 1940 was assassinated on Stalin's orders.

Politburo as well. He was editor of the official newspaper *Pravda,* which in Russian means "Truth." Lenin called Bukharin "the party's most valuable and biggest theoretician."

Bukharin set about solving the task of Russia's single greatest problem: how could Russia, crippled by poverty, find enough capital to industrialize? Insisting on the need for long-term economic planning, Bukharin counted on a prosperous and contented peasantry as the mainstay of his policy. Retail prices must be lowered, overhead must be reduced, and productivity must be improved to accelerate commodity turnover. Bukharin was strongly interested in the possibility of attracting foreign investment to Soviet endeavors as a way of ensuring future productivity.

Bukharin planned to keep the Russian peasants happy. At base he appreciated the importance of landholding to Russian peasants and defended a system of individual farms and private accumulation. Agriculture would operate through a market system, and the peasants would have the right to control their own surpluses. Bukharin never intended to create a wealthy class of peasants but instead to transform the very culture of the countryside by promoting new cultural values of work and progress. He realized that this transformation would take time—at least a generation. Because agriculture was such an overwhelmingly important sector of the economy, rural prosperity would generate profits that could be used for gradual industrial development. Bukharin's policy stood in stark contrast to Stalin's later plan to feed industry by starving agriculture.

To later generations the NEP marked the golden age of the Soviet state. The Bolshevik party monopolized political power, while a pluralistic approach was tolerated in the society and the economy. Peace, stability, and recovery all seemed possible. The flowering of intellectual and artistic life in the twenties in the Soviet Union paralleled the creativity of Western culture. After its bitter civil war, the Soviet Union seemed well on the road to ensuring its own survival.

Yet the period of the NEP from 1921 to 1928 was a time filled with contradictions and uncertainties. The Soviet Union had returned to some capitalist practices and a limited market economy in the hopes of reestablishing a functioning and eventually prosperous economy. This policy was profoundly at odds with the programs of a Communist state, whose ultimate goal was to pull down the capitalist system and establish socialism. Collective and large-scale farming had to be deferred indefinitely in order to reconcile the peasantry to the state. The success of individual farmers was tolerated and encouraged, amid the suspicion harbored by some members of the Politburo that *kulaks,* the derisive term for wealthy peasants that literally means "the tight-fisted ones," were rural capitalists who threatened the future of the revolution. In 1924 the tax in kind was replaced with a tax in cash. With this shift the state now procured grain through commercial agencies and cooperative organizations instead of directly from the peasants. The move toward Western capitalist models seemed more pronounced than ever to critics of the NEP.

Lenin had reasoned in the early days of the NEP that it was a temporary and strategic measure. Beginning in 1922 Lenin suffered a series of strokes, which virtually removed him from power by March 1923. When he died on 21 January 1924, the Communist leadership split over the ambiguities of the NEP and the future of socialism in Russia. Many Communist revolutionaries believed that the revolution had been sold out for bourgeois liberalism. With Lenin's death the struggle for political dominance intensified.

The backward nature of agriculture did not permit the kind of productivity that the NEP policymakers anticipated. Marketed agricultural surpluses remained below prewar levels. This shortfall made the NEP vulnerable to its critics. Cities demanded more food as their populations swelled with the influx of unskilled workers from rural areas. In 1927 peasants held back their grain. The Soviet Union was then experiencing a series of foreign policy setbacks in the West and in China, and Bolshevik leaders spoke of an active anti-Soviet conspiracy, led by Great Britain, which could lead to an attack by the capitalist powers. The Soviet state lowered the price of grain, squeezing the peasantry. The war scare, combined with the drop in food prices, soon led to an economic crisis.

By 1928 the NEP was in trouble. Stalin, general secretary of the Communist party of the Soviet Union, saw his chance. Under his supervision, the state intervened to prevent peasants from disposing of their own grain surpluses. The peasants responded violently to requisitioning. Rioting erupted in the countryside as peasants continued to hoard their produce. Ostensibly with the limited aim of blocking *kulak* speculators, Stalin in fact set out to shut down the free market in grain. Bukharin and his policy were in danger. Stalin manipulated the political machinery that allowed him to exploit the internal crisis and to manipulate external dangers with the aim of eliminating his political rivals. Trotsky was expelled from the Communist party in November 1927 on Stalin's charges that he had engaged in antiparty activities. Banished from Russia in 1929, he eventually found refuge in Mexico, where he was assassinated in 1940 at Stalin's command.

Bukharin's popularity in the party also threatened Stalin's aspirations. Bukharin was dropped from the Politburo in 1929. Tolerated through the early 1930s, he was arrested in 1937, and tried and executed for alleged treasonous activities the following year. The fate that befell Trotsky and Bukharin was typical of that which afflicted those who stood in the way of Stalin's pursuit of dictatorial control. Stalin was, in a colleague's words, "a grey blur." Beneath his apparently colorless personality, however, was a dangerous man of great political acumen, a ruthless, behind-the-scenes politician who controlled the machinery of the party to his own ends and was not averse to employing violence in order to achieve them.

Stalin's Rise to Power

Joseph Stalin was born Iosif Dzhugashvili in 1879. His self-chosen revolutionary name, Stalin, means "steel" in Russian and is as good an indication as any of his opinion of his own personality and will. Stalin, the man who ruled Russia as a dictator from 1928 until his death in 1953, was not a Russian. He was from Georgia, an area between the Black and Caspian seas, and spoke Russian with an accent. Georgia, with its land occupied and its people subjugated by invading armies for centuries, was annexed to the expanding Russian empire in 1801. Georgians were and remain a separate nationality with their own language and culture.

As the youngest of four and the only surviving child of Vissarion and Ekaterina Dzhugashvili, Stalin endured a childhood of brutal misery. Vissarion was a poor and often unemployed shoemaker who intended that his son be apprenticed in the same trade. Under his mother's protection, young Iosif received an education and entered a seminary against his father's wishes. Iosif's schooling, extraordinary for someone of his poverty-stricken background, gave him the opportunity to learn about revolutionary socialist politics. At the turn of the century, Georgia had a strong Marxist revolutionary movement that opposed Russian exploitation. Iosif dropped out of the seminary in 1899 to engage in underground Marxist activities, and he soon became a follower of Lenin.

Stalin's association with Lenin kept him close to the center of power after the October Revolution of 1917. First as people's commissar for nationalities (1920–23) and then as general secretary of the Central Committee of the Communist party (1922–53), Stalin showed natural talent as a political strategist. Stalin's familiarity with non-Russian nationalities was a great asset in his dealings with the ethnic diversity and unrest in the vast Soviet state. Unlike other party leaders who had lived in exile in western Europe before the revolution, Stalin had little knowledge of the West; he had visited London and Stockholm only briefly in 1905 and 1906 and had spent six weeks before World War I in Vienna and Kraków. Stalin also lacked Lenin's image as the legitimate and charismatic leader. After Lenin's death in 1924, Stalin shrewdly promoted such an image for himself and bolstered his own reputation by orchestrating a cult of worship for Lenin.

Many Bolsheviks disapproved of the almost religious superstition that surrounded the endless lines of people that filed past Lenin's mummified body, which had been placed on permanent view in Moscow. Lenin's widow, Nadezhda

Krupskaya (1869–1939), begged the Russian people not to enshrine her dead husband. In a public letter printed in *Pravda* only days after his death, Krupskaya urged a true memorial: "If you want to honor the name of Vladimir Ilyich (Lenin), build day-care centers, kindergartens, houses, schools, libraries, medical centers, hospitals, and homes for the disabled and, above all, let us put his precepts into practice." Krupskaya voiced her dead husband's wishes for a humble burial, but her request fell on deaf ears. Stalin had his way and gave the Russian people what was in essence an embalmed saint. Lenin's body was placed in a mausoleum erected on Red Square.

In 1929 Stalin used the occasion of his fiftieth birthday to fashion for himself a reputation as the living hero of the Soviet state. Icons, statues, busts, and images of all sorts of both Lenin and Stalin appeared everywhere in public buildings, schoolrooms, and homes. He systematically and ruthlessly began eliminating his rivals, so that he alone stood unchallenged as Lenin's true successor. Stalin, the man of steel, intended to make the Soviet Union in his own image. The Stalin cult consolidated his personal power and prepared the way for his plan of rapid industrialization.

The First Five-Year Plan.   The cult of Stalin coincided with the first Five-Year Plan, which initiated an economic revolution. Between 1929 and 1936, the period covered by the first two five-year plans, truncated because of their proclaimed success, Stalin laid the foundation for an urban industrial society in the Soviet Union. By brutally squeezing profits out of the agricultural sector, Stalin managed to increase heavy industrial production between 300 and 600 percent. A simple slogan summarized the political philosophy that justified Stalin's economic plans: "Socialism in One Country!"

"Socialism in one country" committed the Soviet Union to rapid industrialization as the only way to preserve socialism in the Soviet Union. The failure of revolutionary movements in the West was now used as the stick with which to beat the supporters of the NEP. Socialism meant machines and technology and economic power for Stalin, not just a system of political rule. The NEP guaranteed Russian backwardness and Communist failure, Stalin argued. The revolution was in dan-

A Soviet propaganda poster shows a caricature of the fat capitalist dismissing the Five-Year Plan as "fantasy." Later, the smug capitalist turns green with envy as Soviet industrial might amazes the world.

ger and must be saved. Stalin insisted that only he, as a dynamic leader interpreting the will of the great Lenin, could move the revolution ahead.

"Those who fall behind get beaten." Thus spoke Stalin of the Soviet Union's compelling need to industrialize. "We are fifty or a hundred years behind the advanced countries. We must make good this distance in ten years." Stalin communicated to the Soviet people his sense of urgency by warning them that the Soviet Union's survival as a nation was at stake. "Do you want our socialist fatherland to be beaten and to lose its independence? If you do not want this, you must put an end to its backwardness in the shortest possible time and develop a genuine Bolshevik tempo in building up its socialist economy."

Stalin, true to his name, focused on steel and iron as the essential metals in industrial development. Just as he had created a cult around Lenin and himself, he made steel the idol of the new age. The Soviet Union needed heavy machinery to build the future. An industrial labor force was created virtually overnight as peasant men and women were placed at workbenches and before the vast furnaces of modern metallurgical plants. The number of women in the industrial work force tripled in the decade after 1929. The reliability of official indices varied, but there is little doubt that heavy industrial production soared in the first Five-Year Plan (1929–32). The Russian people were constantly reminded that no sacrifice could be too great in producing steel and iron.

When he first began to deal with the grain crisis of 1928, Stalin did not intend collective agriculture as a solution. But by the end of 1929 the increasingly repressive measures instituted by the state against the peasants had led both to collectivization and to deportation of *kulaks*. There were in fact few *kulaks*, and repressive measures most often affected the vast majority of rural dwellers, who had hoped to hold on to their piece of land and to control their own produce. Stalin achieved forced collectivization by confiscating land and establishing collective farms run by the state. Within a few months, half of all peasant

By 1932, the process of collectivization of Soviet agriculture was nearly complete, but some of the farms needed more workers. Appeals went out to urban industrial laborers for help. This photo shows Komsomol members at the Moscow Brake plant signing up for a tour of duty in the countryside.

farms were collectivized. By 1938 private land was virtually eliminated. The state set prices, controlled distribution, and selected crops with the intention of ensuring a steady food supply and freeing a rural labor force for heavy industry.

State propaganda showed tractors and automobiles rolling off the production lines. Few consumers actually saw the new machines, which nevertheless became symbols of the Soviet Union's commitment to heavy industry. More as a publicity ploy than a statement of fact, the Five-Year Plan was declared a success after only three years. It was a success in one important sense: it did lay the foundations of the Soviet planned economy, in which the state made all decisions about production, distribution, and prices. The leap forward toward urban industrial society had been taken. Still, the first Five-Year Plan did not last five years and was, in fact, not much of a plan. It was more a groping toward a plan, a series of experiments among competing groups without much effective direction.

Enormous human cost was the price of the rapid changes that occurred under the first Five-Year Plan. Collectivization meant misery for the 25 million peasant families who suffered under it. At least 5 million peasants died between 1929 and 1932. Peasants who resisted collectivization retaliated by destroying their own crops and livestock. Collectivization ripped apart the fabric of village life, destroyed families, and sent homeless peasants into exile. Rapid industrial development shattered the delicate shells of the lives of millions of people. Stalin considered collectivization of agriculture the only way to develop an industrial sector overnight. He, as tsars before him, saw that Russia could be carried into the future only on the backs of its peasants.

The Comintern and World Politics.   In addition to promoting its internal economic development, the Soviet Union had to worry about survival in a world political system composed entirely of capitalist countries. After the Bolshevik revolution in 1917, Lenin had fully expected that other socialist revolutions would follow throughout the world, especially in central and western Europe. These revolutions would destroy capitalism and secure Russia's place in a new world order. But as the

prospects for world proletarian revolution evaporated, Soviet leaders sought to protect their revolutionary country from what they saw as a hostile capitalist world. They used diplomacy for this purpose. The end of the Allied intervention and blockade of Russia allowed the Bolshevik state to initiate diplomatic relations with the West, beginning with the Treaty of Rapallo signed with Germany in 1921. By 1924 all the major countries of the world—with the exception of the United States—had established diplomatic relations with the Soviet Union. In 1928 the USSR cooperated in the preparation of a world disarmament conference to be held in Geneva and joined western European powers in a commitment to peace. The United States and the Soviet Union exchanged ambassadors for the first time in 1933.

In their diplomatic relations with Europe, Soviet leaders tried to make their country secure by preventing the formation of any anti-Soviet coalitions that might intervene militarily or impose economic boycotts against the USSR. They also promoted trade with the industrialized countries of Europe in order to import the technology necessary for rapid industrialization. The USSR refused, however, to pay any debts incurred by the tsarist regime and refused to return to foreign owners properties nationalized during the Bolshevik revolution. In response, the European powers withheld the long-term loans that the Soviet Union so badly needed for its industrialization. The lack of foreign loans was one reason why Stalin chose to squeeze surplus from the peasants.

In addition to diplomatic relations, the Soviet state in 1919 encouraged various national Communist parties to form an association for the purpose of promoting and coordinating the coming world revolution. This Communist International, or Comintern, was based in Moscow and included representatives from thirty-seven countries by 1920. As it became clear that a world revolution was not imminent, the Comintern concerned itself with the ideological purity of its member parties. Under Lenin's direction, the Soviet Communist party determined policy for all the member parties.

In the early 1920s the Comintern employed a strategy of cooperation with non-Communist socialist parties and even with some "bourgeois" nonworker movements and organizations. These collaborative ventures were called "united fronts." In Europe Communists now cooperated with moderate democratic socialist parties and with trade unions. In Asia and the Middle East Communists supported movements of national liberation that opposed colonial rule. Bukharin and Stalin shared a view of the Comintern that prevailed from 1924 to 1929: the Comintern must take as its starting point the fact that Western capitalist societies were, for the moment at least, stable. Since the collapse of capitalism was not imminent, the Comintern should work to promote the unity of working classes everywhere and should cooperate with existing worker organizations.

In 1929, however, Stalin argued that advanced capitalist societies were teetering on the brink of new wars and revolutions. As a result, the Comintern must seek to sever the ties between foreign Communist parties and social democratic parties in the West in order to prepare for the revolutionary struggle. Stalin purged the Comintern of dissenters, and he decreed a policy of noncooperation in Europe from 1929 to 1933. As a result, socialism in Europe was badly split between Communists and democratic socialists precisely at the moment when new right-wing and fascist groups were making their bid for power. The image of the Comintern as a Moscow-controlled fomenter of revolution, instructing its puppet national Communist parties, further eroded the confidence of the European Left as it confronted fascism. The Right was able to exploit successfully the fear of the spread of Communist revolution. When Stalin finally reversed Comintern policy in 1933, the German Left had been devastated and the National Socialists under Adolf Hitler were in power.

Women and the Family in the New Soviet State

The building of the new Soviet state exacted high costs from the Russian people, in particular from women. In 1926 a Bolshevik woman, Alek-sandra Kollontai (1872–1952), wrote *The Autobiography of a Sexually Emancipated Communist Woman.* The work encapsulates some of the problems that women experienced in the new Soviet state. Kollontai championed woman's right to economic independence and control of her own income, freedom for women in marriage, and state-sponsored communal child-rearing. A member of Lenin's first revolutionary council, the first Soviet commissar of social welfare, the first woman ambassador in the world from any country, Kollontai had a full and rich life worthy of attention, even in an age of such revolutionary change. Kollontai was neither a woman of the working class nor a peasant. As an educated member of the upper middle class, she enjoyed privileges and opportunities before and after the revolution unknown to the great majority of Russian women. Yet she appeared to be a symbol of the new status of women in Soviet society.

Russian women had been active in the revolution from the beginning. Lenin and the Bolshevik leaders were committed to the liberation of women, who, like workers, were considered to be oppressed under capitalism. Lenin denounced housework as "barbarously unproductive, petty, nerve-wracking, stultifying, and crushing drudgery." The "new woman," as Kollontai identified her, was to enjoy full and equal rights before the law, in the workplace, and in education. In its early days the Soviet state pledged to protect the rights of mothers without narrowing women's opportunities or restricting women's role to the family. After the October revolution of 1917, the Bolsheviks passed a new law establishing equality for women within marriage. In 1920 abortion was legalized. New legislation established the right to divorce and removed the stigma from illegitimacy. Communes, calling themselves "laboratories of revolution," experimented with sexual equality. Russian women were enfranchised in 1917, the first women in the major countries to win this right in national elections. The Russian revolution went further than any revolution in history toward the legal liberation of women within such a short span of time.

These advances, as utopian as they appeared to women in the West, did not deal with the problems faced by the majority of Russian

The Soviets waged a vigorous campaign against illiteracy. This picture shows Muslim women of the northern Caucasus region learning to read and write. The poster in the background is written in Russian and Arabic script.

financial responsibility toward their offspring in terminating a marriage. Even as legislation was being passed in the early days of the new Soviet state, women were losing ground in the struggle for equal rights and independent economic survival.

Women's membership in the Communist party doubled from 8 percent in 1925 to 16 percent in 1932. But women were never among the top leadership. The high demand for labor enabled women to move into a variety of new occupations and some women reached supervisory positions. Yet child-care facilities in the factories were poor or nonexistent. Shortages in materials and bottlenecks in production meant that resources were seldom redirected to care for the children of working mothers.

By the early 1930s, reforms affecting women were in trouble due in large part to a plummeting birthrate. This decline created special worries for Soviet planners, who forecast doom if the rate was not reversed. In 1936, women's right to choose to end a first pregnancy was revoked. In the following decade all abortions were made illegal. Sexuality was a state concern and homosexuality was declared a criminal offense. The family was glorified as the mainstay of the socialist order and the independence of women was challenged as a threat to Soviet productivity. While motherhood was idealized, the Stalinist drive to industrialize could not dispense with full-time women workers. The "new woman" of the revolutionary period gave way to the post-1936 woman, who was depicted as the perfect mother who equaled her husband's productivity in the workplace, ran the household, and raised a large family.

Stalin emphasized motherhood as a patriotic duty not least because of his concern to maintain a large industrial work force for future productivity. Large families were encouraged and rewarded. Women who had seven children were decorated with the Order of Maternal Glory. Those with ten or more children received the highest accolade, the designation of Mother Heroine. This emphasis on woman's reproductive role in the family paralleled recognition of woman's role in the workplace as a productive worker. Stalin left no doubt about the political significance of the family:

women. Bolshevik legislation did little to address the special economic hardships of peasant and factory women. Paid maternity leaves and nursing breaks were required by law. But these guarantees became a source of discrimination against women workers who, under the NEP, were the last hired and first fired by employers trying to limit expenses. Antagonisms festered among male co-workers because women were more costly to employ. Divorce legislation was hardly a blessing for women with children, since men incurred no

The State cannot exist without the family. Marriage is a positive value for the Socialist Soviet State only if the partners see in it a lifelong union. So-called free love is a bourgeois invention and has nothing in common with the principles of conduct of a Soviet citizen. Moreover, marriage receives its full value for the State only if there are children, and the husband and wife experience the highest happiness of parenthood.

Stalin's assessment differed widely from Kollontai's pioneering feminist view. For both Stalin and Kollontai, woman's role was centrally important to the smooth functioning of the new Soviet state. Instead of the freedom that Kollontai foresaw, however, women's double burden in the home and workplace became heavier during Stalin's reign. Most Russian women held full-time jobs in the factories or on the farms. They also worked what they called a "second shift" in running a household and taking care of children. In the West, the growth of a consumer economy lightened women's labor in the home to some extent. In Russia procuring the simplest necessities was woman's work that required waiting in long lines for hours. Lack of indoor plumbing meant that women spent more hours hauling water for their families at the end of a working day. In such ways, rapid industrialization exacted its special price from Soviet women.

The Promise of Fascism

The experiences of the war and postwar conditions were the catalysts for the emergence of the new mass movement of fascism in Europe. The Great War had created a political vacuum caused by the crisis in liberal values. In condemning the war and its costs, new fascist leaders, who tended to start their political careers as social reformers and even socialists, proposed a radical reformation of the status quo.

In the Soviet Union, Bolshevik leaders reassured their people that socialism was the only way of dealing with the weaknesses and inequities of the world capitalist system laid bare in the world war. In its initial condemnations of the capitalist economy and liberal political institutions and values, fascism sounded very like socialism. Fascists employed revolutionary language similar to that of the Left, while manipulating the political symbols of the Right—the nation, the flag, and the army—in radically new ways. Fascism promised to steer a course between the uncertainties and exploitation of a liberal capitalist system and the revolutionary upheaval and expropriation of a socialist system. Fascism was ultranationalist, and the use of force was central to its appeal.

The word *fascism* is derived from the Latin *fasces*, the name for the bundle of rods with ax head carried by the magistrates of the Roman Empire. The *fasces* signified a band of comrades, a brotherhood of those sharing similar beliefs. Fascism was rooted in the mass political movements of the late nineteenth century, which emphasized nationalism, antiliberal values, and a politics of the irrational. The electoral successes of the German variant, National Socialism, or nazism, were just beginning in the late 1920s. In the same period, fascist movements were making their appearance in England, Hungary, Spain, and France. But none was more successful and none demanded more international attention than the fascist experiment in Italy that inspired observers throughout the West to consider emulation.

Mussolini's Italy

Being on the side of the victors in World War I did not alter the fact that Italy was a poor nation. The peace settlement of 1919 had resulted in a sense of disillusionment and betrayal for many Italians, who felt they had not received what they were promised for entering the war. A recently created electoral system based on universal manhood suffrage had produced parliamentary chaos and ministerial instability. The lack of coherent political programs only heightened the general disapproval with government that accompanied the peace negotiations. People were beginning to doubt the parliamentary regime's hold on the future. It was under these circumstances that the Fascist party, led by Benito Mussolini (1883–1945), entered politics in 1920 by attacking the large Socialist and Popular (Catholic) parties.

Named after the Mexican revolutionary Benito Juarez, Mussolini was instructed by his blacksmith father in the tenets of radical socialist politics and he had begun his political career before the war as a Socialist. The young Mussolini earned certification as an elementary-school teacher but did not pursue education as a career. Instead, he left school to engage in Socialist political activities for which he was arrested numerous times and placed under state surveillance. An ardent nationalist, Mussolini volunteered for combat in World War I and was promoted to the rank of corporal. Injured in early 1917 by an exploding shell detonated during firing practice, he returned to Milan to continue his work as editor of *Il Populo d'Italia* (People of Italy), the newspaper he founded in 1914 to promote Italian participation in the war.

Mussolini left the war behind to take up a new cause on the home front: "We, the survivors, we who have returned, demand the right to govern Italy." He yearned to be the leader of a revolution in Italy comparable to that directed by Lenin in Russia. Although his doctrinal allegiance to socialism was beginning to flag, Mussolini recognized, like Lenin, the power of the printed word to stir political passions. Emphasizing nationalist goals and vague measures of socioeconomic transformation, Mussolini identified a new enemy for Italy, bolshevism. The vehemence of his nationalist politics and demands for a bolder foreign policy went beyond the programs of existing political parties. He organized his followers into the Fascist party, a political movement that by utilizing strict party discipline quickly developed its own national network.

Many Fascists were former socialists and war veterans like Mussolini who were disillusioned with postwar government. They dreamed of Italy as a great world power, as it had been in the days of ancient Rome. Their enemies were not only Communists with their international outlook but also the big businesses, which they felt drained Italy's resources and kept its people poor and powerless. Panicky members of the lower middle classes sought security against the economic uncertainties of inflation and were willing to endorse violence to achieve it. Unions were to be feared because they used strikes to further their demands for higher salaries and better working conditions for their members while other social groups languished. Near civil war erupted as Italian Communists and Fascists clashed violently in street battles in the early 1920s. The Fascists succeeded in overthrowing city governments and began entering national politics. In spite of its visibility on the national political scene, the Fascist party was still very much a minority party when Mussolini refused to serve as a junior minister in the new government in 1922.

His refusal to serve as representative of a minority party reflected Mussolini's belief that the Fascists must be in charge. On 28 October 1922, the Fascists undertook their famous March on Rome, which followed similar Fascist takeovers in Milan and Bologna. Mussolini's followers now occupied the capital. This event marked the beginning of the end of parliamentary government in Italy and the gradual emergence of Fascist dictatorship and institutionalized violence. Rising unemployment and severe inflation contributed to the politically deteriorating situation that helped bring Mussolini to power.

Destruction and violence, not the ballot box, became fascism's most successful tools for securing political power. *Squadristi*, armed bands of Fascist thugs, attacked their political enemies, both Catholic and Socialist, destroyed private property, dismantled the printing presses of adversary groups, and generally terrorized both rural and urban populations. By the end of 1922, Fascists could claim a following of 300,000 members, who endorsed the new politics of intimidation.

The Fascists achieved their first majority in the Chamber of Deputies by using violent tactics of intimidation to secure votes. One outspoken Socialist critic of Fascist violence, Giacomo Matteotti (1885–1924), was murdered by Mussolini's subordinates. The deed threatened the survival of Mussolini's government as 150 Socialist, Liberal, and Popular party deputies resigned in protest. Mussolini chose this moment to consolidate his position by arresting and silencing his enemies to preserve order. Within two years, Fascists were firmly in control, monopolizing politics, suppressing a free press, creating a secret police force, and transforming social and economic policies. Mussolini destroyed political parties and fashioned Italy into a one-party dictatorship.

In 1925 the Fascist party entered into an

Benito Mussolini (center foreground) at the time of the March on Rome. Il Duce himself did not participate in the march, but after his Fascist followers had taken over the capital, King Victor Emmanuel asked Mussolini to form a government.

agreement with Italian industrialists that gave industry a position of privilege protected by the state in return for its support. Mussolini presented this partnership as the end to class conflict, but in fact it ensured the dominance of capital and the control of labor and professional groups. A corrupt bureaucracy filled with Mussolini's cronies and run on bribes took shape to organize the new relationship between big business and the state. With the Fascist party, Mussolini spoke of creating a "corporativist" economy, that is, one that eliminated the free market, and through planning and management, reallocated economic activities for maximum efficiency. Corporativism was used for rhetorical effect, while big business controlled economic organization on its own terms. Workers gained little from corporativist rhetoric and in fact lost representation with the weakening of trade unions.

Fascist images plastered billboards all over Italy. Radio and film announced the arrival of a new age. *Il Duce,* or the leader, as Mussolini preferred to be addressed, established a ministry for propaganda that devised such memorable slogans as "Mussolini is always right." Mussolini cultivated his own cult of leadership, just as Stalin would do at the end of the decade in the Soviet Union. Mussolini, himself an atheist, recognized the importance of the Catholic church in securing his regime. In 1870 when Italy had been unified, the pope was deprived of his territories in Rome. This event, which quickly became known as the "Roman Question," proved to be the source of ongoing problems for Italian governments. In February 1929 Mussolini settled matters with Pope Pius XI in the Lateran Treaty and the accompanying Concordat, which granted to the pope sovereignty over the territory around St. Peter's Basilica and the Vatican. The treaty also protected the role of the Catholic church in education and guaranteed that Italian marriage laws would conform to Catholic dogma. Tensions resurfaced in the 1930s, when the pope condemned the "pagan intentions" of fascism. For the most part, however, the Lateran Treaty laid to rest an important problem plaguing Italian rule.

By 1929 Mussolini was at the height of his popularity and his power. Apparent political harmony had been achieved by ruthlessly crushing fascism's opponents. The agreement with the pope, which restored harmony with the Church, was matched by a new sense of order and accomplishment in Italian society and the economy. The Duce succeeded in presenting to the world the image of a dynamic and progressive Italy where, as tourists claimed, "the trains ran on time." When asked to define his movement, Mussolini had, with his characteristic egomania, responded, "I am fascism." The importance of the dictator to the movement gave a measure of accuracy to his definition. But as Europe and the world were to learn, fascism did not stop in Italy and did not depend on the person of Benito Mussolini for its success. Fascism appealed to frightened middle classes outside of Italy who were losing their footing in a world they no longer comprehended.

The Failure of Democracy in Germany

In September 1918 the leaders of the German High Command, Erich Ludendorff (1865–1937) and Paul von Hindenburg (1847–1934), knowing that the German war effort was a lost cause, decided that a constitutional monarchy must be introduced in Germany. Their intention was to save the throne of Emperor Wilhelm II and to save themselves by handing the responsibility for the government over to the socialist and liberal politicians who were dedicated to ending the war, getting German soldiers home, and demobilizing the army. Popular uprisings in the navy and in urban areas followed, forcing the emperor to abdicate. In spring 1919, a national assembly meeting in the city of Weimar produced Germany's first democratic constitution. The Weimar Republic was

born. The leaders of the new republic bore the responsibility for accepting the Treaty of Versailles.

The Weimar Republic was in trouble from the start. Germany's first democracy came into existence saddled with a harsh peace. Many Germans identified the new government with defeat and humiliation. A false belief that the Germany military had never really been defeated but rather had been betrayed by the new government came to be

In this satirical painting, The Pillars of Society, *George Grosz caricatures the society of the Weimar Republic as composed of corrupt judges, petty bourgeoisie, militarists, and hypocritical pacifists.*

known as the legend of "the stab in the back." Rumors spread that Communists and Jews associated with the new government invited the Allies to stab the German army in the back with the armistice. The harsh terms of the Treaty of Versailles compounded the negative image of the Weimar Republic. Lost territory and people, destroyed markets, a vastly reduced military force, and reparations payments were the legacy of the new democratic experiment.

Born of political revolution and social upheaval, the Weimar Republic faced the challenges of establishing its legitimacy and main-

The runaway inflation of the 1920s is dramatized by this photo of a German housewife who is lighting the cooking fire with millions of marks. She declared that it was cheaper to use the worthless currency for kindling than to buy wood with it.

taining social peace. Yet it lacked a democratic tradition on which to draw. The German nation before the war had been associated with military power, and the very birth of the unified German nation had resulted from military victories over Austria and France. Traditional ruling groups—the Prussian military, and agrarian and bureaucratic elites—preserved their power and privileges even as democratic institutions struggled for existence. Political as well as economic power continued to be concentrated in the hands of the privileged elite that had ruled the Second Reich.

Repeated economic, political, and diplomatic crises of the 1920s buffeted Germany's internal stability. Most Germans considered reparations to be an unfair burden, so onerous that payment should be evaded and resisted in every way possible. The German government did not actually promote inflation in order to avoid paying reparations but it did do so to avoid a postwar recession, revive industrial production, and maintain high employment. But the moderate inflation that stimulated the economy spun out of control into destructive hyperinflation. Weimar bore a burden of blame for that disaster, too.

The fiscal problems of Weimar obscure the fact that, in the postwar period, Germany experienced real economic growth. German industry advanced, productivity was high, and German workers flexed their union muscles to secure better wages. Weimar committed itself to large expenditures for social welfare programs, including unemployment insurance. By 1930 social welfare was responsible for 40 percent of all public expenditures, compared to 19 percent before the war. All these changes, apparently fostering the well-being of the German people, aggravated the fears of German big businessmen, who resented the trade unions and the perceived trend toward socialism. The lower middle classes felt cheated and economically threatened by inflation. They were a politically volatile group, susceptible to the anti-democratic appeals of some of Weimar's critics.

In the years from 1924 to 1929, after the inflation ended and before the Depression began, Germany prospered. But the real economic growth of this period was not without problems. Wages outpaced productivity. Germans spent and consumed rather than saved and invested. Consumer expectations increased after the deprivation of

During the years of the Weimar Republic, thousands of middle-class people were ruined by inflation and the continuing depression. The humiliating experience of standing in line for bread made such people susceptible to the message of Adolf Hitler, who promised a return to prosperity.

the war. Inflation increased the emphasis on spending, since people were not sure how much money would be worth from day to day. Haunting memories of inflation and hyperinflation also discouraged Germans from investing. Huge American investments often ignored industry and were used instead for civic improvements, such as public swimming pools and concert halls.

Constitutional provisions that allowed for the constant wrangling of a multiparty system divided the Weimar Republic. Political parties formed and destroyed cabinet after cabinet while Germany's real problems remained—the humiliating peace treaty, reparations, and a weak economic structure. As a result, growing numbers of Germans expressed disgust with parliamentary

democracy. The Weimar Republic's claim to legitimacy was staked on its ability to deliver economic prosperity and progressive socialist policies, including unemployment insurance. The so-called golden years of the late 1920s silenced antidemocratic complaints but only temporarily.

The Depression dealt a staggering blow to the Weimar Republic in 1929 as American loans were withdrawn and German unemployment skyrocketed. The government could not fulfill its commitment to supporting the unemployed in hard times. By 1930 the antagonisms among the parties was so great that the parliament was no longer effective in ruling Germany. As chancellor from 1930 to 1932, Centrist leader Heinrich Brüning (1885–1970) attempted to break this impasse by overriding the Weimar constitution. This move opened the door to enemies of the republic, and Brüning was forced to resign.

Everyone with a grievance now blamed the Weimar Republic. German industrialists denounced the high costs of social welfare and reparations. Other Germans saw their savings and their income dwindling, first in the inflation and then in the Depression. Germany's first experiment in democracy was collapsing. The Depression and the harsh Versailles Treaty gave ammunition to Weimar's enemies. One man in particular knew how to exploit Weimar's weaknesses for his own political ends. That man was Adolf Hitler.

The Beginnings of the Nazi Movement

Just as Stalin was born a Georgian and not an ethnic Russian, Adolf Hitler (1889–1945) was born an Austrian outside the German fatherland he came to rule. Hitler, the son of a customs agent who worked on the Austrian side of the border with Germany, came from a middle-class family with social pretensions. Aimlessness and failure marked Hitler's early life. Denied admission to architecture school, he took odd jobs to survive. Hitler was truly grateful for the outbreak of war in 1914 that put an end to his self-described sleep-walking. He volunteered immediately for service in the German army. Wounded and gassed at the front, he was twice awarded the Iron Cross for bravery in action and rose, like Benito Mussolini in the Italian army, to the lowest rank for a noncommissioned officer, that of corporal.

Hitler's war experiences were not unique. He later described what he had learned from war in terms of the solidarity of struggle against a common enemy and the purity of heroism. The army provided him with a sense of security and direction. What he learned from the peace that followed was an equally powerful lesson and determined his commitment to a career in politics. Hitler profoundly believed in the stab-in-the-back legend: Germany had not lost the war, it had been defeated from within. The army had been on the verge of victory when a revolution took place, led, Hitler believed, by Jews and Communists, people

This photographer of Hitler miming to a recording of one of his speeches was one of a series he commissioned to help improve his hold over an audience. His remarkable oratorical skills contributed greatly to his success with a disillusioned public.

he called "the November Criminals." It was they who asked the Allies for an armistice and signed the humiliating Treaty of Versailles. It was they who stabbed the German army in the back, Hitler raged. The Weimar Republic that resulted from their revolution continued to betray the German people by taxing wages to pay reparations. His highly distorted and false view of the origins of the Republic and its policies was the core of Hitler's propaganda against Weimar. It was the basis for his demand that the "Weimar System" must be abolished and replaced by a Nazi regime.

Hitler had become the chief of the National Socialist German Workers' party and surrounded himself with men who shared his hatred of Weimar and his political programs—Joseph Goebbels (1897–1945), a master of mass propaganda; Hermann Göring (1893–1946), an air force squadron commander during World War I; and Ernst Röhm (1887–1934), who formed the private army known as the SA (Sturmabteilung), which was to become famous as Hitler's Brown Shirts.

Prominent among Hitler's followers were army veterans who felt frustration over German military defeat and the postwar economic hardships of inflation and unemployment. Soldiers brought their battlefront experiences home with them. Some committed themselves to idealism and peace, as seen in the Bauhaus community of architects and artists. The attitude of other "front fighters" was shaped by the violence, brutality, and slaughter of the "steel bath." Some of these young ex-servicemen did not readjust to the civilian life of Weimar and were eager to hear Hitler's promises.

Hitler believed that Weimar was ready to be overthrown in 1923, as Germany was buffeted by French occupation and hyperinflation. Hitler's willingness to use violence for political ends surfaced when he and General Erich Ludendorff, German Quartermaster General in World War I, carried out the Beer Hall Putsch in Munich in 1923. Hitler's plan was to seize control of local government in Munich, take over the leadership of all right-wing nationalist, racist organizations in Bavaria, march on Berlin, and do away with the Weimar Republic. Hitler tried to signal the beginning of "the national revolution" by firing a revolver into the ceiling of a Munich beer hall. He and his small band of followers then marched toward the center of the city but were stopped by the rifles of the army.

For his activities Hitler served nine months of a 5-year sentence. In jail he began writing the first volume of his autobiography, *Mein Kampf* (My Struggle). In the turgid work, he condemned the decadence of Western society and singled out for special contempt Jews, Bolsheviks, and middle-class liberals, who he believed had betrayed Germany and were preventing it from becoming strong again.

Hitler had failed in his attempt to seize power at about the time that Mussolini's Fascists were succeeding in Italy. Critical in sustaining the Weimar Republic after 1923 was the influx of American money that reduced the burden of reparations and helped stabilize the economy. Hitler learned one important lesson from his failed attempt. He learned that he could succeed against the German republic only from within, by coming to power legally. By 1928 he had a small party of about 100,000 Nazis. Hitler had modified his anticapitalist message, appealed to the discontented small farmers, and tailored his nationalist sentiments to a frightened middle class.

The commitment to electoral gains guided the organization of the Nazi party in its bid for parliamentary power in the late 1920s. Although the Nazi party never controlled a majority of parliamentary seats, it had become the single largest party by 1932. It appeared to be the only mass party that could form a government that would engineer a way out of the crisis of the Great Depression. The great irony of fascism in Germany was that as an antidemocratic and anti-parliamentary movement, it successfully manipulated democracy and parliamentary politics for its own ends to ensure the destruction of the Weimar Republic between 1930 and 1933.

Cultural Experimentation and Economic Collapse

The events of the 1920s proved that Western civilization is not a concept defined by geography alone. As the center of power shifted to the new giant across the Atlantic, the concept of Western civilization expanded to take into account the presence of the United States. It became impossible in the 1920s to talk about civilization in the West without including the United States in the discussion. Observers at that time and since have feared the consequences of American dominance of European values. The benefits and the costs of U.S. dominance may be debatable, but there can be no disputing that after World War I the United States emerged as an important force in Western affairs.

In the cultural realm, European artists, musicians, and writers made the 1920s an exceptionally rich period of creativity and experimentation. Some American writers and artists moved to Europe, and especially to Paris, in a self-conscious search for the unconventional. Western men and women formed artistic communities that became international in composition and outlook. Economic collapse in 1929 put a halt to one of the richest periods in the cultural history of the West, a period that determined the future of art in the twentieth century.

Cultural Experimentation in the 1920s

The Great War brought in its wake a sense of disillusion and loss. The blood of war baptized those who survived in the 1920s as the "Lost Generation." The American-born poets Thomas Stearns (T. S.) Eliot (1888–1965) and Ezra Pound (1885–1972) lamented the waste and destruction and barbarism that afflicted civilization in the West. Yet these years have also been characterized as the "Roaring Twenties," a creative and vital time in the West. The postwar years were called the "Golden Twenties," especially in a recovering Germany where cultural life was marked by innovation. This was the Jazz Age, everywhere characterized by a style that characterized more than the music of Duke Ellington and Scott Joplin.

The cultural experimentation of the 1920s had its roots in the period before the war, when an avant-garde of artists and intellectuals took shape. In many ways the 1920s were a continuation of prewar experiments. Freud's earlier discovery of the unconscious found a ready audience after the war was over, just as Einstein's discoveries of relativity in physics found wider applications in the 1920s. Many artists active before the war continued to dominate the postwar scene: the Spanish painter Pablo Picasso (1881–1973), the Russian composer Igor Stravinsky (1882–1971), and the French painter Henri Matisse (1869–1954) are a few notable examples. The war itself gave a new direction to cultural development and a new orientation to artistic vision.

The Bauhaus movement founded by Walter Gropius in Germany stressed the social responsibility of art and an awareness of a new age. As Gropius explained, "This is more than just a lost war. A world has come to an end. We must seek a radical solution to our problems." One of the radi-

cal solutions found while the war still raged was the movement known as dada. Dada, a nonsensical term deliberately resembling childlike babble, was devised by an international group of artists in Zurich, Switzerland, in 1916 to indicate an artists' rebellion against art. Rejecting the horrors of war, dadaists set out to embody the chaos of the world around them in their art. The Romanian poet Tristan Tzara (1896–1963) joined forces with the German painter George Grosz (1893–1959), the French artists Marcel Duchamp (1887–1968) and Francis Picabia (1879–1953), the American expatriate Man Ray (1890–1976), and a host of other European artists to produce creations that appeared to be meaningless and random. Duchamp's *Mona Lisa* (1919) was a canvas of the celebrated subject sporting a mustache and goatee.

Dada was succeeded in 1924 by another avant-garde movement, surrealism, which was founded by the French dadaist André Breton (1896–1966). Like dada, surrealism emphasized the irrational roots of artistic expression. Heavily influenced by Freudian thought, surrealists concentrated on the content of dreams and unconscious desires. "Automatic writing" allowed surrealists to produce literary works in an unreflected trance. Jean Cocteau (1889–1963) wrote and directed surrealistic films in France, and Salvador Dali (1904–89) of Spain and Max Ernst (1891–1976) of Germany created canvases filled with fantastical images of melting watches and eerie moonscapes. Committed to improving humanity through a revolutionary artistic perception that would liberate and integrate the unconscious, surrealists in France briefly and disastrously allied with the Communist party in the hopes of putting their artistic revolution into political action.

Attempts to combine art and politics in dramatically new ways were most far-reaching in the Soviet Union. The Proletkult movement emerged from the Russian revolution committed to the creation of a new cultural order built on a proletarian class spirit. With the utopian vision that every worker was a poet, advocates devised community programs to open up the arts to workers. The movement clashed with Leninist policies and its original mass support dwindled. By the late

1920s state-sponsored utopian programs re-placed the Proletkult's grass-roots vision of a new proletarian art.

Weimar Germany became synonymous with cultural experimentation. Bauhaus artists, archi-tects, and craftworkers united their creative vision with technological advances to produce a new functional art. German theater burgeoned. The most famous playwright of the period, Bertolt Brecht (1898–1956), connected politics and art in plays infused with a Marxist vision of exploitation and alienation. *Threepenny Opera* (1928) satirized middle-class society run by a mixture of gangsters and officials. In his critique of capitalism, Brecht used hyperbole in breaking down the distance between the audience and what was happening on the stage.

The Irish novelist James Joyce (1882–1941) revolutionized the presentation of consciousness in novels like *Ulysses* (1921) through new literary techniques and experiments with language. Joyce revealed the inner life of his characters through a stream-of-consciousness technique that gave ver-bal expression to the most random thoughts. The result was a complex and intricately structured novel that greatly influenced other twentieth-cen-tury writers. Feminism also transformed art in new ways in the 1920s. Virginia Woolf (1882–1941), one of the great literary figures of the twen-tieth century, used stream of consciousness to unravel the daily life experiences of her characters in such novels as *Jacob's Room* (1922), *Mrs. Dalloway* (1925), *Orlando* (1928), and *The Waves* (1931). In her brilliant essay, *A Room of One's Own* (1929), Woolf presents an assessment of women's intellectual activity and independence, while crit-icizing the cultural dominance of male values.

Perhaps the greatest cultural innovation of the period was the emergence of film as a mass medium. Throughout Europe but especially in Weimar Germany, the motion picture became a serious art form whose popularity as entertain-ment grew with the availability of leisure time. Expressionism, the distorted representation of reality to tap inner feelings, dominated the early German cinema in such masterpieces as *The Cab-inet of Dr. Caligari*. Spanish and French surrealists experimented with the visual techniques of film to produce disorienting images of experience. The English film actor Charlie Chaplin (1889–1977) became an internationally recognized figure in his baggy trousers, derby hat, and mustache.

A new morality pervaded cultural changes. Women's sexuality was widely discussed and dis-played in the media. In her image as a cabaret singer wearing shorts and silk stockings, Marlene Dietrich (b. 1901), star of the film *The Blue Angel* (1930), became a sex symbol of an age. In *The Blue Angel*, the woman, Lola Lola, transcends gender roles and, in her pursuit of sexual pleasure, behaves as a man. Women wore shorter skirts and appeared to lead freer lives. Young, single women known as "flappers" became identified through-out the Western world with a new freedom that was condemned by its critics as promiscuity and abandonment of traditional morality. The birth-rate dropped throughout Europe in the 1920s, due to the decline in the active male population because of war in countries like France, and to the spread of information about control of family size and birth-control technology. By the late 1920s, a rhetoric of decadence and the disintegration of

Marlene Dietrich in The Blue Angel

values emerged among critics who saw in the cultural experimentation of the age a rejection of traditional values.

Those who felt that art should buttress traditional values rather than point the way to a new world intensified their attacks in the late 1920s. In Germany, the Militant League for German Culture was founded in 1929 by Nazi disciple Alfred Rosenberg (1893–1946). Hitler himself spoke of the need for an eternal German art to replace the degenerate "modern art" of Germany's enemies. Artists and intellectuals who refused to toe the line were regarded as enemies of the state and persecuted. In the Soviet Union in the 1930s the Communist party under Stalin's tutelage directed Soviet artists to produce "socialist realism" in service to the regime. Economic collapse in 1929 exacerbated fears that Western society was in a crisis that changing moral values and innovative artistic vision may have helped to create.

The Great Depression

In the history of the Western world the year 1929 has assumed mythic proportions. During one week in October of that year, the stock market in the United States collapsed. This crash set off the Great Depression in an international economic system already plagued with structural problems. It also marked the beginning of a long period of worldwide economic stagnation and depression. The Great Depression did not begin at the same time throughout the world nor did it affect all countries in the same way. Rural areas isolated from market economies had not experienced the prosperity of the 1924–29 period, and they managed to ride out the Depression with relatively little change in living standards. The Soviet Union had been excluded from the international system during the 1920s. After 1929 it remained isolated because of its single-minded dedication to industrialization through a controlled economy. It too escaped the effects of the Great Depression.

A confluence of factors made Europe and the rest of the world vulnerable to reversals in the American economy. Heavy borrowing and reliance on American investment throughout the 1920s contributed to the inherent instability of European economies. Even Great Britain, itself a creditor, relied on short-term loans; "borrowing short and lending long" proved to be disastrous when loans were recalled. Excessive lending and leniency were fatal mistakes of creditor nations, especially the United States. When in the summer of 1929 American investors turned off the tap of the flow of capital to search for higher profits at home, a precarious situation began to get worse.

A depression is a severe downturn marked by sharp declines in income and production, as buying and selling slow down to a crawl. Depressions were not new in the business cycles of modern economies, but what happened in October 1929 was more serious in its extent and duration than any depression before or since. The bottom was not reached until three years after it began. In 1932 one in four American workers was without a job. One in three banks had closed its doors. People lost their homes, unable to pay their mortgages; farmers lost their land, unable to earn enough to survive. The great prosperity of the 1920s had vanished like a vapor. Full employment and high consumption were now just memories as people everywhere tightened their belts.

The plight of the United States rippled through world markets. Americans stopped buying foreign goods. The Smoot-Hawley Tariff Act, passed by the U.S. Congress in 1930, created an impenetrable tariff fortress against agricultural and manufactured imports and hampered foreign producers. The major trading nations of the world, including Great Britain, enacted similar protectionist measures. American investment abroad dried up, as the lifelines of American capital to Europe were reeled in or cut.

European nations tried to staunch the outward flow of capital and gold by restricting the transfer of capital abroad. Large amounts of foreign-owned gold ($6.6 billion from 1931 to 1938) nevertheless were deposited in American banks. In 1931 President Herbert Hoover supported a moratorium on the payment of reparations and war debts. The moratorium, combined with the pooling of gold in the United States, led to a run on the British pound sterling in 1931 and the collapse of Great Britain as one of the world's great financial centers. Britain was forced to repudiate both the gold standard and its preeminent position as a world financial power.

The gold standard disappeared from the international economy, never to return. So too did reparations payments and war debts when the major nations of Europe met without the United States at a special conference held in Lausanne, Switzerland, in 1932. Something else died as the 1920s ended: confidence in a self-adjusting economy, an "invisible hand" by which the business cycle would be righted, was attacked at its liberal foundations. In 1932–33, the Depression, showing no signs of disappearing, reached its nadir and became a global phenomenon. Economic hardship transformed political realities. The Labour cabinet in Great Britain was forced to resign, and a new national government composed of Conservative, Liberal, and Labour leaders was formed to deal with the world economic emergency. Republican government was torn by bitter divisions in France. In the United States the Republican party, which had been in power since 1920, was defeated in 1932. Franklin D. Roosevelt, a Democrat, was elected president in a landslide victory and with a mandate to transform the American economy. But in no place did the Great Depression have more dramatic political consequences than in Germany, where democratic institutions were pulled down in favor of fascist dictatorship.

The period from 1921 to 1932 is one of the most difficult decades in the history of the West to characterize. Many today look on these years as a period of holding one's breath, part of an interlude between two world wars, a time-out in the thirty years of war (1914-45) in the first half of the twentieth century. It is undoubtedly true that the problems that brought about the war in 1914 were still in place throughout the 1920s. Nationalist feelings had intensified, nationalist conflicts had proliferated. Geopolitical grievances were worse than ever as new borders delineated new animosities, especially in central and eastern Europe.

Yet the 1920s was also a time of great idealism and greater hope that the horrors of war might teach a lasting commitment to peace and that technology could be used to create a better and brighter future. Economic productivity in the late 1920s created a new and deceptively secure prosperity.

Those who probed beneath the surface could find the signs that existing political and economic structures were inadequate to deal with new problems of inflation, depression, and economic collapse. Old problems were demanding new solutions—often violent ones. Empty statements about commitments to peace were matched by secret plans for rearmament. Fascism proposed a third way, not liberalism's way and not communism's way, to address the challenges of power and stability in the modern state. By 1932 the world system was in shambles, with Western economies at the depth of depression and Western political solutions challenged or defeated.

In the first third of the twentieth century, Western men and women grew accustomed to applying the word "great" to disasters. "Great," of course, was used to mean "worst," as in the Great War, the Great Crash, and the Great Depression. But among those who lived through these "great" events, the fear gradually grew that the worst had not yet been experienced. It lay ahead.

Suggestions for Further Reading

Mapping International Politics in 1920s Europe

Marshall M. Lee and Wolfgang Michalka, *German Foreign Policy, 1917–1933: Continuity or Break?* (Leamington Spa, England: Berg, 1987). A solid and synthetic treatment of Weimar diplomacy that takes into account the historiographical debates over revisionism and expansion.

Melvyn P. Leffler, *The Elusive Quest: America's Pursuit of European Stability and French Security, 1919–1933* (Chapel Hill, NC: University of North Carolina Press, 1979). Examines the economic and financial imperatives guiding U.S. foreign policy after World War I and identifies a particular Republican party approach labeled "economic diplomacy." Special attention is paid to European stabilization, French security, and Germany's rehabilitation.

Joseph Rothschild, *East Central Europe Between the Two World Wars* (Seattle: University of Washington Press, 1983). A balanced survey of interwar developments in Poland, Czechoslovakia, Hungary, Yugoslavia, Romania,

Bulgaria, Albania, and the Baltic states, highlighting internal weaknesses and external vulnerabilities. A concluding chapter covers cultural contributions.

Economic Nationalism in the 1920s

Derek H. Aldcroft, *From Versailles to Wall Street, 1919–1929* (Berkeley, CA: University of California Press, 1977). Traces the recovery of the international economy and the systemic forces of its disintegration in the 1920s, with special attention to such areas as war debts, reparations, the gold standard, the agricultural sector, and patterns of international lending.

William R. Keylor, *The Twentieth-Century World: An International History* (New York: Oxford University Press, 1984). Chapter 3 of this work provides a fine and challenging synthesis of recent work on economy and security in the Western world in the 1920s.

Stephen A. Schuker, *The End of French Predominance in Europe: The Financial Crisis of 1924 and the Adoption of the Dawes Plan* (Chapel Hill, NC: University of North Carolina Press, 1976). Locates the decline of France as a great power in the financial crisis of 1924 and the diplomacy of reparations and examines the domestic bases for French powerlessness.

The Soviet Union's Separate Path

Stephen F. Cohen, *Bukharin and the Bolshevik Revolution: A Political Biography, 1888–1938* (Oxford: Oxford University Press, 1980). This milestone work is a general history of the period as well as a political and intellectual biography of Bukharin, "the last Bolshevik," who supported an evolutionary road to modernization and socialism and whose policies were an alternative to Stalinism.

Sheila Fitzpatrick, *The Russian Revolution, 1917–1932* (Oxford: Oxford University Press, 1985). Arguing from the premise that the revolutionary upheaval did not end with the Bolshevik seizure of power in November 1917, Fitzpatrick interprets the developments of the 1920s and early 1930s, including the NEP and the first Five-Year Plan, as stages in a single revolutionary process.

Hiroaki Kuromiya, *Stalin's Industrial Revolution, Politics and Workers, 1928–1932* (Cambridge: Cambridge University Press, 1988). Asks the important question of how Soviet leaders mobilized resources for massive industrialization in the first Five-Year Plan through a political rhetoric of class war and shows how workers' resistance and support enabled the Stalinist regime to survive.

Robert C. Tucker, *Stalin as Revolutionary, 1879–1929: A Study in History and Personality* (New York: Norton, 1973). Traces Stalin's development from his Georgian childhood to his fiftieth year, when he established himself as the new hero of the Soviet state. Tucker uses Freudian terms of analysis in considering Stalin's hero-identification with Lenin.

The Promise of Fascism

Volker R. Berghahn, *Modern Germany: Society, Economy and Politics in the Twentieth Century* (Cambridge: Cambridge University Press, 1987). Considers the particular challenges of rapid industrialization faced by Germany and how they interacted with social tensions and political conflict.

Alan Cassels, *Fascism* (Arlington Heights, IL: AHM Publishing Corporation, 1975). A synthetic overview of fascism as a European movement, with special attention to the "prototypes" of Mussolini's Italy and Nazi Germany.

Eberhard Kolb, *The Weimar Republic*, translated from the German by P. S. Falla (London: Unwin Hyman, 1988). An introduction to the history of Germany's first republic both as a historic survey and as an examination of the basic problems and trends in research.

Adrian Lyttelton, *The Seizure of Power: Fascism in Italy, 1919–1929* (New York: Scribners, 1973). Addresses the question of why fascism first took root in Italy.

Cultural Experimentation and Economic Collapse

Peter Gay, *Weimar Culture: The Outsider As Insider* (New York: Harper & Row, 1968). Traces Weimar culture to its prewar roots, and relates it to the unstable political universe of Germany from 1919 to 1933.

Lynn Mally, *Culture of the Future: The Proletkult Movement in Revolutionary Russia* (Berkeley: University of California Press, 1990). Demonstrates the centrality of cultural issues to the Russian revolutionary experience by examining the institutional history of the Proletkult movement from its origins just before the Bolshevik revolution of 1917 to its virtual collapse in 1923.

John Willett, *Art and Politics in the Weimar Period: The New Sobriety, 1917–1933* (New York: Pantheon Books, 1978). A beautifully illustrated study, which roots the experimental art, theater, and architecture of the 1920s—cubism, expressionism, symbolism, constructivism, and futurism—in political and economic changes and demonstrates the international connections among European artists.

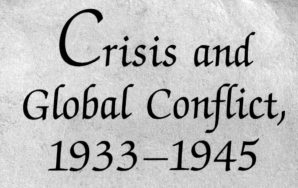

28

Crisis and Global Conflict, 1933–1945

The Screams From Guernica

Rarely does a piece of art scream out. The mural *Guernica* is different. *Listen* to the painting shown here. It is a painting whose images convey sounds, the shrieks of terror, fear, suffering, and death. There is a chaos of noise here that seems at odds with the drab greys, black, and white, the monochromatic colorlessness of the artist's pallet. But no, the lack of color only heightens the noise and allows us to focus on the sound, the screams that come from open mouths of human and beast on the canvas. Death and brutality reverberate throughout the painting. The open mouths of the dead baby's mother, the bull standing behind her, the small bird to the right of the bull, and the wounded horse at the center of the canvas emit fear like projectiles, beak and tongues thrusting forth in pointed daggers.

Pablo Picasso (1881–1973) painted this great mural in May and June 1937 for the Spanish Pavilion of the International Exhibition to be held in Paris. He called it *Guernica* in commemoration of the bombing of the small Basque town in Spain by German and Italian planes at the end of April 1937. The destruction of Guernica was an event that shocked the world and that devastated the Spanish artist, then living in France. Working in collaboration with the insurgent forces of Francisco Franco (1892–1975), German planes dropped bomb after bomb on the ancient city, destroying it in three and a half hours. Their purpose was to cut off the retreat of opposing troops and to terrorize civilians through saturation bombing. Noncombatants were no longer just hapless bystanders but were, in fact, the very targets of indiscriminate killing. Picasso demonstrates this well in the women and children depicted in his painting.

Guernica is a huge canvas, measuring over 11 feet high and 25 feet long. It dwarfs spectators who stand before it, enveloping them in a modern-day apocalypse of contorted bodies. Picasso was well aware of Poussin's *Massacre of the Innocents* (see introduction to chapter 15) and deliberately used the traditional religious symbols of the Madonna and Child and the Pietà as models for his terrifying image of maternity.

We do not look at war directly in the mural but at the terror it creates in this modern-day version of needless slaughter. The lips of the baby, who hangs like a limp rag doll in the arms of its despairing mother on the far left of the canvas, are sealed in the silence of death. The mother finds her counterpoint in the figure of the limping woman in the right foreground, who drags behind her a wounded arm and a swollen knee. Above her a woman, gaping in disbelief and clutching her breasts in anguish, raises a lamp over the scene. On the far right is a fourth woman, trapped in the flames of a burning building. She appears to be exploding upward in terrified petition. On the ground under the horse lies a dead man with his

head and arm severed from his body, clutching a broken sword and flower whose petals wait to be picked in his right hand. The presentation of his head as a piece of statuary fallen from its pedestal reinforces the bloodless horror of his death. His left palm is crisscrossed with the lines of fate or perhaps marked with the toil of heavy labor. Suspended over the scene like a huge eye is a naked lightbulb, symbol of technology, illuminating the timelessness of the theme of the horror of war.

In one of his rare moments of self-interpretation, Picasso explained to a public eager to grasp the mural's symbolism that the horse whose side is opened by a terrible gash is "the people," victimized by incomprehensible cruelty. The bull is an enigmatic figure symbolizing, Picasso tells us, darkness and brutality. The horned beast appears as a powerful and vulnerable witness to this scene of needless destruction.

No matter how you read the individual symbols in the painting, *Guernica* is above all a condemnation of war. In its classic simplicity, Picasso's drama is cartoonlike in stripping images down to their essences of suffering and grief. *Guernica* has been hailed as the most significant painting of the twentieth century. His greatness as an artist, Picasso claimed, derived from his ability to understand his time. In *Guernica* he presents us with a picture of Western civilization that is brutal and horrible. Subsequent events made Germany's actions in the Spanish Civil War seem like a dress rehearsal for atrocities and destruction, when Germany bombed the population centers of Warsaw, Rotterdam, and London. Some years later, during the Second World War, a Nazi official challenged Picasso with a photograph of the great mural, "So it was you who did this." The artist answered, "No, you did."

Political Polarization in the 1930s

The fragile postwar stability of the 1920s crumbled under the pressures of economic depression, ongoing national antagonisms, and insecurity in the international arena. Europe after 1932 was plagued by the consequences of economic collapse, fascist success, and the growing threat of armed conflict. Parliamentary institutions were fighting—and losing—a tug-of-war with authoritarian movements. A fascist regime was in place in Italy. Political and electoral defeats eroded democratic and liberal principles in Germany's Weimar Republic. Dictatorships triumphed in Spain and in much of eastern and central Europe. Liberal parliamentary governments were failing to solve the economic and social challenges of the postwar years.

In the democratic nations of France, Great Britain, and, during the brief period from 1931 to 1936, Spain, parliamentary institutions appeared to be persevering. But even here, polarization and increasing intransigence on both the Left and the Right threatened the future of democratic politics. The particular challenges each nation faced highlighted a general crisis in parliamentary institutions that plagued capitalist nations.

The exclusion of the Soviet Union from Western internationalism both reflected the crisis and exacerbated it. The Bolshevik revolution had served as a political catalyst among workers in the West, attracting them to the possibility of radical solutions. That potential radicalization aggravated class antagonisms where mass politics prevailed and drove political leaders to seek conservative solutions as a means of stabilizing class politics.

Dictatorships in Control

Dictatorships were the most prevalent form of government in interwar Europe. The values of nineteenth-century liberalism that had produced parliamentary institutions, constitutions, and representative government based on elections offered no quick solution to the problems of economic depression and the violence of political extremism. Men who ruled by virtue of charismatic appeal and armed force promised an escape from parliamentary chaos, party wranglings, and the threat of communism. Dictatorships appealed to middle classes who feared loss of their property to socialists and loss of their money to the vagaries of international markets.

The move toward dictatorship appeared relentless in the interwar period. In 1920, of the twenty-eight states in Europe, twenty-six were parliamentary democracies. By the end of 1940, only five democracies remained: the United Kingdom, Ireland, Sweden, Finland, and Switzerland. The rest of Europe was under dictatorial rule. The European dictatorships of the 1930s displayed a variety of forms. On the Left, the "dictatorship of the proletariat" in the Soviet Union was in fact a regime driven by the ruthless brutality of Joseph Stalin toward the goal of building socialism. Other dictatorships were on the Right. Italy and Germany each constructed fascist dictatorships that regarded Soviet communism as their mortal enemy. The Soviet Union, in turn, saw fascism as a serious threat.

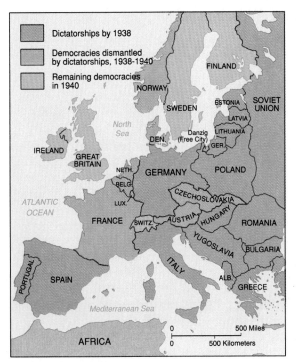

Europe: Types of Government

The fascist regimes in Italy and Germany shared a common ideological orientation and common structures. An imperialist drive characterized Mussolini's involvement in Ethiopia and aspirations in southern Europe; Hitler's desire for living space in eastern Europe was equally expansionist. Italian Fascists and German Nazis were opposed to working-class organizations and were antagonistic to Marxist, socialist, and Communist thought. Both regimes relied on cooperation with conservative nationalists. Both undermined democratic institutions. In neither country did fascism produce a social revolution.

Mussolini and Hitler were charismatic leaders whose political appeal to the masses enabled them to promote war as a goal of the state. Both leaders were ruthless in their use of violence against their opponents. Fascism in both instances stood for a regime that attacked the liberal tradition of individual rights and made a *total* claim on the loyalty of its citizens.

Stalin's Plans and Purges. In 1933 Joseph Stalin announced the second Five-Year Plan, which lasted until 1937. The success of this plan—especially in the areas of heavy industry, machinery, and metal works—reduced considerably the Soviet Union's dependence on foreign imports. The basic physical plant for armaments production was in place by 1937. Advances were also made in consumer industries, but they were well below goals and were considered a lesser priority in relation to defense industries. Resources continued to be shifted away from consumer goods to heavy industrial development. This industrial development, and the collectivization of agriculture, brought growing urbanization. By 1939 one in three people were living in cities, compared to one in six in 1926.

In his commitment to increased production, Stalin introduced into the workplace incentives and differential wage scales at odds with the principles and programs of the original Bolshevik revolution. Stricter discipline was enforced; absenteeism was punished with severe fines or loss of employment. Workers who exceeded their quotas were rewarded and honored. In 1935, a coal miner by the name of Alexei Stakhanov produced 1400 percent more than what was considered normal output. Because of his staggering

Two Soviet bricklayers enjoy a simple lunch of soup and black bread under a poster that exhorts them to accelerate production. By the end of the second Five-Year Plan in 1937, Soviet industrial production was second in the world.

achievement, his name was used to identify a movement. Stakhanovism spread throughout the economy, with the goal of making the USSR the most prosperous country in the world. As a result, work norms were raised for all workers. Some Stakhanovites who exceeded these even higher norms were threatened, beaten, or killed by their fellow workers who resented the relentless push toward greater production.

Amid this rapid industrialization, Stalin inaugurated the Great Purge, actually a series of purges lasting from 1934 through 1938. Those whom Stalin believed to be his opponents—real and imagined, past, present, and future—were labeled "class enemies." The most prominent of them, including leaders of the Bolshevik revolution who had worked with Stalin during the 1920s, appeared in widely publicized "show trials." They were intimidated and tortured into false confessions of crimes against the regime, humiliated by a brutal prosecutor, and condemned to death or imprisonment. Stalin wiped out the Bolshevik old guard, Communist party members whose first loyalty was to the international Communist movement rather than to Stalin himself, and all potential opposition within the Communist party. Probably 300,000 people were put to death, among whom were engineers, managers, technologists, and officers of the army and navy. In addition, 7 million people were placed in labor camps. Stalin now had unquestioned control of the Party and the country.

The purges dealt a severe blow to the command of the army and resulted in a shortage of qualified industrial personnel, slowing industrial growth. As scapegoats, the victims of the purges, however, contributed to the state's ability to sustain economic expansion. These "class enemies" helped Stalin channel discontent away from the Soviet state and helped him maintain absolute power. If the Soviet people did not have eggs, it was because of the evil plotting of these "spies," "traitors," and "wreckers," who smashed eggs and exploited worker discontent. The Great Purge coerced the Soviet people at a time when they were being asked to make great sacrifices in the drive for industrialization. It prevented any possible dissension or opposition within the USSR at a time when the "foreign threat" posed by Nazi Germany was becoming increasingly serious. Stalin was able to maintain loyalty to his personal authority. His personal dictatorship was assured.

The human suffering associated with the dislocation and heavy workloads of rapid, coerced industrialization cannot be measured. Planned growth brought with it a top-heavy and often inefficient bureaucracy, and that bureaucracy ensured that the Soviet Union was the most highly centralized of the European states. In 1939 Stalin's dictatorship could not rest on its laurels. The growing threat of foreign war meant an even greater diversion of resources from consumer goods to war industries, beginning with the third Five-Year Plan in 1938. Stalin was well aware of the Soviet Union's backwardness in preparations for war. He was also aware that time was running out.

Mussolini's Plans for Empire.   In spite of official claims, Fascist Italy had not done well in riding out the Depression. A large rural sector masked the problems of high unemployment by absorbing an urban work force without jobs. Corporatism, a system of economic self-rule by interest groups, was a sham promoted on paper by Benito Mussolini that had little to do with the dominance of the Italian economy by big business. Mussolini was playing a kind of shell game to hide the fact that Italy was ruled increasingly by business cartels that guarded profits at the expense of workers' wages. By lending money to Italian businesses on the verge of bankruptcy, the government acquired a controlling interest in key industries, including steel, shipping, heavy machinery, and electricity.

As fascism failed to initiate effective social programs, Mussolini's popularity plummeted. In the hope of boosting his sagging image, the *Duce* committed Italy to a foreign policy of imperial conquest. Italy had conquered Ottoman-controlled Libya in North Africa in 1911. Now in the 1930s Mussolini targeted Ethiopia for his expansionist aims and ordered Italian troops to invade that east African kingdom in October 1935. Using poison gas and aerial bombing, the Italian army defeated the native troops of Ethiopian emperor Haile Selassie (1930–74). Western democracies, under the pressure of public opinion, cried out against the wanton and unwarranted attack, but Mussolini succeeded in proclaiming Ethiopia an Italian territory. He justified the Ethiopian campaign in terms of Italy's destiny to be a great empire once again with the motto, "Italy, a people without land; Ethiopia, a land without people!"

The invasion of Ethiopia exposed the ineffectiveness of the League of Nations to stop such flagrant violations. Great Britain and France took no action other than to express their disapproval of Italy's conquest. Yet a rift opened up between these two western European nations and Italy. Mussolini had distanced himself from the Nazi state in the first years of the German regime's

The Nazis used pageantry and pomp to telling effect. Masses of banners and thousands of marchers contributed to the mystique of overwhelming unity and power. In this scene Adolf Hitler ascends the steps at a giant party rally.

existence and he was critical of Hitler's plans for rearmament. Now, in light of the disapproval of Britain and France, Mussolini turned to Germany for support. In the summer of 1936, Mussolini supplied military assistance to Francisco Franco and his insurgents in Spain, an act that Hitler seconded. A few months later, in October 1936, Italy aligned itself with Germany in what Mussolini called the "Rome-Berlin Axis." Germany and Italy agreed to offer support in any offensive or defensive war; the agreement, known as the Pact of Steel, in fact bound Italy militarily to Germany. There could be no doubt that this partnership of ideologically similar fascist states threatened the peace of Europe.

Mussolini pursued other imperialist goals within Europe. The small Balkan nation of Albania entered into a series of agreements with Mussolini beginning in the mid-1920s that made it dependent financially and militarily on Italian aid. By 1933 Albanian independence had been undermined by this "friendship" with its stronger neighbor. In order not to be outdone by Hitler, who was at the time dismantling Czechoslovakia, Mussolini invaded Albania in April 1939, overthrew the monarchical regime, and annexed Albania, ending the fiction that Albania was an Italian protectorate.

Hitler and the Third Reich

The state created by Adolf Hitler—what he called the Third Reich—fascinates, perplexes, and shocks those trying to understand how one of the world's most advanced industrial countries turned from a parliamentary democracy into a dictatorship. Hitler's rise to power in the 1930s attracted admirers as well as critics in western Europe and the United States. For many, the supposed efficiency and organization of Hitler's regime outweighed the suspension of civil liberties and the high social costs, the extent of which few understood at the time.

The person of Adolf Hitler mocked the ideal of honorable and reasonable leadership. With his magnetic appeal, Hitler inspired and manipulated the devotion of nearly all who heard him speak. Leni Riefenstahl, a young filmmaker working for Hitler, made a documentary of a National Socialist, or Nazi, party rally at Nuremburg. In scenes of swooning women and cheering men, the film, called *Triumph of the Will*, recorded the dramatic force of Hitler's rhetoric and his ability to move the German people. Hitler's public charisma masked a profoundly troubled and incomplete individual capable of irrational rage and sick hatred of his fellow human beings. His warped views of the world were responsible for the greatest outrages committed in the name of legitimate power. Hitler was charismatic and megalomaniacal, a most dangerous combination in the leader of one of the world's most powerful nations.

Adolf Hitler became chancellor of Germany in January 1933 by legal, constitutional, and democratic means. The Nazi party was supported by farmers, small businessmen, civil servants, and young people. In the elections of 1930 and 1932, the voters made the Nazi party the largest party in the country—although not the majority. A few conservative, nationalist politicians believed that Germany needed a stronger, more stable political system than the one offered by the Weimar Republic. They convinced President Otto von Hindenberg to invite Hitler to form a government. Once Hitler was in office, they expected to be able to control Hitler and use him for their own purposes.

They were mistaken. Hitler claimed that Germany was on the verge of a Communist revolution, and he persuaded Hindenberg and the Reichstag to consent to a series of emergency laws, which the Nazis used to establish themselves firmly in power. These laws outlawed freedom of the press and public meetings, and approved of the use of violence against Hitler's political enemies, particularly the Socialists and the Communists. Within two months after Hitler came to office, Germany was a police state and Hitler was a "legal" dictator who could issue his own laws without having to gain the consent of either the Reichstag or the president. After carrying out this "legal revolution" incapacitating representative institutions and ending civil liberties, the Nazis worked to consolidate their position and their power. They abolished all other political parties, established single-party rule, dissolved trade unions, and put their own people into state governments and the bureaucracy.

Many observers at the time considered the new Nazi state to be a monolithic structure, ruled and coordinated from the center. This was not, however, an accurate observation. Hitler actually issued few directives. Policy was set by an often chaotic jockeying for power among rival Nazi factions. Moreover, Hitler was careful not to alienate the non-Nazi conservative and nationalist pol-

iticians, landowners, industrialists, and military men who supported the Nazi regime and continued to hold positions of power in it until 1936–37. His political alliance with these right-wingers helped give the Third Reich an element of continuity with the past and make it seem less alarming and more normal to both the German people and to foreigners.

Hitler ruled by eliminating his enemies. This might be a quite literal elimination of opposition leaders, especially Communists, who were dragged from their beds in the middle of the night and imprisoned. Or it might mean preventing public discussion and closing public forums by both physical intimidation and decree. Hitler also purged the ranks of his friends and supporters, if he feared they were becoming a challenge to his power. Key to Hitler's success was his ability to marshal the use of violence to achieve his ends. For this purpose, paramilitary forces were the right arm of the Nazi party.

The first of the paramilitary groups was the SA (*Sturmabteilung*), or the storm troopers, under Ernst Röhm (1877–1934), who helped Hitler achieve electoral victories by beating up political opponents on the streets and using other thuglike tactics. The group was organized in 1921 as the gymnast and sports division of the Nazi party, and its membership consisted of a large number of army veterans. Adopting a military appearance for their terrorist operations, SA members were also known as Brown Shirts. By the beginning of 1934, there were 2.5 million members, vastly outnumbering the regular army of 100,000 soldiers.

Heinrich Himmler (1900–1945) headed an elite force of the Nazi party within the SA called the SS (*Schutzstaffel*, or protection squad), a group whose members wore black uniforms and menacing skull-and-crossbone insignia on their caps. Himmler seized control of political policing and now stood as Röhm's chief rival. The SS became indispensable to the success of the Nazi party. As Hitler explained it, "Terror is the most effective political instrument." In 1934 with the assistance of the army, Hitler and the SS purged the SA and executed Röhm. The leaders of the army feared Röhm's demands that the SA become the core of a new, enlarged army of the Third Reich. Hitler saw Röhm's demands for a "second revolution" and a more radical Nazi regime as a threat to his leadership of the Nazi movement. The SS rid itself of its rival organization and became Hitler's exclusive elite corps, responsible for carrying out his extreme programs and responsible later for the greatest atrocities of the Second World War.

Nazi Goals. Hitler identified three organizing goals for the Nazi state: *Lebensraum,* or living space; rearmament; and economic recovery. These goals were the basis of the new foreign policy Hitler forged for Germany. And they served to fuse that foreign policy with the domestic politics of the Third Reich.

Key to Hitler's worldview was the concept of *Lebensraum,* which he considered the right and the duty of the German master race. The term *Lebensraum* embodied the concept that the Third Reich would be the world's greatest empire, one that would endure for a thousand years. Hitler first stated his ideals about living space in *Mein Kampf,* where he argued that superior nations had the right to expand into the territories of inferior states. Living space meant for him German domination of central and eastern Europe at the expense of Slavic peoples. The Aryan master race would dominate inferior peoples. In order for the German population to expand, Germany needed more land. Colonies were unacceptable because they weakened rather than strengthened national security. Germany must expand within Continental Europe. Hitler's primary target was what he called "Russia and her vassal border states." But his aspirations stretched beyond the European continent to include German domination of the entire world. He considered the United States to be a racially mongrel state that could be defeated by a strong and racially pure Germany at some future and unspecified time. His idea of world mastery always held out the promise of a future Aryan utopia.

Hitler also committed the Nazi state to the rearmament of Germany. He withdrew Germany from the world arena to prepare the German nation for war. By postponing his rearmament plans for the first year of his rule and then by using devious bookkeeping practices to bury his budgetary expenditures, he managed to obscure from the world his massive commitment to rearmament. In 1933 the German state was illicitly spending one billion Reichsmarks on arms. By 1939 annual expenditures to prepare Germany for war had climbed to thirty billion.

Hitler knew that preparation for war meant more than amassing weapons. One of Germany's great weaknesses in World War I had been its dependence on imports of raw materials and foodstuffs. Dependence on other nations for raw materials had crippled the German war effort by 1918. To avoid this problem again, Hitler instituted a program of *autarky,* or economic self-sufficiency, by which Germany aimed to produce everything that it consumed. He encouraged the efforts of German industry to develop synthetics, including petroleum, rubber, metals, and fats.

Autarky, as a rearmament measure, contributed to Hitler's third goal for the Nazi state: economic recovery from the Great Depression. The state pumped money into the private economy, creating new jobs and achieving full employment after 1936, an accomplishment unmatched by any other Western nation. Recovery was built on armaments as well as consumer products. The Nazi state's concentration of economic power in the hands of a few strengthened big business. The victims of corporate consolidation were the small firms that could no longer compete with government-sponsored corporations like the chemical firm of I. G. Farben.

Some of the non-Nazi conservative and nationalist leaders who supported the Nazi regime thought that the emphasis on rearmament was potentially dangerous. Economists feared that it would cause serious inflation. Even some generals thought that Hitler was rearming Germany in a too rapid and disorderly manner. Hitler prevailed in 1936–37, when he introduced his Four-Year Plan dedicated to the goals of full-scale rearmament and economic self-sufficiency.

National Income of the Powers in 1937 and Percentage Spent on Defense

	National Income (billions of dollars)	Percentage on Defense
United States	68	1.5
British Empire	22	5.7
France	10	9.1
Germany	17	23.5
Italy	6	14.5
USSR	19	26.4
Japan	4	28.2

Before the third year of the Four-Year Plan, however, Hitler was aware of the failure to develop synthetic products sufficient to meet Germany's needs. In order to preserve his commitment to military and economic recovery, he found another path to self-sufficiency. If Germany could not create substitutes, it could control the territories that provided fuel, metals, and foodstuffs. Germany had been importing raw materials from southeastern Europe and wielding increasing economic influence over the Balkan countries. Hitler now realized that economic self-sufficiency could be directly linked to the main goal of the Nazi state: *Lebensraum.* Acquiring new lands would solve Germany's supply needs.

Hitler was, thus, committed to territorial expansion from the time he came to power. He rearmed Germany for that purpose. When economists and generals cautioned him, he refused to listen. Instead he informed them of his commitment to *Lebensraum* and of his intention to use aggressive war to acquire it. He removed his critics from their positions of power and replaced them with Nazis loyal to him. Massive and rapid rearmament continued after 1937, now based on a drive for economic self-sufficiency. The growing economic costs did not cause Hitler to slow down or retreat from his programs. Instead under Hitler Germany rushed forward into a war for conquest.

Organizing Loyalty. For Hitler to pursue successfully the goals of the Nazi state, he had to have the loyalty and obedience of the German people. To realize his desire for the *total state,* a term he used to describe the absolute regulation of the German people, he set about destroying the rights of the individual: "We must develop organizations in which an individual's entire life can take place." The Nazi party was the preeminent organization. It coordinated the activities of approved groups of all sorts whose chief purpose was to inspire adherence to Nazi ideology. The organized terror of the SS and the Gestapo, the secret state police, silenced opposition.

To reinforce his personal power, Hitler created a Ministry of Propaganda to be headed by Joseph Goebbels (1897–1945), a former journalist and district Nazi party leader in Berlin. Goebbels was a master of manipulating emotions in mass demonstrations held to organize enthusiasm for Nazi policies. Flying the flag and wearing the swastika signified identification with the Nazi state. Every aspect of daily life, even the new form of greeting, "Heil Hitler!" was meant to indicate a new mentality and a new commitment.

Family life, too, was carefully regulated. Loyalty only to the state meant less loyalty to the family. Special youth organizations indoctrinated boys with nationalistic and military values. Hitler Youth comprised 82 percent of all young people in 1939. Children all over Germany recited the slogans of the organization: "Führer, command— we follow!" "We are born to die for Germany." Hitler's stated goal was to have all children in organizations by the age of ten and "not be free again for the rest of their lives."

Organizations for girls were intended to mold them into worthy wives and mothers. Teenage girls were required to join a Nazi organization called Faith and Beauty, which taught them etiquette, dancing, fashion consciousness, and beauty care. Woman's natural function, Hitler argued, was to serve in the home. Education for women beyond the care of home and family was a waste. Adult women had their own organizations to serve the Nazi state. The German Women's Bureau under Gertrud Scholtz-Klink instructed women in their "proper" female duties. Single women were urged to stop working, get married, and have children. In an effort to promote large families, the state paid allowances to couples for getting married, subsidized families according to their size, and gave tax breaks to large families. Hitler created the German Mother's Cross in 1938 to honor mothers of four or more children for their service to the state. Abortion and birth control were outlawed and women who sought such measures risked severe penalties and imprisonment.

By 1937 the need for women workers conflicted with the goals of Nazi propaganda. With the outbreak of war in 1939, women were urged to work, especially in jobs like munitions manufacture, formerly held by men. For working women with families, the double burden was a heavy one, as women were required to work long shifts— sixty-hour work weeks were not unusual—for low wages. Many women resisted entering the work force if they had other income or could live

A recruiting poster bearing the slogans "Youth serves the Führer" and "All ten-year-olds in the Hitler Youth" urges young boys to join the paramilitary youth organization.

on the cash payments they received as the wives of soldiers. At the beginning of 1943, the German people were ordered to make sacrifices for a new era of "total war." Female labor became compulsory and women were drafted into working for the war.

Racism and Culture. Mickey Mouse was declared "a dangerous foreigner" in Germany in the 1930s. Nazi propaganda was directed toward excluding outsiders—even cartoon characters—because they were deemed a threat to Hitler's New Order. Purging foreign influences meant purging political opponents, especially members of the Communist party, who were rounded up and sent to concentration camps in Germany. Communism was identified as an international Jewish conspiracy to destroy the German *Volk*, or people. Nazi literature also identified "asocials," those who were considered deviant in any way, including homosexuals, who were likewise to be expelled. Euthanasia was used against the mentally ill and the mentally disabled in the 1930s. Concentration camps were expanded to contain enemies of the state. During the 1930s foreigners, the mentally deficient, and the politically unacceptable were all targets of policies of containment and removal. Later, when concentration camps became sites of extermination and forced labor, gypsies, homosexuals, criminals, and religious offenders had to wear triangles of different colors to indicate their basis for persecution. But no group received greater attention for exclusion from Nazi Germany, and then from Europe, than did the Jews.

Racism was nothing new in European culture. Nor was its particular variant, anti-Semitism—hatred of the Jews—the creation of the Third Reich. The link the Nazis cultivated between racism and politics was built on cultural precedents. In the 1890s in France and Austria and elsewhere in Europe, anti-Semitism was espoused by political and professional groups that formed themselves around issues of militant nationalism, authoritarianism, and mass politics. Hitler himself was both a racist and an anti-Semite and he placed theories of race at the core of his fascist ideology.

Racist theories came to justify more than displacement and exclusion. "Experts" decided sterilization was the surest way to protect "German blood." In 1933, one of the early laws of Hitler's new Reich decreed compulsory sterilization of "undesirables" in order to "eliminate inferior genes." The Nazi state decided who these "undesirables" were and forced the sterilization of 400,000 men and women. Sexual relations between Aryans and Jews were prohibited as "racial defilement." In his pursuit of racial purity, Hitler justified the invasive role of the state in people's lives and the state's control over people's bodies: "*We* will regulate the relations between the sexes. *We* will form the child."

The battleground for racist theories became

the human body. Conceiving and bearing children were no longer matters of free choice. Procreation was to be directed by the state. Government agencies promoted a cult of masculinity and fatherhood. Motherhood was to serve the needs of the state and thus must be controlled by the state. The *Lebensborn* program directed the mating of women with SS officers, who were considered to be the flower of German manhood, for the purpose of producing a superior Aryan race. The program did not signify the sanctification of motherhood, as the Nazis proclaimed, but meant rather the transformation of women into breeders for the fatherland. Although only 12,081 children were born of these matings, the program indicated the nature of the Nazi commitment to racist theories.

Democracies in Crisis

Democracies in the 1930s turned in on themselves in order to survive. In contrast to the fascist mobilization of society and the Soviet restructuring of the economy, Western democracies took small steps to respond to the challenges of the Great Depression. Parliamentary political systems foundered, and parties bound to ideological programs failed to reach consensus on solutions to the economic crisis. Democratic leaders lacked creative vision or even clear policy. Both France and Great Britain were less successful than Germany in responding to the challenges of the Depression. France paid a high price for parliamentary stalemate and was still severely depressed on the eve of war in 1938–39. Great Britain maintained a stagnant economy and stable politics under Conservative leadership. Internal dissension, however, ripped Spain apart. Its civil war assumed broader dimensions as the Soviet Union, Italy, and Germany struggled over Spain's future, while Europe's democratic nations stood by and accepted defeat.

The Failure of the Left in France. France's Third Republic, like most European parliamentary democracies in the 1930s, was characterized by a multiparty system. Genuine political differences often separated one party from another. The spectrum of political views in the Third Republic

often meant stalemate. This situation was aggravated by the Depression and by the increasingly extremist politics on both the Left and the Right in response to international developments in the Soviet Union and Germany.

The Great Depression arrived later and lasted longer in France than anywhere in the Western world. The belief of the French people in a private enterprise economy was shaken but no new unifying belief replaced it. Some felt that state planning was the answer; others were sure that state intervention had caused the problem. Distrusting both the New Deal model of the United States and the Nazi response to Depression politics, the Third Republic followed a haphazard, wait-and-see policy of insulating the economy, discouraging competition, and protecting favored interests in both industry and agriculture. To protect the sacred cow of a balanced budget, the government spent less and less until 1936. Stimulating the economy by deficit spending was considered anathema. Devaluation of the franc, which might have helped French exports, was regarded by policymakers as an unpatriotic act. France stood fast as a bastion of liberal belief in the self-adjusting mechanism of the market and it suffered greatly for it. Party politics worked to reinforce the defensive rather than offensive response to the challenges of depression and a sluggish economy.

In 1936 an electoral mandate for change swept the Left into power. The new premier, Léon Blum (1872–1950), was a Socialist. Lacking the votes to rule with an exclusively Socialist government, Blum formed a Popular Front of Left and Center parties intent on economic reforms. Before the new government could take power, a wave of strikes swept France. Though reluctant to intervene in the economy, the Popular Front nevertheless was pushed into some action. It promised wage increases, paid vacations, and collective bargaining to French workers.

Problems plagued Blum's Popular Front. German rearmament, now publicly known, forced France into rearmament, which France could ill afford. The economic policies of the Left aggravated the problems they set out to solve. The reduced work week of forty hours caused a drop in productivity, as did the short-lived one-month vacation policy, which was eventually suspended until after World War II. The government did nothing to prevent the outflow of investment capital from France. Higher wages failed to generate increased consumer demand because employers raised prices to cover their higher operating costs. Blum's government failed in 1937, with France still bogged down in a sluggish and depressed economy. The last peacetime government of the 1930s represented a conservative swing back to laissez-faire policies that put the needs of business above those of workers and brought a measure of revival to the French economy.

The radical Right drew strength from the Left's failures. Right-wing leagues and organizations multiplied, appealing to a frightened middle class. The failure of the Socialists, in turn, drove many sympathizers further to the Left to join the Communist party. A divided France could not stand up to the foreign policy challenges of the 1930s posed by Hitler's provocations. Just as economic policy had no direction, foreign policy too lacked the sharp focus necessary to deal with the growing German threat. The slogan of the Right, "Better Hitler than Blum!" conveyed at least a confusion about what France's leadership should be doing.

Muddling Through in Great Britain.   Great Britain was hard hit by the Great Depression of the 1930s; only Germany and the United States experienced comparable economic devastation. The socialist Labour government of the years 1929 to 1931 under Prime Minister Ramsay MacDonald (1866–1937) was unprepared to deal with the 1929 collapse and lacked the vision and the planning to devise a way out of the morass. It took a coalition of moderate groups from the three parties—Liberal, Conservative, and Labour—to address the issues of high unemployment, a growing government deficit, a banking crisis, and the flight of capital. The National Government (1931–35) was a nonparty, centrist coalition whose members included Ramsay MacDonald, retained as prime minister, and Stanley Baldwin (1867–1947), a Conservative with a background in iron and steel manufacturing.

The National Government undertook measures that had been unpopular only a decade earlier. In response to the endemic crisis, the government took Britain off the international gold standard and devalued the pound. In order to protect domestic production, tariffs were established. Production was generally reduced, as planned production levels—especially in shipbuilding and the iron and steel industries—replaced competition in the marketplace. The British economy showed signs of slow recovery, probably due less to these government measures than to a gradual improvement in the business cycle. The government had survived the crisis without resorting to the kind of creative alternatives devised in the Scandinavian countries where, for example, consumer and producer cooperatives provided widespread economic relief. Moderates and classical liberals in Great Britain persisted in defending the nonintervention of the government in the economy, despite new economic theories, such as that of John Maynard Keynes (1883–1946), who urged government spending to stimulate consumer demand as the best way to shorten the duration of the Depression.

Another alternative to the British approach of muddling through came from Sir Oswald Mosley (1896–1980), a wealthy and prominent former Conservative who had recently become a socialist. He presented his radical economic proposals to his colleagues in the Labour Party in 1930, when the government's failure was apparent. Mosley recommended deficit spending in order to stimulate purchasing power and reduce unemployment. For him, unemployment was a pressing problem that must be solved. His Labour colleagues perceived his proposals as extreme and expelled him from the party. Bitterly denouncing the shortsightedness of Labour, the fiercely ambitious Mosley decided to create his own party, the New Party, which in its first electoral endeavor in 1931 gained no seats in Parliament. At this point Mosley showed the first signs of a total break with parliamentary politics. In 1932 he founded the British Union of Fascists (BUF), a group with its own goon squads of bodyguards. BUF was opposed to free-trade liberalism and communism alike. Mosley developed a corporate model for economic and political life in which interest groups rather than an electorate would be represented in a new kind of parliament. His policies favored, above all, national solutions by relying on imperial development; he rejected the world of international finance as corrupt.

The BUF shared similarities with European fascist organizations. Its members adopted a uniformed military look and identified themselves as the Blackshirts. At their mass meetings, they waved the black flag of the movement. Like fascists on the Continent, BUF squads beat up their political opponents and began attacking Jews, especially the eastern European émigrés living in London. Increasingly, inflammatory anti-Semitic rhetoric characterized the harangues of Mosley and other Blackshirt leaders. The British fascists struck a responsive chord among the poorest working classes of London's East End; at its peak the group claimed a membership of 20,000. Public alarm converged with parliamentary denunciation. Popular support for the group was already beginning to erode when the BUF was outlawed in 1936. By this time, anti-Hitler feeling was spreading in Great Britain.

Mosley's response to harsh economic times had proven to be no match for the steady and reassuring strength of Stanley Baldwin's National Government, which seemed to be in control of an improving economic situation. The traditional party system prevailed not because of its brilliant solutions to difficult economic problems but because of the willingness of moderate parliamentarians to cooperate and to adapt, however slowly, to the new need for economic transformation. The spirit of the "Victorian Compromise," by which reforms had been hammered out by competing parties in the third quarter of the nineteenth century, helped Britain to ride out the great economic and politic challenges of the 1930s.

The Spanish Republic As Battleground.

In 1931 Spain became a democratic republic after cen-

Members of the British Union of Fascists kneel to salute the grave of the Unknown Warrior in the courtyard of Westminster Abbey, 1922. The popularity of the BUF declined sharply in the mid-1930s. Oswald Mosley's continued support for Hitler and Nazi Germany led to his imprisonment during World War II.

Spanish refugees stream into France after the Republican defeat and the fall of Barcelona. More than two hundred thousand refugees and troops were interned in France.

turies of Bourbon monarchy and almost a decade of military dictatorship. Within five years, the voters of Spain had elected a Popular Front government. The Popular Front in Spain was more radical than the one in France: it unleashed a social revolution. The property of aristocratic landlords was seized; revolutionary workers went on strike; the Catholic church and its clergy were attacked. Three years of civil war followed. On one side were the Republicans, the Popular Front defenders of the Spanish Republic and of social revolution in Spain. On the other side were the Nationalists, those who sought to overthrow the Republic—aristocratic landowners, supporters of the monarchy and the Catholic church, and much of the Spanish army. In this civil war foreign powers—Italy, Germany, and the Soviet Union—intervened in what became a dress rehearsal for World War II. Spain became the battleground of the great ideological conflict of the period between the two world wars, a conflict between fascism and democracy.

The Spanish Civil War

The Spanish Civil War began in July 1936 with a revolt against the Republic from within the Spanish army. It was led by General Francisco Franco, a tough, shrewd, and stubborn man, a nonideological conservative nationalist allied with the Falange, the fascist party in Spain. The conflict soon became a bloody military stale-

mate, with the Nationalists controlling the more rural and conservative south and west of Spain and the Republicans holding out in the cities of the north and east—Madrid, Valencia, and Barcelona.

Almost from the beginning, the Spanish Civil War was an international event. Mussolini sent ground troops, "volunteers," to fight alongside Franco's forces. Hitler dispatched technical specialists, tanks, and the Condor Legion, an aviation unit. The Germans treated Spain as a testing ground for new equipment and new methods of warfare, including aerial bombardment. The Soviet Union intervened on the side of the Republic, sending armaments, supplies, and technical and political advisers. No democratic nation came to the aid of the Spanish Republic. Because the people of Britain and France were deeply divided in their attitudes toward the war in Spain, the British government stayed neutral, and the government of France was unable to aid its fellow Popular Front government in Spain. The American government did not prevent the Texas Oil Company from selling 1.9 million tons of oil to Franco's insurgents, nor did it block the Ford Motor Company, General Motors, and Studebaker from supplying the rebels with army trucks. There were similar sales to Hitler's Germany that continued even after the outbreak of war in 1939.

The Spanish government pleaded, "Men and women of all lands! Come to our aid!" In response, 2,800 American volunteers, among them college students, professors, intellectuals, and trade unionists, joined the loyalist army and European volunteers in defense of the Spanish Republic. The American battalion was called the Abraham Lincoln Brigade, a name that reflected its idealism and commitment to the defense of democratic ideals. Most American volunteers died in Spain and those who survived were wounded. Britons and antifascist émigrés from Italy and Germany also joined international brigades, which were vital in helping the city of Madrid hold out against the Nationalist generals. About one-half of the fighters in these brigades were Communists when they arrived. Many more became so after indoctrination by Stalin's advisers. In the minds of the members of the brigades and those who learned of them through the efforts of sympathetic writers, the Spanish Civil War became a great struggle for democracy. It was also a struggle of those trained by and increasingly controlled by Communists against those supplied and supported by fascists.

The Russians withdrew from the war in 1938, disillusioned by the failure of the French, British, and Americans to come to the aid of the Republicans. Madrid fell to the Nationalists in March 1939. The government established by Franco sent one million of its enemies to prison or concentration camps.

Ranks of seamstresses churn out Nazi flags in 1933 Berlin. The swastika—das Hakenkreuz—was a ubiquitous Nazi symbol that has come to stand for bigotry and religious and racial oppression throughout the world.

The Coming of World War II

The years between 1933 and 1939 marked a bleak period in international affairs when the British, the French, and the Americans were unwilling or unable to recognize the dire threat of Hitler and his Nazi state to world peace. The leaders of these countries did not comprehend Hitler's single-minded goal to extend German living space eastward as far as western Russia. They failed to understand the seriousness of the Nazi process of consolidation at home. They took no action against Hitler's initial acts of aggression. When war began in Europe in 1939 it eventually became a great global conflict that pitted Germany, Italy, and Japan—the Axis Powers—against the British Empire, the Soviet Union, and the United States—the Grand Alliance.

Even before war broke out in Europe, there was armed conflict in Asia. The rapidly expanding Japanese economy depended on Manchuria for raw materials and on China for markets. Chinese boycotts against Japanese goods and threats to Japanese economic interests in Manchuria led to a Japanese military occupation of Manchuria and the establishment of a Japanese puppet state there in 1931–32. When the powers of the League of Nations, led by Great Britain, refused to recognize this state, Japan withdrew from the League. Fearing that the Chinese government was becoming strong enough to exclude Japanese trade from China, Japanese troops and naval units began an undeclared war in China in 1937. Many important Chinese cities—Peking, Shanghai, Nanking, Canton, and Hankow—fell to Japanese forces. Relentless aerial bombardment of Chinese cities and atrocities committed by Japanese troops against Chinese civilians outraged Europeans and Americans. The governments of the Soviet Union, Great Britain, and the United States, seeking to protect their own ideological, economic, and security interests in China, gave economic, diplomatic, and moral support to the Chinese government of Chiang Kai-shek. The stage was set for a major military conflict in Asia and in Europe.

Hitler's Foreign Policy and Appeasement

For Hitler a war against the Soviet Union for living space was inevitable. It would come, he told some of his close associates, in the years 1943–45. However, he wanted to avoid refighting the war that had led to Germany's defeat in 1914–18. World War I was a war fought on two fronts—in the east and in the west. It was a war in which Germany had to face many enemies at the same time, and a war that lasted until German soldiers, civilians, and resources were exhausted. In the next war, Hitler wanted, above all, to avoid fighting Great Britain while battling Russia for living space. He convinced himself that the British would remain neutral if Germany agreed not to attack the British Empire. Would they not appreciate his willingness to abolish forever the menace of communism? Were they not Aryans also?

From the time he assumed power in 1933, Hitler began to prepare the German nation for war. He continued the secret rearmament of Germany begun by his Weimar predecessors in violation of the restrictions of the Treaty of Versailles. He withdrew Germany from the League of Nations and from the World Disarmament Conference, signaling a new direction for German foreign policy. Hitler vastly expanded the rearmament program. In 1935 he publicly renounced the Treaty of Versailles and announced that Germany was rearming. The following year he openly defied the French and moved German troops into the Rhineland, the demilitarized security zone that separated the armed forces of the two countries. Hitler also reversed the cooperative relationship his nation had established with the Soviet Union in the 1920s. He maintained a consistently anti-Soviet stance until just before war began in 1939.

Beginning in 1938, with the non-Nazi conservatives removed from positions of power in Germany, Hitler alone determined foreign policy. He became increasingly impatient. He considered time his greatest enemy: Germany could fail by waiting too long to act. And he became more aggressive and willing to use military force as he set out to remove the obstacles to German domination of central Europe—Austria, Czechoslovakia, and Poland. In March, he annexed Austria to the German Reich. Many Austrians wished to be united with Germany; others had no desire to

A triumphant Hitler enters Austria in 1938. The union of his native country with the German Reich had long been a cherished goal of the Nazi Führer.

be led by Nazis. Using the threat of invasion, he intimidated the Austrian government into legalizing the Nazi party, bringing pro-Nazis into the Cabinet, and finally inviting German troops into their country. Encouraged by his success, Hitler provoked a crisis in Czechoslovakia in the summer of the same year. He demanded "freedom" for the German-speaking people of the Sudetenland area of Czechoslovakia. His main objective, however, was not to protect the Germans of Czechoslovakia but to smash the Czech state, the major obstacle in central Europe to the launching of an attack on living space farther east.

Western statesmen did not understand Hitler's commitment to destroying Czechoslovakia or his willingness to fight a limited war against the Czechs to do so. Hitler did everything possible to isolate Czechoslovakia from its neighbors and its allies. France, an ally of Czechoslovakia, appeared distinctly unwilling to defend it against Germany's menaces. Britain, seeking to avoid a war that the government did not think was necessary and for which the British were not prepared, sent Prime Minister Neville Chamberlain (1869–1940) to reason with Hitler. Believing that transferring the Sudetenland, the German-speaking area of Czechoslovakia, to Germany was the only solution—and one that would redress some of the wrongs done to Germany after World War I—Chamberlain convinced France and Czechoslovakia to yield to Hitler's demands.

Chamberlain's actions were the result of British self-interest. British leaders agreed that their country could not afford another war like the Great War of 1914–18. Defense expenditures had been dramatically reduced in order to devote national resources to improving domestic social services, protecting world trade, and fortifying Britain's global interests. Britain understood well its weakened position in its dominions. In the British hierarchy of priorities, defense of the British Empire ranked first, above defense of Europe; and Britain's commitment to western Europe ranked above the defense of eastern and central Europe.

Hitler's response to being granted everything he requested was to renege and issue new demands. His desire for war could not have been more transparent, nor could his unwillingness to

play by the rules of diplomacy have been clearer. One final meeting was held at Munich to avert war. On 29 September 1938, one day before German troops were scheduled to invade Czechoslovakia, Mussolini and the French prime minister, Edouard Daladier (1884–1970), joined Hitler and Chamberlain at Munich to discuss a peaceful resolution to the crisis.

At Munich, Chamberlain and Daladier again yielded before Hitler. The Sudetenland was ceded to Germany and German troops occupied the area. The policy of the British and French was dubbed *appeasement* to indicate the willingness to concede to demands in order to preserve peace. *Appeasement* has become a dirty word in twentieth-century European history, taken to mean weakness and cowardice. Yet Chamberlain was neither weak nor cowardly. His great mistake was in assuming that Hitler was a reasonable man, who like all reasonable persons wanted to avoid another war.

Chamberlain thought his mediation at Munich had won for Europe a lasting peace—"peace for our time," he reported. The people of Europe received Chamberlain's assessment with a sense of relief and shame—relief over what had been avoided, shame at having deserted Czechoslovakia. In fact, the policy of appeasement further destabilized Europe and accelerated Hitler's plans for European domination. Within months, Hitler cast aside the Munich agreement by annihilating Czechoslovakia. German troops occupied the western, Czech part of the state including the capital of Prague. The Slovak eastern part became independent and a German satellite. At the same time, Lithuania was pressured into surrendering Memel to Germany, and Hitler demanded that Germany control Danzig (Gdansk) and the Polish Corridor. No longer could Hitler be ignored or appeased. No longer could his goals be misunderstood.

Hitler's War, 1939–41

In the tense months that followed the Munich meeting and the occupation of Prague, Hitler readied himself for war in western Europe. In order to strengthen his position, in May 1939 he formed a military alliance with Mussolini's Italy, the Pact of Steel. Then, Hitler and Stalin shocked the West by uniting their two nations in a pact of mutual neutrality, the Non-Aggression Pact of 1939. Opportunism lay behind Hitler's willingness to ally with the Communist state that he had denounced throughout the 1930s. A German alliance with the Soviet Union would, Hitler believed, force the British and the French to back down and to remain neutral while Germany conquered Poland—the last obstacle to a drive for living space—in a short, limited war. Stalin recognized the failure of the West to stand up to Hitler. There was little possibility, he thought, of an alliance against Germany with the virulently anti-Communist Neville Chamberlain. The best Stalin could hope for was that the Germans and the Western powers would fight it out while the Soviet Union waited to enter the war at the most opportune moment. As an added bonus, Germany promised not to interfere if the Soviet Union annexed eastern Poland, Bessarabia, and the Baltic republics of Latvia and Estonia. The prospect of regaining territory lost from the Russian Empire in the aftermath of the Russian Revolution of 1917 cinched the deal.

Finally recognizing Hitler's intent, the British and the French also signed a pact in the spring of 1939, promising assistance to Poland in the event of aggression. Tensions mounted throughout the summer. On 1 September 1939 Germany attacked Poland. By the end of the month, in spite of valiant resistance, the vastly outnumbered Poles surrendered. Although the German army needed no assistance, the Russians invaded Poland ten days before its collapse, and Germany and Russia divided the spoils. Almost immediately, Stalin took measures to defend Russia against a possible German attack. The Soviet Union assumed military control in the Baltic states and demanded of Finland territory and military bases from which the city of Leningrad could be defended. When Finland refused, Russia invaded. In the snows of the "Winter War" of 1939–40, the Finns initially fought the Russian army to a standstill, much to the encouragement of the democratic West. The Finns, however, were eventually defeated in March 1940.

Hitler's war, the war for German domination of Europe, had begun. But it had not begun the way he intended. Great Britain and France, true to their alliance with Poland, and contrary to Hitler's expectations, declared war on Germany on 3 September 1939, even though they were unable to give any help to Poland. In the six months after the fall of Poland, no military action took place between Germany and the Allies, because Hitler postponed offensives in northern and western Europe due to poor weather conditions. This strange interlude that became known as "the phony war" was a period of suspended

A German motorized detachment rides through a bomb-shattered town during the Nazi invasion of Poland in 1939. The invasion saw the first use of the Blitzkrieg—lightning war—*in which air power and rapid tank movement combined for rapid victory.*

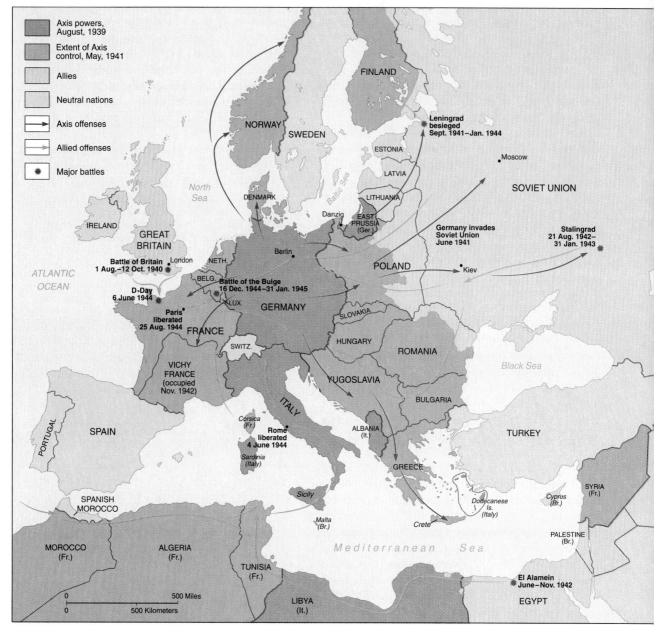

Legend:
- Axis powers, August, 1939
- Extent of Axis control, May, 1941
- Allies
- Neutral nations
- Axis offenses
- Allied offenses
- Major battles

World War II in Europe

reality in which France and Great Britain waited for Hitler to make his next move. Civilian morale in France deteriorated among a population that still remembered the death and destruction that France had endured in the Great War. An attitude of defeatism germinated and grew before the first French soldier fell in battle.

With the arrival of spring, Germany attacked Denmark and Norway in April 1940. Then on 10 May 1940, Hitler's armies invaded the Netherlands, Belgium, and Luxembourg. By the third week of May, German mechanized forces were racing through northern France toward the English Channel, cutting off the British and Belgian troops and 120,000 French forces from the rest of the French army. With the rapid defeat of

Belgium, these forces were crowded against the Channel and had to be withdrawn from the beaches of Dunkirk. France, with a large and well-equipped army, was in a desperate situation with the loss of Allied support.

In France, the German army fought a new kind of war called *Blitzkrieg*, or lightning war, so named because of its speed. The British and the French had expected the German army to behave much as it had in World War I, concentrating its striking forces in a swing through coastal Belgium and Holland in order to capture Paris. With stunning speed, Germany drove their tanks—*Panzers*—through the French defenses at Sedan in eastern France. French strategists believed that France was safe because of the hilly and forested terrain they thought was impassable. They also counted on the protection of the fortress wall known as the Maginot Line that France had built in the interwar period. The Maginot Line stretched for hundreds of miles but was useless against mobile tank divisions that outflanked it.

The French could have pinched off the advance of the overextended *Panzers*, but the French army, suffering from severe morale problems, collapsed and was in retreat. On 17 June 1940, only weeks after German soldiers had stepped on French soil, Marshal Henri-Philippe Pétain, the great hero of the Battle of Verdun in World War I, petitioned the Germans for an armistice. Three-fifths of France, including the entire Atlantic seaboard, was occupied by the German army and placed under direct German rule. In what remained, Pétain created a collaborationist government that resided at Vichy, a spa city in central France, and worked in partnership with the Germans for the rest of the war. General Charles de Gaulle (1890–1970) withdrew to London, where he set up a Free French government in exile.

French capitulation in June 1940 followed Italian entry into the war on the side of Germany in the same month. The British were now alone in a war against the two Axis powers as Germany made plans for an invasion of the British Isles from across the English Channel. To prepare the way, the German air force under Reich Marshal Hermann Goering (1893–1946) launched a series of air attacks against England—the Battle of Britain. The German air force first attacked Brit-ish aircraft, airfields, and munitions centers and then shifted targets to major population centers like London and industrial cities like Coventry. Between 7 September and 2 November 1940, the city of London was bombed every night, inflicting serious damage on the city and killing 15,000 people.

The British resisted these attacks under the leadership of Winston Churchill, who had succeeded Chamberlain as prime minister in 1940. Churchill was a master public speaker who, in a series of radio broadcasts, inspired the people of Britain with the historic greatness of the task confronting them—holding out against Nazism until the forces of the overseas British Empire and the United States could be marshaled to liberate Europe. The British Royal Air Force inflicted serious losses on German aircraft while British industry was able to maintain steady production of planes, bombs, and armaments. Civilians endured the nightly destruction and air raids in what Churchill termed Britain's "finest hour." Recognizing his lack of success in establishing air superiority in the skies over the Channel or in breaking the will of the British people, Hitler

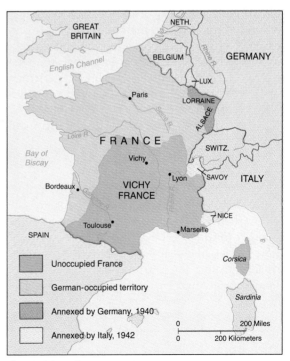

The Division of France, 1940–44

abandoned the Battle of Britain and canceled the invasion.

By the middle of the year 1941 Hitler controlled a vast continental empire that stretched from the Baltic to the Black Sea and from the Atlantic Ocean to the Russian border. In addition to occupied territories and satellites, he had the support of collaborationist governments. Some collaborators served in puppet governments out of an ideological commitment to fascism. They were hostile to communism and believed that Hitler's Nazism was far preferable to Stalin's communism. They saw in the German victory the chance to put their beliefs into practice. Some governments collaborated with the Germans out of national self-interest. The government of Hungary allied with Germany in the hope of winning back territory lost at the end of World War I. Romania hoped to gain territory from Russia. The government of Slovakia was loyal to the Third Reich because Hitler had given it independence from the Czechs. A German puppet state was set up in the Yugoslav province of Croatia. Other collaborators were pragmatists who believed that by taking political office they could negotiate with the German conquerors and soften the effects of the Nazi conquest on their people. Hitler had little affection for local ideological fascists and sometime smashed their movements. He preferred to work with local generals and administrators. Pragmatic collaborators often could not or would not negotiate with the German authorities very well. The help they gave in rounding up opponents of Nazi Germany—resistance fighters and Jews—resulted in their punishment after the war.

Resistance against German occupation and collaborationist regimes took many forms. Resisters wrote subversive tracts or distributed them, gathered intelligence information for the Allies, sheltered Jews or other enemies of the Nazis, committed acts of sabotage or assassination or other violent acts, and carried on guerrilla warfare against the German army. Resisters ran the risk of endangering themselves and their families, who, if discovered, would be tortured and killed. Resistance movements developed most strongly after the German attack on the Soviet Union in 1941, when the Communist parties of occupied Europe formed the core of the violent resistance against the Nazi regime. Resistance grew stronger when the Germans began to draft young European men for work on German farms and in German factories. Many preferred to go underground rather than to Germany.

The greatest resistance fighter of the Second World War, or perhaps of any war, was Josip Broz (1892–1980), alias Tito. He was a Croatian Communist and a Yugoslav nationalist. Instead of waiting to be liberated by the Allies, his partisans fought against Italian and German troops. Ten or more German divisions which might otherwise have fought elsewhere were tied up combating Tito's forces. He gained the admiration and the support of Churchill, Roosevelt, and Stalin. After liberation, Tito's organization won 90 percent of the vote in the Yugoslav elections, and he became the leader of the country in the postwar era. Resistance entailed enormous risks and required secrecy, moral courage, and great bravery. But, on the whole, the actions of resistance fighters were militarily insignificant in changing the course of the war.

Racism and Destruction

War, as the saying goes, is hell. But the horrors perpetrated in World War II exceeded anything ever experienced in Western civilization. Claims of racial superiority were invoked to justify inhuman atrocities. The Germans and Japanese used spurious arguments of racial superiority to fuel their war efforts in both the European and Asian theaters of battle. In Asia the subjugation of inferior peoples became a rallying cry for conquest. But the Germans and the Japanese were not alone in using racist propaganda. The United States employed racial stereotypes to depict the inferiority of the enemy and interned Japanese-Americans living on the West Coast to camps and seized their property.

Nowhere, however, was the use of racism by the state more virulent than in Germany. German racist ideology distorted pseudoscientific theories for the purpose of separating the racially superior from the racially inferior. Those human beings worthy of living were the master race; those not worthy were deemed "subhuman." Hatred of certain groups fueled both politics and war. Hitler promised the German people a purified Reich of Aryans "free of the Jews" and the racially and mentally inferior. Slavic peoples—Poles and Russians—were designated as subhumans who could be displaced in the search for *Lebensraum* and German destiny. With the war in eastern Europe, anti-Semitism changed from a policy of persecution and expropriation in the 1930s into a program of systematic extermination beginning in 1941.

The Destruction of Europe's Jews

Although anti-Semitism was an integral part of Hitler's view of the world, he did not think the peoples of Germany or of Europe were ready for harsh measures against the Jews. The Nazis did not have a blueprint for the destruction of Europe's Jews when they came to power in 1933; the anti-Semitic policies of the Third Reich evolved incrementally in the 1930s and 1940s. The first measures against the German Jews, such as

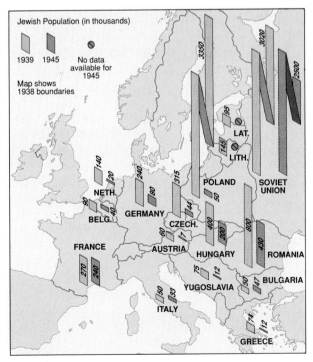

The Holocaust

their exclusion from public employment and higher education, began almost immediately in 1933. In 1935 the Nuremberg Laws were enacted to identify Jews, to deprive them of their citizenship, and to forbid marriage and extramarital sexual relations between Jews and non-Jews. Jews were defined as an inferior and alien presence in the German community.

Massive public violence against Jews took place five years after the Nazis came to power. On the night of 9 November 1938, synagogues were set afire and books and valuables owned by Jews were confiscated throughout Germany. Jews were beaten, about 91 were killed, and 20,000 to 30,000 were imprisoned in concentration camps. The night came to be called *Kristallnacht,* meaning "night of broken glass," which referred to the Jewish shop windows smashed by the Brown Shirts under orders from Goebbels. The government claimed that *Kristallnacht* was an outpouring of the German people's will. An atmosphere of state-sanctioned hate prevailed. German citizens acquiesced, sometimes silently and in many cases vociferously.

In the aftermath of *Kristallnacht,* civil servants expropriated Jewish property as the rightful property of the state. When the war began, Jews were rounded up and herded into urban ghettos, both in Germany and in the large cities of Poland. For a time the German foreign ministry considered the possibility of deporting the more than three million Jews under German control to Madagascar, an island off the southeast coast of Africa. Until 1941, Nazi policies against the Jews were often uncoordinated and unfocused.

The "Final Solution." Confinement in urban ghettos was the beginning of a policy of concentration that ended in annihilation. After having identified Jews, seized their property, and then confined them to ghettos, German authorities began to implement a step-by-step plan for extermination. There appears to have been no single order from Hitler that decreed what became known to German officials as the "Final Solution"—the total extermination of European Jews. But Hitler's recorded remarks make it clear that he knew and approved of what was being done to the Jews. A spirit of shared purpose permeated the entire administrative sys-

The "Final Solution" in the Death Camps

Camp	Main Geographic Origins of Victims	Principal Time Spans of Systematic Killings	Number Killed
Kulmhof	Wartheland Reich, via Łódź	December 1941 to September 1942 and June-July 1944	150,000
Bełżec	Galicia Kraków district Lublin district (including Reich deportees)	March–December 1942	550,000
Sobibór	Lublin district Netherlands Slovakia Reich-Protektorat France Minsk	April–June 1942 and October 1942 to October 1943	200,000
Treblinka	Warsaw district Radom district Białystok district Lublin district Macedonia-Thrace Reich Theresienstadt	July 1942 to October 1943	750,000
Lublin	Lublin district Warsaw district France	September 1942 to September 1943 and November 1943	50,000

tem from the civil service through the judiciary. Administrative agencies competed to interpret the Führer's will. SS guards in the camps and police in the streets embraced Hitler's "mission" of destruction. Those involved in carrying out the plan for extermination understood what was meant by the Final Solution and what their responsibilities were for enforcing it. To assure that the whole process operated smoothly, a planning conference for the Final Solution was conducted by Reinhard Heydrich (1904–42), leader of the *Sicherheitsdienst* (SD), or Security Service of the SS, for the benefit of state and party officials at Wannsee, a Berlin suburb, in January 1942.

Mass racial extermination began with the German conquest of Poland, where both Jews and non-Jews were systematically killed. It continued when Hitler's army invaded the Soviet Union in 1941. This campaign, known as Operation Barbarossa, initiated the mass execution of eastern Europeans declared to be enemies of the Reich. Its tactics pointed the way to the Final Solution. To the Nazi leadership, Slavs were "subhuman." Russian Jews were, by extension, the lowest of the low, even more despised than German Jews. Nazi propaganda had equated Jews with Communists,

and Hitler had used the single word *Judeocommunist* to describe the most dangerous criminal and enemy of the Third Reich, the enemy who must be annihilated at any cost.

The executions were the work of the SS, the elite military arm of the Nazi party. Special mobile murder squads of the SD under Heydrich were organized behind the German lines in Poland and Russia. Members of the army were aware of what the SS squads were doing and participated in some of the extermination measures. In the spring of 1941 Hitler ordered a massive propaganda campaign to be conducted among the armed forces. The army was indoctrinated to believe that the invasion of the Soviet Union was more than a military campaign; it was a "holy war," a crusade that Germany was waging for civilization. SS chief Heinrich Himmler, probably responding to oral orders from Hitler, set about to enforce the Führer's threats with concrete extermination policies. Fearful that the SS would be outstripped by the regular army in the Führer's favor, Himmler exhorted his men to commit the worst atrocities.

Firing squads shot Russian victims en masse, then piled their bodies on top of one another in open graves. Reviewing these procedures for mass killings, Himmler—ever competitive with other Nazi agencies—suggested a more efficient means of extermination that would require less manpower and would enhance the prestige of the SS. As a result, extermination by gas was introduced, using vans whose exhaust fumes were piped into the enclosed cargo areas that served as portable gas chambers. In Poland, Himmler replaced the vans with permanent buildings housing gas chambers using Zyklon B, a gas developed by the chemical firm I. G. Farben for the purpose. The chambers could annihilate thousands at a time.

The Third Reich began erecting its vast network of death in 1941. The first extermination camp was created in Chelmno, Poland, where 150,000 people were killed between 1941 and 1944. The camps practiced systematic extermination for the savage destruction of those groups deemed racially inferior, sexually deviant, and politically dangerous. The terms *genocide, judeocide*, and *holocaust* have been used to describe the mass slaughter of the Jewish people, most of which took place in the five major killing centers in what is now Polish territory—Chelmno, Belzec, Sobibor, Treblinka, and Auschwitz.

Many victims died before ever reaching the camps, transported for days in sealed railroad cars, without food, water, or sanitation facilities. Others died within months as forced laborers for the Reich. People of all ages were starved, beaten, and systematically humiliated. Guards taunted their victims verbally, degraded them physically, and tortured them with false hope. Promised clean clothes and nourishment, camp internees were herded into "showers," which dispensed gas rather than water. Descriptions of life in the camps reveal a systematized brutality and inhumanity on the part of the German, Ukrainian, and Polish guards toward their victims. In all, eleven million people died by the extermination process—six million Jews and almost as many non-Jews, including Slavic slave laborers, Soviet prisoners of war, Communists, members of the Polish and Soviet leadership, various resistance elements, gypsies, Jehovah's Witnesses, and homosexuals.

Work Makes Free. The words *Arbeit Macht Frei* ("Work Makes Free") were emblazoned over the main gate at Auschwitz, the largest of the concentration camps. It was at Auschwitz that the greatest number of persons died in a single place, including more than one million Jews. The healthy and the young were kept barely alive to work, including to transfer bodies from the gas chambers to the ovens. Hard labor, starvation, and disease—especially typhus, tuberculosis, and other diseases that spread rapidly because of the lack of sanitation—claimed many victims.

These women and children, many wearing the yellow star that identified them as Jews, were photographed minutes before they entered the gas chambers at Auschwitz.

On entering the camps, the sick and the aged were automatically designated for extermination because of their uselessness as a labor force. Many children were put to work, but some were designated for extermination. Many mothers chose to accompany their children to their deaths to comfort them in their final moments. Pregnant women too were considered useless in the forced labor camps and were sent immediately to the "showers." The number of German Jewish women who died in the camps was 50 percent higher than the number of German Jewish men. Starvation diets meant that women stopped menstruating. Women who showed signs of menstruation were killed immediately. The Nazis worried that women of child-bearing age would continue to reproduce. Women who were discovered to have given birth undetected in the camp were killed, as were their infants. Family relations were completely destroyed, as inmates were segregated by sex. It soon became clear that even those allowed to live were only intended to serve the short-term needs of the Nazis.

Resisting Destruction. Could the victims of extermination have resisted? The answer is no. The impossibility of any effective resistance was based on two essential characteristics of the process of extermination. First, the entire German state and its bureaucratic apparatus were involved in the policies, laws, and decrees of the 1930s that singled out victims, and most Germans stood silently by. There was no course of appeal and no place to hide. Those who understood early what was happening and who had enough money to buy their way out emigrated to safer places, including Palestine and the United States. But most countries blocked the entry of German and eastern European refugees with immigration quotas. Neither Britain nor the United States was willing to deal with the mass influx of European Jews. Jews in the occupied countries and the Axis nations had virtually no chance to escape. They were trapped in a society where all forces of law and administration worked against them.

A second reason for the impossibility of resistance was the step-by-step nature of the process of extermination, which meant that few understood the final outcome until it was too late. Initially in the 1930s, many German Jews believed that things

could get no worse and obeyed the German state as good citizens. Even the policy of removing groups from the ghetto militated against resistance because the hope was that sending 1,000 Jews to "resettlement" would allow 10,000 Jews remaining behind to be saved. The German authorities deliberately controlled information to cultivate this misunderstanding of what was happening.

Isolated instances of resistance in the camps—rioting at Treblinka, for example—only highlight how impossible rebellion was for physically debilitated people in these heavily guarded centers. In the Warsaw ghetto, a resistance movement was organized with a few firearms and some grenades and homemade Molotov cocktails in April 1943. Starvation, overcrowding, and epidemics made Warsaw, the largest of the ghettos, into an extermination camp. As news reached the ghetto that "resettlement" was the death warrant of tens of thousands of Polish Jews, armed rebellion erupted. It did not succeed in blocking the completion of the Final Solution against the Warsaw ghetto the following year when the SS commandant proclaimed, "The Jewish Quarter of Warsaw is no more!" Polish and Russian Jews account for 70 percent of the total Jewish deaths.

Who Knew?

It is impossible that killing on such a scale could have been kept secret. Along with those who ordered extermination operations, the guards and camp personnel involved in carrying out the directives were aware of what was happening. Those who brought the Jews to the camps, returning always with empty railroad cars, knew it too. Neighbors who saw Jews disappearing for a time believed that they were being resettled in the east. But as news got back to central and western Europe, it was harder to sustain belief in this ruse. People who lived near the camps could not ignore the screams and smells of gas and burning bodies emitted from the camps.

Although never publicly announcing its extermination program, the German government convinced its citizens that the policies of the Nazi state could not be judged by ordinary moral standards. The benefits to the German state were

Rows of dead slave laborers await burial by U.S. troops at Nordenhausen concentration camp in 1945. They died from starvation, overwork, and beatings while working on the V-1 and V-2 bombs.

justification enough for the annihilation of eleven million people. Official propaganda successfully convinced millions that the Reich was the supreme good. Admitting the existence of the extermination program carried with it a responsibility on which few acted, perhaps out of fear of reprisals. There were some heroes like Raoul Wallenberg of Sweden, who interceded for Hungarian Jews and provided Jews in the Budapest ghetto with food and protection. The king of Denmark, when informed that the Nazis had ordered Danish Jews to wear the yellow star, stated that he and his family would also wear the yellow star as a "badge of honor." Heroic acts, however, were isolated and rare.

Collaborationist governments and occupied nations often cooperated with Nazi extermination policies. The French government at Vichy introduced and implemented a variety of anti-Jewish measures. All of this was done without German orders and without German pressure. By voluntarily identifying and deporting Jews, the Vichy government sent 75,000 men, women, and children to their deaths.

As the war dragged on for years, internees of the camps hoped and prayed for rescue by the Allies. But such help did not come. The U.S. State Department and the British Foreign Office had early and reliable information on the nature and extent of the atrocities. But they did not act. American Jews were unable to convince President Franklin D. Roosevelt to intercede to prevent the slaughter. Appeals to bomb the gas chambers at Auschwitz and the railroad lines leading to them were rejected by the United States on strategic grounds. Yet American planes were bombing the region within fifty miles of Auschwitz and had come as close as five miles from the gas chambers in striking industrial targets. Diverting essential air power away from key targets would not have been involved since these bombers were already so close to the camp. This action, which could have saved perhaps hundreds of thousands of lives, was never taken. Those trying to survive in the camps and the ghettos despaired at their abandonment.

The handful of survivors found by Allied soldiers who entered the camps after Germany's defeat presented a haunting picture of humanity. A British colonel who entered the camp at Bergen-Belsen in April 1945 gave a restrained account of what he found:

> As we walked down the main road of the camp, we were cheered by the internees, and for the first time we saw their condition. A great number were little more than living skeletons. There were men and women lying in heaps on both sides of the track. Others were walking slowly and aimlessly about, vacant expressions on their starved faces.

The haunting sight of corpses piled on top of one another lining the roads, the piles of shoes, clothing, underwear, and gold teeth extracted from the dead shocked those who came to liberate the camps. One of the two survivors of Chelmno summed it all up: "No one can understand what happened here."

The Final Solution was a perversion of every value of civilization. The achievements of twentieth-century industry, technology, state, and bureaucracy in the West were turned against millions to create, as one German official called it, murder by assembly line. Mass killing was not prompted by military or security concerns. Nor was the elimination of vital labor power consistent with the needs of the Nazi state. The international tribunal for war crimes that met in 1945 in the German city of Nuremberg attempted to mete out justice to the criminals against humanity responsible for the destruction of eleven million Europeans labeled as demons and racial inferiors. History in the end must record, if it cannot explain, such inhumanity.

Allied Victory

The situation at the end of 1941 appeared grim for the British and their dominions and the Americans who were assisting them with munitions, money, and food. Hitler had achieved control of a vast land empire covering all of continental Europe in the west, north, south, and center. This empire, which Hitler called his "New Order" included territories occupied and directly administered by the German army, satellites, and collaborationist regimes. It was fortified by alliances with Italy, the Soviet Union, and Japan. Hitler commanded the greatest fighting force in the world, one that had knocked France out of the war in a matter of weeks, brought destruction to British cities, and conquered Yugoslavia in twelve days. Much of the world was coming to fear German invincibility.

Then in June 1941, Hitler's troops invaded the Soviet Union, providing the British with an ally. In December the naval and air forces of Japan attacked American bases in the Pacific, providing the British and the Russians with still another ally. What was a European war became a world war. This was the war Hitler did not want and which Germany could not win—a long, total war to the finish against three powers with inexhaustible resources—the British Empire, the Soviet Union, and the United States.

The Soviet Union's Great Patriotic War

Hitler had always considered the Soviet Union Germany's primary enemy. His hatred of communism was all-encompassing: Bolshevism was an evil invention of the Jewish people and a dangerous ideological threat to the Third Reich. The 1939 Non-Aggression Pact with Stalin was no more than an expedient for him. Hitler rebuked a

The Jewish Population Loss 1939–45

	1939	1945
Austria	60,000	7,000
Belgium	90,000	40,000
Bulgaria	50,000	47,000
Czechoslovakia	315,000	44,000
Denmark	6,500	5,500
France	270,000	200,000
Germany	240,000	80,000
Greece	74,000	12,000
Hungary	400,000	200,000
Italy	50,000	33,000
Luxembourg	3,000	1,000
Netherlands	140,000	20,000
Norway	2,000	1,000
Poland	3,350,000	50,000
Romania	800,000	430,000
USSR	3,020,000	2,500,000
Estonia	4,500	
Latvia	95,000	
Lithuania	145,000	
Yugoslavia	75,000	12,000

Men and women on a Ukrainian collective farm labor to erect huge antitank traps during the German invasion of the Soviet Union. The steadfast courage of the civilian population contributed greatly to the defeat of Hitler's quest for "Lebensraum" in the east.

Swiss diplomat in 1939 for failing to grasp the central fact of his foreign policy:

> Everything I undertake is directed against Russia. If those in the West are too stupid and too blind to understand this, then I should be forced to come to an understanding with the Russians to beat the West, and then, after its defeat, turn with all my concentrated force against the Soviet Union.

That is exactly what happened on 22 June 1941 when German armies marched into Russia. They found the Soviet army larger but totally unprepared for war. In contrast to German soldiers, who had fought in Spain, Poland, and France, Soviet troops had no firsthand battle experience. Nor were they well led. Stalin's purges of the officer corps in the late 1930s removed 35,000 officers from their posts by dismissal, imprisonment, or execution. Many of the men who replaced them were unseasoned in the responsibilities of leadership.

Russian military leaders were sure they would be ready for a European war against the capitalist nations by 1942, and Stalin refused to believe that Hitler would attack the Soviet Union before then. British agents and Stalin's own spies tried to warn him of German plans for an invasion in the spring of 1941. When the Germans did invade Russian territory, Stalin was so overwhelmed that he fell into a depression and was unable to act for days.

In his first radio address after the attack on 3 July 1941, Stalin identified his nation with the Allied cause: "Our struggle for the freedom of our country will merge with the struggle of the peoples of Europe and America for their independence, for democratic liberties." He accepted offers of support from the United States and Great Britain, the two nations that had worked consistently to exclude the Soviet Union from European power politics since the Bolshevik Revolution in 1917. With France defeated and Great Britain crippled, the future of the war depended on the Soviet fighting power and American supplies.

Hitler's invasion of Russia, involved 3 million soldiers from Germany and Germany's satellites, the largest invasion force in history. It stretched along an immense battlefront from the Baltic to the Black Sea. Instead of exclusively targeting Moscow, the capital, the German army concentrated first on destroying Soviet armed forces and capturing Leningrad in the north and the oil-rich Caucasus in the south. In the beginning the German forces advanced rapidly in a *Blitzkrieg* across western Russia, where they were greeted as liberators in the Ukraine. The Germans took 290,000 prisoners of war and massacred tens of thousands of others in their path through the Jewish settlements of western Russia. The devastation they left in their wake was staggering.

Within four months, the Germany army had advanced to the gates of Moscow, but they concentrated their forces too late. The Red Army rallied to defend Moscow, as thousands of civilian women set to work digging trenches and antitank ditches around the city. The Soviet people answered Stalin's call for a scorched-earth policy by burning everything that might be useful to the advancing German troops. German troops had also burned much in their path, depriving themselves of essential supplies for the winter months ahead. The German advance was stopped, as the best ally of the Red Army—the Russian winter—settled in. The first snow fell at the beginning of October. By early November, German troops were beginning to suffer the harsh effects of an early and exceptionally bitter Russian winter.

Hitler promised the German people that "final victory" was at hand. So confident was Hitler of a speedy and decisive victory that he sent his soldiers into Russia wearing only light summer uniforms. Hitler's generals knew better and tried repeatedly to explain military realities to the Führer. General Heinz Guderian (1888–1954), commander of the tank units, reported that his men were suffering frostbite, tanks could not be started, and automatic weapons were jamming in the subzero temperatures. Back in Germany, the civilian population received little accurate news of the campaign. They began to suspect the worst when the government sent out a plea for woolen blankets and clothing for the troops.

By early December, the German military situation was desperate. The Soviets, benefiting from intelligence information about German plans and an awareness that Japan was about to declare war on the United States, recalled fresh troops from the Siberian frontier and the border with China and Manchuria and launched a powerful counterattack against the poorly outfitted German army outside Moscow. Under the command of General Gyorgi Zhukov (1896–1974), Russian troops, dressed and trained for winter warfare, pushed the Germans back in retreat across the snow-covered expanses. By February, 200,000 German troops had been killed, 46,000 were missing in action, and 835,000 were casualties of battle and the weather. Thus, the campaign cost the German army over a million casualties. It probably cost the Soviets twice that number of wounded, missing, captured, and dead soldiers. At the end of the Soviet counterattack in March, the German army and its satellite forces were in a shambles reminiscent of Napoleon's troops, who 130 years earlier had been decimated in the campaign to capture Moscow. An enraged Hitler dismissed his generals for retreating without his permission, and he himself assumed the position of commander-in-chief of the armed forces.

Hitler was not daunted by the devastating costs of his invasion of Russia. In the summer of 1942, he initiated a second major offensive, this time to take the city of Stalingrad. Constant bombardment gutted the city, and the Soviet army was forced into hand-to-hand combat with the German soldiers. But the German troops, once again inadequately supplied and unprepared for the Russian winter, failed to capture the city. The Battle of Stalingrad was over in the first days of February 1943. Of the original 300,000 members of the German Sixth Army, fewer than 100,000 survived to be taken prisoner by the Soviets. Of those, only 5,000 returned to Germany in 1955, when German prisoners of war were repatriated.

The Soviets succeeded by exploiting two great advantages in their war against Germany: the large Soviet population and their knowledge of Russian weather and terrain. There was a third advantage that Hitler ignored: the Soviet people's determination to sacrifice everything for the war effort. In his successive Five-Year Plans, Stalin had mobilized Soviet society with an appeal to fulfill and surpass production quotas. In the summer of 1941, as Hitler's troops threatened Moscow, he used the same rhetoric to appeal to his Soviet "brothers and sisters" to join him in waging "the Great Patriotic War." The Russian people shared a sense of common purpose, sacrifice, and moral commitment in their loyalty to the nation.

The advancing Germans themselves intensified Soviet patriotism by torturing and killing tens of thousands of peasants who might have willingly cooperated against the Stalinist regime. Millions of Soviet peasants joined the Red Army. Young men of high-school age were drafted into the armed forces. Three million women became wage earners for the first time as they replaced men in war industries. Women who remained on the land worked to feed the townspeople and the soldiers. Because the Red Army had requisitioned horses and tractors for combat, grain had to be sown and harvested by hand—and this often meant women's hands. Tens of thousands of Russians left their homes in western Russia to work for relocated Soviet industries in the Urals, the Volga region, Siberia, and Central Asia. More than 20 million Soviet people, soldiers and civilians, died in the course of World War II. In addition to those killed in battle, millions starved as a direct result of the hardships of war. In 1943, food was so scarce that seed for the next year's crops was eaten. One in every three men born in 1906 died in the war. But Soviet resistance did not flag.

The Great Patriotic War had a profound impact on Soviet views of the world and the Soviet Union's place in it. The war left the Soviet people with an enduring fear of invasion. The official falsification of all published maps of the Soviet Union in order to mislead spies and foreign armies is just one indication of the Russian expectation of treachery. (This practice is as recent as 1988.) Today, a visitor to Stalingrad, renamed Volgograd, can still find old tanks in city parks and on streets as reminders of the front line of the Red Army in the Great Patriotic War. Ruins of buildings have been left standing as grim monuments of the need for continued preparedness. The absence of trees is another indication of past devastation. The few surviving trees bear plaques that make of their survival a memorial.

The Soviet Union sacrificed 10 percent of its population to the war effort, incurring well over 50 percent of all the deaths and casualties of the war. Few families escaped the death of members in the defense of the nation. Soviet citizens correctly considered that they had given more than

any other country to defeat Hitler. For the Soviet people, their suffering in battle made World War II the Soviet Union's war and their sacrifice made possible the Allied victory. But victory still eluded the Allies in western Europe, where now another nation, the United States, had entered the fray.

The United States Enters the War

Although a neutral power, the United States began extending aid to the Allies after the fall of France in 1940. Since neither Britain nor the Soviet Union could afford to pay the entire costs of defending Europe against Hitler, the United States Congress passed the Lend-Lease Act in 1941. This act authorized President Roosevelt to provide armaments to Great Britain and the Soviet Union without payment. America became "the arsenal of democracy." The United States and Britain sent 4,100 airplanes and 138,000 motor vehicles as well as steel and machinery to the Soviet Union for the campaign of 1943. In all, America pumped $11 billion worth of supplies and equipment into the Soviet war effort between 1941 and 1945. Stalin later told Roosevelt that

Russian villagers search for loved ones among civilians slain by German troops. Noncombatants were frequent victims of the Nazi policy of enslavement or annihilation.

the USSR would have lost the war with Germany without the help of the Americans and the British.

President Roosevelt and his advisers considered Germany, not Japan, to be America's primary target for a future war. Japan nevertheless had been threatening American trade interest in Asia and had embroiled the United States in disputes over Japanese imperialist expansion in the late 1930s. In the summer of 1941 Japanese-American relations appeared to be deteriorating following the Japanese invasion of Indochina and Thailand. The United States insisted that Japan vacate China and Indochina and reestablish the open door for trade in Asia. But Japan held fast and in September 1940 joined forces with the Axis Powers of Germany and Italy in the Tripartite Pact, in which the signatories promised mutual support against aggression. The United States knew that it was only a matter of time until Japan attacked but was uncertain about where that attack would take place.

On Sunday morning, 7 December 1941, Japan struck at the heart of the American Pacific Fleet stationed at Pearl Harbor, Hawaii. The fleet was literally caught asleep at the switch: 2,300 people were killed, and eight battleships and numerous cruisers and destroyers were sunk or severely damaged. The attack crippled American naval power in the Pacific as the American navy suffered its worst loss in history in a single engagement. The attack on Pearl Harbor led to the United States' immediate declaration of war against Japan. In President Roosevelt's words, 7 December 1941 was "a date which will live in infamy." In the next three months, Japan captured Hong Kong, Malaya, and the important naval base at Singapore from the British, taking 60,000 prisoners. They drove the Dutch from all of Indonesia but New Guinea, pushed American forces in the Philippines into the Bataan Peninsula, occupied Burma, and inflicted severe defeats on British, Dutch, and American naval power in East Asia. With the armies of Germany deep in Russian territory, Australia now faced the threat of a Japanese invasion.

Hitler praised the Japanese government for its action against the British Empire and against the United States and its "millionaire and Jewish backers." Germany, with its armies retreating

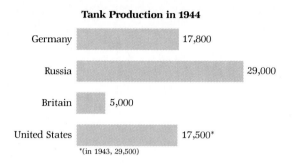

Tank Production in 1944

Germany	17,800
Russia	29,000
Britain	5,000
United States	17,500*

*(in 1943, 29,500)

from Moscow, nevertheless declared war against the United States on 11 December 1941. Hitler, in fact, considered that the United States was already at war with Germany because of its policy of supplying the Allies. Within days the United States, a nation with an army smaller than Belgium's, had gone from neutrality to a war in two theaters. Although militarily weak, the United States was an economic giant, commanding a vast industrial capacity and access to resources. America grew even stronger under the stimulus of war, increasing its production by 400 percent in two years. It now devoted itself to the demands of a total war and the unconditional surrender of Germany and then Japan.

The Allies, however, did not always share the same strategies or concerns. President Roosevelt and Prime Minister Churchill had already discussed common goals in the summer of 1941 before U.S. entry into the war. The United States embraced the priority of the European war and the postponement of war in the Pacific. Stalin pleaded for the Anglo-Americans to open up a second front against Germany in western Europe in order to give his troops some relief and save Soviet lives. Anglo-American resources were committed to the Pacific in order to stop the Japanese advance, and the Americans and the British disagreed as to where a second front in Europe might be opened.

Because of British interests in the Mediterranean, Churchill insisted on a move from North Africa into Sicily and Italy. This strategy was put into effect in 1942. The Italian government withdrew from the war in September, but German troops carried on the fight in Italy. The Anglo-American invasion of Italy did little to alleviate Russian losses, and the Soviet Union absorbed almost the entire force of German military power until 1944. Stalin's distrust of his allies increased. Churchill, Roosevelt, and Stalin met for the first time in late November 1943 at Teheran, Iran. Roosevelt and Churchill made a commitment to Stalin to open a second front in France within six months. Stalin, in turn, promised to attack Japan in order to aid the United States in the Pacific. The great showdown of the global war was at hand.

On 6 June 1944, Allied troops under the command of the American general Dwight D. Eisenhower (1890–1969) came ashore on the beaches of Normandy in the largest amphibious landing in history. In a daring operation identified by the code name Operation Overlord, 2.2 million American, British, and Free French forces, 450,000 vehicles, and 4 million tons of supplies poured into northern France. Allied forces broke through German lines to liberate Paris in late August. The Germans launched a last-ditch counterattack in late December 1944 in Luxembourg and Belgium. This Battle of the Bulge only slowed the Allied advance; in March 1945 American forces crossed the Rhine into Germany. Hitler,

meanwhile, refused to surrender and insisted on a fight to the death of the last German soldier. Members of his own High Command had attempted unsuccessfully to assassinate Hitler in July 1944. The final German defeat came in April 1945, when the Russians stormed the German capital of Berlin. Hitler, living in an underground bunker near the Chancellery building, committed suicide on 30 April 1945.

In the Pacific, the planned Japanese invasion of Australia was thwarted. Fighting in the jungles of New Guinea, Australian and American troops under the command of General Douglas MacArthur (1880–1964) turned back the Japanese army. U.S. Marines did likewise with a bold landing at Guadalcanal and months of bloody fighting in the Solomon Islands. In June 1942, within six months of the attack at Pearl Harbor, American naval forces commanded by Admiral Chester Nimitz (1885–1966) inflicted a defeat on the Japanese navy from which it could not recover. In the battle of Midway Japan lost 4 aircraft carriers, a heavy cruiser, over 300 air planes, and 5,000

Supplies for the Allied forces pour ashore at the beachheads of Normandy during Operation Overlord in 1944. The invasion began the opening of the second front that Stalin had been urging on the Allies since the German armies thrust into Russia in 1941.

men. Midway was the Pacific equivalent of the Battle of Stalingrad.

In the summer of 1943, as the Soviet Union launched the offensive that was to defeat Germany, America began to move across the Pacific toward Japan. Nimitz and MacArthur conceived a brilliant plan in which American land, sea, and air forces fought in a coordinated effort. With a series of amphibious landings, they hopped from island to island. Some Japanese island fortresses like Tarawa were taken; others like Truk were bypassed and cut off from Japanese home bases. With the conquest of Saipan in November 1944 and Iwo Jima in March 1945, the United States air force acquired bases from which B-29 bombers could strike at the Japanese home islands. In the summer of 1945, in the greatest air offensive in history, American planes destroyed what remained of the Japanese navy, crippled Japanese industry, and mercilessly firebombed major population centers. The attack ended with the dropping of atomic bombs on the cities of Hiroshima and Nagasaki. (See Special Feature, "The Atomic Wasteland," pp. 922–923.) The Japanese government accepted American terms for peace and

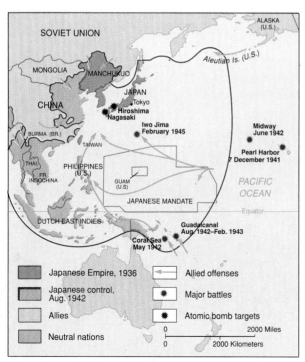

World War II in the Pacific, 1941-45

surrendered unconditionally on 2 September 1945 on the battleship *Missouri* in Tokyo Bay. Four months after the defeat of Germany the war in Asia was over.

The Fate of Allied Cooperation: 1945

The costs of World War II in terms of death and destruction were the highest in history. Fifty million lives were lost. Most of the dead were Europeans, and most of them were Russians and Poles. The high incidence of civilian deaths distinguished the Second World War from previous wars—well over 50 percent of the dead were noncombatants. Deliberate military targeting of cities explains this phenomenon only in part. The majority of civilian deaths were the result of starvation, enslavement, massacre, and deliberate extermination.

The psychological devastation of continual violence, loss, injury, and rape of survivors cannot be measured. Terrorizing citizens became an established means of warfare in the modern age. Another phenomenon not matched in the First World War emerged in 1945: mass rape. The Soviet officer corps encouraged the advancing Russian army in the use of sexual violence against German women and girls. The Russians, brutally treated by Hitler's army, returned the savagery in their advance through eastern and central Europe. Rape became a means of direct retaliation. The Great Patriotic War reached its nadir in central Europe with collective rape as a form of war against civilians.

Material destruction was also great. Axis and Allied cities, centers of civilization and culture, were turned into wastelands by aerial bombing. The Germans bombed Rotterdam and Coventry. The British engineered the fire-bombing of Dresden. Warsaw and Stalingrad were destroyed by the German army. Hiroshima and Nagasaki were leveled by the United States. The nations of Europe were weakened after World War I; after World War II, they were crippled. Europe was completely displaced from the position of world dominance it had held for centuries. The United States alone was undamaged and stronger after the war than before, its industrial capacity and production greatly improved by the war.

Churchill, Rossevelt, and Stalin—the Big Three—at the Yalta Conference. Stalin invoked the Yalta agreements to justify the Soviet Union's control over Eastern Europe after the war.

What would be the future of Europe? The leaders of the United States, Great Britain, and the Soviet Union—the Big Three as they were called—met three times between 1943 and 1945: first at Teheran; then in February 1945 at Yalta, a Russian Black Sea resort; and finally in July and August 1945 at Potsdam, a suburb of Berlin. They coordinated their attack on Germany and Japan and discussed their plans for postwar Europe. After Allied victory, the governments of both Germany and Japan would be totally abolished and completely reconstructed. No deals would be made with Hitler or his successors; no peace would be negotiated with the enemy; surrender would be unconditional. Germany would be disarmed and denazified and its leaders tried as war criminals. The armies of the Big Three would occupy Germany, each with a separate zone, but the country would be governed as a single economic unit. The Soviet Union, it was agreed, could collect reparations from Germany. With Germany and Japan defeated, a United Nations organization would provide the structure for a lasting peace in the world.

Stalin expected that the Soviet Union would decide the future of the territories of eastern Europe that the Soviet army had liberated from Germany. This area was vital to the security of the war-devastated Soviet Union; Stalin saw it as a protective barrier against another attack from the west. Romania, Bulgaria, Hungary, Czechoslovakia, and Poland, the Big Three decided, would have pro-Soviet governments. Since Soviet troops occupied these countries in 1945, there was little that the Anglo-Americans could do to prevent

Russian control unless they wanted to go to war against the USSR. Churchill realistically accepted this. But, for Americans who took seriously the proclamations of President Roosevelt that their country had fought to restore freedom and self-determination to peoples oppressed by tyranny, Soviet power in eastern Europe proved to be a bitter disappointment.

The presence of Soviet armies in eastern Europe guaranteed that communism would prevail there after 1945. In western Europe the American and British presence fostered the existence of parliamentary democracies. Germany was divided. A similar pattern emerged in Asia. The United States forces of occupation in Japan oversaw the introduction of democratic institutions. The USSR controlled Manchuria. Korea was divided. The celebration of victory after a war in which 50 million people died did not last long. Nor did the Anglo-American cooperation with the Soviet Union endure. With the defeat of Germany and Japan, two ideological systems stood facing each other suspiciously across a divided Europe and a divided Asia.

Suggestions for Further Reading

Political Polarization in the 1930s

Richard F. Kuisel, *Capitalism and the State in Modern France: Renovations and Economic Management in the Twentieth Century* (Cambridge: Cambridge University Press, 1981). Surveys twentieth-century French economic history with special attention to the role of technocracy and planning. The intersection of politics and economics and the failure of liberal solutions is treated in chapter 4.

Claudia Koonz, *Mothers in the Fatherland: Women, the Family, and Nazi Politics* (New York: St. Martin's Press, 1987). A pioneering history of women's choices and women's actions in the Third Reich in which the author analyzes the importance of middle-class women's organizations that supported Nazism.

Maurice Larkin, *France Since the Popular Front: Government and People, 1936–1986* (Oxford: Clarendon Press, 1988). A work of total history that situates French political developments in the history, traditions, social structure, and economy of France. Separates the legend from the legacy of the Popular Front.

Ian Kershaw, *The "Hitler Myth": Image and Reality in the Third Reich* (New York: Oxford University Press, 1987).

The Atomic Wasteland

The sixth of August 1945 was a typical summer day in southwestern Japan. In the city of Hiroshima at 8:15 A.M. people were walking to work, sitting down at office desks, riding buses, weeding gardens, and clearing away breakfast dishes. Suddenly a noiseless flash lit the sky over the city and environs for miles. A mammoth column of smoke in the shape of a mushroom cloud ballooned up. The United States had dropped history's first atomic bomb.

The explosion had the intensity of a huge blast furnace. In some areas, the brilliant light created by the explosion bleached everything it touched. Near the epicenter of the blast, human bodies were charred to cinders or turned into frightening statues. Elsewhere, flesh melted and bones fused. Buildings were reduced to ashes. Stones bled. The world had never seen a bomb like this. Hiroshima, a city renowned in prewar Japan for its relaxed and agreeable atmosphere, was leveled by the terrifying force of a single atomic bomb.

There were 78,000 dead in Hiroshima on 6 August. By December the number had reached 140,000 as the sickness caused by radioactive poisoning continued to take its toll. Rescue workers inhaled the dense dust and became contaminated by radioactivity. Surviving victims often lost their hair and eyebrows, experienced nausea, vomiting, diarrhea, and bleed-

ing. Others suffered from internal hemorrhaging, blindness, chronic weakness, fatigue, and leukemia. Many developed cancer, sometimes years later. The bomb scarred and disfigured. Atomic radiation released by the bomb caused unseen damage by attacking the lungs, heart, bone marrow, and internal organs. It poisoned the lymph glands. It worked unobserved to alter genetic structure, deforming unborn babies and those not yet conceived.

Harry Truman, who became president of the United States on 12 April 1945, following the death of Franklin D. Roosevelt, later spoke of his decision to drop the atomic bomb in order to bring about a speedy end to the war. In July 1945 Truman issued an ultimatum to Japan to surrender immediately or face dire consequences. The Japanese ignored the warning. Hiroshima was targeted, according to Truman, in order to make a point to the Japanese, to demonstrate the unimaginable force of this new American weapon. The city was a military center, a major storage and assembly point that supplied the armed forces. Nagasaki, bombed three days after Hiroshima with an experimental plutonium bomb, was targeted as an industrial center and the place where the torpedoes that had destroyed American ships were manufactured.

It is undoubtedly true that the bombings were responsible

for the Japanese surrender that followed a few days later. The atomic bomb did bring the Asian war to an immediate end. But critics of the bombings pointed out that Japan was already close to defeat. Secret U.S. intelligence studies that came to light in the 1980s indicate that American leaders knew that Japan had been weakened by intense American incendiary bombing of its cities. Twenty-six square miles of the working-class and industrial section of Tokyo had been burned at the cost of well over 100,000 lives. Many refugees from other Japanese cities had fled to Hiroshima to live with relatives. The Sea of Japan had been heavily mined, cutting off Japan from its armies on the Asian mainland. Some young radical officers of the Japanese army were preparing to kidnap Emperor Hirohito in order to keep him from capitulating. The planned American landing on Japan was expected to be costly. U.S. forces had already suffered over 100,000 casualties in the conquest of the Japanese island of Okinawa in April. Truman and his advisers were now prepared to use any means possible to prevent further American casualties. Defenders of the decision have argued that any responsible American leader would have made the same decision to use the atomic bomb. Modern total wars acquire a life of their own, and desperate nations use the science, technology, and weapons available to them.

In the summer of 1945, General Dwight D. Eisenhower, then the victorious Supreme Allied Commander in the European theater of war, was informed by U.S. Secretary of War Henry L. Stimson of what was about to take place in Hiroshima. Eisenhower voiced his "grave misgivings" based on his "belief that Japan was already defeated and that the dropping of the bomb was completely unnecessary" to end the war. He was not alone among military men in questioning the use of nuclear force on strategic and moral grounds. Strong opposition to nuclear weapons began to surface among scientists working on the bomb. In opposition to many of their colleagues, they warned that the atomic bomb was an undiscriminating weapon that could not pinpoint supply depots and military targets but would destroy entire civilian populations. The peace movement based on banning nuclear weapons actually began among horrified scientists who were aware, before the rest of the world could know, of the terrible force that they had helped to create.

At the Potsdam Conference in July 1945 Stalin had informed President Truman and Prime Minister Winston Churchill that the Soviet Union was about to invade Manchuria, honoring the promise he had made at Teheran in 1943 to join the war against Japan after Germany was defeated. The Soviet Union would now play a role in determining the future of Asia.

Truman told Stalin of the powerful new weapon America had developed. Stalin seemed unimpressed. Secretary of War Stimson was aware that the atomic bomb would be an important weapon to have in the American arsenal when the time came to negotiate a post-war world settlement with the Russians. Truman and his advisers, however, never deviated from their insistence that saving the lives of thousands of American and Japanese soldiers was their only consideration in dropping the bomb.

An American observer called the bombing of Hiroshima "the immersion in death." Survivors repeatedly described Hiroshima after the "flash" as what hell must be like. Photographs of the city record the total devastation to buildings and vegetation. Japanese cameramen avoided photographing the devastation to human bodies, believing that what they saw was too horrible to record. Yet the brutality of nuclear war could not be ignored. It has become a central issue of international politics in the second half of the twentieth century. The decision to drop the atomic bomb has had enduring moral and political consequences. On that August morning in 1945, the world had its first terrifying glimpse of the power of total annihilation. In an instant—0.3 second— Hiroshima became an atomic wasteland. The world now lived with the knowledge that it could happen again.

Examines the power of the "Hitler" myth created by the German Propaganda Ministry, the German people, and Hitler. The myth accounted for the stability of the Third Reich throughout the thirties and in the first years of the war.

MacGregor Knox, *Mussolini Unleashed, 1939–1941: Politics and Strategy in Fascist Italy's Last War* (Cambridge: Cambridge University Press, 1982). Argues that Mussolini had a consistent and planned foreign policy in the Mediterranean and a genuine program for living space in the Mediterranean and the Middle East. In his bid for power and prestige, Mussolini was willing to risk war and short-term instability at home.

Detlev Peukert, *Inside Nazi Germany: Conformity, Opposition, and Racism in Everyday Life* (New Haven, CT: Yale University Press, 1987). Discusses the informal modes of resistance among the German people.

The Coming of World War II

Andreas Hillgruber, *Germany and the Two World Wars*, translated by William C. Kirby (Cambridge, MA: Harvard University Press, 1981). A series of clear and concise lectures by a leading scholar of the period.

Eberhard Jäckel, *Hitler's World View: A Blueprint for Power*, translated by Herbert Arnold (Cambridge, MA: Harvard University Press, 1972). Argues for the intentionality of Hitler's plan for world domination and his persecution of the Jews by examining Hitler's writings and actions before and after he came to power.

Paul Kennedy, *The Realities Behind Diplomacy: Background Influences on British External Policy, 1865–1980* (London: Allen & Unwin, 1981). Essays dealing with the continuity of appeasement in British foreign policy across two centuries.

Ian Kershaw, *The Nazi Dictatorship* (London: Edward Arnold, 1985). A fine synthesis of key problems of interpretation regarding the Third Reich. Special attention is paid to the interdependence of domestic and foreign policy and the inevitability of war in Hitler's ideology.

Donald Cameron Watt, *How War Came: The Immediate Origins of the Second World War* (London: Heinemann, 1989). An international historian chronicles the events leading to the outbreak of the war.

Racism and Destruction

Renate Bridenthal, Atina Grossmann, and Marion Kaplan, eds., *When Biology Became Destiny: Women in Weimar and Nazi Germany* (New York: Monthly Review Press, 1984). A volume of essays pursuing common themes on the relation between sexism and racism in interwar and wartime Germany.

Raul Hilberg, *The Destruction of the European Jews* (New York: Holmes and Meier, 1985), 3 volumes. An exhaustive study of the annihilation of European Jews

beginning with cultural precedents and antecedents. Examines step-by-step developments that led to extermination policies and contains valuable appendices on statistics and a discussion of sources.

Gerhard Hirschfield, ed., *The Policies of Genocide: Jews and Soviet Prisoners of War in Nazi Germany* (London: Allen & Unwin, 1986). A collection of essays by leading specialists of the Third Reich dealing with controversial issues of intentionality, participation, and resistance in the "final solution."

Claude Lanzmann, director, *Shoah*, 4-volume videocassette; *Shoah: The Complete Text of the Claude Lanzmann Film*, with a preface by Simone de Beauvoir (New York: Pantheon Books). *Shoah* is a nine-and-a-half-hour video archive that documents the experiences of concentration camp survivors and features interviews with Poles and Germans who lived in the vicinity of the camps between 1941 and 1945.

Charles S. Maier, *The Unmasterable Past: History, Holocaust, and German National Identity* (Cambridge, MA: Harvard University Press, 1988). A thoughtful discussion of the historical debate over the Holocaust and the comparative dimensions of the event. Especially valuable in placing the Holocaust within German history.

Michael R. Marrus, *The Holocaust in History* (New York: New American Library, 1987). A comprehensive survey of all aspects of the Holocaust, including the policies of the Third Reich, the living conditions in the camps, and the prospects for resistance and opposition.

David S. Wyman, *The Abandonment of the Jews: America and the Holocaust, 1941–1945* (New York: Pantheon Books, 1984). A damning account with documentation of the failure of the United States to act on its certain knowledge of the Holocaust.

Allied Victory

John Campbell, ed. *The Experience of World War II* (New York: Oxford University Press, 1989). This richly illustrated work provides an overview of the Second World War in both the Asian and European theaters, in terms of origins, events, and consequences.

Akira Iriye, *The Origins of the Second World War in Asia and the Pacific* (London: Longman, 1987). Examines the events of the 1930s leading up to hostilities in the Pacific theater, with a special focus on Japanese isolation and aggression.

John Keegan, *The Second World War* (New York: Viking, 1990). Provides a panoramic sweep of "the largest single event in human history," with special attention to warfare in all its forms and the importance of leadership.

Susan J. Linz, *The Impact of World War II on the Soviet Union* (Totowa, NJ: Rowman & Allanfied Publishers, 1985). Fourteen scholars in the field of Soviet studies evaluate World War II and its effects on society, politics, and the economy.

29

Postwar Recovery and Crisis: From the Cold War to the New Europe, 1945–1968

Sex and Drugs and Rock 'N' Roll

"I Wanna Hold Your Hand" seems an unlikely anthem for a generation. Yet this song, performed by the British rock group the Beatles was known around the world in the early 1960s by an entire generation of the young. Youth screamed and swooned and danced to it. Parents and educators screamed, too, but out of fear that "Beatlemania" signaled the decline of the younger generation in Western societies. Adults worried that young people were being caught up in hedonism, sexual pleasure, and mind-numbing drugs, all because of this loud, cacophonous music.

Young people of the fifties and sixties saw the advent of rock 'n' roll differently. Rock 'n' roll emerged as a national phenomenon in the United States in the mid-1950s, firmly rooted in the black music of rhythm and blues. White country and western music was also influential in shaping the new sound. Titles like "Rock Around the Clock," "Shake, Rattle, and Roll," "Keep A-Knockin'," and "Blue Suede Shoes," captured the attention of a generation. The experiences of teenagers were at the center of the new rhythms, confronted in the lyrics and amplified with electric guitars. Rock 'n' roll appealed to the young because it dealt openly with the issues of sex and young love and was aimed at the hypocrisy of the adult white world. Even the sound was revolutionary. It became "the music of the young," something that accentuated their differences from the adult world and their commonalities with each other.

Babies born after World War II began entering adolescence

near the end of the 1950s, constituting a new audience for mass entertainment. They were also an important international mass market for music, as popular recordings began selling in the millions for the first time in history on such a scale. Music was now an important consumer product. Elvis Presley, a white country blues singer from Memphis, Tennessee, emerged as the greatest figure on the rock 'n' roll scene in the late 1950s. His overt and androgynous sexuality, gyrating hips, and explicit lyrics made him an object of adult fears about loss of control of their children. He quickly developed a worldwide following of devoted fans, who hailed him "the King" and who continue to honor his memory years after his death.

In the 1960s, British groups such as the Beatles from Liverpool entered the international rock scene. Dubbed "the mop tops" because of their long hair, they were condemned for transgressing sex roles in their appearance. Millions of boys copied their idols as hair became a political issue, a symbol of rebellion. Billboards appeared across the United States that proclaimed, "Beautify America—Get A Haircut!" With the new music came a new style of dressing, what adults saw as a uniform of disrespect for traditional values and parental authority. The British group Rolling Stones, who introduced electronic innovations to rock music, was considered more outrageously

sexual, vulgar, and lewd than their countrymen the Beatles. Antirock movements cited "specialists" who warned that the new, amplified music caused deafness, drug addiction, and excessive sexual activity.

The gap between the generations yawned into a gulf as rock music became political in the mid-1960s. Bob Dylan, an American rock performer, introduced folk music to the genre with songs of social protest like "Blowin' in the Wind" and "Only a Pawn in Their Game." Rock music was denounced as a communist plot, as performers urged their audiences to "Make Love, Not War." Dylan's "Subterranean Homesick Blues" targeted the hypocrisy of his society:

> Ah get born, keep warm
> Short pants, romance, learn
>   to dance
> Get dressed, get blessed
> Try to be a success
> Please her, please him, buy
>   gifts
> Don't steal, don't lift
> Twenty years of schoolin'
> And they put you on the
>   day shift
> Look out kid
> they keep it all hid

Although rock music served as a rallying cry for a generation who opposed war and exploitation, its frankness about sexuality did not result in a reformulation of gender roles. Woman's place in rock music was usually as an object of desire. Few of the major rock stars were women. The American artist Janis Joplin

was a striking exception. What was known in the rock world as "girl groups"—the Ronettes and the Shangri-Las are two examples—reinforced predominantly male views of sexuality both by their dress and by the lyrics of their songs. The female body was treated as a commodity itself in the fashions associated with the new youth culture, such as the miniskirt and the bikini. Girls and young women were important consumers of the new music and the values it communicated.

Rock music quickly became an international phenomenon, spreading from the United States and Great Britain to appeal to the young throughout the world. Rock stars were the new self-made millionaires, often from working-class backgrounds, who were able to benefit from advertising innovations and mass-marketing techniques in a new age of consumption. The postwar generation that grew into adulthood beginning in the late 1960s shared a common musical culture. Student protest movements spread throughout Europe and the United States, and in the same period rock music gained acceptance as a legitimate and important musical genre. Through radio, television, and the international distribution of recordings, an international youth culture linked European and American youth together with common symbols and a common language of protest.

Regulating the Cold War

With the cessation of the "hot" war that had ripped Europe apart from 1939 to 1945, the armies of the United States and the Soviet Union met on the banks of the Elbe River in 1945. Greeting each other as victors and allies, the occupying armies waited for direction on how to conduct the peace. Europe and Japan were destroyed, leaving the United States and the Soviet Union as indisputably the two richest and strongest nations in the world. The Soviets understood that they ran a sorry second to American military superiority—the United States was alone in possessing the atomic bomb—and to American wealth, which, measured in GNP, was 400 percent greater than that of the Soviet Union. War had made these two superpowers allies; now the peace promised to make them once again into wary foes. In the three years that followed the war, a new kind of conflict emerged between the two superpower victors, a war deemed "cold" because of its lack of military violence, but a bitter war nonetheless.

The Cold War emerged as an ideological opposition between communism and capitalist democracies, dominated by the two superpowers, the Soviet Union and the United States, and affecting the entire globe. Drawing on three decades of distrust between the East and the West, the Cold War was related to the economic and foreign policy goals of both superpowers.

Cold War conflict initially developed because of differing Russian and American notions regarding the economic reconstruction of Europe. The Soviet Union realized that American aid to Europe was not a primarily humanitarian program. It was part of an economic offensive in Europe that would contribute to the dominance of American capital in world markets. The United States recognized that the Soviet Union hoped to achieve its own recovery through outright control of eastern Europe. Needing the stability of peace, the Soviets saw in eastern Europe, hostile as the area may have been to forced integration, a necessary buffer against Western competition. The Soviet Union feared U.S. intentions to establish liberal governments and capitalist markets in these states bordering its own frontiers and

viewed such attempts as inimical to Soviet interests. For these reasons, Stalin refused to allow free elections in Poland and by force of occupying armies annexed neighboring territories that included eastern Finland, the Baltic States, East Prussia, eastern Poland, the Subcarpathian Ukraine (Ruthenia), and Bessarabia. With the exception of East Prussia, these annexations were all limited to territories that had once been part of tsarist Russia.

Winston Churchill captured the drama of the new international order in a speech he delivered in Missouri in 1946: "From Stettin in the Baltic to Trieste in the Adriatic an iron curtain has descended across the continent." The term *iron curtain* described graphically for many the new fate of Europe, rigidly divided between East and West, a pawn in the struggle of the superpowers.

Atomic Politics

The nuclear arms race began in earnest during World War II, well before the first atomic bomb was dropped in August 1945. The Germans, the Russians, and the British all had teams exploring the destructive possibilities of nuclear fission during the war. But the Americans had the edge in the development of the bomb. Stalin understood the political significance of the weapon and committed the Soviet Union to a breakneck program of development following the war. The result was that the USSR ended the American monopoly and tested its first atomic bomb in 1949. Both countries developed the hydrogen bomb almost simultaneously in 1953. Space exploration by satellite was also deemed important in terms of detection and deployment of bombs, and the Soviets pulled ahead in this area with the launching of the first satellite, *Sputnik I* in 1957. Intercontinental ballistic missiles (ICBMs) followed, further accelerating the pace of nuclear armament.

The atomic bomb and thermonuclear weapons contributed greatly to the shape of Cold War politics. The incineration of Hiroshima and Nagasaki sent a clear message to the world about the power of total annihilation available to those who controlled the bombs. The threat of such total destruction made full and direct confronta-

Territorial Gains of the USSR

public addresses throughout the fifties. Traitors were publicly tried, while espionage was sponsored by the state.

The first nuclear test-ban treaty, signed in 1963, banned tests in the atmosphere. Arms limitation and nonproliferation were the subjects of a series of conferences between the United States and the Soviet Union in the late 1960s and pointed the way to limitations eventually agreed on in the next decade. The United Nations, created by the Allies immediately following World War II to take the place of the defunct League of Nations, established international agencies for the purpose of harnessing nuclear power for peaceful uses. On the whole, however, the arms race persisted as a key continuity in Cold War politics. The race required the dedication of huge national resources to maintain a competitive stance. Conventional forces, too, were expanded to protect Eastern and Western bloc interests. With the aim of containing the USSR, the United States entered into a series of military alliances around the world. In order to provide mutual assistance should any member be attacked, the United States joined with Belgium, Britain, Canada, Denmark, France, Iceland, Italy, the Netherlands, Norway, and Portugal in 1949 to form the North Atlantic Treaty Organization (NATO). Greece and Turkey became members in 1952, West Germany in 1955, and Spain in 1982. The potential military threat of the Soviet Union in western Europe prompted this peacetime military alliance. The Southeast Asia Treaty Organization (SEATO) in 1954 and the Baghdad Pact of 1955 (known as CENTO in 1959) followed. The United States strengthened its military presence throughout the period by acquiring 1,400 military bases in foreign countries for its own forces. The Soviet Union countered developments in the West with its own alliances and organizations. In 1949, the USSR established the Council for Mutual Economic Assistance, or Comecon, with bilateral agreements between the Soviet Union and eastern European states. Comecon was Stalin's response to the U.S. Marshall Plan in western Europe. Rather than providing aid, however, Comecon benefited the Soviet Union at the expense of its partners and sought to integrate and control the economies of eastern Europe for Soviet gain. In 1955, Albania, Bulgaria, Romania, Czechoslo-

tion with an equally armed enemy impossible. Both the United States and the Soviet Union, the first two members of the nuclear "club," knew that they had the capability of obliterating their enemy but not before the enemy could respond in retaliation. They also knew that the technology necessary for nuclear arms was available to any industrial power. By 1974 the "nuclear club" included Great Britain, France, the People's Republic of China, and India. These countries joined the United States and the Soviet Union in spending the billions necessary every year to expand nuclear arsenals and to develop more sophisticated weaponry and delivery systems.

A new vocabulary transformed popular attitudes and values. "Missile gaps," "deterrence," "first strike," "second strike," "radioactive fallout," and "containment" were all terms that colored popular fears. Citizens in the Soviet Union learned of American weapons stockpiling and American deployment of military forces throughout the world. Americans learned that the Russians had the ability to deliver bombs that could wipe out major U.S. cities. Paranoia on both sides was encouraged by heads of state in their

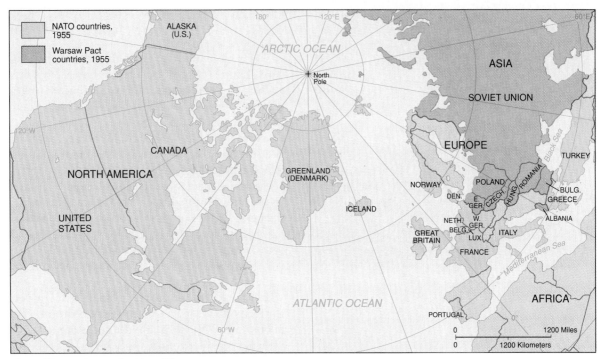

The Cold War: U.S. and Soviet Alliances

vakia, Hungary, Poland, and East Germany—all Comecon members—joined with the Soviet Union to form a defensive alliance organization known as the Warsaw Pact. The USSR intended its eastern European allies to serve as a strategic buffer zone against the NATO forces.

Atomic politics encouraged brinksmanship, a term coined by John Foster Dulles (1888–1959), U.S. secretary of state from 1953 to 1959. Brinksmanship referred to a confrontationist foreign policy that brought the superpowers repeatedly to the edge of armed conflict. It also encouraged a new kind of global politics in which the superpowers vied with each other to find new partners, especially in formerly colonized areas, to join their camps.

Decolonization

By the end of the Second World War, European colonial empires had been weakened or destroyed by the ravages of battle, by occupation, and by neglect. The United States, committed to free and open markets, pushed its advantage at the conclusion of the peace by insisting on the disman-

tling of the empires of its Allies as well as those of its enemies. The Soviets, preoccupied with their own recovery, were in no position to assert a global policy at the end of the war.

Nationalist movements had been growing in power in the 1930s, and many nationalist leaders saw the war as a catalyst for independence, especially in Asia. Great Britain knew that it no longer commanded the resources to control India, historically its richest colony, which under the leadership of Mohandas Gandhi (1869–1948) had been agitating for independence since 1920. Given the title of "Mahatma" or "great-souled" by his people, Gandhi advocated passive resistance to achieve independence. He campaigned by means of civil disobedience, boycotts, and public fasts instead of violence to bring pressure on the colonizers. The British granted self-government to India in 1946 with the proviso that if the bitter conflict between Hindus and Muslims was not settled by mutual agreement, Great Britain would decide on the division of power. As a result, Muslim and Hindu representatives agreed to the division of British India into the independent states of India and Pakistan in 1947. Ceylon (now

Sri Lanka) and Burma (now Myanmar) achieved full independence in 1948.

In its march through Asia during the war, Japan had smashed colonial empires. Japan's defeat created a power vacuum that nationalist leaders were eager to fill. Civil wars erupted in China, Burma, Korea, and Indochina. Anti-colonial resistance opened the way to Communist insurgence. Indochina declared its independence in 1945 and waged war with France until 1954. South Vietnam was declared a republic, and the United States sponsored a regime that was considered favorable to Western interests. The North Vietnamese state was established under the French-educated leader, Ho Chi Minh. The civil war continued, with the North Vietnamese backing the National Liberation Front in the South. After almost two decades of escalating involvement, in 1973 American troops were finally withdrawn from a war they could not win. Cold War politics had enmeshed the United States in Southeast Asia and Cold War imperatives had kept it there.

The first wave of decolonization after 1945 had been in Asia. A second wave crested and crashed in the late 1950s and early 1960s in Africa, another ready battleground for Cold War dominance. During the Second World War, North Africa had served as a theater of military action, while South Africa was a source of supplies and troops. Wartime experiences and rapid economic development fed existing nationalist aspirations and encouraged the emergence of mass political demands for liberation. A new generation of leaders, many of them educated in European institutions, moved from cooperation with home rule to demands for independence by the early 1960s. British prime minister Harold MacMillan (1894–1986) spoke of "the winds of change" in 1960, the year that proved to be a turning point in African politics. Britain and Belgium yielded their colonies. In 1960 Patrice Lumumba (1925–61) became the first prime minister of the Republic of the Congo (present-day Zaire). White European rule continued in Rhodesia (now Zimbabwe) and South Africa, despite continued world pressure.

French troops move into the Catholic town of Bui Chu in Vietnam during the war to regain the French colonies in Indochina.

The French, having faced what its officer corps considered a humiliating defeat in Indochina, held on against the winds of change in North Africa. France's problems in Algeria began in earnest in 1954 when Muslims seeking independence and self-rule revolted. Although the Algerian rebels successfully employed terrorist and guerrilla tactics, European settlers and the French army in Algeria refused to accept defeat. The Fourth Republic was on the verge of collapse when General Charles de Gaulle (1890–1970), leader of the Free French resistance in World War II, stepped in to establish the Fifth Republic with a strong executive. He ended the war and agreed to Algeria's independence, which was achieved in 1962.

One supporter of the Algerian revolution, Frantz Fanon (1925–61), was working as a French-trained psychiatrist in Algeria when the revolution began. In his writings, especially his book *The Wretched of the Earth* (1961), he argued in favor of national liberation movements and for the necessity of violence. Fanon described the trap of dependence of colonized countries: "We go on

sending out raw materials; we go on being Europe's small farmers; we specialize in unfinished products."

Decolonization meant continued dependence for many Third World countries, as they were now known. First World nations were identified as the advanced industrial countries; Second World countries were those whose lower level of prosperity indicated a transition from agricultural to industrial production. Third World nations were suppliers of raw materials and food to the countries of the First World. These countries were no longer directly controlled as colonies but continued to be dominated by the Western capitalist powers and Japan, on whom they relied for their markets and trade. As Frantz Fanon had described it, these newly independent countries had to continue doing what they had done as colonies: supplying raw materials to their former masters.

African leader Kwame Nkrumah (1909–72) of Ghana denounced this situation of dependence as "neocolonialism" and called for a united Africa as the only means of resistance. Nkrumah argued that "aid" was merely a "revolving credit" plan

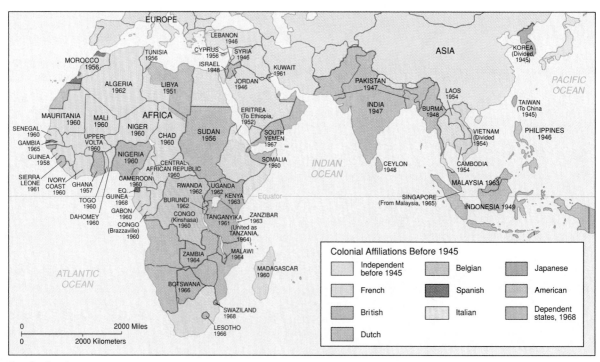

Decolonization

Jubilant Algerians celebrate the granting of independence to their country on 3 July 1962, after a bloody seven-year war. Many Europeans whose families had been settled in Algeria for generations fled during the fighting or left after independence was won.

that returned increased profits to the former colonial masters while extracting wealth from African nations. He led Ghana in a policy of nonalignment in the Cold War. With Jomo Kenyatta (1894–1978) of Kenya, he founded the Pan-African federation, which promoted African nationalism.

Soviet leader Joseph Stalin limited the Soviet Union's foreign involvement following the Second World War to communist regimes that shared borders with the USSR in eastern Europe and Asia. After Stalin's death in 1953, the Soviet Union

turned to the Third World. Former colonies played an important new role in the Cold War strategies with the accession to power of Nikita Khrushchev (1894–1971) in the mid-1950s. The Soviet Union abandoned its previous caution and assumed a global role in offering "friendship treaties," military advice, trade credits, and general support for attempts at national liberation in Asia, Africa, and Latin America. Cold warriors took advantage of tribalism and regionalism, which mitigated against the establishment of strong central governments. Military rule and fragmentation often resulted. Instability and acute poverty continued to characterize former colonies after emancipation, regardless of which camp the new leaders joined.

The Two Germanies and the World in Two Blocs

In central Europe Cold War tensions first surfaced over the question of how to treat Germany. The United States and the Soviet Union had very different ideas about the future of their former enemy. In fostering economic reconstruction in Europe, the United States counted on a German economy transfused with American funds that would be self-supporting and stable. To the contrary, the Soviet Union, blaming Germany for its extreme destruction, was explicit in its demands: German resources must be siphoned off for Soviet reconstruction. Stricken as the Soviets were with twenty million dead, millions of homeless refugees surviving in dire poverty, and 1,700 cities in ruins, commandeering German labor and stripping Germany of its industrial plant seemed to them only fair.

With Germany's defeat, its territory had been divided into four zones, occupied by American, Soviet, British, and French troops. An Allied Control Commission consisting of representatives of the four powers was to govern Germany as a whole in keeping with the decisions made at Yalta before the end of the war. As Soviet and American antagonisms over Germany's future deepened, however, Allied rule polarized between East and

German children (above) climb atop a pile of rubble left from the wartime bombing of Berlin as they cheer on an allied plane bringing supplies to the beleaguered city during the airlift. A brother and sister (right) on the way home from school walk down a deserted street in a bombed-out section of Berlin. They carry tin cans for the hot meal they receive in school.

West, with the internal politics of each area determined by the ideological conflicts between communism and capitalist free enterprise.

Allied attempts to administer Germany as a whole faltered and failed in 1948 over a question of economic policy. The zones of the Western occupying forces (the United States, Great Britain, and France), now administered as a single unit, issued a uniform and stable currency that the Russians accurately saw as a threat to their own economic policies in Germany. The Soviets blockaded the city of Berlin which, although behind the frontier of the Russian sector, was being administered in sectors by the four powers and whose western sector promised to become a successful enclave of Western capitalism. With the support of the people of West Berlin the Allies responded by airlifting food and supplies into West Berlin for a period of almost a year, defending it as an outpost that must be preserved from the advance of communism. The Russians were forced to withdraw the blockade in the spring of 1949. The Berlin blockade hardened the commitment on both sides to two Germanies.

The two new states came into existence in 1949, their origins separated by less than a month. The Federal Republic of Germany, within the American orbit, was established as a democratic, parliamentary regime. Free elections brought the Christian Democrat Konrad Adenauer to power as chancellor. The German Democratic Republic was ruled as a single-party state under Walter Ulbricht, who took his direction from the Soviet Union.

The division of Germany became a microcosm of the division of the world into two armed camps. With the support of local Communist parties, Soviet-dominated governments were established in Poland, Hungary, Bulgaria, and Romania in 1947. The following year Czechoslovakia was pulled into the Soviet orbit. Czechoslovakia serves as a significant marker in the development of

Cold War confrontation. The tactics of the Communists in Czechoslovakia taught the West that coalition governments were unacceptable and undoubtedly hardened the resolve of U.S. policymakers in support of two Germanies.

In 1953 the man who had ruled the Soviet Union in his own image for almost three decades died. The death of Joseph Stalin unleashed a struggle for power among the Communist party leadership. It also initiated almost immediately a process of de-Stalinization and the beginnings of a thaw in censorship and repression. A growing urban and professional class expected improvements in the quality of life and greater freedoms after years of war and hardship. In 1956, at the Twentieth Party Congress, Nikita Khrushchev, as head of the Communist party, denounced Stalin as incompetent and cruel. After five years of jockeying for power among Stalin's former lieutenants, Khrushchev emerged victorious and assumed the office of premier in 1958.

De-Stalinization also blossomed in eastern Europe. Discontent over collectivization, low wages, and the lack of consumer goods fueled a latent nationalism among eastern European populations resentful of Soviet control and influence. Violence erupted in 1953 in East Berlin as workers revolted over conditions in the workplace, but it was quickly and effectively suppressed. Demands for reforms and liberalization in Poland also produced riots and changes in Communist party leadership. Wladislaw Gomulka (1905–82), a Communist with a nationalist point of view who had survived Stalin's purges, aimed to take advantage of the power vacuum created by the departure of Stalinist leaders. Gomulka refused to back down in the face of severe Soviet pressure and the threat of a Soviet invasion to keep him from power. Elected as the first secretary of the Communist party in Poland, Gomulka sought to steer his nation on a more liberal course.

Hungarians followed suit with their demands for diversity and for the withdrawal of Hungary from the Warsaw Pact. On 23 October 1956, inspired by the events in Poland, Hungarians rose up in anger against their old-guard Stalinist rulers. Imre Nagy (1896–1958), a liberal Communist, took control of the government, attempted to introduce democratic reforms, and relaxed economic controls. The Soviets, however, were unwilling to lose control of their sphere of influence in Eastern Bloc nations and to jeopardize their system of defense in the Warsaw Pact. Moscow responded to liberal experimentation in Hungary by sending tanks and troops into Budapest. Brutal repression and purges followed. The Hungarian experience in 1956 made clear that too much change too quickly would not be tolerated by the Soviet rulers. The thaw following Stalin's death had promoted expectations among eastern Europeans that a new era was dawning. The violent crushing of the Hungarian revolution reminded everyone of the realities of Soviet control and the Soviet Union's defense priorities in eastern Europe.

East Berlin in the late 1950s and early 1960s posed a particular problem for Communist rule. Unable to compete successfully in wages and standard of living with the western, capitalist sector of the city, East Berlin saw increasing numbers of its population, especially the educated and professional classes, crossing the line to a more prosperous life. In 1961 the Soviet Union re-

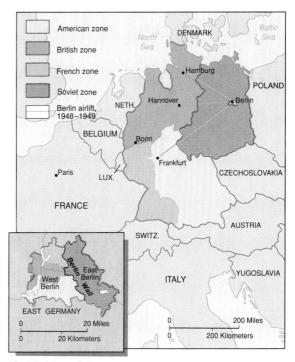

The Division of Germany

sponded to this problem by building a wall that cordoned off the part of the city that it controlled. The Berlin Wall eventually stretched for 103 miles, with heavily policed crossing points, turrets, and troops and tanks facing each other across the divide that came to symbolize the Cold War.

The process of liberalization that had begun after Stalin's death and continued under Khrushchev certainly experienced its setbacks and reversals in the case of Budapest and Berlin. But it was

Angry citizens of Budapest rip up portraits of Matyas Rakoski (First Secretary of the Workers' Party) and throw them on a fire during the Hungarian uprising of 1956. The revolt did not bring freedom to Hungary, but it helped cut short the Stalin era in the Soviet Union.

in 1968 that the policy of de-Stalinization reached a critical juncture in Czechoslovakia. Early in 1968, Alexander Dubček, Czech party secretary and a member of the younger, educated generation of technocrats, supported liberal reforms in Czechoslovakia that included decentralization of planning and economic decision-making, market pricing, and market incentives for higher productivity and innovation. He acted on popular desires for nationalism, the end of censorship, and better working conditions. Above all, he led the way to democratic reforms in the political process that would restore rule to the people. Dubček spoke of "socialism with a human face," although, unlike the Hungarians in 1956, he made no move to withdraw his country from the Warsaw Pact or to defy Soviet leadership. Moscow nevertheless feared the erosion of obedience within the Eastern Bloc and the collapse of one-party rule in the Czech state, and sent in thousands of tanks and hundreds of thousands of Warsaw Pact troops to Prague and other Czech cities to reestablish control. The Czechs responded with passive resistance. The Soviet invasion made clear that popular nationalism was intolerable in an Eastern Bloc nation.

Alone among eastern European leaders, Josip Broz (1892–1980), better known as Marshal Tito, of Yugoslavia resisted Soviet encroachment. As a partisan leader of the Communist resistance during World War II, Tito had heroically battled the Germans. Ruling Yugoslavia as a dictator after 1945, he refused to accede to Soviet directives to collectivize agriculture and to participate in joint economic ventures. For its defiance of Soviet supremacy, in 1948 Yugoslavia was expelled from the Cominform, the Soviet-controlled information agency that replaced the Comintern after 1943.

No part of the globe escaped the tensions generated by the Cold War. Asia was the next arena for the development of Cold War antagonisms. In 1950 the United States and the United Nations intervened when North Korea attacked South Korea. Korea, formerly controlled by Japan, had been divided following the war as a result of the presence of Russian and American troops. Communist-dominated North Korea refused to

Soviet tanks rumbled through Prague as troops from the Warsaw Pact countries invaded the Czechoslovakian capital in 1968, bringing an end to Alexander Dubček's reform movement. Dubček was rehabilitated in the liberalization of 1989 and elected chairman of the parliament.

accept the artificial boundary between it and Western-dominated South Korea. China, a Communist state following the victory of Mao Ze-dong (1893–1976) in 1949, intervened in the Korean conflict when American troops advanced on Chinese frontiers in October 1950. After three years of military stalemate, Korea was partitioned on the 38th parallel in 1953. The Soviet Union was not party to the conflict in Korea, but the United States considered China to be in the Soviet camp rather than an independent contender for power.

The Middle East was another theater of confrontation between the superpowers. The United States and the Soviet Union used aid to win support of "client" states. The withdrawal, sometimes under duress, of British and French rule in the Middle East and North Africa, and the crea-

tion of the new state of Israel in 1948 destabilized the area and created the opportunities for new power alliances. Egypt and Syria, for example, sought Soviet support against the new Israeli state, which had been formed out of the part of Palestine under British mandate from 1920 and was dependent on U.S. aid.

Oil, an essential resource for rapid industrialization, was the object of Soviet politicking in Iran after the war. Western oil companies, long active in the area, had won oil concessions in Iran in 1946, but such rights eluded the Soviets. In 1951, a nationalist Iranian government sought to evict Westerners by nationalizing the oil fields. The British blockaded Iranian trade in the Persian Gulf, and the newly formed American espionage organization, the Central Intelligence Agency

(CIA), subverted the nationalist government and placed in power the Shah of Iran, a leader favorable to American interests.

A crisis came in 1956 in Egypt. Egyptian president Gamal Abdel Nasser (1918–70), a nationalist in power by virtue of a military coup d'état in 1952, oversaw the nationalization of the Suez Canal. British and French military forces attacked and were forced to withdraw by pressure from both the Soviet Union and the United States, which cooperated in seeking to avert a disaster. The Middle East, however, remained a Cold War powder keg, with Israeli and Arab nationalist interests and Soviet and American aid running on a collision course. The expansion of the Israeli state at the expense of its Arab neighbors further exacerbated tensions.

The United States was heavily committed as a military presence in Southeast Asia after the French withdrawal from Indochina caused by its defeat at Dien Bien Phu in 1954. Arguing the domino theory—that one Southeast Asian country after another would fall like a row of dominoes to Communist takeover—the United States also intervened in Laos and Cambodia. Between 1961 and 1973, the United States committed American troops to a full-scale war—though officially termed only a military action—against Communist guerrilla forces throughout the region.

The United States was also experiencing Cold War problems closer to home. In 1954 the CIA plotted the overthrow of Guatemala's leftist regime in order to keep Soviet influence out of the Western Hemisphere. In 1958, President Dwight Eisenhower sent his vice-president, Richard Nixon, on a tour of Latin American countries. Crowds everywhere jeered the American vice-president and hurled stones and eggs at his motorcade, in response to U.S. policies. In 1959 a revolution in Cuba, an island nation only ninety miles off the American coast, resulted in the ejection of U.S. interests and the establishment of a Communist regime under the leadership of a young middle-class lawyer, Fidel Castro. In 1962 a direct and frightening confrontation occurred between the United States and the USSR over Soviet missile installations in Cuba. Following the Russian withdrawal from the island, both U.S.

president John F. Kennedy and Soviet leader Nikita Khrushchev pursued policies of "peaceful coexistence," intent on averting nuclear confrontation. Both sides recognized how close they had come to mutual annihilation in the showdown over Cuba.

Another kind of challenge to Cold War power politics came from within the NATO alliance. General Charles de Gaulle, as president of the French Fifth Republic, rejected the straitjacket of American dominance in Western Europe and asserted his country's independent status by exploding the first French atomic bomb in 1960. Refusing to place the French military under an American general who served as Supreme Allied Commander for NATO, de Gaulle completely withdrew France from participation in NATO by 1966. He forged an independent French foreign policy, taking advantage of the loosening of bloc politics around the mid-1960s.

In May 1965 U.S. secretary of state Dean Rusk observed, "This has become a very small planet. We have to be concerned with all of it—with all of its land, waters, atmosphere, and with surrounding space." Atomic politics in the Cold War era had helped to shrink the globe by bringing the threat of destruction closer to home. In the mid-1960s leaders of the two great blocs of East and West began to realize that peaceful coexistence was the only reasonable outcome of the atomic age and that alternatives to the arms race must be found.

Reconstructing Europe

Europe faced peace in 1945 politically disorganized and economically crippled. Allied and Soviet occupation forces carved Germany into zones and its capital, Berlin, into sectors. In the international arena, growing antagonism marked relations between the United States and the Soviet Union, the two nations that controlled the future of Europe.

When the dust from the last bombs settled over Europe's cities, the balance sheets of destruction were tallied. Millions of survivors found themselves homeless, having lost their loved ones, often all of their personal belongings, and the roofs over their heads. Millions returned home to rubble from battlefronts and concentration camps with wounds beyond healing. There were no jobs; there was nothing to eat. Peacetime rationing dipped below wartime levels. What was not measured in the statistics on physical and human destruction, at least immediately, was the psychological devastation that succeeded such loss. There could be no returning to life as normal. For many the war was far gentler than the peace. For these combatants of peacetime, often women and children, digging out and surviving were the greatest battles of all.

The Problem: Europe in Ruins

An American observer wrote back to his government in 1947 that "Europe is steadily deteriorating. The political position reflects the economic. One political crisis after another merely denotes the existence of economic distress. Millions of people in the cities are slowly starving." Even the winners were losers as survivors experienced a level of human and material destruction unknown in the history of warfare. Economists judged that Europe would need at least twenty-five years to regain its prewar economic capacity. The worst was also feared: that Europe would never recover as a world economic power.

Large-scale population movements made matters worse. Displaced persons by the millions moved across Europe. The release of prisoners of war and slave-workers imprisoned during the Third Reich strained already weak economies. Germans were expelled from territories that Germany had controlled before the war. Soviet expansionist policies forced others to flee Estonia, Latvia, and Lithuania. Jews who survived the concentration camps resettled outside Europe, primarily in Palestine and the United States.

Industrial production in 1945 was a third of its level in 1938. Housing shortages existed everywhere. France had lost one-fifth of its housing during the war years; Germany's fifty largest cities had seen two-fifths of their buildings reduced to rubble. Frankfurt, Düsseldorf, Dresden, Warsaw,

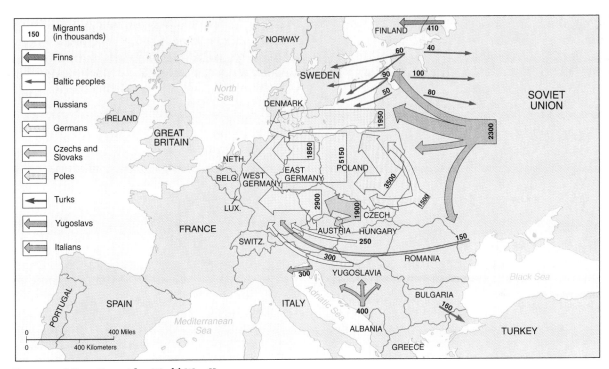

European Mirgrations After World War II

and Berlin were virtually destroyed. The transportation infrastructure was severely damaged: railways, roads, and bridges were in shambles all over Europe. Communications networks were in disarray. In some cases, industrial plants had not been as adversely affected as urban centers. Yet machinery everywhere had been worn out in wartime production and replacement parts were nonexistent. German equipment was dismantled and seized by Soviet soldiers to be used in Russia in place of what the Germans had destroyed.

Agriculture, too, suffered severe reversals in wartime economies and was unable to resume prewar production in 1945. In general, European agriculture was producing at 50 percent of its prewar capacity. Livestock had been decimated during the war years—in France, for example, 50 percent of all farm animals had been killed—and it was estimated that restoring herds would take decades. Italy suffered greatly, with one-third of its overall assets destroyed. The scarcity of goods converged with ballooning inflation. Black markets with astronomical prices for necessities flourished, as currency rates plummeted. Everywhere the outlook was bleak. Yet in less than a decade, the situation had been reversed. The solution came from outside of Europe.

The Solution: The Marshall Plan

The Soviet Union implemented an expansion of its territorial boundaries as a way of reversing some of its drastic losses in the war. Above all, it wanted a protective ring of satellite states as security from attack from the west. Stalin also was eager to see the Soviet Union surrounded by "friendly" governments in eastern Europe to replace the hostile regimes with which the Soviets had had to contend in the interwar period. Picking up territory from Finland and Poland, parts of East Prussia and eastern Czechoslovakia, forcibly reincorporating the Baltic states of Estonia, Latvia, and Lithuania, and recovering Bessarabia, the Soviet Union succeeded in acquiring sizable territories. In addition, the Soviet state dedicated itself to economic reconstruction behind a protective buffer of satellite states—Poland, East Germany, Czechoslovakia, Hungary, Romania, Bulgaria—over which Soviet leaders exercised strong control. Yugoslavia and Albania chose to follow a more independent Communist path. Lacking the capital necessary to finance recovery, the Soviets sought compensation from eastern and central European territories.

In contrast to the Soviet Union, the United States had incurred relatively light casualties in World War II. Because the fighting had not taken place on the North American continent, U.S. cities, farmlands, and factories were intact. As the chief producer and supplier for the Allied war effort, even before its entry into the conflict, the United States had benefited from the conflict in Europe and actually expanded its economic productivity during the war. In 1945 the United States was producing a full 50 percent of the world's gross national product—a staggering fact to a displaced Great Britain, whose former trade networks were permanently destroyed. Furthermore, the United States held two-thirds of the world's gold. A United States bursting with energy and prosperity was a real threat to the Soviet Union viewing the rubble of its destroyed cities and counting the bodies of its dead.

The United States knew that it lacked one important guarantee to secure its growth and its future prosperity: adequate international markets for its goods. After World War I, American officials and businessmen understood that America's productive capacity was outpacing its ability to export goods. In the 1920s the United States had exported capital to Europe in the form of private loans with the hope that trade would flourish as a result. The decade following the Great Depression of 1929 witnessed the search for a policy to expand  U.S. markets. Both Europe and Japan were recognized as potential buyers for American goods, but both areas parried with protectionism to foster their own postdepression recovery. World War II facilitated the success of an international economic policy consistent with U.S. economic goals since 1920. In both Europe and Japan, the United States intervened to aid reconstruction and recovery of war-torn nations. These economies, hungry for capital, no longer opposed U.S. intervention or erected trade barriers against American goods. The prospect of a Europe in chaos economically, socially, and politically and on the verge of collapse justified immediate action by the United States.

By the spring of 1947 it was clear to American policymakers that initial postwar attempts to stabilize European economies and promote world recovery were simply not working. The United States had, earlier in the same year, engineered emergency aid to Turkey and Greece, both objects of Soviet aspirations for control. President Truman articulated a "doctrine" bearing his name: "I believe that it must be the policy of the United States to support free people who are resisting attempted subjugation by armed minorities or by outside pressures." The aid emerged in an atmosphere of opposition between the United States and the Soviet Union over issues of territorial control in eastern and southern Europe. The Cold War coincided with and reinforced the U.S. need to reconstruct Western Europe.

On 5 June 1947, Secretary of State George C. Marshall (1880–1959) delivered the commencement address at Harvard University. In his speech Marshall introduced the European Recovery Act, popularly known as the Marshall Plan, through which billions of dollars in aid would be made available to European states, both in the east and in the west, provided that two conditions were met: (1) the recipient states must cooperate with one another in aligning national economic policies and improving the international monetary system; (2) they must work toward breaking down trade barriers.

Participating countries included Austria, Belgium, Denmark, France, West Germany, Great Britain, Greece, Iceland, Italy, Luxembourg, the Netherlands, Norway, Sweden, Switzerland, and Turkey. Russia and eastern European countries were also eligible for aid under the original formulation. But Russia opposed the plan from the first, wary of U.S. intentions to extend the influence of Western capitalism. Soviet opposition encouraged members of the U.S. Congress, afraid

This West German poster says "Clear the road for the Marshall Plan." The truck is flying the flags of many of the Euopean nations that were recipients of Marshall Plan aid.

of a Communist takeover in Europe, to support the plan.

Like the United States, the Soviet Union had its own economic imperatives that dictated its attitudes toward European economic development. Under Stalin's direction, the Soviet Union concentrated all its efforts on reconstructing its devastated economy and, to this end, sought integration with eastern European states, whose technology and resources were needed for the rebuilding of the Soviet state. U.S. dominance threatened the vital connection with eastern Europe that the Soviet Union was determinedly solidifying in the postwar years.

The amount of U.S. aid to Europe was massive. Over $23 billion was pumped into Western

Europe between 1947 and 1952. By every measure the Marshall Plan was judged a success in the West. American foreign aid restored western European trade and production, while at the same time controlling inflation. Dean Acheson (1893–1971), Marshall's successor as secretary of state, described the plan in terms of "our duty as human beings" but nevertheless considered it "chiefly as a matter of national self-interest." Soviet critics and Western observers differed dramatically in describing the relationship between self-interest and philanthropy as motives for the plan.

Administering the Plan

As significant as the gift of funds to European states undoubtedly was, no less important was the whole administrative apparatus that American money brought in its wake. In order to expend available monies most effectively and comply with stipulations for cooperation and regulation, the states of western Europe resorted to intensified planning and limited nationalization. These ideas were not new in the experience of European states: Vichy France, for example, had emphasized the importance of planning and specialization in its corporatist approach to economic development and social-welfare policies. Regulation and state intervention dominated the formulation of economic policy. Special attention was given to workers' welfare through unemployment insurance, retirement benefits, public health, and housing policies. European states recognized the need to provide a safety net for their citizens in order to avoid the disastrous depression and stagnation of the 1930s, while attempting to rebuild their shattered economies. These were lessons that had been learned as much from the attempts at recovery before 1939 as from the experiences of running wartime economies.

The economic theory of John Maynard Keynes (1883–1946), applied successfully by neutral Sweden to its economic policies during the war, came into vogue throughout Europe in 1945, and the postwar era saw the triumph of Keynesian economics. Keynes favored macroeconomic policies to increase productivity and argued for an active role for government in "priming the pump" of economic growth. The government should be responsible, according to Keynes, for the control and regulation of the economy with the goal of ensuring full employment for its people. Governments could and should check inflation and eliminate boom-and-bust cycles, incurring deficits by spending beyond revenues if necessary.

U.S. foreign aid contributed mightily to the extension of central planning and the growth of the welfare state throughout Western Europe. But money alone could not have accomplished the recovery that took place. The chief mechanism for administering Marshall Plan aid was the Office of European Economic Cooperation (OEEC). This master coordinating agency made the requirements for recovery clear. European states had to stabilize their own economies. Cooperation between the public and private sectors was intended to free market forces, modernize production, and raise productivity. Planning mechanisms, including transnational organizations and networks, resulted in the modernization of production and the assimilation of new techniques, new styles of management, and innovative business practices from the United States. This modernization of economies through centrally coordinated planning made Europe once again a major contender in the international economic arena.

The major exception to the establishment of central planning agencies and the nationalization of key industries was West Germany. Deciding against the British and French models of planned growth, the West Germans endorsed a free-market policy that encouraged private enterprise while providing state insurance for all workers. What has been described as "a free enterprise economy with a social conscience" produced the richest economy in Western Europe by the mid-1950s. Some West German industries had been dismantled, but much of West Germany's productive capacity remained intact in the late 1940s. The wealth of great industrialists like Krupp, serving prison sentences as war criminals, was not expropriated and their commercial empires stood ready to direct the economic revival. The Krupp and I.G. Farben empires were successfully broken up into smaller units. Industries forced to start afresh benefited from the latest technology.

Japanese economic challenges in the postwar era were similar to those of western Europe. As a defeated and occupied nation in 1945, Japan faced a grim future. U.S. aims for Asia were similar to those for Europe: American policymakers sought to create a multilateral system of world trade and preserve America's sphere of influence against communist encroachment. The American general Douglas MacArthur (1880–1964) was appointed the Supreme Commander for the Allied Powers and the head of occupation forces in Japan. His mission in Japan was to impose rapid economic change from above. The occupation government set out to erect institutions to promote political democratization and to eliminate militaristic institutions, official patronage, and censorship. Planning, both formal and informal, reshaped the economy as U.S. aid flowed into Japan during the late forties and early fifties. These changes in Japan, as in western Europe, took place alongside growing American fears of communism in the region.

Japan turned its wartime devastation into an advantage by replacing destroyed, obsolete factories with the latest technology obtained by license from foreign firms. Through a combination of bureaucracy and patronage devoted to planned growth, Japan's GNP reached prewar levels by 1956. By 1968, Japan had turned defeat into triumph and stood as the third largest industrial nation in the world. Japanese growth paralleled the "economic miracle" of West Germany, with the Japanese economy growing at a rate three times faster than that of the United States between 1954 and 1967.

The abolition of the army and navy was a boon for the Japanese economy, since 16 percent of prewar GNP had been devoted to support of the military. Postwar demilitarization freed Japan of the financial exigencies of the arms race. Funds formerly used for arms now flowed into investment and new technology. Slowed population growth after 1948 and increased volume in foreign trade contributed to Japanese prosperity. In the 1960s, Japan emerged as an affluent society undergoing a revolution in consumer durables including televisions, washing machines, refrigerators, and family automobiles.

The United States had succeeded in exporting aspects of its own economy abroad. Through management and planning, recipients of American aid surpassed U.S. goals. A multilateral system of world trade emerged out of the ashes of war. The effects of the Depression, which the world had been unable to shake throughout the 1930s, had been laid to rest by global war and its consequences.

Western European Economic Integration

European integration, discussed before and during the war, received added impetus in the postwar period. The Marshall Plan reconciled western Europe with West Germany through economic cooperation, although that was by no means its original purpose. Realizing that Europe as a region needed the cooperation of its member states if it was to contend in world markets, associations dedicated to integration began to emerge alongside economic planning mechanisms. The Council of Europe dealt with the "discussion of questions of common concern and by agreements and common action in economic, social, cultural, scientific, legal, and administrative matters and in the maintenance and further realization of human rights and fundamental freedoms." Although not itself a supranational institution with its own authority, the Council of Europe urged a federation among European states. Britain alone rejected all attempts to develop structures of loose, intergovernmental cooperation.

Belgium, the Netherlands, and Luxembourg were the first European states to establish themselves as an economic unit—the Benelux. Internal customs duties were removed among the three states and a common external tariff barrier was erected. The Schuman Plan joined France and West Germany in economic cooperation by pooling all coal and steel resources beginning in 1950. Creators of the plan, Jean Monnet (1888–1979) and Robert Schuman (1886–1963) of France, saw it as the first step toward the removal of all eco-

A train carrying iron ore crosses the Franco-Luxembourg border, celebrating the joint community in coal and steel that became effective in 1953. The European Coal and Steel Community was the first step in the economic integration of Europe.

the beginning of what became known as the Common Market.

The Common Market aimed to establish among its member states a free movement of labor and capital, the elimination of restrictions on trade, common investment practices, and coordinated social-welfare programs. National agricultural interests were to be protected. Great Britain was initially a vocal opponent of the Common Market and continued to defend its own trading relationship with its Commonwealth countries, eventually founding its own free trade association in 1959. In 1973 Great Britain became a member of the Common Market and joined with other European nations in defining common economic policies. The EEC meanwhile achieved the support of the United States in its transitional period, in which it had fifteen years to accomplish its aims.

European union was a phenomenon of exclusion as much as inclusion. It sharpened antagonisms between the West and the East by its very success. While promoting prosperity, European economic unification favored concentration and the emergence of large corporations. Vast individual fortunes flourished under state sponsorship and the rule of the experts. National parliaments were sometimes eclipsed by superfluous new economic decision-making organizations that aimed to make Western Europe into a single free-trade area. The Soviet Union, too, relied on state planning to foster rapid economic growth, but it was central planning emanating from Moscow, based on different assumptions and directed toward different ends.

Creating the Welfare State

The welfare state, a creation of the post-World War II era throughout Europe, grew out of the social welfare policies of the interwar period and out of the war itself. Welfare programs aimed to protect citizens through the establishment of a decent standard of living available for everyone. The experiences of the Great Depression had done much to foster concern for economic security. In France, the primary concern of the welfare state was the protection of children and

nomic barriers among European states and as a move toward eventual political integration. In 1951 the Netherlands, Belgium, Luxembourg, France, Italy, and West Germany formed the European Coal and Steel Community (ECSC). While constantly confronting domestic opposition on nationalist grounds, the ECSC succeeded in establishing a "common market" in coal and steel among its member states. In 1957 the same six members created the European Economic Community (EEC) and committed themselves to broadening the integration of markets. This was

This free bathhouse for babies was set up near East Berlin in 1946 in response to chronic shortages of soap and fuel in the Eastern Bloc.

the issue of family allowances. In Great Britain, as in Germany, emphasis was placed on unemployment insurance and health care benefits. Everywhere, however, the welfare state developed a related set of social programs and policies whereby the state intervened in the cycles of individual lives to provide economic support for the challenges of birth, sickness, old age, and unemployment. (See Special Feature, "Utopia Lost," pp. 946–947.)

Protection of citizenry took varied forms according to Cold War politics. In the Warsaw Pact countries, the need to industrialize rapidly and to dedicate productive wealth to armament and military protection resulted in a nonexistent consumer economy in which the issues of quality of life and protection took a very different direction. Based on a concept of equal access to a minimum standard of living, welfare states did not treat all its members equally. Women were often disadvantaged in social welfare programs, as family needs, men's rights, and the protection of children led to different national configurations.

Prosperity and Consumption in the West

Despite the different paths toward reconstruction following World War II, every western European nation experienced dramatic increases in total wealth. Per capita income was clearly on the rise through the mid-1960s, and there was more disposable wealth than ever before. Prosperity encouraged new patterns of spending based on confidence in the economy. This new consumerism, in turn, was essential to economic growth and future productivity.

The social programs of the welfare state played an important role in promoting postwar consumption. People began to relax about their economic futures, more secure because of the provisions of unemployment insurance, old-age pensions, and health and accident insurance. The state alleviated the necessity of saving for a rainy day by providing protection that was formerly covered out of the savings of workers. In the mid-1950s all over western Europe people began to spend their earnings, knowing that accidents,

Utopia Lost

The pig's name is Napoleon. The farmer who drinks too much and loses control of his animals is named Jones. In his "fairy tale" entitled *Animal Farm*, George Orwell (pseud. of Eric Arthur Blair, 1903–1950) gives us a deceptively simple and frightening tale of rebellion and tyranny. The farmyard animals of Mr. Jones know they are exploited by their human masters. When they can stand it no longer, they rise up against their oppression. Their revolution succeeds only when one animal, a pig, emerges as the revolutionary leader, the consolidator of revolutionary aims. It is he who is named Napoleon.

The animals' cause is just: they want equality and fair treatment for their labors. They dream of a world that is a utopia, a place free of care and filled with comforts. But in the process of wresting power and consolidating it, their paradise is lost, their utopia distorted. The seven commandments of the animal revolution are rewritten in such a way that all power resides in the dictator pig. All principles are reduced to one commandment: "All animals are equal, but some animals are more equal than others." A desire for a better life has produced a dictatorship that is far worse than the human tyranny the animals overthrew.

George Orwell created a *dystopia*, a utopia turned inside out, a dream that ends as a nightmare, a paradise lost in a new hell of oppression. Working in the same tradition as Thomas More's sixteenth-century masterpiece, *Utopia*, Orwell uses his fable to criticize contemporary institutions and events. In his parable of farmyard life, Orwell intended to "fuse political purpose and artistic purpose into one whole" in an assault on totalitarianism. Orwell's novel appeared in 1946. *Animal Farm* is recognizably an indictment of the Russian Revolution, an event that Orwell considered had soured under Stalinist rule and one that had colored the politics of the twentieth century with false hope. It served as a fitting herald to Cold War politics in the West.

Yet *Animal Farm* indicts more than communist rule in one country. It is a fairy tale without a moral, a profoundly cynical appreciation of the advances of civilization in the twentieth century. The civilization that Orwell judged so negatively had made important advances in science, technology, state organization, and a rhetoric of equality and welfare. For the donkeys, horses, and chickens of the farmyard—as for people in his own society—liberal and democratic values shrivel when squared off against the realities of power and force. In the end, the farm grows richer but the animals do not. The dreams of a better life, of the luxuries that electric power could bring, fade. The pigs become the ruling class, controlling information in mysterious files, memoranda, and reports. Neither technology nor government bureaucracy has improved animal life. The animals now work harder to support a greedy and parasitic ruling class.

Most unsettling of all, the animals lack their own history, remembering only what they are told was their past. In the concluding pages of the work, an old donkey by the name of Benjamin, who has lived through the pre revolutionary and revolutionary periods and who is now under the yoke of the new tyrant pig, declares that things are little different from the old days: hunger, hardship, and disappointment are the unalterable laws of life. His memory serves as the only historical record. Napoleon now lives in farmer Jones' house, sleeps in his bed, wears his clothes, and drinks his whiskey. In the greatest perversion of the transfer of power, the pig now walks on his two hind legs, terrifyingly humanized.

Orwell's fusion of politics and art did not stop with *Animal Farm*. In *Nineteen Eighty-Four* (1949), he created an equally horrifying picture of the future, one that does not resort to animal parables but instead portrays a mechanized kind of inhuman tyranny, that of Big Brother, a force that sees all and controls all, down to what people think. Both works were

banned in the Soviet Union and in communist eastern Europe. Many intellectuals of the post-war period shared Orwell's concern for what they saw as the erosion of personal freedom. For Orwell, the liberal traditions of the West were as hollow as the socialist promises of the Soviet world were dangerous. The great principle of equality, the cornerstone in the Western political tradition, served as the instrument of a new oppression.

Standing on the edge of the abyss of war, revolution, and human suffering in the twentieth century, Orwell peered into the future and saw ahead only what he was trying to leave behind.

disasters, and sicknesses would be taken care of by the state.

The main items in the new consumption were consumer durables, above all, televisions and automobiles. Refrigerators and washing machines also developed mass markets, as did the increased consumption of liquor and cigarettes. Increased leisure resulted in the mass consumption of vacation travel. In addition to spending their salaries, western Europeans began to buy on credit, spending money they had not yet earned. This, too, was an innovation in postwar markets. People sought immediate gratification through consumption now by means of delayed payment against future earnings.

Welfare programs could be sustained only in an era of prosperity and economic growth, since they depended on taxation of income for their funds. Such taxation did not, however, result in a redistribution of wealth. Wealth remained in the hands of a few and became even more concen-

trated as a result of phenomenonal postwar economic growth. In West Germany, for example, 1.7 percent of the population owned 35 percent of the society's total wealth.

Just as the welfare state did not redistribute wealth, neither did it provide equal pay for equal work. In France, women who performed the same jobs as men in typesetting, for example, and who on average set 15,000 keystrokes per hour at the keyboards compared to 10,000 by men, earned 50 percent of men's salaries and held different titles for their jobs. Separate wage scales for women drawn up during the Nazi period remained in effect in West Germany until 1956. The skills associated with occupations performed by women were downgraded, as were their salaries. Women earned two-thirds or less of what men earned throughout western Europe. Welfare state revenues were a direct result of pay-scale inequities. Lower salaries for women meant higher profits and helped make economic recovery possible.

A traffic jam on the Place de la Concorde in Paris in 1962. Western Europeans learned that prosperity has its price, as ninteenth-century cities were thrust into the automobile age.

The Eastern Bloc and Recovery

In the years before his death in 1953, Joseph Stalin succeeded in making the Soviet Union a vital industrial giant second only to the United States. The Soviet economy experienced dramatic recovery after 1945, in spite of the severe damage inflicted on it during the war. The production of steel, coal, and crude oil skyrocketed under state planning. Heavy industry was the top priority of Soviet recovery, in keeping with prewar commitments to rapid modernization. In addition, the postwar Soviet economy assumed the new burdens of the development of a nuclear arsenal and an expensive program for the exploration of space. Stalin maintained the Soviet Union on the footing of a war economy, restricted occupational mobility, and continued to rely on forced-labor camps.

The Soviet Union's standard of living remained relatively low in these years when western Europe was undergoing a consumer revolution. Soviet consumption was necessarily stagnant, as profits were plowed back as investments in future heavy industrial expansion. In the Soviet Union and throughout the Eastern Bloc countries, women's full participation in the labor force was essential for recovery. In spite of their presence in large numbers in highly skilled sectors like medicine, Soviet and Eastern Bloc women remained poorly paid, as did women in the West. Soviet men received higher salaries for the same work on the grounds that they had to support families.

With Stalin's death, new leaders recognized the need for change, especially with regard to the neglected sectors of agricultural production and consumer products. The Soviet population was growing rapidly, from 170 million in 1939 to 234 million in 1967. Khrushchev promised the Russian people lower prices and a shorter work week but in 1964, when he fell from power, Russians were paying higher prices for their food than before. With a declining rate of development, the Soviet economy lacked the necessary capital to advance the plans for growth in all sectors. Defense spending nearly doubled in the short period between 1960 and 1968.

The nature of planned Soviet growth exacted heavy costs in the Eastern Bloc countries. Adher-

Women worked alongside men in heavy industrial jobs to implement the Soviet Five-Year plans. This woman welder is working on the construction of a giant tractor factory in Byelorussia.

ing to the Soviet pattern of heavy industrial expansion at the expense of agriculture and consumer goods, East Germany nearly doubled its industrial output by 1955, despite having been stripped of its industrial plant by the Soviet Union before 1948. Czechoslovakia, Bulgaria, Romania, and Yugoslavia all reported significant industrial growth in this period. Yet dislocations caused by collectivization and heavy defense expenditures stirred up social unrest in East Germany, Czechoslovakia, Poland, and Hungary. The Soviet Union responded with some economic concessions but on the whole stressed common industrial and defense pursuits, employing ideological persuasion and military pressure to keep its reluctant partners in line. The slowed growth of the 1960s, the delay in development of consumer durables, and the inadequacy of basic foodstuffs, housing, and clothing were the costs that Eastern Bloc citizens paid for their inefficient and rigid planned economies dedicated to the development of heavy industry. In eastern Europe and the Soviet Union, poverty was virtually eliminated, however, as the state subsidized housing, health care, and higher education, which were available to all.

Family Strategies

The pressures on European women and their families in 1945 were often greater than in wartime. Severe scarcity of food, clothes, and housing required careful management. Women who during the war held jobs in industry and munitions plants earned their own money and established their own independence. After the war in victorious and defeated nations alike, women were moved out of the work force to make room for returning men. Changing social policies affected women's lives in the home and in the workplace and contributed to the politicization of women within the context of the welfare state.

Demography and Birth Control. Prewar concerns with a declining birth rate intensified after World War II. In some European countries the birth rate climbed in the years immediately following the war, an encouraging sign to observers who saw in this trend an optimistic commitment to the future after the cessation of the horrors of war. The situation was more complicated in France and the United States, where the birth rates began to climb even before the war was over. Nearly everywhere throughout Europe, however, the rise in the birth rate was momentary, with the United States standing alone in experiencing a genuine and sustained "baby boom" until about 1960. In Germany and in eastern Europe (Poland and Yugoslavia, for example) the costs of the war exacted heavy tolls on families long after the hostilities ended. On average, women everywhere were having fewer children by choice.

Technology had expanded the range of choices in family planning. In the early 1960s, the birth-control pill became available on the Euro-

pean and American markets, primarily by middle-class women. Europeans were choosing to have smaller families. The drop in the birth rate had clearly preceded the new technological interventions that included intrauterine devices (IUDs), improved diaphragms, sponges, and more effective spermicidal creams and jellies. The condom, invented a century earlier, was now sold to a mass market. Controversies surrounded the unhealthy side effects of the pill and the dangerous Dalkon shield, an IUD that had not been adequately tested before marketing and that resulted in the death or sterilization of thousands of women. Religious leaders spoke out on the moral issues surrounding sexuality without reproduction. Information about their reproductive lives became more accessible to young women. Illegal abortions continued to be an alternative for women. In France and Italy birth control information was often withheld from the public. Abortion was probably the primary form of birth control in the Soviet Union in the years following the war.

The Family and Welfare. Concurrent with a low birth rate was a return to family life and family values in the years after the war. Those who had lived through the previous twenty years were haunted by the memories of the Great Depression, severe economic hardships, destructive war, and the loss of loved ones. Women and men throughout western Europe and the United States embraced family values and a return to normal life, even if they did not opt for large families. Expectations for improved family life placed new demands on welfare state programs. They also placed increased demands on mothers, whose presence in the home was now seen as all-important for the proper development of the child. Handbooks for mothers proliferated, instructing them in the "science" of child-rearing. The bestseller *Baby and Child Care* by Dr. Benjamin Spock was typical of such guides.

European states implemented official programs to encourage women to have more children and to be better mothers. "Pronatalism," as this policy was known, resulted from an official concern over low birth rates and a decline in family size. It is unlikely that pronatalism was caused by a fear of a decline in the labor force, since the influx of foreign workers, refugees from eastern Europe, and migrant laborers from poorer southern European nations provided an expanding labor pool. Other considerations about racial dominance and woman's proper role seem to have affected the development of policies. In 1945, Lord Beveridge (1879–1960), the architect of the British welfare state, emphasized the importance of women's role "in ensuring the adequate continuance of the British race" and argued that women's place was in the home: "During marriage most women will not be gainfully employed. The small minority of women who undertake paid employment or other gainful employment or other gainful occupations after marriage require special treatment differing from that of single women."

Welfare state programs differed from country to country as the result of a series of different expectations of women as workers and women as mothers. Konrad Adenauer, chancellor of West Germany, spoke of "a will to children" as essential for his country's continued economic growth and prosperity. In Great Britain, the welfare system was built on the ideal of the mother at home with her children. With the emphasis on the need for larger families—four children was considered "desirable" in England—English society focused on the importance of the role of the mother. Family allowances determined by the number of children were tied to men's participation in the work force; women were defined according to their husbands' status. The state welfare system strengthened the financial dependence of English wives on their husbands.

Women entered law enforcement in Paris in 1964 as auxiliary police charged with traffic control. In this photograph, a policewoman receives instruction from a male police officer. As a concession to traditional ideas of female roles, policewomen were assigned to work mostly near junior schools and kindergartens.

In Great Britain, anxiety over the low birth rate was also tied to the debate over equal pay for women. Opponents of the measure argued that equal pay would cause women to forgo marriage and motherhood and should, therefore, be avoided. There was a consensus about keeping women out of the work force and paying them less in order to achieve that end.

The French system of *sécurité sociale* defined all women, whether married or single, as equal to men; unlike the British system, all French women had the same rights of access to welfare programs as men. This may well have reflected the different work history of women in France and the recognition of the importance of women's labor for reconstruction of the economy. As a result, family allowances, pre- and postnatal care, maternity benefits, and child care were provided on the assumption that working mothers were a fact of life. French payments were intended to encourage large families and focused primarily on the needs of children. More and more women entered the paid labor force after 1945, and they were less financially dependent on their husbands than were their British counterparts.

Both forms of welfare state, the British that emphasized women's role as mothers, and the French that accepted women's role as workers, were based on different attitudes about the nature of gender difference and equality. Women's political consciousness developed in both societies. The women's liberation movements of the late sixties and early seventies found their roots in the contradictions of differing welfare policies.

The Beginnings of Women's Protest.

The 1960s was a period of protest in Western countries as people demonstrated for civil rights and free expression. The movement against U.S. involvement in Vietnam was fueled by the activism of the black civil rights movement. Pacifist and antinuclear groups united to "Ban the Bomb." Women participated in all of these movements, and by the end of the 1960s had begun to question their own place in organizations that did not acknowledge their claims to equal rights, equal pay, and liberation from the oppression of male society. A new critique began to form within the welfare state that indicated there were cracks in the facade.

French novelist and feminist Simone de Beauvoir participated in demonstrations for women's issues such as family planning. Her armband advocates the free use of abortion and contraception for birth control.

One book in particular, written after World War II, captured the imagination of many women who were aware of the contradictions and limitations placed on them by state and society. *The Second Sex* (1949), written by Simone de Beauvoir (1908–86), a leading French intellectual, analyzed women in the context of Western culture. By examining the assumptions of political theories, including Marxism, in the light of philosophy, biology, history, and psychoanalysis, de Beauvoir uncovered the myths governing the creation of the female self. By showing how the male is the center of culture and the female is "other," de Beauvoir urged women to be independent and to resist male definitions. *The Second Sex* became the handbook of the women's movement in the 1960s.

A very different work appeared in 1963, *The Feminine Mystique.* In this work author Betty Friedan voiced the grievances of a previously politically quiescent group of women. Friedan was an American suburban homemaker and the mother of three children when she wrote about what she saw as the schizophrenic split in her own middle-class world between the reality of women's lives and the idealized image of the perfect homemaker. After World War II women were expected to find personal fulfillment in the domestic sphere. Instead Friedan found women suffering from "the sickness with no name" and "the nameless desperation" of a profound crisis in identity.

A new politics centered on women's needs and women's rights slowly took root. The feminist critique did not emerge as a mass movement until the 1970s. Youth culture and dissent among the young further informed growing feminist discontent. But the agenda of protest in the sixties accepted gender differences reinforced by social policies as normal and natural.

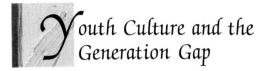

Youth Culture and the Generation Gap

Youth culture was created by outside forces as much as it was a self-creation. Socialized together in an expanding educational system from primary school through high school, the young came to see themselves as a social force. They were also socialized by marketing efforts that appealed to their particular needs as a group.

The prosperity that characterized the period from the mid-fifties to the mid-sixties throughout the West provided a secure base from which radical dissenters could launch their protests. The young people of the 1960s were the first generation to come of age after World War II. Though they had no memory themselves of the destruction of that war, they were reminded daily of the imminence of nuclear destruction in their own lives. The combination of the security of affluence and the insecurity of Cold War politics

The cover of the Beatles' album Sergeant Pepper's Lonely Hearts Club Band. *The cover was designed by pop artist Peter Blake. It featured the four members of the goup in nineteenth-century regimental army uniforms, along with a photomontage of famous faces.*

created a widening gap between the world of decision-making adults and the idealistic universe of the young. To the criticisms of parents, politicians, and teachers, the new generation responded that no one over thirty could be trusted.

New styles of dress and grooming were a rejection of middle-class culture in Europe and the United States. Anthropologists and sociologists in the 1960s began studying youth as if they were a foreign tribe. The "generation gap" appeared as the subject of hundreds of specialized studies. Adolescent behavior was examined across cultures. Sexual freedom and the use of drugs were subjected to special scrutiny. But it was above all the politics of the young that baffled and enraged many observers. When the stable base of economic prosperity began to erode as a result of slowed growth and inflation in the second half of the sixties, first in western Europe and then in the United States, frustrated expectations and shrinking opportunities for the young served as a further impetus for political action.

Sex and Drugs and Protest

Increased emphasis on fulfillment through sexual pleasure was one consequence of the technological revolution in birth-control devices, and it led to what has been called a revolution in sexual values in Western societies in the 1960s. The sexual revolution drew attention to sexual fulfillment as an end in itself. Women's bodies were displayed more explicitly than ever before in mass advertising to sell products from automobiles to soap. Sex magazines, sex shops, and movies were part of an explosion in the marketing of male sexual fantasies in the 1960s.

Sweden experienced the most far-reaching reforms of sexual mores in the 1960s. Sex education became part of every school's curriculum, contraceptive information was widely available, and homosexuality was decriminalized. Technology allowed women and men to separate pleasure from reproduction but did nothing to alter men's and women's domestic roles. Pleasure was also separated from familial responsibilities, yet the domestic ideal of the woman in the home

remained. Some women were beginning to question their exploitation in the sexual revolution. In the early 1970s that this issue became the basis of mass feminist protest.

Just as sexuality was invested with new meaning within the context of protest, so was the use of drugs. Drug use was not new in history: through the ages drugs have been taken as painkillers or pleasure enhancers, and used in religious and cultural rituals. Soldiers in nineteenth-century

Many critics perceived a connection between the rise of rock music in the 1960s and the growing use of drugs by young people. This newspaper exhorts the popular rock group The Beatles to speak out against drugs to their millions of fans.

wars in Europe and America returned home addicted to opium and morphine, which they were given when treated for their wounds. In the 1960s American soldiers in Vietnam turned to drugs as an escape from the horrors of war.

Drugs began to pervade Western cultures in apparently harmless ways. At the end of the nineteenth century in the United States, the newly created Coca-Cola was actually made with cocaine, a drug derived from the coca shrub. Another ingredient in the soft-drink formula was the kola nut, which contains the stimulant caffeine. In the 1950s and 1960s, chemical technology made possible the manufacture of synthetic drugs. Pharmaceutical industries in Europe and the United States expanded by leaps and bounds with the mass marketing of amphetamines, barbiturates, and tranquillizers. Doctors prescribed these new drugs for a variety of problems from obesity to depression to sleeplessness. People discovered that these drugs had additional mood-altering effects.

Marijuana grew in popularity as a safe "recreational" drug, especially among college and university students in the 1960s. In fact, young people were the primary users of drugs of all sorts, including synthetic drugs like the hallucinogen LSD (lysergic acid diethylamide). Hallucinogens were considered by their proponents to be mind-expanding drugs that permitted the achievement of new levels of consciousness. Drugs used by young people affluent enough to afford them served to widen the gap between the generations still further.

The Protests of 1968

Student protest, which began at the University of California at Berkeley in 1964 as the Free Speech movement, by the spring of 1968 had become an international phenomenon that had spread to other American campuses and throughout Europe and Japan. A common denominator of protest, whether in New York, London, or Tokyo, was opposition to the war in Vietnam. Growing numbers of intellectuals and students throughout the world condemned the U.S. presence in Vietnam as an immoral violation of the rights of the Vietnamese people and a violent proof of U.S. imperialism.

Student protesters shared other concerns in addition to opposition to the war in southeast Asia. The growing activism on American campuses was aimed at social reform, student self-governance, and the responsibilities of the university in the wider community. In West Germany, highly politicized radical activists, a conspicuous minority among the students at the Free University of Berlin, directed protest out into the wider society. Student demonstrations met with brutal police repression and violence, and rioting was common.

European students, more than their American counterparts, were also experiencing frustration in the classroom. European universities were unprepared to absorb the huge influx of students in the 1960s. The student-teacher ratio at the University of Rome, for example, was 200 to 1. In Italian universities in general, the majority of over half a million students had no contact with their professors. The University of Paris was similarly overcrowded.

For the most part, student protest was primarily a middle-class phenomenon. In France, for example, only 4 percent of university students came from below the middle class. Higher education had been developed after World War II to serve the increased needs of a technocratic society. Instead of altering the social structure, as politically committed student protesters had hoped, mass education served as a certifying mechanism for bureaucratic and technical institutions. Many of the occupations that students could look forward to were in dead-end service jobs or in bureaucratic posts.

Student dissent reflected the changing economy of the late 1960s. Inflation, which earlier in the decade had spurred prosperity, was spiraling out of control in the late sixties. In the advanced industrial countries of western Europe and later in the United States, the growth of the postwar period was slowing down. Economic opportunity was evaporating and jobs were being eliminated. One survey estimated that only one in three Italian university graduates in 1967 was able to find a job. The dawning awareness of shrinking opportunities in the workplace, once students had

*Students riot in Paris in 1968. The student protests of the late 1960s were sparked in part
by the war in Vietnam and by disallusionment with the present and uncertainty about
the future.*

attained their degrees and been properly certified, further aggravated student frustration and dissent. Anger about the uncertainties of their future mixed with the realization of the boredom of the careers that awaited them upon graduation.

By the late sixties, universities and colleges provided the forum for expressing their discontent in advanced industrial societies. In their protests, student activists rejected the values of consumer society. The programs and politics of the student protesters aimed to transform the world in which they lived. Student protesters in France chanted, "Métro—Boulot—Dodo," a slang condemnation of the treadmill-like existence of those who spent their lives in a repetitive cycle of subway riding (Métro), mindless work (Boulot), and

sleep (Dodo). The spirit of protest was captured in the graffiti and posters that seemed to appear overnight on Paris walls.

> "Action must not be a reaction—but a creation"
> "Power to the Imagination"
> "The revolution will be won when the last bureaucrat is strangled in the entrails of the last cop"
> "The state is each one of us"

In May 1968 in France, protest spread beyond the university when workers and managers joined students in paralyzing the French economy and threatening to topple the Fifth Republic. Between 7 and 10 million people went on strike in support of worker and student demands. White-collar employees and technicians joined blue-collar factory workers in the strike. Student demands, based on a thoroughgoing critique of the whole society, proved to be incompatible with the wage and consumption issues of workers. But the unusual if short-lived alliance of students and workers shocked those in power and induced reforms.

The division of the world into two camps framed the recovery of combatant nations dealing with the losses of World War II. The Cold War instilled fear and terror in the populations who lived on both sides of the divide. Yet the Cold War also created the terms for stability following the upheaval of war. It promoted prosperity that preserved the long-term policies of both the United States and the Soviet Union in the twentieth century. The Soviet Union had buffered itself from the West by creating a ring of friendly nations on its borders and had continued its race to industrialize. The belief that the USSR had won the war for the Allies and the sense of betrayal that followed the war determined the outlook of grim distrust shared by postwar Soviet leaders who had survived the years from 1939 to 1945.

The United States, on the other hand, found itself playing the role of rich uncle in bankrolling the European recovery. Its long-term commitment to promote its own economic interests by helping future trading partners led it also into playing the role of policeman throughout the world. The escalating war in Vietnam made America vulnerable to growing world criticism and to growing domestic discontent.

The gains of economic recovery began to unravel in the mid-1960s. In the West, rising expectations of consumer societies came up against the harsh realities of slowed growth. In the East, frustrated nationalism, the lack of consumer goods, and repressive conditions resulted in low morale, demonstrations, and outright conflict. After Stalin's death resources were diverted to consumer goods, but there was little measurable improvement in the quality of life.

The nations of Europe and the United States sensed that they stood at a crossroads in 1968. Whether the future inspired confidence or fear remained to be seen. The threat of nuclear annihilation had considerably diminished. The euphoria of students in the West and the Prague springtime in the East seemed to be more an interlude than a turning point. If the rivalry between East and West no longer dominated the international arena, what lay ahead?

Suggestions for Further Reading

Regulating the Cold War

Franz Ansprenger, *The Dissolution of the Colonial Empires* (London: Routledge, 1989). An analysis of Europe's withdrawal from Asia and Africa following the Second World War, beginning with an examination of post–World War I imperialism.

Walter Lafeber, *America, Russia, and the Cold War, 1945–1966* (New York: John Wiley and Sons, Inc., 1978). A Cold War revisionist interpretation of American foreign policy in the two decades after World War II. Lafeber examines the influence of Soviet and American domestic policies on the two nations' foreign policies.

William Roger Louis and Roger Owen, eds., *Suez 1956: The Crisis and Its Consequences* (New York: Oxford University Press, 1989). A series of essays resulting from new research into the origins and consequences of the Suez crisis.

Charles S. Maier, ed., *The Origins of the Cold War and Contemporary Europe* (New York: Franklin Watts, 1978). A series of essays considering the origins of the Cold War and its impact on the political economy of Europe.

Charles S. Maier, *In Search of Stability: Explorations in Historical Political Economy* (Cambridgeshire: Cambridge University Press, 1987). Covers a wide variety of issues affecting twentieth-century Europe, including the foundation of American international economic policy after World War II and the conditions for stability in Western Europe after 1945.

Bruce D. Porter, *The USSR in Third World Conflicts: Soviet Arms and Diplomacy in Local Wars, 1945–1980* (Cambridgeshire: Cambridge University Press, 1984). A case study approach to the Soviet Union's changing postwar policies toward the Third World that centers on local wars in Africa and the Middle East.

Tony Smith, ed., *The End of the European Empire: Decolonization After World War II* (Lexington, MA: Heath, 1975). A collection of articles dealing with the rapid decolonization of the overseas holdings of Great Britain, France, the Netherlands, and Belgium, and the growing agitation and organization of nationalist movements.

Reconstructing Europe

Stanley Hoffman and Charles Maier, *The Marshall Plan: A Retrospective* (Boulder, CO: Westview Press, 1984). Based on a commemorative conference held at Harvard University, thirty-five years after George C. Marshall's address at that university, this collection assembles the work of specialists and actual participants in the plan's implementation.

Michael J. Hogan, *The Marshall Plan: America, Britain, and the Reconstruction of Western Europe* (Cambridgeshire: Cambridge University Press, 1987). A thoroughly researched argument on the continuities of U.S. economic policy in the twentieth century. Hogan counters the interpretation that the Marshall Plan was merely a response to the Cold War.

Derek W. Urwin, *Western Europe Since 1945: A Political History*, 4th ed. (London: Longman, 1989). An updated general survey of postwar politics with a special focus on the problems of reconstruction and the role of the resistance after 1945.

Creating the Welfare State

Simone de Beauvoir, *The Second Sex* (New York: Knopf, 1963). The author, one of France's leading intellectuals in the twentieth century, describes the situation of women's lives in the postwar West by placing them within the context of the history and myths governing Western culture.

Betty Friedan, *The Feminine Mystique* (New York: Norton, 1963). Captures the essence of the fifties' image of American middle-class women as perfect mothers and homemakers and chronicles the high social and emotional costs for women of the new feminine ideal.

Jane Jenson, "Both Friend and Foe: Women and State Welfare," *Becoming Visible: Women in European History*, edited by Renate Bridenthal, Claudia Koonz, and Susan Stuard (Boston: Houghton Mifflin, 1987). This essay illuminates the mixed blessing of the welfare state for women after 1945 by focusing on the experiences of women in Great Britain and France.

Walter Laqueur, *Europe Since Hitler: The Rebirth of Europe* (New York: Penguin Books, 1982). Surveys politics, economy, society, and culture in order to explain Europe's postwar resurgence.

Denise Riley, *War in the Nursery: Theories of the Child and Mother* (London: Virago Press, 1983). Treats social policies of postwar pronatalism within the context of the popularization of developmental and child psychologies in Europe, with special attention to Britain and the United States, and emphasis on the postwar period as a turning point in attitudes toward women and the family.

Mary Ruggie, *The State and Working Women: A Comparative Study of Britain and Sweden* (Princeton, NJ: Princeton University Press, 1984). A sociological study comparing the economic status of women in two European welfare states.

Youth Culture and Youth Dissent

David Caute, *The Year of the Barricades: A Journey Through 1968* (New York: Harper and Row, 1988). More than its title suggests, this work is an overview of postwar youth culture on three continents. The politics of 1968 is featured, although other topics regarding the counterculture, life-styles, and cultural ramifications are considered.

John R. Gillis, *Youth and History: Tradition and Change in European Age Relations, 1770–Present* (New York: Academic Press, 1981). Connects the history of European youth to broad trends in economic and demographic modernization over the last two hundred years.

Margaret Mead, *Culture and Commitment: The New Relationships Between the Generations in the 1970s* (New York: Columbia University Press, 1978). This series of essays, written by one of America's premier anthropologists, explores the origins and the consequences of the generation gap with special attention to Cold War politics, historical conditions, and technological transformations.

30

Europe Faces the Future: Hope and Uncertainty, 1968 to the Present

Toppling Communism

"Nothing Lasts Forever." Such was the wisdom of Western women and men at the end of the twentieth century as they faced cataclysmic changes in their world. After over forty years of relative postwar stability, the year 1989 marked a period of rapid political transformations. In February the Soviet Union withdrew its troops from an increasingly unpopular war in Afghanistan, paralleling the U.S. experience in Vietnam in the 1970s. In the spring of 1989 the Soviet people participated in elections. That indicated a new democratic process and popular debate challenged the Communist party rule. Reformers ousted by party leaders appealed directly to the electorate; one such reformer, Boris Yeltsin, dismissed as the head of the Moscow party in 1987 garnered 89 percent of the popular vote in the elections for the Congress of People's Deputies. Soviet citizens looked forward to democratic reforms. Soviet leader Mikhail Gorbachev took the measure of popular opinion and channeled it by championing free enterprise, individual initiative, open markets, and self-determination of peoples.

The apparent democratization of Soviet political life in 1989 was matched by dramatic transformations in central and eastern Europe among the Warsaw Pact nations that had been allied with the Soviet Union since 1955. In April, Hungarians disinterred the body of Imre Nagy, leader of the 1956 anti-Soviet uprising. He was declared a state hero and reburied with full funeral honors. The Western world was stunned, but this was just the beginning. In June, after a number of political reversals in the 1980s, democratic rule was established in Poland.

Symbols of freedom and democratic cooperation appeared everywhere in 1989. One million people joined hands to form a 370-mile-long human chain that stretched across the Soviet Baltic republics of Estonia, Latvia, and Lithuania in protest against Soviet annexation in 1940. In September 1989 East German citizens flooded into Hungary at the rate of 300 people an hour with the hope of escaping to West Germany and political and economic freedom. Soon thereafter the German borders were opened to the free movement of people. The 35-year reign of Todor Zhivkov, dictator of Bulgaria, was ended as Bulgarians endorsed parliamentary government.

Throughout central and eastern Europe people were successfully rejecting Communist values in favor of democratic free institutions. In November 1989 Czechoslovakia embraced pluralist politics and democratic rule. Tens of thousands of Czech demonstrators in the capital city of Prague sang songs about freedom and cheered their new heroes, dissidents persecuted and jailed under the former Communist regime. Communism itself had been toppled by a mass movement reminiscent of the Prague Spring of 1968, when demands for greater freedom, national autonomy, and improved economic conditions were heard and brutally repressed.

In the illustration here, a nicked and battered bust of the long-reigning Soviet dictator Joseph Stalin (1928–1953) is being carried through the streets of Prague. The placard around the neck of the bust is a reminder of the impermanence of all things: translated, it reads, "Nothing Lasts Forever." Stalinism had been long dead by 1989 even within the Soviet Union, where it was criticized and buried by Stalin's successors. Yet the bust of Stalin was an easily recognizable symbol of the worst aspects of communist rule: dictatorship, repression, and denial of individual liberties and civil rights. To the Czech people, the bust stood for communism controlled from the center by a bureaucratic elite that they were intent on overthrowing.

For many, the most dramatic moment in the collapse of communism came in November 1989 as bulldozers moved against the Berlin Wall, the tangible symbol of Cold War politics that had been erected through the center of Berlin in 1961. As the barrier came down, so too did the 18-year-old government of Communist leader Erich Honecker, who was forced to resign. The East German Communist party, confronted with popular discontent and charges of corruption, decided to change both its tune and its name.

Poland, Hungary, Bulgaria, Czechoslovakia, and East Germany all underwent what were consid-

ered to be "velvet revolutions," characterized by a lack of violence and smooth passage to a new order. The year 1989 did not end, however, without bloody upheaval. In December 1989, Nicolae Ceaucescu, Communist dictator of Romania, ordered his troops to fire on demonstrators. Thousands of men, women, and children were killed and buried unceremoniously in mass graves. The slaughter set off a revolution in which Ceaucescu and his wife and co-ruler Elena were captured, tried, and executed by a self-identified revolutionary tribunal. Their declared crimes were genocide—the slaughter of 64,000 people—and the mismanagement of the economy. In the days that followed, Romanians interviewed by the international media spoke of their newly won freedom, as videotaped images of the slain leaders were broadcast to the world.

Any one of these events by itself could have commanded world attention and shocked international opinion. Combined, they spelled the end of an era. The Eastern Bloc under Soviet control was disintegrating and communism as an ideology was crumbling. No one was sure what the future held, as changes brought instability and cut eastern and central European states free of their Soviet protector. "Nothing Lasts Forever" was a sign of the times. It reflected the optimism of hundreds of thousands of people who saw democracy, nationalism, and free markets as guarantees of a better future. Few recognized that the aphorism was a double-edged one that contained also the cynical recognition, perhaps forgotten in the euphoria of the moment, that change, even the toppling of communism, did not guarantee stability.

Ending the Cold War

The Soviet action against Czechoslovakia and other expressions of dissent in eastern Europe in 1968 seemed to affirm the power of communist unity in the Eastern Bloc. The use of military intervention to resolve the Czech crisis opened a new era governed by what came to be known as the Brezhnev Doctrine. Leonid Brezhnev (1906–82), General Secretary of the Communist party and head of the Soviet Union from 1966 to 1982, established a policy whereby the Soviet Union claimed the right to interfere in the internal affairs of its allies in order to prevent counterrevolution. Brezhnev was responsible for the decision to intervene in Czechoslovakia, arguing that a socialist state was obliged to take action in another socialist state if the survival of socialism was at stake. The Brezhnev Doctrine influenced developments in eastern Europe through the next decade. After 1968, rigidity and stagnation characterized the Soviet, East German, and Czechoslovak governments, as well as rule in other east European states.

Within the Soviet Union, meanwhile, dissent appeared to be growing, and Soviet dissidents were commanding international attention. Criticism of the Soviet Union by its own citizens was at first strongly repressed. In 1985, the accession to power of Mikhail Gorbachev as General Secretary ushered in a new age of openness in the Soviet Union. By the end of 1989, leaders in both the East and the West declared that the Cold War was over and that a new and permanent détente was now possible. Gorbachev commanded center stage as a leader with international appeal. The dismantling of the Berlin Wall was the most visible sign that the Cold War was indeed ended.

Soviet Dissent

In December 1989 Andrei Sakharov was buried with full state honors in the Soviet Union. Soviet president Gorbachev hailed him as a hero, "a man of conviction and sincerity." In terms of Sakharov's early career, such a description would hardly have been surprising. Much decorated as the father of the Soviet hydrogen bomb, Sakharov was a Russian scientist of great eminence. But he was also one of the leading dissidents of the Soviet Union.

The funeral of Andrei Sakharov. The scientist-dissenter was eulogized at a public service held in Lenin Stadium at Luzhniki Complex in Moscow.

During the Brezhnev years, dissidence took on new forms in response to state repression. Growing numbers of Soviet Jews sought to emigrate to Israel, in an attempt to escape anti-Semitism within the Soviet Union and to embrace their own cultural heritage. Some of the 178,000 who were allowed to emigrate found their way to western Europe and the United States.

In May 1976 a number of Soviet dissidents, many of them Jewish, declared themselves united for the purpose of securing human rights. Some of the leading organizers were charged with anti-Soviet propaganda and given harsh prison sentences. Outside the Soviet Union protest against Soviet repression and violations of civil liberties began to mount.

Samizdat, the Russian word for self-published, privately circulated manuscripts, became the chief vehicle of dissident information. For the most part, dissidents came from an educated elite with professional and university training. Sakharov was joined by other figures of stature including novelist Alexander Solzhenitsyn and historian Roy Medvedev. In his novels, such as *Gulag Archipelago* and *One Day in the Life of Ivan Denisovich*, Solzhenitsyn showed the abuses of Soviet bureaucracy. For his writings he was forced into exile in the West. Medvedev criticized Stalinism and continued to speak out in favor of peace and democratic principles in the Gorbachev years.

For three decades Sakharov and other dissidents waged a lonely battle within the Soviet Union for civil liberties, democratic rights, and the end of the nuclear arms race. For his efforts, Sakharov won international acclaim abroad and was awarded the Nobel Peace Prize in 1975. But at home he was a prophet without honor. Sakharov endured internal exile for six years in the closed city of Gorki, one of Russia's great industrial cities east of Moscow, where inhabitants were not allowed freedom to enter or leave without permission and from which members of the foreign press corps were excluded. He never stopped agitating for peace and human rights. He continued his campaign against Soviet policies when he returned to Moscow in 1986.

In the few years before his death, Andrei Sakharov was reinstated as a public figure. He took his seat as a member of the Soviet Parliament. At his death, public opinion polls showed him to be the most respected individual in the Soviet Union. The changing fate of dissidents like Sakharov was one of the best barometers of the social revolution that was transforming Soviet politics in the late 1980s.

Détente: The Soviets and the West

The Nuclear Test Ban Treaty of 1963 inaugurated a period of lessening tension between the Eastern and Western Blocs. By the early 1970s both the United States and the Soviet Union recognized the importance of a rapprochement between the superpowers. The USSR and the United States had achieved nuclear parity: from positions of equality, both sides expressed a willingness to negotiate. The 1970s became a decade of détente, a period of cooperation between the two superpowers. The Strategic Arms Limitation Treaty, known as SALT I, signed in Moscow in 1972 limited defensive antiballistic missile systems.

The refusal in 1979 of the United States to sign SALT II to limit strategic nuclear weapons ushered in "the dangerous decade" of the 1980s, when the possibility of peaceful coexistence seemed crushed. U.S. president Ronald Reagan, during his first term in office, revived traditional Cold War posturing. In many of his speeches, he pitted capitalism against communism and denounced the Soviet Union as "the evil empire." Nuclear strategists on both sides were once again talking about nuclear war as possible and winnable. Popular concern over the nuclear arms race intensified in the United States, the Soviet Union, and throughout Europe. U.S. plans for the Strategic Defense Initiative (SDI), popularly called the "Star Wars" defense system, promised an escalation in nuclear defense spending in an attempt to end the parity between the United States and the Soviet Union.

On balance, however, East-West relations after 1983 were characterized by less confrontation and more attempts at cooperation between the Soviet Union and the United States. The world political system itself appeared to have stabilized with a diminution of conflict in the three main arenas of superpower competition—the Third World, China, and western Europe. The changing political situation in central and eastern Europe among Soviet satellites gave to those who longed for peace the best hope that the Cold War was truly over.

The Gorbachev Phenomenon

Mikhail Sergeyevich Gorbachev's life is the ultimate Soviet success story. He was born in 1931 on a collective farm near Stavropol, on the plains south of the Caucasus Mountains. His grandfather enjoyed high status in the community as the founder and chairman of the area's collective farm. Gorbachev's official biography describes Mikhail as a model student who, at the age of fourteen, began working at a machine tractor station. At the age of nineteen he traversed the great social distance from the collective farm to Moscow and entered Moscow University to study law. In 1952, while still a student, Gorbachev joined the Communist party. He graduated with distinction in 1955 and returned to his hometown of Stavropol, which he used as a base for his steady, almost meteoric rise through the Party hierarchy. At the unusually young age of 39, he was elected to the central committee; he achieved the status of the central committee's secretary in charge of agriculture and then, in 1980, he became a voting member of the Politburo.

When Yuri Andropov (1914–84), head of the KGB, the Soviet secret police controlled by the Communist party and responsible for internal intelligence-gathering and surveillance, succeeded Brezhnev as General Secretary in 1983, Gorbachev found that he had a friend in a very high place indeed. Andropov recognized Gorbachev's abilities as a problem-solver and a politician. Typical of a new generation in Western Europe as well as the Soviet Union, Gorbachev was above all a technocrat, someone who could apply specialized knowledge to the problems of the Soviet economy. In the 1960s, he returned to college to take a degree in agronomy to complement his initial degree in law. The two degrees gave him an unbeatable combination of expertise in a country plagued in the early 1980s by problems of collectivization and low productivity.

Gorbachev became Andropov's principal deputy and, following the brief regimes of Andropov and then Konstantin Chernenko (1911–85), Gorbachev assumed party leadership in 1985. Gorbachev's story is, however, more complicated than that of an individual man of exceptional ability and ambition making it to the top. His rise to political power was part of a general phenomenon in which social changes—urbanization, education, and increased communication—fostered the emergence of a generation of leaders committed to finding new and better ways of doing things. The Soviet Union had undergone dramatic changes after Stalin's death in 1953. In 1961 Stalin's corpse was removed from its place of honor beside Lenin's tomb in Red Square and many Stalinist policies were repudiated. The sixties was a period of increasing prosperity, as the population became more urban (180 million people lived in cities by mid-1970) and more literate (the majority of the population stays in school until the age of 17 or 18). Reaching his thirties in the 1960s, Gorbachev was undoubtedly influenced by his country's changing fortunes in that era.

Gorbachev's life reflects the changing outlook and experiences of an educated urban elite. The Gorbachevs were an example of an upwardly mobile middle class of professionals. Gorbachev chose to study law, an unusual choice in the Soviet Union until the 1950s, when lawyers experienced an explosive growth in their ranks. His wife, Raisa, was a sociological researcher who lectured in philosophy at Moscow University. Their daughter, licensed as a doctor, worked as a medical researcher; her husband was a surgeon. As one Soviet journalist explained the new style of leadership to his Western counterpart after Gorbachev assumed power, "We have our Kennedy." The Gorbachevs were typical of a social revolution that had produced an educated professional middle-class elite. Gorbachev himself was the first Soviet leader since Lenin to have received a university education.

Gorbachev and the Soviet Economy. Soviet citizens of the 1960s and 1970s were better fed, better educated, and in better health than their parents and grandparents had been. When people grumbled over food shortages and long lines, the Soviet state reminded its citizens of how far

Mikhail Gorbachev, General Secretary of the Communist Party of the Soviet Union, meets with potato farmers in the Ramanskoye District of the Moscow Region in 1987. A persistent shortage of food is one of the most recalcitrant problems of the troubled Soviet economy.

they had come and told them that Soviet economic planning was not a failure. Yet while growth continued throughout the postwar years, the rate of growth declined in the 1970s. Some planners began to fear that the Soviet Union would never catch up to the economies of the United States, Japan, and West Germany. Citizens, too, were increasingly aware of the sacrifices and suffering that economic development had cost the Soviet people in the twentieth century and of the disparities in the standards of living between the capitalist and communist worlds. Due to outmoded technology, declining older industries, pollution, labor imbalances, critical shortages of foodstuffs and certain raw materials, and a significant amount of hidden unemployment in unproductive industries, discontent mounted.

When Gorbachev assumed power in 1985, he promised to address the economic discontent of Soviet citizens. Consumer products were either of poor quality or unavailable. People queued on the average of two hours every day to purchase food and basic supplies. Workers shopped during their lunch breaks and even during working hours, undercutting their productivity. Housing, when it was available, was inadequate, and there were long waiting lists for vacancies. The black market flourished, with high prices on everything from Western blue jeans to Soviet automobiles. People could look around them and see corruption in their ruling elite, who wore Western clothes, had access to material goods not available to the general population, and lived in luxury in large apartments and vacationed in dachas, second homes in the country.

Workers were well paid, with more disposable income than ever before and that was, ironically, a key to the problem. People had money to

Russian shoppers queue outside the state butcher shop. Long lines for scarce products and produce are a grim reality of Soviet life.

spend. In fact, purchasing power far outstripped supplies. The state system of production, which emphasized quantity, resulted in overproduction of some goods—shoes for example—and under-production of others like soap. Soviet shoes produced in the 1980s were neither of the style nor the quality that people wanted to buy, so hundreds of millions of them moldered in state warehouses. The state kept prices low in order to control the cost of living, but low prices did not provide incentives for the production of better-quality goods. A typical example of the state system at its worst was the official quota for the chandelier industry. Quotas in this area were met by weight: manufacturers produced chandeliers so heavy that they pulled down ceilings and ripped out beams. In spite of the fact that they were cheap, no one bought them.

Gorbachev was well aware of these problems, but his programs between 1985 and 1988 promised more than they delivered. Modest increases in output were achieved, but people's expectations regarding food and consumer goods were, thanks to Gorbachev's rhetoric, rising faster than they could be met. The Soviet Union did not increase imports of consumer durables or food to meet

demand, nor did quality improve appreciably. Gorbachev realized that meeting consumer demand was both desirable and necessary in order to provide incentives for workers to increase productivity. Rising wages only gave them more money that they could not or would not spend on Soviet products.

The black market was a symbol both of the economic failures of the state and of the growing consumerism of Soviet citizens. Rather than purchase poor-quality goods, Soviets purchased foreign products at vastly inflated prices. A black market in Soviet goods, like automobiles, also developed, with people paying more for used cars rather than waiting years to buy a new one. The most common car in the Soviet Union, the Zhighuli, cost 9,000 rubles new in 1989. Because of inadequate supply and the cumbersome allocation system, prospective buyers had to wait years to be eligible to buy one. A used Zhighuli, five days old on the second-hand market, cost 12,000 rubles. A five-year-old car cost the same as a new car bought in the state system.

Gorbachev was candid about his economic policies. He warned that there would be no consumption revolution in the near future but that a greater degree of consumer satisfaction and technological innovations in factory production could be achieved in the short run. His economic reforms broke sharply with the centralized economy established by Stalin in the 1930s. In its place, Gorbachev proposed a limited open market free of state controls for manufacturing enterprises organized on a cooperative basis and for light industry. He loosened restrictions on foreign trade, encouraged the development of a private service sector, and, as in Lenin's New Economic Policy of the 1920s, decentralized economic decision-making for agriculture and the service sector.

Price increases and imports of foreign goods, the two essential measures necessary for progress in the Soviet consumer economy, had been resisted by Gorbachev's predecessors as politically explosive. The state kept prices down in order to maintain the low cost of living. But prices of raw materials and energy were kept so low that they discouraged increased productivity, efficiency, and quality. In both the economy and in politics Gorbachev wanted to usher in a period of change and greater freedom. In contrast to the ingrained conservatism of his predecessors, Gorbachev represented experimentation, innovation, and vitality. For him, economic and political reforms had to be accomplished in concert; the economy could only be restructured by "a democratization of our society at all levels."

Gorbachev's foreign policy served his economic goals. Military participation in decision-making declined, as state expenditures on defense were decreased. Moscow had always borne larger military costs than Washington. Gorbachev recognized that Cold War defense spending must decline, if the Soviet Union was to prosper. Consumer durables had to take the place of weapons on the production lines.

Gorbachev and Soviet Politics. From the beginning of the twentieth century, Soviet leaders had dealt with a vast array of crises from civil war, world war, collectivization, rapid industrialization, purges, and massive social dislocations. Stalin's planning had created a rigidly centralized bureaucracy that had proven itself incapable of meeting the consumer needs of the Soviet people in the late twentieth century. By the time Gorbachev came to power, Soviet citizens had enjoyed forty years of peace and were demanding a change from the decades of sacrifice for defense.

Gorbachev was not the first to emphasize the need for change. In the early 1960s some reformers began talking about the importance of profits instead of quotas, but the inertia of the bureaucracy prevailed. Khrushchev had questioned the inefficiencies caused by the distribution of power in the Soviet Union, but his inattention to the dominance of the Communist party spelled an end to his regime. Brezhnev reasserted the commitment to bureaucratic socialism and the stability—even stagnation—of Party cadres. Under Brezhnev the Party bureaucracy was associated with corruption as shortages provided opportunities for hoarding, bribery, and black-market activities.

The Communist party, set in place as a disciplined body of cadres by Lenin, operated on the principle that power must flow from the top in order to preserve and advance the revolution. In the late 1980s, grass-roots movements responding to Gorbachev's rhetoric of reform and democracy asserted that they should have a political voice.

The Big Mac comes to Moscow. McDonald's opened its first Soviet fast-food outlet in 1990, just a few blocks from the Kremlin. Muscovites stood in long lines for milkshakes, fries, and the "Bolshoi Mak."

On coming to power, Gorbachev could blame his predecessors for the Soviet Union's problems, but this defense had its limits, as people began demanding results. Tensions became most apparent over how Party rule and centralization could be coordinated with the demands for freedom and autonomy that Gorbachev's own reforms fostered.

In the 1980s the growing participation of the masses was a fact of Soviet political life. A larger urban elite provided a mass audience for Gorbachev's reforms. Highly educated groups of professionals and managers constituted a significant 22 percent of the population by the 1980s. The Soviet Union was no longer a nation of villages and semiliterate peasants. "Public opinion" was now a reality, with various interest groups forming successful coalitions over issues that included the environment and preservation of historical monuments. Gorbachev addressed these groups directly with his programs of *perestroika* (restructuring) and *glasnost* (openness).

Gorbachev possessed a fine instinct for managing public opinion. Gorbachev was able to manipulate the sense of impending crisis to pro-

mote change. As General Secretary, Gorbachev removed his political rivals from positions of power, replacing one-third of the government's ministers and one-fourth of the party's first secretaries. In 1988 he engineered his election as president. Andrei Gromyko, a Soviet foreign-policy veteran, observed of Gorbachev's desire to run things his way, "He may have a nice smile but he has teeth of steel." (See Special Feature, "Television and Revolutions," pp. 972–973.)

Gorbachev benefited initially from favorable public opinion to reshape the Party to his own ends. In the 1920s Lenin had tolerated disagreement and pluralism within the Party to a degree greater than Gorbachev seemed willing to accept in the 1980s. There was fear that decentralization of the economy would dilute the Party's monopoly on political power. Gorbachev's aim was to preserve socialism through democracy. As one Soviet editor explained the reforms, "We must...do something more human, more democratic. This is the only way to live in the modern world."

In 1979 the Soviet Union listed 102 nationalities in its census. Twenty-two of those nationalities had populations of a million or more peo-

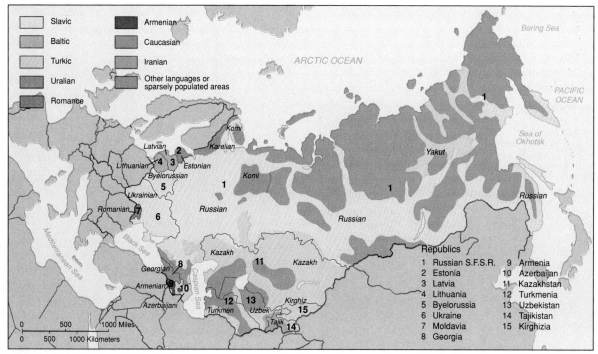

Republics of the Soviet Union

Armenians gather in Yerevan, the capital of Soviet Armenia, to demonstrate for the annexation of a predominately Armenian area now attached to the neighboring Soviet republic of Azerbaijan.

ple. Some Western observers predicted that this diversity would destroy the Soviet Union, that the Soviet empire was crumbling from within. Others wondered how Gorbachev could support the demands for self-determination in eastern European states and deny it in the Soviet republics. For many, the nationalities problem posed the single greatest threat to Gorbachev's regime, even more challenging than the establishment of a free-market economy.

The nationalities problem in the Soviet Union was in fact shaped by the very social forces that brought Gorbachev to power. The three major areas of nationalist conflict—central Asia, Armenia, and the Baltic states—had had grievances against the Soviet state since the 1920s. What was different about the protests of the 1980s was the emergence of a new and educated urban elite, formed after World War II, as the driving force behind nationalist reform. Moscow relied on these groups of university-educated and upwardly mobile professionals to further economic reforms. Gorbachev's challenge was to harness nationalist protest without undermining the Party's authority in favor of local organizations. He had to make the Party responsible to these new social groups and to local needs.

Ethnic minorities in the Soviet Baltic republics of Latvia, Lithuania, and Estonia, in particular, threatened the dominance of Party rule in favor of self-determination. Large-scale riots in Lithuania erupted over demands for nationalist rights. Nationalist awareness was not unprecedented in the Baltic in the 1980s—but the context of *perestroika* in which nationalist demands were now being voiced posed a serious challenge to Gorbachev's democratic reforms. In 1988 Estonians demanded the right of veto over any law passed in Moscow. Russians, who were a minority in Estonia, protested attacks and prejudicial treatment at the hands of Estonians.

Endorsing diversity of opinion and individual rights and freedom as the basis of good government, Gorbachev now had to deal with vocal nationalist awareness in the Baltic states and the republic of Georgia and with outright violence in Azerbaijan. In 1988 tens of thousands of Armenians took to the streets to demand the return of the Armenian enclave of Nagorno-Karabakh, incorporated into Azerbaijan in 1921. In the Azerbaijan capital of Baku, the center of Russia's oil-producing region, demonstrators demanded greater autonomy for their republic and the accountability of their deputies in Moscow. Violence between Azerbaijanis and Armenians resulted in thirty-two deaths and the displacement of tens of thousands. Gorbachev and his advisers were blamed for the failure to anticipate the problem and prevent the violence. The situation of upheaval climaxed in December 1988 when an earthquake in Armenia killed 25,000 people. Soviet troops were placed in the area, ostensibly to deal with the aftermath of the natural disaster.

In 1986 university students in the central Asian republic of Kazakhstan incited two days of demonstrations and rioting over the removal of a corrupt local leader who was replaced with a Russian. The Soviet government's attempt to clean up politics in the area betrayed a clumsy disregard for ethnic issues and seemed at odds with Gorbachev's commitment to decentralization. Crimean Tatars, who had been exiled in Islamic fundamentalist Kazakhstan since World War II, agitated for return home. Unlike the treatment of its own ethnic policy, the Soviet Union pursued a policy of recognition of the self-determination of peoples in Eastern and central Europe.

*E*astern and Central Europe Since 1968

The dramatic upheavals in eastern Europe in the late 1980s had been in the making for over two decades. Czechoslovakia's attempt in 1968 to strike out on a more independent path to socialism only strengthened the Soviet Union's hold on Warsaw Pact nations. The Soviet Union's use of troops had sent a clear message that it would not tolerate deviation. When the dust of tens of thousands of Soviet-led troops settled in the Czech capital of Prague, one-party rule was reestablished and a more democratic socialism based on freer markets and individual initiative had failed.

The demands for consumer goods and national autonomy behind the protests of 1968 were effectively quelled in the seventies by the memory of Soviet invasion, but they did not disappear. The recurrent crises over oil prices and the greater hardships inflicted on eastern European consumers fanned the embers of unsettled issues in the 1980s. Incidents of protest and resistance began to mount.

Solidarity in Poland

Poland was especially important to the Soviet Bloc both because it was Eastern Europe's most populous country and because of its strategic location. Poland provided a corridor for supplies to the Soviet Union's 380,000 troops in East Germany. In Poland, as in Czechoslovakia, demonstrations against Soviet dominance and one-party rule by the Communists had been brutally repressed. Poland entered the 1970s economically handicapped. In December 1970 the Polish government instituted major price increases for food. Workers spontaneously struck in protest, with demonstrations beginning in the shipyards of Gdansk, the Baltic seaport in northern Poland, and spreading to other cities. The Polish government responded by sending the militia to tear-gas the workers. People were killed and injured but protest was not silenced.

Wladislaw Gomulka, who had been head of the Polish government since 1956, was replaced by Edward Gierek in hopes of improving the economic situation. More protests followed before prices were rolled back and the Soviet Union provided economic aid. Throughout the 1970s one-party rule prevailed, as workers attempted to maintain forms of permanent organization. The Polish government drew loans from abroad for investment in technology and industrial expansion. The government increased its foreign indebtedness rather than raise prices at home. In 1976, however, Gierek could no longer avoid price increases. A new wave of spontaneous strikes erupted, forcing the government to rescind the increases.

Poland's indebtedness to the West rose from $2.5 billion in 1973 to $17 billion in 1980. Poland was sinking into the mire of ever higher interest payments that absorbed the country's export earnings. At the beginning of July 1980 the government was forced once again to raise food prices. Shipyard workers in Gdansk were ready, solidly organized in a new noncommunist labor union

Three metal crosses over 130 feet high mark the place outside the Lenin Shipyard in Gdansk, where Polish workers were shot by the militia in 1970. Bronze relief at the bases of the crosses depict scenes from the workers' lives. Atop the crosses are giant anchors, symbols of hope.

called Solidarity (Solidarnosc), under the leadership of a politically astute electrician named Lech Walesa. The union staged a sit-down strike that paralyzed the shipyards. Union committees coordinated their activities from one factory to the next and succeeded in shutting down the entire economy. The government agreed to a series of union-backed reforms known as the Gdansk Accords, which, among other measures, increased civil liberties and acknowledged Solidarity's right to exist.

Within a year Solidarity had an astounding 8 million members out of a population of 35 million. The Catholic church lent important support to those who opposed communist rule. Dissident intellectuals also cast their lot with the organized workers in demanding reforms. General Wojciech Jaruzelski became prime minister in February 1981, but the situation of shortages did not change appreciably. Jaruzelski attempted to curb the union's demands for democratic government and participation in management by harsh measures: he declared martial law on 13 December 1981. Jaruzelski was trying to save the Polish Commu-

nist party by using the Polish military to crack down on the dissidents. The Soviet response was to do nothing. Poland was left to Polish rule. Soviet leaders knew that the size of Polish protest required a massive retaliation, which they were unwilling to undertake, especially since to do so would fly in the face of Western opinion which supported the Solidarity movement. In addition, the Soviet Union had other problems in this period: in 1979 it began a war in Afghanistan to secure communist rule. Moscow feared the Islamic fundamentalism at its border threatened to stir up the rapidly growing Muslim populations in six Soviet republics—Azerbaijan, Kazakhstan, Uzbekistan, Tadzhikistan, Turkmenistan, and Kirgizia.

Martial law in Poland produced military repression. Solidarity was outlawed and Walesa was jailed. The West did not lose sight of him: in 1983 the union leader was awarded the Nobel Peace Prize for his efforts. After years of negotiations and intermittent strikes, Solidarity was legalized once again in 1989. The economy was in dire straits and Jaruzelski knew he needed Soli-

Television and Revolutions

Television became the principal means of communicating current events to mass populations in the second half of the twentieth century. It was one of the chief consumer durables purchased by the newly prosperous populations of the United States and Europe beginning in the 1950s. Many intellectuals in the West feared that television, because of its uninspired programming, would dull the sensibilities of the masses and serve as a kind of opiate to cloud political judgment. Yet the role of television in politics was more complex, as events after 1968 made clear.

As East Germans in large numbers began buying televisions in the 1960s and 1970s, they faced a dilemma. Should they heed the prohibition of the East German government against watching West German television programs, whose signals were so easily accessible to them, or should they disobey the law and take advantage of the varied entertainment that West German television afforded? East German leaders feared the "corrupt" and "decadent" images of West Germany that might attract their citizens. The East German head of state Walter Ulbricht warned ominously in 1961 that "The enemy of the people stands on the roof." He was talking about television antennas. The East German ban was, however, impossible to enforce. Millions of East German viewers tuned in daily to West German programs and were able to compare the different standards of living in the two German nations and to learn of their own deprivation. The irony of awareness was that as East Germans achieved a higher standard of living and were able to buy more televisions, they became more and more discontented over their relatively low standard of living. Television contributed to rising expectations and the exodus of East Germans to the West.

Television played a central role in the Romanian revolution of 1989, spreading information and encouraging coordinated action throughout the country. One of the first acts of the Bucharest revolutionaries was to seize the headquarters of the state television station in order to transmit their own view of the conflict. When Nicolae and Elena Ceaucescu were executed, the event was videotaped for broadcast to the Romanian nation and the world. In a still heavily rural society undergoing modernization, television provided the essential link between city and countryside. Television promoted concerted action. Simultaneously Romanians in Timósoara, a small city near the Hungarian border, and Bucharest, the nation's capital, espoused the same revolutionary program and adopted the

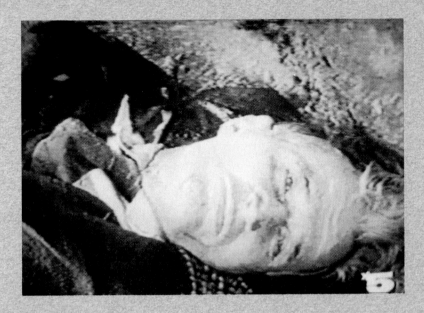

same symbols, as similarly doctored national flags made clear. The new regime governed by means of the television screen.

Politicians on both the left and the right used television for political ends. The political utility of television was exploited in France, where 60 percent of the population owned TV sets in 1968. Charles de Gaulle, president of the Fifth Republic, used the medium to appeal directly to the French people against the student-worker revolt that began in Paris in May 1968. Television was decisive in maintaining de Gaulle in power and mobilizing conservatives against the activists.

No one in the late twentieth century was better at grasping the power of the televised image than the Soviet leader Mikhail Gorbachev, who from the very beginning used the small screen to appeal directly to the Soviet people. He carefully cultivated his own image and used televi-

sion to build a personal power base outside of the Communist party. Gorbachev was so successful in creating his own televised publicity that he became a popular figure within the Western capitalist world as well as within Soviet Bloc countries. Crowds everywhere greeted him with the affectionate nickname "Gorby"; he was as easily recognizable in the streets of New York and Paris as in the streets of Moscow. Even the new revolutionaries in eastern Europe, who were intent on breaking their bonds with the Soviet state and who espoused democracy and capitalism, saw in Gorbachev the guarantee of their aspirations. Romanians chanted his name in public squares as they set about pulling down the communist regime that ruled them.

Above all, television contributed to the revolution in expectations in communist countries in the last quarter of the twen-

tieth century. The contrast between the quality of life in the East and the West became inescapable for many educated east European and Soviet men and women, who had access to travel and to television. Modern video technology did not cause revolutions but it did convey information and provide political platforms. Television also publicized revolutions and, in some cases, sold dreams.

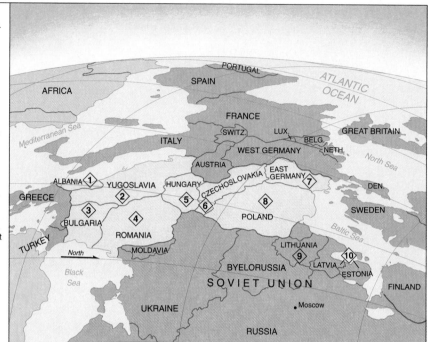

1. **Albania.** Communist Party still retains Leninist orientation, Jan. 1990. Parliament backs liberal reforms, May 1990.
2. **Yugoslavia.** Government decides to hold free elections, Dec. 1989.
3. **Bulgaria.** Government disavows "dominant role" for Communist Party; pledges free elections and new constitution in 1990.
4. **Romania.** Communist dictator Ceausescu overthrown and executed, Dec. 1989; Salvation Front led by dissident former Communists wins elections, May 1990.
5. **Hungary.** Free election sweeps non-Communists into power, April 1990.
6. **Czechoslovakia.** Communist leadership ousted, Nov. 1989; Vaclav Havel named president, Dec. 1989.
7. **Germany.** Berlin Wall breached, Nov. 1989. Re-unification of East and West Germany, Oct. 1990.
8. **Poland.** Solidarity Party sweeps elections, June 1989.
9. **Lithuania** declares independence, March 1990; Moscow calls move illegal.
10. **Latvia and Estonia** begin process of separation from Soviet Union, April 1990.

Events in Eastern Europe, 1989–90

darity's cooperation: he agreed to open elections. At the polls, Solidarity candidates soundly defeated the Communist party. Poland was the first country anywhere to turn a Communist regime out of office peacefully. Yet Poland did not pull out of the Warsaw Pact. As Lech Walesa explained it in 1989 on West German television, "Poland cannot forget where it is situated. You know we are in the Warsaw Pact. That cannot be changed." Poland needed above all its own *perestroika*, its own restructuring of its economy and administration.

The great challenge before the new Solidarity government, as for the Communist regime that preceded it, was economic recovery. Inflation drove food prices up at the rate of 50 percent a month. The Polish government committed itself to freeing the *zloty* from state control and making it a convertible currency, one that could be bought and sold for other currencies on the international currency market, so that Polish goods could compete on world markets. Poland faced the task of earning enough foreign trade credits to alleviate its indebtedness and to justify foreign investment. In the midst of euphoria, the leaders of the new government spoke of the need for

patience and discipline. Economists wondered if that would be enough.

Gennady Gerasimov, a high-ranking Soviet official to the United States, explained that the Brezhnev Doctrine of total Soviet control over eastern European economies had been replaced by what he called the Sinatra Doctrine. The reference was to the song "My Way," the signature theme of singer Frank Sinatra. The Soviet official was explaining that eastern Europeans were on their own, free to reform their economies "their way."

Emancipation in Eastern Europe

The total control advocated by the Brezhnev Doctrine was crumbling well before 1989. In the 1970s, Hungarians began to experiment cautiously with free markets and private control. Romania under Nicolae Ceaucescu appeared to be successful in evading its military responsibilities in the Warsaw Pact. It alone of the member states had refused to participate in the Czechoslovak intervention of 1968. The East German government tolerated the Lutheran church's criticism of the Soviet military presence in East Germany in the 1970s. Deviation was not punished by Soviet repression but quietly and carefully pursued in an age colored by Soviet attempts at détente with the West.

The Soviet example and Gorbachev's calls for reforms and openness gave the lead to eastern Europe. In 1988 Gorbachev, speaking before the United Nations, assured the West that he would not prevent eastern European satellites from going their own way: "Freedom of choice is a universal principle," the Soviet head of state declared. Poland's first free elections in forty years were part of a vast mosaic of protest from which a pattern began to emerge in the spring of 1989. The barbed-wire fences on Hungary's Austrian border were dismantled; all of its borders to the West were opened in September 1989. East German vacationers in Hungary poured across the frontiers, creating an international crisis. People wanted freedom of movement and freedom of expression. Everywhere east Europeans demanded democratic institutions modeled on those of Western nations. "People power" swept away Communist leaders and ousted the Communist party, many felt for good. The leader of the New Socialist party in Hungary, Imre Pozsgay, declared that "Communism does not work. We must start again at zero."

Czechoslovakia's revolution began with angry university students. Singing Czech versions of protest songs like "We Shall Overcome," student protesters were reminiscent of the student movements of 1968. They tried to give flowers to police, who responded by bludgeoning them. This spark touched off a mass movement that within days drove out the Czech Communist party. Idealism and growing public sympathy were on the side of the protesters. The dissident playwright Vaclav

Czech students wearing headbands proclaiming "democracy" hold a solidarity march in support of the ill-fated Chinese pro-democracy movement, which was crushed when the tanks of the Communist government rolled into Tiananmen Square in Peking.

Havel, released from jail just before the demonstrations began, emerged as the leader of the democratic opposition and was elected president of the new government.

The iceberg of communism was melting. As dictators were replaced by democrats, some observers wondered if counterrevolution was waiting in the wings, should the new capitalist experiments fail. At the end of 1989, British prime minister Margaret Thatcher warned that when ice begins to break up, "it can be very dangerous."

The Two Germanies Since 1968

The German Democratic Republic (East Germany) and the German Federal Republic (West Germany) continued to develop after 1968 as two separate countries with different social, economic, and political institutions. On the surface, their differences seemed insurmountable. The Berlin Wall, erected in 1961, divided the former German capital; the Wall served its intended purpose of keeping East Germans confined behind it, but it could not contain the hostile rhetoric of the communist state against its capitalist counterpart.

From the 1960s through the 1980s East Germany underwent a series of economic transformations. Under the leadership of Walter Ulbricht (1893–1973), East Germans achieved their own version of recovery, the "other economic miracle," and overcame their severe economic handicaps after World War II. Ulbricht committed the German Democratic Republic to an economic policy in which performance was measured in terms of profits rather than quotas. Individual initiative and market incentives replaced Soviet-style central planning and bureaucratic decision-making. Ulbricht's programs were out of step with Soviet directives, although they foreshadowed the changing emphasis on local control among Eastern Bloc countries that took place in the late 1980s. By 1969 East Germany's economy was the strongest among Eastern Bloc nations, and East Germans enjoyed the highest per capita output.

In spite of his economic successes, Ulbricht fell from power in 1971. An important factor in his removal was his support for rule by government bodies rather than Communist party control. Party members eagerly seized on economic reversals in 1970 to promote Moscow's disfavor with Ulbricht. In addition to his arrogance toward Soviet leaders, Ulbricht's opposition to improved relations between the Soviet Union and West Germany after 1969 gave Soviet leaders cause for complaint. Ulbricht felt that such a Soviet course of détente would only retard East Germany's chance for full recognition in the West.

Erich Honecker, who succeeded Ulbricht, had the mission of bringing the German Democratic Republic back into the fold of Soviet economic policy. Honecker rejected Ulbricht's emphasis on profitability and committed East Germany to centralized planning. By 1972 virtually all privately held businesses had been converted to state enterprises. Private enterprise was also eliminated in agriculture. Honecker's policies were not a return to Stalinism but were built on an awareness of the consumer expectations of the East German population. Honecker's "consumer socialism" gave top priority to consumer goods and housing. But the oil crisis of the 1970s undermined this orientation by driving up the costs of production, so dependent on foreign fuel, and thereby driving up consumer prices. Trade deficits soared and consumer industries slowed.

In West Germany politics took a new direction in 1969. For the first time since 1930, the Social Democrats were back in power, displacing the more conservative Christian Democrats. An era of social-liberal cooperation between the leftist Social Democrats and the centrist Free Democrats began. Under the chancellorship of Social Democrat Willy Brandt, the new government promised to make the welfare state more responsive to social needs, to involve labor more directly in economic decision-making, and to attend to feminist demands regarding abortion, divorce, and pornography.

Brandt was equally committed to changes in foreign policy. From the first, he set out to improve relations with eastern Europe and the Soviet Union. Repudiating the policy that refused recognition to any eastern European country that had diplomatic relations with East Germany, West Germany established trade missions in Poland,

West German chancellor Willy Brandt visited the Soviet Union in 1970 to sign a treaty to relax tensions between Moscow and Bonn. In this photograph, Brandt, on the right, reviews a Red Army honor guard with the Soviet premier, Alexei Kosygin.

Hungary, Bulgaria, and Romania—everywhere in eastern Europe except for Albania.

While maintaining West Germany's commitment to NATO and western European integration, Brandt pursued a new cooperation with the Soviet Union through a nonaggression pact. Negotiated in 1970, the pact renounced territorial claims and the use of force. A treaty with Poland accepted the status quo of existing borders in return for Polish exit visas for ethnic Germans. In a dramatic gesture of reconciliation, Brandt traveled to Warsaw and knelt before a memorial to Jewish victims of Nazi atrocities in World War II. Still without the official recognition of East Germany, West Germany agreed to normalized relations in 1972 in the Basic Treaty, which permitted West German citizens easier movement to visit relatives in East Germany. In 1973 both Germanies successfully applied for membership in the United Nations.

Willy Brandt captured international acclaim with his bold foreign policy of *Ostpolitik*, the establishment of cooperative politics with the East, for which he was awarded the Nobel Peace Prize in 1971. Brandt reminded Germans that they could once again be proud of their country. Ostpolitik was a clear break with superpower hegemony, as Brandt, in his own version of détente, seized the initiative without waiting for directions from the United States. At home, however, he was not always a hero, as his domestic policies underwent reversals and the fabric of the social-liberal coalition began to fray. The 1973 oil crisis brought about rising unemployment and a decline in consumer demand. Shrinking tax revenues undermined Brandt's plans to expand the welfare state. Expenditures on existing state programs placed a heavy burden on the state's budget and contributed to the highest inflation rate in West Germany since 1948.

Added to these challenges at home was an espionage scandal in which a close aide of Chancellor Brandt's was discovered to be an East German spy. Cold War paranoia flared. Brandt resigned in 1974 and was succeeded by Social Democrat Helmut Schmidt, who continued Brandt's policies of rapprochement with the East. In 1981 Honecker, head of the East German state, and Schmidt, head of the West German state, sat down together to discuss common concerns. Bonn and East Berlin were engaging in their own détente.

When he came to power in 1974, Schmidt found that he had inherited a recession that became more severe over the next year. Necessary compromises with the Free Democrats in the 1970s produced growing dissension within the Social Democratic party and eroded Schmidt's support as chancellor. Taking advantage of the split between the Free Democrats and the Social Democrats and growing concern over the economic situation, the Christian Democrats displaced the Social Democrats with their candidate, Helmut Kohl, in 1982. Kohl stressed the importance of individual enterprise and competition and ran a winning campaign with the slogan, "Less State, More Market."

Toward One Germany

The two Germanies were linked economically, if not politically, throughout most of the postwar period. When the Federal Republic of Germany entered the European Community in 1957, it insisted that in matters related to trade the two Germanies were to be treated as one country. As a result, the German Democratic Republic benefited from its free-trade relationship with West Germany. This advantage provided an important part of East Germany's prosperity since the 1960s. West Germany, in turn, achieved much of its prosperity though export-led growth and found markets in the German Democratic Republic. The trade terms that the Federal Republic extended to East Germany served as a form of assistance during the oil crisis of the 1970s. West Germany also made lump-sum payments to East Germany in order to free visitors

"There Are No Better-Fed Refugees"	
East Germany has built the strongest economy in the Soviet Bloc, but its standard of living lags far behind that of West Germany.	
Federal Republic of Germany (West)	German Democratic Republic (East)
Population: 61 million	**Population:** 17 million
Life Expectancy: For men, 71.2 years; for women, 78.1 years	**Life Expectancy:** For men, 69.5 years; for women, 75.4 years
Gross National Product: $1.12 trillion	**Gross National Product:** $207.2 billion
Public Spending on Education: 9.4% of all government expenditures	**Public Spending on Education:** 5.5% of all government expenditures
New Books Published: 50,903 volumes	**New Books Published:** 5,636 volumes

Source: Statistical Yearbook, Unesco 1988; Demographic Yearbook, United Nations; CIA World Factbook, 1988

from paying travel fees required by the German Democratic Republic. These payments provided a ready source of convertible currency that the East Germans needed to compete in world markets.

East Germany continued to emphasize its differences from West Germany through a policy of "delimitation." Nevertheless, in the 1980s it began to accept its common cultural heritage with Germans in the West. In 1983 East Germany celebrated the 500th anniversary of Martin Luther's birth in Saxony. Until this event Luther had been officially denounced by East Germany as a religious fanatic. Biographies of Bismarck, the founder of the German Empire, appeared for the first time in East Germany. Such instances indicated an attempt to recapture a common German past.

West Germany stood in the 1980s as an economic giant, second only in foreign trade to the United States and far ahead of Japan. With its economic opportunities and advanced social welfare programs, West Germany exerted considerable attraction for East Germans. East Germany, too, established itself as an important trading nation—fifteenth in the world in 1975. East Germany's number one problem was the exodus of skilled workers and professionals in search of a better life in the West. The flow of emigration throughout the 1950s turned into a torrent in the first eight months of 1961 when the number of refugees fleeing from East to West Germany reached 160,000 people. The total number of those who emigrated since the division of Germany following World War II had reached nearly three million. The Berlin Wall was, more than anything else, an effort to keep the East German labor force, so expensive to train and so necessary for economic recovery, in the German Democratic Republic.

Applications for authorized immigration increased in the 1980s, and in 1984 East Germany allowed 30,000 citizens to emigrate to the West. The application procedure led to panic among the tens of thousands of applicants whose expectations had been raised but who had not been granted the right to leave. Some East Germans whose requests had not been approved camped out at West German offices in East Berlin and at the West German embassy in Prague. The incident was settled when the East German government promised West German officials that there would be no reprisals against aspiring émigrés. Throughout the late 1980s the emigration rate remained high with an average exodus of 20,000 a year. In 1989 trainloads of East Germans were allowed to enter West Germany and to claim full citizenship. Germans entered the last decade of the twentieth century with an increased awareness of their shared destiny and common interests and with mounting hope about the possibility of a united Germany.

Some politicians in the German Federal Republic had never completely abandoned the idea of a single German nation. Germans are the largest nationality in Europe west of Russia. Other Europeans, particularly the French, have feared the prospect of a united Germany, although publicly they endorse the principle of the self-determination of peoples. A unified Germany as "the

East Berliners stream through a breach in the Berlin Wall in November 1989. One Western wag summed up the occasion: "They came; they saw; they shopped."

land of the middle" at the heart of Europe seemed to be an imminent reality when East and West Germans danced together in 1989 on the crumbled remains of the Berlin Wall that had separated them for nearly thirty years.

Unity and Diversity in Western Europe

The events of 1968 in eastern Europe sent a negative message to western European communists, who were intent on adopting a more liberal and cooperative stance with both parliamentary institutions and capitalism. By the end of the 1960s the fate of communist parties in the West appeared uncertain. The events of the Prague spring catalyzed a new kind of communism, dubbed Eurocommunism, among western European communist parties in the 1970s.

United Germany

Western European nations had met the challenges of wartime devastation with miraculous economic recoveries in the 1950s and 1960s. A key component in achieving growth was the availability to western European economies of a floating labor pool of workers from southern Europe and from former colonies in Asia and Africa. The phenomenal growth and prosperity in western Europe came up against a new set of harsh realities in the 1970s with skyrocketing oil prices, inflation, and recession. The permanent presence of foreign workers, many of them unemployed or erratically employed in the economic downturns of the 1970s and 1980s, came to be seen as a problem by welfare-state leaders and politicians of the new Right. Europe's new working class became the brunt of racist antagonisms.

With the goal of reviving the economy, in the 1980s the twelve member states of the European Economic Community devoted themselves to making western Europe competitive as a bloc in world markets. At the same time that Russian satellites in eastern Europe were breaking free of Soviet control and attempting to strike out on their own, the nations of western Europe were negotiating a new unity based on a single market and centralized policymaking.

Eurocommunism

Divisions among the Left excluded the western European Communists from wielding political power in the early 1970s. Then in 1973 the international politics of oil prices provoked an economic crisis, followed by a recession. The Organization of Petroleum Exporting Countries (OPEC) raised prices and cut back production. Western European countries depended heavily on imported oil, which they used to fuel their prosperity through the early 1970s. Poor Soviet economic performance in the postwar era offered no model for action, especially for dealing with Western economies after 1973. European Communists decided to cooperate with other Leftists and moderates in a new electoral politics.

The Italian Communist party, the largest in Europe, led the way under the leadership of Enrico Berlinguer, who became the spearhead for Eurocommunism in Western Europe. Eurocommunism, a designation resisted by its practitioners, was a response to the dual influences of democratic institutions and Western economies that combined free enterprise and state control. It was above all a recognition that revolution was not likely—at least in the near future—in western Europe. Eurocommunists accepted the European Community and membership in NATO. After 1973, communists, first in Italy and then in Spain and France, moved from a position of opposition to partnership with liberal and Left-wing reformers. With the move, communists became Eurocommunists, rejecting unquestioned allegiance to Soviet policies and trying to become a mainstream electoral party.

In Spain, the death of General Francisco Franco in November 1975 ended the authoritarian regime set in place in the 1930s. The Spanish Communist party was granted legal status in 1977 and its leader, Santiago Carrillo, returned from exile in France to establish a Spanish version of Eurocommunism under a constitutional monarchy headed by King Juan Carlos. Moderates prevailed, with reformist Socialists coming to power in 1982.

Eurocommunism also helped to bring a Socialist president to power in France in 1981. The French Communist party had maintained its loyalty to Moscow longer than had its counterparts in Italy and Spain. Conservatives had controlled French politics since 1958 when Charles de Gaulle became president of the Fifth Republic. De Gaulle's successors, Georges Pompidou and Valéry Giscard d'Estaing made it clear to the Left that they needed to cooperate with each other if they were to wrest power from the conservatives. In the late 1970s the Communist party threw in its lot with the French Socialists, and their coalition resulted in the election of Socialist François Mitterrand as president. Yet at the moment of victory, the Communist party was in decline, and a reformist Left was taking its place in electoral politics.

Eurocommunism's influence diminished in the 1980s as moderate politics maintained its appeal to voters. Eurocommunism had been a creative attempt to meet the challenge of preserving socialist goals in capitalist democracies. It paralleled attempts at democratic reforms in Czechoslovakia and Poland in the 1960s, except that the Eastern Bloc revisionists were met with repression and control rather than with electoral failures. Eurocommunism's attempt at adaptation actually marked the demise of communism's appeal in western Europe. By criticizing Soviet actions, western communists had abandoned their self-imposed isolation within Western democracies. There appeared to be no turning back. But either in isolation or in cooperation, it appeared that the power of western European Communist parties was on the decline.

A New Working Class: Foreign Workers

Foreign workers played an important role in the industrial expansion of western Europe beginning in the 1950s. Western European nations needed cheap unskilled laborers. Great Britain, France, and West Germany were the chief labor-importing countries, whose economic growth in the fifties and sixties was made possible by readily available pools of cheap foreign labor. The chief labor-exporting countries included Portugal, Turkey, Algeria, Italy, and Spain, whose sluggish economic performance spurred workers to seek employment opportunities beyond national borders. Great Britain imported workers from the West Indies, Ireland, India, Pakistan, Africa, and southern Europe. Migrant employment was by definition poorly paid, unskilled or semiskilled, manual work. Italian workers in West Germany, for example, commonly worked the night shifts in factories that German workers refused. France employed a high number of foreign laborers in agriculture, public works, commerce, and engineering. Foreign male workers found employment on construction sites all over western Europe. Foreign women worked in domestic service, personal care, and factories.

Foreign workers came for the most part from the less developed countries of southern Europe or from developing former colonies in Africa and Asia. Commonly, married men migrated without their families with the goal of earning cash to send home to those left behind. Switzerland actu-

Indian immigrants in France sewing in a "sweat shop." Immigrant workers in European countries took low-paying menial jobs. They faced resentment form xenophobic native Europeans.

ally discouraged family migration with restrictions on income and housing. Nevertheless, prosperous and underpopulated Switzerland had Europe's highest percentage of foreign workers—16 percent of the total Swiss population in 1975. The inability of people to put down roots, however, hampered assimilation among this sizable percentage of foreign workers.

Most immigrants who came looking for jobs carried with them the "myth of return," the belief that they would some day go back home. For the most part, however, foreign workers stayed in the host country. Irish workers were alone in following the pattern of return to the home country.

The lot of foreign workers was difficult and sometimes dangerous. Onerous and demanding labor was common. Foreign workers were often herded together in crowded living quarters, socially marginalized, and identified with the degrading work they performed. Street cleaning and refuse collection in France were jobs typically performed by black Africans. Foreign workers were frequently denied the rights of citizenship and subjected to vagaries of legislation. In economic downturns they were the first to be laid off. Yet the obligations of foreign workers to send money back home to aged parents, spouses, children, and siblings persisted. The children who resided in the host country with their foreign-worker parents could suffer from severe identity problems, experiencing discrimination in schooling in the countries in which they were born and with which they identified. A rising incidence of violence among second-generation Algerian adolescents in France, for example, indicated tensions and a new kind of rebellion among migrant populations in the 1970s and 1980s. Third and fourth generations of foreign workers born on West German soil were refused the rights of citizenship and denied the possibility of naturalization.

Women endured special problems within the foreign work force. Between 1964 and 1974 the majority of Portuguese immigrants to France came with families, but there was little in the way of social services to support them on their arrival. Dependable child care was either too expensive or unavailable to female workers with children. Increasing numbers of single women began migrating to western Europe independently of households and male migrants. Like men, they worked in order to send money back home. Often housed in dormitories provided by their employers, Spanish and Portuguese women factory workers in Germany and France were isolated from the communities of their compatriots.

Opposition to the presence of foreign workers was often expressed in an ultranationalist rhetoric and usually flared up in periods of economic reversals. Right-wing politicians sometimes complained that foreign workers deprived native workers of jobs. This argument seemed unlikely since many of the jobs filled by migrants were spurned by native workers as too menial or too poorly paid or too physically demanding. Opposition nonetheless became virulent. In 1986 in France the xenophobic National Front campaigned on a platform of "France for the French" and captured 10 percent of the vote in national elections. Racism was out in the open in Western countries that had depended on a foreign labor force for their prosperity. Arab and black African workers in France resorted to work stoppages to protest police discrimination and identity controls that they likened to the yellow Stars of David that Jews had been required to wear in Nazi Germany. Riots in Great Britain in 1980 and 1981, particularly in the London ghetto of Brixton, were motivated by racial discrimination against blacks, severe cuts in social welfare spending, and deteriorating working conditions.

Before 1973 most countries in Western Europe, including Great Britain, actively encouraged foreign labor. After that date restrictions became the order of the day. It is no coincidence that restrictions on foreign labor followed the 1973 oil crisis. Western governments enforced new conservative policies throughout the 1970s and 1980s aimed at keeping out Third World refugees. Exceptions were made for political refugees from eastern Europe. Racial considerations lay beneath the surface of discussions about political asylum. In 1989 the British government sent back to Vietnam the "boat people" who had escaped to Hong Kong in search of a better life in the West. Britain earned the condemnation of other Western governments and humanitarian groups for its refusal to provide a haven for Asian refugees, many of whom were children.

On the whole, restrictions failed to achieve what they set out to do.—remove foreign workers from Western countries by repatriation. Foreign workers in West Germany learned to get around the restrictions and sent for their families to join them. British laws also had the effect of converting temporary migration by single men into permanent family migrations, actually increasing the total annual rate of migration. In 1974 the French government halted immigration altogether. The state withdrew subsidies from businesses employing large numbers of foreign workers and instituted police identity controls two years later. In 1977 foreign workers were offered cash incentives to encourage them to return to their home countries, but to little avail. Governments refused to acknowledge the reality of the plight of foreign workers.

By the end of the 1970s there were 10 million foreign workers settled in Europe. Their presence heightened racism and overt antagonism from a resurgent extreme Right. At the moment in the late 1980s when movements for democratic freedom and human rights were being endorsed in

Britain became the scene of racial unrest as increasing numbers of people from former British colonies in Africa, the West Indies, and the Indian subcontinent entered the country as immigrants.

eastern Europe, the problem of permanent resident "aliens" was without a solution in western Europe. Those who advocated extreme measures of removal seemed to be gaining ground in European states.

Women's Changing Lives

During the last quarter of the twentieth century, the lives of Western women reflected dramatic social changes. Women were more educated than ever before. Access to institutions of higher learning and professional schools allowed women to participate in the work force in the areas of education, law, medicine, and business throughout the world, whether it was in France, the United States, or the Soviet Union. Women had been active in the politics of liberation of peoples in the 1960s. These activities served to heighten women's collective awareness of the disparities between their own situations and the role of men in Western societies: women worked at home without pay; in the workplace women received less than men for the same work.

In this period of increased educational and work opportunities an international women's movement emerged. International conferences about issues related to women were media events in the 1970s. In 1975 the United Nations Conference on the Decade for Women was convened in Mexico City. Women activists felt that something more was needed than this conference, which was accused of seeking only to integrate women into existing social structures dominated by men. On 8 March 1976—International Women's Day—the International Tribunal of Crimes Against Women was convened in Brussels.

Modeling the conference on tribunals like the Nuremburg Commission, which dealt with Nazi atrocities in World War II, the feminists who convened in Brussels concentrated on crimes against women for the purpose of promoting greater political awareness and action. Fertility and sexuality were at the center of the new politics of the women's movement, justified in the slogan "The personal is political." Rape and abortion were problems of international concern. "Sisterhood is powerful!" gave way to a new organizing cry that "International Sisterhood is *More* Powerful!"

In Italy women's political action yielded a new law in 1970 that allowed divorce under very restricted circumstances. Italian feminists used the legal system as a public forum. In France the sale of contraceptives was legalized in 1968. French feminists, like their Italian counterparts, worked through the courts to make abortion legal: they achieved their goal in 1975. Important in the victory were two manifestos, one signed in 1971 by 343 French women, many of them prominent, who acknowledged having had an abortion; the other signed in 1975 by 345 French doctors who acknowledged having performed abortions.

This 1971 photograph shows a Women's Liberation March in London. The women hold aloft a symbol of the cross they refuse to bear, adorned with the symbols of women's enslavement: shopping bag, washing, apron, and a female torso in chains.

Deputy Tatyana Koryagina asks for the floor at the opening sitting of the First Congress of the People's Deputies of the Russian Federation on 16 May 1990. The Congress marked a new wave of liberalization for Soviet communism.

Widespread opposition from religious and conservative groups did not reverse the legal gains.

The feminist movement also created a new feminist scholarship that sought to incorporate women's experiences and perspectives into the disciplines of history, humanities, and the social sciences. Women's studies courses, which emphasized the history of women and their contributions to civilization, became part of university and college curricula throughout Europe and the United States. Reformers also attempted to transform language, which, they argued, had served as a tool of oppression.

In addition to promoting political action throughout Europe, issues of domestic violence, incest, and heterosexuality entered the political arena. In 1970 Western feminism was discovering that "socialism was not enough," and that women had to address problems of discrimination in terms of gender as much as class. As two French feminists explained it in 1974: "If we maintain that our sex unites us across all class differences because we are oppressed as women, regardless of class, race, and age, then even those men who serve the revolution start to react violently and brutally against us. Since we conceive of ourselves as an oppressed sex, we naturally resist those who oppress us." This was a declaration of war between the sexes. In its most radical form lesbian separatism meant a total rejection of men as enemies. Separatists provoked a rift in the women's movement.

Feminists continued to be politically active in the 1970s and 1980s in the peace movement, antinuclear protests, and in ecological groups concerned with protecting the environment. As Petra Kelly, the West German leader of the Green party, an ecological and pacifist coalition, described it, "... women all over the world are rising up, infusing the antinuclear, peace, and alternative movements with a vitality and creativity never seen before."

The women's movement recognized that women in socialist and capitalist countries alike shared similar problems. Increasingly, well-educated Soviet women demanded reforms, and the beginnings of a women's protest literature in the 1970s indicated an awakening concern for women's issues. Soviet women enjoyed more representation in parliamentary bodies than women in the West. More than half of the 2.3 million deputies to the local Soviets in the 1980s were women. One-third of the 1,500 members of the Supreme Soviet were women. Gorbachev appointed a woman as one of the twelve Central Committee secretaries—the most politically influential people in the country. In spite of greater participation, women enjoyed little real authority in the higher echelons of political life and most Soviet women rejected feminism as a political movement.

The same pattern held true for women in the work force. Over 85 percent of Soviet women worked, compared to about 60 percent of women in the West. Seventy percent of doctors and 73 percent of teachers were women, but women hold few positions of authority. Both their pay and status were lower than men's as the example of primary school teaching reveals: 80 percent of primary school teachers were women but two out of three head teachers were men.

Unlike Western women, many Soviet women—two out of three on average, according to censuses in the 1970s—performed heavy manual labor. Older women, for example, still chopped ice from Soviet streets. This practice began forty years earlier in World War II because of the heavy losses of men—15 million died in the war. In her doctoral dissertation on the sociology of the rural village of Stavropol, Raisa Gorbachev, wife of the Soviet leader, argued that while men were trained to run machines and tractors, women were expected more and more to perform the heavy physical labor associated with farm work.

Birth rates fell in the Soviet Union as in Western countries as women were bearing fewer children. Technology had made controlled fertility possible in safer, more dependable ways but most birth-control devices remained unavailable to Soviet women and what was available was often unreliable. Abortion continued to be a common form of birth control in the Soviet Union with two abortions for every live birth. Women were also choosing to have their children later, often because of work and financial considerations, with a growing percentage delaying childbearing until their thirties. Women complained of lack of quality in maternity hospital care. As one young mother explained, "The only experience worse than an abortion is having a baby in a Soviet hospital."

Gorbachev made direct appeals for women's support by promising preschool nurseries and kindergartens for every child. Gorbachev also committed himself to support increased sick leave for mothers of sick children, and paid maternity leave for a period of eighteen months, increased child-care allowances, and shorter work days for women who work at home. In support of women's voice in the workplace, women's councils were to be revived.

Women's work experience in the East and the West varied in degree, but a startlingly similar pattern of home and work life prevailed in the late twentieth century. Neither state institutions nor the law met the needs of women.

Terrorism and Contemporary Society

Terrorism persisted as a force of political violence in the second half of the twentieth century. The Middle East, Latin America, Africa, and Asia all witnessed growing terrorist opposition to enemies described as imperialists and colonizers. The creation of Israel in 1948 affected the territory of five Middle Eastern nations—Palestine, Libya, Jordan, Egypt, and Syria. Israel became the source of terrorist opposition that radiated out from the Middle East among the Palestinian dispossessed. Having lost all of their territory by 1967, Palestinian guerrillas decided that the best way to attack Israel and its protectors was with a global strategy of terrorist violence.

The first Palestinian highjacking took place in the summer of 1968. Ejected from Jordan, Palestinian guerrillas set up their headquarters in Syria and Lebanon in order to continue their terrorist activities. By the late 1970s terrorism appealed to European Revolutionaries and intensified with political killings in western Europe. A small group of left-wing radicals known as the Red Army Faction executed key industrial, financial, and judicial leaders in West Germany. The Red Army Faction was also responsible for a number of bombings, including that of the West German embassy in Stockholm. In Italy, a small group known as the Red Brigades, which claimed to represent the masses, was responsible for violent incidents, including the "kneecapping"—that is, crippling people by shooting them in the knees—of leading Italian businessmen and the kidnapping and murder of the former Italian prime minister Aldo Moro. In 1981, the Red Brigades targeted the United States for their terrorist reprisals when they abducted an American general, James Dozier.

Terrorism was heir to an anarchist tradition in Western society. Anarchism in nineteenth-century Europe fought against the rise of the state and in favor of an older way of life that existed before central control and industrialization. Anarchism was also a tool of oppressed nationalist minorities: the assassination of the Archduke Ferdinand in 1914 was the single most consequential act of an anarchist-nationalist—it started World War I. Although modern-day terrorists did not share a single political program, they were alike in their desperation, as graffiti scrawled on the wall of a French university in the late 1970s explained, "Hope betrayed arrays itself in bombs." Terrorists lacked access to channels of peaceful change and shared a utopian vision of a better world, which could be achieved only by the use of violence for political ends. Groups as disparate as the Provisional Wing of the Irish Republican Army (IRA), the West German Baader-Meinhof gang, and the Palestine Liberation Organization (PLO) shared these common features.

An ancient Chinese proverb captures well terrorism's strategic rationale: "Kill one, frighten ten thousand." Terrorism meant politically motivated violence and performed by groups claiming to represent some greater political cause. Victims were targeted by terrorists not because they merited any punishment themselves but as a means of attracting international attention to the terrorists' cause. Victims—whether American tourists or German capitalists—were considered symbols of a greater oppression.

Western Europe served as an important arena for terrorist acts. In order to succeed—that is, to terrify—terrorism had to be publicized: terrorists relied on media exposure and claimed responsibility for their acts after they had been successfully completed. In September 1972 members of the Palestinian Black September movement kidnapped eleven Israeli athletes at the Olympic Games in Munich. An estimated 500 million people watched in horror as all eleven were slaughtered during an American sports broadcast. In a dramatic televised shoot-out five of the terrorists also died. Later in the decade OPEC oil ministers were held hostage in Vienna.

A hooded Arab terrorist stands on a balcony during the attack on the Israeli Olympic team headquarters at the Munich Olympics in 1972.

In 1981 a Turkish fascist attempted to kill the pope. In 1983 a Lebanese Shiite guerrilla blew up the American garrison in Beirut, taking hundreds of American lives along with his own. In October 1985, the cruise ship *Achille Lauro* was highjacked by a Palestinian ultranationalist group. One aged American passenger, confined to a wheelchair, was killed. In 1985, Palestinian terrorists bombed the airports in Vienna and Rome. All of these highly publicized acts of violence were part of a larger pattern of terrorism throughout the 1980s.

The Provisional Wing of the IRA justified its bombing of Christmas crowds in London with the need to unite Northern Ireland with the independent Irish Republic. Like the Provisional Wing of the IRA and the Palestine Liberation Organization, many terrorists saw themselves as representing nationalist liberation movements: "One man's freedom fighter is another man's terrorist." Resistance fighters in World War II had used bombs and assassinations as their means of fighting a more powerful enemy. Seeing themselves engaged in wars of liberation, revolution, and resistance, terrorists argued that they used the only weapons at their disposal against the great imperialist powers: plastic explosives in suitcases, nearly impossible to detect by available technology in the 1980s, became the weapon of choice. If all was fair in war—and World War II demonstrated that both sides bombed innocent civilian victims in pursuit of victory—then, terrorists countered, they were fighting the war with the only weapons and in the only arena at their disposal.

Terrorism was not a single movement but a variety of groups and organizations on both the Left and the Right. Some organizations were Marxist, as was the Popular Front for the Liberation of Palestine (PFLP); some were nationalist, as was the PLO. All defined the enemy as an imperialist and a colonizer. Western capitalist nations, and especially the United States and Israel, were common targets of terrorist attacks. Terrorists all shared a utopian vision of the world based on the commonly held belief that the destruction of the existing order was the only way of bringing about a more equitable system. The Japanese Red Army, in support of the PLFP, massacred 24 passengers at Lod Airport in Israel in 1972. At his trial, the only surviving Red Army terrorist made the following statement:

> Revolutionary warfare is warfare for justice, which I define as creating a society with no class struggle. War involves killing and destruction. We cannot limit warfare to the destruction of buildings. We believe that the killing of human beings is inevitable ... The Arab world lacks spiritual fervor, so we felt that through this attempt we could probably stir up the Arab world.

Although motivated by different political agenda, terrorist groups often formed cooperative networks on an international basis, sharing training, weapons, and information. The shadowy figure of the terrorist "Carlos" is one such example of the networks of cooperation established among a variety of groups in the mid-1970s. "Carlos," a Latin American by the name of Ilyitch Ramirez Sanchez, worked with a German group of anarcho-communist terrorists, trained with the PFLP, was supported by Syrian and Libyan agencies, and cooperated with the Russian KGB.

By 1990 terrorism challenged the tranquillity of Western capitalist nations in effective ways. One reason for terrorism's success was the vulnerability of advanced industrial societies to random terror. Modern terrorists were able to evade policing and detection. Surveillance has not prevented terrorists from striking at airplanes and cruise ships. In December 1988 hundreds of people died when a Pan American flight was bombed over Lockerbie, Scotland, probably in retaliation for the accidental downing of an Iranian passenger airliner by the U.S. Navy in the Persian Gulf. Yet terrorism accomplished little by way of bringing about political change or solutions to problems like the question of a Palestinian homeland in the Middle East.

West European governments often refused to bargain with terrorists. Yet at times European nations have been willing to negotiate for the release of kidnapped citizens. They have also been willing to use violence themselves against terrorists. Israel led the way in creating antiterror squads. In 1976 Israeli commandos succeeded in freeing captives in Entebbe in Uganda. The following year specially trained West German troops freed Lufthansa passengers and crew held hostage at Mogadishu in Somalia on the east coast of Africa. The Arab kidnappers had hoped to bargain for the release of the imprisoned leaders of the Red Army Faction; the West German government refused. In 1986 the United States bombed Libya, long recognized as a training ground for international terrorist recruits, in retaliation for the bombing of a discotheque frequented by American service personnel in West Germany. Israel bombed refugee camps to retaliate against Palestinian nationalists. The goal of this "counterterrorism" was the undermining of support for terrorists among their own people, which made it very similar in tactics and ends to the terrorism it was opposing.

Toward a Single European Community: Europe 1992

In 1957, the founders of the European Economic Community, Robert Schuman and Jean Monnet, envisioned the idea of a United States of Europe. Both men perceived that Europe's only hope of competing in a new world system was through unity. The European Community was created in 1967 by merging the three transnational European bodies—the European Coal and Steel Community, the European Economic Community, and Euratom. It operated with its own commission, parliament, and council of ministers, although it had little real power over the operations of member states. In 1974 a "European Council" was created within the European Community, made up of heads of government who met three times a year. Almost since its inception the European Community has been committed to European integration.

The oil crisis of the 1970s encouraged isolationism among the members of the EEC and eroded foreign markets, with growing dependence on national suppliers thereby undercutting the goals of the Common Market. As the crisis abated, competition and efficiency reemerged as priorities within the European Community. Europeans were well aware that the United States and Japan had surged ahead after the 1973 crisis. They also recognized that the Common Market

had been successful in promoting European growth and integration since 1958. They now realized that integration was the only defense against the permanent loss of markets and dwindling profits. In unity there was strength, as the aggregate economic indicators for 1987 made clear.

In 1985 the European Community negotiated the Single European Act, which was ratified by the parliamentary bodies of the member nations by 1987. Final steps were initiated to establish a fully integrated market by 31 December 1992. In 1989 there were 320 million European citizens of the twelve countries of the European Community: the original Common Market six of France, West Germany, Belgium, the Netherlands, Luxembourg, and Italy were joined by Britain, Denmark, and Ireland in 1973, Greece in 1981, and Portugal and Spain in 1986. The goal behind the planning for 1992 was to make the European Community think and act as a single country. Supporters compared it to the fifty individual American states participating in the single U.S. nation. There would eventually be a single currency (based on the European Currency Unit, or ECU), a single central banking system, and a common European defense system. Many feared that the long histories, traditions, and national identifications of the individual member states might stand in the way of a single market.

As the core of the 1992 plan, the twelve members of the European Community intended to eliminate internal barriers and to create a huge open market among the member states with common external tariff policies. In addition, the elimination of internal frontier controls, with a single-format European Community passport was intended to make travel easier and to elimi-

Aggregate Economic Indicators for 1987			
1987	Population	GNP (in ECUs*)	% of World Trade
EC	320 mil	380 bil	18%
USSR	275 mil	N/A	N/A
USA	234 mil	370 bil	17%
Japan	119 mil	200 bil	9%

* European Currency Unit

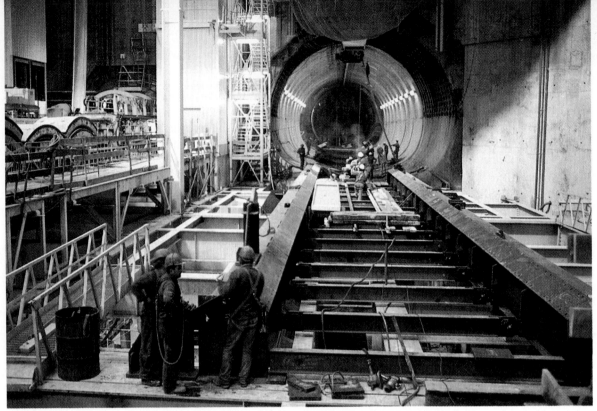

In 1986, Great Britain and France began the construction of a twin-tube railway tunnel under the English Channel. The "chunnel" will enable passengers to avoid the chronically rough weather of the Channel crossing while cutting travel time between England and the Continent to thirty minutes.

nate shipping delays at frontiers, thereby lowering costs. An international labor market based on standardized requirements for certification and interchangeable job qualifications would result. The easier movement of capital was encouraged to areas were profitability was greatest. All aspects of trade and communication, down to electrical plugs and sockets, were intended to be standardized.

Britain was the most reluctant of the member states at the prospect of European integration. Prime Minister Margaret Thatcher expressed the British concern over how a single European market would affect national industries and finance, as well as how it would alter concepts of national sovereignty. Thatcher emphasized the unworkability of a European Central Bank, which she dismissed as "airy-fairy" in the 1989 public discussions of the process. Nonetheless, Thatcher solidly committed Great Britain to the European Community: "Britain does not dream of an alternative to the European Community, of some cozy isolated existence on its fringes. Our destiny is in Europe, as part of the

Community." British critics insisted, however, that economic power and political power were not separable and that there would be negative political consequences to unified economies.

Neither Helmut Kohl, the Christian Democratic chancellor of West Germany, nor Michel Rocard, the French Socialist prime minister, shared Thatcher's concerns in 1988. Rocard called Thatcher's views of federation "archaic" and prophesied that "if we [Europeans] are not federated within twenty or thirty years, our generation will be guilty in front of the world." At the end of 1988 President François Mitterrand of France endorsed the goals of the 1992 integration: "One currency, one culture, one social area, one environment."

The plan for a single European market affected more than just economics. Education, too, faced standardization of curricula and requirements for degrees. There were proposals for a common European history textbook that, in place of national perspectives, would emphasize the values of a single political entity in its discussion of battles, wars, social change, and culture.

Some planners were wary about the prospect of including all of eastern Europe, whose troubled economies, they feared, would dilute the economic strength of the European Community. Nevertheless, even before the freedom movements of 1989 and the disintegration of the Eastern Bloc, some economists were predicting a fully integrated Europe, including the eastern European nations, by the year 2014.

Other world trading powers fear "Fortress Europe," that is, Europe as a global trading bloc with a common external tariff policy that would exclude them. United Europe would constitute a formidable presence in the world arena with the world's largest volume of trade and highest productivity. The move might easily place Europe at the center of world politics, as the Cold War thawed and the bloc politics of East versus West no longer dominated the international system.

Nationalist feelings were intensifying within eastern Europe at the very moment of integration in the west. Demands for autonomy lay behind the revolutionary events in Poland, the Baltic Soviet states, Hungary, Bulgaria, and Romania. Meanwhile in western Europe, planners spoke of a European Community in which national differences would be muted for the common good. Europeans were assured that the federal solution would preserve national identities, culture, and language, and that the new federal government would only make those decisions not better made on the local and regional levels.

At the end of the twentieth century Western women and men faced the future filled with uncertainty. Social change threatened to wither without producing fruit, as governments cut free of the security of old ways grappled with new political challenges and economic uncertainties. Yet there was hope, too, as both Mikhail Gorbachev and Margaret Thatcher spoke of a common European destiny for Communist and democratic nations who had once been enemies. On New Year's Day 1990, an international orchestra led by the American conductor Leonard Bernstein gathered at the Berlin Wall to celebrate the new era that seemed to be dawning in Europe. For the event, Bernstein chose Beethoven's Ninth Symphony, "Ode to Joy," which he took the liberty of recasting as "Ode to Freedom." The symphony rang out as an anthem for the aspirations of Europeans facing the twenty-first century.

Europe 1992

Suggestions for Further Reading

Ending the Cold War

Stephen F. Cohen, *Rethinking the Soviet Experience: Politics and History Since 1917* (New York: Oxford University Press, 1985). Offers a revisionist analysis of the historiographical debates in Soviet studies with the intention of casting light on contemporary Soviet politics.

Patrick Cockburn, *Getting Russia Wrong: The End of Kremlinology* (London: Verso, 1989). A Moscow correspondent takes the measure of the politics of the Gorbachev era, while attempting to uncover the shortcomings of Western misconceptions about the Soviet Union.

Geoffrey Hosking, *The Awakening of the Soviet Union* (Cambridge, MA: Harvard University Press, 1990). Published in the midst of the dramatic changes taking place in the Soviet Union, this study emphasizes the social bases of reform and the challenges to Soviet leadership.

Brian McNair, *Images of the Enemy: Reporting the New Cold War* (London: Routledge, 1988). Focuses on the importance of television in conveying the East-West debate to a mass audience in the 1980s. McNair demonstrates that the Soviets learned in the 1980s to manage communication techniques to their own advantage.

Adam B. Ulam, *Dangerous Relations: The Soviet Union in World Politics, 1970–1982* (New York: Oxford University Press, 1983). Discusses the making of détente and the relationship between internal developments in the Soviet Union and their impact on foreign policy.

Eastern and Central Europe Since 1968

Teresa Rakowska-Harmstone and Andrew Gyorgy, eds., *Communism in Eastern Europe* (Manchester, England: Manchester University Press, 1984). Provides a comprehensive country-by-country approach with consideration of nationalism and shared regional problems.

Joseph Rothschild, *Return to Diversity: A Political History of East Central Europe* (New York: Oxford University Press, 1989). A historical and analytical survey of Poland, Czechoslovakia, Hungary, Yugoslavia, Romania, Bulgaria, and Albania that appeared just before the great changes that swept eastern Europe in 1989. Rothschild highlights the tensions between nationalist aspirations and communist rule.

Henry Ashby Turner, Jr., *The Two Germanies Since 1945* (New Haven: Yale University Press, 1987). A political history from the postwar division of Germany until 1987 that bridges a period that the author contends was one of increasing involvement and underlying mutual interests between the two nations.

Unity and Diversity in Western Europe

J. Bowyer Bell, *Transnational Terror* (Washington, DC: American Enterprise Institute, 1975). Presents a compelling argument about the social revolutionary origins of terror and its threat to Western democracies.

Richard Clutterbuck, *Guerrillas and Terrorists* (London: Faber and Faber, 1977). Clutterbuck considers terrorism as a kind of war rooted in historical experience and global in nature. His purpose is to consider protection against terrorists by examining the roles of the media, the police, and the public.

Michael Emerson, et al., *The Economics of 1992: The E.C. Commission's Assessment of the Economic Effects of Completing the Internal Market* (Oxford: University Press, 1988). A work replete with empirical data that gives a comprehensive assessment of the potential impact of establishing a single internal market in the European Economic Community.

Wolfgang Mommsen and Gerhard Hirschfeld, eds., *Social Protest, Violence and Terror in Nineteenth- and Twentieth-Century Europe* (London: The MacMillan Press Ltd., 1982). Places terrorism within a historical context in Europe over the last century and a half in a series of articles that proceed with a national, case-history approach.

Richard E. Rubinstein, *Alchemists of Revolution: Terrorism in the Modern World* (New York: Basic Books, 1987). Examines the local root causes of terrorism in historical perspective and argues that it is a social and moral crisis of a disaffected intelligentsia.

MAP CREDITS
602 Cereal Crops
646 Population Growth in Europe, 1800-1850
648 The European Linen Industry Based on information from Norman J. G. Pounds, *An Historical Geography of Europe, 1500-1840* (New York: Cambridge University Press, 1980).
733 Russian Serfs
939 European Migrations After World War II Based on information from *The New Cambridge Modern History Atlas* (Cambridge: Cambridge University Press, 1979).
802 European Foreign Investments, ca. 1878 Based on information from *The Times Atlas of World History* (Maplewood, NJ: Hammond, 1985).
844 Revolution and Civil War in Russia, 1914-20 Based on information from Andrew Wheatcroft, *The World Atlas of Revolutions* (New York: Simon and Schuster, 1983).
909 The Holocaust Based on information from Raul Hilberg, *The Destruction of European Jews* (New York: Holmes and Meier, 1985).

PHOTOGRAPH CREDITS
Positions of the photographs are indicated in the abbreviated form as follows; top (t), bottom (b), center (c), left (1), right (r). Unless otherwise acknowledged, all photographs are the property of Scott, Foresman.

TABLE OF CONTENTS
iii National Portrait Gallery, London
iv The British Library
v The British Library
vi Museum of London
vii Kunsthistorisches Museum, Vienna
viii (t) UPI/Bettmann

CHAPTER OPENERS
Chapter 15, p. 450 *Massacre of the Innocents* by Nicolas Poussin. Musee' Conde', Chantilly/Giraudon/Art Resource, NY
Chapter 16, p. 482-483 Versailles as it looked in 1722 by Pierre Denis Martin. Bulloz
Chapter 17, p. 515 *The Anatomy Lesson of Dr. Nicolaes Tulp* by Rembrandt van Rijn, 1632. Photograph © Mauritshuis, The Hague
Chapter 18, p. 546-547 *Das Flotenkonzert* by Adolph von Menzel, 1852. Staatliche Museen Preussischer Kulturbesitz, Nationalgalerie, Berlin
Chapter 19, p. 578 *The Visit to the Nursery (A Visit to the Wet Nurse)* by Jean-Honore Fragonard, painted before 1784. National Gallery of Art, Washington; Samuel H. Kress Collection
Chapter 20, p. 610 *Marie Antoinette à la Rose* by Elisabeth Vigée-Lebrun. Lauros-Giraudon/Art Resource, NY; p. 611 A sketch of Marie Antoinette on her way to the guillotine by Jacques Louis David. Giraudon/Art Resource, NY
Chapter 21, p. 642 *Saint-Lazare Train Station, the Normandy Train (La Gare Saint-Lazare, le Train de Normandie)* by Claude Monet., 1877, oil on canvas. 59.6 x 80.2 cm. Mr and Mrs. Martin A. Ryerson Collection, 1933.1158. Photograph © 1990, the Art Institute of Chicago. All Rights Reserved.
Chapter 22, p. 681 *Potato Planters* by Jean Francois Millet. Gift of Quincy Adams Shaw through Quincy A. Shaw, Jr. and Mrs. Marian Shaw Haughton. Courtesy, Museum of Fine Arts, Boston
Chapter 23, p. 714 *Proclamation of the German Empire at Versailles*,; 1871 by Anton von Werner, 1885. Staatliche Museen Preussischer Kulturbesitz, Berlin
Chapter 24, p. 750 *Riot in the Galleria* by Umberto Boccioni, 1910. Bridgeman/Art Resource, NY
Chapter 25, p. 783 Map of the British Empire in 1886. Mansell Collection
Chapter 26, p. 816 *Take Up the Sword of Justice* by Sir Bernard J. Partridge, England, 1915; p. 817 *Deutsche Frauen Arbeitet im Heimat-Heer! Kriegsamtstelle Magdeburg* (German *Women Work in the Home-Army! Magdeburg War Office*) by Georg Kirchbach, Germany, 1914-18. (both) From copy in Bowman Gray Collection, Rare Book Collection, UNC Library, Chapel Hill, North Carolina
Chapter 27, p. 850 *Project for a Glass Skyscraper* by Ludwig Mies van der Rohe, 1921, model-no longer extant. Photograph Courtesy The Museum of Modern Art, New York; p. 851 *Armchair (B3)* by

Marcel Breuer, late 1927 - early 1928, chrome-plated tubular steel with canvas slings, 28⅛ x 30¼ x 27¾". Collection, The Museum of Modern Art, New York. Gift of Herbert Bayer
Chapter 28, p. 888-889 *Guernica* by Pablo Picasso, 1937. Museo del Prado, Madrid. Copyright 1990 ARS N.Y./SPADEM
Chapter 29, p. 926 The poster scene, 1967. Topham/The Image Works
Chapter 30, p. 961 Protest in Prague, November 1989. AP/Wide World

CHAPTER 15
457 National Portrait Gallery, London 470 Reproduced by Courtesy of the Trustees of the British Museum 472 Musée de Strasbourg

CHAPTER 16
485 National Portrait Gallery, London 487 (t) Reproduced by courtesy of the Trustees, The National Gallery, London (b) Courtesy of The Hispanic Society of America 488 National Portrait Gallery, London 493 The Bettmann Archive 496 Cliché des Musées Nationaux, Paris 500 By permission of the Earl of Rosebery. On loan to the Scottish National Portrait Gallery 510 Scala/Art Resource, NY

CHAPTER 17
518 The British Library 520 Biblioteca Nazionale Centrale, Florence 523 National Library of Medicine 526 Städelsches Kunstinstitut, Frankfurt am Main. Photo: Blauel-Gnamm/Artothek 536 National Maritime Museum Greenwich

CHAPTER 18
551 Giraudon/Art Resource, NY 554 Central Naval Museum, Leningrad 561 State Russian Museum , Leningrad 562 Private Collection 563 Staatliche Museen Preussischer Kulturbesitz, Kunstbibliothek, Berlin 566 Kunsthistorisches Museum, Vienna

CHAPTER 19
582 Giraudon/Art Resource, NY 585 (r) Scottish National Portrait Gallery 587 Giraudon/Art Resource, NY 593 Staaatliche Museen Preussischer Kulturbesitz, Gemaldegalerie, Berlin 595 Scala/Art Resource, NY 597 Alinari/Art Resource, NY 607 The Metropolitan Museum of Art, Harris Brisbane Dick Fund, 1932

CHAPTER 20
616 Bulloz 621 Bibliothèque Nationale, Paris 623 Giraudon/Art Resource, NY 624 Bulloz 625 Cliché: Musées de la Ville de Paris © SPADEM 1990 626 Bulloz 630 Library of Congress 635 Scala/Art Resource, NY 636 *Neither Do These (Ni Por Esas)* by Francisco Goya, 1863, etching, 16 x 21 cm. Gift of J./C. Cebrian, 1920. 1316. Photograph © 1990, The Art Institute of Chicago. All Rights Reserved 638 Musée des Beaux-Arts, Rouen

CHAPTER 21
647 Reproduced by Courtesy of the Trustees of the British Museum 651 Bulloz 652 Musée de l'Art Wallon, Liège 655 Mansell Collection 656 National Museums and Galleries on Merseyside (Walker Art Gallery, Liverpool) 657 National Portrait Gallery, London 659 Museum of American Textile History 661 Bridgeman/Art Resource, NY 664 Victoria and Albert Museum/Art Resource, NY 665 Reproduced by kind permission of New Lanark Conservation Trust 667 John Freeman/Fotomas Index 671 Bulloz 675 Ullstein Bilderdienst 677 Free Library of Philadelphia

CHAPTER 22
687 Bettman/Hulton 690 Historisches Museum der Stadt Wien 691 The Royal Collection. Copyright Reserved to Her Majesty Queen Elizabeth II 693 The British Library 695 Scala/Art Resource, NY 697 Giraudon/Art REsource, NY 698 Reproduced by Courtesy of the Trustees of the British Museum 703 Weidenfeld & Nicolson Archives 706 Scala/Art Resource, NY 710 Historisches Museum der Stadt Wien

CHAPTER 23
717 Reproduced by Courtesy of the Trustees of the British Museum 719 Museo del Risorgimento e Raccolte Storiche, Milan 721

INDEX

Abortion, 950, 986, 872, 873, 950, 986
Abraham Lincoln Brigade, 901
Absolutism, 503, 504-512
    collapse of in Prussia, 709-710
    French Revolution and, 617-618
Acheson, Dean, 942
Achille Lauro, 988
Act of Succession, 570
Adam brothers, 582
Adenauer, Konrad, 934, 951
Advancement of Learning [Bacon], 524
Afghanistan, Soviet withdrawal from, 960
Africa
    decolonization in, 931-932
    exploration of, 787, 792
    Germany and, 793
    slaves from, 530-531
    western imperialism and, 790-794, 804-805
Afrikaans language, 797
Agricultural Revolution, 645, 649-652
Agriculture
    Austrian, 565
    eighteenth-century, 645-646
    enclosure vs. open-field, 645, 649-650, 652
    French, in the industrial age, 670-671
    German, in industrial age, 673
    overproduction in, 753
    rotation in, 650
    Russian, 557
    seventeenth-century, 494, 646
    in Soviet Union, 867, 870-871
    in World War I, 834-835
    post World War II, 940
    eighteenth-century, 596, 599-603
Aix-la-Chapelle, 567
Alba, Duke of, 457, 463-464
Albania, 893
Albert, Charles, 710
Albert, Prince, 691
Alchemy, 519, 522
Alexander I (Russia)
    Congress of Vienna and, 685
    Holy Alliance and, 686
    Napoleonic era and, 636, 637-638
Alexander II (Russia), 718, 733-735
Alexandra (Russia), 841
Alexis I (Russia), 555, 556
Algeciras, Act of, 799
Algeria, 707, 709, 787, 788
    independence of, 932
All Quiet on the Western Front [Remarque], 824
Alliance system, 686, 809, 810-811
    in 1914, 819-820
Allies
    Anti-Bolshevik forces assisted by, 846
    France after Napoleon's defeat and, 683-684
    Italy convinced to join, 831
    joined by United States, 836-837
    reparations and war debts and, 859-865
    Talleyrand and, 685
    United States and, 917-920
    in World War I, 823, 827, 831
    in World War II, 914-921

Almanacs, 606
Alsace, 538, 548, 550
Alsace-Lorraine, 827, 838, 839
Amadeus II, 552
Amboise, Edict of, 454, 455
America. *See* North America; United States
Americas, African slaves imported into, 530-531
Amsterdam, 514-515, 528, 532
An Essay Concerning Human Understanding [Locke], 584
Anabaptists, in Netherlands, 462, 463
Anarchy, 769-771, 987
Anatomy, study of, 514-515, 517, 522-523
Anatomy Lesson of Dr. Nicolaes Tulp, The [Rembrandt], 514
Andropov, Yuri, 964
Angell, Norman, 847
Anglo-Dutch wars, 536-537
Animal Farm [Orwell], 946-947
Animal husbandry, 650-651, 673
Anjou, Duc d', 458
Anne (England), 488, 496, 540
Anti-semitism, 767-769
    Austrian, 763
    French, 761-762
    in World War II, 909-914
Anti-Socialist Law, 758-759
Antwerp, 464
ANZACS, 831
April Theses, 845
Arabs
    Israelis vs., 938
    terrorism and, 989
    in World War I, 835
Archangel, 469
Architecture, twentieth-century, 850-851
Aristocrats
    Austrian, 763
    Enlightenment and, 617
    French Revolution and, 616-617
    Lithuanian, 466
    sixteenth-century French, 453-454
    Spanish, 901
    eighteenth-century, 580-582
Aristotle, new science vs. theories of, 517, 518, 520
Arkwright, Richard, 658-660, 664
Armenians, 969, 970
Art
    depicting royalty, 484
    Dutch, 514
    French impressionists, 751
    futurist, 750-751
    Hitler and, 884
    in the 1920s, 881-884
    romanticism in, 695-696
    sixteenth- and seventeenth-century, 484
    twentieth-century, 850
    Victorian, 740-742
Artisans' Dwelling Act, 731
tist's Studio, The [Courbet], 741
Asia
    Cold War and, 936-938
    decolonization in, 931
    European trade with, 529-531, 543
    imperialism in, 794-797
    Japanese imperialism in, 800-801
    post World War II, 921
    western imperialism and, 790
Astrology, astronomy and, 519
Astronomy, 517-519
Astrophysics, 773

Athletics, eighteenth-century, 606
    See also Sports
Atom, structure of, 773
Atomic bomb, 920, 922-923, 928
Auschwitz, 911-912
Austen, Jane, 689, 740
Australia, 807, 831
Austria, 538, 540, 562, 565-567
    annexed by Hitler's Germany, 903-904
    Bismark and, 723-725
    Congress of Vienna and, 684-685
    eighteenth-century, 552
    Enlightenment in, 583, 589
    France and, 626
    Frederick the Great and, 567
    in the industrial age, 675, 677
    liberalism defeated in, 762-764
    Napoleon and, 635-636
    nineteenth-century revolution iin, 710, 711
    Prussia and, 711
    separated from Germany, 548-549, 568
Austria-Hungary
    after 1871, 810, 812
    in World War I, 822, 828, 829
Autarky, 895
Autobiography of a Sexually Emancipated Communist Women [Kollontai], 872
Axis Powers, 918
Azerbaijan, 969, 970

Baader-Meinhof gang, 987
Baby and Child Care [Spock], 950
Bacon, Sir Francis, 524
Bagehot, Walter, 809
Baghdad, in World War I, 831
Baghdad Pact (CENTO), 929
Baku, 969
Bakunin, Mikhail, 770
Balaklava, battle of, 718
Baldwin, Stanley, 899, 900
Balfour, Arthur, 835
Balkans
    after 1871, 811, 812
    pre World War I, 822
    reconquest of from Ottoman Empire, 549
Baltic States, 846, 969
Bank of Amsterdam, 528
Bank of England, 654
Banking, 754-755
    British, 654-655, 801
    Dutch, 532
    during 1870-1914, 754-755
    U.S., in the 1920s, 864
Barbados Island, 530
Barbarini, Cardinal, 520
Barbarossa, Operation, 910
Barbusse, Henri, 829
Barcelona, 494, 495
Basic Treaty, 977
Bastille, storming of, 622-623
Bataan Peninsula, 918
Bauhaus, 850-851, 882, 883
    Hitler's followers and, 881
Bavaria, during Thirty Years' War, 476-477
Beatles, 926, 927
Bebel, August, 758
Beccaria, Cesare, 583, 585, 589
Beer Hall Putsch, 881
Belgian Congo, 789, 790, 793, 804-805
Belgians, Netherlands and, 700

Belgium, 548
  in World War I, 826-827
  in World War II, 906, 919
  post World War II, 931
Bellarmine, Cardinal, 521
Belorussia, 846
Benelux, 943
Bentham, Jeremy, 692, 693
Bergen-Belsen, 914
Berkeley, 955
Berlin
  in World War II, 919
  post World War II division of, 934
Berlin Act, 793
Berlin Congress, 811
Berlin Opera House, 593
Berlin Wall, 936, 976
  removal of, 960, 991
Berlioz, Louis Hector, 695
Bernstein, Eduard, 759
Bernstein, Leonard, 991
Besant, Annie, 756, 775
Beveridge, Lord, 951
Bible, Galileo and, 519, 521
Biedermeier style, 690
Big Five, 809
Binet, Alfred, 774
Biology, 517, 772
Bismark, Otto von, 714-715, 723,
  735-736
  Africa and, 793
  Berlin Congress and, 811
  Big Five and, 809
  East Germany and, 978
  newspapers and, 789
  and parliamentary German govern-
    ment, 758
  resignation of, 812
  siege of Paris and, 745
Black Friday, 765
Black Hand, 822
Black September, 987
Blackshirts, 900
Blair, Eric Arthur, 805
Blanc, Louis, 709
Blenheim, 540
Blenheim Palace, 582
Blitzkrieg, 907, 915
Bloody Sunday, 840
Blucher, General, 706
Blue Angel, The, 883
Blum, Leon, 898
Boccioni, Umberto, 751, 752
Bodin, Jean, 485
Boer War, 789, 798
Boers, 797-798
Bohemia
  Protestants in, 565
  during Thirty Years' War, 473-477
Bohr, Niels, 771
Bologna, Concordat of, 453
Bolsheviks, 845-847
  Hitler's contempt for, 881
  in the 1920s, 854, 865-866
  Stalin and, 892
Bombay, 550
Bonald, Louis de, 696
Book of Household Management
  [Beeton], 737
Bosnia, 812
Bossuet, Jacques, 504
Boston Tea Party, 575
Boulanger Affair, 760-761
Boulton, Matthew, 657
Bourbons, 454-460, 540, 551

  end of restoration of, 699
  after Napoleon's defeat, 683, 684
Bourgeoisie, 590-596
  Austrian, 762-763
  French, 707, 708
  French Revolution and, 616, 617-618,
    629
  Russian, 841
Bouvard et Pecuchet [Flaubert], 741
Boxer Rebellion, 796
Boycotts, aganst Great Britain, 575
Boyle, Robert, 522, 524
Boyle's Law, 522
Brahe, Tycho, 518
Brandenburg, 473, 476, 505
Brandenburg-Prussia, 548, 553, 563-565
Brandt, Willy, 976-978
Brazil, 530-531, 549
Brecht, Bertolt, 883
Brest-Litovsk, Treaty of, 846
Breton, Andre, 882
Breuer, Marcel, 850
Brezhnev, Leonid, 962, 967
Brezhnev Doctrine, 962, 974
Briand, Aristide, 858
Bridgewater, Duke of, 654
Britain, Battle of, 908
British Constitution, 569, 570-571
British Light Brigade, 718
British Museum, 547
British North America, 543
British Royal Air Force, 907
British Union of Fascists (BUF), 899-900
Brixton, 983
Broca, Paul, 774-775
Brown Shirts, 881, 909
Broz, Josip, 908
Bruning, Heinrich, 879-880
Brusilov, Aleksei, 829
Brussels, 464
Buckingham, Duke of, 486, 488
Budapest, 710
Bukharin, Nikolai, 866-868, 872
Bulgaria, 811, 812
  Communist party in, 934
  late twentieth-century, 960
  in the 1920s, 854
Bulge, Battle of the, 919
Burial at Ornans [Courbet], 741
Burke, Edmund, 696
Burma, 797, 931
Byron, Lord, 700

Cabinet of Dr. Caligari, The, 883
Caillaux, Joseph, 835
Calculus, 516
Calcutta, 550
Calicoes, 529. *See also* Cloth production
Calonne, Charles Alexandre de, 615
Calvin, John, 453
Calvinism
  in France, 454
  in Netherlands, 462-463
  Philip II and, 461
  sixteenth-century, 453
  of William Laud, 497
Calvinists
  Dutch, Boers as, 797
  Frederick William as one of, 563
  Lutherans united with, 475
  after Thirty Years' War, 479
Cambodia, 797, 938
Canada, 543, 549
Candide [Voltaire], 584, 588
Canning, George, 686

Cape of Good Hope, 797
Capitalism, 808-809
Caribbean islands, 549, 808
Carlo-Alberto, 719
"Carlos,"988
Carlos, Juan, 981
Carrillo, Santiago, 981
Cartels, 754
Cartesianism, 525
  Hume and, 585
  Voltaire and, 583
Cartwright, Major John, 663
Castile, seventeenth-century, 488
Castlereach, 682, 686
Castro, Fidel, 938
Cat and Mouse Act, The, 766
Catalonia
  in the industrial age, 675, 677
  Philip IV and, 495
  rebellion in, 490, 492, 495
Catherine de' Medici, 453, 454-459
Catherine II,"the Great,"558-562
  eighteenth century and, 588-589
Catholic League, 458-459
Catholicism
  Philip II's, 461
  vs. Protestantism in sixteenth century,
    452-460
  vs. Protestantism during Thirty Years'
    War, 472-479
Catholics
  eighteenth-century, 589
  French Revolution and, 625
  under James II, 503
Cavaignac, Louis, 709
Cavour, Camillo di, 716, 719-723,
  735-736
Ceaucescu, Nicolae and Elena, 961, 972
Central America, United States and,
  808, 836
Central Intelligence Agency (CIA),
  937-938
Central Powers, 825, 831
Ceramics, Dutch, 532
Cervantes, Miguel de, 460
Ceylon, post World War II, 930
Chadwick, Edwin, 665, 666-667, 727,
  728
Chamberlain, Neville, 904
Chaplin, Charlie, 883
Charcot, Jean Martin, 776
Charles, Archduke, 540
Charles I (England)
  art depicting, 484
  Duke of Buckingham and, 488
  execution of, 499, 500-501
  religious reform and, 497
  Scotland and, 498
  Spanish Armada and, 491
  William Harvey and, 523
Charles II (England), 502
Charles II (Spain), 539, 540a
Charles VI (Austria), 565, 565-566
Charles IX (France), 454, 455, 457, 470
Charles X (France), 699
Chartists, 702-708
Chelmno, 911, 914
Chemistry, 516, 522
Chevalier-Cobden Treaty, 729
Chiang Kai-shek, 902
Child labor, 690
Children
  in the industrial age, 663, 664-665,
    668-669
  in Nazi Germany, 896

nineteenth-century, 688, 689, 690
  welfare state and, 951
eighteenth-century, 590, 594-595, 596
China
  Japan and, 800-801
  Japan's undeclared war on, 902
  opium and, 795
  tea from, 530
  United States and, 797
  western imperialism and, 790,
    795-796
Chios, 700
Chlorine gas, 826
Cholera, 706-707, 718
Chopin, Frederic, 695, 700
Christian IV, 470, 475
Christianity
  Africa and, 790-791, 804-805
  Enlightenment and, 585-586
  Russian, 465-466, 508, 555, 556, 589
  See also Orthodox (eastern) Chris-
    tianity; Roman Catholic church
Church
  Enlightenment and, 584
  French Revolution and, 625
  reform in England, 497
  See also specific types
Church of England, Gladstone and, 731
Churchill, John, 540, 582
  See also Marlborough, Duke of
Churchill, Winston, 831, 907-908
  post World War II, 928
  Roosevelt and, 918-919
Cities/towns
  nineteenth-century, 687-688, 702, 707
  eighteenth-century, 598
Civil War
  Asian, post World War II, 931
  Korean, 936-937
  Russian, 846-847, 852
  Spanish, 901-902
  of United States, 725
Clemenceau, Georges, 835, 838, 839
Clement VIII, 452
Clerke, Agnes Mary, 773
Cloth production, 533, 795
  Indian, 529
  in Industrial Revolution, 658-660
Coal, 654, 655-657
  France and, 672
  railroads and, 662
Coca-Cola, 955
Cocceji, Samuel von, 588
Cocteau, Jean, 882
Coffee, 529-530
Colbert, Jean-Baptiste, 509, 533, 537
Cold War, 928-938
  Asia during, 936-938
  ending the, 962-970
  former colonies and, 933
  Ronald Reagan and, 963
Coleridge, Samuel Taylor, 694
Cologne, 538
Colonial America, 541, 543, 549
Colonial trade, 533
Colonization
  by Great Britain, 790-794
  See also Decolonization; Imperialism
Comecon, 929-930
Common Market, 944, 989-991
Communications, 786
Communism
  "Eurocommunism," 980-981
  failure of, 960-961, 975-976, 981
  post World War II, 831

United States' fear of, 864
Communist Manifesto, The [Marx], 698
Communist party
  death of Stalin and, 935
  in late twentieth-century Germany,
    960
  in late twentieth-century Italy, 981
  in late twentieth-century Poland,
    971-974
  in late twentieth-century Soviet
    Union, 967-968
  in Russia in the 1920s, 865-874
  Soviet women and, 873
  Stalin and, 892
  surrealist artists and, 882
Communists
  vs. Fascists in Italy, 875
  Hitler and, 894, 910
  in Nazi Germany, 897
Concordat, Mussolini and, 876
*Condition of the Working Class in
  England in 1844, The* [Engels], 668,
  674, 690, 743
Condor Legion, 901
Condorcet, Marquis de, 584, 585, 630
  women and, 628
Congo, Republic of the, 931
Congo. *See* Belgian Congo
Conservatism/Conservatives, 696
  British, 757
  nineteenth-century British, 730-732
  nineteenth-century compared with
    nineteenth-century, 732
Constantinople, 700
Constitution, French, 625-626, 627-628,
  633
Contagious Diseases Act, 665
Continential System, 636, 638, 671
Cook, Thomas, 662
Copernicus, Nicolaus, 517-518
Copernicus, Galileo, 520-521
Corn Laws, 681
Cossacks, 555, 559, 846
Cottage industry, 647
Cotton, British production of, 658-660,
  795
Cotton gin, 660
Counter-Reformation, Austria and, 565
Courbet, Gustave, 740-741
Crete, 773
Crime and Punishment [Dostoyevsky],
  742
Crimean Tartars, 467
Crimean War, 716-718, 719
  and reform in Russia, 733
Crimes and Punishments [Beccaria], 584
Criminal Man, The [Lombroso], 774
Croatia, 908
Croats, 854
Crompton, Samuel, 659
Cromwell, Oliver, 499, 502
  Navigation Ordinance and, 535-536
Crystal Palace, 669, 788
Cuba, 938
Curie, Marie, 771
Czechoslovakia, 854
  Brezhnev and, 962
  Communist party in, 934-935
  Hitler and, 904
  in the 1920s, 854
  nineteenth-century, 710
  late twentieth-century, 960, 970,
    975-976

Dadaists, 882

Daladier, Edouard, Hitler and, 904
Dali, Salvador, 822
Dalmatian islands, 831
Danes
  Sweden and, 469, 472, 553
  during Thirty Years' War, 475
Danton, George-Jacques, 633
Darby, Abraham, 657
Dardanelles, Straits of, 831
Darnley, Lord, 457
Darwin, Charles, 742, 774-775, 802
  Karl Marx and, 742-743
Darwinists, social, 775
Das Kapital [Marx], 743
Davison, Emily Wilding, 766
Dawes, Charles G., 860
Dawes Plan, 860, 861, 864
de Beauvoir, Simone, 952
De Beers Consolidated Mining, 798
De Gaulle, Charles, 907, 932, 938
  television and, 973
De Quincey, Thomas, 643
Declaration of Independence (U.S.), 584
Declaration of Rights (England), 503
*Declaration of the Rights of Man and
  Citizen*, 627
*Declaration of the Rights of Woman and
  Citizen* [Gouges], 628
Declaratory Act, 575
Decolonization, 930-933
Dee, John, 525
Defense of Liberty Against Tyrants, A
  [Duplessis-Mornay], 494
Defoe, Daniel, 532
Deforestation, 692
Degas, Edgar, 751
Delacroix, Eugene, 695
Democracy
  blocked in early twentieth-century
    Germany, 758
  failure of in Germany, 877-880
  French Revolution and, 618, 627-634
  in Great Britain, 730
  in the late twentieth century, 960
  Napoleon and, 637
  in the 1930s, 898-902
  in nineteenth-century France, 708
  rise of in Europe, 752
Denmark
  Jews and king of, 913
  nineteenth-century, 723
  in World War II, 906
Depression, Great, 753, 884-885
  in France, 898
  in Germany, 863, 879
  in Great Britain, 899
  Hitler and, 895
Descartes, Rene, 525, 582
Descent of Man, The [Darwin], 774
d'Estaing, Giscard, 981
Detente, 963-964, 975
*Dialogue Between the Two Great Systems
  of the World, A* [Galileo], 518, 521,
  525
Diamond mines, 792, 798
Dickens, Charles, 612, 741
Dictatorships, 890-893
Dictionary of Accepted Ideas [Flaubert],
  741
Diderot, Denis, 558, 583, 585
Dietrich, Marlene, 883
Dimitris, 468
Directory, 633-634, 637
Disasters of War, The [Goya], 636
Discourse on Method [Descartes], 524

Disraeli, Benjamin, 730-731, 788, 794
Divine right of kings, theory of, 492
    revived, 503
Doll's House, A [Ibsen], 775
Don Quixote [Cervantes], 460
Donne, John, 516
Dostoyevsky, Fyodor, 742
Dreyfus Affair, 760, 761-762
Drugs, 954-955
Dual Alliance, 811
Dubcek, Alexander, 936
Duchamp, Marcel, 882
Dunkirk, 907
Duplessis-Mornay, Philippe, 494
Durkheim, Emile, 774
Dutch Boers, 797
Dutch East India Company, 532, 534
Dutch Protestants, 494
Dutch Republic, 472, 514-515, 550
    Descartes and, 525
    end of golden age of, 550
    England and, 532-538
    prosperity of, 531-533, 550
    trading by, 532-533, 535-538
Dutch Revolt, 505
Dylan, Bob, 927

East Berlin, 934, 935, 978
East Germany, 949, 960, 976-980
    Lutheran church in, 975
    television and, 972
Easter Rebellion, 835
Eastern Europe
    eighteenth-century, 548, 552-553
    Industrial Revolution and, 670
    late twentieth-century, 970-980
    in the 1920s, 853-854
    postwar recovery of, 949-950
    northeastern Europe, 465-472
Economy
    early twentieth-century, 778-779
    1870-1914 imperialism and world,
        801-802
    eighteenth-century European, 644
    of Europe, 1870-1914, 752-764
    French, in the industrial age, 672
    late twentieth-century Soviet, 965-967
    in the 1920s, world, 858-865, 884-885
    nineteenth-century European,
        729-730
    Polish, 974
    in postwar Germany, 878-879
    regulation of, 1870-1914, 754-755
    seventeenth-century, 490-493, 533-544
    single European market (1992) and,
        991
Edinburgh, 497
Education
    eighteenth-century, 589
    nineteenth-century French, 691
    Russian, 556
    single European market (1992) and,
        990
Edward VII (England), 753
Egmont, Count, 463
Egypt
    Great Britain and, 788
    post World War II, 937, 938
Eiffel Tower, 779
Eighty Years' War, 536
Einstein, Albert, 771, 772, 1920s and,
    882
Eisenhower, Dwight D., 919, 923
Electricity, 786
Eliot, George, 742

Eliot, T. S., 882
Elizabeth (Russia), 567
Elizabeth I (England), 456, 457, 497
    art depicting, 484
    Philip II and, 461
Ellington, Duke, 882
Ellis, Havelock, 778
Emile [Rousseau], 585, 632, 694
Emma [Austen], 689
Encyclopedia [Diderot], 583
Engels, Friedrich, 666, 674, 690, 698
    Karl Marx and, 742-744
Engineering, nineteenth-century, 785
England
    eighteenth-century, 581
    civil wars of, 497-499
    Dutch and, 532-538
    eighteenth-century France and, 539
    as "Great Britain," 541, 550
    liberalism challenged in, 755-757
    nineteenth-century, 689
    and Scotland joining together, 550,
        570
    seventeenth-century trade by, 528,
        529-530
English East India Company, 532, 533,
    795
English Revolution, 499-503, 505
English Royal African Company, 534
Enlightenment, 579, 582-590
    aristocrats and, 580
    France in, 612
    French nobility and, 617
    French Revolution and, 614-615
    liberalism based on rationalism of,
        692
    salons and, 582
Enquiry Concerning Human Under-
    standing [Hume], 585
Entebbe, 988
Epidemics
    of cholera in Paris, 706-707
    in Russia, 865
    See also Plague
Ernst, Max, 882
Essay on Population [Malthus], 742
Essay on the Principles of Population, An
    [Malthus], 597
Estates-General, 485
    Louis XVI and, 615, 618, 620-622
Esterhazys, 580, 581
Estonia, 553, 905
    late twentieth-century, 960, 969
Ethiopia, 790, 892
Euclid, 525
Europe
    in 1815, 682-686
    in 1850, 711
    during 1850-1871, 714-748
    during 1870-1914, 750-780
    eighteenth-century, 548-562, 579-607
    industrial age of, 642-677
    Industrial Revolution in, 652-677
    late twentieth-century, 960-991,
        960-991
    during 1920-1932, 850-885
    during 1933-1945, 888-924
    in 1945, 938-944
    in 1960s, 955-957
    nineteenth-century, 679-748
    nineteenth-century revolutions,
        699-712
    northeastern, 465-472
    reform in, 726-736
    seventeenth-century, 482-512

seventeenth-century absolutism in,
    504-508
"single," in 1992, 989-991
after Thirty Years' War, 479
warfare of 1555-1648, 451-480
post World War II reconstruction of,
    938-944
youth culture in, 953-957
European Coal and Steel Community
    (ECSC), 944
European Community, 989-991
European Currency Unit (ECU), 989
European Economic Community (EEC),
    944, 989
European Recovery Act, 941
Evans, Mary Ann, 741-742
Evans, Sir Arthur, 773
Evolutionary theory, 742

Fabians, 756-757
Factories, 752
    British nineteenth-century, 688
    children in, 688
    German, 673-674
    in the industrial age, 669, 688
    Russian, 556
    women in, 690
Factory Act, 665, 688, 731
Fairfax, Sir Thomas, 499
Fairy Tales [Grimm], 693
Falkenhayn, Erich von, 829, 830
Famine
    in China, 796
    potato, 681, 688
    in Russia, 847, 865
    seventeenth-century, 598
Fanon, Frantz, 932
Farmers
    Dutch, 531-532
    eighteenth-century, 645-646
    French, 671-673
    German, and Hitler, 881
    South African, 797-798
Farnese, Alexander, 465
Fascism, 874-881, 891
    in Great Britain, 899-900
Fashoda, 793
Faust [Goethe], 695
Feminine Mystique, The [Friedan], 953
Feminists
    early twentieth-century, 764-767, 775
    late twentieth-century, 985-986
    in the 1920s and art, 883
Ferdinand, Archduke, 821
Ferdinand I (Austria), 711
Ferdinand II (Bohemia), 473-477
Ferry, Jules, 793
Fichte, Johann, 693
Ficino, Marsilio, 519
"Final Solution," 909-911, 914
Finland, 553
    famine in, 598
    Russia and, 846
    Soviet Union vs., 905
First Futurist Manifesto, 752
Fitzgerald, F. Scott, 830
Flanders
    Louis XIV and, 550
    in World War I, 830
Flappers, 883
Flaubert, Gustave, 741
Florence, eighteenth-century, 552
Foch, Ferdinand, 837
Ford Motor Company, 901
Four Ordinances, 699

Fourier, Charles, 691, 697
Fourteen Points, 838-839
Fragonard, Jean-Honore, 579
France
    Africa and, 793
    Austria and, 626
    Britain and, 793
    Canada and, 543
    civil wars of, 452-455, 452-460
    colonial America and, 543
    decolonization by, 932
    Dutch and, 537
    early twentieth-century, 760-762
    eighteenth-century, 549, 550-551, 579, 550-551, 612-618
    eighteenth-century agriculture in, 646
    eighteenth-century England and, 539
    Enlightenment in, 583
    Fifth Republic of, 932, 938, 956
    Fourth Republic of, 932
    Free French government of, 907
    Hitler and, 899, 905-906
    in the industrial age, 671-673
    late twentieth-century, 981, 982-983
    under Louis XIV, 482-483, 511
    in the 1920s, 856-857
    Provisional Government of, 708-709
    Prussia and, 724-725, 745
    racism in, 982
    railroads in, 670
    reform in, 726-730
    reparations and war debts of, 859-860
    revolution of 1832
    Second Empire of, 708, 711, 726-730, 745-747
    Spanish Civil War and, 901
    television and politics in, 973
    Third Republic of, 760-762, 770, 898
    during Thirty Years' War, 475, 477-478
    twentieth-century, 898-899
    welfare state in, 952
    women's rights in, 690
    women's suffrage granted in, 767
    in World War I, 829-830, 834
    post World War I, 847
    in World War II, 907
Francis I
    court of, 486
    Lutheranism and, 453
Francis II, 453-454
Franco, Francisco, 893
    death of, 981
    Spanish Civil War and, 901, 902
    United States and, 901
Franco-Dutch war, 538, 539
Franco-Prussian War, 724-725, 729
Frankfurt parliament, 709-710
Franz Josef I (Austria), 711
Frederick the Great, 546-547, 563
    Frederick William and, 564
Frederick V, 474, 475
Frederick William, 505, 563-564
Frederick William III, 685
Fredrich Wilhelm IV, 709, 710
French (Great) Revolution, 618-639
    industrialization and, 670, 671
    liberalism as result of, 692
    nationalism as result of, 693
    nineteenth-century labor and, 704
    and revolutions of 1832, 702
    voting rights mandated during, 702
French (Great) Revolution
    convening of Estates-General, 620-622
    end of, 633-634
    events preceding, 610-618

storming of Bastille, 622-623
    and the "three estates," 615-618
French impressionists, 751
French language
    as universal European language, 511
    in Belgian Congo, 805
    French Revolution and changes in, 627
French Plan XVII, 820
French Revolution of 1848, 708-709, 712
Freud, Sigmund, 769, 773, 776-777, 776, 1920s and, 882
Friedan, Betty, 953
Fry, Elizabeth, 721
Furs, 531, 543
Futurists, 750-752

Galapagos Islands, 742
Galen, 522
Galicia, 569
Galileo, 516, 518-519, 520-521
    Descartes and, 525
    theory of inertia developed by, 523, 524
Gallipoli Peninsula, 831
Galton, Francis, 773-774, 803
Gandhi, Mohandas (Mahatma), 930
Garibaldi, Giuseppe, 710, 719-722
Gdansk, 467
Gdansk Accords, 971
General Electric, 864
General Motors, 901
Generation gap," 954
Genetics, study of, 772, 603-606
Gentleman's Magazine, 594
Geopolitics, 787-788, 809-810
George, David Lloyd, 757, 834, 835, 838
George I (England), 572
George II (England), 547, 572
George III (England), 573
George of Hanover, 550
Georgia, 969
Gerasimov, Gennady, 974
German Confederation, 684, 696
German states
    sixteenth-century, 452
    after Thirty Years' War, 479, 480
Germany
    Africa and, 793
    Alsace-Lorraine and, 827
    declaration of war on United States by, 918
    early twentieth-century, 757
    during 1850-1871, 714-748
    after 1871, 809-810, 812
    eighteenth-century, 551
    Enlightenment in, 583
    failure of democracy in, 877-880
    France and, 820
    Great Depression in, 885
    under Hitler, 880-881, 891
    Industrial Revolution in, 673-674
    Mussolini's Italy and Nazi, 892-893
    in 1914, 822
    in the 1920s, 852, 854-856
    nineteenth-century, 690, 708, 709-710
    nineteenth-century unification of, 723-725
    railroads in, 670, 675
    reparations and war debts of, 859-865
    reunification of in late twentieth-century, 960
    Schlieffen Plan of, 820
    Second Reich of, 714, 878
    Soviet Union and, 905, 910-911, 914-917

under Stalin, 891-892
    Sweden and, 472
    Third Reich of, 893-898
    during Thirty Years' War, 475-477
    unified, 548, 568
    women's suffrage granted in, 767
    in World War I, 827-829, 834, 835, 836-837
    in World War I, turning point of, 836-837
    post World War I, 837, 839-840, 847
    post World War I inflation in, 862-863
    in World War II, 908-909, 910-911, 914-917
    post World War II, 921, 939-940
    post World War II division of, 933-938
    See also Prussia
Gestapo, 896
Ghana, 932-933
Ghent, 464, 550
Gibraltar, 540, 542, 550
Gierek, Edward, 970
Girondins, 629
Gladstone, William Ewart, 730-731
Glasnost, 968
Glass, Venetian, 533
Glorious Revolution, 503
Goebbels, Joseph, 880-881, 896, 909
Goering, Hermann, 907
Goethe, Johann Wolfgang von, 695
Gold, in South Africa, 798
Gold standard, 865, 885
Golden Twenties, 882
Gomulka, Wladislaw, 935, 970
Gorbachev, Mikhail, 960, 962, 964-970
    public image of, 973
    single European market (1992) and, 991
    women and, 986
Gorbachev, Raisa, 964, 986
Goring, Hermann, 881
Gorki, 963
Gouges, Olympe de, 628, 632
Government
    British, 569-572, 755-757
    British under Gladstone, 731
    liberal view of, 692
    Russian, 558
    seventeenth-century English, 512
    seventeenth-century French, 512
    western, 1870-1914, 788
    in World War I, 836
Goya, Francisco, 636
Grand Alliance, 539, 540
Great Britain, 541, 550, 569-575
    Agricultural Revolution in, 645
    Boers and, 798
    Colonial America revolt against, 573-575
    Congress of Vienna and, 685-686
    creation of United Kingdom of, 681
    decolonization and, 930-931
    Egypt and, 788
    during 1870-1914, 755-757
    after 1871, 812
    eighteenth-century, 653-654
    France and, 793
    Hitler and, 905-906
    imperialism in India by, 794-797
    imperialism in South Africa by, 797-799, 804-805, 927
    Industrial Revolution in, 652-669
    Napoleon and, 635, 636, 638, 671
    in 1914, 822
    in the 1920s, 853

political parties of, 571-572
racism in, 982-983
railways in, 661-662
reform in, 665-669, 690, 702-703, 726.
    See also Victorian Age
riots in nineteenth-century, 699
Spanish Civil War and, 901
twentieth-century, 899-900
welfare state in, 951
women's rights in, 691
in World War I, 830
post World War I, 840, 847
in World War II, 907-908
post World War II, 940
Great Elector, 505, 511
"Great Hunger,"668, 680, 682
Great Illusion, The [Angell], 847
Great Northern War, 552, 553, 555
Great Powers, 682, 700
    and alliance system, 809, 810-811
    and beginning of World War I, 822
    after 1871, 809-812
    France after Napoleon's defeat and,
        683-684
    Ottoman Empire and, 716
    revolutions of 1832 and, 700, 701
    United States becomes one of, 847
    post World War I, 840
Great Purge, 891-892
Great Reform Bill of 1832, 702, 730
Great Revolution
Great Trek, 797
Great War of 1914, 811
Greece
    in the 1920s, 854
    nineteenth-century, 700
    in World War I, 831
Greek Orthodox Christians, 716
Green party, 985
Grey, Sir Edward, 822
Grimm brothers, 693, 695
Gromyko, Andrei, 968
Gropius, Wlater, 850-851, 882
Grosz, George, 882
Guatemala, 938
Guderian, Heinz, 916
Guernica [Picasso], 888-889
Guiana, 807
Guilds, French, in industrial age, 671
Guillotine, 630-631, 632
Guises, 454-460
Guizot, Francois, 702
Gulag Archipelago [Solzhenitsyn], 963
Gustavus Adolphus, 471-472, 475-477
    Frederick William and, 505
Gustavus Vasa, 469

Habsburg, Ferdinand, 473
Habsburgs
    Austrian, 473, 474
    Bohemia and, 473-474
    in the eighteenth century, 551-552
    Hungary and, 565
    Louis XIV and, 537, 538, 539, 550
    nineteenth-century, 710, 723, 762
    after Thirty Years' War, 479
    Valois and 550
Haig, Douglas, 830
Haiti, 543
Hall of Mirrors, 714
Hamlet [Shakespeare], 485
Handel, Georg Friedrich, 592
Hanover, 553, 567
    Zollverein and, 674
Hard Times [Dickens], 741

Hardie, James Keir, 756
Hargreaves, James, 658
Harmonious Fists, 796
Harvey, William, 523
Haussmann, Georges, 727
Hawaiian Islands, 808
Hay, John, 797
Haydn, Joseph, 580
Hegel, George Wilhelm Friedrich, 693,
    743
Henrietta Maria, 474
Henry Bourban, 454
Henry Cort, 658
Henry Guise, 459
    See also Guises
Henry II (France), 457
Henry III (France), 458, 459
Henry IV (France), 459-460, 472
    assassination of, 495, 508
Henry of Navarre, 458, 459
Henry V [Shakespeare], 485
Henry VI [Shakespeare], 485
Herder, Johann Gottfried, 693, 695
Hermes Trimegistus, 519
Hermeticism, 519
Hermitage, 547
Herzegovina, 812
Herzl, Theodor, 769
Heydrich, Reinhard, 910
Himmler, Heinrich, 894, 911
Hindenberg, Otto von, 894
Hindenburg, Paul von, 828, 877
Hindus, in India, 930
Hiroshima, 920, 922-923, 928
Hitler, Adolf, 863, 864, 891
    appeasement of, 904
    collaborationist governments and,
        908, 913
    Comintern and, 872
    death of, 919
    foreign policy of, 903-904
    Mussolini and, 893
    rise of, 880-881
    Spanish Civil War and, 901
    Third Reich and, 893-898
    Weimar Republic and, 880
    during World War II, 904-914
Ho Chi Minh, 931
Hobbes, Thomas, 504, 519
Hobson, J. A., 789, 809
Holland, 464, 465, 472, 477
    Britain and, 550
    eighteenth century in, 591
    Frederick William and, 505
Holy Alliance, 686
Holy Land, Ottoman Empire and, 716
Holy Roman Empire
    Bohemia and, 473
    Burgundy and, 462
    Congress of Vienna and, 684
    decline of, 548, 551
    eighteenth-century, 551
    Peace of Westphalia and, 479
    after Thirty Years' War, 479
    Thirty Years' War and, 562
Honecker, Erich, 960, 976
Hong Kong, 797
Hostages, 987, 988, 989
Hugenberg, Alfred, 834
Hugo, Victor, 695, 707
Huguenots, 454-460
    Cardinal Richelieu and, 508
    divine right of kings theory and, 494
    Louis XIV and, 511
    Philip II and, 461

Hume, David, 583, 585-588
Hungary
    Austria (Hungary), 565
    Communist party in, 934, 935
    in the industrial age, 677
    late twentieth-century, 960, 975
    in the 1920s, 854
    nineteenth-century, 710
    sixteenth-century, 452
Hutcheson, Francis, 584
Hydrogen bomb, 928, 962

Ibsen, Henrik, 775
Illiteracy, in the industrial age, 677
Immanuel Kant, 583, 584-585
Immigrants, late twentieth-century,
    981-984
Imperialism, A Study [Hobson], 809
Imperialism, 1870-1914, 784-813
*Imperialism the Highest Stage of
    Capitalism* [Lenin], 809
India
    British and, 550
    calico cloth from, 529
    post World War II, 930
    sugar from, 530-531
    western imperialism and, 790,
        794-797
Indochina
    France and, 797, 932
    independence of, 931
Industrial age, 642-677
Industrial Revolution, 652-677
    beginning of, 653
    in Britain, 652-669
    in France, 671-673
Industry, heavy, 752, 754-755, 788
    post World War II, 942-943
Inflation
    in the 1920s, 858, 862-863, 878-879
    postwar, 954
    in West Germany, 977
Inner Circle, 779
Instruction [Catherine the Great], 559
Interpretation of Dreams [Freud], 776,
    778
*Introduction to the Principles of Morals
    and Legislation* [Bentham], 692
Iran, oil trade and, 937-938
Iranian airliner, accidental destruction
    of, 988
Ireland
    early twentieth-century, 757
    in World War I, 836
Irish Home Rule, 757, 812
Irish Poor Law system, 682
Irish Republican Army (IRA), Provi-
    sional Wing of, 987, 988
Iron
    Industrial Revolution and, 656-657,
        658
    railroads and, 662
Iron Curtain, 928
Israel
    late twentieth-century, 986
    recognized as Jewish state, 769
    terrorism in, 986, 988
Israelis
    Arabs vs., 938
    Olympic athletes, 987
Italy
    Enlightenment in, 583, 591
    in the industrial age, 675, 677
    late twentieth-century, 981, 981
    under Mussolini, 874-877, 891,

892-893
nationalism in, 694
in the 1920s, 854
nineteenth-century revolution in, 701, 708
seventeenth-century, 493-494
Triple Alliance and, 811
unification of, 548, 719-723
in World War I, 831
in World War II, 918
Ivan the Terrible, 467-468

Jacob's Room [Woolf], 883
Jacobins, 629, 632, 635
Jacobs, Aletta, 775
Jamaica, 531
James I (England), 472-473, 497
  conspiracy against, 495
  wife of, 488
  views on divine right of kings, 485, 486
  William Harvey and, 523
James II (England), 503
James VI (Scotland), 485
Jameson Raid, 798
Japan
  decolonization and, 931
  imperialism in Asia by, 800-801, 807-808
  undeclared war on China by, 902
  United States and, in World War II, 918-920
  in World War II, 908
  post World War II, 921, 943
Japanese-Americans, internment of, 908
Jarry, Alfred, 752
Jaruzelski, Wojciech, 971-974
Java, 530, 550
Jazz Age, 882
Jeanne d'Albret, 454, 456, 457
Jenkins, Robert, 542
Jenny (machine), 658
Jerusalem, in World War I, 831
Jesuits, 462
  Austria and, 565
  Enlightenment and, 584, 589
  expelled from Germany, 758
  seventeenth-century, 524, 525
  Sigismund II and III, 466, 467
Jewish State, The [Herzl], 769
Jews
  French Revolution and, 628
  Hitler and, 881, 897
  post World War II, 939
  Soviet, 963
  in World War I, 835
  in World War II, 908-914
Jingoism, 789
Joffre, Joseph, 829, 833
Johnson, Samuel, 605, 663
Jones, Inigo, 485
Jonson, Ben, 484
Joplin, Scott, 882
Joseph II (Austria), 566, 589-590
Josephine, 637
Joyce, James, 883
Juarez, Benito, 729, 875
Judaism, Zion and, 769
July Monarchy, 699, 702, 704
  overthrow of, 709
  Paris and, 707
  revolution of 1848 and, 708
Junkers, 723
Jutland, Battle of, 832

Kandinski, Vasili, 850
Kant, Immanuel, 694
Kautsky, Karl, 758
Kay, John, 658
Kellog-Briand Pact, 858
Kellogg, Frank B., 858
Kelly, Petra, 985
Kemble, Fanny, 643
Kennedy, John F., 938
Kenya, 933
Kenyatta, Jomo, 933
Kepler, Johannes, 518
  Hermeticism and, 519
  Newton and, 524
Kerenski, Aleksandr, 846-847
Keynes, John Maynard, 847, 899, 942
King and the Education of the King, The [Mariana], 494
Kingdom of the Two Sicilies, 710
Kings, divine right of, 484-486
Kipling, Rudyard, 802, 803
Kitchener, Horatio H., 793, 798, 827
Klee, Paul, 850
Knights of the Teutonic Order, 466, 469
Knox, John, 456
Kohl, Helmut, 978, 990
Kollantai, Aleksandra, 872, 874
Korea
  Japan and, 801
  post World War II, 921, 937
Kossuth, Lajos, 710
Kowloon, 797
Krafft-Ebing, Richard von, 778

La Nouvelle Heloise [Rousseau], 632
Labor movements, 704-705
  in World War I, 836
Labour party, British, 756-757
Ladies Diary, The, 594
Lafayette, Marquis de, 620, 622
LaGare Saint-Lazarre [Monet], 642
Lamartine, Alphonse de, 708
Laos, 797, 938
Lateran Treaty, Mussolini and, 876-877
Latvia, 905, 960, 969
Laud, William, 497, 498
Law
  English, 569, 570-571
  Enlightenment and, 588
  Napoleonic, 637
  Russian, 559
  seventeenth-century English, 489
  seventeenth-century French, 488-489
  seventeenth-century Spanish, 489-490
Le Bon, Gustave, 774
Le Feu [Barbusse], 829
League of Nations, 838, 839, 857
  Hitler's Germany and, 903
  Japan and, 902
  and Mussolini's invasion of Ethiopia, 892
  replaced by United Nations, 929
Left (origin of term), 629
Legouve, Ernest, 764
Lend-Lease Act, 917
Lenin (Vladimir Ilich Ulyanov), 809, 871
  in the 1920s, 865-866
  repudiated in Soviet Union, 964
  in Russian Revolution, 845, 846-847
  Stalin's honoring of, 868-869
  widow of, 868-869
  women and, 872
  in World War I, 836
Leo XIII, Germany and, 758
Leopold I (Austria), 538-539, 540, 552

Lepanto, 460, 461
Les Miserables [Hugo], 695, 707
Lesseps, Ferdinand di, 785-786
Leviathan [Hobbes], 504
Lewis, 457
Liaotung peninsula, 801
Liberalism, 691, 692-693
  Austrian, 762-764
  English, 755-757
  in 1914, 818
Liberals
  British, 756-757
  Junkers and, 723
  nineteenth-century British, 730-732
  nineteenth-century compared with twentieth-century, 732
Liberia, 790
Liberty Leading the People [Delacroix], 695
Lincoln, Abraham, 725
List, Georg Friedrich, 694
Liszt, Franz, 695
Literature
  futurist, 750-751
  glorifying monarchy, 484
  in the 1920s, 881, 882-884
  nineteenth-century, 695, 741-742
  romanticism in, 694-696
  sixteenth- and seventeenth-century, 484-485
  eighteenth-century, 605-607
Lithuania
  Hitler and, 904
  late twentieth-century, 960, 969
  in the 1920s, 854
  sixteenth-century, 457
Livingstone, David, 787
Livonia, 469, 553
Locarno, 855, 864
Locke, John, 503, 504
  Enlightenment and, 584
Logarithms, 516
Lombardy
  joined to Piedmont-Sardinia, 719
  nineteenth-century, 710
Lombroso, Cesare, 774
London, 687
  Industrial Revolution and, 654-655
Lorraine, 538, 548, 550
"Lost Generation," 882
Louis, Antoine, 630
Louis XIII (France), 474, 508
Louis XIV (France), 482, 496, 509-512
  absolutism and, 504, 505
  continuing influence of, 582
  death of, 541
  Dutch trading superiority and, 535, 537
  eighteenth century and, 590
  Netherlands and, 537-539
  wars of, 537-541, 550
Louis XV (France), 612-613
Louis XVI (France), 613-618, 626
  Estates-General and, 615, 618, 620-622
  French women and, 625
  results of arrest, trial, and execution of, 629
Louis XVII (France), 683, 699
Louis-Philippe, 699, 708
Louisiana, 549
Louvois, Marquis de, 509-510
Luck, Lucy, 739, 740
Luddism, 704
Luddites, 660

Ludendorff, Erich, 829, 877, 881
Ludendorff offensive, 837
Lueger, Karl, 763
Lufthansa, 989
Lumumba, Patrice, 931
Lusitania, 817
Luther, Martin, East Germany and, 978
Lutheranism
    in Netherlands, 462, 463
    in Sweden, 466
Lutherans, Calvinists united with, 475
Luxembourg, 548, 906, 919
    in World War II, 906, 919
Luxembourg Commission, 709
Lyrical Ballards [Wordsworth and
    Coleridge], 694

MacArthur, Douglas, 919, 920, 943
Macbeth [Shakespeare], 485
MacDonald, Ramsay, 899
Machiavelli, 457
Machine gun, 825
MacMillan, Harold, 931
Madagascar, 909
Madame Bovary [Flaubert], 741
Madras, 550
Madrid, 902
Magazines, 593-594
Magdeburg, 476
Magenta, battle of, 719
Maginot Line, 907
Magyars, 710
Maistre, Joseph de, 696
Malay Peninsula, 549
Malthus, 742
Malthus, Thomas, 597-598, 688
Manchuria, 801, 902, 921, 923
Manet, Edouard, 751
Manufacturing
    eighteenth-century, 644, 646-649
    French, 672
    middlemen in, 705
    minerals and metals in, 655-658
    nineteenth-century, 704-705
    rural, 646-649
    Russian, 556
Mao Ze-dong, 937
Mapmaking, 782-783
Marat, Jean Paul, 630
March on Rome, 875
Marchand, J. P., 793
Margaret of Parma, 456, 457, 462, 463
    Duke of Alba and, 464
Marguerite of Navarre, 454, 457
Maria Theresa (Austria), 565-566, 567,
    610
Mariana, Juan de, 494-495
Marie Antoinette, 610-611, 626
Marie de Medicis, 484, 487
Marijuana, 955
Marinetti, Emilio, 750
Maritime Provinces, 797
Marlborough, Duke of, 540, 582
    See also Churchill, John
Marne, Battle of the, 826-827, 834
Marshall, Alfred, 773
Marshall, George C., 941
Marshall Plan, 940-944
Martineau, Harriet, 721
Marx, Karl, 698, 742-745
    Bakunin and, 770
    Louis Napoleon and, 726-727
    Paris Commune and, 747
Marxism
    Bismark and, 759

Social Democratic party and, 758
Marxists, 745, 845
Mary, Queen of Hungary, 456, 457
Mary, Queen of Scots, 454, 456, 457
Mary I (England), 456
    Philip II and, 461
Mary Stuart, 503
Mary Tudor, 457
Maryland, 531
Massachusetts, 574
Massacre of the Innocents [Poussin], 451
Materialism, 516, 736, 744
*Mathematical Principles of Natural
    Philosophy* [Newton], 523
Mathematics
    advances in, 516, 519
    Descartes and, 525
    Newtonian, 523-524
Mathias, 473, 474
Matisse, Henri, 882
Matteotti, Giacomo, 875
Maupeou, Rene de, 613
Maximilian (Austria), 476, 729
Maxwell, James Clerk, 771
Mazarin, Jules, 496, 509
Mazzini, Giuseppe, 693-694, 710,
    719-722
Measure for Measure [Shakespeare], 485
Medici, Catherine de', 453, 454-457
Medici, Marie de, 484, 487
Medicine
    advances in, 514, 523
    Florence Nightingale and, 718,
        720-721
    forensic, 774
    nineteenth- to twentieth-century, 772;
        773, 786
    Paracelsus and, 522
    twentieth-century, 955
    eighteenth-century, 600-601
Medvedev, Roy, 963
Meiji, 807-808
Mein Kampf [Hitler], 881, 895
Mendel, Gregor, 772
Mensheviks, 845
Mercantilism, 533-535
Metric system, 637, 782, 783
Metternich, Klemens von, 686, 696, 699,
    708
Mexico
    France and, 729
    Germany and, 836
Michael (Russia), 468
Michelet, Jules, 704
Mickiewicz, Adam, 700
Middle class
    early twentieth-century, 778-779
    in 1914, 818
    Hitler's contempt for, 881
    in the industrial age, 669
    liberalism among European, 692
    nineteenth-century German, 690
    postwar U.S., and women, 953
    Victorian women, 740
Middle East
    Cold War and, 937-938
    late twentieth-century, 986
Middlemarch [Eliot], 742
Midland Revolt, 493
Midway, 919-920
Military
    British, 569
    western, during 1870-1914, 788
    western, in 1914, 820-821
Mill, James, 693

Mill, John Stuart, 691, 693, 764-765
Millet, Jean-Francois, 681
Milton, John, 495
    Galileo and, 519
Mines Act, 665
Minoans, 773
Minorca, 540, 550
Mirabeau, Honore de, 621
Missouri, 920
Mitterand, Francois, 981, 990
Mogadishu, 989
Mohacs, battle of, 457
Molotov cocktails, 912
Mommsen, Theodor, 768
Mona Lisa [Duchamp], 882
Monet, Claude, 642, 751
Money
    early twentieth-century, 778-779
    in the 1920s, 862-863
    single currency forecasted for EEC,
        989-990
Monnet, Jean, 943, 989
Monopolies, 533-534
Montesquieu, Baron de, 559, 584-588
Moro, Aldo, 987
Morocco, 799-800
Morphine, 955
Moscow
    eighteenth-century, 554
    in the industrial age, 675
    Napoleonic era and, 638
    Poland and, 468
    in World War II, 915-916
Mosley, Sir Oswald, 899-900
Mother Goose nursery rhymes, 596
Motion pictures, 883
Mozart, Wolfgang Amadeus, 580
Mrs. Dalloway [Woolf], 883
Mule (machine), 659
Munich, 881
Munich agreement, 904
Muscovy
    Orthodox (eastern) Christianity of,
        465-466
    Poland and, 467, 468
    Sweden and, 470-471
    after Thirty Years' War, 479
Music
    eighteenth-century, 580
    Jazz Age, 882
    in the 1920s, 882
    rock 'n' roll, 926-927
    romanticism in, 695
Muslims, 930, 932
Mussolini, Benito, 874-877, 891
    Hitler and, 893, 904
    plans for empire of, 892-893
Mustard gas, 826
Myanmar, 931

Nadaud, Martin, 706
Nagasaki, 920, 922-923, 928
Nagy, Imre, 935, 960
Nairobi, 807
Nanking, Treaty of, 796
Nantes, Edict of, 457, 459
    Louis XIV and, 511
Naples, seventeenth-century, 494
Napoleon, Bonaparte, 25, 634-639
    Paris and, 706
Napoleon III (Louis Napoleon), 719, 722,
    726-736
    Prussia and, 724, 745
Napoleonic Code, 637
Nasser, Gamal Abdel, 938

Natal Republic, 797-798
National Front, 982
National Insurance Act of 1911, 757
National Socialists, 863, 864
  Comintern and, 872
  as Fascists, 874
  Hitler becomes chief of, 880-881
Nationalism, 693-694, 708, 710
  African, 933
  imperialism and, 788-790
  post World War II, 930-933
  romanticism and, 695
Native Americans, 543, 808
Navarre, 456
Navigation Acts, 534, 535, 536, 654
Nazis, 894-898
  goals of, 895-896
  rise of, 880-881
Necker, Jacques, 614-615, 637
Neoplatonism, during Renaissance, 519
Netherlands, 452, 456, 457
  Belgians and, 700
  Calvinism in, 462-465
  Charles V and, 461-462
  in the industrial age, 675
  Louis XIV and, 537-539
  Philip II and, 460, 461-465
  Spain and, 463-465, 479
  in World War II, 906
New Caledonia, 807
New France, 549
New Guinea, 919
New Lanark, 664-665
New Orleans, 549
New World, trade with, 533
New Zealand, 831
Newbery, John, 596
Newcomen, Thomas, 656, 657
Newfoundland, 531, 540
Newspapers, 593-594, 788-789
Newton, Sir Isaac, 523-524
  Voltaire's views on, 582-583, 587
Nicholas I (Russia), 717-718
Nicholas II (Russia), 840, 843
Nietzsche, Friedrich, 752
Nightingale, Florence, 718, 720-721, 740
Nijmegen France, Treaty of, 538
Nimitz, Chester, 919, 920
Nine Years' War, 538-539, 540
Nineteen Eighty-Four [Orwell], 946-947
Nivelle, Robert Georges, 830
Nixon, Richard, 938
Nkrumah, Kwame, 932
Nobel, Alfred, 773
Nobel Prizes, 773
Non-Aggression Pact, 905
North Africa
  France and, 793
  in World War II, 931
North America, 543
  British, 543, 549
  eighteenth-century, 549
  French, 549
  revolt against Britain, 573-575
  Spanish, 549
North Atlantic Treaty Organization
  (NATO), 929, 930, 938
Norway, in World War II, 906
Notre Dame Cathedral, 632, 637
Notre-Dame de Paris [Hugo], 695
Nova Scotia, 540
November Criminals, 880
Nuclear arms race, 928-930, 963
  women's protests against, 952
Nuclear Test Ban Treaty, 963

Numerology, 519
Nuremberg Laws, 909
Nuremberg trials, 914
Nystad, Treaty of, 548, 552

O'Brien, James Bronterre, 703
O'Connor, Feargus, 703
Oath of the Tennis Court, 621, 623
Obstetrics, 601
October Revolution, 868
Office of European Economic Coopera-
  tion (OEEC), 942
Oil crisis, 937-938, 989
Okinawa, 922
Old Believers, 589
Oligarchy
  in Holland, 503
  Whig, 572
Olivares, Count-Duke, 486, 487, 488-489
Olmutz, 711
Olympic Games, 779
On Liberty [Mill], 693
*On the Excellence of the Kings and the
  Kingdom of France*, 484
*On the Origin of Species by Means of
  Natural Selection* [Darwin], 742
*On the Revolutions of the Heavenly
  Spheres* [Copernicus], 517
One Day in the Life of Ivan Denisovich
  [Solzhenitsyn], 963
OPEC, 987
Open Door policy (in China), 797
Opium, 795, 955
Orange Free State, 798
Orlando, Vittorio, 838
Orlando [Woolf], 883
Orthodox (eastern) Christianity, Rus-
  sian, 508
Orwell, George, 805, 946-947
Ostpolitik, 977
Ottoman Empire
  after 1871, 810
  nineteenth-century, 700, 716-717
  in World War I, 831
Ottoman Turks
  Philip II and, 460-461
  Poland and, 553
Owen, Robert, 664, 665

Pact of Steel, 893, 904
Pakistan, 930
Palatinate, 474
Palermo, 493-494
Palestinians, 986, 988
Palestine, emigration of Jews to, 769
Palestine Liberation Organization
  (PLO), 987, 988
Pamela [Richardson], 594
Pan American airline, bombing of, 988
Pan-African federation, 933
Panama Canal, 786, 808
Pankhurst, Emmeline, 766
Pankhurst, Sylvia, 767
Papacy, Philip II and, 462
Papal States
  eighteenth-century, 552
  Congress of Vienna and, 684
  nineteenth-century revolution in, 701,
  710
Paracelsus, 519-522
Paris
  American artists and writers moving
  to, 881
  Louis XIV and, 496
  nineteenth-century, 687-688, 706-707

  rebuilding of, 728
  salons of, 582
  siege of, 745-747
Paris Commune, 747, 770
Parliament Bill of 1911, 757
Parliamentarians, 498
Passcheddaele offensive, 830-831
Pasteur, Louis, 772
Pavlov, Ivan, 773
Peace Conference, 839
Peace of Augsburg, 452, 462, 473
  after Thirty Years' War, 479
Peace of Paris, 543, 683
  Russia and, 718
Peace of Ryswick, 539
Peace of Westphalia, 452, 479, 538
Pearl Harbor, 918-920
Peary, Robert E., 772
Peasants
  Austrian, 566
  in Catalonia, 495
  eighteenth-century, 645-646
  in the industrial age, 671-673, 677
  French Revolution and, 617, 623-624
  Russian, 557
  Russian, revolts of, 733
  seventeenth-century French, 493
  in Soviet Union, 866, 867-868, 871
  See also Serfs
Penck, Albrecht, 783
Peninsular War, 637-638
People's Charter, 702-703
Perestroika, 968, 969
Perry, Matthew C., 807
Pershing, John "Black Jack," 836
Persian Gulf, 937-938, 988
Persian Letters [Montesquieu], 584, 586,
  587
Petain, Henri-Philippe, 830, 907
Peter III (Russia), 558, 559
Peter the Great, 506-508, 511, 553, 554
  the West and, 555-556
Petition of Right (England), 497
Petrograd, 840
Philip II (Spain), 457, 460-461
Philip III (Spain), 472, 474, 477
Philip IV (Spain), 495, 539
  art depicting, 484
  Olivares and, 489
Philip of Anjou, 540
Philip V (Spain), 540, 582
Philippines, 550
*Philosophical Letters Concerning the
  English Nation* [Voltaire], 582-583
Philosophical Letters [Voltaire], 587
Philosophy
  French, 752
  German, 752
  nineteenth-century, 692-698
Physicians, 514
Physics, 517, 771
Picabia, Francis, 882
Picasso, Pablo, 882, 888-889
Pico della Mirandola, 519
Piedmont, 710
Piedmont-Sardinia, 718, 719-723
Piracy, 541
Pitt, Sir William, 542
Pius IX, 710-711
  Germany and, 758
Pius VI, 625
Pius VII, 637
Pius XI, 876-877
Place, Francis, 606
Plague, European

eighteenth-century, 598, 599
seventeenth-century, 493
after Thirty Years' War, 480
See also Epidemics
Planck, Max, 771
Planting Potatoes [Millet], 680, 682
Plastic, 772
Platonic Academy, 519
Plombieres, Treaty of, 719
Poetry
    in the 1920s, 882
    romanticism in, 694, 700
Poincare, Raymond, 859
Poland
    Catherine the Great and, 559, 568-569
    Fredrick the Great and, 568-569
    Communist party in, 934, 935
    Congress of Vienna and, 684-685
    eighteenth-century, 552, 553
    extermination camps in, 911-912
    Hitler and, 904, 905
    late twentieth-century, 960, 970-974
    Muscovy and, 468
    nineteenth-century revolution in,
        700-701, 708
    Russia and, 569
    Russian peasants escaping to, 557
    sixteenth-century, 452, 466-467
    Soviet Union and, 905
    Sweden and, 469-470
    Wilson's Fourteen Points and, 838
Poland-Lithuania
    Protestantism in, 465
    Roman Catholicism in, 465-466
    sixteenth-century, 452, 465-467
Polish Diet, 467, 568
Polish University of Krakow, 517
Political Testament [Richelieu], 508
Politics
    late twentieth-century Soviet, 967-970
    in the 1930s, 890-902
    television and, 972-973
    transformation of, 752-753
Politiques, 458, 459
Poltava, battle of, 507
Pomerania, 553, 563
Pompidou, Georges, 981
Pope, Alexander, 590
Popular Front for the Liberation of
    Palestine (PFLP), 988
Porcelain, Dutch, 532
Portugal
    eighteenth-century, 549
    Philip II and, 460
    rebellion in, 492, 495
Potato famine, 681, 688
Potsdam Conference, 923
Pottery
    Dutch, 532
    industrial age, 660, 664
    Wedgwood, 664
Pound, Ezra, 882
Poussin, Nicolas, 451
Pozsgay, Imre, 975
Pragmatic Sanction, 565-566, 567
Prague
    Defenestration of, 473
    Hitler and, 904
    late twentieth-century, 960
    nineteenth-century revolution in, 710
Prague Spring, 960
Pravda, 867
Presbyterians, 499
Presley, Elvis, 927
Pride and Prejudice [Austen], 689

Prince, The [Machiavelli], 457
Princip, Gavrilo, 821
*Principles of Political Economy and Tax-
    ation* [Ricardo], 692, 693
Printing press, at Moscow, 556
Progress of the Human Mind, The
    [Condorcet], 584
Proletkult, 882-883
Protectionism
    French, 533
    U.S., 865
Protestantism
    vs. Catholicism in sixteenth century,
        452-460
    vs. Catholicism during Thirty Years'
        War, 472-479
    in Poland-Lithuania, 465
Protestants
    Austria and, 565
    Bohemia and, 473, 565
    Dutch, 494
    in the eighteenth century, 589
    French Revolution and, 628
    persecution of under Louis XIV, 511
Proudhon, Pierre-Joseph, 696-697, 770
Prussia, 472, 505-506, 548, 562-565
    agriculture in, 646
    Austria and, 711
    Austria invaded by, 566-567
    Bismark and, 723-725
    Congress of Vienna and, 684, 685
    eighteenth-century, 552, 553
    Enlightenment in, 583, 588-589
    France and, 724-725, 745
    Grand Alliance and, 540
    in the industrial age, 674
    Napoleon and, 636, 638
    in the 1920s, 854
    nineteenth-century, 709-710
    Peter the Great and, 507
    Seven Years' War and, 568
Psychology of Crowds [Le Bon], 774
Psychology of Jingoism [Hobson], 789
Ptolemic theory, 521
    debates on, 517-519
Public Health Act, 665, 731
Pugachev's revolt, 559-562
Punjab, 795
Puritans
    Cromwell as one of, 502
    in England, 497
Putting-out system, 647-648, 658

Quadruple Alliance, 686
Quakers, in the industrial age, 663
Quantz, Johann, 546
Queens, 456-457
Quinine, 786-787
Quintuple Alliance, 686

Radioactivity, 771
Radziwills, 581
Railroads, 661-662, 670, 675, 677
    China and, 796
    French, 729
    in World War I, 829
Ramillies, 540
Ranke, Leopold von, 773
Rapallo, Treaty of, 871
Rasputin, 841
Rathenau, Walter, 834
Rationale of Punishments and Rewards
    [Bentham], 693
Ravachol, 769
Ray, Man, 882

Reagan, Ronald, 963
Realism, 740-742
Realpolitik, 723, 736
Red Army, 866, 915-916
    Japanese, 988
Red Army Faction, 986
Red Guards, 846
Redshirts, 719, 722
Reflections on the Revolution in France
    [Burke], 696
Reflections on Violence [Sorel], 770
Reform Bill of 1832, 702, 730
Reign of Terror, 630, 632-633
Reinsurance Treaty, 811
Religion
    in early twentieth-century Germany,
        758
    Enlightenment and, 583, 584, 589-590
    freedom of, in Holland, 514
    French Revolution and, 625, 628, 632
    nineteenth- to twentieth-century, 771
    sixteenth-century wars of, 452-460
    and eighteenth-century tracts, 606
Remarque, Erich Maria, 824
Rembrandt van Rijn, 514
Renaissance, Hermetic thinking arising
    in, 519
Renoir, Pierre-Auguste, 751
*Report on the Sanitary Condition of the
    Laboring Population in Britain*
    [Chadwick], 665
Revisionism, German, 759
Revolutions of 1832, 699-702
Revolutions of 1848, 705-711, 712
Rhineland, Industrial Revolution in, 673
Rhodes, Cecil, 798-799
Rhodesia, 931
Ricardo, David, 692, 694
Rice, 531
Richard II [Shakespeare], 485
Richardson, Samuel, 594
Richelieu, Cardinal, 451, 477, 486, 489
    life of, 487
    Louis XIII and, 508-509
    quote regarding tyranny, 495
Riefenstahl, Leni, 893
Riga, Treaty of, 854
Right (origin of term), 629
Riot in the Galleria [Boccioni], 751
Roaring Twenties, 882
Robespierre, Maximilien, 629-633
Rocard, Michel, 990
Rocroi, 478
Rohe, Ludwig Mies van der, 850
Rohm, Ernst, 881, 894
Rolling Stone, 927
Roman Catholic church
    Descartes and, 525
    Galileo and, 518-519, 520-521
    Germany and, 758
    in late twentieth-century Poland, 971
    Mussolini and, 876-877
    science and, 524
    in Spain during 1930s, 901
Romances (literature), 606
Romania, 718, 831
    Communist party in, 934
    Gorbachev and, 973
    late twentieth-century, 961, 972
    in the 1920s, 854
Romanov, Michael, 468
Romanov dynasty, 840
Romanticism, 694-696, 741
Rome, Republic of, 710
Rome-Berlin Axis, 893

Room of One's Own, A [Woolf], 883
Roosevelt, Franklin D., 885
  Stalin and, 917
  in World War II, 913, 918-920
Rosenberg, Alfred, 884
Rothschild, Baron de, 769
Rousseau, Jean-Jacques, 585
  influence on Germaine de Stael,
    694-695
  Robespierre and, 632
Royal Greenwich Observatory, 783
Royalists, 498
Rubens, Peter Paul, 484
Rusk, Dean, 938
Russia
  Congress of Vienna and, 685
  Crimean War and, 716-718
  after 1871, 811, 812
  eighteenth-century, 552-562
  Enlightenment in, 583, 589
  Hitler's view of, 895
  in the industrial age, 675, 676
  Japan and, 801
  in 1914, 822
  in the 1920s, 852-853, 865-874
  Napoleonic era and, 637-638
  Ottoman Empire and, 700, 716-717
  Paris Commune and, 747
  Poland and, 569
  Provisional Government in, 841-847
  reform in, 726, 732-735
  seventeenth-century, 506-508
  Spanish Civil War and, 902
  Whites and Reds in, 846
  pre World War I, 820
  in World War I, 827-829, 835
  post World War I, 838, 840-847, 840
  See also Muscovy
Russian Civil War, 846-847, 852
Russian Orthodox Church, 508, 556, 589
  eighteenth century and, 589
Russian Revolution, 809, 840-847
Russo-Japanese War, 801, 808
Rutherford, Ernest, 771

Sahara, sub-, 790
St. Bartholomew, 455
St. Bartholomew's Day massacre, 455,
  458
St. Domingue Island, 531, 543
St. Giles Cathedral, 497
St. Peter's Basilica, 876
St. Peter's Field, 698
St. Petersburg, 557, 840
Saint-Just, Louis de, 579
Saint-Simon, 483
  Henri de, 696, 697
Sakharov, Andrei, 962, 963
Salons, 582
Samoa, 808
Samsonov, Aleksandr, 828
Sanchez, Ilyitch Ramirez, 988
Sanger, Margaret, 775
Sarajevo, 821
Sardinia, 552
  See also Piedmont-Sardinia
Savoy, 552
Saxony, 473, 476
  Frederick the Great and, 567
  Industrial Revolution in, 673
  Zollverein and, 674
Sceptical Chymist, The [Boyle], 522
Schleswig, 723
Schlieffen, Alfred von, 820
Schliemann, Heinrich, 773

Schmidt, Helmut, 978
Schonerer, Georg von, 768
Schopenhauer, Arthur, 752
Schuman, Robert, 943
Schuman Plan, 943, 989
Schutzstaffel, 894
Science
  advances in, 514-525
  Darwin and, 742
  Napoleon and, 637
  nineteenth- to twentieth-century,
    771-773
  seventeenth-century, 524-525
  social, 773-774
  women and, 775-778
Scotland
  and England joining together, 550,
    570
  Enlightenment in, 583
  invasion of England by, 497
  John Knox and, 456
  religion in, 498
Scouting, 779
Second Sex, The [de Beauvoir], 952
Secondat, Charles-Louis, 586
  See also Montesquieu, Baron
Selassie, Haile, 892
Serbia, 812, 822
  in World War I, 828, 831
Serbs, 854
Serfs
  Austrian, 565, 566
  Russian, 557
  Russian, liberation of, 733
Seven Weeks' War, 723, 729
Seven Years' War, 543, 567, 568
  French trade and, 671
  Great Britain and, 573
  Louis XV and, 613
Sex education, 954
Sexual revolution, 954-955
Shakespeare, William, 485
Shanghai, 795, 796
Shaw, George Bernard, 756
Shelley, Percy Bysshe, 700
Ship Money, 491
Ships, iron steamers, 785
Siberia, 557, 916
Sicherheitsdienst (SD), 910
Sicily
  eighteenth-century, 552
  seventeenth-century, 493
Sieyes, Abbe Emmanuel Joseph, 621
Sigismund II, 466
Sigismund III, 467, 470
  Muscovy and, 468
Silesia, 566-567, 568
  Industrial Revolution in, 673
Sinatra, Frank, 974
Single Europe in 1992, 989-991
Single European Act, 989
Sino-Japanese War, 800-801, 808
Six Books of the Commonwealth, The
  [Bodin], 485
Skepticism, 583
Skyscrapers, 851
Slavery
  abolition of by Great Britain, 790, 797
  British, 541
  seventeenth-century, 526, 534
  South African, 797-798
Slaves
  African, Brazil and, 531
  African, England and, 530-531
Slavs, Hitler's view of, 895, 909, 910

Slovakia, 908
Slovaks, 854
Slovenes, 854
Smith, Adam, 525, 534, 583, 585, 590
Smoot-Hawley Tariff Act, 884
Smuggling, 541, 573
  in the industrial age, 676
Social Contract, The [Rousseau], 585
Social Contract [Rousseau], 632
Social Darwinists, 775
Social Democratic party (Germany),
  758, 976
Social Democratic party (Russia), 845
Social reform
  in Britain, 665-669, 690, 702-703
  early twentieth-century women and,
    767
  of Europe, 726-736
Social sciences, 773-774
Socialism, 696-698, 709
  German, 758-760
Socialists
  Fascists as former, 875
  women as, 767
  in World War I, 836
Solferino, battle of, 719
Solidarity, 970-974
Solzhenitsyn, Alexander, 963
Somme Valley, 829, 830
Sophie of Anhalt-Zerbst, 560-561
Sorel, Georges, 752, 770
Soup kitchens
South Africa
  diamond mines in, 792, 798
  formation of Union of, 798
  western imperialism in, 797-799
  in World War II, 931
Southeast Asia, 931, 938
Southeast Asia Treaty Organization
  (SEATO), 929
Soviet Union, 854
  art and politics combined in,
    882-883, 884
  Cold War and, 928-938
  Comintern in, 871-872
  communes in, 872
  effect of World War II on, 917
  Germany vs., 903, 910-911, 914-917
  Germany's invasion of, 910-911,
    915-916
  invasion of Czechoslovakia, 936, 970
  invasion of Hungary, 935
  late twentieth-century, 962-970
  Nazi Germany and, 892, 905
  New Economic Policy (NEP) in,
    866-867, 869
  in the 1920s, 865-874
  post World War II, 921, 940, 949-950
  Third World and, 933
Soviets, 845, 846
Space exploration, 928
Space satellites, 928
Spain
  Dutch and, 477
  eighteenth-century, 549, 551, 581, 582
  France and, 472, 477-478
  under Franco, 893
  in the industrial age, 675, 677
  late twentieth-century, 980
  Netherlands and, 457-465, 477, 479
  Napoleonic era and, 637
  Philip II and, 460-461
  sixteenth-century, 452
  twentieth-century, 900-902
Spanish Armada, 461

Elizabeth I and, 456
and English Ship Money, 491
Spanish Civil War, 901-902
Spanish Inquisition, Netherlands and, 463
Spectator, The, 594
Spencer, Herbert, 802
Spices, Dutch Republic and, 532
Spirit of the Laws [Montesquieu], 586, 587
Spock, Benjamin, 950
Sports, 606, 779
Sputnik I, 928
Sri Lanka, 931
Stael, Germaine de, 694-695
Stakhanov, Alexei, 891
Stalin, Joseph, 865, 866-868, 891-892
    Allies and, 915
    Churchill and Roosevelt's commitment to, 919
    death of, 935, 949
    Great Purge of, 891-892
    Hitler and, 905, 916
    rise to power of, 868-872
    Truman and, 923
    views on art of, 884
    women and, 873-874
Stalingrad, 916, 917
Stamp Act, 573, 574, 575
Stanley, Henry M., 787
"Star Wars,"963
Starry Messenger [Galileo], 520
Steam engine, 657-658, 661
Steamships, 785
Stephenson, George, 661, 662, 675
Stephenson, Robert, 662
Stettin, 563
Stimson, Henry L., 923
Stock market, 865
Stone Breakers [Courbet], 741
Storm troopers, 894
Strael, Germaine de, 637
Strafford, Earl of, 497
Strasbourg, 538, 550
Strategic Arms Limitation Treaty (SALT I), 963
Strategic Defense Initiative (SDI), 963
Stravinsky, Igor, 882
Stresemann, Gustav, 855-856
Strikes
    Chartist, in Great Britain, 703
    early twentieth-century, 757
    in twentieth-century France, and student protests, 956-957
    in nineteenth-century France, 704
    Polish, 970-971
    in World War I, 836
Stuarts, 498, 502-503
Studebaker, 901
Student protests, 955-956, 970
Sturm und Drang, 695
Sturmabteilung, 881
Sturmabteilung (SA), 894
Submarines, 832, 836
Subway, 779
Sudetenland, 904
Suez Canal, 729, 785-786, 788
    Nasser and, 938
    in World War I, 831
Sufffragettes, 766-767
Sugar, 530-531, 532, 537
    Britain and, 541
Sugar Act, 573, 575
Surgeons, 514
Surrealism, 882

Swahili language, 804-805
Sweden, 466
    Congress of Vienna and, 685
    eighteenth-century, 552, 553
    Muscovy and, 468
    Poland and, 467
    rise of, 469-472
    Russia and, 507
    sexual mores in, 954
    during Thirty Years' War, 475-476, 476
Switzerland
    Congress of Vienna and, 684
    1920s' artists in, 882
    nineteenth-century, 699
    after Thirty Years' War, 479
Syria, post World War II, 937
Systemic Dictionary of the Sciences, Arts, and Crafts [Diderot], 583

Table of Ranks, 555-556
Talleyrand, 685
Tannenburg, 827
Tariffs, 533, 537
    Benelux and, 943
    during 1870-1914, 755
    Gladstone and, 731
    Great Depression and, 884
    in the industrial age, 676
Tartars, 467, 555
Taylor, Harriet, 693
Tea, 530, 795
Technology
    during 1870-1914, 784-787
    in industrial age, 663
    postwar, 950
    in World War I, 823-826
Teheran, 919, 923
Telegraph, 786
Television (political impact of), 972-973
Tempest, The [Shakespeare], 485
Ten Hours age, 665
Tender Is the Night [Fitzgerald], 830
Tennyson, Alfred, Lord, 718
Tenure of Kings and Magistrates, The [Milton], 495
Terrorism, late twentieth-century, 986-989
Texas Oil Company, 901
Thatcher, Margaret, 976, 990, 991
The Waves [Woolf], 883
Theater, 883
Theory of the Leisure Class, The [Veblen], 778
Third Reich, 893-898
Third World, 932-933
    refuges from, 983
Thirty Years' War, 472-479, 492
    Austria and, 565
Three Emperors' League, 809-810, 811
Threepenny Opera [Brecht], 883
Time of Troubles, 468
Time zones, 782-783
Tito, 908
Tobacco, 531, 532
    Britain and, 541
Toleration Act, 503
Tolstoy, Leo, 778
Tories, 571-572
    Gladstone and Disraeli as, 732
Tour de France, 779
Townsend, Charles"Turnip,"650
Trade and commerce
    British imperialism and, 792
    China and Britain, 795-796
    Dutch, 526, 529, 532-533, 535

during 1870-1914, 792, 801-802
    English, 528, 529-530
    between Europe and Asia, 529-531, 543
    in the industrial age, 676-677
    nineteenth-century French, 729
    seventeenth-century, 525-544
    single European market (1992) and, 991
    western, in the 1920s, 858-865
    See also Industrial Revolution
Trade Unions Act of 1913, 731, 757
Transportation
    early twentieth-century, 779
    during 1870-1914, 785-786, 801
    industrial age, 660-662
    eighteenth-century, 582
Transvaal Republic, 798
Treatise of Human Nature, A [Hume], 585
Treblinka, 912
Trent, Council of, 463
Trevithick, Richard, 661
Tripartite Pact, 918
Triple Alliance, 811, 812
Triple Entente, 811. *See also* Allies
Tristan, Flora, 691, 705
Triumph of the Will [Riefenstahl], 893
Trotsky, Leon, 843, 846, 866
    expelled from Communist party, 868
True Law of Free Monarchies, The [James VI], 485
Truman, Harry, 922, 923
Truman Doctrine, 941
Turgot, Anne-Robert-Jacques, 590, 614
Turkey, Russia and, 700
Turks, in World War I, 835
    See also Ottoman Empire; Ottoman Turks
Turner, J. M. W., 695
Tuscany, 552, 710
Twelve Years' Truce, 465, 472, 473
    expiration of, 477
Two New Sciences, The [Galileo], 521
Two Treatises on Civil Government [Locke], 503
Typhus, 718
Tyrants, 494-495
Tzara, Tristan, 882

U-boats, 832, 836
Uganda, 988
Uitlanders, 798
Ukraine, 846, 854
Ulbricht, Walter, 934, 972, 976
Ulysses [Joyce], 883
Union of Soviet Socialist Republics, 857
Unions, labor, 705
    early twentieth-century British, 756, 757
    French, 770
    German, 759
    See also Labor movements
United Nations, nuclear power and, 929
United States
    Cold War and, 928-938
    Great Depression in, 885
    Hitler's view of, 895
    imperialism by, 808
    late twentieth-century, 963
    League of Nations and, 839, 857
    in the 1920s, 852, 853, 857-858
    in 1960s, 955-957
    Spanish Civil War and, 901-902
    women's suffrage granted in, 767

in World War I, 836-837
post World War I, 840, 847
in World War II, 908, 913, 917-920
post World War II, 921, 940
youth culture in, 953-957
Universities
European, in 1960s, 955-956
U.S., 955-956
See also Student protests
Urals, 916
Urban VIII, 520, 521
Utopia [More, compared with Orwell's
Animal Farm, 946
Utrecht, Treaty of, 540, 541, 542, 548
Dutch gain from, 550

Vaccination Act, 665
Valois, Habsburgs and, 550
Van Dyck, Sir Anthony, 484
Vatican, Mussolini and, 876
Veblen, Thorstein, 778
Velazquez, Diego, 484
Venice, nineteenth-century, 710
Verdun, 829, 830
Versailles, 482-483, 510
Bismark at, 714-715
convening the Estates-General at,
620-622
Marie Antoinette and, 610-611
Versailles, Treaty of, 856, 857
Hitler and, 880
Vichy, 907, 913
Victor Emmanuel II, 719, 722
Victoria (England), 691, 753
Disraeli and, 732
as Empress of India, 794
suffragettes and, 767
Victorian Age, 714-748
Vienna, Congress of, 683-686
nineteenth-century revolution iin, 710,
711
rebuilding of, 762
Vietnam, 931
Vietnam War, 955
Virchow, Rudolf, 772
Virginia, 531
Visit to the Wet Nurse, A [Fragonard],
579
Volga region, 916
Volgograd, 917
Voltaire, 580, 582-588
the bourgeoisie and, 592
Voting rights, 702
British, 730
in Western Europe, 753
of women, 766-767

Walesa, Lech, 974
Wallace, A. R., 742
Wallenberg, Raoul, 913
Wallenstein, Albrecht von, 475, 476-477
Walpole, Sir Robert, 572, 573, 575
War of Jenkins' Ear, 542
War of the Austrian Succession, 567
War of the Spanish Succession, 540, 550,

552
Austria and, 565
Prussia and, 563
Warfare
British, 543
colonial, 541-544
over commerce, 535-544
Dutch, 531
English civil, 497-499
French civil, 452-455
from 1555 to 1648, 451-480
of Netherlands, 463-465
seventeenth-century, 490-491, 493
eighteenth-century, 599
Wars of Liberation, 696
Warsaw, Grand Duchy of, 685
Warsaw, Jewish ghetto in, 912
Warsaw Confederation, 467
Warsaw Pact, 935, 936
Waterloo, 638-639
Watt, James, 657
Wealth of Nations, The [Smith], 525
Weapons
during 1870-1914, 787
nuclear, 928-930
of World War I, 823-826
Webb, Beatrice, 756
Webb, Sidney, 756
Wedgwood, Josiah, 664
Weimar Republic, 854, 877-880
art and, 883
destruction of, 881
U.S. support of, 881
Welfare state, 944-953
Wells, H. G., 756
Werner, Anton von, 715
Wesley, John, 595
West Africa
France and, 793
Germans and, 792
West Berlin, 934
West Germany, 942-943, 951, 960
East Germany and, 976-980
television and, 972
West Indies, 542
Western Europe
eighteenth-century, 548, 549-552
Industrial Revolution and, 670
late twentieth-century, 980-991
in the 1920s, 856-857
post World War II, 921, 945-948
warfare of 1555-1648, 452-465
women's suffrage in, 767
What Is Property? [Proudhon], 696-697
Whigs, 571-572
White Mountain, battle of, 474, 475
Whitney, Eli, 660
Wilhelm II (Kaiser), 758-760, 796, 798,
806
Schlieffen Plan and, 820
Wilkes, John, 575
Wilkinson, John, 657
William III (England), 537, 538-540
William of Orange, 463, 464, 503, 537
Wilson, Woodrow, 836, 838, 853

Women
early twentieth-century, 753, 779
eighteenth-century, 589, 595-596,
598-599, 600-601
during 1870-1914 imperialism,
803-806
as feminists, 764-767
in French Revolution, 624-625, 628,
632
Gorbachev and, 986
in industrial age, 668, 690
late twentieth-century, 982, 984-986
Napoleonic Code regarding, 637
in Nazi extermination camps, 912
in Nazi Germany, 896
and new morality of 1920s, 883-884
nineteenth-century, 690-691, 720-721,
737-740
nineteenth-century labor and,
704-705
postwar protests by, 952-953
rock music and, 927
Russian, 558
in Russian Revolution, 841, 842-843,
844
science and, 775-778
as sixteenth-century rulers, 456
as socialists, 767
in Soviet Union, 872-874, 986
in welfare state, 948, 951
in World War I, 833-834, 845
Women's rights, 690-691, 697
in early twentieth-century Germany,
758
suffrage in Britain, 730
See also Suffragettes
Wool production, 533, 795
Woolf, Virginia, 883
Wordsworth, William, 694
World Disarmament Conference, 903
World Exposition, 779
World War I, 816-848
aftermath of, 838-847, 854
on eastern front, 827-829
food rationing in, 834
governments during, 835
Industrial Revolution and, 677
Israel and, 769
Lenin and, 809
reparations and debts of, 859-865
start of, 821-822
turning point of, 836-837
weapons of, 823-826, 832
on western front, 829-831
World War II, 767, 902-923
aftermath of, 920-921
concentration camps in, 912-914
end of, 920
internment of Japanese-Americans in,
908
Jews in, 908-914
navies in, 832
Nazi collaborators in, 908, 913
resistance fighters in, 908
SS in, 895